PUBLIC ADMINISTRATION

AN
ACTION
ORIENTATION

BROOKS/COLE SERIES IN PUBLIC ADMINISTRATION

PUBLIC ADMINISTRATION

AN ACTION ORIENTATION

ROBERT B. DENHARDT
UNIVERSITY OF COLORADO AT DENVER

BROOKS/COLE PUBLISHING COMPANY
PACIFIC GROVE, CALIFORNIA

Brooks/Cole Publishing Company
A Division of Wadsworth, Inc.

Printed in the United States of America

10 9 8 7 6 5 4 3 2 1

Library of Congress Cataloging-in-Publication Data
Denhardt, Robert B.
    Public administration : an action orientation / Robert B. Denhardt.
      p. cm.
    Includes bibliographical references and index.
    ISBN 0-534-13182-4
    1. Public administration. I. Title.
JF1351.D45 1991
350—dc20
                                          90-21346
                                            CIP

Sponsoring Editor: *Cynthia C. Stormer*
Editorial Assistant: *Cathleen S. Collins*
Production Editor: *Penelope Sky*
Production Assistant: *Micky Lawler*
Manuscript Editor: *Molly Kyle*
Permissions Editor: *Marie DuBois*
Interior and Cover Design: *Lisa Berman*
Art Coordinator: *Cloyce J. Wall*
Interior Illustration: *Cloyce J. Wall, Kristen Y. Calcagno*
Typesetting: *Execustaff*
Cover Printing: *Phoenix Color Corporation*
Printing and Binding: *Arcata Graphics/Fairfield*

FOR MICHAEL AND CARI

Robert B. Denhardt teaches in the Graduate School of Public Affairs at the University of Colorado at Denver. He is a recent past president of the American Society for Public Administration, the leading national organization devoted to advancing excellence in public service. Dr. Denhardt served for six years as chair of the Governor's Advisory Council on Productivity for the state of Missouri, and was awarded the prestigious Stephen B. Sweeney Award by the International City Management Association for Excellence in Urban Management Education.

Dr. Denhardt has taught at the Universities of Missouri, Kansas, and New Orleans, and has served in a variety of administrative capacities, most recently as Vice Provost at the University of Missouri–Columbia. His publications include *In the Shadow of Organization* and *Theories of Public Organization*, and more than fifty articles in professional journals.

Public Administration: An Action Orientation contains subtle but telling differences from other books in the field. I assume that students in an introductory course in public administration don't want to learn about the profession only in the abstract, but are interested in influencing the operations of public agencies, as a manager from the inside or as a citizen from the outside. They want to acquire the skills necessary to changing things for the better. It is thus important that the text introduce students to the scholarly literature of public administration, but also help them develop the insights and abilities that will make them more effective and responsible actors. This book contains a good deal of material that is basic to working in or with public organizations; at the same time, the discussion attends to the complex and often confounding values that distinguish work in the public sector. Most significant, however, is the focus on the technical expertise and interpersonal skills that are crucial to effecting change in public organizations.

    I give balanced attention to the work of managers at all levels of government, and in nonprofit organizations. Although the federal government is a powerful model for the study of public administration, managers of state and local agencies are important actors in the governmental process, and their work is acknowledged and examined as well. Similarly, I show how managers of associations, nonprofit and "third sector" organizations, and even traditionally private organizations are now confronting the same issues faced by administrators in the public sector. In fact, I use the term "public organizations" to describe all such groups.

    In *Public Administration: An Action Orientation* students will find (1) a broad base of knowledge about public agencies at all levels: history, structure, and operation; (2) extensive discussion of the moral and political context of public organizations; and (3) new material and fresh perspectives on the real world of public administration. Again, most important is *action*, the actual experiences of administrators, and the skills necessary to success in that arena.

    In this text I talk about action, but I also invite students to act. At the end of each chapter are self-diagnostic material and exercises (cases, simulations, discussion points, and so on) designed to supplement students' cognitive learning with behavioral practice. These activities impart a sense not only of what public administration looks like to the impartial observer, but also what it *feels like* to the manager

ix

or private individual engaged in public action. Students have opportunities to test, practice, and improve their skills. Each chapter also contains a list of key terms and definitions (which reappear in the Glossary), and recommendations for further reading.

There are very exciting possibilities in public administration today. Working to solve important public problems, sensing the human drama involved in such work, and gaining the satisfaction of doing something really worthwhile make being involved in public organizations quite fascinating. The perspective I have adopted here, focusing on the experiences of people acting in the real world of public organizations and on the skills needed for managerial success, permits a lively and interesting presentation of the field. I particularly hope to convey, in a personal and direct manner, the challenges and rewards of public service.

Acknowledgments

Many people contributed to this book. From my work with members of the American Society for Public Administration, I gained special appreciation of the complexity of public management and of the dedication and hard work required for public service. I hope I have conveyed the commitment and concern that guide the work of the best public managers in the country; they deserve great credit and tremendous respect. My colleagues in the Department of Public Administration at the University of Missouri–Columbia were a great source of help and support; I especially acknowledge the contributions of Stan Botner and Ed Jennings. Kathy Denhardt and Allen Bluedorn contributed material in Chapters 4, 10, and 11; their help was invaluable.

For the past decade I've had the pleasure of working with Lil Lynn, a real professional whose work continues to amaze me; her contribution to the preparation of the manuscript was superb as always. Along the way, I was assisted in various ways by Norma Meyer, Ken Wilson, Jana Knudson, and especially Juli Schmidt. Cindy Stormer, Penelope Sky, and others at Brooks/Cole have been delightful colleagues throughout the project. Finally, I want to express my appreciation to those who reviewed drafts of the text and made useful suggestions: Robert Bartlett, Purdue University; Dennis Daley, North Carolina State University; Mark Huddleston, University of Delaware; Arthur Johnson, University of Maryland–Baltimore; Richard C. Kearney, University of Connecticut; J. Edward Kellough, University of Georgia; Harvey Lieber, American University; Wilbur Rich, Wayne State University; William West, Texas A & M University; and Gordon Whitaker, University of North Carolina–Chapel Hill.

While I have been going forward with this work, others have provided balance in my life, and their help in maintaining my sanity should be acknowledged. I especially want to say thanks for the warmth and support of the poets and pickers of the Tyree Basement String Band; I've never met a better group of people, except for our neighbors on Hickory Hill. Most important is a special word of recognition to the family: to Kathy, who keeps it all together, and to two great kids, Michael and Cari. We did it!

Permissions

Several parts of this book were adapted from my previously published works. The material on strategic planning in Chapter Seven was revised from "Strategic Planning in State and Local Government," *State and Local Government Review, 17* (Winter, 1985), 174–179. By permission of the Carl Vinson Institute of Government, University of Georgia. A part of Chapter Eight originally appeared as "Implementing Quality Circles in State Government," *Public Administration Review, 47* (July–August, 1987), 304–309 (with James Pyle and Allen Bluedorn). © 1987 by the American Society for Public Administration. All rights reserved. Chapter Twelve draws on material from "Image and Integrity in the Public Service," *Public Administration Review, 49* (January–February, 1989), 74–77 (with Edward T. Jennings, Jr.), and "Frontiers of Public Service," *American Review of Public Administration, 16* (March, 1988), 1–7.

Robert B. Denhardt

PART ONE

THE
EXPERIENCE
OF
PUBLIC
ADMINISTRATION

PERSONAL
ACTION
IN
PUBLIC
ORGANIZATIONS

Public administration is concerned with the management of public programs. Public administrators work at all levels of government, both at home and abroad, and they manage not-for-profit organizations, associations, and interest groups of all kinds. The substantive fields within which public managers work range across the varied interests of government and public affairs, from defense and national security to social welfare and environmental quality, from the design and construction of roads and bridges to the exploration of space, and from taxation and financial administration to personnel and human resources management. Though public administration varies tremendously in its scope and substance, however, those who work in public organizations share certain commitments. Among these, none is more important than a commitment to *public service.*

In this book, we will examine the work of public administrators in many different kinds of organizations. We will seek a clear understanding of the political and historical context within which public organizations operate; we will examine the commitments that underlie the notion of public service and the opportunities and constraints they place on public action; we will examine the many technical fields, such as planning, budgeting, personnel, and evaluation, with which public administrators must be familiar; and we will consider the personal and interpersonal talents needed by successful public managers. Most importantly, we will emphasize the knowledge, skills, and values that *you* will need to be both effective and responsible as you act in the public interest.

Although we will introduce you to many different areas of public administration, we will do so from a particular point of view that will provide a unifying theme in our examination of administrative work in public organizations. Briefly stated, that point of view is that there is something very special about public administration—that your work in public organizations is distinguished by its pursuit of democratic values and that this concern affects nearly everything you do as a public manager. As a public administrator, you are obligated not only to achieve efficiency and effectiveness, but to be responsive to the many bodies that help define the public interest—elected officials, members of the legislature, client or constituent groups, and the public generally. This special obligation requires that you be ever mindful of managerial concerns, political concerns, and ethical concerns, and that you develop structures and processes that take into account all three. The result is a particularly complicated approach to getting things done, but one that has special rewards. From service to the public, you may gain a very special sense of accomplishment and personal satisfaction, one that comes from helping others and from pursuing the public interest.

WHY STUDY PUBLIC ADMINISTRATION?

Students come to introductory courses in public administration for many different reasons. Many students recognize the vast array of positions in government (and elsewhere) that require training in public administration and hope that the course will provide some of the basic information and skills that will move them toward careers as public managers. These students seek to understand the field of public administration, but also to sharpen their own skills as potential administrators.

Other students, whose interests lie in technical fields as wide-ranging as engineering, teaching, natural resources, social work, and the fine arts, recognize that at some point in their careers their jobs may involve management in the public sector. The engineer may become director of a public works department, the teacher may become school principal, the natural resources expert may be asked to run an environmental quality program, the social worker may administer a welfare program, the fine arts major may direct a publicly supported gallery or museum. In these cases and others like them, the individual's technical expertise may need to be complemented by managerial training.

Other students may have no expectation whatever of working in a public agency, but recognize that, either as corporate executives, as business people, or merely as citizens, they are likely to be called upon to interact with those in public organizations. Someone who owns a small business might wish to sell products or services to a city, a county, or some other governmental body; partners in an accounting firm might seek auditing contracts with a local or state government; a construction firm might bid on the design and construction of a new public building. In each case, knowledge of the operations of public agencies would not only be helpful, it would be essential.

A final group of students, a group overlapping with any of the previous three, might simply recognize the importance of public agencies in the governmental process and the impact of public organizations on their daily lives. They might wish to acquire the knowledge and skills that would enable them to more effectively analyze and influence public policy. Some will find the world of public administration a fascinating field of

4

study in its own right and pursue academic careers in public affairs. Because understanding the motives for studying public administration will also give us a more complete view of the variety and the importance of managerial work in the public sector, we will examine each in greater detail.

Preparing for Administrative Positions

You may be among those who wish to use the introductory public administration course as a stepping-stone to a career in the public service. If so, you will find that these careers take many forms; for example, we sometimes make distinctions among program managers, staff managers, and policy analysts. **Program managers** range from the executive level to the supervisory level and are in charge of particular governmental programs, such as those in environmental quality or transportation safety. Their job is to allocate and monitor human, material, and financial resources to meet the service objectives of their agency. **Staff managers,** on the other hand, support the work of program managers through budgeting and financial management, personnel and labor relations, and purchasing and procurement. Meanwhile, **policy analysts** provide important information about existing programs through their research into the operations and impacts of the programs; moreover, analysts help bring together information about new programs, assess the possible effects of different courses of action, and suggest new directions for public policy. Managers and analysts may work with the chief executive, with the legislature, with officials at other levels of government, and with the public in framing and reframing public programs.

5

As we will see, the work of public organizations also encompasses a wide variety of substantive areas. Think for a moment of the range of activities the federal government engages in; as we see in Box 1.1, the federal government touches upon nearly every aspect of American life, from aeronautics to waste management to help for the homeless. In each area, skilled managers are called upon to develop, to implement, and to evaluate government programs. But the work of managers at the federal level represents only a part of the work of those trained in public administration.

BOX 1.1

SOME AREAS OF
FEDERAL INVOLVEMENT

Abaca production and sale, abortion, adult education, advertising, aeronautics, age discrimination and aging, agency procurement, aging persons, agriculture, including the subsidization and regulation of the production of specific crops, marketing, and

(continued)

(continued)

farmers in general, air pollution, air transportation, alcohol, alcohol and tobacco, alcohol fuels, alcoholism, aliens, allergies and infectious diseases, apprenticeship programs, architecture, armed forces and defense, arthritis, the arts, astronomy, athletics, atmospheric sciences, atomic energy, auto and no-fault insurance, automobiles, and aviation.

Balance of payments, banks and financial institutions, battle monuments, bilingual education, biology, birds, bituminous coal, the blind, blood, boating safety, bonds, botany, breakfast and school lunch programs, broadcasting and films, building of dams, business, and business and tax law.

Cable television, campaign financing, capital punishment, career education, census, chemistry, child development, child nutrition, children, cities, citizenship education, civil defense, civil rights, claims against the government, coal, coast guard, coins and currency, college accreditation, colleges and community development, community and conservation of soil, construction, consumer affairs, consumer education, copyrights, corporations, corrections, cosmetics, cost of living, cotton, credit practices, crime, and customs and tariffs.

Dairy industry, dance, data processing and telecommunications, day care, the deaf, defense policy, dental health, design arts, disability, disadvantaged education, disadvantaged persons, disarmament and arms control, disaster assistance and federal insurance, discrimination, and drugs.

Earthquakes, economic development assistance, economic growth and stability, the economy, education, electric power, emergencies, emergency preparedness, employment, energy, energy use (conservation, engineering, environmental quality), equal opportunity, equal rights (minorities, women, equal time/fairness doctrine), exchange programs, exports, and extradition.

Fabrics, families, families with dependent children, family planning and population, farm supplies, federal aid to states, fellowships, fertilizer, financial aid to students, firearms, fire prevention and control, fish, fishing/law of the sea, fish resources, fitness, flammable products, floods, folk and nature arts, food and nutrition, food stamps, foreign investment, foreign policy, foreign trade impact, forest and rangeland resources, and freedom of information.

Genealogy, general insurance, geographic names, geology and earth sciences, geothermal energy, gifted and talented education, gold and precious metals, government contracts, government personnel, government publications, government recordkeeping, grain, grazing, and gun control.

The handicapped, handicapped employment, handicapped-learning disabilities education, hazardous and solid waste, hazardous substances, health, health maintenance organizations, health planning, health research, highways, historic preservation, holidays and celebrations, the homeless, hospitals, housing, housing construction standards and materials, housing (government assisted), human rights, and hydroelectric power.

Icebreakers, immigration and naturalization, imports, Indians, insects, intergovernmental relations, internal affairs, internal security, international communications, international education, international law, international organizations, international trade, international trade and cooperation, interstate compacts, and irrigation.

Judicial appointments, justice, juvenile delinquency, and juvenile justice.

Labeling and packaging, labor, labor-management policy, land, land resources, law enforcement, libraries and information science, livestock, and loans.

7

Mail, maintenance of an air force, malpractice, manpower, maps, maritime activities, maritime safety, maritime transportation, mathematical, computer, and physical sciences, mediation, medical and medicare, medical matters, mental health, mentally retarded, metabolic and digestive diseases, metal resources, Mexicans, migrant and seasonal farm workers, migrants, military assistance, military history, mine leasing, mineral resources, minimum wages, mining health and safety, minorities, minority business, mortgage banking, motor vehicles, motor vehicle transportation, museum programs, and music.

Narcotics, national debt, national forests, national health insurance, national parks, naval matters, newsmen's privilege, nuclear energy, nuclear weapons and power, and nutrition.

Occupational health and safety, oceanography, ocean resources, oceans, offshore resources, oil, oil shale and tar sands, organized crime, outdoor recreation, outer continental shelf, outer space, and overseas investment.

Pardons, parks and recreation, passports, patents, copyrights and trademarks, pay and employee benefits, pensions and retirement, physical education, physically handicapped, pipelines, plants, policy, pollution, postal service, power, prayer in schools, prenatal, maternal, and child health care, prices, print media,

(continued)

(continued)

private radio services, product safety and testing, public and subsidized housing, and public utilities.

Radiation, radiation protection, radio and television, railroad transportation, rat control, reading, reclamation of sand, refugees and repatriated Americans, rent, retirement and survivors' benefits, revenue sharing, rights for mental patients, rivers, rubber, and rural areas.

Safety and health, satellite communications, savings, scholarships, sexual assault and domestic violence, small business, social sciences, stamps, standards and measures, statistical data and projections, stocks, bonds, and securities, subversive activities, sugar, and supply shortages and industrial production.

Tariffs and taxes, taxes, teachers' education, technology, telephone and telegraph, textiles, theatre, tobacco, tourism, trade, trademarks, transportation, and treaties and executive agreements.

Underemployment, unemployment, unemployment benefits, unions, urban planning, and urban redevelopment and relocation.

Veterans, visual arts, visual disorders, vocational affairs, and vocational education.

Wages, wage standards, war, waste management, water, water quality, waterways, weather, weights and measures, welfare, welfare recipients, wildlife and marine mammals, women, and workers compensation.

Youth.

Zoology.

SOURCE: Adapted from the U.S. Government Manual, Washington, D.C., 1989.

At the state and local levels, even more opportunities exist. As we will see in chapter 2, whereas there is only one federal government in this country, there are over eighty thousand state and local governments! (These include cities, counties, and special districts.) Consequently, state and local government employment in this country amounts to over thirteen million persons (compared to just under three million civilians employed at the federal level).

Obviously, the work of government at the state and local levels is different from that at the federal level. State and local governments, for example, do not directly provide for the national defense; however, most have police forces, which the federal government does not. There are also positions at the state and local levels that do not have exact counterparts at the federal level. For example, consider the president or chancellor of your state university—a public administrator with significant and unusual responsibilities— or consider the city manager in a local community, a professional administrator appointed by a city council to manage the various functions of local government.

Work in public organizations, however, is not limited to work in government. Beyond working in federal, state, or local government, those trained in public administration will find many other opportunities. Directors of nonprofit organizations at the state and local levels, as well as those in similar associations at the national level, often find that the skills required for their jobs—skills that combine managerial training with an understanding of the political system—are the skills developed in public administration courses. Again, to demonstrate the breadth of these activities, we might note that there are large numbers of nonprofit associations at the national level alone, ranging from well-known groups like the American Medical Association or the American Bar Association, to trade groups such as the American Frozen Food Institute and the National Association of Bedding Manufacturers, to professional associations such as the American Society for Public Administration and those representing a particular field of interest, such as the Metropolitan Opera Guild. There is even an association of association executives—the American Society of Association Executives! Beyond these groups at the national level, there are numerous nonprofit groups operating at state and local levels; examples include the local United Way organization, an art league, or a historic preservation group.

Finally, those with training in public administration may work in a private corporation's public affairs division. Because of the increasing interaction between business and government, corporations often need special assistance in tracking legislation, developing and monitoring government contracts, and influencing the legislative or regulatory process. Thus, the combination of managerial and political skills possessed by someone with training in public administration can be highly valuable. The career possibilities in the field of public administration are seemingly endless.

Combining Technical and Managerial Training

Many students seek positions in the public service as a primary career objective, but there are many others who see the possibility of work in public administration as secondary to their main field of interest, but nonetheless important. As noted, the work of government spans many areas; consequently, the people who work for government (one out of every six people in this country) come from a wide variety of professional backgrounds. There are engineers who work in the Defense Department and for NASA at the federal level, in state highway departments, and in local public works departments. There are persons interested in natural resources who work for the U.S. Forest Service and the Environmental Protection Agency, in state conservation departments, and local parks departments. There are medical personnel who work for the Veterans Administration or the National Institute for Mental Health, for state health departments, and for local hospitals and health offices.

Governments at all levels hire social workers, planners, personnel specialists, accountants, lawyers, biologists, law enforcement officers, educators, researchers, recreation specialists, and agricultural specialists, just to mention a few. To illustrate the magnitude of government employment of technical specialists, some 154,000 engineers and architects, 134,000 medical personnel, and 123,000 accountants and budget specialists work for the federal government alone.

People who have worked for some time within a technical field in a public organization are often promoted to managerial positions. A surgeon may become Chief of Surgery, a water pollution specialist may be asked to direct a pollution control project, or a teacher may become a school principal. Despite having started out in a technical field, these individuals find themselves in a managerial position; they are public administrators. Some people may desire promotion to a managerial position; others may not. (There are some jurisdictions in which continued advancement practically requires moving to an administrative position.) But whatever one's motivation, a new administrator soon discovers a completely new world of work. Now the most pressing questions are not the technical ones, but rather those having to do with program planning and budgeting, with supervision and motivation, with balancing scarce resources. Often the situation is quite bewildering; it's almost as if one has been asked to change professions in midcareer— from technical expert to public manager.

The fact that so many people from technical fields eventually find themselves in managerial positions in the public sector has led many of them to seek training in public administration. For this reason, it is no longer unusual for students majoring in technical fields to take courses in public administration or for students to combine undergraduate training in a technical field with graduate training in public administration (even at midcareer). This, then, is a second reason for studying public administration—to prepare for the eventuality that work in a technical field of interest might lead you to a managerial position in the public sector.

10

Interaction of Business and Government

Even for students who never work for a public agency of any type, understanding the processes of policy formulation and implementation can be enormously helpful. One of the most important trends in American society is the increasing interaction of business and government. Clearly, the decisions of government affect the environment within which business operates, but government also specifically regulates many businesses, and, of course, serves as the biggest single customer of business.

Those in business recognize that governmental decisions affect the economic climate. Most obvious are the effects of governmental decisions at the federal level; note, for example, the impact of government economic pronouncements on the stock market. But state and local governments also affect the business climate. The governors of many states have begun major campaigns to attract industry to their states, providing not only information and advice, but specific incentives for plants and industries that might relocate. Similar activities are being undertaken in more and more local communities, as cities recognize that they are in competition for economic development. At a minimum, business recognizes that the political climate of any locality directly affects the area's economic climate.

But the influence of government on business is more specific. At the federal level, major regulatory agencies, such as the Federal Communications Commission and the Federal Trade Commission, provide specific guidelines within which certain businesses must operate. Moreover, requirements of agencies such as the Environmental Protection Agency and the Occupational Safety and Health Administration restrict the operations of business so as to assure the quality of air and water and the safety of working conditions. Similarly, at the state level, some agencies directly regulate specific businesses, while others act more generally to prevent unfair or unsafe practices. Even at the local level, through licensing and zoning practices, public organizations directly regulate business practice.

Government is also important as a consumer of business products and services. At the federal level, over $116 billion is spent each year on goods and services; in the Defense Department alone, the figure is over $85 billion per year. Similarly, at the state and local levels, expenditures for products and services amount to $176 billion. Business is attentive to its customers, so it is not surprising that business is attentive to government!

For all these reasons, people in business are becoming increasingly aware of the need to understand in detail the work of government—how policies are made, how they are implemented, and how they may be influenced. Not only are more and more businesses developing public affairs offices to specialize in governmental operations, to track policy developments, and to try to influence policy, but they are placing a greater premium upon having executives at all levels who understand how government agencies operate. Even if you plan a career in business, understanding the work of public organizations is an essential part of your training.

Influencing Public Organizations

Any of the motives for studying public administration we have discussed so far may bring you to an introductory course; however, there is another more general reason you may wish to study public administration—to understand one important aspect of the governmental process so as to be able to deal effectively with public issues that directly affect your life. We are all affected by the work of government, so it is helpful, and sometimes even essential, to understand the operations of public organizations.

We have become so accustomed to the pervasiveness of government and the range of its influence that we sometimes forget just how often our lives are touched by government. Imagine a typical day: we awake in the morning to the sounds of a commercially regulated radio station or National Public Radio coming over a patented and FCC–registered clock radio operating on power supplied either by a government regulated power company or by a public utility. We brush our teeth with toothpaste produced under a government patent and trust that it has been judged safe (if not effective) by a federal agency. We use municipally operated water and sewer systems without thinking of the complexity of their operation. We dress in clothes produced under governmental restrictions and eat food prepared in accord with government regulations and inspected by the government. We drive on a public highway, following government enforced traffic laws, to a university substantially funded by federal, state, and sometimes local dollars to study from books copyrighted and catalogued by the Library of Congress. Though the day has hardly started, our lives have been already touched by government in many, many ways.

The importance of government and public administration in daily life is tremendous; consequently, the decisions made by governmental officials (and not just elected officials) can affect us quite directly. Imagine, for example, that one day you discover that the loan program that is helping to finance your college education is being reviewed and will likely be revised in such a way that you will no longer be eligible for funding. In such a case, you might well want to take some action to try to maintain your eligibility.

Obviously, knowing something about the operations of government agencies, especially some of the ways administrative decisions can be influenced, would be of great help.

As citizens affected by government, understanding the operations of public organizations is helpful; it is even more important if one becomes personally involved in some aspect of the governmental process. For those reading this book, such involvement is actually rather likely. Indeed, if you are a college graduate, regardless of your field of interest, chances are quite good that at some point in your life you will engage in some kind of formal governmental activity. You may be elected to local, state, or national office; you may be asked to serve on a board or commission; or your advice concerning government operations in your area may be sought in other ways. You may also become involved in the work of nonprofit organizations or charities in your local community. In any of these cases, a thorough knowledge of the structure and processes of public organizations, both government and nonprofit organizations, will be of great importance.

Finally, those who are interested in understanding the work of public organizations may indeed find the field of public administration interesting from a more academic standpoint: studying and commenting upon the operations of government and nonprofit organizations contribute to our understanding of the process of policy development and support the work of those in public organizations. The opportunities for academic careers in public administration—positions involving teaching and research—are many, and you may find yourself drawn to those opportunities; even here, however, one begins with a concern for action.

Making Things Happen

Of the many reasons to learn about public organizations, one theme seems to tie together the various interests—an interest in making things happen. Whether you are preparing for a career in the public sector, covering the possibility that you might someday manage a public agency, or simply preparing to affect the course of public policy and its implementation as it directly affects you or your business, your interest is in taking action, in influencing what goes on in public organizations. It's one thing to gain knowledge of the field in the abstract; most students want to learn those things that will make them more effective *actors* in the governmental process.

This book is oriented toward action, toward how to make things happen in public organizations. Our perspective will be that of the actor not the scholar, although an understanding of the world of administrative action is the basis for good scholarship as well. Action first requires a base of knowledge; there are certain things that you simply need to know about government and the administrative process to be effective. There are also value questions that must be settled in the course of making and carrying out public decisions. And, finally, there are both technical and interpersonal skills you must acquire to be effective in working with others in your chosen field. Selecting an action orientation, therefore, commits you to emphasizing all three areas—the knowledge, values, and skills that will help you to become more effective and responsible in your work in and with "real life" public organizations.

WHAT IS PUBLIC ADMINISTRATION?

We have described public administration as the management of public programs; to elaborate on this definition, it helps to know a little history. Happily, there's only a little history to learn, for public administration—at least in the U.S.—is a relatively new field of study. Of course, people have been engaged in the management of public programs for thousands of years (imagine, for example, the administrative headaches involved in building the Egyptian pyramids!). The self-conscious study of public administration is a fairly recent development, however, often dated to the work of French and German scholars in the late nineteenth century.

Public administration as we know it today in the U.S. began as the study of government administration, and that study began as part of late-nineteenth century efforts to reform governmental operations. Most scholars and practitioners date the beginnings of the study of public administration to an 1887 essay by Woodrow Wilson. While some have recently questioned Wilson's influence on the field, there is no question his essay marks the symbolic beginning of American public administration.

Wilson's essay was basically reformist in nature and highly practical. It was designed to address the inefficiency and open corruption that had become a part of government during the late 1880s and to suggest certain remedies within the administration of government. Wilson argued that, whereas scholars and practitioners had focused on political institutions (such as Congress or the presidency), too little attention had been paid to administrative questions, the questions of how the government actually operates. The result, according to Wilson, was that it was becoming "harder to run a constitution than to frame one" (Wilson, 1887, p. 200).

Wilson's recommendations involved first isolating the processes of administration from the potentially corrupting influences of politics, then conducting the administration of government following the model of business. With respect to the first issue, Wilson wrote, "Administration lies outside the proper sphere of politics. Administrative questions are not political questions. Although politics sets the tasks for administration, it should not be suffered to manipulate its offices" (Wilson, 1887, p. 210). In other words, although policies were to be debated and decided by politicians, they were to be carried out by a politically neutral, professional bureaucracy. In this way, the everyday conduct of government would be isolated from the potentially corrupting influence of politics.

But Wilson also wanted the work of government agencies to be accomplished more effectively. He felt that such organizations would operate best if they pursued the private sector's commitment to efficient or "businesslike" operations. Wilson, of course, wrote during a period in which business, industry, and technology were developing in rapid and surprising new ways. Like others, he admired the managerial philosophies that business seemed to be developing. Among these notions, Wilson particularly favored the idea of concentrating power in a single authority atop a highly integrated and centralized administrative structure. His recommendation of a strong chief executive has been echoed by writers (and chief executives!) even to the present.

The men and women who followed Wilson in discussions of what came to be called public administration were practical people, concerned with reforming governmental structures and making them more efficient. But they were also careful to place these concerns within the context of democratic government. How might the principles of democracy, including such lofty ideals as liberty and justice, be extended throughout government and throughout society? Indeed, Leonard D. White, one of the most thoughtful of the early writers, commented that "the study of public administration . . . needs to be related to the broad generalizations of political theory concerned with such matters as justice, liberty, obedience, and the role of the state in human affairs" (White, 1948, p. 10).

The Values of Democracy

Nothing more clearly affects the work of those in public organizations than their commitment to democratic values. For this reason, it is helpful to review some of the key commitments we associate with democratic governance. The term *democracy* well reflects its roots—the Greek words *demos*, meaning *people*, and *kratis*, meaning *authority*. Generally, **democracy** refers to a political system in which the interests of the people at large prevail. It is clear, however, that within these broad parameters there are many different conceptions of democracy. As one illustration, at the end of World War II, when representatives of the U.S., Great Britain, France, and Russia met to consider the "democratization" of Germany, it soon became apparent that the Russian idea of democracy was quite different from the Western view. Whereas Westerners associated democracy with ideas such as free elections, freedom of the press, freedom of movement, and the freedom to criticize the government, the Russians had quite a different conception. For them, democracy did not necessarily mean government by or of the people, but rather, whether government policy is carried out *in the interest* of the people.

Even today, *democracy* is used in many different ways by many different people. Yet, in the American experience, there is general agreement that democracy refers to a political system—a way of ordering power and authority—in which decision-making power is widely shared among members of the society. Or, to put it in terms of control, democracy is a system in which many ordinary citizens exercise a high degree of control over their leaders. (In either case, the opposite would be **oligarchy**—government by the few—or **autocracy**—government by one.)

But democracy is defined not only in terms of processes or procedures but by several important cultural values that are typically pursued in a democratic society. Among these, three have been of special importance to those who have helped shape the American idea of democracy. The first is **individualism,** the idea that the dignity and integrity of the individual is of supreme importance. Individualism suggests that achieving the fullest potential of each individual is the best measure of the success of our political system. It is the idea of individualism that is reflected in the familiar phrasing of the Declaration of Independence—that all persons are endowed by their Creator with certain inalienable rights and that it is the purpose of government to secure those rights.

Second is the idea of **equality**—not the notion that all persons are equal in talents or possessions, but that each individual has an equal claim to life, liberty, and the pursuit of happiness. In this view, each person should be seen as an end, not a means; no one should be merely a tool of another. Moreover, equality in the field of government would suggest that differences in wealth or position are not sufficient reasons for giving one group preference over another. In a democracy, each one has an equal claim to the attention of the system and should be able to expect just outcomes.

14

A third central value of a democratic society is **liberty** or *freedom*—the concept that the individual citizen of a democracy should have a high degree of self-determination. You should have the maximum opportunity to select your own purposes in life and to choose the means to accomplish these. Liberty is more than just the absence of constraints; it suggests the freedom to act positively in pursuit of one's own ends. Only by allowing individuals the freedom to choose, it is argued, will social progress occur. Whereas authoritarian regimes are static and unchanging, those that value liberty are creative and dynamic.

Contrasting Business and Public Administration

Obviously, work in public organizations is guided by commitments to democratic ideals. But because it also involves management, public administration is often confused with business management. Indeed, such confusion has occasionally been quite prominent in the field of public administration. (As we have already seen, early writers in the field often suggested that government should become more like business, a phrase heard even today.) Certainly there are similarities between business and public administration: managers in both sectors are involved in questions of organizational design, allocation of scarce resources, and management of people. But most observers agree that the context of public management significantly alters the work itself (see Box 1.2). Three differences are most apparent: ambiguity, pluralistic decision making, and visibility.

15

BOX 1.2

PUBLIC SERVICE: A DISTINGUISHED PROFESSION

"I want to echo the words of President Bush when he delivered the first speech of his presidency, most appropriately, to a government employee group in Washington this past January. 'Government service is a noble calling and a public trust,' the President said. '. . . There is no higher honor than to serve free men and women, no greater privilege than to labor in government. . . . You work hard, you sacrifice, you deserve to be recognized, rewarded, and appreciated.'

"For my part, when I think of government service, in uniform and out, I think of individual men and women of genuine distinction who have served this country over the years—and also of the amazing diversity of a service that can range from defending our borders to delivering our mail, curing disease to

(continued)

(continued)

exploring outer space. I was looking at a civil service publication the other day containing an alphabetical list of well known employees through the years . . . and found it began with a career civil servant named Neil Armstrong who went on TDY to the moon . . . and concluded several pages later with Walt Whitman, the poet, who worked in the Department of the Interior and the U.S. Attorney General's office. How's that for diversity?

"Incidentally, the group also included four Nobel Prize winners and several important inventors, including Alexander Graham Bell, who among his other associations worked for the Census Bureau. There also were some other familiar names of people who shared your proud profession: Clara Barton, Washington Irving, Abraham Lincoln, Charles Lindbergh, Knute Rockne, Harry Truman, and James Whistler, to name but a few.

"In my own experience, as one who served the federal government for some years, I look back on those periods as among the most exciting, challenging, and thoroughly demanding in my life. I have often said, and still say, that I never worked harder than I did in my years as a public servant. I worked alongside some of the finest, most competent, thoroughly committed people I have ever known. I realize this does not comport with everything that you read in the papers or see on television— but I never miss a chance to point it out.

"My own experience in government left me with an abiding respect for the men and women who serve this nation as public employees."

SOURCE: Norman R. Augustine, Chairman and Chief Executive Officer of Martin Marietta Corporation. Address to the Federal Executive Board, Denver, Colorado, April 26, 1989. Text provided by The Council for Excellence in Government, Washington, D.C.

16

Ambiguity   A first difference between government and business lies in the purposes to be served. In most businesses, even those with service objectives, the bottom line— profit—is the basic measure for evaluating how good a job the organization is doing. In turn, the performance of individual managers can, in many cases, be directly measured in terms of their units' contribution to the overall profit of the company. The same is not true in public agencies, where the organizations' objectives may be much more ambiguous and where making or losing money is not the main criterion for success or failure.

The objectives of public organizations are often stated in terms of service; for example, an agency's mission may be to protect the quality of the environment or to provide an adequate level of rehabilitative services to the disabled. Yet such service objectives are much harder to specify and to measure. What does "quality" mean with respect to the environment? What level of service to the disabled is "adequate"? The difficulty of specifying objectives such as these makes it harder to assess the performance of government agencies and, in turn, their managers. Moreover, most businesses would not tolerate a money-losing operation in a depressed area, but a public organization, though equally attentive to the money being spent, might well consider meeting a human need in an area more important than the financial "bottom-line."

Pluralistic decision making   A second difference between work in government and in business is the fact that government, at least in a democratic society, requires that many groups and individuals have access to the decision process. As a result, decisions that one individual or a small group might quickly make in a business may, in a public organization, require input from many diverse groups and organizations. Consequently, it is difficult to speak of specific decision centers in government. W. Michael Blumenthal, a business executive who became Secretary of the Treasury in the Carter administration, described the situation in this way:

> If the President said to me, you develop (an economic policy toward Japan), Mike, the moment that becomes known there are innumerable interest groups that begin to play a role. The House Ways and Means Committee, the Senate Finance Committee, and every member on them and every staff member has an opinion and seeks to exert influence. Also the Foreign Relations Committee, the oversight committees, and then the interest groups, business, the unions, the State Department, the Commerce Department, OMB, Council of Economic Advisers, and not only the top people, but all their staff people, not to speak of the President's staff and the entire press. (Blumenthal, 1983, p. 30)

The pluralistic nature of governmental decision making has led many business executives who have worked in government to comment that this feature of the public service makes government management much more difficult than management in the private sector. But, as Blumenthal points out, "the diversity of interests seeking to affect policy is the nature and essence of democratic government" (Blumenthal, 1983, pp. 30–31). Many have also found this aspect of government service particularly challenging and rewarding.

Visibility   Finally, managers in government seem to operate with much greater visibility than their counterparts in industry. The work of government in a democratic society is subject to constant scrutiny by the press and by the public. Donald Rumsfeld, another who has worked in both government and business, once commented that "In government, you are operating in a goldfish bowl. You change your mind or make a blunder, as human beings do, and it's on the front page of every newspaper" (Rumsfeld, 1983, p. 36). Media coverage of everything one does may be a mixed blessing. On the one hand, media coverage enables organization leaders to communicate rapidly to both external and internal audiences; on the other hand, the media's constant scrutiny of policy positions and their labeling inconsistencies as weaknesses can somewhat limit free discussion of issues in the formulation stage. And, of course, press intrusions into even the most mundane personal matters can be excessive; one local newspaper reported that a new city manager who had just moved to the community was having a problem with his new refrigerator! Yet executives in government realize that it is essential to a democratic society that their work be visible to the public and subject to the interest and control of the citizenry.

An Action Orientation to Public Administration

With this background, we can now think more carefully about how the field of public administration has traditionally been described and how we might develop an action orientation toward its study. In terms of definition, many early writers spoke of administration as a function of government, something that occurred in many shapes and forms throughout government. There were obviously administrative activities performed in the executive branch, but there were also administrative functions performed in the legislative and judicial branches. Some even noted that, from time to time, any single official might engage in both legislative and administrative functions.

Somewhat later, public administration came to be viewed as concerned merely with the activities of the executive agencies of government. In the words of an early text, public administration is concerned with the "operations of the administrative branch only" (Willoughby, 1927, p. 1). By the 1950s, such a perspective was so firmly entrenched that the leading textbook of that period stated, "By public administration is meant, in common usage, the activities of the executive branches of national, state, and local governments; independent boards and commissions set up by Congress and state legislatures; government corporations; and certain other agencies of a specialized character" (Simon, Smithburg, & Thompson, 1950, p. 7).

More modern definitions of public administration tend to return to the traditional view, including attention to administrative officials in all branches of government and focusing even on those in nonprofit organizations. For our purposes, a formal definition of the field may be less important than trying to discover how public administration is experienced by those in the "real world" and determining the kinds of activities public administrators engage in and the environmental factors that help to shape their work. We have already seen how the ambiguity of service objectives, the pluralistic nature of governmental decision making, and the visibility of management in the public sector create a context in which managerial work differs significantly from that in other settings. From the standpoint of the "real-world" administrator, the things that really make the difference in how you operate are not whether you are employed by a government agency but rather whether you work under circumstances that feature an ambiguity of objectives, a multiplicity of decision centers, and high public visibility.

These features derive in turn from the simple fact that the public manager is pursuing public purposes. In terms of the public administrator's actions and experiences, therefore, we may say that it is the "publicness" of the work that distinguishes public management from other similar activities. Thus, as a public manager, you must operate with one eye toward managerial effectiveness and the other toward the desires and demands of the public. This view recognizes that you are likely to experience an inevitable tension between efficiency and responsiveness, a tension that will be absolutely central to your work.

Let us point out some of the implications of this orientation. Many commentators point out that the distinction between public and private management is no longer simply between business and government or between profit and service. In fact, more and more frequently, we encounter situations in which traditionally public organizations are pursuing enhanced revenues (profits?) and traditionally private organizations are concerned with providing services. What is important is not merely what is sought, but whose interest is served. On this basis, a private enterprise would be one in which private interests privately arrived at are paramount; a public organization, on the other hand, would be one in which public interests publicly arrived at are paramount.

There is a trend in our society for greater openness and responsiveness on the part of many organizations. Most associations and nonprofit organizations would fit this mold, and managers in those organizations must certainly be attentive to both efficiency and responsiveness. But many corporations as well are now finding it important to open their decision-making processes to public scrutiny and involvement. The range of public organizations (and the applicability of public management) seems ever increasing.

On the other hand, our understanding of the public manager's role suggests that managers in government agencies could also be pursuing interests other than those of the public. Certainly, those who operate agencies in totalitarian countries could hardly be considered to be pursuing publicly defined values; they would more likely be pursuing the privately defined interests of a political elite. Similarly, we might question from time to time whether all managers in our democratic society have a proper concern for the public interest. When managers pursue their own personal agendas, as in cases of empire-building, we would question the "publicness" of their actions.

We now have a notion of the complexity of work in the public sector—the complexity inherent in the technical work of public agencies, but, even more important, the complexity of the political and ethical context in which public managers operate. Indeed, as noted, this complexity provides a theme that ties together many aspects of your work as a public manager. The way you set objectives, the way you develop budgets and hire personnel, the way you interact with other organizations and with your own clientele, the way you evaluate the success or failure of your programs—all these aspects of your work as a public manager, and many more, are directly affected by the fact that you will be managing in the public interest.

19

WHAT DO PUBLIC ADMINISTRATORS DO?

An action orientation to public administration requires that we focus on what public managers actually do—how they act in "real world" situations. How do they spend their time? What skills do they require to do their work well? What are the rewards and frustrations of public service? From the perspective of the administrator, we can ask: What characterizes the most effective and responsible public management? What are the demands on administrators? What are the satisfactions that public managers draw from their work?

We will approach these issues by concentrating on the skills managers need to accomplish their work. A 1974 article in *Harvard Business Review* provided the first major description of the general types of skills all managers need: conceptual, technical, and human (Katz, 1974).

Conceptual skills include the ability to think abstractly, especially in regard to the manager's concept of the organization. This category also involves the ability to see the organization as a whole, how all the parts or functions work and fit together, and how making a change in one part will affect other parts. Conceptual skills also include the ability to see how the organization, or parts of it, relate to the organization's environment. *Technical skills* refer to an understanding of and proficiency in the methods, processes, and techniques for accomplishing tasks. These are, for example, the skills of an accountant who can conduct an audit or develop an income statement or the skills of a mechanic who can repair an engine. *Human skills* involve the capacity to work effectively as a member of a group, or the ability to get others to work together effectively. ("Others" may include subordinates, superiors, managers at the same level—virtually anyone with whom one might work on a given project or assignment.)

All these skills are important to managers, but not equally important to all managers. Katz makes a strong argument that technical skills are most important to managers at the supervisory level who manage day-to-day operations but become less and less important as the level of management increases. On the other hand, conceptual skills are most important to top-level managers who must deal with the organization as a whole rather than with just one or a few parts of it. Conceptual skills are less important at the middle-management level and least important at the supervisory level.

Human skills, however, maintain a constant, high level of importance; they are critical regardless of one's level. How managers' human skills are employed may vary from level to level (e.g., top managers lead more meetings than supervisory managers), but as a category, human skills remain the one constant for managerial success. In this book, we will consider the knowledge and values associated with public management (conceptual skills), the techniques public managers require in such areas as budgeting and personnel (technical skills), and the personal and interpersonal qualities that help managers work effectively with others (human skills).

An Inventory of Public Management Skills

One way to elaborate on an action approach is to create an inventory of the skills and competencies required for successful public management. There are many ways such an inventory can be constructed; one of the best ways is to talk with public managers about their work. But a number of research studies have sought to identify the skills that are critical to managerial success. Of these studies, research by the federal government's Office of Personnel Management (OPM) is particularly helpful (Flanders & Utterback, 1985). The OPM study was based on information gathered from a large number of highly effective federal managers and produced a description of the broad elements of managerial performance at all levels—supervisory, managerial, and executive. These sets of competencies were divided into two subcategories: (1) management functions (the "what" of management, its content responsibilities) and (2) effectiveness characteristics (the "how" of management, the style found most effective). (See Appendix 1.A at the end of this chapter.)

According to the OPM study, the competencies of public managers include such things as being sensitive to agency policies and national concerns; representing the organization and acting as a liaison to those outside the organization; establishing organizational goals and the processes to carry them out; obtaining and allocating necessary resources to achieve the agency's purposes; effectively utilizing human resources; and monitoring, evaluating, and redirecting the work of the organization. But the OPM researchers recognized that managerial excellence requires not merely doing the job, but doing it well. For this reason, they developed a set of skills, attitudes, and perspectives that seemed to distinguish the work of highly successful managers.

Displaying these characteristics in terms of several concentric circles (see Box 1.3) makes a point about their importance at different organizational levels—that as managers move up the organizational ladder, they must accumulate broader and broader sets of skills. The researchers suggest, for example, that first-line supervisors must apply communication skills, interpersonal sensitivity, and technical competence to assure effective performance on their own part and within the work unit. In addition, their actions must begin to

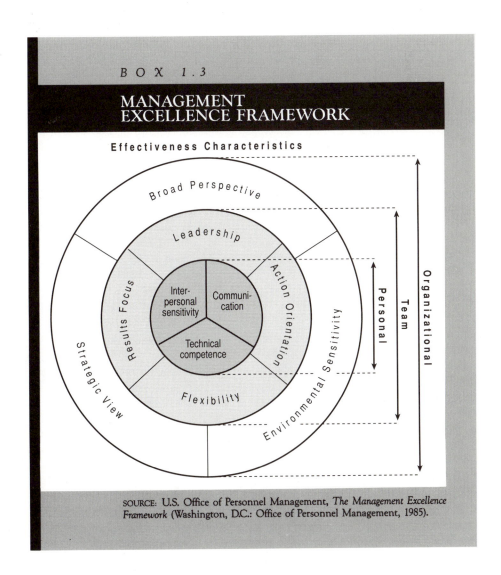

BOX 1.3

MANAGEMENT EXCELLENCE FRAMEWORK

Effectiveness Characteristics

Broad Perspective

Leadership

Action Orientation

Interpersonal sensitivity

Communication

Technical competence

Results Focus

Flexibility

Strategic View

Environmental Sensitivity

Personal

Team

Organizational

SOURCE: U.S. Office of Personnel Management, *The Management Excellence Framework* (Washington, D.C.: Office of Personnel Management, 1985).

21

reflect those characteristics in the next ring—leadership, flexibility, an action orientation, and a focus on results.

Midlevel managers, on the other hand, must demonstrate all these characteristics of effectiveness and begin to acquire the skills listed in the outer ring—a broad perspective, a strategic view, and environmental sensitivity. Executives at the highest levels of government who are responsible for the accomplishment of broad agency objectives must demonstrate the full complement of effectiveness characteristics to be most successful. Clearly, a wide diversity of skills, regardless of how the job is constructed or of the style with which it is executed, will be essential to your success as a public manager.

Voices of Public Administrators

Studies such as that of the OPM are helpful in understanding what you need to know and what you must be able to do to be successful in public management. But how does it actually "feel" to work in a public organization? The best way to answer this question is to let some public administrators speak for themselves. Recently, we spoke to three young professionals in the field of public administration about their views of the field and their feelings about their work. The following accounts are based on those interviews.

Jan C. Perkins is City Manager of Morgan Hill, California. When asked about her motivations for entering the field of public administration, she replied:

"I was interested in improving the quality of life for all people and increasing the access of women and minorities. I believed that I could have the most impact by being involved in local government at a management level.

"The most rewarding aspects of my work have been being able to articulate the mission of the city and focus our resources and efforts in effectively meeting that mission, solving the problems of residents, and seeing employees grow and develop.

"Those considering public service careers should understand that managing in the public arena is different than in a private corporation. It requires a commitment to values of providing quality services for all and dealing with all people on an equal level. It is very important that people who enter the public service do so with a high standard of ethical behavior and an ability to deal honestly and directly with all people."

Michael Stahl works for the federal government in the Environmental Protection Agency:

"I entered public service because I viewed (and still do) government as an instrument to solve social problems. Democratic government can be a tremendous positive force in society, and in spite of recent political rhetoric and prevailing political ideology, I am convinced that the institutions and programs of government are of vital importance to the nation and that public service is a noble calling.

"There is great satisfaction in knowing that your work has made an impact on persons who could only have been helped through the intervention of the government. In my own experience, for example, school children across the country have been helped by elimination of exposure to asbestos in their schools—schools that were unable to remove asbestos materials without federal financial assistance from a program I helped implement. Government service provides opportunities to help people through means that are beyond the capabilities of the private sector.

"If you are considering a career in the public service, take the time to reflect on your motivation for entering the public service, because there are "right" reasons and "wrong" reasons. You are entering for the right reasons if you want to make a contribution to the solution of social problems, promote democratic values and ethical standards on using the powers of government, and if the concept of serving the public good is a passion. You are entering for the wrong reasons if you are looking for public adulation and recognition for your accomplishments, seeking material or financial rewards as compensation for your hard work, or expecting to acquire levels of power and change the world according to your own plan. Those entering for the wrong reasons will be bitterly disappointed. . . . Yet, for those whose passion is to contribute to the public good, government service can represent the single most satisfying way of translating your passion into ideas and events for improving the quality of life for scores of people. Very few professions offer this kind of opportunity and that is why public service will always be an exciting, challenging, and satisfying endeavor."

Cheryle A. Broom is Legislative Auditor for the State of Washington. She describes her reasons for entering the public service:

"I was working in business and felt the need to make a change to a career where my efforts might make more of a difference in terms of addressing public needs. While I had a somewhat idealistic goal to serve the public, I recognized my orientation was not toward professions such as social work or K–12 teaching.

"Problem solving and proposing solutions to significant public issues have been the emphasis of my work. It is particularly rewarding when these efforts influence policy and administrative changes that, hopefully, improve service delivery and cost effectiveness of public programs.

"Individuals with an interest should be encouraged to explore careers in the public service and to develop the skills necessary to be successful in their chosen field. I think it is also important to keep a perspective, i.e., it won't be easy nor will you do it single-handedly, but you can make a difference."

Obviously, these three professionals, as well as Tom Downs, the "public service junkie" (see Box 1.4), take very seriously their commitment to serving others. In making such a

23

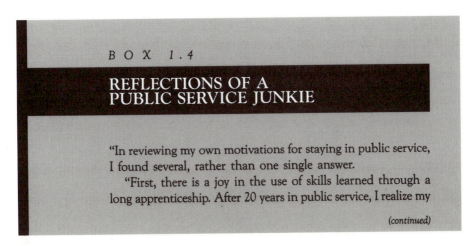

BOX 1.4

REFLECTIONS OF A
PUBLIC SERVICE JUNKIE

"In reviewing my own motivations for staying in public service, I found several, rather than one single answer.

"First, there is a joy in the use of skills learned through a long apprenticeship. After 20 years in public service, I realize my

(continued)

(continued)

skills and abilities were not easily or painlessly acquired. My education in public service has been costly, and I feel an obligation to repay the resources, energy, and interest others have invested in teaching me.

"A second factor is the conviction that the work is important. There is an underlying assumption in public service that we are all part of an effort that leads to a better life for individuals in our society. Public service is ultimately based on the view that the human condition can be improved, an optimism which perhaps forms the core of the motivation for staying in public service. In order to remain in government, you have to believe that your actions can have some small impact on the public good.

"Only in public service can you find the sense of completion that comes from working on a successful program—to reduce infant mortality, for example, and then realizing that 35 more children are alive this year as a result of that effort. Only in public service can you participate in a process that helps move individuals from mental hospitals back into the community. The opportunity to help solve a community problem and then to witness the changes that occur is the cement that binds us to public service.

"A final motivation for public service is the importance of constantly reaffirming the legitimacy and credibility of government services in the public's mind. One vital way to reaffirm our ability to govern ourselves, to control our own fate, is to have government, at all levels, that delivers the services expected of it. This presupposes a cadre of individuals who can understand and manage public institutions. If there is no response when the public demands action, then it confirms our sense of alienation and powerlessness, and we lose our ability to cooperate. If, as public servants, we are rusty, run-down, obsolete tools of government, then there will only be further reaction against the institution of government. The challenge is to be there whether or not we are wanted, to be committed to the public's business whether or not we are noticed, to carry the public trust whether or not we are asked, and to pick up the garbage.

"In the end, regardless of the personal reasons to stay in public service, the process of government demands dedicated professionals to make it work. The ability to continue day-to-day government operations in the face of all difficulties is what public service is about. That ability is what creates a legitimate government, what creates the public trust. If that is too abstract, then let

> us say that public service is about babies living, fires being extinguished, garbage collected, crimes solved, people moved. That is all there is, ever."
>
> SOURCE: Thomas Downs, "Reflections of a Public Service Junkie," *Public Management* 70, (March 1988): 7–8, International City Management Association, Washington, D.C.

commitment, these administrators participate in a long and proud tradition. Indeed, the public service has historically been considered one of the highest callings in our society and has been even more highly regarded in other countries, such as France and Japan.

In the last chapter, we will examine the work of groups such as the American Society for Public Administration's National Campaign for Public Service and the National Commission on the Public Service (the Volcker Commission) to restore an even greater sense of dignity and worth to the idea of public service. For the time being, we should simply note that the idea of serving others has great appeal, in part because of the great joy and satisfaction it brings. Those working in public organizations experience almost daily the rewards of public service.

As noted, our focus will be on the individual administrator or the individual citizen seeking to influence public policy through the agencies of government or through other public organizations. We will consider in some detail the institutions, processes, and techniques required for work in the public sector. But, most importantly, we will examine the "real world" of public administration, the world as it is experienced by the administrator.

That world, as we have seen, is one for which you will need to develop certain capabilities to operate effectively and responsibly. Among these we include an understanding of the institutions and processes of government; an appreciation of the values underlying public service; technical skills in such areas as program design, budgeting, and personnel; interpersonal skills in communications, leadership, and decision making; and a capacity to "put it all together"—to integrate knowledge, skills, and values appropriately.

Ideally, in studying the issues discussed in this book, you will develop a good sense of the political context of public administration; a sound understanding of your role in both policy development and policy implementation; a sensitivity to the moral and ethical questions inherent in the notion of public service; technical competence in such areas as planning and program development, budgeting, personnel, and productivity; facility with interpersonal relationships (including leadership, decision making, and communications), and the self-confidence and self-awareness to act effectively and responsibly in real-life situations. Though public administration in the abstract sometimes appears lifeless and remote, the real world of the practicing public administrator is a quite lively and interesting place, filled with challenging problems and unique opportunities.

TERMS AND DEFINITIONS

Autocracy: Government by one.

Democracy: A political system in which decision-making power is widely shared among members of the society.

Equality: The idea that all persons have an equal claim to life, liberty, and the pursuit of happiness.

Individualism: The idea that the dignity and integrity of the individual is of supreme importance.

Liberty: The idea that individual citizens of a democracy should have a high degree of self-determination.

Oligarchy: Government by the few.

Policy analysts: Persons who provide important information about public programs through research into the operations and impacts of the programs.

Program manager: Persons ranging from the executive level to the supervisory level who are in charge of particular governmental programs.

Public administration: The management of public programs.

Staff managers: Persons who support the work of program managers through budgeting and financial management, personnel and labor relations, purchasing and procurement.

26

STUDY QUESTIONS

1. Discuss some of the career opportunities available to those trained in public administration.
2. "One of the most important trends in American society is the increasing interaction of business and government." This quotation signals the need for better recognition and understanding of the interactions between business and government. Discuss the importance of this interaction and why a clear understanding of the relationship between the public and private sector is necessary.
3. The differences between public administration and business management are profound. Explain how the two fields differ and why the two terms are *not* interchangeable.
4. How did early scholars, such as Woodrow Wilson, view the role of public administration in a democracy?
5. The term *democracy* can be interpreted in a variety of ways. What significant concepts helped form the democratic society within which American government operates?
6. What is the role of "publicness" in defining the work of public managers?

CASES AND EXERCISES

1. Interview a public administrator. Locate one or more people who work as a manager or analyst in a public organization and interview them. The interviewees might work in a public university, a local government, a state or federal agency, or a nonprofit organization. They might be a university department chair, someone working in administrative services at the university, a city manager or department director (public works, parks and recreation, etc.), a county official (such as a county clerk), a manager in state government (perhaps someone in a welfare office or the highway department), a federal government manager (in a local office of a department such as Social Security, Agriculture, or the FAA), or someone such as an association executive. They might be a program manager, a staff manager, or a policy analyst.

Ask the people you interview to describe their jobs, including the range of responsibilities they have, and the knowledge, values, and skills that are important to them in their work. The following are some examples of questions you might want to ask:

Describe the work you do and how you came to this position. What is your educational and work background?

What impact does the work you do have on the community/state/nation/etc.?

What do you find different or unusual about working in a public organization? How do you think your job compares to work at a comparable level in business or industry?

What knowledge, values, and skills are important to your work? For instance, if you were hiring someone to take your place, what would you look for?

2. Consider the following case. As an administrative assistant in the Department of Finance of a mid-sized suburban community, you are asked by the director to contract with an accounting firm to audit the books of the ten major city departments. You develop a request for bids, advertise in the local newspaper, and send written notices to all the local accounting firms. In response, you receive five proposals, four from local firms and one from a Big Eight accounting firm based in the nearby city. The proposals are essentially the same with respect to cost and expected quality of work; however, one firm, Jones and Denham, appears to have considerably more experience, having done similar audits locally in the past. Having gathered all the information you feel you need to make a decision, you make an appointment to report to the director early Tuesday morning. At lunch Monday, however, a friend who knows you are working on the auditing contract casually mentions that a certain Mr. Howard, of the firm T. P. Howard and Co., is the brother-in-law of the mayor. T. P. Howard and Co. is one of the five firms that has submitted bids for the auditing contract. Later that afternoon, you receive a call from the mayor, asking for a report on the auditing contract. What do you say to the mayor? What do you recommend be done about the contract? What does this case say about the relationship between business and government?

3. Consider the following case. There wasn't much that David Wood couldn't do. He was an excellent teacher, a dedicated scholar, and a good department chair. He had been called to the chancellor's office to comment on a new curriculum proposal, one his faculty and he had discussed and one they firmly opposed. The chancellor began the meeting by commenting on the excellent administrative work that David had been doing and on the possibility that he might be considered for a deanship that was coming open soon. David had always wanted to be a dean. He voiced very mild objection to the curriculum proposal, then promised to try to convince his faculty to support it.

27

Moving from an academic position into an administrative position or from any technical position into an administrative position puts you in a different world, one with greater complexity and different pressures. What are some of the factors that affect those holding managerial jobs as opposed to technical jobs?

4. Recently fraternities and sororities at a major midwestern university were informed that the property tax classification for their houses was being changed from "residential" to "commercial," a change that would increase the assessed values of the properties from 19 to 32 percent and would cost the Greek houses thousands of dollars in new taxes. The Greeks felt the change was inappropriate because, as one member stated, "There's not a fraternity or sorority on campus that makes a profit." On the other hand, a county official pointed out that the houses contain more than "four dwelling units," as the law describes it. Moreover, fraternities and sororities are probably not residential enterprises and are definitely not agricultural ones (as specified in the law), so they are relegated to the third "catch-all" category, "commercial and all others."

If you were advising the Greek organizations as to how they might seek relief, what would you recommend? What kind of action should they take? Where should an appeal originate? How might it proceed?

28

FOR ADDITIONAL READING

Doig, Jameson W., and Hargrove, Erwin C. *Leadership and Innovation.* Baltimore, MD: Johns Hopkins University Press, 1987.

Gawthrop, Louis C. *Public Sector Management, Systems, Ethics.* Bloomington: Indiana University Press, 1984.

Hummel, Ralph. *The Bureaucratic Experience.* 2nd ed. New York: St. Martin's Press, 1982.

Lynn, Naomi B., and Wildavsky, Aaron, eds. *Public Administration: The State of the Discipline.* Chatham, NJ: Chatham House, 1990.

Perry, James L., ed. *Handbook of Public Administration.* San Francisco: Jossey-Bass, 1989.

Rabin, Jack, Hildreth, W. Bartley, and Miller, Gerald J., eds. *Handbook of Public Administration.* New York: Marcel Dekker, 1989.

Waldo, Dwight. *The Enterprise of Public Administration.* Novato, CA: Chandler and Sharp, 1980.

OPM Inventory of Management Skills

The "What" of Management: Functions

1. *External awareness:* Identifying and keeping up-to-date with key agency policies and priorities and/or external issues and trends (e.g., economic, political, social, technological) likely to affect the work unit.
2. *Interpretation:* Keeping subordinates informed about key agency and work unit policies, priorities, issues, and trends and how these are to be incorporated in work unit activities and products.
3. *Representation:* Presenting, explaining, selling, and defending the work unit's activities to the supervisor in the agency, and/or persons and groups outside the agency.
4. *Coordination:* Performing liaison functions and integrating work unit activities with the activities of other organizations.
5. *Work unit planning:* Developing and deciding upon longer-term goals, objectives, and priorities; and developing and deciding among alternative courses of action.
6. *Work unit guidance:* Converting plans to actions by setting short-term objectives and priorities; scheduling/sequencing activities; and establishing effectiveness and efficiency standards/guidelines.
7. *Budgeting:* Preparing, justifying and/or administering the work unit's budget.
8. *Material resources administration:* Assuring the availability of adequate supplies, equipment, facilities; overseeing procurement/contracting activities; and/or overseeing logistical operations.
9. *Personnel management:* Projecting the number and types of staff needed by the work unit, and using various personnel management system components (e.g., recruitment, selection, promotion, performance appraisal) in managing the work unit.
10. *Supervision:* Providing day-by-day guidance and oversight of subordinates (e.g., work assignments, consultation, etc.); and actively working to promote and recognize performance.
11. *Work unit monitoring:* Keeping up-to-date on the overall status of activities in the work unit, identifying problem areas, and taking corrective actions (e.g., rescheduling, reallocating resources, etc.).
12. *Program evaluation:* Critically assessing the degree to which program/project goals are achieved and the overall effectiveness/efficiency of work unit operations, to identify means for improving work unit performance.

The "How" of Management: Effectiveness Characteristics

1. *Broad perspective:* Broad, long-term view: balancing short- and long-term considerations
2. *Strategic view:* Collecting/assessing/analyzing information; diagnosis; anticipation; judgment

29

3. *Environmental sensitivity:* "Tuned into" agency and its environment; awareness of importance of non-technical factors
4. *Leadership:* Individual; group; willingness to lead and manage, and accept responsibility
5. *Flexibility:* Openness to new information; behavioral flexibility; tolerance for stress/ambiguity/change; innovativeness
6. *Action orientation:* Independence, proactivity; calculated risk-taking; problem solving; decisiveness
7. *Results focus:* Concern with goal achievement; follow through, tenacity
8. *Communication:* Speaking; writing; listening
9. *Interpersonal sensitivity:* Self-knowledge and awareness of impact on others; sensitivity to needs/strengths/weaknesses of others; negotiation; conflict resolution; persuasion
10. *Technical competence:* Specialized expertise (e.g., engineering, physical science, law, accounting, social science)

SOURCE: Loretta R. Flanders and Dennis Utterback, "The Management Excellence Inventory," *Public Administration Review*, 45 (May/June, 1985): 403–410. Reprinted with permission from *Public Administration Review*, © 1985 by the American Society for Public Administration (ASPA), 1120 G Street NW, Suite 500, Washington, D.C. 20005. All rights reserved.

THE
POLITICAL
CONTEXT
OF
PUBLIC
ADMINISTRATION

Your involvement in public organizations, whether in your career or as a private citizen, will inevitably center on the development and implementation of public policies. You may work for an agency charged with devising new approaches to familiar problems, you may want to see that a particular policy or proposal is framed in a way that is consistent with your beliefs, or you may simply want to better understand the implications of a particular direction in national policy. In any case, it will be helpful for you to know how public policies are developed and implemented.

Talk of public policy is, of course, quite familiar. From one day to another, we hear criticisms of the U.S. policy in Central America, calls for a more effective drug enforcement policy, challenges to a state's policy on AIDS in the schools, ideas for changing a city's policy toward the homeless, or proposals for altering an organization's hiring practices. Our uses of the term *policy* are many and varied, and the process by which policies are developed is even more complex.

We may think of a **policy** as a statement of goals and intentions with respect to a particular problem or set of problems, a statement often accompanied by a more detailed set of plans, programs, or instructions for pursuing those goals. **Public policies** are authoritative statements made by legitimate governmental actors (the chief executive, the legislature, public agencies, etc.) about important, and sometimes not so important public problems. We expect public officials at all levels to spend considerable time and energy dealing with such topics as foreign affairs, health, education, employment, the economy, civil rights, the environment, energy, transportation, housing, agriculture, law enforcement, and a myriad of other areas. But in each of these areas, public policy is simply what an agency or the entire government decides to do or not do.

Public organizations are deeply involved in carrying out public policy—executing or "implementing." But public organizations are also involved in developing policy. The agencies of government are key actors in shaping public policy. Proposals are written and submitted by agency personnel, testimony and other expert advice is presented, and representatives of various agencies, especially political appointees who head agencies, often seek to build public support for particular ideas. Those in governmental agencies are often asked to elaborate or clarify legislative intentions, and, in doing so, they continue the process of policy development.

Moreover, other public organizations, such as nonprofit organizations and associations, not only develop policies that guide their own activities, but also seek to influence the course of public policy in behalf of their members or other constituencies. Many such groups limit their activities to providing public information and seeking to affect indirectly the formation of policies in their area of interest. But others are far more direct, employing lobbyists and others whose specific job is to influence the policy process.

To understand the conduct of public organizations in the policy process, you must have some understanding of the context in which public organizations operate. That context is not merely physical; it includes the beliefs and values that shape our expectations of public organizations as well as the structures we have developed to try to maintain those values. In large part, the complexity of the policy process in this country is the result of the Founding Fathers' fear of concentrated power, a fear they sought to allay by organizing the federal government into three branches—executive, legislative, and judicial—so that no one branch could exert itself above the others. As we will see, our political system has evolved in such a way that the relations between and among the various branches remain a central issue in conducting public programs. This chapter focuses on relations between public administrators and the executive, the legislature, and the judiciary as they work together to seek important policy goals.

ADMINISTRATIVE ORGANIZATIONS AND EXECUTIVE LEADERSHIP

As we saw in chapter 1, public administrators work in the federal, state, and local governments and in nonprofit organizations and associations. But, understandably, the federal government, simply by virtue of its size and the range of its activities, has become the model against which others are often judged. For that reason, we will begin our discussion of the structure of American public administration by examining the development of the national administrative system and the role of the chief executive in that system.

Again it is helpful to begin with a brief historical review, primarily because some of the arguments that characterized discussions of administration in the early days of our nation are quite similar to those that continue to confront us. Take, for example, the difference between the Federalist view, expressed most forcefully by Alexander Hamilton, and that of the Jeffersonians, led by (you guessed it!) Thomas Jefferson. Hamilton and his Federalist colleagues argued for a strong centralized government, staffed and managed by men of wealth, class, and education. "The Federalist preference for the executive branch was a faithful reflection of their distrust of the people. An intelligent perception of sound public policy, in their view, could come only from well-educated men of affairs, men with trained minds and broad experience—in short from the upper classes" (White, 1948, p. 510).

The Jeffersonians, on the other hand, saw the administration of government as intimately connected to the problem of extending democracy throughout the nation. They thus preferred a more decentralized approach to the executive function and sought formal legal controls on the executive so that executive power would not be abused (Caldwell, 1944). These democratic views reached their pinnacle in the administration of Andrew Jackson, known for its openness to the "common man." But the Jacksonian era was also notable for extension and formalization of the administrative apparatus of government; the administration of government began to form "a link between the nation's political authorities and its citizens" (Crenson, 1975, p. 10; see also Nelson, 1982).

Despite these developments, the president's role as chief executive officer, the head of the federal bureaucracy, was not clearly established until well into the twentieth century, when Franklin Roosevelt was able to assert his administrative management of the executive branch and to set a model for all the presidents who have followed him. Some changes were inevitable: the growing size and scope of governmental activity simply required greater attention to management and organization. Others were more reflective of a greater understanding of the administrative process, how the work of government might be accomplished more effectively.

In 1936, President Roosevelt appointed a Committee on Administrative Management, chaired by Louis Brownlow, that included a number of respected scholars and practitioners in the emerging field of public administration. The Brownlow Committee concluded that "the president needs help" and recommended a series of possible steps to improve the president's management of the executive branch (Karl, 1963). Though initially sidetracked in the wake of the president's attempt to "pack" the Supreme Court, the major recommendations of the Brownlow Committee were finally approved in the Reorganization Act of 1939. This act authorized the president to take the initiative in reshaping and reorganizing the executive branch, subject only to congressional veto. The Reorganization Act also allowed President Roosevelt to create the Executive Office of the President, composed of six assistants, to give the president the help he needed. (The Executive Office of the President continues today, though now it employs some 1,500 people.)

All presidents since Roosevelt have continued to assert their executive power in various ways. President Nixon, for example, sought to further centralize managerial power in the White House; President Carter sought greater managerial responsiveness through the Civil Service Reform Act. President Reagan pursued the same ends, by extending political control further into the bureaucracy while also developing programs to reduce costs and increase productivity. President Bush has pursued a more managerial approach, seeking cooperation and quality improvements through the bureaucracy. (The president's policy leadership role is illustrated in Box 2.1.)

One important tool that presidents have employed is the **executive order,** a presidential mandate directed to and governing, with the effect of law, the actions of government officials and government agencies. Over time, the executive order has become a chief

33

BOX 2.1

PRESIDENTIAL LEADERSHIP

Lyndon B. Johnson furnishes yet another example of presidential style in policy making. On November 24, 1963, his first full day in office following the assassination of John F. Kennedy, Johnson was informed by Council of Economic Advisers Chairman Walter Heller that Kennedy had approved Heller's proposal to devise a comprehensive plan to deal with the problem of poverty in America. The idea resonated with Johnson personally and politically, and he told Heller, "I'm interested, I'm sympathetic. Go ahead. Give it highest priority. Push ahead full tilt." In his memoirs, Johnson wrote of his reaction to Heller's idea: "I believed that I could—for a while at least—really get things done." Observes political scientist James L. Sundquist, "The issue itself was peculiarly suited to the personality of Lyndon Johnson, who could talk feelingly of his firsthand knowledge of poverty in the Texas hills and recall his experience as the director of Franklin Roosevelt's National Youth Administration. It gave him the excuse to stand on the same southern courthouse steps where Roosevelt stood and pledge himself to carry on the war on want that FDR had started."

The staff work for devising what became Johnson's War on Poverty was supervised by Heller and Kermit Gordon, director of the Bureau of the Budget. However, Johnson spent many long hours with them at the LBJ ranch during Christmas week 1963, "discussing, planning, and evolving the outlines of a poverty program." Staff members occasionally sat in on these discussions, as did associates from earlier days and a group of Texas cattlemen, invited so that Heller and his colleagues could get a taste of the opposition their plan would later encounter. Johnson recalled how "one evening during those Christmas holidays in 1963, I walked from the main ranch house to a little green frame house we call the 'guest house,' a distance of about two hundred yards. Inside, seated around a small kitchen table, were Walter Heller, Budget Director Kermit Gordon, Bill Moyers, and Jack Valenti (both of Johnson's White House staff). The table was littered with papers, coffee cups, and one ashtray brimming over with cigarettes and torn strips of paper. . . . I sat down at the table to talk about the program they were preparing." Johnson urged them away from considering a demonstration program toward a big and bold program. At his instruction, $500 million, obtained largely through defense department economies, and another $500 million already in the budget for programs that would strike at poverty were incorporated into the new poverty program. Two budget bureau staff members contributed the notion that the funds would be channeled directly to and through local organizations, bypassing the mayors. In this way the Community Action Program was born.

Following his announcement of the War on Poverty in his January 8, 1964, state of the union message, Johnson decided, against the advice of Secretary of Labor Willard Wirtz and Attorney General Robert F. Kennedy, to assign the program to a new agency, as advocated by Heller, Gordon, and economist and Kennedy adviser John Kenneth Galbraith (and much as Franklin D. Roosevelt would have done), rather than to the existing cabinet departments. Johnson chose Sargent Shriver, director of the Peace Corps, to direct the new agency, then closely monitored Shriver and his associates, who would have to run the new program, as they designed the authorizing legislation that would be submitted to Congress. Six weeks later, on March 16, a bill was submitted. In what Johnson himself regarded as a crucial step, he convinced Phil M. Landrum, a conservative Georgia Democrat who had successfully sponsored "right-to-work" legislation, to sponsor the bill in the House, then persuaded George Meany, the powerful head of the AFL-CIO, to cooperate with Landrum.

As the bill was being debated in Congress, according to Johnson's memoirs, "Lady Bird and I made a special trip to the Middle West and through the scarred mountains of Appalachia to focus the nation's attention on the problem of poverty." He repeatedly lobbied delegations of visitors, appealing, for example, to labor editors to help mold public opinion, and ask people to write their congressmen and senators. In making his appeals, however, Johnson "built the rhetoric far beyond that which had been planned by his advisers," a habit that contributed to the disillusionment that would set in when it was realized that the high expectations Johnson helped create could not be met. On August 20, 1965, the Economic Opportunity Act was signed into law.

35

SOURCE: Excerpted from Laurence E. Lynn, Jr. and David deF. Whitman, *The President as Policymaker.* © 1981 by Temple University. Reprinted by permission of Temple University Press.

instrument of presidential power. President Reagan, for example, issued Executive Order 12498, giving his Office of Management and Budget broad authority in eliminating agency regulations found inconsistent with administration policy. In this case and many others like it, the president is essentially making law by decree, occasionally in direct opposition to the wishes of Congress (Cooper, 1986).

The president, as the chief executive officer of the federal government, exercises power over an enormous and wide-ranging set of public organizations. There are some 2.8 million civilians employed by the federal government and another 2.5 million uniformed military personnel. In addition, the federal government supports and pays for the work of a wide variety of activities in which the actual work is performed by someone other than a federal civil servant. The Defense Department, for example, supervises some 3 million persons in private industry involved, directly or indirectly, in defense-related work. Moreover, despite efforts by the Reagan and Bush administrations to reduce the size of the federal government, federal employment has actually gone up seven percent in the past decade (mostly through increases in the Defense Department, the Veterans Administration, and the Post Office).

Administrative Organizations

You are probably already familiar with many of the agencies of government at the federal level; however, several types are particularly important: (1) the Executive Office of the President; (2) the cabinet-level executive departments; (3) a variety of independent agencies, regulatory commissions, and public corporations; and (4) administrative agencies that support the work of the legislature and the judiciary.

The Executive Office of the President   The various administrative bodies located in the Executive Office of the President both advise the president and assist in formulating and implementing national policy. Several offices have come to play especially important policy roles; the *Office of Management and Budget*, for example, assists the president in preparing the budget, submitting it to Congress, and administering it. OMB is also involved in reviewing the management of various agencies, suggesting changes in structures and procedures, and searching out capable executives for service in government. The *National Security Council* is charged with integrating domestic, military, and foreign policy; it is made up of the president, vice-president, and secretaries of State and Defense and is directed by the National Security Adviser. (Recall that in late 1986, charges that John Poindexter and Oliver North, among others on the NSC staff, were exceeding their statutory authority and engaging in covert military operations led to the Iran-Contra affair, and, among other things, a reorganization of the NSC.) Finally, the *Council of Economic Advisers* consists of three economists who develop proposals to "maintain employment, production, and purchasing power." The Council also develops a variety of economic reports.

Obviously, each of these groups, and others in the Executive Office of the President, are used in different ways by different presidents, according to the personality of the president and the particular issues that are most pressing at that time. Some presidents, such as Eisenhower and Reagan, have relied very heavily on their staffs, while others, such as Carter, have been much more personally involved in management and policy development.

Cabinet-Level Executive Departments   These agencies are among the most visible, if not always the largest, of the federal executive agencies. There are currently thirteen cabinet-level departments. In decreasing order of size, they are the Departments of Defense, Health and Human Services, Treasury, Agriculture, Interior, Transportation, Justice, Commerce, State, Labor, Energy, Housing and Urban Development, and Education. Several departments, such as Treasury and State, date back to the nation's founding; others have been created by Congress as needed.

Each cabinet-level department is headed by a secretary, who, along with a group of top-level staff people, is appointed by the president with the approval of the Senate. Each cabinet-level department is organized into smaller units, such as offices, services, administrations, branches, and sections. The Department of Health and Human Services, for example, includes the Public Health Service, which in turn includes the Food and Drug Administration, and so on. Though each department is headquartered in Washington, D. C., their offices are, of course, spread across the country. Indeed, only about eleven percent of the federal work force lives in or around the District of Columbia.

The cabinet-level secretaries, along with a few others, such as the Director of the Office of Management and Budget and the Ambassador to the United Nations, constitute the president's *cabinet,* a group that some presidents have used sparingly and primarily for formal matters and others have employed extensively for help and advice. Conflict occasionally arises between presidential advisers and cabinet officials. Most notable in recent years have been flare-ups between the president's National Security Adviser and the Secretary of State; for example, differences with the National Security Adviser led to the resignation of Secretary of State Cyrus Vance in the Carter administration and Alexander Haig in the Reagan administration.

Independent agencies, regulatory commissions, and public corporations   A variety of **independent agencies** have been created intentionally outside the normal cabinet organization. Some are engaged in staff functions in support of other agencies. The Office of Personnel Management, for example, oversees the federal personnel function, and the General Services Administration oversees the government's property. Other agencies have simply not been viewed as appropriate to include in cabinet-level departments; among these are the Environmental Protection Agency, the Small Business Administration, and the Veterans Administration. With rare exceptions, these independent agencies are directed by persons appointed by the president with the confirmation of the Senate.

Regulatory commissions, which are formed to regulate a particular area of the economy, are structured quite differently. Typically, they are headed by a group of individuals (variously called directors, commissioners, or governors) appointed by the president and confirmed by the Senate. These persons are protected in various ways from removal by the president; in some cases, their terms of appointment overlap presidential terms. Presumably, the regulatory commissions are to perform their tasks independently and objectively, free from undue influence either by the political incumbent or by the affected clientele. As we will see later, however, the nature of regulatory work makes this task exceedingly difficult. (Note that not all regulatory bodies are located outside the cabinet departments; for instance, the Food and Drug Administration is part of the Department of Health and Human Services.)

Public corporations are employed where the objective of the agency is essentially commercial, where the work of the agency requires greater latitude than would be typical, and where the agency will acquire at least a portion of its funding in the marketplace (Walsh, 1978). The Tennessee Valley Authority, which has provided power in the Tennessee Valley for over fifty years, is a classic example of a public corporation. More recent additions to the growing list of government corporations include the U.S. Postal Service and the National Rail Passenger Corporation (AMTRAK), both established in 1970. (The Postal Service was previously a cabinet department, and its somewhat ambiguous current relationship to the president and to Congress has led to occasional suggestions that it be returned to that status.)

Agencies supporting the legislature and the judiciary   Whereas both the legislative and judicial branches require considerable direct administrative support for their members (legislative staff, committee staff, court administrators), there are also several specific agencies attached to the legislative branch that are of special significance. Among these, you are probably familiar with the Government Printing Office and the Library of Congress. But, although less is known about the General Accounting Office (GAO), its duties have become increasingly important. Established in 1921, the GAO is responsible for auditing funds to see that they are properly spent. In recent years, however, the agency's mission has broadened to include formal program evaluations within various agencies (Rourke, 1978). Finally, Congress is supported by the Office of Technology Assessment and the Congressional Budget Office, whose operations we will examine more carefully in chapter 5.

38

The State Level

The organization of state governments varies considerably, according to each state's policy interests and political development; however, there is little question that state government in this country is "big business." One recent study compared the sales of the Fortune 500 companies to the revenues of state governments. It turns out that, on this basis, twenty-four state governments would move into the top one hundred and even the smallest state, Vermont, would rank 383rd on the Fortune 500 list (Behn & Behn, 1986).

Recent efforts to decrease federal involvement in domestic policy have combined with a general growth in the range of activities undertaken at the state level to support a vast increase in state activity. Between 1970 and 1987, state government employment rose from 2.7 million to 4.1 million, with an even more dramatic rise in state expenditures. Moreover, the states are entering into an increasing range of activities (for example, economic development), though their primary areas of emphasis and expenditure continue to be education, social services, and highways.

The organization and structure of state government in many ways mirrors that of the national government, but there are some distinctive features. You should note, for example, the large number of elected administrative officials in most state governments. In most states, the people elect not only the governor and lieutenant governor, but also the attorney general, the secretary of state, and the state treasurer. Many states still elect the head of the department of agriculture by popular vote, and it is not uncommon to have members of various boards and commissions (e.g., the public service commission) elected by the public. Obviously, these latter offices are filled at the federal level by presidential appointment. (The large number of elected officers at the state and local level is a carry-over from a period in which democratic tendencies in this country were especially strong and it was felt that nearly all major officials of government should be elected directly by the people.)

In addition, many state departments do not report directly to the governor, but rather to boards or commissions isolated from executive control in the same way as regulatory commissions at the federal level. For example, a Department of Conservation may report to a commission appointed by the governor for periods exceeding those of the governor and, indeed, may have dedicated sources of revenue essentially outside the governor's budgetary control. Obviously, under such circumstances, the governor's power as chief executive is severely limited.

Despite structural limitations on gubernatorial powers, contemporary governors exercise a broad range of political and executive powers that enable them to play a major, even central role in the operations of state government. Most important, governors play a major symbolic role, helping to set the political agenda and to focus the attention of other political and administrative actors on a limited number of special topics. In addition, most governors have accumulated special powers with respect to the budget process through which they are able to dramatically affect the allocation of state resources and to mediate policy disputes among executive agencies (Bowman & Kearney, 1986, p. 54).

Beyond these somewhat informal powers, the strength of the governor's formal executive powers is often gauged by three measures: the presence or absence of the item veto, the ability of the governor to reorganize state agencies, and the number of other elected officials. In all states but North Carolina, the governor (like the president) has the power to veto legislation. Most states also give the governor the power of *item-veto*, the capacity to veto specific items within an appropriations bill (as opposed to accepting all or nothing), which is a helpful tool in shaping legislation according to the governor's preferences. (President Reagan, himself a former governor, unsuccessfully pursued the idea of an item veto at the federal level throughout his administration.) The gubernatorial power to reorganize is more limited. Roughly half the states require either statutory or even constitutional action to reorganize. Finally, as we have seen, nearly all states have a variety of statewide elected officials in addition to the governor and lieutenant governor. Indeed, most states have between four and eight agencies that are controlled by individuals elected statewide rather than appointed.

The growing importance of state government suggests that governors will likely continue to assert their executive leadership role and will seek greater control by reorganizing the executive branch. So far, however, relatively few structural moves have been made. (In one notable attempt at change, Oklahoma has recently moved to establish a "cabinet" system of governance.) However, some procedural changes have occurred; for example, many states have moved in the direction of more clearly establishing the governor's leading role in the budgetary process and establishing centralized management improvement programs.

Although the organization of government varies considerably from state to state, most states have a variety of substantive agencies concerned with state and local needs (Natural Resources, Highways and Transportation, etc.), as well as several agencies, such as the Department of Social Services, that largely administer programs funded by the federal government. These agencies are likely to be assisted by a central management support unit, called an Office of Administration or some similar title, that provides budget, personnel, and other general services. As mentioned, if there is one trend in the reorganization of state agencies, that trend would seem to be creation of a greater number of state departments devoted to economic development. In some cases, these departments seek to coordinate many economic development activities; in others, there is a more specific focus on small business or on providing incentives for industrial location or relocation.

The Local Level

There are over 80,000 local governments (see Box 2.2). Many of these are municipalities, cities, and towns of varying sizes offering a full range of services; others are counties, typically more limited in their role but still embracing a variety of governmental functions. But most are special districts, created to serve one particular function, such as education, fire protection, or parks and recreation.

B O X   2 . 2

Number of Governmental Units, by Type of Government

Type of government		1987
Federal		1
State		50
Local		83,186
County	3,042	
Municipal	19,200	
Township and town	16,691	
School district	14,721	
Special district	29,532	
Total		83,237

SOURCE: U.S. Bureau of the Census, *Statistical Abstract of the United States.* Washington, D.C.: U.S. Government Printing Office, 1988.

Cities   American cities are organized in three ways. The *mayor–council* form is used by about 54 percent of all municipalities—about 61 percent of those over 250,000 population and nearly all of those with over a million population. In all cases, both the council and the mayor are elected, the latter either by direct popular vote or a council election. One variation of the mayor–council form features a *strong mayor*, with almost total administrative authority, including preparation and administration of the budget. Policy making in this form is a joint endeavor of the mayor and the council. The *weak mayor* type places primary administrative control, including most appointments and development of the budget, in the hands of the council.

The power of the mayor as chief executive is obviously greater in the strong mayor system and, consequently, that system is used in most large, industrial cities. At least in a formal sense, however, several large cities, including Chicago, still maintain a weak mayor system, although even under such circumstances, a particular mayor may assert considerable strength. The legendary Mayor Richard Daley of Chicago, for example, was able to utilize a well-oiled political machine to assert substantial administrative power. Though he operated in a weak-mayor system, Daley was unquestionably a strong mayor.

One interesting recent variation on the mayor–council form is the use of a professionally trained chief administrative officer (sometimes called a "deputy mayor") to oversee the administrative operations of city government (e.g., Los Angeles, New Orleans, Washington, D.C.). We find this administrative arrangement in many big cities, where mayors are often more interested in campaigning and in working with external constituencies and like to have someone else oversee the internal management of the city. But city administrators are also being hired in an increasing number of smaller mayor–council communities as well, mostly in an effort to bring professional expertise to local government.

The *council–manager* form of local government is of special interest in that it represents a structural effort to solve the classic question of the relationship between politics (or policy) and administration. In this form, the city council, usually five to seven people, has responsibility for making policy, including passing appropriations and supervising in a general way the administration of city government. The primary executive responsibility, however, lies with a full-time professionally trained city manager; the mayor has no involvement in the administration of the city and performs primarily ceremonial duties and legislation. In its classic formulation, therefore, the council–manager form is designed so that the council makes policy and the city manager carries it out.

The council–manager plan was first tried in Staunton, Virginia, in 1908, and a few years later was adopted in Dayton, Ohio, with great success. Several reform organizations, such as the National Municipal League, felt the council–manager plan would be a good way to insulate the management of city government from the vagaries of local politics and consequently added their endorsement.

The number of council–manager governments has grown steadily throughout this century. Today, some 36 percent of American communities employ the plan. Where the mayor–council system is associated with larger, industrialized, and heterogeneous cities, the council–manager plan is most frequently found in medium-sized cities. Over 56 percent of American cities between 25,000 and 250,000 operate with the plan, and 26 percent of the cities below 5,000 population have adopted it. Although a number of large cities, such as Dallas, Kansas City, Phoenix, San Antonio, and San Diego, use the plan, it is rare among cities over one million population. The council–manager form continues to grow, however, with the number of council–manager adoptions outrunning those of the mayor–council form by three to one over the past fifteen years (Stillman, 1985). Those favoring the council–manager plan usually argue that it emphasizes professional expertise and administrative accountability; those favoring the mayor–council plan emphasize its adaptability and its responsiveness to community needs.

A small number of American cities use the *commission* form of government. Under this form, the people elect a set of commissioners. Each acts as a council member, but also as director of a particular city department; for example, one commissioner might head the parks department and another the public works department. The commission form is fading; we find it today primarily in smaller rural communities, though it is still found in such cities as Portland, Oregon, and Tulsa, Oklahoma. These larger cities usually hire a chief administrative officer to provide the necessary coordination of city government.

Counties Counties (or variations such as *parishes*, in Louisiana) are found in nearly every state and range in population from very small to huge. Once considered the "dark continent" of local government, counties are emerging as important actors in the modern governmental system. Counties have traditionally provided a range of services in behalf of state government, a role that has expanded considerably in the past few years. In addition, counties have recently assumed a wide range of new services (such as mass transit, mental health, waste disposal, and police services) that, for one reason or another, cannot be offered by individual municipalities (Dodge, 1988, pp. 2–3).

The traditional form of county government has been a combination of a county commission and a series of elected administrative officials, such as sheriff, auditor, treasurer, and so on. An emerging trend in county government, however, is the use of appointed county administrators, similar in many ways to the city manager at the municipal level. Still another type of county government, also increasing in use, involves the combination of a city council and an elected executive. In this system, a chief executive is elected by the people and holds powers similar to that of a governor in a state system. For example, the elected executive often has veto power of council actions (Henry, 1980, pp. 158–164). Trends toward a greater range of activities, especially in the social services, combined with the increasing professionalism of county government, make this often-overlooked area one of the most interesting arenas for public service today.

Special districts Finally, we should note again the large number of special districts that exist at the local level. These limited-purpose districts, which may operate in the areas of natural resources, fire protection, libraries, schools, housing and community development, and so forth, are typically governed by an appointed part-time governing board and a full-time general manager or executive director, who plays the most significant role in the operation of the district. Critics claim the proliferation of special districts causes fragmentation and lack of coordination, but others argue that such districts remain important because they are "close to the people."

Nonprofit Organizations and Associations

A multitude of public organizations fall somewhere between what we think of as the "public sector" and the "private sector." These may be described as belonging to an independent or *third sector* of our economy. For the most part, third-sector organizations do not have producing a profit as one of their major objectives; they exist instead to meet the needs of the public at large, a particular portion of the public, or the needs and interests of their own members (McLaughlin, 1986). Technically, **nonprofit organizations** are defined as those prohibited by law from distributing surplus revenues (profits) to individuals (typically, members). Such organizations may in fact make a profit; however, the profit must be used for the purposes of the organization.

Nonprofit organizations may include churches, civic organizations, schools and colleges, charitable organizations, social and recreational groups, health service organizations, membership organizations (including labor unions and fraternal organizations), conservation and environmental groups, mutual organizations (including farmers' cooperatives), trade associations, community chests, youth activities (such as Boy Scouts), community betterment organizations, advocacy groups of all kinds, and many others. Their numbers range into the millions, depending on how they are counted, and, as noted earlier, include some 18,000 *national* nonprofits (see Box 2.3).

While private nonprofit organizations account for between 6 and 10 percent of employment in the U.S. (depending again on how you count), the voluntary effort that is

BOX   2.3

National Nonprofit Organizations by Specialty, 1985

Category	Number
Trade, business, and commercial organizations	3622
Agricultural organizations and commodity exchanges	832
Legal, governmental, public administration, and military organizations	646
Scientific, engineering, and technical organizations	1170
Educational organizations	1132
Cultural organizations	1548
Social welfare organizations	1333
Health and medical organizations	1805
Public affairs organizations	1795
Fraternal, foreign interest, nationality, and ethnic organizations	480
Religious organizations	894
Veteran, heredity, and patriotic organizations	263
Hobby and vocational organizations	1232
Athletic and sports organizations	707
Labor unions, associations, and federations	249
Chambers of commerce	135
Greek and non-Greek letter societies, associations, and federations	327
Total	18,170

SOURCE: Denise S. Akey, ed., *Encyclopedia of Associations*, 19th ed., vol. 1. Detroit, MI: Gale Research Company, 1984.

expended in support of these groups makes their impact far greater. Some 80 million American adults devote volunteer time to such organizations, an investment of time that has been estimated as the equivalent of over 56 billion dollars a year (Hodgkinson & Weitzman, 1984, pp. 11–13). For most of the 1980s, this third sector was the fastest growing segment of our economy.

Many of these organizations are concentrated in the human services, especially in such important areas as health, education, and welfare. As efforts have been made to "privatize" certain traditionally public functions (a trend we will explore later), nonprofit organizations have come to carry an increasing share of the delivery of major services. Nonprofit organizations are involved in such key service areas as hospitals, museums, colleges and universities, the performing arts, religion, advocacy, and research (Young, 1983, p. 9). It has been estimated that over 50 percent of the human services delivered in major urban areas are delivered not by government but by other groups, mostly nonprofit organizations.

Nonprofits can be categorized in many ways, but perhaps most easily according to their purposes and source of financial support. Some nonprofits are *charitable* or *public benefit organizations*, which provide services to the public at large or to some segment of the public. These organizations, such as social service organizations or art museums, may receive some funding from government and some from private contribution; they are generally tax-exempt under federal statutes. Other nonprofits are *advocacy organizations*, groups that espouse a particular cause and seek to lobby for that cause, or *mutual benefit organizations*, which produce benefits primarily for their members. The former would include groups like Common Cause and the Sierra Club; the latter would include trade associations, professional organizations, labor unions, and others that directly promote the interests of their own members. Obviously, however, from these examples, the line between the two is not completely clear. Finally, *churches* are obviously charitable organizations, but are difficult to classify in the categories mentioned.

Indeed, the entire "third sector" is sometimes confusing to categorize. For one thing, the distinctions among the three sectors are not clear, even to the point that a particular individual might find the same service provided by one or more sectors. For example, you can play golf at a municipal course (public sector), a private driving range (private sector), or a country club (third sector). Moreover, the sources of funding are often intermixed. For example, both governments (public sector) and private corporations (private sector) often contribute financial support to local Chambers of Commerce.

The fact that nonprofit organizations are required to pursue a public interest is reflected in their legal structure (and tax-exempt status). Typically, so that the government can feel that a public purpose is being carried out, there are requirements that the organization be governed by a board of trustees (or directors or commissioners), the purpose of which, at least in legal terms, is to promote and to protect the public interest that is involved (Wolf, 1984, p. 21). Such persons will also likely establish the mission and operating policies, hire an executive director, and generally oversee fiscal and programmatic operations. The executive director is responsible for day-to-day operations and often becomes the organization's chief spokesperson. Most nonprofit associations are highly dependent on their executive director's leadership. More and more, such persons (and other major staff persons in nonprofit organizations) are coming from a background in public administration.

RELATIONSHIPS WITH THE LEGISLATIVE BODY

In examining the political context of public organizations, we have thus far emphasized the importance of executive leadership. For example, we noted the emergence of the president as the chief executive officer of our national government and the pivotal role of the chief executive in state and local governments and in nonprofit organizations and associations. But though we tend to associate public agencies with the executive branch of government, there are numerous administrative bodies associated with the legislative and judicial branches. More important, wherever agencies are located, their role in the policy process will be especially clear in their relationship with the legislature. In discussing the relationship between public agencies and legislative bodies, we will focus much more directly on the policy process.

The Policy Process

Before we examine the role of public organizations in developing public policy, we should review the process by which public policies are developed. We may think of the policy process as involving three stages: agenda setting, policy formulation, and policy implementation (see Box 2.4). Whereas public organizations are the primary actors in implementing public policy (indeed, most of this book focuses on ways to effectively carry out public policy), they are also significant players in the first two phases.

45

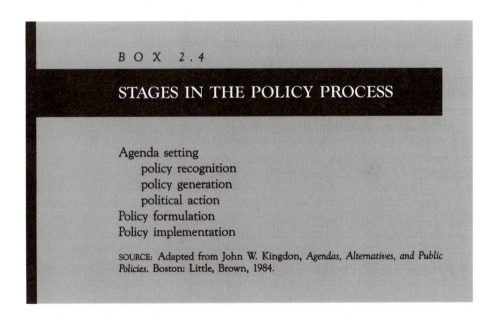

B O X   2 . 4

STAGES IN THE POLICY PROCESS

Agenda setting
    policy recognition
    policy generation
    political action
Policy formulation
Policy implementation

SOURCE: Adapted from John W. Kingdon, *Agendas, Alternatives, and Public Policies.* Boston: Little, Brown, 1984.

Agenda setting   Obviously, before policies are acted upon, they must get the attention of major decision makers. From among all the many and competing claims on their time and interests, decision makers must select issues that will be given priority and those that will be filtered out. Through the **agenda-setting** phase, certain problems come to be viewed as needing action, while others are postponed. Naturally, there is a great deal of ebb and flow in what is considered most important. In the sixties and seventies, U.S. policy in Southeast Asia was of great concern, whereas now attention has shifted to the Middle East and Central America. Similarly, any particular issue area can gain or decline in prominence over time, as has the attention to energy policy over the past fifteen years.

Many people contribute to setting the public policy agenda. The president, for example, has a special claim on the attention of the American people and their elected representatives; a presidential speech or press conference can significantly affect what decision makers see as important. But there are many others whose actions can give certain topics greater or less visibility. Members of Congress, executive branch officials, political parties, interest groups, the media, and the general public can all significantly shape the question of what will be considered important. Think, for example, how concern for the homeless has been recently brought to public awareness. Who have been the leaders in shaping public opinion on this issue?

The agenda-setting process may be viewed as the confluence of three streams of events—policy recognition, policy generation, and political action (Kingdon, 1984). The first, *policy recognition*, has to do with the way certain topics emerge as significant issues that demand action. As you can well imagine, decision makers are subject to many influences in choosing what items are significant. They may respond to particular indicators that come to public view, such as an increase in air traffic problems or a rise in unemployment. Or they may get feedback on current programs that indicates some need to reassess the status of a particular issue. Finally, some items are brought to the policy agenda by events that simply demand attention, such as the taking of hostages in Iran or the emergence of AIDS as a major health hazard.

There are many ways people try to affect the degree of attention given to particular items. Sometimes called **policy entrepreneurs,** those who are willing to invest personal time, energy, and often money in pursuit of particular policy changes can use a variety of personal tactics, such as publicity campaigns, direct contacts with decision makers (letters, phone calls), petition drives, and many others. Or they can involve themselves in major institutions, such as the media, political parties, or interest groups, that provide access to decision makers. Election campaigns, for example, often help clarify or focus the policy agenda.

A second phase of the agenda-setting process may occur almost simultaneously. At the same time that attention is focusing on a particular issue, it is likely that many will be involved in trying to *generate solutions* to the problem. Ideas may come from decision makers themselves, members of their staffs, experts in the bureaucracy, members of the scientific community, policy think-tanks (such as the Brookings Institution or the American Enterprise Association), or from the public generally. Typically, proposed solutions swirl around through speeches and articles, papers, and conversations until a few ideas begin to gain special currency. Most often these will be the ideas that not only seem to correctly address the problem, but seem also to be technically and administratively feasible, as well as politically acceptable.

A third stream of events affecting the policy agenda is concerned with *political action*. For a proposal to reach the top of the policy agenda, it must be consistent with emerging political realities. Items that are consistent with the prevailing political climate, those that are favored by the incumbent administration and legislative majority, and those that have interest group support (or at least lack organized opposition) are more likely to reach the top of the agenda. These political realities, the proposed ideas or solutions, and the recognition of particular topics represent streams that must come together at just the right moment for action to occur. The windows of opportunity for policy action are narrow, and it takes great skill in managing the various streams so that one's interests are best served.

Policy formulation   Formulation of public policy involves development of formal policy statements (legislation, executive orders, administrative rules, etc.) that are viewed as legitimate. Again, we will focus here on policy making by the legislature and on the role of public administrators in the legislative process. The basics of how a bill becomes law are well known. At the federal level and in most state governments, a bill is introduced and referred to a committee (and perhaps a subcommittee), hearings are held, the committee reports to the larger body, a vote is taken in both houses, a conference committee works out any differences in the two versions, and the bill is sent to the chief executive for signature. In most other jurisdictions, a similar, though often simplified, approach is used. In any case, the complexity of the legislative process, and the fact that many different decision points must be passed before anything is final, means there are many occasions when those seeking to shape legislative outcomes can seek to exert their influence.

The president, of course, has both formal and informal means of influencing legislation, most notably through program initiatives and budget proposals. Others in the government, including many agency personnel, interact with Congress on a regular basis and may also affect policy outcomes. At the same time, those outside the government— from individual citizens to well-organized interest groups—also seek access and influence. Agency personnel become involved in the legislative process in several ways. In many cases, agencies actually send program proposals to the legislature for its consideration. Such proposals are usually submitted to the legislative leadership, then passed on in turn to the appropriate committee chairs. Though a member of Congress will actually be the one to introduce the proposed legislation, that person may depend on those in the agency for background information and other support. Whether or not legislation has been submitted by an agency, agency personnel will often be called upon to provide testimony regarding particular proposals. As you might imagine, those who staff major public agencies constitute an important source of expertise concerning public issues. For example, it's hard to imagine a group of people better able to understand the tax laws of a particular state than those who work in the state revenue department.

Over time, the relationship between agency personnel and representatives of Congress (either members or staff) can become quite strong. After all, the two groups share common interests and concerns, along with representatives of certain interest groups. A subcommittee on aging, a senior citizen's lobbying organization, and the Social Security Administration, for example, are likely to agree on the need for more Social Security benefits. When the relationship among such interest groups, agency personnel, and members of Congress becomes especially frequent and intense, the resulting alliances are sometimes called *subgovernments* or **iron triangles.** These coalitions can often exert great, possibly even unwarranted, influence.

47

You should be aware of some of the special considerations facing public administrators at the local level and in nonprofit organizations as they are called upon for advice and help during the process of policy development. As noted, the council–manager form of government was actually founded on a separation of policy and administration—the council made policy and the city manager carried it out. Over time, however, many city managers have become valued by their councils for their expertise in local government and frequently find themselves commenting on or even proposing particular policies. The same is true of executives in nonprofit organizations and associations. Such situations are not without risk, however, for a delicate balance must be maintained between the executive and legislative functions. Council or board members who feel that their policy-making territory has been intruded upon may exercise another of their council prerogatives—firing the manager or executive!

Policy implementation   Members of public organizations play important roles in building the policy agenda and shaping legislative policy, but they are also involved in policy making as part of the implementation process. By its very nature, legislation is general and lacking in detail. Legislators cannot foresee all the individual questions that might come up in implementing a program. Moreover, legislators don't want to tie the hands of program managers by being too restrictive. Consequently, legislation typically leaves a great deal of discretion to public managers in working out the details of a particular program. The Federal Trade Commission, for example, is instructed to prevent deceptive advertising, but has to decide what is deceptive; the Occupational Safety and Health Administration is asked to define and set safety standards for the workplace, but must define more clearly what that means (Meier, 1987, p. 52). In these and many other cases, managers develop administrative rules or policies to give detail to the legislation or to fill in the gaps—and, in effect, they make policy.

A recent case involving the Environmental Protection Agency illustrates the latitude administrators are often given by Congress (and other legislative bodies) and the difficulties they can cause (Reich, 1985). The EPA is required by law to develop national standards limiting the emission of hazardous air pollutants so as to provide an "ample margin of safety" to protect the public health. But there is no definition in the legislation of *ample*. This question was especially problematic in the case of a copper smelter in Tacoma, Washington. The EPA determined that, in the absence of any controls on emissions of arsenic from the plant, four new cases of cancer each year could be expected. Even with the very best control equipment, there would still be one new case each year. On the other hand, requiring actions to eliminate the threat would cost the company so much money that it could not afford to continue operations, and its annual $23-million payroll would be lost to the Tacoma community. Obviously, EPA administrator William Ruckelshaus faced a difficult exercise of discretion. (We'll see in chapter 4 what he did.)

There have been several recent debates concerning the amount of discretion given to administrative agencies. Some analysts argue that broad grants of discretion amount to an abdication of legislative power; others point to the advantages of expertise and flexibility residing in the agencies or with the executive. Currently, the trend appears to be in the direction of greater detail in federal legislation, though occasionally less so at other levels; in any case, there inevitably remain many opportunities for the exercise of administrative discretion.

Types of Policy

The government develops and carries out several different types of policies, and the involvement of public organizations in the policy process varies somewhat according to type. We will examine four types—regulatory, distributive, redistributive, and constituent policy (Meier, 1987). These classifications are not precise, however, and indeed, many agencies work in several different areas at the same time.

Regulatory policy is designed to limit the actions of persons or groups so as to protect the general public or a substantial portion of the public. For example, people are prohibited from selling certain drugs, polluting the air and water, and engaging in monopolistic business practices. One form of regulation simply focuses on illegal criminal activity; it is a crime to do certain things. State and local governments have special responsibilities in this area, and certain federal agencies, such as the Drug Enforcement Administration, are active here as well. Another form of regulation focuses on American business and seeks to assure fair and competitive practices. Indeed, the first major regulatory effort in this country came in 1887, when the federal government created the Interstate Commerce Commission to regulate the railroads. Similar regulatory agencies today monitor securities (Securities and Exchange Commission), commodity exchanges (Commodity Futures Trading Association), and labor relations (National Labor Relations Board), among others.

A more modern regulatory area is concerned with limiting access to certain goods available to the public generally, such as the airwaves (regulated by the Federal Communications Commission) or clean air and water (regulated by the Environmental Protection Agency). Other regulatory bodies focus on protecting health and safety, in such areas as consumer protection (Consumer Product Safety Commission), air travel (Federal Aviation Administration), food (Food and Drug Administration), and workplace safety (the Occupational Safety and Health Administration).

While federal regulation of economic activities has seen several waves of growth through the past century (Ripley & Franklin, 1987), the last decade has been a movement in the opposite direction. Late in the Carter administration and extending through the Reagan administration, there were several efforts to deregulate certain industries. The Civil Aviation Board was disbanded in 1984 and significant areas of transportation, telecommunications, and banking were deregulated. Moreover, regulations were eliminated or enforcement slowed down in areas such as the workplace, auto, and consumer products safety.

Distributive policy, perhaps the most common form of government policy, uses general tax revenues to provide benefits to individuals or groups, often by means of grants or subsidies. If the country faces a large agricultural surplus, for example, the federal government may provide incentive payments to farmers not to produce crops that would add to the surplus. Similarly, the federal government provides direct grants to state and local governments for a variety of purposes. Finally, governments often create "public goods" that all citizens can enjoy. In some cases, such as national defense, the good is provided

49

for all; in others, such as city, state, or national parks, it is anticipated that some citizens will use the benefit and others will not. (In chapter 3, we will examine the growing trend toward employing user fees for certain of these traditionally public goods.)

Unlike regulatory agencies that are often at odds with a clientele group they are seeking to regulate, agencies that carry out distributive policies often develop close relationships with their constituencies and, in turn, with interested members of Congress. The growth of veteran's benefits over the past several decades is an almost classic example of the operation of such a subgovernment. The Veterans Administration is now one of the largest federal agencies and provides a broad range of health benefits, educational assistance, pensions, and insurance for veterans. Such a development would not have been possible without the VA's close relationship with veteran's groups (such as the American Legion and the Veterans of Foreign Wars) and with the veteran's committees in Congress.

Redistributive policies take taxes from certain groups and give them to another group. On rare occasions, redistribution is from the less well off to the better off; many charged that President Bush's capital gains proposal early in his administration was of this type. Redistribution is, however, generally thought of as benefiting less advantaged groups at the perceived expense of the advantaged. Among major redistributive policies are those that deal with (1) income stabilization, helping to support those who are unemployed or retired; (2) social welfare, providing either direct payments to individuals or supporting state and local efforts for the indigent; and (3) health care programs, such as Medicaid and Medicare. Most federal agencies active in the redistributive area, such as the Social Security Administration or the Office of Human Development, are located in the Department of Health and Human Services.

Since redistributive policies are often (though sometimes incorrectly) viewed in win-lose terms—that is, if one group benefits, another will surely lose—they generate perhaps more intense discussion than any other area of public policy. Despite this controversy, every American president since Roosevelt and prior to Reagan has supported some major redistributive efforts. President Reagan, however, took the opposite position, seeking to limit and even reduce redistributive programs. Although support for such programs in the Congress remained substantial, and few programmatic changes came about through legislation, budget reductions and administrative actions substantially diminished social programs.

Constituent policies (Lowi, 1972, p. 300) are intended to benefit the public generally or to serve the government. Foreign and defense policies are good examples of the first set of constituent policies, as well as good examples of the operations of a significant subgovernment. The Air Force had lobbied since the 1960s to build the B-1 bomber as a mainstay of our air defense. In 1978, President Carter was able to "kill" the B-1; however, only three years later, a combination of Defense Department officials, representatives from the defense industry (especially contractors), and congressional supporters of increased military capabilities helped President Reagan resurrect the B-1. Even today the B-1 remains an object of debate and controversy.

The other set of constituent policies are those directed toward the agencies of government itself. Legislation affecting the structure and function of government agencies, as well as policies governing their operations, falls in this area. President Carter was especially interested in this area and was instrumental in such changes as a reorganization of the federal personnel system and a reemphasis on affirmative action in hiring practices. President Reagan was more interested in matters of technical efficiency in government and appointed the Grace Commission to locate alleged problems of waste in government. Early in his term, President Bush showed a special interest in the ethical posture of governmental agencies as well as a willingness to work within the governmental system rather than to confront established powers in Washington.

Sources of Bureaucratic Power

There are several reasons governmental agencies have become so influential in the policy process. First, those who staff the agencies constitute an enormous source of expertise with respect to their areas of interest. No president, governor, mayor, or legislator could ever be expected to gain comparable expertise in all areas. Consequently, to make informed decisions, elected officials must often rely on those in the various agencies. It is often said that information is power; the information that is stored in government agencies is a distinct source of power.

Second, as noted earlier, legislation is often both inevitably and intentionally vague, leaving considerable discretion to the administrator. In some cases, legislators simply wish to defer to the expertise of those in the agencies to provide detailed rules and interpretations. In others, they are recognizing the necessity of some flexibility in administering public programs. In still others, they are responding to the pressures of the legislative process itself, where specificity leads to disputes and vagueness can often promote agreement.

Administrative discretion is also necessary because changing conditions necessitate changing policies, and it is not always possible to wait for new laws to be passed. In the 1960s, for example, the Department of Agriculture sought to maintain farm income by lowering the supply of agricultural products. Following shortages in the seventies, the department sought increased production. In the eighties, the policy once again became one of limiting production (Anderson, Brady, & Bullock, 1984). Flexibility is also needed as new information is discovered; for example, a few years ago, the Surgeon General sent a brochure to all households in the country outlining the latest information about AIDS—an action not mandated by Congress but, in the judgment of the Surgeon General, required by emerging events.

Through their expertise and discretionary power, those in public agencies help shape public policy. But there are more active and more political ways in which certain agencies become involved in the policy process. Whereas all agencies participate in making policy at some level, some agencies clearly are more politically adept than others. The Defense Department and the Veterans Administration, for example, both wield considerable power, whereas the Government Printing Office has little.

The power, influence, and, in turn, the resources an agency is able to generate depend on several factors, some external to the agency, some internal (Meier, 1987, pp. 54–72). Obviously, shifts in public opinion concerning the agency's task are likely to affect the support the agency receives. The National Aeronautics and Space Administration has experienced wide variations in public support over the years, riding a crest of popularity with the first lunar landing, but later coming under special scrutiny in the wake of the Challenger disaster. Not surprisingly, there seems to be a close correlation between

51

favorable public opinion concerning an agency's area of interest and the support it receives from Congress.

More specific support comes from clientele groups, members of the legislature, and others in the executive branch. We have already noted the support certain agencies receive from clientele groups who benefit from the agencies' actions. Obviously, the larger and more powerful the supporters of the agency, the more powerful the agency is likely to be. But agencies also develop opposition, which can be damaging to the agency's programs. The Environmental Protection Agency, for example, interacts with many different groups, including businesses, state environmental agencies, members of the scientific community, and groups like the Sierra Club or the National Wildlife Federation; the EPA is likely to receive support from some groups and opposition from others.

Special support can also come from individual members of the legislature who decide, for whatever reason, to champion an agency's cause. Rep. Claude Pepper, for instance, became associated with improved benefits for older Americans and, in that role, worked closely with the Social Security Administration and related social welfare agencies. As we have seen, the combination of congressional and clientele support can lead to the development of "subgovernments" within particular policy areas. These subgovernments come about, in part, because each group has something to give and something to gain from the relationship. The agency can provide quick and favorable responses to congressional requests for help as well as rulings favorable to clientele groups. In return, the agency might receive support for expansion of its budget and programs.

52   Support may also come from other members of the executive branch. Presidential support is obviously important, whether it is diffuse support of the general area of the agency's work or specific, as in a president's support for AIDS research, increased drug enforcement, or a particular new weapons system. But agencies are also attentive to their relationships with other agencies. The development of a new state park may raise environmental issues, economic development issues, and health issues. The Parks Department will clearly fare better if all the relevant groups and agencies are "on-board."

In addition to the external sources of bureaucratic power, there are several internal sources of power (Meier, 1987, pp. 66–72). We have already noted the importance of the *information* and expertise of agency personnel. Especially in highly technical areas, such as medicine or agricultural economics, those in the agencies are likely to be far more knowledgeable than many others involved in setting policies and priorities. If they can employ their expertise credibly, demonstrating effective performance over time, the agency will surely benefit.

Agencies are also likely to benefit by their **cohesion,** the degree to which members are uniformly committed to the organization and its goals. An agency that is seen as divided over major issues will suffer a loss of credibility. Conversely, a sense of unity within an agency is likely to make the agency more effective, both internally and externally.

Finally, agencies benefit from strong and effective *leadership.* Caspar Weinberger, whether in the Federal Trade Commission, the Office of Management and Budget, or the Department of Defense, was generally perceived to be a capable spokesperson for his agency's position, as well as a highly competent internal manager able to lead the organization in new directions. The impact of effective versus ineffective leadership is illustrated by the change in the EPA under the highly effective William Ruckelshaus and the ineffective Anne Burford.

The power of particular agencies, therefore, is the result of interaction between the agency and its environment, a process to which the agency brings certain strengths, but must also exercise considerable skill to reach its goals. The external support an agency can generate and the internal combination of its knowledge, cohesion, and leadership affect the amount of power and influence it can command. Whatever an agency's degree of power and influence, however, that power and influence must be exercised judiciously. The agency is a creation of the legislature, and its programs are always subject to the legislature's review, alteration, and even termination.

Legislative Supervision: Structural Controls

Obviously, most governmental programs (and the agencies that administer them) first take shape in the legislative process. In response to public demands and perhaps also executive leadership, the Congress or a state legislature or a city council or a board of directors passes legislation to correct a particular problem. The problems vary widely, from federal environmental policy to state education requirements to local trash collection practices to the establishment of local health centers, but in most cases legislation authorizes the program. Typically, especially in larger jurisdictions, money to operate the program is separately authorized through an appropriations process. With a program authorized and money appropriated, the building (or expansion) of a public organization can commence.

Legislation is, however, somewhat limited as a device for controlling the day-to-day   53
activities of public organizations, especially at the federal and state levels. (Remember that legislation is usually intentionally vague at some points.) But legislation can be used as a control device. After a program is underway, legislation may be passed to prevent members of the executive branch from taking certain actions (Meier, 1987, pp. 140–141). For example, the Boland amendment sought to prevent covert action in support of the Contras in Nicaragua in the mid-1980s. Whereas legislation authorizing programs must inevitably be somewhat general, legislative prohibitions on administrative actions can be quite specific. (However, as in the Iran–Contra scandal, members of an administration may go to great lengths to reinterpret legislation so as to avoid those prohibitions.)

One specific device legislatures employ to control public agencies is the **legislative veto,** a statutory provision that essentially says that any action proposed by the executive (or administrative agency) under provisions of a particular piece of legislation is subject to the approval or disapproval of Congress (or some portion of Congress), usually within thirty to ninety days. For example, legislation might authorize a new highway program, but require legislative consent to undertake specific projects. The legislative veto was first used in the 1930s to permit the president to reorganize, subject to review by Congress. In the seventies and early eighties, however, the legislative veto began to be used in many other areas, most notably in the War Powers Resolution of 1973, which required the president to notify Congress of military action and to cease such action within sixty days unless Congress acts to continue it.

The effect of a legislative veto provision on a public agency is illustrated in the experience of the Federal Trade Commission in the late seventies and early eighties. An aggressive consumer protection effort by the FTC in the late seventies was countered by business groups in Congress, who successfully passed legislation to the effect that

Congress could disapprove any FTC rules it didn't like. Congress used that provision in 1982 to disapprove an FTC rule, which had been developed over a ten-year period, requiring used-car dealers to disclose defects in cars they sold (Ripley & Franklin, 1987, pp. 141–142). In a similar case that found its way to the Supreme Court as *Immigration and Naturalization Services v. Chadha* (1983), the Court ruled the legislative veto unconstitutional. The Court's argument was that the constitutional process for passing legislation requires the involvement of the president, and actions under a legislative veto provision fail to involve the executive.

Despite the unconstitutionality of the legislative veto, the interest of the Congress in controlling the work of administrative agencies has not diminished. Indeed, Congress has found a variety of ways to get around the Chadha ruling, either informally, or by adding detailed rules to legislative authorizations, or by simply continuing to include veto provisions in legislation despite the court's ruling (Fisher, 1985). Some have even charged that congressional involvement in the details of administration (sometimes called *micromanagement*) has increased as a result of the Chadha ruling (P.A. Times, 29 April 1988, p. 1). According to this argument, Congress, lacking the legislative veto, has sought to exert its influence through increasingly detailed legislation, which may unduly limit administrative flexibility. (The Chadha ruling in a federal case does not itself limit the use of the legislative veto at the state level, where use of the veto has been rapidly growing. Those few cases that have been decided in state courts, however, have followed the Chadha lead in ruling the legislative veto unconstitutional [Johnson, 1983]. At the same time, state legislatures have also continued vetolike actions.)

Another control device that legislatures employ, to assess the performance of agencies and to eliminate those that are not successful, is the **sunset law.** Sunset laws are based on the assumption that certain governmental programs should periodically terminate, to continue only after an evaluation of the program's effectiveness and a specific vote by the legislature. "The objective is to replace the assumption that every program automatically continues unless there is a specific vote to terminate it, with the assumption that every program automatically terminates unless there is a specific vote to continue it" (Behn, 1977, p. 104). Sunset laws became popular in the late seventies and early eighties, after the state of Colorado, at the urging of Common Cause, passed a set of laws requiring that certain regulatory agencies be terminated at a given point unless given new life by the legislature. Soon dozens of other states and many municipalities passed general sunset laws, applying termination dates to a set of programs, or included sunset provisions in legislation creating new programs. Proposals containing sunset provisions were also presented at the federal level.

The purpose of specifying a particular life span for a program is to force careful evaluation of the program at some future point. Critics of automatic terminations point out several problems, not the least of which is the cost of evaluations and the burden to the legislature and legislative staff if all programs were periodically evaluated in great detail. Questions also arise about whether sunset legislation actually changes our assumptions about continuing most programs; for example, no one would seriously anticipate that a police or fire department would be eliminated. Finally, critics point out that most programs are reviewed periodically anyway and that highly ineffective programs are often eliminated even without "sunset" provisions.

54

A final mechanism through which legislative bodies formally exert control over administrative agencies is passage of broad legislation to govern agency conduct. Such legislation, applicable to all agencies, might affect administrative procedures, contracting or purchasing arrangements, human resources management, or other areas. A good example is the continuing congressional interest in access to governmental information. Following World War II, governmental agencies, probably in keeping with the military mentality of the war years, could legally classify as "confidential" all records for which there was "good cause" to hold secret. As you can imagine, it was not difficult to come up with all kinds of "good causes" or reasons to withhold records. The practice of keeping secrets became so widespread that one congressional investigating group found that the Pentagon had classified as secret the construction of the bow and arrow and the fact that water runs downhill! Similarly, the General Services Administration had decided photographs could not be taken in federal buildings without permission of the janitor (Archibald, 1979, p. 314).

As a result of findings such as these, and in the belief that the public has the right to information gathered by the government, Congress passed the Freedom of Information Act in 1966. The law was based on the assumption that the public has the right to know, except in clearly defined and exceptional cases; in other words, it limited those in the executive branch from classifying documents for ill-defined purposes. Implementation of the new law was hindered by confusion about certain of its parts and by some agency officials who still tried to maintain as much secrecy as possible. These problems were addressed in a series of amendments passed over the veto of President Ford in 1974. The amendments required agencies to respond to inquiries quickly and even sought to penalize government officials who hid government records from the public (Archibald, 1979). Although problems with the act have persisted, nearly all federal agencies have now implemented the Freedom of Information provisions.

These examples of constraints on the operation of government agencies are closely related to **sunshine laws** that require various agencies, especially regulatory agencies, to conduct business in public view (except under specific conditions). All fifty states now have "sunshine" provisions for their own legislative bodies, for administrative agencies, and for local governments. In all these cases, the legislative body, in expressing its concern for the public's right to be informed about the public's business, has exercised control over a broad range of administrative agencies.

Legislative Supervision: Oversight

In addition to the "structural" mechanisms for legislative control, the legislature also exercises continuing supervision of administrative agencies through what is called the *oversight* function. Each house of Congress has a government operations committee charged with overseeing the activities of all government agencies, including their relationships with other levels of government. In addition, each of the other congressional committees exercises oversight responsibility with respect to its particular area of interest and expertise (e.g., defense, welfare, the post office). Oversight is especially connected to the legislative and appropriations processes, but may occur at any time. For this reason, it is not unusual to see a cabinet secretary, complete with charts and documents, testifying before a congressional committee that is interested in his or her programs.

Holding hearings is probably the most visible oversight activity of Congress, at times assuming a circuslike atmosphere. The Iran–Contra hearings, for example, were essentially an investigation of the activities of the National Security Council, an executive agency, but they became the arena for considerable political in-fighting concerning the Reagan administration's conduct of foreign policy. (They were also noteworthy for their revelations of intentional efforts by Col. Oliver North and Undersecretary of State Elliot Abrams to deceive Congress in the course of normal oversight activities.)

The exposure that hearings provide members of Congress is obvious. Politicians from Harry Truman to Sam Ervin to Daniel Inouye have built national reputations through their involvement in congressional hearings. But hearings can also provide excellent opportunities for administrative officials—at the federal, state, and local levels, and in nonprofit organizations—to tell their side of the story, to help educate members of the legislature and the public generally, and to build support for their programs. Consequently, most agencies devote considerable time and attention to legislative relations, often, at the federal level, working through a legislative liaison office, or, at the state and local levels, on a more individual basis.

Nationally, Congress can also exercise oversight through its staff agencies, most of which were significantly enhanced by legislation in the early 1970s that created the Congressional Budget Office and charged it with furnishing certain program information to Congress, and also shifted the focus of the General Accounting Office from its traditional financial auditing to program evaluations. Now, in addition to holding hearings, Congress can exercise oversight responsibility through staff evaluations of agency operations, by requesting information from the Congressional Budget Office, or by initiating audits or program evaluations by the General Accounting Office. Although staff capabilities at the state and local levels are considerably less, and often more focused on policy development than oversight, all levels of government have witnessed a general increase in legislative staff over the past twenty years.

Despite the array of oversight activities available to members of Congress and despite devoting increased staff resources to oversight, questions remain concerning the effectiveness of legislative oversight of executive branch operations. Part of the problem is simply that many legislators have relatively little interest in oversight activities. Instead, they tend to focus on policy issues, recognizing that they are much more likely to build their reputations in the policy arena than in oversight. Moreover, interest in oversight activities is likely to vary from time to time, increasing in times of crisis or public outcry, when new and different program requests are forthcoming from an agency, or when a member feels a particular agency has not been responsive to constituent groups. Generally, when a member has high confidence in a set of leaders and tends to agree with policies, the motivation for oversight decreases (see Box 2.5); conversely, when trust is low or when the member's favored policies are being ignored, the incentive for oversight is greater (Ogul, 1976).

Legislative Supervision: Casework

Legislators also interact with those in public agencies on an individual basis, usually in behalf of their constituents. Obviously, legislators who wish to be reelected must be attentive to requests for information or influence from those in their districts. And,

BOX 2.5

TESTIFYING BEFORE THE APPROPRIATIONS COMMITTEE

"The most important thing in a Committee hearing is creating an atmosphere of confidence—so that you have confidence in the Committee and they have confidence in you. I tell my people to be perfectly honest and to have a full, free, and frank discussion with the Committee, even if it hurts you a little bit. That will mean more than anything else in getting your money. Nobody likes to admit things and cast reflections on his own shop, but don't try to fool the congressmen. You can't. They have a sixth sense when someone is not talking freely and frankly. If you have a perfectly open discussion, they'll have more confidence in you, and your appropriations troubles will be minimized."

SOURCE: An agency budget officer quoted in Richard F. Fenno, Jr., *The Power of the Purse.* Boston: Little, Brown, 1966, p. 298.

57

on the other side of the coin, individual citizens have come to expect that they can and should receive help from their senator or representative in dealings with government. Thus, members of the legislature receive a multitude of requests for assistance, from someone who needs help to collect Social Security benefits to someone who hopes to influence the award of a particular governmental contract. Intervention in behalf of individuals or groups that need assistance with or access to government agencies is called legislative *casework.*

At the federal level, providing services for constituents has become one of the most time-consuming and important activities for Congress members. Requests for assistance are typically handled by congressional staff members who specialize in casework. If the request requires an inquiry into an agency activity, the staffer will likely approach the agency's congressional liaison office or perhaps go directly to the agency head or a regional office. In most instances, inquiries are responded to promptly, and information about the case and any necessary explanations of the agency's action are returned quickly to the member of Congress.

Federal officials, in both the legislature and the agencies, feel the process is useful not only in providing a mechanism for review, but in clarifying agency policies and procedures and assessing agency performance (Johannes, 1984). Occasionally, however, pressure to "bend the rules" or to play political favoritism occurs. Several years ago, for example, Congressman Daniel Flood of Pennsylvania was charged with conspiracy, bribery, and perjury in connection with his efforts to obtain certain federal grants and loans for a hospital in his district.

Casework activities seem less routine and institutionalized at the state and local levels. Here there appear to be both benefits and costs (Elling, 1980). On the one hand, casework activities serve to "humanize" the bureaucracy; on the other, there are disadvantages in the disruption of administrative processes and in the possibility of political influence. Certainly in the more highly professionalized governmental agencies, agency heads view legislators' involvement positively (Abney & Lauth, 1982).

In many European countries, and in some American states and localities, the legislature's casework function has been paralleled or even turned over to the office of the **ombudsman,** a permanent office that receives complaints and acts on behalf of citizens in securing information, requesting services, or pursuing grievances. Many other jurisdictions have created similar, though less formal, structures, such as public advocates, citizen's assistance offices, and so on (Hill, 1982).

RELATIONSHIPS WITH THE JUDICIARY

The relationship between administrative agencies and the judiciary derives, as you might expect, from the legal foundations of administrative actions, some of which are quasi-legislative and others of which are quasi-judicial. Those that are *quasi-legislative* elaborate the details of legislation. As we have noted, most legislation is necessarily and intentionally general, leaving considerable room for interpretation or discretion on the part of the administrator. For example, an agency might be required by law to set safety standards for nuclear-powered electric utilities, but receive little guidance about which specific standards should be employed. The agency would seek to determine appropriate standards, then develop rules to govern implementation of the legislation. **Rule making** is concerned with establishing general guidelines that would apply to a class of people or a class of actions in the future.

At the federal level, rule making by administrative agencies, as well as many other aspects of administrative law, is governed by the Administrative Procedures Act. (Similar statutes exist in each state to provide the legal framework for administrative actions.) The act seeks to assure that rules are based on proper legal authority, that there are both adequate notice of the rule making and an opportunity for citizens to be heard, that the rule is clear and unambiguous, and that people are given sufficient advance warning that the new rule will take effect. In most cases, rule making is fairly straightforward, involving notice, comment, and steps to assure an adequate record; in others, legislation requires greater detail and great formality in the rule-making process. Food and Drug regulations and others that involve high risks require a formal rule-making process, which includes a trial-type hearing, and often takes years to resolve (Cooper, 1983).

Other administrative actions are *quasi-judicial* in that they produce orders relating to individual cases. For example, following the issuance of safety standards for nuclear power plants, an administrator might have to decide if a particular plant has met those standards. Similarly, an administrator might have to decide if a specific individual is eligible for worker's compensation. In such cases, the administrator is making decisions that determine one's status under the law. The substantive decisions are obviously important, but so are the procedures under which they are resolved. For example, a woman denied welfare support might request a hearing to argue her case before a final decision is made. The administrator's decision to grant or refuse the hearing represents another kind of quasi-judicial administrative action.

In quasi-judicial administrative actions, often called *adjudication*, procedural issues such as those just mentioned are of special importance. There is a desire that citizens be treated fairly and not subjected to arbitrary decisions. Consequently, where standards of due process are applied, notice of the proposed action must be given, there must be a chance for the affected party to respond, and there must be an independent decision maker and an opportunity for appeal (Cooper, 1983).

The courts may review administrative actions (in rule making, adjudication, or other areas) through *judicial review*. Such review typically occurs when a party "suffering legal wrong because of agency action, or adversely affected or aggrieved by agency action" seeks judicial remedy (5 U.S.C., Section 702). The court reviews the case in light of constitutional, statutory, and executive provisions and determines the appropriateness of the administrative action. Generally speaking, courts may find unlawful and set aside agency actions that are unconstitutional, that extend beyond the limits of statutory authority, that are "arbitrary, capricious, or an abuse of discretion," that are procedurally unfair, or without substantive justification (5 U.S.C., Section 706).

Of special interest are those cases in which the court determines that the administrative agency has misinterpreted (or gone beyond) the intent of the legislature. As an example, the statute creating the Occupational Safety and Health Administration (OSHA) in the Department of Labor charged the agency with developing a standard for toxic substances in the workplace "which assures, to the extent feasible . . . that no employee will suffer material impairment . . . even if such employee has regular exposure to the hazard . . . for the period of his working life" (quoted in Cooper, 1983, p. 192). After extensive studies, OSHA determined that exposure to the toxic substance benzine created a risk of cancer and other health hazards and set a standard accordingly.

The American Petroleum Institute sought judicial review that led the courts to a discussion of two rather interesting issues. One aspect of the case had to do with legislative intent. The Fifth Circuit Court focused on this issue, finding that the phrase "to the extent feasible" in the legislation meant that a standard had to be both technologically and economically feasible. For this reason, the court set aside the OSHA standard. The Supreme Court concentrated more on the health aspects of the case, with the majority concluding that existing standards were not dangerous and the new standard was not necessary. The justices who dissented argued that the court should not substitute its own judgment on the technical merits of the case for that of experts within the agency. The benzine case illustrates several of the most important difficulties that face the courts in reviewing administrative actions.

The courts lately have more frequently acted not only to review agency actions, but to compel agency action "unlawfully withheld or unreasonably delayed" (5 U.S.C., Section 706). A few years ago, the Food and Drug Administration received a petition from a group of death row inmates to determine whether the materials used for lethal injections were safe and painless or whether they might leave the prisoner conscious but paralyzed, a witness to his or her own slow death. The FDA responded that it did not have jurisdiction to review the practices of state corrections systems in cases such as this; however, on review, the Circuit Court concluded that the FDA did indeed have jurisdiction. The court wrote, "In this case FDA is clearly refusing to exercise enforcement discretion

59

because it does not wish to become embroiled in an issue so morally and emotionally troubling as the death penalty. As a result of the FDA's inaction, appellants face the risk of cruel execution . . ." (quoted in Cooper, 1985, p. 649).

Closely related to the FDA's failure to undertake an investigation are cases in which the agency refuses to make rules or delays the issuance of rules required by statute. But there have also been several recent cases where agencies have been found to have exceeded their authority in rescinding previously established rules. The Department of Transportation recently withdrew mandatory passive restraint rules as part of a general effort toward deregulation of the automobile industry. The Supreme Court found that this action was not fully justified by the record and remanded the case to the agency for further exploration.

Concerns for Due Process

At the heart of our system of jurisprudence is the assurance that people will be treated fairly, that they have a right to present arguments and evidence in their own behalf, and that those who make the decisions will be unbiased and impartial. As with administrative adjudication in issues of due process—whether a hearing is required, at what point, and the format of the hearing—some patterns have emerged in the Supreme Court's evaluation of administrative matters. During the fifties, sixties, and early seventies, the Court sought to protect the rights of citizens from arbitrary action on the part of administrative agencies by requiring that, before a person could be made to suffer serious harm, that person should be allowed an opportunity to challenge the proposed action. The Court would not allow cost or inconvenience to the agency as an excuse for causing harm to an individual.

Through the seventies and eighties, however, the Supreme Court, under the leadership of Chief Justice Warren Burger, began to alter its approach to administrative due process, treating administrative hearings not as a means of protection but as devices for fact-finding. Most frequently, the Court has employed a "balancing test," weighing the interests of the individual (rather narrowly defined), the value of additional safeguards, and the government's interest (including the fiscal and administrative burdens that additional procedural safeguards might impose). As a result, it has become much more difficult for someone who feels that adequate protections have not been provided to prevail in the courts (Cooper, 1982).

The Courts and Agency Administration

Over the past twenty years, one of the most dramatic developments in the relationship between administrative agencies and the judiciary is the direct involvement of federal district courts (and some state courts) in agency administration, including decisions on spending, personnel, organization, and management. This involvement has come about through court rulings in *administrative equity cases*, wherein individual rights, such as the prohibition against cruel and unusual punishment, have been violated by state and local administrative organizations.

Two landmark cases in the early seventies set precedents for such rulings. In the first, prisoners in the Arkansas Penitentiary System alleged a large number of abuses, including dangerous and unhealthy conditions in the prisons. The court ruled that confinement in the Arkansas system amounted to cruel and unusual punishment and ordered corrections officials to devise a plan to remedy the problems. Similarly, in Alabama, a federal district court judge found "intolerable and deplorable" conditions in that state's largest mental health facility and ordered corrective actions. The court also established a constitutional right to treatment, detailing actions required to meet that constitutional standard (Gilmour, 1982, pp. 26–29).

The involvement of courts in the management of public agencies is especially well illustrated in a federal judge's order demanding reform of the New Orleans Parish Prison. In addition to ordering adequate medical services, improved security, and development of recreational facilities, the judge directed that "the management and operation of the prison be improved immediately," that a professional penologist be hired to manage the prison, and that personnel practices (filling vacancies, raising wages, etc.) be improved in specific ways. Although court actions such as this have obviously corrected constitutional inequities, there are questions as to whether the courts are well suited for involvement in the details of administration (see Box 2.6). Moreover, many states and localities argue that court-ordered expenditures of funds on projects such as desegregation or prison reform take money away from other needed services, such as education, social welfare, or mental health. Indeed, for these various reasons, the Supreme Court has recently taken steps to limit the involvement of courts in the work of administrative agencies, requiring carefully tailored plans of limited duration based on specific constitutional violations.

61

B O X   2 . 6

THE FEDERAL COURTS AND STATE ACTION

"The U. S. Supreme Court has let stand a ruling requiring Alaska to collect rent or royalties from miners of gold, silver, and other hard rock, despite the fact that collections will be so low that the money won't even cover state paper-work costs.

"Under the Alaska Statehood Act, the state received more than 100 million acres of land and was directed to devise a system to protect its mineral rights. The Legislature decided to collect royalties from companies involved in the lucrative search for oil, gas, and coal, but waived the requirement for the mining of gold, silver, and other hard rock because it did not generate much money.

"Alaska received more than $1 billion a year in royalties from companies that mine for oil and gas, the state's major resources. The state has argued that royalties for hard rock mining would

(continued)

(continued)

amount to only $100,000 a year, not enough to make the paper work worthwhile.

"A coalition of environmental, fishing and native Alaskan groups had originally filed suit to force the state to collect fees for the mining for hard rock, accusing Alaska of violating the Alaska Statehood Act."

SOURCE: *City and State* 5 (June 6, 1988): 4. Reprinted by permission.

SUMMARY AND ACTION IMPLICATIONS

This chapter has explored the political context of public administration, including things you will simply need to know to operate effectively in or with public organizations. The material in this chapter (and in chapter 3) constitutes a knowledge base on which to build your action skills. Understanding the political context of work in the public sector will enhance the effectiveness of your actions.

62   Public managers work in many different institutional settings, but those institutions all reflect important political values that lie at the heart of a democratic system. Whether at the federal, state, or local level, in government or in the nonprofit sector, a democracy's values, especially a concern for operating in the public interest, affect the structure of public organizations. For example, the division of powers at the federal level expresses a fear of concentrated power; similarly, the council–manager plan expresses one way to view the relationship between politics and administration. Finally, the structure of non-profit organizations reflects their operation in the public interest. Knowing something about how democratic values are reflected in the structure of public organizations and knowing something about the role of executive leadership in administrative organizations will enable you to act with greater confidence and authority.

As a public manager, you may have important interactions with a legislative body, either the national Congress, a state legislature, a local city council, or a nonprofit organization's board of directors. Those in public organizations participate in one way or another in nearly all policy areas—a situation that our political system encourages. The distinction Woodrow Wilson suggested between politics (or policy) and administration no longer accurately describes the relationship between the legislative and the executive branch. Today, the legislature and the various agencies of government share in the policy process, either working together in developing policy or making separate decisions in different realms.

As a public manager, you will also deal with the legislature in many other ways. Most importantly, the legislature will establish the tasks your agency or association will undertake and provide human and financial resources to carry them out. Moreover, the legislative body will exercise continuing, though sometimes intermittent, supervision over your work. Thus, you may spend a great deal of time developing effective working relationships with those in the legislature.

The involvement of the courts in the work of administration is both intense and inevitable. For this reason, your understanding of the legal system and your ability to interact with legal and judicial officers will improve your effectiveness as a public manager. Whether you are dealing with the legislative body or the courts, your relationship with either need not be adversarial. Indeed, in many cases, the legislature and the courts can help to substantially improve administrative practices.

By now you should be coming to realize that your behavior as a public manager is bounded by a vast and complicated network of relationships in which you are but one of many players. Within this network, you must be attentive to questions of executive leadership, legislative intent and oversight, and judicial interpretation. The world of the public administrator is indeed complex!

TERMS AND DEFINITIONS

Agenda setting: Phase in public policy process when certain problems come to be viewed as needing attention.

Cohesion: Degree to which members of a group are uniformly committed to the group and its goals.

Constituent policy: Policy designed to benefit the public generally or to serve the government.

Distributive policy: Policy involving use of general tax funds to provide assistance and benefits to individuals or groups.

Executive order: A presidential mandate directed to and governing, with the effect of law, the actions of government officials and agencies.

Independent agencies: Agencies intentionally created outside the normal cabinet organization.

Iron triangle: Term given to a coalition of interest groups, agency personnel, and members of Congress created to exert influence on a particular policy issue.

Legislative veto: Statutory provision that gives Congress the authority to approve or disapprove certain executive actions.

Nonprofit organizations: Organizations prohibited by law from distributing surplus revenues to individuals.

Ombudsman: Permanent office that receives complaints and acts on behalf of citizens to secure information, request services, or pursue grievances.

Policy: Statement of goals and intentions with respect to a particular problem or set of problems.

Policy entrepreneur: A person willing to invest personal time, energy, and money in pursuit of particular policy changes.

Public corporations: An essentially commercial agency where work requires greater latitude and acquires at least a portion of its funding in the marketplace (e.g., Tennessee Valley Authority).

Public policy: Authoritative statements made by legitimate governmental actors about public problems.

Redistributive policy: Policy designed to take taxes from certain groups and give them to another group.

Regulatory commission: Group formed to regulate a particular area of the economy; usually headed by a group of individuals appointed by the president and confirmed by the Senate.

Regulatory policy: Policy designed to limit actions of persons or groups to protect all or parts of the general public.

Rule making: Administrative establishment of general guidelines for application to a class of people or a class of actions at some future time.

Sunset law: Provision that sets a specific termination date for a program.

Sunshine law: Provision that requires agencies to conduct business in public view.

STUDY QUESTIONS

1. What do we mean by the term *public policies?*
2. Describe how the president's role in the administration of government has changed since the framing of the Constitution.
3. Describe the administrative system at the federal level.
4. State and local governments have been designed to operate similarly to the national level; however, both have distinct structures for administering government initiatives. Explain each level's structure and the different approaches to operating the government bureaucracy.
5. Describe the policy process and actors who play significant roles in shaping administrative issues.
6. What are the four types of policy? Define and give examples.
7. How do agencies maintain a power base within the government?
8. Describe some of the structural controls on bureaucratic power and how government, as a whole, benefits from these controls.
9. Discuss several ways the legislative and judicial branches interact with the bureaucracy. Explain why these interventions are necessary and useful.

CASES AND EXERCISES

1. We have discussed the various powers, both formal and informal, that affect the governor's ability to exercise executive power in the administration of state government. Among the informal powers that governors exercise are political powers (including agenda setting), budgetary powers, and executive leadership. Among the formal powers are the presence or absence of an item veto, the ability of the governor to reorganize state agencies, and the number of other elected statewide officials. Analyze the power of the governor in *your* state, giving special attention to the governor's power to exercise executive leadership over the agencies of state government. How do your governor's executive powers compare to those of the president of the United States? How do they compare to those of your local mayor?

2. The *United States Government Manual* is the handbook or encyclopedia of federal government programs and activities. It contains descriptions of the many programs the federal government operates, as well as information about how the government is organized to conduct those programs. Obtain a copy of the *Manual* and analyze the organization and structure of one cabinet-level department, such as transportation or health and human services. Then, using local sources, try to develop similar information about how your state and your local government are organized to deal with the same subject matter. What are the similarities and what are the differences? How do you explain them?

3. Attend a meeting of a congressional or state legislative committee, of your local city council, or of the board of directors of a local nonprofit organization. Watch the pattern of interaction between elected members of the legislative body and full-time administrators. (The latter may be agency staff called to testify, legislative support staff, a city manager or executive director, or many others.) What strengths does each side bring to the exchange? What is the level of cooperation or competition? If possible, try to follow up with the administrator to see how he or she felt about the interchange. To what extent did the legislative body set a clear direction for the administrator's ensuing actions? What discretion did the administrator have (or claim to have) following the meeting?

65

4. Consider the following case: Billie Jackson was city manager of a small community in Colorado. For six years, Billie had been trying to interest members of her city council in purchasing an abandoned downtown hotel for conversion to a city-owned long-term care facility. Billie felt strongly that the community needed such a facility and that the city had a golden opportunity to meet that need through purchase of the hotel. The problem was that several extremely conservative members of the council felt differently. In their view, the city shouldn't get into providing social services, especially where the need might be met by a private firm at some point in the future. Moreover, they felt the cost of the purchase and renovations would be more than the community could bear.

The hotel issue was once again on the council agenda, and Billie was determined to make the strongest appeal possible. With the help of a nearby university, she had prepared a lengthy report documenting the need for the facility and the desirability of purchasing the hotel. Just as she was beginning her presentation, one of the conservative council members said, "Mrs. Jackson, we have heard more on this topic than we care to. I just don't want to go through all this again. I move to table the issue indefinitely." The motion to table carried by a quick and somewhat confused voice vote.

Assume the role of Billie Jackson. What is your immediate response? What would you do in the days and weeks that followed? Would you consider resignation? Why or why not?

5. Reread the Alaska case in Box 2.6. Discuss your response to this case. Under what circumstances, if any, do you think it is appropriate for a federal court to order a state or locality to undertake an action it has chosen not to take and that will cost the state or locality to administer?

FOR ADDITIONAL READING

Bowman, Ann O'M., and Kearney, Richard C. *The Resurgence of the States.* Englewood Cliffs, NJ: Prentice-Hall, 1986.

Cooper, Phillip J. *Public Law and Public Administration.* Palo Alto, CA: Mayfield, 1983.

Gies, David L., Ott, J. Steven, and Shafritz, Jay (eds.). *The Nonprofit Organization.* Pacific Grove, CA: Brooks/Cole, 1990.

Kingdon, John W. *Agendas, Alternatives, and Public Policies.* Boston: Little, Brown, 1984.

Mazmanian, Daniel A., and Sabatier, Paul. *Implementation and Public Policy.* Glenview, IL: Scott, Foresman, 1983.

McLaughlin, Curtis. *The Management of Nonprofit Organizations.* New York: Wiley, 1986.

Meier, Kenneth J. *Politics and the Bureaucracy,* 2nd ed. Pacific Grove, CA: Brooks/Cole, 1987.

Palumbo, Dennis J. *Public Policy in America.* Englewood Cliffs, NJ: Prentice-Hall, 1988.

Ripley, Randall B., and Franklin, Grace A. *Congress, the Bureaucracy, and Public Policy,* 4th ed. Pacific Grove, CA: Brooks/Cole, 1987.

Seidmen, Harold, and Gilmour, Robert. *Politics, Position, and Power,* 4th ed. New York: Oxford University Press, 1986.

Wolf, Thomas. *The Nonprofit Organization.* Englewood Cliffs, NJ: Prentice-Hall, 1984.

Young, Dennis R. *If Not for Profit, for What?* Lexington, MA: Lexington Books, 1983.

CHAPTER THREE

THE
INTERORGANIZATIONAL
CONTEXT
OF
PUBLIC
ADMINISTRATION

As a public manager, you will interact not only with many
others at your level of government, but also with your counterparts
at other levels of government, to say nothing of those in client groups,
businesses, interest groups, and associations of all types. More and
more, public administrators recognize that managing an agency requires
paying attention to what happens in other organizations and that
relations with those outside the agency are just as important as relations
with those inside. This chapter will examine the interorganizational
context in which public administrators operate.

The traditional focus in public administration has been the agency,
and that is the focus we have largely taken so far. In many cases,
however, especially those involving various levels of government, those
involving both the public and private sector, and those that bring
together many different organizations in the delivery of human services,
it may be more helpful to focus not on the individual agency but on
the *relationships* among many different groups. Today, the effectiveness
of public programs depends on the ability of various agencies to
cooperate in delivering services.

Federal grant money, whether in housing, social services, transportation, or other areas, goes to states and localities to fund particular
programs. This funding is typically accompanied by specific guidelines
and reporting requirements to assure that the money is properly spent.
In turn, the states and localities may either develop their own
capabilities to run the programs or they may rely on other groups,
including nonprofit organizations or even private businesses.

The Job Training Partnership Act, for example, designed to help the unemployed prepare for the world of work, provides for grants to the states to conduct job-related training and development. The states, in turn, are required to create Private Industry Councils composed of public and private sector representatives at the local level to serve as a board of directors for developing training programs. The Councils then rely on a variety of other groups to actually run the programs—city or county governments, community action programs, councils of government, private nonprofit organizations, and even Chambers of Commerce. These administrative bodies deliver some services themselves, but also contract with other organizations, such as public school systems, private vocational schools, or private businesses to operate specific programs. The job training a particular individual receives may well be the product of work at all levels of government and perhaps the public, private, and nonprofit sectors.

This example illustrates complexity of the interactions triggered by federal policies. But equally complex relationships can grow from the bottom up as well. A local community that wants to attract new industry might develop a coalition of government, business, labor, and education groups to promote the city's image and to work with groups at other levels of government. These groups might include a state Department of Economic Development to help contact prospective employers wishing to relocate. Or the city might request that the state or federal government designate a particular area in the city as an *enterprise zone*, thus permitting special tax incentives and other benefits for businesses willing to locate there. Again, a variety of government and nongovernment entities are involved in the task of economic development.

One can easily understand why the effectiveness of many public programs depends on the quality of the relationships among various organizations. For this reason, some analysts emphasize the importance of the **interorganizational networks** that develop in various policy areas. Obviously, the various groups and organizations involved in any policy arena do not report to a single director, nor are they structured in a typically hierarchical fashion. Rather, they are loosely joined systems that often have overlapping areas of interest, duplication of effort, and lack of coordination (Milward, 1982, p. 464).

Whether the growing dependence on such systems is a helpful development is a matter of some debate. Many experts have suggested that the use of intermediaries in the delivery of services is a major reason for the difficulties many programs encounter (Kettl, 1988). On the other hand, many such networks have proven enormously stable over time, while others have capitalized on the inherent flexibility and adaptability of such systems. In any case, because interorganizational networks are such an important part of the management of public programs, they deserve our attention.

THE DEVELOPMENT OF INTERGOVERNMENTAL RELATIONS

In terms of your ability to operate public programs effectively and responsibly, you must understand the relationships among levels of government. There are various ways to describe the relationship between a larger comprehensive unit of government and its constituent parts. A *confederation*, for example, is a system in which the constituent units grant powers to the central government, but do not allow it to act independently.

A *unitary* system is one in which all powers reside with the central government and various units derive their powers from that unit. France and Sweden, for instance, are characterized by unitary systems. And the relationship between states and localities in the U.S. is unitary; localities hold only those powers specified or permitted by the state.

The relationship between our national government and the states, is *federal* in that it involves a division of powers between the two levels of government—federal and state/local. Some powers are granted specifically to the central government (to conduct foreign relations, to regulate interstate commerce, etc.); some are reserved by the states (to conduct elections, to establish local governments, etc.), and some are held by both levels (to tax, to borrow money, to make laws, etc.). (This system of governance is also referred to as "federalism.") A federal structure has many advantages, in that it allows for diversity and experimentation, but it has also led to the development of a highly complex intergovernmental system, a fact of life with important implications for the management of public programs.

The term **intergovernmental relations** is often used to encompass all the complex and interdependent relationships among those at various levels of government as they seek to develop and implement public programs. The importance of intergovernmental relations has been recognized in several structural developments. At the federal level, a permanent Advisory Commission of Intergovernmental Relations was established in 1959 and continues to operate. All states and nearly all major cities have a coordinator for intergovernmental relations (though the specific titles vary). Finally, many scholars and practitioners have begun to emphasize the managerial processes involved in intergovernmental relations by employing the term *intergovernmental management*.

A key to understanding intergovernmental relations in this country is understanding the changing patterns used to fund public programs. Although intergovernmental relations involves much more than money, financial questions are inevitably at the core of the process, so definitions of various types of **grants,** transfers of money (and property) from one government to another, are a helpful starting place.

Some grants give more discretion to the recipient than do others. **Categorical grants or project grants** may be spent for only a limited purpose, such as building a new sewage treatment plant. Categorical grants have historically been the predominant form of grants in this country; however, in recent years, many categorical grants have been consolidated into **block grants,** which may be used for nearly any purpose within a specific functional field, such as housing, community development, education, or law enforcement. The recipient government might spend a law enforcement grant on police training, new equipment, or crime prevention programs. Finally, **revenue sharing,** when it has been used, has made funds available for use by the recipient government in any way its leaders choose (within the law).

Grants may also be classified in terms of how they are made available. A **formula grant** employs a specific decision rule indicating how much money any given jurisdiction will receive. Typically, the decision rule is related to the purpose of the grant (for example, money for housing might be distributed to qualified governments based on the age and density of residential housing). A project grant, on the other hand, makes funds available on a competitive basis. Those seeking aid must submit an application for assistance for review and approval by the granting agency.

Grants may also be categorized as to the purposes they serve. **Entitlement grants** provide assistance to persons meeting certain criteria, such as age or income; for example, aid to families with dependent children or Medicaid. **Operating grants** are for use in the development and operation of specific programs, such as those in education or employment and job training. **Capital grants** are for use in construction or renovation, as in the development of the interstate highway system.

Finally, grants may vary according to whether they require matching funds from the recipient agency. Some federal grants require the state or locality to put up a certain percentage of the money for the project; in the case of the interstate highway system, states contribute one dollar for every nine dollars of federal money. Other grants require different matching amounts, and some will require no matching at all. Note that the different types may be combined in different ways to create quite a variety of grant possibilities. A specific grant might be made available on a competitive basis strictly for use in programs for job training and may require local matching funds.

Dual Federalism

Historically, the various grant types have been employed in different ways and in different times. The earliest period in our country's intergovernmental history, a period that lasted well into this century, was characterized by what has been called **dual federalism,** a pattern in which the federal and state governments both sought to carve out their own spheres of power and influence and during which there was relatively little intergovernmental cooperation—indeed, there was substantial conflict.

However, some programs cut across the strict divisions of federal, state, and local responsibility associated with dual federalism. A notable example is the Morrill Act of 1862, which granted land to universities to establish agricultural programs and was the basis for the eventual development of "land-grant" colleges. It was important in the development of higher education, but it was also precedent-setting in terms of the structure of its grants (Nathan, Doolittle, et al., 1987). No longer were grants made in a fairly open-ended fashion; specific instructions were attached, requiring that they be used for "agriculture and the mechanical arts." In addition, new reporting and accounting requirements were added as a condition of receiving the grants.

The adoption of grant programs such as the Morrill Act was accompanied by considerable anguish, because some saw such programs as a drastic departure from the dual federalism they preferred. The Morrill Act itself, signed by President Lincoln, had previously been vetoed by President Buchanan, who commented: "Should the time arrive when the State governments shall look to the Federal Treasury for the means of supporting themselves and maintaining their systems of education and internal policy, the character of both Governments will be greatly deteriorated" (quoted in Nathan et al., 1987, p. 25).

In any case, the period of dual federalism was marked by considerable conflict among the various levels of government. The federal government sought to deal effectively with the increasingly broad issues being raised in a more complex, urbanized society by developing new grant programs in such areas as highway construction and vocational education. The states, though they appreciated federal money, were cautious of federal

70

interference in their spheres of responsibility. The localities, though creatures of the state and dependent on state grants of authority or money, sought to build their own political bases. The resulting pattern of federalism resembled a layer cake, with three levels of government working parallel to one another but rarely together.

Cooperative Federalism

If the layer cake was the prevailing image associated with dual federalism, the marble cake was the image for the period that followed, notable for its increasing complexity and interdependence. As opposed to the conflict and division of the earlier period, the emerging era of **cooperative federalism** was characterized by greater sharing of responsibilities. The marble cake image implied a system in which roles and responsibilities were intermixed in a variety of patterns—vertical, horizontal, and even diagonal.

The great impetus for the development of cooperative federalism was the Roosevelt program for economic recovery following the Great Depression. Although the majority of President Roosevelt's programs were national in scope and could have been national in execution, a political choice was made to operate many of the programs through the states and their localities. The pattern of intergovernmental relations that emerged revealed a dramatically increased federal role, accompanied almost paradoxically by greater federal/state/local sharing of responsibilities. In addition, there was greater attention to vertical relationships within functional areas such as social welfare or transportation.

The pattern of federal/state/local relations that emerged from the New Deal is illustrated by several key programs. The first was the Federal Emergency Relief Administration, which provided grants to states for both direct relief and work relief and was able to revitalize many rather weak state relief agencies. A variety of public works and employment security programs were also attempted to supplement relief efforts; the best known was the Works Progress Administration (WPA), a program that used federal money to hire state-certified workers for locally initiated construction projects. Finally, the Social Security Act of 1935 brought the federal government to an even greater degree into the area of direct relief for the poor, disabled, and unemployed, an area that had previously been reserved for the states and cities.

Through the middle part of this century, the structure of the various grant programs initiated at the federal level featured

1. Federal definition of the problem
2. Transfer of funds primarily to the states (rather than localities)
3. A requirement that plans for use of funds be submitted to the federal government
4. A requirement for state matching funds
5. A requirement for federal review and audit of the programs (Nathan et al., 1987, p. 31)

For the most part, these grant programs were categorical—that is, directed to a particular category of activity, such as public works. Indeed, the use of categorical grants as the primary mechanisms for federal/state transfers continued until the 1970s. Throughout this period, various groups appointed to review the state of intergovernmental relations returned the same verdict—that the federal government and the states should begin "cooperating with or complementing each other in meeting the growing demands on both" (quoted in Nathan et al., 1987, p. 33). Today, the principle of cooperative federalism is well established.

More Recent Developments

Over the past thirty years, there have been dramatic shifts in the pattern of intergovernmental relations. Nowhere are these shifts more striking than in the contrast between the activism of the Kennedy-Johnson years and the cutbacks of the Reagan years. President Johnson used the phrase *creative federalism* to describe his approach to intergovernmental relations, which included a huge increase in the number and amounts of federal grants available to states, localities, and other groups. Over three years, the number of available grants from the federal government grew from about fifty to nearly four hundred. Federal aid to states and localities rose from $7 billion in 1960 to $24 billion in 1970 (Wright, 1987, p. 236). Interestingly, state aid to local governments also nearly tripled during this period.

The new federal programs focused mainly on urban problems and problems of the disadvantaged. Medicaid, for example, the largest of the new grant programs, provided funds to states to assist in medical care for low-income people. (Medicaid is largely administered by the states [eligibility requirements vary from state to state], but it also requires state matching funds, which became a fiscal problem for many states.) But there were also new programs in education aimed directly at school districts, new programs in employment and training run by cities and other independent providers, and new programs in housing and urban development in major metropolitan areas.

Probably the most publicized domestic program of the Johnson years was the "War on Poverty," launched with the passage of the Economic Opportunity Act of 1964. The War on Poverty and other Johnson programs were significant for both their size and shape. Substantially more aid was aimed directly at local governments, school districts, and various nonprofit groups, as opposed to the previous pattern of aid primarily to states. Second, there were requirements for detailed planning and for streamlined budgeting systems, as well as demands for public participation in management of the programs. Third, and most important, the majority of the new programs involved project grants, requiring grant applications for specific purposes. States and localities began to spend enormous amounts of time playing the federal grant game—trying to obtain grants, searching for matching funds, and trying to meet planning and reporting requirements. As a result, intergovernmental relations took on an increasingly competitive tone (Wright, 1988, pp. 81–90).

Through this period, the intergovernmental system was becoming dominated more and more by the relationships among professionals within various substantive areas at various levels of government. In a particular program area, the relationship among mayor, governor, and president might be less important than that involving a local health department official, someone from a state department of health, and the manager of a federal program in health care. A new image emerged, replacing the "cakes" of earlier periods, that of **picket fence federalism.** The horizontal bars of the fence represented the levels of government, and the vertical slats represented various substantive fields, such as health, welfare, education, employment, and training (see Box 3.1).

President Nixon's administration brought about a reaction against many of the developments we have just described. Claiming that the programs of the Great Society

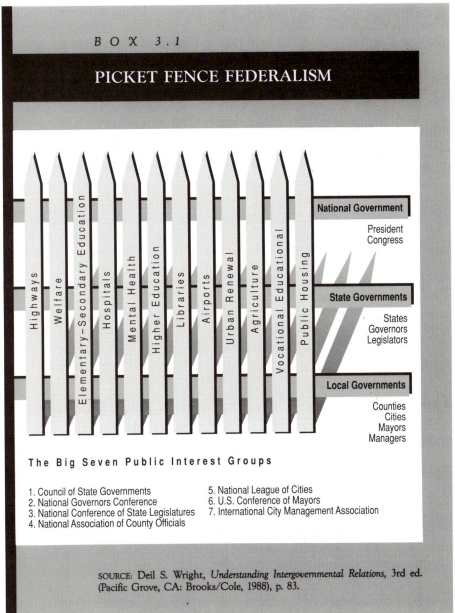

BOX 3.1

PICKET FENCE FEDERALISM

The Big Seven Public Interest Groups

1. Council of State Governments
2. National Governors Conference
3. National Conference of State Legislatures
4. National Association of County Officials
5. National League of Cities
6. U.S. Conference of Mayors
7. International City Management Association

SOURCE: Deil S. Wright, *Understanding Intergovernmental Relations*, 3rd ed. (Pacific Grove, CA: Brooks/Cole, 1988), p. 83.

were simply too detailed in their requirements to administer effectively at the local level and that subgovernments within particular substantive areas were coming to dominate the intergovernmental system, Nixon proposed what he termed a *New Federalism* that would reestablish greater local autonomy in the use of federal funds. Although a part of his program involved administrative changes, lessening certain requirements, the most notable changes President Nixon proposed involved changes in the structure of grant programs.

One way to return power to state and local leaders, especially elected leaders as opposed to program professionals, was through general revenue sharing. The Nixon plan for general revenue sharing involved transfers of money from the federal government to states and localities, to use for any purpose they wished. The funds were distributed based on a complex formula, but once in the hands of the state or local political leadership, they could be used for tax reduction, transportation, community development, law enforcement, or any other area. First passed in 1972, the Nixon revenue sharing program provided approximately $6 billion a year for five years and was continued through the Nixon, Ford, Carter, and early Reagan years, before being eliminated in 1986.

The Nixon administration also sought to consolidate large numbers of categorical grants into block grants, two of which were passed. The Comprehensive Employment and Training Act (CETA) provided funds to local "prime sponsors," usually a local government or group of governments, for manpower training. Which specific programs would be developed was up to the prime sponsor at the local level. Similarly, two weeks after President Nixon resigned, President Ford signed the Community Development Block Grant program (CDBG) consolidating several categorical grant programs, including **urban renewal** and the model cities program. Despite these successes in altering the pattern of federal grants, the Nixon-Ford years actually increased the total amount of aid available to states and localities.

The dependency of state and especially local governments on federal aid became more apparent during the administration of President Carter. The Carter years saw few dramatic departures in intergovernmental relations, continuing the general revenue sharing and block grants of the Nixon administration, though there was a greater tendency to target funds through categorical grants. Among the more important initiatives were expansion of public service employment under CETA, so that local government jobs would be filled by the unemployed, and passage of the Urban Development Action Grant program to stimulate economic development in especially distressed cities.

As a former governor, President Carter was attentive to the needs of state and local governments to more effectively operate intergovernmental programs, so he proposed a series of administrative steps for improving intergovernmental management. (In this effort, he worked closely with a group of seven major Public Interest Groups, known as the PIGs, that had come to be increasingly active in the intergovernmental system. These included such groups as the Council of State Governments, the National League of Cities, the National Governor's Association, and others; see Box 3.1.) Later in the Carter years, however, a new mood of fiscal restraint combined with Carter's own fiscal conservatism to limit the amount of money available, something states and localities found difficult to handle. But, from the standpoint of state and local governments, the reductions of the late Carter years were just the beginning.

The Reagan Years

The Reagan administration brought major structural changes in the pattern of fiscal federalism, including elimination of general revenue sharing and a reworking of the block grant system; however, the Reagan years were more significant (in intergovernmental terms) for the administration's efforts to reduce the size of the federal government through a variety of tax and spending cuts and to return responsibility for major areas, especially social welfare, to the states.

A strong ideological commitment undergirded President Reagan's efforts to eliminate federal funding and federal regulation of state and local activity wherever possible. In his inaugural speech, the president stated, "It is my intention to curb the size and influence of the federal establishment and to demand recognition of the distinction between the powers granted the federal government, those reserved to the states or to the people" (Reagan, 1981). One way he proposed to do so was by turning back responsibility for a variety of federal programs, and the resources to pay for them, to the states.

Proposals along these lines, however, quickly became intertwined with the president's 1981 efforts to reduce taxes and spending under the banner of **supply-side economics,** an approach that holds that decreased taxes and spending will stimulate capital investment and in turn economic growth (Stone & Sawhill, 1984). The defense budget was protected by the Reagan administration, so the majority of cuts were sought in federal grant programs and general government operations. Indeed, during 1981, the Reagan administration achieved the first absolute decline in federal expenditures in decades. As part of these reductions, federal grants were lowered from about $95 billion in fiscal year 1981 to about $88 billion in fiscal year 1982, with a major portion of the cuts coming in employment and training programs (Beam, 1984, p. 420).

Meanwhile, state and local officials decried the depth of the cuts and the administration's failure to make available any revenue sources to pick up the slack, especially as the tax cuts failed to produce the expected economic growth. Attention turned to the mounting federal deficit, which was so large that interest payments alone soon exceeded all federal aid to state and local governments. Moreover, concerns were increasingly voiced that efforts to balance the budget had been especially damaging to the poor—for example, by reducing eligibility for AFDC payments (Nathan et al., 1987, pp. 52–57). Whereas the public was apparently concerned about excessive spending, it became clear that neither the Congress nor the public always considered spending for social welfare, environmental protection, and infrastructure maintenance excessive.

Thus, by the middle of the second Reagan term, eligibility requirements in AFDC were restored; the environmental Superfund, designed to clean up toxic wastes and repair leaking underground tanks, was funded by Congress at a significantly higher level than the president requested; use of the Highway Trust Fund for improved highways, including urban mass transit, was passed over Reagan's veto. (This final piece of legislation also raised the highway speed limit to 65 mph on selected interstate highways.) The decline in federal grant dollars that had begun in 1979 was reversed in 1985, and federal programs increased again in 1986 (Rafuse, 1987).

On the other hand, reductions continued in specific areas, most notably in general revenue sharing. Recall that the Nixon general revenue sharing program had been continued through the Carter administration; however, early in the Reagan years, revenue sharing for states was eliminated. Finally, in 1986, revenue sharing for local governments was also ended. Many saw general revenue sharing as a way to equalize the disparity between rich and poor communities and allow greater flexibility at the local level; others saw revenue sharing as providing too much money and too much discretion, especially to wealthy communities.

But whatever the reasons for terminating general revenue sharing, many of the affected governments suffered serious losses. Many cities had become quite dependent on federal assistance; in some poorer communities, revenue sharing amounted to as much as two-thirds of total revenue. With the loss of revenue sharing, many local communities experienced serious financial difficulties and found it necessary to cut important services, including police and fire, city streets and drainage, parks and recreation, and general administration (Forester, 1988, p. 10). Because eighty-five percent of general revenue sharing went to cities under 10,000 population, the impact was especially severe among these communities. Indeed, many small cities found that their only source of federal funding had been cut off.

Other communities, however, were able to avail themselves of another Reagan administration change in the structure of intergovernmental relations, a revamping of the federal block grant program. Early in his administration, President Reagan proposed grouping nearly a hundred categorical grant programs into seven block grants. Congress gave him part of what he wanted, passing legislation that created nine block grant programs. Some consolidated many existing programs; others merely continued existing efforts in block grant format (Peterson et al., 1986). These nine areas were selected for block grants:

1. Social services
2. Low income energy assistance
3. Small city community development
4. Elementary and secondary education
5. Alcohol, drug abuse, and mental health
6. Maternal and child care
7. Community services
8. Primary health care
9. Preventive health and health services

These areas were supplemented by four other block grants during the Reagan administration. Although provisions in each area varied, most programs faced reduced funding levels, which the president justified as easy to absorb through savings in the cost of operating the programs. Most also targeted states rather than local governments as recipients of the aid programs. Two programs illustrate the changes that occurred. One of the biggest areas of budget reductions in the early Reagan years was employment and job training, especially the elimination of public-sector employment programs. In 1982, Congress enacted a replacement program, the Job Training Partnership Act, to give states a major role in employment training and to involve the private sector in job training efforts. Similarly, community development funds for small cities had previously been administered through the Department of Housing and Urban Development directly to local communities. New legislation permitted the states to assume responsibility for administering such programs, and most states did so (Jennings, Krane, Pattakos, & Reed, 1986).

The Reagan years were certainly dramatic in terms of changes in the structure of intergovernmental relations. There is no question that the Reagan administration pursued a highly ideological position in its approach to federalism, arguing that "the primary challenge to federalism comes from the policy-making process of the government in Washington" (Meese, 1987, p. 10). Overall, the burdens of the reductions fell disproportionately on the poor, because of changes in funding and requirements for various welfare programs, but also through reductions in public service jobs, aid to large cities, community development, and public housing (Nathan et al., 1987, pp. 65–66).

There have also been important shifts in the structure of intergovernmental relations (see Box 3.2). Some have argued that the Reagan programs amounted to a return to dual federalism, a clearer division of responsibilities between the nation and the states, and, to some extent, this conclusion is valid. Across the board, however, one continues to find numerous instances of federally-initiated programs continuing to operate only through the efforts of state and local governments (Derthick, 1987). How this will change during the Bush administration is still unclear. On the one hand, the enormous federal deficit combined with economic uncertainty will limit possibilities for new grant programs; on the other hand, a lessening of East–West tension may permit some restructuring of the federal budget, by limiting defense spending.

BOX 3.2

THE STATE OF AMERICAN FEDERALISM

How can one characterize the state of American federalism . . . ? Perhaps the code words are frustration and anticipation. There is frustration over the fiscal crisis of the federal government and the degree to which that crisis is driving intergovernmental policy making. There is frustration over the inability to achieve a significantly "new federalism" as a deliberate constitutional and legislative process rather than as a de facto outcome of a multitude of discrete policy developments. There is frustration over the lack of consensus about the nature and future of federalism.

This frustration is due in part, however, to the ending of a two-term presidency and to what may have been an era in the

(continued)

78

(continued)

history of American federalism. During that passing era, the federal government developed into a powerful engine pulling state and local governments uphill into the twentieth century. The little engine that could became the big engine that did. Meanwhile, the passengers in the rear were busy rebuilding their own engines and raising their fares. Ever confident that it could reach new speeds and round sharp economic curves, the big engine neglected its own fare structure and overrode standing rules of the railway. The big engine that did make it up the hill became the runaway engine that can't find the next station stop. The little engines that couldn't, however, are becoming the bigger engines that can. Even the caboose seems ready to take on new passengers. Thus, the much-noted resurgence of the states presents opportunities for fashioning a new consensus on federalism. It is in this respect that there can be said to be anticipation, and the raising of constitutional issues, even if there is no basic constitutional change, signals the need to reconstitute agreements on the nature and future of the federal system.

SOURCE: Excerpted from John Kincaid, "The State of American Federalism," *Publius* (Summer 1988); 14–15. Used with permission.

John Shannon, director of the Advisory Council on Intergovernmental Relations, described recent intergovernmental relations this way: "The changing fiscal fortunes of the national government now stand as the single most important factor in reshaping relations between Washington and the 50 state–local systems. It has transformed the expansive 'Great Society' of federalism of the 1960s into the fairly austere and competitive fend-for-yourself federalism of the 1980s" (quoted in Beckman, 1988, p. 438). Under these conditions, the ability of state and local governments as well as nonprofit organizations to be effective in pursuit of grant funding will be especially important, and **grantsmanship,** the ability to play the grants "game" successfully, will be an important and highly valued skill.

THE STATE AND LOCAL PERSPECTIVE

We have described the system of intergovernmental relations primarily from the federal perspective, but states and localities are also major actors in the intergovernmental system, both as they participate in federal programs and as they interact with one another— state to state, state to locality, and locality to locality. Here also intergovernmental relations have been changing. The budgetary reductions of the eight Reagan years, along with outright elimination of general revenue sharing, created serious problems for state and local governments. At the same time, state governments especially have proven remarkably well equipped to deal with these problems, both financially and administratively.

Funding Patterns

It is clear that the federal government is a major source of funds for state and local governments. Near the end of the Reagan administration, there were 422 categorical grant programs and thirteen block grants, for a total of 435 grant programs. Over the last thirty years, the total amount of federal money transferred to state and local governments has grown from $7 billion to $124 billion. From the point of view of state and local governments, however, these figures fail to indicate the dramatic decreases in federal aid. In the late seventies, aid to state and local governments amounted to over 15 percent of the total federal budget; by the late eighties, aid to states and localities was under 11 percent of the total.

The impact on state and local governments, as well as other service delivery organizations, has been severe. As we see in Box 3.3, in 1980, the federal government provided over 25 percent of the money spent by state and local governments. By 1988, only about 18 percent of state and local spending was supported by federal funding. Consequently, it was necessary to curtail or even terminate many state and local programs while, at the same time, trying to develop new sources of revenue.

B O X   3 . 3

Federal Grants-in-Aid (Current Dollars) as a Percentage of Total State/Local and Total Federal Outlays

Year	Total state/ local outlays	Total federal outlays
1955	10.2%	4.7%
1960	14.5	7.6
1965	15.1	9.2
1970	19.0	12.3
1975	22.6	15.0
1980	25.8	15.5
1981	24.7	14.0
1982	21.6	11.8
1983	21.3	11.4
1984	20.9	11.5
1985	20.9	11.2
1986	20.5	11.3
1987	18.3	10.8
1988	18.2	10.8

SOURCE: ACIR, *Significant Features of Fiscal Federalism*, vol. II (Washington, D.C.: Advisory Commission on Intergovernmental Relations, 1989), p. 18.

To illustrate the impact of these changes at the state and local levels, let's look at the experience of Newark, New Jersey, one of the nation's poorer cities and one highly dependent on federal assistance. From 1980 to 1988, federal and state aid to Newark was cut by more than half. The city government, with the support of outside funding, employed some 10,000 people in 1980; in 1988, only about 4,000. As a consequence, many services were reduced or eliminated. According to Newark business administrator Richard Monteilh, "The problems have gotten worse. You have a higher incidence of teen-age pregnancy, day care, welfare, remedial education, drug problems, housing problems. People are beating on our doors to provide some relief" (Kurtz, 1988, p. 31).

One way that Newark sought to cope with reduced federal assistance was by developing public-private partnerships, useful in rebuilding certain commercial areas. But even these efforts were stimulated by federal assistance, primarily through the Urban Development Action Grant program. The city secured some $40 million in UDAG funds, which it used to attract $182 million in private funds. The result was construction of several major new shopping areas and office complexes. Mayor Sharpe James, however, calls even these efforts a "Band-Aid approach." "We feel we're not getting our fair share," he says. "Our doing more with the private sector does not excuse government from helping" (Kurtz, 1988, p. 31).

The city also sought to cope with reduced federal assistance through state aid and help from nonprofit organizations and private businesses. For example, state aid for mass transit permitted modernization of the bus fleet and led to increased ridership. State aid also helped sustain the Newark public schools, where federal aid increased only slightly during the eighties. Finally, private funding, such as major grants from the Robert Wood Johnson Foundation for health care for the homeless and social services to AIDS victims, allowed the city to offer some important new services. On the other hand, some programs, such as public housing, still have severe problems. The waiting list for public housing in Newark recently had 11,000 names. All in all, the Reagan administration's reductions in federal aid to urban areas were extremely difficult for Newark to sustain.

Without question, the Reagan years presented a variety of fiscal challenges to state and local governments. It was, of course, President Reagan's intention to shift a great deal of responsibility for domestic programs to the states and indeed that occurred, though far more incrementally than envisioned in the early Reagan proposals for "turning back" whole programs to the states (Nathan et al., 1987). One surprising development, however, is that the states have proven able to manage their new responsibilities far better than many predicted.

Once considered a weak link in the federal system, the states have been able, over the past twenty years, to dramatically increase their capacities (Stenberg, 1985). Although there are still considerable variations in the capacities of the states, most states have undertaken important institutional reforms (such as developing legislative audits), have expanded the scope and professionalism of their operations (to include new services in areas such as energy planning and conservation or new programs in areas such as productivity improvement), and have demonstrated remarkable fiscal restraint (Bowman & Kearney, 1986, pp. 22–31). Indeed, while the national government has a $2 trillion debt, the states are operating balanced budgets, and some are even making investments for the future (Beckman, 1988, p. 438).

The states are thus moving into areas of responsibility once thought to rest at the federal level. The field of international trade is one area where some shifting in roles already seems to be taking place. Whereas the federal government has traditionally played the leading (if not exclusive) role in foreign affairs, economic forces are precipitating much greater state and local activity in the international arena. For example, all states have offices of economic development involved in some way with international economic development. Indeed, in 1984, the states collectively spent over $21 million on international trade, by way of opening offices in other countries, conducting trade fairs or language seminars, and hosting business groups from around the world (Bowman & Kearney, 1986, pp. 194–195). Working closely with local governments, the states have come to play a significant role in international trade.

Nonfiscal Patterns in Federal/State/Local Interaction

Federal grants are not merely sources of revenue; they act as a stimulus to state and local action in many other ways. In addition to providing financial assistance to supplement limited local resources, federal grants seek the following objectives:

1. *To establish minimum national standards:* Particular programs vary widely from state to state. Federal action in enforcing clean water standards or requirements for workplace safety, for example, can assure that special interests at the local level do not endanger the public health.
2. *To equalize resources:* States and localities differ widely in their economic bases and their capacity to raise revenues. Like Robin Hood, many federal programs take from the rich (states with the highest per capita incomes) and give to the poor (those with lower income levels).
3. *To improve the performance of state and local governments:* Traditionally, states and localities have not been able to attract the same level of professional talent as has the federal government. Consequently, in reviewing state and local grant applications or project implementation, the federal government has been able to provide added technical expertise. (The increased professionalization of state and local government over the past twenty years, however, has now made this a two-way street, with expertise and advice flowing in both directions.)
4. *To concentrate resources:* No state alone could undertake a comprehensive program of research into air pollution standards or other environmental policy questions, nor would we want the duplication of effort in having fifty (or more) similar types of research going on at the state or local level.
5. *To stimulate experimentation:* Federal grant programs can stimulate states and localities to develop new and innovative approaches to local problems that, if successful, can later be transferred to other jurisdictions. Similarly, the "carrot" of federal funds often stimulates governments to act in areas that would not otherwise have high priority—for example, in waste water treatment or urban mass transit.
6. *To improve the administration of state and local governments:* Many federal grant programs lead to changes in state and local administrative operations—for example, through requirements for planning systems, merit personnel plans, or new budgeting and accounting procedures.
7. *To encourage general social objectives:* Requirements for nondiscriminatory hiring have been a major stimulus to affirmative action efforts in state and local

81

governments; similarly, requiring environmental impact statements prior to federally funded projects helps assure important environmental objectives.

Regulation and Mandating

The requirement of specific state or local actions as a precondition for receiving federal funding has become a significant concern. Although our federal system of government establishes certain federal powers, reserves certain powers to the states, and permits certain actions at both levels, there has long been controversy about the exact definition of these categories. This controversy has been especially intense where the question concerns the power of the federal government to coerce states and localities into doing (or not doing) particular things.

As a case in point, the Fair Labor Standards Act of 1938 set the minimum wages and maximum hours that could be worked before overtime pay was required. Whereas the Act originally applied only to the private sector, 1974 amendments applied its provisions to all state and local governments. Many state and local officials argued against the amendments, citing the difficulties in applying the standards to government; for example, how do you measure the hours a fire fighter works in off and on shifts of several days duration? Soon the amendments were challenged in court and, in the case of *National League of Cities v. Usery* (1976), the Supreme Court decided that the functions of "general government" were part of the powers "reserved" to the states by the Tenth Amendment and therefore could not be regulated by the federal government. Consequently, the FLSA did not apply.

Confusion remained, however, about which areas were included in the phrase "general government." The confusion persisted until, nearly ten years later, the Court reviewed a case that sought to determine whether the San Antonio transit authority was performing "general government" functions and was therefore exempt from the Fair Labor Standards Act. In *Garcia v. San Antonio Metropolitan Transit Authority* (1985), however, the Court went beyond the narrow question of whether transit is a general government function and decided that Congress did in fact have the power, under its responsibilities to regulate commerce, to intervene in the affairs of state and local governments.

The effect of *Garcia*, a direct reversal of the Court's earlier position in the Usery case, was to remove questions about the scope of the federal government's powers from the realm of judicial inquiry. The Court essentially held that the states have sufficient input into the national legislative process, through the election of members of Congress and the influence of their governors and mayors, to be able to protect themselves politically from burdensome legislation. That being the case, the question of whether the federal government could act in areas previously believed reserved to the states should be decided through legislation rather than judicial action. The rights of the states were, therefore, viewed as raising political rather than judicial questions (Howard, 1985).

The Garcia case potentially opens the door for the federal government to move into more areas once thought to be the province of state and local governments. Certainly state and local officials, who have seen the federal government act in areas from rat control to minimum drinking ages, have been skeptical of the self-restraint of Congress. At a minimum, *Garcia* sets a precedent for expanded federal action directed at state and local governments.

Whereas the Garcia case deals with the powers of the federal government over states and localities, similar but somewhat less complex issues have been raised with respect to the powers of the states over local governments. As noted, our intergovernmental system does not allocate separate spheres of power to state and local governments, but rather treats local governments merely as "creatures of the state," having only those powers granted by the state. In what has come to be known as **Dillon's Rule,** Judge John Dillon declared in 1911 that municipalities had only those powers granted in their charters, those fairly implied by the expressed powers, and those essential to the purposes of their being granted a charter. In other words, Dillon's Rule allowed for state control over all but a narrow range of local activities. Dillon's Rule has been somewhat relaxed, especially in states that permit cities greater autonomy through *home-rule* provisions, but the powers of local government continue to derive directly from the actions of the state.

The Garcia case deals with what are called **direct orders**—requirements or restrictions enforced by one government upon another (the federal government on states and localities, the states on the cities). Direct orders might include a federal requirement that cities meet certain clean water standards or a state requirement that a city pay part of the costs of certain welfare programs. Another way control may be exercised over another government is through *conditions* tied to grants-in-aid. These conditions are typically of the type parents use with children: "You can go outside to play, if you first clean up your room." Conditions of aid might require land use planning prior to a capital construction project or making facilities accessible to the handicapped.

Because cities derive their powers from the states, most state requirements are in the form of direct orders. But most federal requirements are conditions-of-aid tied to a particular grant program (Lovell & Tobin, 1981, pp. 319–320). "Conditions-of-aid" are of two varieties. **Cross-cutting requirements** are rules that apply to most, if not all, grant programs; for instance, the federal government requires environmental impact statements before undertaking capital projects, certain personnel provisions in agencies receiving grant funds, and compliance with civil rights legislation. Other conditions-of-aid are *program specific,* applicable only to the particular program. They may include rules about program planning, implementation, and evaluation; for example, a particular program might prescribe certain maximum salaries for individuals employed under the grant or some form of citizen participation in program design (most federal programs have this latter requirement) (Kettl, 1983).

The term **mandate** has been used to embrace both "conditions-of-aid" and "direct orders," in either case an order requiring a government to do something it might not otherwise do. Mandates often require states or localities to spend money they would not otherwise spend. Meeting new clean water standards, for example, has been estimated to require some $3 billion nationally in capital outlays for new sewage treatment facilities (Rafuse, 1987, p. 52). Moreover, states and cities claim that mandates unduly impinge upon the autonomy of their level of government. Consequently, mandates have become a source of considerable frustration for those on the receiving end.

In 1980, New York City's Mayor Edward Koch wrote that "a maze of complex statutory and administrative directives has come to threaten both the initiative and the financial health of local governments throughout the country." Koch estimated that compliance with forty-seven federal and state mandates over the next four years would cost the city of New York $711 million in capital expenditures, $6.25 billion from the city's operating budget, and $1.66 billion in lost revenues (Koch, 1980, p. 42). Koch was joined in his argument by mayors and governors across the country—the mayors concerned with both federal and state mandates, the governors concerned primarily with federal mandates.

At the federal level, every president since Nixon has pledged to reduce the burden of mandates on states and local governments, and certain administrative reforms have occurred in each administration. The Reagan administration proposed deregulation of states and localities in addition to the deregulation of private businesses; however, while the issuance of new regulations slowed, efforts to remove major regulations met with limited success. A requirement that transit systems be made accessible to the handicapped was targeted for elimination by the Reagan administration; however, public outcry was so great that the regulation was not only reinstated, it was rewritten so as to include more people in the handicapped category and therefore to cost transit systems more money (Beam, 1984, pp. 438–439).

States and localities have discovered, however, that they have some leeway in adherence to certain regulations. (The Reagan administration's less active enforcement of regulations in civil rights, environmental health, and workplace safety was probably its most significant change in patterns of federal regulation.) Still, calls for reform of the mandate system continue. Among the proposals now under consideration is a requirement for identifying and reimbursing costs incurred by state and local governments in carrying out activities mandated by the federal government. Parallel proposals have been suggested for state reimbursements to local governments.

84

Subnational Relationships

Even focusing on state and local activities, we find the federal government involved in some way—at a minimum, in providing funds for states and localities. But important intergovernmental activity also occurs at the subnational level: state to state, state to local, and local to local.

State to state   Relationships between and among states are mentioned several times in the U.S. Constitution, most notably in the requirement that states recognize the rights and privileges of citizens of other states and give "full faith and credit" to the public acts and legal proceedings of other states. Some of the most important intergovernmental relationships involving various state governments are not based in constitutional doctrine, however, but are rather the result of political practices over the years.

Relationships among states are not without conflict. States may differ over census counts (important in determining the number of representatives in Congress), dispute shifting state boundaries (as when a river changes course), and debate a variety of substantive policy issues (such as the rights to underground water or the degree to which dumping pollutants into a river affects water quality in states downstream). In addition, states must increasingly compete with one another for economic development; for example, when General Motors announced its plans to build a major new plant to produce the Saturn, many states entered an intense bidding war, each hoping GM would locate the plant within its boundaries.

States also cooperate. There are many opportunities for officials in one state to seek the advice of those in other states with respect to policy alternatives or new administrative arrangements. Many organizations, including the Council of State Governments, the National Governor's Association, the National Council of State Legislators, and groups that bring together state officials in personnel, budgeting, purchasing, social welfare, health, and so forth, have been created to help officials share information and expertise. These groups, along with the Washington offices of various states, constitute an important lobbying group in Washington.

One way the states come together to resolve potential disputes or work together on common problems is through *interstate compacts*. These agreements have historically been bilateral, involving only two states; however, increasingly, compacts are being developed to involve a number of states within a region or even all fifty states. Originally used to resolve boundary disputes, interstate compacts today cover a wide variety of topics, most arising from the fact that today's policy problems do not confine themselves neatly to the borders of one state. Imagine, for example, the common interests of people in several states sharing the same underground water supply. Think also of the problems that are of interest to all who live in metropolitan areas, such as Cincinnati or Kansas City, that cross the boundaries of two or even more states. It is not uncommon in such areas to find interstate compacts covering air and water pollution, transportation, law enforcement, and so on.

States may also use interstate compacts to symbolize their agreement to cooperate in especially important policy areas. For example, Maryland, Delaware, Virginia, West Virginia, New York, and the District of Columbia recently entered into a compact that essentially declared a regional "war on drugs." Although the compact calls for information sharing and cooperative research and training, its primary value is clearly symbolic—a recognition of the importance of the drug issue. In all cases, an interstate compact provides a way to formalize resolution of a dispute or to arrange to work together without involving the federal government.

State to local   We have seen that the relationship between states and localities is unitary—that is, local governments have only those powers granted by the state. However, the nature of the powers may vary considerably. Most cities operate under some form of **charter,** the local government equivalent of a constitution. But a state may grant charters in several ways. Some states develop *special charters* for each individual local government; others take exactly the opposite approach and grant a *general charter* for all local governments. The *classified charter* approach seeks to avoid the restrictive nature of the special charter and the rigidity of the general charter by granting charters to various classes of cities. For example, all cities over a million in population might be designated Class A and have one set of charter provisions, while cities from 250,000 to a million might be in Class B and have a different set of provisions. A final means of chartering cities, called **home rule,** permits cities to write their own charters, within very broad state guidelines and generally subject to voter approval.

Home rule obviously provides the greatest flexibility for local governments in terms of basic structure; however, even under home rule, there is substantial state involvement in local government affairs. For one thing, the states are an important source of funding for local activities. Indeed, at a time when federal aid has leveled somewhat, state aid to local governments has increased dramatically. Between 1984 and 1986, for instance, state aid to localities increased 22 percent, from $107 billion to $130 billion, with most

85

of that aid targeted for education and lesser amounts for welfare, highways, and other purposes (Kane, 1988, p. 451).

But states not only provide money; they also regulate local government activities. State governments tell local governments what taxes they can levy, what services they can provide, and what types of management systems they must employ. In doing so, states provide needed uniformity, as in the case of highway signs, as well as assure minimum standards of performance, as in education or welfare programs.

But just as states complain about federal mandates, many local officials view state mandates as unnecessary intrusions on local prerogatives and may require local expenditures that might not otherwise be made. Recently, localities have complained especially about *sneaky mandates*, actions that are required of local governments by the inaction of state governments. For example, Georgia failed to pick up prisoners housed "temporarily" in county jails, resulting in overcrowding in the prison system, to say nothing of the additional financial burden on the counties (Zimmerman, 1988, p. 448).

But localities are not powerless in their relationship with the states, especially as they are an important base of political support for those in the legislatures. Local representatives and senators can and often do voice the local message loudly and clearly in the state legislature. Moreover, various patterns of state/local cooperation have emerged in the past several years. Many states, for example, have developed state-level equivalents of the federal Advisory Commission on Intergovernmental Relations. These state commissions bring together state and local officials to discuss problems in the intergovernmental system and devise ways to work together more effectively. Among the recommendations that have emerged are suggestions for greater local discretionary authority and for reductions in the number of state mandates. Despite these recommendations, the states still maintain a dominant position in their relationships with cities.

Local to local   In discussions of intergovernmental relations, there is an understandable tendency to focus on national patterns, but for those who work at the local level, relationships with other local governments are extremely important. One reason is that many citizens live in one jurisdiction, work in another, shop in another, and pay taxes to several. They naturally expect services, such as the quality of the streets or law enforcement, to remain fairly constant as they move from one place to another.

From a political standpoint, the fragmentation of government, especially in urban areas, often means that problems are separated from the resources that might be employed to solve them. Wealthier cities have the money; poorer cities have the problems. But even where resources are fairly evenly distributed, it is difficult to get several local governments together to resolve common problems. Where this is the case, citizens often turn to higher-level governments for help, thus taking the problem (and its solution) out of the hands of local authorities (Nice, 1987, p. 191).

But many interlocal problems are resolved at the local level. Natural, though informal, patterns of cooperation develop, especially in the relationships among local professionals. The police chief in one community talks with other police chiefs, the health officer talks with other health officers, and so on. More formally, one government may actually purchase services from another, contracting for police or fire protection, waste water treatment, or trash collection. The County of Los Angeles, for example, provides a variety of services to local governments through contract arrangements. Similarly, Allegheny

County (in Pennsylvania) began offering police detective services when distressed munici-palities could no longer do so. Additionally, **councils of government** (COGs), over-sight bodies representing various localities, may be created to help coordinate local affairs.

Finally, special districts may be created to solve problems that cross governmental boundaries. As mentioned, **special districts** are local governments created for a specific purpose within a specific area (not necessarily coinciding with the boundaries of a city or county). Although special districts may promote coordination of health, education, or other services, they also add to the number of governments within a particular area. Thus, one city block may be governed by the city, a county, and several special districts; a resident may have difficulty figuring out which government can help with a particular problem. The difficulties in coordinating efforts are substantial, as are the problems of holding the various governments accountable.

WORKING WITH NONGOVERNMENTAL ORGANIZATIONS

It is not unusual for one level of government to make use of another in carrying out its policies—the federal government uses the states to carry out programs in transportation, criminal justice, and health and human services; the states use local governments to carry out policies in education and human services. But governments at all levels may also utilize private and nonprofit organizations to help carry out their policies. The National Aeronautics and Space Administration, for example, contracts with private companies to build space shuttles; state governments use both private and nonprofit organizations to conduct job training and provide employment services; local governments often contract with private firms for trash collection or towing services. In each case, the interorganizational relationships that arise are important to the success or failure of public programs. For this reason, many argue that looking solely at intergovernmental relations is insufficient; it is better to use the more inclusive term *interorganizational relations.*

The use of private and nonprofit organizations in the delivery of public services has grown markedly in the last several years. Box 3.4 compares, at the federal level, civilian employment and overall governmental expenditures. Between 1950 and 1987, government spending increased by over 300 percent, even holding inflation constant, but government employment grew only about 25 percent, with practically no growth in the last twenty years. This substantial growth in federal programs, occurring without comparable growth in federal employment, is explained by the fact that parties other than the federal govern-ment are actually conducting the programs and delivering the services. Federal money, for example, goes to private firms, such as defense contractors or banks that administer school loan programs, and to nonprofit organizations, especially those that provide human services such as care for the homeless or disabled.

Privatization

The movement toward greater involvement of private and nonprofit organizations in the delivery of public services is partly ideological. Some people simply feel that services should be provided by those outside government wherever possible. But the movement has also been stimulated by recent restrictions on government spending and a resulting effort

87

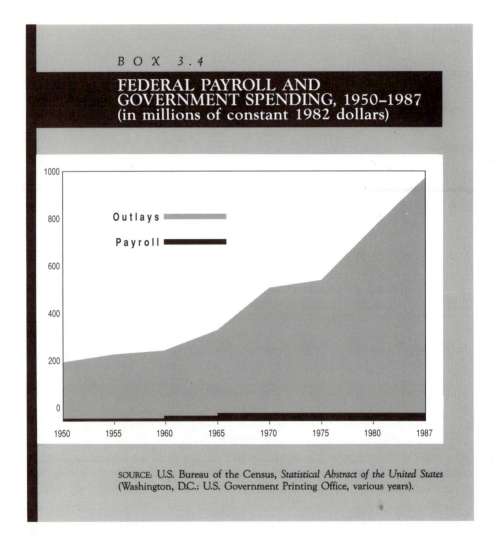

BOX 3.4

FEDERAL PAYROLL AND
GOVERNMENT SPENDING, 1950–1987
(in millions of constant 1982 dollars)

SOURCE: U.S. Bureau of the Census, *Statistical Abstract of the United States*
(Washington, D.C.: U.S. Government Printing Office, various years).

88

to find more efficient ways to conduct the public's business. Both motives have been discussed under the heading **privatization**—the use of nongovernmental agencies to provide goods or services previously provided by government—but since the term is used several different ways, it is important to be clear about its various meanings (Kolderie, 1986).

In its broader sense, privatization refers to efforts to remove government from any involvement in either the design or conduct of a particular service. In Great Britain, for example, major industries such as steel or coal, once nationalized, are returning to private control, typically through direct sales to individuals, firms, or other groups. In the U.S., most such major industries, including most utilities, are already in private hands, so there are relatively few examples of such magnitude (the sale of Conrail and certain petroleum reserves are exceptions). There are many more limited examples of privatization, however; a city might, for example, sell a golf course to a country club development, thus ending the government's involvement in golf.

The rationale for removing government from a particular area varies. In some cases, people may feel that clients will receive more personal attention from a nongovernmental group, such as one that operates a drug abuse program or a day care center. Other governmental programs may be turned over to private firms because the programs seem inappropriate to government or because the private firm can operate more efficiently; for example, the Hospital Corporation of America at one point owned or leased more than twenty-five hospitals previously owned or controlled by municipalities (Hatry, 1983, p. 70).

Privatization is used in a more narrow sense (and more frequently) to refer to various devices through which a government retains a policy role regarding a particular service but engages someone else to actually deliver the service. A federal agency might decide to contract with a private firm rather than handle all its computer programming itself; a state might contract with a nonprofit organization to deliver services to welfare recipients; or a local government might lease a public hospital to a private firm. In each case, the services would be spelled out in detail by the government and some, if not all, funding might be provided, but day-to-day operation of the program would be the responsibility of the private or nonprofit agency.

Contracting

There are various mechanisms through which relationships are established among government agencies and private and nonprofit organizations. By far the most common way to involve nongovernmental bodies in the conduct of public business is by *contracting* for goods or services. A decision to contract for goods or services may arise for several reasons. The government agency may not have (or wish to develop) the capacity to produce certain items—it may be easier to purchase a hammer, automobile, or tank from a private firm than to build one. Or those in the agency may feel that a private firm would be able to produce a good or deliver a service more efficiently, given their greater flexibility, different labor costs, or economies of scale.

On the other hand, private firms may become more concerned with profit than with the quality of service and, similarly, may neglect values such as equity in their pursuit of efficiency. Moreover, it is not always certain that the private firm will operate more efficiently. Mayor George Lattimer of St. Paul has commented,

> The private sector also has its problems in delivering expensive and desirable products: the private sector has had a decline in productivity, slackening investment in research and development, an unwillingness to consider external effects of private actions, a lack of capital investment, a trend to see short-term benefits, resistance to experiment with creative management, a loss of competitive strength . . ., and problems with the public sector contracting out enormous sums of dollars to private businesses where we have seen delays, cost overruns, and sometimes frauds. (quoted in Hatry, 1983, pp. 8–9)

Interestingly, after allowing public and private groups to bid on service contracts, jurisdictions have found that sometimes the private group wins and sometimes the public group wins!

Defense contracting The most notable example of government contracting in recent years has been the Defense Department's procurement of new weapons systems. The Pentagon oversees contracts totaling more than $160 billion a year and, perhaps not

89

surprisingly, has had its share of problems with these contracts. Several aspects of the procurement process have proven especially troublesome. First, there may be difficulties in identifying exactly what the government wants. Detailed specifications may be required even for simple items. The contract specifications for fruitcakes that are fed to military personnel are eighteen pages long and describe such things as the size of the nuts and the types of raisins that are allowed (Kettl, 1988, p. 35)! But as the requested items become more complex, the process of writing specifications also becomes more difficult. The Pentagon has its own experts who are responsible for writing specifications; however, since the size of Pentagon procurement offices was reduced during the eighties, outside help has become necessary. The drafting of specifications is increasingly done by technical consultants hired by the government for their expertise in weapons technology. This arrangement has led to difficulties when consultants "rigged" specifications in favor of particular contractors or wrote specifications for the government, then helped contractors respond to the specifications.

Second, there is the question of government oversight of the contractor's performance. Recent investigations reveal a variety of abuses by contractors, including the widely publicized $700 pliers and $600 toilet seats. Oversight has also revealed other questionable items charged to the government, such as country club dues, corporate parties, and even boarding an executive's dog (Carrington & Pound, 1988, p. 4). Although these investigations have demonstrated abuse of the system, contractors often complain that government oversight has become too detailed and hinders the contractor in getting the job done. Sanford McDonnell, head of McDonnell–Douglas, cited thousands of visits by government auditors and accused the federal government of "overmanaging, overspecifying, and overscrutinizing" defense contractors (quoted in Kettl, 1988, p. 40).

Third, recent policies that sought to create more competition for defense contracts have run into unexpected difficulties. In the past, the Pentagon worked closely with single contractors on a *sole-source* basis to develop new systems, but now competitions are held to determine who will receive a contract. Whereas competition has generated some savings on major items such as attack submarines and fighter plane engines, it has also created a new market for "inside" information that would give companies an edge in the competition. "Operation Ill Wind," a 1988 investigation into defense procurement practices, revealed that a combination of consultants, government officials, and contractors apparently conspired to exchange information that would give certain companies an advantage in the bidding process.

Human services   A quite different set of issues has emerged as states and localities have contracted for human services. One motive for contracting out is to obtain reductions in cost; however, in the social services, other motives also enter in. Most state social service agencies use federal Title XX funds to contract with private and nonprofit organizations for services, but competition for the funds is rare, because the number of agencies that operate in any one field—say, geriatric day care—is small. Moreover, groups that provide social services have not traditionally considered themselves subject to the same pressures for profit making as others, such as trash collection services. Quite appropriately, they have been more concerned with changing the lives of their clients than meeting some "bottom line" financial figure (DeHoog, 1984, p. 134). The determining factor in a contract for human services is likely to be the capacity of the organization to effectively deliver high-quality services.

90

Even the operation of correctional facilities has been contracted to private and non-profit organizations. Prison services, such as medical care or drug treatment programs, have been contracted for many years. More recently, however, as incarceration rates have soared and the cost of operating prisons has risen, entire prisons have been contracted to outside organizations. The Illinois Department of Corrections contracted eight of its twenty community correctional centers to nonprofit organizations such as the Salvation Army (Hatry, 1983, p. 21). Many other states have passed legislation permitting privately run jails and prisons, but the moral and philosophical questions raised by such efforts are both obvious and complex—for example, how can a jurisdiction be sure that the rights of prisoners will not be violated by private entrepreneurs seeking higher profits?

Equity in delivery of services is important in the human service areas. Sylvester Murray, former City Manager of Cincinnati, describes contracting for garbage collection: one particular area of the city, "Over the Rhine," according to Murray, deserved garbage collection two or three times a week rather than once a week. As he put it, poor people accumulate more trash because they don't have garbage disposals and don't buy packaged goods as often. "The richer person will buy one giant-sized box of Tide and use that for three weeks. In the lower-income area, a person buys a small box every week . . ." (Murray, 1985, p. 4). An equitable solution would be to collect garbage more often from poorer neighborhoods than from richer neighborhoods. According to Murray, "What frightens us . . . about contracting out (for trash collection) is that the independent entrepreneur may not even think about (the equity issue). He may not even consider it something that we ought to be concerned about, because he is so particularly interested in just the input and the output" (Murray, 1985, p. 4).

Through the eighties, of course, one problem facing governments and their contractors was how to effectively—and equitably—cut back on existing services. Connecticut, for example, faced nearly a one-third reduction in funds for social services, with the decision about what to eliminate left to the state (Kettl, 1988, pp. 66–68). In making its decisions, the state followed a recommendation of the Kettering Foundation and used what is called a **negotiated investment strategy,** bringing together representatives of all the affected groups to set priorities for funding under the remaining block grant. Representatives of the fourteen state agencies involved, of nearly 1,000 nonprofit groups involved in grant activity, and of the local governments affected by the grants met with skilled mediators to try to reach an agreement that all could sign. The questions were obviously difficult: Is child care more important than family planning? Is emergency shelter more important than recreation? (In both of these areas, the group answered "yes.") After an extended period of bargaining and negotiation, an agreement was reached that participants felt represented a fair and equitable solution to the state's funding dilemma.

Local government contracting   Over the past couple of decades, local governments have been especially interested in contracting for services. In St. Paul, Minnesota, private groups provide sanitation, street paving, lighting improvements, and other services. Scottsdale, Arizona, has a privately run and highly regarded fire department, while Newark, New Jersey, contracts for sewer cleaning, vehicle maintenance, printing, data processing, and street repair. Overall, local governments have contracted out some sixty different services (Seader, 1986, pp. 6–7).

The experience of one city, Rochester, New York, illustrates some of the forces driving privatization efforts in American communities (Doherty, 1985). During the seventies,

91

Rochester experienced severe economic decline and a consequent loss of city revenue; one study ranked Rochester as the sixth most distressed central city in America. A reduction in city expenditures was inevitable; however, citizens still wanted the full range of municipal services. One way the city sought to cope with this problem was through contracting out for various services.

Prior to the mid-seventies, Rochester had used private contracts for residential snowplowing and street lighting, but over the next ten years, the city initiated nearly eighty new contracts, ranging from operation of major city facilities to maintenance of street malls. Among the major contracts were several entrepreneurial activities, including the city's sports arena, stadium, and parking facilities. The contracts were based partly on percentages of revenues, thus providing a market incentive for the contractor. Additionally, Rochester contracted for various human services (housing, employment and training, etc.), professional services (engineering, computer programming, etc.), and even trade services (painting, roofing, etc.). The city also contracted with neighborhood organizations for the maintenance of neighborhood parks and street malls.

As a result of contracting for services such as these, the city was able to reduce its 1984–1985 budget by $3.1 million. But cost savings are not the only issue; one must consider as well the quality and equity of services. During one of the city's largest snowfalls, for example, the private contractor failed to plow several areas of the city, leaving residents of those neighborhoods "snowed in" for days. The city also encountered a storm of protests when a regional high school basketball tournament could not afford the rates set by the arena's new operator. Though in each case the contractor was responsible, the protests were directed at the city. Edward Doherty, the city's Director of Budget and Efficiency, notes that, "In emergencies, the public has traditionally turned to government and expected a response regardless of cost. This simply cannot be expected of private companies" (Doherty, 1985, p. 33).

Rochester contracted out a variety of services, but one municipal service, street lighting, which had previously been handled privately, was brought back under the city's ownership and operation—at a substantial savings and an improvement in quality. Whereas savings may be generated by contracting out, you cannot assume that private companies will always operate more efficiently than government. Indeed, the Rochester experience (and that of other cities) indicates that a careful assessment of costs and quality is necessary in any decision to contract for municipal services.

Other Mechanisms for Privatization

Contracting is the most common technique for privatizing public services, but a variety of other mechanisms are used as well (Hatry, 1983). A **franchise** can be awarded to a private firm to perform a certain service within a state or locality. The firm charges citizens directly for the services it provides. Typically, rates and performance standards are established by the government and there is often some continuing regulation of the firm. Examples include electric power, taxi services, cable television, and emergency ambulance services. Similarly, governments may provide *grants* or *subsidies* to private or nonprofit organizations that are performing needed public services. The government provides full or partial support for activities that will benefit the community but which the local government, for financial or other reasons, does not wish to operate on its own. Examples include local government support for the arts, child care, or shelter for the homeless.

All levels of government have experimented with the use of *vouchers*. In a voucher system, citizens receive vouchers or coupons to redeem for goods or services from a variety of suppliers. The federal food stamp program, for example, provides recipients with coupons with which to purchase food, but permits the individual to choose both the supplier and the items to be purchased (within stated limits). At the local level, several cities have experimented with voucher systems for taxis to provide transportation to elderly citizens. This kind of system is considered more cost effective than providing more extensive mass transit.

Another means of privatizing public services is through the involvement of citizens in activities that were previously the work of government. **Coproduction,** as this technique is known, involves supplementing or perhaps supplanting the work of government officials with local residents' volunteer activity (Brudney & England, 1983). Private citizens and government workers share in providing a particular service. Many cities, for example, have called on volunteers to assist in police, fire, parks and recreation, and education. Others have asked citizens to "adopt a park" or "adopt a highway" and to share in its maintenance.

What is important in all of these efforts to privatize public services is that they bring government officials into new relationships with nongovernment agents, whether contractors, service providers, or volunteers. Thus, it is no longer sufficient to focus on intergovernmental relations alone; we must now speak of the importance of interorganizational relations. Moreover, these new circumstances raise important value questions. Where government programs are run directly by government, responsibility for their success lies squarely with the government agency. But where such programs are actually delivered by those in the private or nonprofit sector, traditional mechanisms for control and accountability may not work. Maintaining a proper concern for democratic values such as equity and responsiveness may, in the long run, prove more difficult than the managerial challenges of creating appropriate interorganizational policy networks.

SUMMARY AND ACTION IMPLICATIONS

Given the complexity of modern society, your work as a public administrator will likely involve a complex set of relationships with all kinds of external groups. Many of these groups will be agencies at other levels of government. Our federal system has evolved from a pattern in which the various levels of government were relatively distinct to a pattern in which funding and programmatic relationships are extremely intense. Especially with the reductions in federal funding during the Reagan years, the previous pattern of cooperative federalism has been replaced by a highly competitive federalism. Under these conditions, those who work at the state and local levels and in nonprofit organizations are increasingly attentive to grant possibilities and are in need of individuals who can not only track grant possibilities but can successfully apply for federal (and other) dollars. Grantsmanship is becoming an especially valuable skill; Box 3.5 lists guidelines for successful grant writing.

The fact that public programs today operate through vast and complex networks of people and organizations—public, private, and nonprofit—means that new skills are required of the public manager. Any particular program may involve various levels of government, organizations from all sectors of society, and clients or citizens with many

BOX 3.5

GRANT WRITING

The following criteria for evaluating grant proposals will help in writing grant proposals.

1. *Clarity:* The proposal must be clearly written and organized so that it can be readily followed and easily understood. The style of writing and organization of material should be as simple as possible.
2. *Responsiveness:* Proposals must be responsive to the requirements of the funding agency and must also be responsive to a documented problem and need.
3. *Internal consistency:* All parts of the proposal should be related to and consistent with each other. For example, the kinds of activities proposed should be logically consistent with the objectives that are set forth. Similarly, the proposed staff should be of sufficient size and quality to deliver the proposed services.
4. *External consistency:* The proposal should recognize both the generally known and accepted ideas in the particular field and the program approaches, activities, and methods that are believed to be effective.
5. *Understanding of the problem and service methods:* It is important to indicate a thorough understanding of the nature of the problem that the program addresses. In addition, the proposal should show one's understanding of the way in which the proposed services must be delivered. Most importantly, it must have an effective plan to carry out the proposed activities.
6. *Capability:* A major criterion to funders is evidence of the capability of the organization to successfully carry out the activities it promises to implement in its written proposal.
7. *Efficiency and accountability:* Funders want to be assured that programs will be efficiently managed and effectively executed. Plans for the administration and organization of the program activities, staff, and committees are ways to indicate ability to efficiently implement the program.

> 8. *Realism:* A proposal should be realistic. No more than can really be achieved and delivered in the way of objectives and program activities should be promised.
>
> SOURCE: From the book, *Getting a Grant in the 1980s*, 2nd ed. By Robert Lefferts © 1982. Used by permission of the publisher, Prentice-Hall, Inc., Englewood Cliffs, N.J.

different interests and concerns. As a public manager, you must be able to identify the network that is or should be involved in a particular situation and assess the effectiveness of that network.

To make that judgment, you will need to consider several factors. The first is *communications*, the type of information that goes from one organization to another and how it is transmitted. Second, you might focus on *exchanges* of goods and services, money, and personnel among the organizations involved. Third, you might examine the *normative* aspect of the relationship—that is, what each organization expects of the other and what each is willing to contribute to the relationship (Aldrich & Whetten, 1981). Examining these same categories may also suggest ways to improve the effectiveness of interorganizational networks.

The interorganizational nature of modern public administration also has interesting implications for the interpersonal skills you must bring to the job. Increasingly, the government official responsible for a given program must be skilled in negotiating relationships with those outside the agency to ensure that the program proceeds effectively and responsibly. More and more, the public administrator works in a world in which older images of organizational hierarchy and control are quickly giving way to newer images of "managing in ambiguity" and "negotiating organizational boundaries." The interorganizational nature of public administration today has a direct effect on what skills managers need.

TERMS AND DEFINITIONS

Block grants: Grants in which the money can be used for nearly any purpose within a specific functional field.

Capital grants: Grants for use in construction or renovation.

Categorical or project grants: Grants requiring that the money may be spent for only a limited purpose; typically available on a competitive basis.

Charter: Local government's equivalent of a constitution.

Cooperative federalism: Greater sharing of responsibilities between federal and state governments.

Coproduction: Using volunteer activity to supplement or supplant the work of government officials.

Councils of government: Oversight bodies representing various localities to help coordinate local affairs.

Cross-cutting requirements: Rules that apply to most grant programs.

Dillon's Rule: Municipalities have only those powers granted in their charters; cities are creatures of the state.

Direct orders: Requirements or restrictions that are enforced by one government over another.

Dual federalism: Pattern in which federal and state governments are struggling for power and influence with little intergovernmental cooperation.

Entitlement grants: Grants that provide assistance to persons who meet certain criteria.

Formula grants: Grants that employ a specific division rule to indicate how much money any given jurisdiction will receive.

Franchise: Exclusive award to one firm (or a limited number) to operate a certain business within the jurisdiction.

Grants: Transfers of money (and/or property) from one government to another.

Grantsmanship: Skills needed to compete successfully in the grant process.

Home rule: Provision allowing cities greater autonomy over local activities.

Intergovernmental relations: A term encompassing all the complex and interdependent relations among those at various levels of government.

Interorganizational networks: Pattern of relationships within and among various groups and organizations working in a single policy area.

Mandate: Order requiring a government to do something.

Negotiated investment strategy: Bringing together representatives of all affected groups to set priorities for funding.

Operating grants: Grants for use in development and operation of specific programs.

Picket fence federalism: Pattern of intergovernmental relations in which the horizonal bars represent levels of government and the vertical slats represent various substantive fields.

Privatization: Use of nongovernmental agencies to provide goods and services previously provided by government.

Revenue sharing: Grant pattern in which the money can be used any way the recipient government chooses.

Special districts: Local governments created for a specific purpose within a specific area.

Supply-side economics: Argument that decreased taxes and spending will stimulate capital investment and economic growth.

Urban renewal: Government program designed to provide cities with money for public housing and urban redevelopment.

96

STUDY QUESTIONS

1. Although intergovernmental relations involve more than financial matters, funding programs have a significant role in the process. Define and give examples of the various kinds of grants and funding programs.
2. Compare and contrast "dual federalism" and "cooperative federalism."
3. In the last decade, states and localities have faced significant changes in funding from the federal government. Discuss the reasons for the changes and how they affect relations among the various levels.
4. How do governmental mandates and regulations affect operations at the state and local levels?
5. Government has been moving to "privatization" of some goods and services. How will this trend affect intergovernmental relations?
6. Explain the importance and use of contracting for services and goods.

CASES AND EXERCISES

1. Analyze the relationship between state and local governments in your state. What legal requirements govern state/local relationships? What, if any, bodies exist to help in intergovernmental cooperation? What kinds of mandates has the state imposed on local governments? What has been the reaction to these? How do you think state/local relations could be improved?

2. Assume the role of a member of a task force that has been asked to consider ways your local parks and recreation services could be delivered at less cost to the city government. (You may be able to obtain a budget, a list of services, and existing fees from the Parks and Recreation Department.) Consider alternatives such as special charges, citizen involvement in service delivery, and limitations on services. At the same time, consider what minimal level of parks and recreational services the city should provide as part of its general operations.

3. Deil S. Wright, a prominent student of intergovernmental relations, offers a list of major trends affecting intergovernmental relations in the 1980s. Discuss each trend and predict its impact on the future of intergovernmental relations.

- Decreased flow (especially in relative terms) of federal aid to state and local governments
- Doubling of the national debt, from $1 trillion to over $2 trillion
- Growing trade deficit and decline of U.S. competitiveness internationally
- Burnout of the tax revolt and continued state activism in raising taxes
- Rise of "fee fever"—resort to charges and user fees by local and state governments
- Spread of privatization in a variety of forms and types

- Increasing significance of "regulatory federalism"
- State governments actively pursue economic development strategies, often consciously linked to educational policy changes

SOURCE: Deil S. Wright, *Understanding Governmental Relations*, 3rd ed. (Pacific Grove, CA: Brooks/Cole, 1988), p. 456.

4. Divide the class into several groups of six to eight students each. Have one group assume the role of a granting agency charged, by legislation, with providing funds to local communities to help in projects that "improve the economic potential of the community and assist low-income and disadvantaged groups in the community." Assume that the agency has $25 million dollars to distribute, but that the legislation has given the granting agency the authority to determine all other details of the grant program.

The agency group must first define as clearly as possible the intent of the legislation, then prepare guidelines outlining the types of projects that will be funded under the program. A written Request for Proposals (RFP) should then be prepared and distributed to a set of potential applicant communities, each represented by one of the other groups in the class. The RFP should contain, at a minimum, a description of the program, criteria by which proposals will be evaluated, examples of projects that might be funded, and instructions for submitting proposals for funding (including a deadline for applications).

Each community group will then prepare a grant application to support a project or projects it wants for its community. Members of each community group may communicate with one representative of the agency designated as liaison to that community, but should not talk with other agency members. Community groups can communicate with one another if they wish. By the deadline contained in the RFP, all proposals should be submitted to the agency. The agency will then determine which, if any, projects will be funded and at what levels. The results should be communicated to all the communities.

Following the exercise, the class as a whole should discuss the entire process. You might want to focus on issues such as these:

- What is the role of the agency in defining the kinds of projects that will be funded?
- What types of instructions are necessary to enable communities to compete fairly and effectively?
- What was most attractive about the proposals that were funded?
- For what reasons were other proposals not funded?
- What effect on the final decisions did communications between the community and the liaison from the agency have?
- Did "politics" play any role?

FOR ADDITIONAL READING

DeHoog, Ruth Hoogland. *Contracting Out for Human Services.* Albany: State University of New York Press, 1984.

Howitt, Arnold M. *Managing Federalism.* Washington, DC: Congressional Quarterly Press, 1984.

Jennings, Edward T., Jr., Krane, Dale, Pattakos, Alex N., and Reed, B. J. (eds.). *From Nation to States.* Albany: State University of New York Press, 1986.

Kettl, Donald F. *Government by Proxy.* Washington, DC: Congressional Quarterly Press, 1988.

Kettl, Donald F. *The Regulation of American Federalism.* Baton Rouge: Louisiana State University Press, 1983.

Nathan, Richard P., Doolittle, Fred C., and Associates. *Reagan and the States.* Princeton, NJ: Princeton University Press, 1987.

Nice, David C. *Federalism: The Politics of Intergovernmental Relations.* New York: St. Martins Press, 1987.

Reagan, Michael D., and Sanzone, John G. *The New Federalism,* 2nd ed. Oxford: Oxford University Press, 1981.

Walker, David B. *Toward a Functioning Federalism.* Cambridge, MA: Winthrop, 1981.

Wright, Deil S. *Understanding Intergovernmental Relations,* 3rd ed. Pacific Grove, CA: Brooks/Cole, 1988.

99

THE
ETHICS
OF
PUBLIC
SERVICE

S o far we have focused on the context of public administration—the values, structures, and relationships you need to understand to act effectively and responsibly in public organizations. Now we begin a transition to more skill-based issues by exploring the ethical issues raised in public service. An ethical posture toward work in public organizations requires not only knowing the right answers, but being willing and able to do what is right. You must be prepared to act.

Over the last several years, there has been a surge of interest in ethical issues in public organizations. A set of *Time* cover stories in 1987 asked the question, "What Ever Happened to Ethics?" The articles commented on ethical dilemmas in business, education, and even religion, but gave special attention to the ethics of those in government. In one article, Sissela Bok, a philosophy professor at Brandeis University, stressed that moral leadership must come first from those in public office. "Aristotle said that people in government exercise a teaching function. Among other things, we see what they do and think that is how we should act. Unfortunately, when they do things that are underhanded or dishonest, that teaches too" (*Time*, May 25, 1987).

Certainly the concerns Bok and others expressed about the ethical behavior of public officials have been triggered by such dramatic public events as Watergate and the Iran-Contra scandal. But in fact, ethical issues permeate public organizations—as they do all organizations. Every action of every public official—whether in the formulation or implementation of public policy—carries value implications.

In turn, as a public manager, you will often face difficult ethical choices. These choices may present themselves in several ways. "Dilemmas arise for decision makers when responsibilities conflict, when the obligations they undertake or the rules to which they are subject are unclear, or when they are unsure how to weigh their responsibilities against personal needs or desires" (Fleishman & Payne, 1980, p. 17). Understanding the moral implications of your actions and resolving the dilemmas they pose is one of the most difficult problems you will face working in the public sector. Consequently, your ability to understand the context in which public problems arise and to work them out in a careful, reasoned, and ethical fashion will be essential to your success (and your own sense of personal well-being).

In this chapter we examine a variety of ethical issues faced by public managers. Some involve concerns that might arise in any organization—cases of lying, cheating, or stealing, or questions about what to do when you feel impelled to refuse an order from your boss. Others are more directly connected to the special values that underlie public service, involving the relationship between political leaders and career civil servants or between competing demands for efficiency and responsiveness.

APPROACHES TO ETHICAL DELIBERATION

Ethics is, of course, a branch of philosophy and is concerned with the study of moral principles and moral action. To properly define *ethics*, therefore, we must first understand the meaning of morality. **Morality** is concerned with those practices and activities that are considered right or wrong; it is also concerned with the values those practices reflect and the rules through which they are carried out within a given setting (DeGeorge, 1982, p. 12). The morality of a society, a political system, or a public organization concerns what is considered to be right or wrong within that group. Morality expresses certain values that members of the group hold to be important and is reflected in laws, rules, and regulations, or in policies and procedures. Moral action, in turn, is action that is consistent with the group's morality—that which expresses the group's most basic commitments about what is right and what is wrong.

Ethics, on the other hand, can be defined as "a systematic attempt through the use of reason to make sense of our individual and social moral experience in such a way as to determine the rules which ought to govern human conduct . . ." (DeGeorge, 1982, p. 12). Ethics is concerned with the process by which we clarify what is right and wrong and by which we act on what we take to be right; ethics involves the use of reason in determining a proper course of action. Ethics is the search for moral standards.

Though we have defined ethics as the study of morality, the two terms are often used almost interchangeably. For example, we often call an action that is morally correct an ethical action. Similarly, we speak of codes of moral conduct as codes of ethics. Despite the overlapping uses of the terms, the distinction between morality and ethics is important not only for philosophical reasons, but because focusing on ethics emphasizes the individual's active involvement in searching out morally correct positions. Ethics calls us into action; it requires us to reason, to analyze, and to seek guidance as to the proper course of action.

This deliberative aspect of ethics is important because the issues you will face in public organizations are rarely black or white. Should you lie to a legislator so as to carry out a policy you think is correct? Should you bend the rules to benefit a client in need? Should you follow orders from an organizational superior even if you know you are being asked to do something wrong? These questions and the thousands of others you may encounter in public organizations don't have easy answers. To act properly, you must be able to sort through the many and often competing values that underlie your work, and you must be able to come to a reasoned conclusion that will form the basis for action.

It's not enough to simply say, "It depends," and go about your business—though such a position has gained widespread currency in our society. **Ethical (or moral) relativism** is the belief that actions that are immoral in some places or circumstances are moral in others and that one can make moral judgments only by taking into account the context in which an action occurs. According to this view, there are no universal rules of conduct that apply in all situations. A defense of the relativist position is that different cultures have different rules of conduct. One culture may consider it proper to leave old people to die alone, while another may give the elderly considerable care and attention.

Such arguments, however, often fail to take into account larger and more unifying moral principles, such as respect for the elderly. Furthermore, the relativist position seems at odds with our moral experience. When we make the judgment that murder is immoral, we don't mean that it is immoral for some individuals and not others. We don't even mean that murder is immoral in some countries and not in others. We claim that murder is immoral for all people at all times—and we can defend our statement on both rational and emotional grounds. This position suggests that there is really only one right answer to moral questions (even though that answer may be hard to find!). Nevertheless, by understanding the context in which an action occurs, working through the various arguments in behalf of one position or another, and arriving at a set of guidelines for action, one can at least act with greater clarity and confidence.

What are the steps in ethical deliberation? First, you should attempt to *clarify the facts*. Although most ethical issues involve both facts and values and the facts alone are not likely to resolve the issue, it is important to establish the facts as clearly as possible. A pollution control policy may require precise measurements of pollutants released into the air; knowing the exact measurements, rather than speculating about them, may resolve the issue. In other cases, merely becoming clearer about the facts will help resolve certain ethical problems.

Second, it is easier to resolve ethical issues if those involved come to some agreement about *basic principles*. These may be broad moral standards (such as freedom or justice); they may be laws or other rules accepted by the society; or they may be standards of behavior appropriate to a particular group or organization. These ideas are, of course, deeply held by members of any society or organization, so disagreements may be marked. For example, two detectives may have dramatically different views about how to treat criminals, but if they clarify their agreement on the basic goal of fighting crime, they may be able to reconcile their differences. Generally speaking, any progress you can make in establishing a common ground or in bringing about agreement on basic principles will help resolve the issue.

Third, one of the central aspects of ethical deliberation is the *analysis of arguments* presented in behalf of various viewpoints. The arguments may be articulated by different individuals or different groups, or they may simply be arguments and counterarguments you think through yourself. In either case, you will need to consider the evidence presented, the justifications for various viewpoints, and possible fallacies of the justifications. Throughout the process of argumentation, dialogue is extremely helpful in clarifying one's position. (If the problem is one you are considering alone, finding someone to talk through the issues with you is a good idea.) Ultimately, however, you will need to make a decision and act on it. Ethical deliberation will lead you to a decision, but acting in a way that is consistent with that decision is also important, though often difficult.

Reasoning, Development, and Action

You will be better prepared to deliberate if you become familiar with some basic approaches to ethical reasoning: moral philosophy, moral psychology, and moral action. In each case, we will present only a brief overview. You should be aware that there are many varying and sometimes conflicting interpretations of these issues, and you may find others (perhaps including your teacher) who disagree with the formulation presented here. Consider this material merely an invitation for further learning!

Moral philosophy Regarding *moral philosophy*, we can ask: given a particular set of circumstances, how do we determine what is right and what is wrong? In other words, how do we go about figuring out the proper course of action? One approach is to consider who will benefit and who will suffer from each of various alternative actions, then ask which course of action provides the greatest benefit at the least cost. Another approach is to search for a moral principle or rule against which to measure aspects of the particular case. In the first approach, one focuses on the consequences of the action; in the second, one looks for universal rules of conduct.

103

One of the most common forms of ethical deliberation, which focuses on the consequences of actions, is utilitarianism. **Utilitarianism** holds that an action is right, compared to other courses of action, if it results in the greatest good for the greatest number of people (or at least the minimum harm). Proponents of this view contend that there are no universal principles that can guide action, but rather that the likely benefits and costs associated with any action must be calculated to judge that practice either moral or immoral.

Obviously, this view leans toward relativism; according to a utilitarian, telling the truth cannot be judged a priori either right or wrong—rather, the rightness or wrongness of telling the truth depends on a calculation of who is helped and who is harmed by the act. Only then can a moral judgment be rendered. In the utilitarian view, "Actions themselves have no intrinsic values. They are simply means to attain things which do have value" (DeGeorge, 1982, p. 40).

An administrator employing a utilitarian approach to moral reasoning in a specific situation would ask what the likely outcomes of one course of action or another might be. If building a new highway through a particular neighborhood would inconvenience a few people but benefit many others, then building that highway in that location would be considered a proper course of action. The administrator would not follow any predetermined moral principle, such as that citizens should not be arbitrarily displaced, but would calculate costs and benefits relative to the specific case. Moreover, the administrator would not generalize beyond the specific case; each act would be judged on its own merits (Denhardt, 1988, pp. 50–51).

A contrasting approach to moral reasoning based on the search for general rules or principles of conduct is often called deontological. **Deontology** holds that broad principles of rightness and wrongness can be established and that these principles are not dependent on the consequences of a particular action. Those who hold this view tend to focus on duties or responsibilities (*deontology* derives from the Greek word for "duty"). Quite simply, one's duty is to do what is morally correct and to avoid doing that which is morally wrong, regardless of the consequences of one's actions (DeGeorge, 1982, p. 55). Deontologists thus tend to focus on broad principles of right and wrong, such as those embodied in concepts like "rights" or "justice."

Using the deontological approach, an administrator would seek to act in accord with generally accepted moral precepts, such as honesty or benevolence. Administrators are expected, for example, to tell the truth, keep their promises, and respect the dignity of the individual. Their doing so does not derive from laws or codes of ethics but from generally accepted moral principles. In particular situations, these actions might even be harmful to the overall interests of the organization or the society, but, because the actions could be justified as consistent with a shared sense of moral order, the administrator should feel strongly compelled to act in that way (Denhardt, 1988, p. 46).

One contemporary deontological theory that has received considerable attention is that of philosopher John Rawls. His approach emphasizes fairness or equity in policy decisions (Rawls, 1971). An interesting argument that Rawls develops to explain his theory suggests that if decisions were made under conditions in which the decision makers had no knowledge of whether they would personally accrue harm or benefit by choosing one way or another, then fairness would likely prevail. Imagine a city council committee deciding where to spend a million dollars on street improvements. If all members of the committee acted in their own interest, they might spend the money in their own neighborhoods (and those would likely be the more affluent neighborhoods). On the other hand, if all members of the committee acted under a "veil of ignorance," not knowing where they lived or whether or not they were affluent, they would most likely spend the money so as to bring the poorer streets up to some standard level (and in doing so, they would likely spend more in less affluent neighborhoods). If all public decisions were rendered by acting out of concern for fairness rather than self-interest, Rawls argues, a far different moral order would prevail—one that was much more consistent with the basic principles of liberty and justice.

Moral psychology   The psychologist Lawrence Kohlberg devised a scheme outlining three levels of moral development through which people pass—the preconventional, conventional, and postconventional stages (Kohlberg, 1971). According to Kohlberg, most people operate on one of the first two levels of moral development, and no one operates exclusively on the third level.

At the *preconventional level,* children begin to develop certain ideas about right and wrong. They interpret these ideas in terms of the consequences of their actions or the physical power of those around them. At an early stage, the ideas are associated with punishments; for example, if the child writes on the wall with a crayon, the child will be scolded. To avoid the negative consequences associated with writing on the wall, the child avoids that behavior. Later on, the child begins to behave in certain ways to receive rewards, such as parental praise. Whether to avoid negative consequences or to receive praise, the child begins to behave in ways that we characterize as right rather than wrong. Of course, from the child's point of view, there is no moral code; the child is merely doing things to avoid punishments or to seek rewards. At this level of moral development, therefore, the consequences of our actions—the rewards or punishments we receive—determine whether we consider our actions right or wrong. The preconventional orientation is, of course, one that we all carry into adulthood.

At the *conventional level* of moral development, people behave morally in terms of conformity to various standards or conventions of the family, group, or nation. The individual seeks to conform to given moral standards and, indeed, to actively support and maintain those standards. This level involves two stages. Kohlberg calls the first the "Good Boy/Nice Girl" stage, at which we conform to expectations of parents or teachers or peers and to the norms we learn at home, in church, or at school. We come to develop moral rules or codes, standards of right and wrong, though what we think of as good behavior is really just that which meets the expectations of others.

A second stage in the conventional level of moral development is the "Law and Order" orientation. At this stage, we develop an orientation toward authority and the social order; we learn what it means to be a "good citizen"; and we come to accept the importance of living by the conventional rules of the society. Notions of duty and honor tend to dominate one's moral perspective at this level. We recognize that certain behaviors are wrong—lying, cheating, stealing—but if asked why, we can only answer, "Because everyone knows they are wrong" (DeGeorge, 1982, p. 25). Most adults continue to operate, at least in part, at this level of moral development.

Few adults reach the final level, the *postconventional*, but some do. At this level, people accept moral principles and behave according to those principles, not merely because someone says they should, but because they know themselves what makes these principles right. The individual seeks to define moral principles for himself or herself and to understand how those values operate independently of any group or society. A first postconventional stage is called the "social-contract" or "legalistic" stage, which has a strong utilitarian bias. The individual recognizes the rights of other individuals, including the right to one's own beliefs and values, and how societies are constituted to support those rights. The result is a legalistic viewpoint, though it recognizes the possibility of changing the legal order (rather than freezing it, as in the previous level). Changes of this sort are often supported based on the greatest good for the greatest number.

The second stage of the postconventional level represents the highest stage of moral development. At this stage, the individual freely chooses to live by a particular set of abstract moral principles, such as justice, equality, and respect for individual dignity. One chooses to follow these precepts not for rewards or punishments and not to meet others' expectations, but because one understands why the principle should be supported and freely chooses to live by that standard. The actual standards one follows may be the same in both level two and level three, but there is an important difference in the *reason* one holds an action to be right or wrong.

As you work in and with public organizations, you will come to recognize that many of the ethical decisions you make are based in one or another level of moral development. We do certain things because they will lead to rewards or punishments and we do other things because we must adhere to laws or organizational standards of conduct. For example, you may obey an order from a superior so that you won't be fired, or you may purchase a new piece of equipment through a bidding process rather than from a friend because that's the law. But you will also encounter cases that will require you to think much more carefully and much more personally about the standards you are willing to live by. For example, purchasing a piece of equipment might be complicated by the fact that your supervisor *ordered* you to purchase the equipment from a friend without other bids. In cases such as these, postconventional or "principled" reasoning may be essential. Certainly if you recognize that not all the answers can come from the power or expectations of others and that careful deliberation concerning moral principles is often quite appropriate, you will be better positioned to make the correct ethical decisions, time after time.

Moral action   Knowing the proper and correct course of action is not enough. You must indeed act in a way that is consistent with what you consider to be right. (After all, we describe people as having "integrity" not merely on the basis of what they believe, but on the basis of how they act.) This concern is especially significant for a public manager (or, for that matter, any other professional) who wishes to act ethically. Questions of ethics in the public service are not abstract; they are real. And they have immediate and sometimes serious human consequences. It is thus important to consider how we can assure moral actions in public organizations.

106   A long philosophical tradition holds that putting principles (whether utilitarian, deontological, or otherwise) into action requires the development of "character" on the part of the individual. In other words, it is necessary to apply a complex set of general principles to specific cases—something that requires more than abstract knowledge. Aristotle spoke of the importance of gaining "practical wisdom" so as to make morally correct judgments in specific situations. This practical wisdom or "virtue" requires that the individual not simply know how to apply given principles, but rather why to do so. That is, to bring moral knowledge to bear in the "real world," the individual needs a strong sense of what is ideal in human conduct.

This "ethics of virtue," then, is not merely another philosophical approach but a way of developing the skills one brings to the problem of ethical decision making. Aristotle speaks of developing the skills of virtue in the same way we develop other skills, that is, by practice: "The virtues we get first by exercising them . . . for the things we have to learn before we can do them, we learn by doing them . . . we become just by doing just acts, temperate by doing temperate acts, brave by doing brave acts" (McKeon, 1941, p. 952).

But what are the virtues that we must practice? Obviously, this question has challenged philosophers over the centuries. Answers range from honesty, courage, and trustworthiness to kindness, fairness, and dependability, but most seem to center around concerns for *benevolence* and *justice*. If this is the case, then all persons should practice these virtues, while members of specific professions (such as public administrators) should practice applications of these virtues in their specific situations (Tong, 1986, pp. 91–92).

How, then, does one sort out the various philosophical and psychological approaches one might employ to make ethical choices in the "real world"? First, if you set about solving difficult moral problems through the application of broad moral principles in specific situations, you need to understand the principles and moral reasoning that underlie them. Second, you must engage in careful and consistent ethical deliberation, through self-reflection and dialogue with others. Third, you must understand how virtues such as benevolence or justice are played out in public organizations; that is, you must recognize the political and ethical context that conditions the moral priorities of the public service (Bailey, 1965, p. 285).

As you approach particular questions, it may be helpful to consider first the utilitarian position—what are the costs and benefits and which alternative will bring the greatest benefits? Next, you might ask whether the alternative you chose will infringe upon the rights of others and, if so, whether there are overwhelming factors that justify such an outcome. You might next ask whether the chosen alternative violates principles of equity and fairness and, if so, whether again there are overwhelming factors that would justify the outcome. Finally, you might ask whether the alternative is consistent with your ideals with respect to human conduct (especially the conduct of public affairs) and whether by choosing this alternative you will be acting in a way you consider to be virtuous. At any point, you may find that the alternative comes up short, and you must search for another. Remember that your ultimate goal is the development of virtue and the application of sound ethical reasoning to public problems.

ISSUES OF ADMINISTRATIVE RESPONSIBILITY

People who work in or with public organizations face literally dozens of ethical dilemmas. Some, like lying, cheating, or stealing, are the same problems that many others face. But some, like the public manager's commitment to democratic standards or feelings about the political involvement of public employees, are peculiar to public organizations.

One of the most troublesome "broad-range" issues in the field of public administration is that of administrative responsibility. (In the section that follows, we focus much more specifically on issues where personal values, such as honesty, equity, and justice, become deeply intermingled with the broader values of public service.) As a public manager, you may often confront the potentially conflicting demands of operating as efficiently as possible while, at the same time, being fully responsive to administrative superiors, to the legislature, to the citizenry, and to the principles of democratic governance generally. This tension between *efficiency* and *responsiveness* characterizes many of the problems public managers face.

Basically, the tension between efficiency and responsiveness grows from two other issues that are deeply rooted in the history of public administration—the issue of politics and administration and the issue of bureaucracy versus democracy. As we have seen, early writers in the field sought a clear distinction between *politics* and *administration*, arguing that, wherever possible, administrative activities should be insulated from the potentially corrupting influence of politics. Obviously, this idea was based on the assumption that policy making could be distinguished from policy implementing. Making such an assumption allows easy resolution of questions of democratic responsibility—the legislature, charged with making policy, should be responsive to the people; the administrative agencies, charged with implementing policy, should be responsive to the legislature. The requirements of democracy will be met by a neutral and competent public bureaucracy that follows the mandates of the legislative body; this is called the doctrine of **neutral competence.** Most writers and practitioners clearly preferred this somewhat narrow view of administrative responsibility. Indeed, the doctrine of neutral competence, and the politics-administration dichotomy on which it is based, continues to influence the field. But there were and are many who recognize the difficulty of maintaining a neutral public bureaucracy. Some even argue that the role administrative agencies play in the policy process is not only inevitable, but proper.

A second theme that grew from the earliest discussions of public administration had to do with the potential for conflict between *democracy* and *bureaucracy*. First, democratic principles assume that the *individual* is the primary measure of human value, and that development of the individual is the primary goal of a democratic political system. Second, democratic morality suggests that all persons are created *equal*—differences in wealth, status, or position should not give one person or group an advantage over another. Third, democratic morality emphasizes widespread *participation* of the citizens in making major decisions (Redford, 1969, p. 8).

Set against these tenets of democracy are the ideals of bureaucratic management. The early scholars and practitioners in public administration wrote, of course, at a time when businesses were growing rapidly and were beginning to use both new and more complicated technologies and new ways of organizing that were appropriate to those technologies. The growth of large-scale business led to the development of large and complex bureaucratic organizations that were built around values quite different from those of a democracy. (The term *bureaucracy* is often used in a pejorative sense, as in "bureaucratic red tape"; we use it in its more neutral and scientific sense, as one of many ways of organizing work.)

The values of bureaucracy included first the need to bring together the work of many individuals to achieve purposes far beyond the capabilities of any single individual. Second, bureaucratic systems were to be structured hierarchically, with those at the top having far greater power and discretion than those at the bottom. Third, bureaucratic organization generally assumes that power and authority flow from the top of the organization to the bottom. (We will examine the concept of bureaucracy in greater detail in chapter 9.)

In contrast to the democratic value of individuality, there stood the bureaucratic value of the group or organization; in contrast to the democratic values of equality, there stood the bureaucratic hierarchy; and in contrast to the democratic values of participation and involvement, there stood the bureaucratic value of top-down decision making and authority.

How to reconcile these values became a difficult issue for early scholars and practitioners, as it continues to be today. A variety of questions arise. For example, is it proper for a democratic government to carry out its work through basically authoritarian organizations? But the key issue turns out to be emphasis on efficiency as the sole measure of agency success.

Many early writers took the position that government administration should be measured strictly in terms of efficiency: "The objective of public administration is the most efficient utilization of the resources at the disposal of officials and employees" (White, 1948, p. 2). Making the parallel to business, Gulick argued that "In the science of administration, whether public or private, the basic 'good' is efficiency" (Gulick, 1937, p. 192). In the view of many, public administration came to be the study and practice of making more efficient the operations of those executive agencies charged with carrying out the decrees of the legislature.

But not all the early writers fully concurred with the preoccupation with administrative efficiency. Marshall Dimock, for example, argued that efficiency is "coldly calculating and inhuman," where "successful administration is warm and vibrant. It is human" (Dimock, 1936, p. 120). Dimock, as well as others, held that a more sensitive under-standing of management was especially required in the public sector where objectives were less easily measured and where service to the public was what really counted. Most important was the question as to whether an agency that concentrated all its energies on efficiency could be fully responsive to the needs of citizens and to other principles such as equity and justice.

Efficiency versus Responsiveness: A Case Study

As those in public administration have wrestled with the issues of politics and administra-tion and democracy and bureaucracy, public managers have begun to experience day-to-day problems more often in terms of efficiency versus responsiveness. On the one hand, there is the hope that public organizations will operate as efficiently as possible, getting things done quickly and with the least cost to taxpayers. On the other hand, public managers must be constantly attentive to the demands of the citizenry, whether the demands are expressed through the chief executive, through the legislature, or directly. The following case study, based on a real-life situation, shows a practical and contemporary expression of this difficulty.

109

John Taylor and Carol Langley worked for a local community development agency. Following a rather massive reorganization of the agency in which a number of new programs were taken on, John was asked to supervise a new housing loan program, and Carol was asked to assist him. The program was designed to provide low-interest loans to help people rehabilitate housing in certain parts of the city. Although John and Carol had experience in related areas, neither was familiar with this particular program. To make matters worse, seminars to provide help in establishing such programs had been held some months earlier. John and Carol were simply given a manual and told to begin.

The program involved a number of new activities and took considerable time to set up. For example, it was necessary to train new housing inspectors to coordinate their inspection activities with those provided by the city, and relationships had to be estab-lished with the many agencies that would provide information about the applicants being processed.

John soon began receiving considerable pressure to complete the processing of the first group of applications within a brief period. For one thing, the first groups of applicants consisted of some forty persons who had originally applied for other programs but had been turned down. Since their applications had been on file in the agency for as long as a year, they were quite anxious to have their applications processed quickly. Initial visits and phone calls from several of the applicants made John quite aware of their feelings. John was also aware, however, that this particular loan program would have a significant impact on the community and that, consequently, his doing an efficient job under these difficult circumstances would be important to the agency and in turn important to his own future in government service.

Carol recognized the need to do the work as quickly as possible, but she also felt a special obligation to the applicants themselves. She took seriously the director's comment that the agency could use this opportunity to help "educate" the applicants about the procedures involved in such projects. She felt that it was important to check periodically on the inspections, cost estimates, loan amounts, financial information, and terms and conditions of the loans. Unlike John, who spent most of his time in the office, she talked frequently with the applicants, many of whom she knew personally from her previous position in the agency.

For each applicant, John and Carol were to accumulate a complete file of information about financial status and what kind of rehabilitation project the applicant had in mind. This file was to be sent to and signed by the applicant, then forwarded to the federal regional office of HUD for its action on the loan.

John felt the process could be completed more quickly if Carol would simply get the applicants to sign a blank set of forms that could be kept at the office. When information was received regarding a loan, the appropriate items could be entered on the signed forms, bypassing the time involved in reviewing each form with the applicant. Also, this procedure would eliminate the often lengthy process of coordinating several office visits to discuss the material.

When John asked Carol to obtain the signed forms, she refused. Not only was she concerned that the applicants see and understand the materials before signing, she was afraid that getting people to sign blank forms might be illegal. When she talked with John's supervisor about the request, she was told that the procedure was not illegal and had even been used before by persons in the regional office.

Although this case presents several different issues, most students who review it focus on the different interpretations that John and Carol have of their work. At first glance, John appears to be interested solely in doing things efficiently, while Carol appears to be much more concerned with responding to the needs of the client group. The case appears to be a classic illustration of the tension between efficiency and responsiveness; but, at a deeper level, it also illustrates how complex the issues really are. You might say, for example, that John was trying to be efficient *in response to* the demands of those clients who had been waiting for their loans to be processed. You might also say that Carol, through her educational efforts, was helping to assure a *more efficient* long-term operation.

The main point, of course, is that, in public organizations, you may quite frequently encounter difficulties in reconciling efficiency and responsiveness. A key to resolving the ethical questions in situations such as John and Carol faced is first to understand the various moral values represented on each side of the equation, and second, to engage in ethical deliberation (and perhaps dialogue) to arrive at a proper approach to the problem. Interestingly enough, in this particular case, the real-life characters represented by John and Carol got together and talked through the differences in their respective approaches. The result was a course of action they both agreed upon, which they felt met their obligations to be both efficient and responsive. In the real world, dialogue sometimes works!

The Limits of Administrative Discretion

Two other questions are closely related to the efficiency-responsiveness issue: the limits of administrative discretion and avenues for public participation in administrative decision making. We have noted that administrators take their primary cues from the actions of legislatures that initiate programs and from executives who are charged with carrying out the programs. If you are hired to manage a new agency, one of your first priorities will be to familiarize yourself with the legislation that created the agency and with any executive orders or other directives outlining the agency's responsibilities. But if your situation is typical, you will find that neither the legislation nor the directions you receive from the executive are sufficiently detailed to answer all the questions your work raises. There will be a need to develop policies regarding these issues; policies that are, in effect, merely more detailed pieces of "legislation." In addition, as you get into the work, you may find it necessary to ask the legislature or the chief executive to make certain changes in the rules and regulations under which you operate.

The problem, of course, is to make sure that your policies or recommendations for change are consistent with the wishes of the citizenry. In most jurisdictions, of course, the legislature and the chief executive are popularly elected, and their reelection depends on their response to the public's perceived needs and interests. For them, the electoral process assures responsiveness, at least in theory. As long as you are acting in a way that is clearly consistent with legislative intent, you are likely to be considered appropriately responsive. But because most situations aren't that clear, the question becomes, "How can we assure that the administrator is exercising discretion in a way consistent with the will of the people, whether expressed in the Constitution, the laws of the land, or the preferences of citizens?" (see Box 4.1).

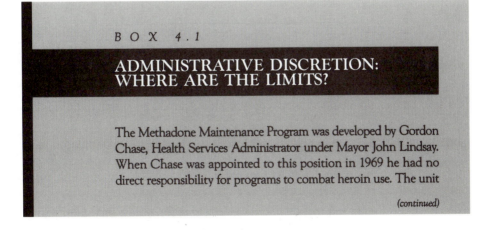

BOX 4.1

ADMINISTRATIVE DISCRETION: WHERE ARE THE LIMITS?

The Methadone Maintenance Program was developed by Gordon Chase, Health Services Administrator under Mayor John Lindsay. When Chase was appointed to this position in 1969 he had no direct responsibility for programs to combat heroin use. The unit

(continued)

(continued)

then responsible for addicts was the Addiction Services Agency (ASA). Its approach was to encourage abstinence from heroin through supervised voluntary therapeutic communities operating under strict discipline. Another agency, the State Narcotics Addiction Control Commission, forcibly confined addicts in expensive treatment centers. There were also two private programs that tried to shift the addict's craving from heroin to an inexpensive synthetic drug called methadone. One was located at the Beth Israel Hospital, the other at the Addiction Research and Treatment Corporation (ARTC).

Shortly after taking office Gordon Chase decided that not enough was being done to treat the 100,000 or more heroin addicts on the streets of New York. Lacking formal authority to undertake new programs but believing that he personally should take action to fill the treatment gap, Chase resolved to establish a methadone maintenance treatment program. His first move was to send the Mayor's Narcotics Control Council a proposal to treat 15,600 addicts in less than a year. This number was inflated, but Chase thought that his memorandum would help to get key officials to think in terms of large programs and would create momentum. Then even before the mayor authorized him to do so and before funds were available, he began to recruit a dynamic and capable staff. The head of the new Bureau of Methadone Maintenance was Dr. Robert Newman, who was handpicked by Chase. Newman kept up the momentum by opening clinics in existing institutions, maintaining control and accountability through a tight monitoring and reporting system, pressing to meet deadlines, and working to overcome community opposition to clinics for "junkies." By June 1971, the city's methadone programs had treated 6,000 addicts, and by January of 1974 the figure had risen to over 20,000. Moreover, the apparent success of this effort had stimulated the Beth Israel Hospital to expand its intake of patients.

SOURCE: Excerpted from Donald P. Warwick, "The Ethics of Administrative Discretion," in *Public Duties: The Moral Obligations of Government Officials*, ed. Joel Fleishman, Lance Liebman, and Mark Moore (Cambridge, MA: Harvard University Press, 1981), pp. 94–95.

Historically, two answers have been posed to this question. In an important debate in the pages of the *Public Administration Review* and other journals some forty years ago, Herman Finer argued that, to maintain responsiveness to the public, managers in public organizations should be subjected to strict and rigid controls by the legislature.

His question was straightforward (though perhaps overdrawn): "Are the servants of the public to decide their own course, or is their course of action to be decided by a body outside themselves?" (Finer, 1972, p. 328). His answer was equally direct: only through specific and detailed legislation carefully limiting the work of public managers could responsiveness to the legislature be maintained. This interpretation of how to assure responsiveness is often called **objective responsibility,** depending as it does on objective external controls.

Carl Friedrich, on the other hand, argued that the increasing complexity of modern society made such detailed legislation difficult, if not impossible; consequently, Friedrich felt that the administrator's own concern for the public interest was often the only real assurance that his or her actions would be responsive to the electorate. Fortunately, wrote Friedrich, the growing number of professionals in government increases the likelihood that a sense of democratic responsibility will be a part of the administrator's makeup (Friedrich, 1972).

Others, following Friedrich's lead, noted the growing number of governmental officials receiving training in schools of public affairs and public administration. These schools take quite seriously the need to expose students to the ethical issues they may encounter in public organizations and to ways these issues might be resolved. This way of assuring responsiveness is often called **subjective responsibility,** depending as it does on the subjective nature of the individual.

One approach to assuring responsiveness that cuts across the objective/subjective distinction is *representative bureaucracy*—the idea that public agencies whose employees reflect certain demographic characteristics of the population as a whole are likely to operate more in line with the policy preferences of the general citizenry. According to this view, an agency with a substantial number of women or minority employees is more likely to take into account the views of women and minorities in the population than would an agency of white males. Experience with representative bureaucracy has produced mixed results. Whereas we might indeed expect greater responsiveness with respect to race and gender in the example, there is no reason to think that such an agency would be more or less representative on other types of issues. Moreover, there is no real assurance that a person from one particular group would necessarily or always reflect that group's policy preferences. Those preferences might well be displaced by the professional or bureaucratic norms that person adopts.

Avenues for Public Participation

Another way to assure that public managers and employees act in a way consistent with the desires of the public is to involve citizens directly in the decision-making process, through membership on advisory boards, open hearings, or direct polling. Such techniques, which have now become widespread, took their initial impetus from passage of the Economic Opportunity Act of 1964, legislation that required the "maximum feasible participation" of the poor in the design and conduct of antipoverty programs. In this case, the question of involvement itself became quite an issue, especially as the representatives of the poor came into direct confrontation with those holding established positions of power in local communities. The movement toward widespread citizen participation was soon well-established, however, and spread quickly to local school boards, universities, and a variety of other government agencies. Today, for example, the practice of holding hearings prior to administrative decisions is commonplace at all levels of government.

There are questions, of course, as to whether real power is transferred to the citizens or whether citizen involvement is merely a device for defusing protests. Some use the term **cooptation** to describe situations in which citizens are given the feeling of involvement but little real power. On balance, it is probably accurate to say that there are some cases in which citizens have been coopted through involvement in advisory boards or even public hearings, but in most cases, administrators are truly interested in receiving input from the public that will help them make difficult decisions.

The complexities of public involvement in administrative decision making are illustrated in the following case, actually a continuation of one we encountered in chapter 2. As we learned, the Clean Air Act required EPA to set national emissions standards for hazardous air pollutants to protect the public health. But no definition was given as to what would be considered "an ample margin of safety."

> The issue received national attention in 1983 when EPA was trying to decide what, if anything, should be done about inorganic arsenic, a cancer-causing pollutant produced when arsenic-content ore is smelted into copper. The problem was particularly serious in the area around Tacoma, Washington, where the American Smelting and Refining Company (ASARCO) operated a copper smelter. The EPA had concluded that, in the absence of any controls on ASARCO's arsenic emissions, approximately four new cases of lung cancer would be contracted each year in the Tacoma area. Even after installation of the "best available" pollution-control equipment, there would still be one new case of cancer per year. But there was an important consideration on the other side of the issue as well. If the EPA were to impose any more onerous conditions on ASARCO—requiring, for example, that it use ore containing less arsenic or install a new and far more expensive electric smelter—the company could not afford to continue to operate the plant. ASARCO employed 570 workers, with an annual payroll of approximately $23 million; the company bought an additional $12 million worth of goods from local suppliers. Closing the plant therefore would pose serious economic problems for the local economy.
>
> William Ruckelshaus, then Administrator of the EPA, decided that the citizens of the Tacoma area ought to wrestle with the problem. Accordingly, Ruckelshaus flew to Tacoma to announce a series of three public workshops to be held during the summer of 1983. The purpose was to acquaint residents with the details of the pollution problem, help them prepare for subsequent formal hearings, and enable them to deliberate about what should be done.
>
> Some questions concerned technical matters, like the reliability of the proposed control equipment and the risk figures and epidemiological studies on which the EPA had based its estimates. Other questions revealed the inadequacy of the EPA's explanation of the relative health risk posed by the smelter: One resident asked whether that risk was greater than the risk posed by auto emissions.
>
> Residents were not solely concerned, however, with the factual basis for the agency's claims. Several residents wanted to discuss the effects of the arsenic emissions on their gardens, their animals, and on the overall quality of life. Several residents expressed hostility toward the EPA for involving them in this difficult decision making in the first place. These issues are very complex and the public is not sophisticated enough to make

these decisions. This is not to say that EPA doesn't have an obligation to inform the public, but information is one thing—defaulting its legal mandate is another.

These numerous workshops, together with the national attention that Ruckelshaus had deliberately drawn to them by traveling to Tacoma to announce them, created considerable and often unfavorable press coverage. In an editorial on July 16, 1983, entitled "Mr. Ruckelshaus a Caesar," the *New York Times* argued that "Mr. Ruckelshaus has it all upside down. . . . What is inexcusable is for him to impose such an impossible choice on Tacomans." An article in the *Los Angeles Times* pointed out the difficulties "in taking a community's pulse. . . . [Should one] poll the community . . . [or] count the pros and cons at the massive hearing?" Ruckelshaus was not surprised by the controversy. He said, "Listen, I know people don't like these kinds of decisions. . . . [W]elcome to the world of regulation. People have demanded to be involved and now I have involved them, and they say, 'Don't ask that question.' What's the alternative? Don't involve them? Then you are accused of doing something nefarious." (Reich, 1985)*

The outcome of the case is anticlimactic: before the EPA promulgated its regulations, declining copper prices led to the closing of the ASARCO smelter anyway. The case does, however, point out some of the difficulties in designing adequate programs for public participation. Certainly there is every reason to think that Secretary Ruckelshaus really wanted to test the pulse of the citizens before making regulations. But his attempt was met not only with ambivalence, as is often the case, but with outright hostility. Moreover, despite his efforts, there were few clear signals to the agency with respect to what to do. The ethical issues posed by the requirements of administrative responsibility are indeed complex.

115

The Ethics of Privatization

We noted in chapter 3 the increasing involvement of private and nonprofit organizations in the delivery of public programs. Especially as governments have contracted for or otherwise sought to "privatize" services, private and nonprofit organizations have become major providers of public services. But, as we also saw, transfer of responsibility may raise significant ethical questions regarding equity and accountability. The government might find it necessary or expedient to contract out for garbage collection, for example, but neither necessity nor cost savings would justify allowing contractors to engage in discrimination or other unethical practices.

The issue is particularly critical for private sector providers, who could have a tendency to maximize profits even at the sacrifice of some other public value. A private organization might be tempted to provide either more services than necessary for clients (to increase payments and therefore revenues) or less services than necessary (to cut costs). Actions such as these, clearly motivated by concern for profit, are less likely to occur in service delivery by nonprofit organizations, simply by virtue of their service "ethos," but even they require mechanisms to assure equity and accountability (Rubin, 1990).

In any privatization arrangement, the government's responsibility is not only to assure quality and cost consistent with stewardship of public resources, but also to promote

*SOURCE: Reprinted by permission of the Yale Law Journal Company and Fred B. Rothman & Company from *The Yale Law Journal*, Vol. 94, pp. 1617-1641.

democratic ideals and assure constitutional protections. There are at least two different types of delegation to consider: those that involve no transfer of discretionary authority and those that do. Obviously, many contracts involve no transfer of authority; public works contracts, for example, can usually be standardized and highly specified so as to grant virtually no discretionary public authority to contractors (though even here there are exceptions, as we saw with Rochester). The government retains responsibility for exercising public authority (e.g., determining eligibility for and frequency of garbage collection or street repair) and for holding contractors accountable for quality, quantity, and cost of work.

Other arrangements may involve transfer of discretionary authority; for example, the authority to determine details of eligibility requirements for student loans or the authority to decide what services to provide to inmates of a privately operated prison. In situations such as these, appropriate accountability structures must be in place to assure responsiveness to the government agency that administers the contract as well as to the public generally. Developing contractual arrangements that fully incorporate appropriate concerns for the public interest presents one of the most significant challenges of efforts to privatize public services.

ETHICAL PROBLEMS FOR THE INDIVIDUAL

116

Even the most straightforward ethical problems may be problematic, especially in the context of work in public organizations. Think for a moment about telling the truth. At first glance, nothing could seem more obvious than to tell "the truth, the whole truth, and nothing but the truth." But is that really the proper ethical position (outside a courtroom)? Should you be prepared to lie to protect matters vital to the national defense? Should you tell the whole truth in response to questions from the press about confidential matters affecting your clients? Is it proper to "stretch" research findings so they better support a policy position you feel is in the public interest? These are just a few of the most pressing and difficult questions you may face that will test not only your principles but also your willingness to act in accord with those principles.

Interacting with Elected Officials

The relationship between public managers and elected officials, either chief executives (such as mayors or governors) or members of a legislative body, presents a unique but nearly pervasive set of issues for the public manager. Whether as a department head working with a legislative committee, a city manager working with a city council, or an executive director working with the board of a nonprofit organization, the relationship between manager and the legislative body presents special problems.

We have examined some of the implications of this relationship for the development of public policy; but we should also be aware of possible ethical implications. On the one hand, an administrator should be accountable to the legislative body; on the other hand, responding blindly to legislative decree may not always be in the public interest.

The latter situation might arise in several ways. Certainly, differing strongly with members of the legislature on policy questions presents great difficulties. As an administrator, to what extent should you seek to persuade the legislature to your position? Is it proper for a manager to try to build a power base in the legislature to enable special consideration of legislation favorable to the agency? If the legislature acts contrary to your strong beliefs, should you continue in your position or should you resign? If you continue, is it proper to try later to shape implementation of the legislation to fall more closely in line with your beliefs?

Similarly difficult questions might arise if the manager is asked to do something improper. For instance, what would you do if a legislator asked you to do something illegal, such as permitting health care payments to an ineligible client? How would your decision change if the legislator only asked you to "bend the rules" a little bit? How would your decision change if the legislator chaired the committee that passed on your agency's appropriation?

These issues may arise in any public organization; however, they are especially well illustrated at the local level with the council–manager form of government, which is built around the distinction between policy and administration. Theoretically, the council is responsible for determining policy and the manager is responsible for carrying it out. In practice, however, the line between policy and administration is never so clear; inevitably, the manager becomes involved in policy matters and the council in administrative matters.

Because of this overlap, the Code of Ethics of the International City Management Association contains several statements that bear on the council–manager relationship. The Code's first item emphasizes the manager's dedication to "effective and democratic local government *by responsible elected officials*" and recognizes the contribution profes-   117
sional management can make in this regard. More specifically, on the manager's policy role, the Code suggests that the manager "submit policy proposals to elected officials; provide them with facts and advice on matters of policy as a basis for making decisions and setting community goals, and uphold and implement municipal policies adopted by elected officials." Similarly, the manager is advised to "recognize that elected representatives of the people are entitled to the credit for the establishment of municipal policies; (while) responsibility for public execution rests with the members."

Despite these helpful guidelines, city managers often face difficulties in relationships with city councils. One city manager disagreed strongly with a council move to limit widening a particular city street, an improvement the manager felt was essential to local economic development; another city manager felt that a council member was acting irresponsibly in proposing legislation that would help his contracting business; still another city manager was asked to process travel vouchers that included payment for personal vacation expenses. Simply figuring out how to respond effectively to these situations is hard enough, but the problem is even greater when you remember that the city manager who forces an issue of policy or ethics may be seen as "attacking" his or her bosses—and may, at any time, be summarily fired. It's no wonder that the average tenure of city managers in this country is only between four and five years!

Following Orders

Another problem has to do with limits to organizational authority. What would you do if your boss asked you to do something you felt was morally wrong? Suppose you are asked to "bury" a report on toxic wastes you consider potentially dangerous to the public, or that, under pressures of time, you are asked to give quick approval to a piece of equipment that might be unsafe. Or imagine that you are asked to approve an expense reimbursement for your boss, when you know the amount has been "padded."

In cases such as these, you face difficult choices—choices made even more difficult by the very logic that causes us to employ bureaucratic means of organizing. Bureaucratic organizations are attractive because they enable people to accomplish large-scale tasks they would not otherwise be able to undertake, but bureaucracy as a social form also demands a certain amount of obedience to authority. Presumably, if orders are not obeyed, the whole system falls apart—so there are strong pressures for individuals to follow orders rather than their consciences.

The most dramatic historical example of the problem of unquestioning obedience to authority comes from Hitler's attempt to exterminate the European Jews during World War II. Although the killings were ordered by political leaders, they were carried out through the German bureaucracy. The problem faced not only those at the top of the organization; rather, it extended throughout. Raul Hilberg, author of a classic study of the holocaust, writes:

> Most bureaucrats composed memoranda, drew up blueprints, signed correspondence, talked on the telephone, and participated in conferences . . . . However, these men were not stupid; they realized the connection between their paperwork and the heaps of corpses in the East. And they realized, also, the shortcomings of those rationalizations which placed all evil on the Jew and all good on the German. That was why they were compelled to justify their individual activities. The first rationalization was the oldest, the simplest, and therefore the most effective: the doctrine of superior orders. First and foremost there was duty. No matter what objections there might be, orders were given to be obeyed. A clear order was like an absolution; armed with such an order, a perpetrator felt that he could pass his responsibility and his conscience upward. (Hilberg, 1961, p. 649)

This manner of justifying one's actions became central to the defense of those accused at the Nuremberg trials. Many defendants argued, as did General Alfred Jodl, that it is "not the task of a soldier to act as a judge over his superior commander" (Arendt, 1963, p. 133). But despite the rationale of "superior orders," for the German bureaucrats and for their more contemporary counterparts, the moral dilemma posed by such orders remains.

One might argue, of course, that the German example is overdrawn—that such a thing could never happen in a democratic society such as ours. But perhaps it could. Indeed, a remarkable series of studies conducted by Yale psychologist Stanley Milgram several years ago suggests that Americans are often quite willing to obey, even where doing so causes them extreme moral discomfort. In an elaborate series of experiments, Milgram asked subjects to administer shocks to a person supposedly involved in a memory experiment. Even though the person receiving the shocks writhed in pain (he was actually an actor and an accomplice), the subjects continued to follow Milgram's orders to administer the painful shocks—simply because they were told to do so! Milgram concluded that "a substantial proportion of people do what they are told, irrespective of the content of the act and without limitations of conscience, so long as they perceive that the command comes from a legitimate authority" (Milgram, 1974, p. 189).

Contemporary examples of problems with orders from above are perhaps less dramatic than the German illustration, but they present equally difficult choices for the individual.

118

You may, of course, protest the action, either directly to your superiors or more indirectly, though in doing so, you may place yourself in jeopardy. Or you may leave the organization, resigning in protest, even though the available alternatives—such as unemployment—may not be attractive. Or you may simply keep quiet and do what you are told. The latter alternative is certainly the easiest in most cases—by obeying orders, you feel you have someone else (your superior) to blame if something goes wrong—and, in any case, there is a strong feeling that if people in large organizations fail to follow orders, things won't get done. Unfortunately, rationalizations such as these don't allow you to escape the moral consequences of your actions.

Conflicts of Interest

Another area of potential ethical difficulties for public officials involves conflicts of interest. Finding ways to avoid conflicts of interest, especially financial, has been central to federal, state, and local ethics legislation for the past twenty-five to thirty years. At the federal level, legislation proscribing the ethical behavior of public officials has deep historical roots; however, the tone of modern ethics legislation was set by Executive Order 11222 issued by President Johnson in 1965. In part, the policy reads as follows:

> Where government is based on the consent of the governed, every citizen is entitled to have complete confidence in the integrity of his government. Each individual officer, employee, or advisor of government must help to earn and must honor that trust by his own integrity and conduct in all official actions.

The Executive Order then provides a set of "Standards of Conduct" that covers such topics as accepting gifts, financial conflicts of interest, misuse of federal property, and limitations on outside employment. The policy also bars use of public office for personal gain or for the gain of those with whom the individual has family, business, or financial ties.

The Johnson Policy also initiated public disclosure of financial statements, something that was given greater prominence in the Ethics and Government Act of 1978. This act codified many of the previously established standards and created the Office of Government Ethics to establish more detailed regulations to monitor the behavior of public servants and provide ethics training for managers and other officials.

President Bush, in keeping with his desire to set a high moral tone for his administration, used his first executive order to establish a Commission on Federal Ethics Law Reform. In establishing the Commission, the president sought four key principles: "(1) ethical standards for public servants must be exacting enough to ensure that the officials act with the utmost integrity and live up to the public's confidence in them; (2) standards must be fair, they must be objective and consistent with common sense; (3) the standards must be equitable across all three branches of the federal government; finally we cannot afford to have unreasonably restrictive requirements that discourage citizens who are able from entering public service" (President's Commission, 1989, p. 2). Central to the Bush recommendations were provisions dealing with conflicts of interest.

Under existing legislation, officers of the executive branch of the federal government are required to refrain from participating "personally and financially" in deciding, approving, recommending, or advising with respect to matters in which they or family members or close associates have a financial interest. An official facing a possible conflict of interest has a number of avenues available. First, the official can simply withdraw from partici-pating in the particular case. Second, the official may seek a waiver, especially when his or her interest is not considered substantial or the relationship is too remote to affect the integrity of the action. Third, the employee may choose to place his or her assets in a "blind trust"; or fourth, the official can sell, give away, or otherwise divest himself or herself of the financial interest in question.

Other parts of the federal ethics legislation restrict outside income and the acceptance of gifts or favors. For example, as a federal employee, you are prohibited from accepting any salary or contribution from any source other than the federal government. The law also limits the acceptance of meals, entertainment, and gifts; for example, meals can usually be accepted if offered during the course of a working meeting, but there are prohibitions on "one-on-one" meals in which you are being treated.

There are also prohibitions on what a federal employee can do after leaving govern-ment. Sections of the Ethics and Government Act prohibit former officials from repre-senting outside parties before the federal government with respect to matters in which they had some personal involvement or official responsibility for a period of two years. There is also a one-year "cooling-off period," during which you cannot represent parties before your agency even on matters that were not your responsibility while working for the government. The Bush Commission recommended strengthening provisions dealing with activities of former federal officials by requiring a prohibition not only against personally representing outside interests before government agencies but also "aiding or advising any other person." The proposal would eliminate not only direct representa-tion, but "behind the scenes" advice and counsel as well.

Legislation such as this is obviously intended to prevent "influence peddling" by those who have recently left government and to limit the "revolving door" phenomenon, wherein persons move in and out of government to acquire knowledge and information valuable to external groups. This issue became particularly prominent during the Reagan administration, when several officials, such as Michael Deaver and Lynn Nofziger, were accused of using their previous contacts to unduly influence the governmental decision process. Moreover, the defense procurement scandals of the Reagan years underlined the need for stricter controls on information exchange that could influence purchase of defense materials or contracts.

Finally, the potential for conflicts of interest is decreased by requirements for financial disclosure on the part of executive officials. The Bush Commission, for example, wrote "financial disclosure has been variously described as the lynch pin of the ethical enforce-ment system, as the disinfectant sunlight which makes possible the cleaning up of abusive practices" (President's Commission, 1989, p. 5). Though financial reporting requirements have sometimes been criticized as excessively detailed and intrusive, they have been, in the view of most ethics experts, highly valuable in maintaining public confidence in the integrity of government. If nothing else, the reports have meant that individuals are forced to carefully review potential conflicts of interests that they may bring with them to government and thus be more aware of those interests should conflicts arise.

Many of the same provisions for preventing conflict of interest in federal ethics legisla-tion have been paralleled at the state level. Many states have passed detailed ethics legislation, often using financial disclosure as a chief mechanism for preventing abuse. Indeed, all but seven states have some form of financial disclosure provision for some state employees (Burke & Benson, 1989, p. 196). In addition, thirty-five states have established ethics commissions to provide oversight of ethical behavior in state government and, in most cases, local government as well. Such commissions have the power to investigate violations of the state's ethics law and, usually, to impose administrative fines (Burke & Benson, 1989, p. 197). There are great variations among the states, however, in terms of number and type of officials covered (elected, appointed, etc.) and the number of jurisdictions included (legislature, all state officials, local officials, etc.). Although many local officials are covered under state ethics provisions, local governments have also been increasingly interested in developing and enforcing their own codes of ethics.

Whistle Blowing

There has been a marked increase over the last twenty years in employee disclosure of problems in public organizations. Public employees have exposed defense contract overruns, spoken out against corruption in local police departments, and revealed abuses of the merit system, improper enforcement of toxic waste legislation, and other matters. Alan Campbell, Director of the Office of Personnel Management during the Carter administration, described these public disclosures, or "whistle blowing," in this way: "Quite simply, I view whistle blowing as a popular short-hand label for any disclosure of a legal violation, mismanagement, a gross waste of funds, an abuse of authority, or a danger to public health or safety, whether the disclosure is made within or outside the chain of command" (Bowman, 1983, p. 91). In other words, the *whistle blower* reveals information about fraud, waste, or abuse in government, including actions that might endanger the safety or liberty of other government employees or citizens at large.

121

Generally, employees who decide to blow the whistle move through several stages. First, the employees become aware of an organizational practice that is unethical or dangerous; second, they express concern to their immediate supervisor or those further up in the hierarchy; and, third, unsatisfied that anyone in the organization will take appropriate action, they take the issue outside, either through "leaks" to the press or to external public interest groups. (The press, of course, may play an important role in revealing instances of wrongdoing.)

Unfortunately, whistle blowers in both government and in industry have often been subjected to abuse and retaliation by superiors. One study of whistle blowers shows a large number who were fired or forced to resign or retire, as well as others who were refused promotions or given less desirable work assignments. Others felt excluded from communication within the organization and were avoided by both supervisors and co-workers (Truelson, 1986, p. 9). Studies show that, as a result, many public employees who have knowledge of corruption don't bother to report it, and many who do report abuses suffer reprisals (Bowman, 1983, p. 272).

Obviously if you discover improper actions on the part of persons in your organization, you have a strong obligation to report those actions; however, you should be careful that your allegations are based on fact and are properly reported. Norman Bowie suggests that an act of whistle blowing can be justified

1. If it is done with an appropriate moral motive;
2. If all internal channels of dissent have been exhausted;

3. If it is based on evidence that would persuade a reasonable person;
4. If analysis has been made of the seriousness, immediacy, and specificity of the problem;
5. If it is commensurate with one's responsibility; and
6. If it has some chance of success. (Bowman, 1983, p. 91)

At the federal level, codes of conduct have encouraged public servants to expose corruption wherever it is discovered, and protection for whistle blowers has been provided through the Civil Service Reform Act. Moreover, some agencies have established formal *dissent channels*, confidential patterns of communications outside the normal chain of command, that allow a potential whistle blower or someone who merely disagrees with a proposed policy to express a dissenting opinion without fear of reprisal. Consequently, whistle blowing has become somewhat more common at the federal level. But wherever you work, if you decide to blow the whistle, you should be fully aware not only of potential dangers, but also of the protection available to you based on rights of free speech and of prohibitions against discriminatory actions. Encouraging greater communication by providing freer and more open channels of dissent is one way to assure more ethical behavior in public organizations (see Box 4.2).

B O X   4 . 2

WHISTLE BLOWING

The following is a resolution passed by the American Society for Public Administration:

The American Society for Public Administration endorses the growing public demand for improved accountability of government employees in order to achieve more efficient, effective, and ethical enforcement of the laws, and more competent conduct of the public business, recognizing that most whistle blowing results from different perceptions of accountability.

Therefore, in order to improve accountability at all levels of government, ASPA recommends that federal, state and local governments take the following actions:

1. *Establish and enforce policies and procedures that clearly describe the ethical bases for public employment and the penalties for violating them.*

Adherence to such codes would result in improved accountability by public employees, especially managers, for their decisions and actions. This should result in a concomitant decrease in the need for whistle blowing aimed at exposing criminal activity, abuse of process, waste, withholding or distortion of information, and other unethical or illegal behavior.

2. Establish and enforce policies and procedures for more adequately communicating to each public employee the expectations of the governmental employer with respect to job performance, ethics, accountability, rewards, penalties, and regulations.

Since well-informed and well-supervised employees reflect good management practices, individual employees who know what is expected of them may be more likely to meet accountability standards and less likely to refuse responsibility for their performance— or to choose *nonlegitimate* whistle blowing as a vehicle for communicating. Workshops and other forms of training programs are useful in helping managers and their employees cope with dissent and change.

3. Establish and enforce policies and procedures for internally reporting, investigating, assessing, and acting on allegations of illegality, mismanagement, waste, or unethical behavior.

Complaint handling offices such as inspectors general and other appropriate mechanisms should be created and adequately supported to receive, and promptly and objectively, investigate internal allegations of wrongdoing in order to diminish the need for the public gesture of whistle blowing. To be effective as well as efficient, such offices must inspire the trust and confidence of both managers and employees to avoid the aura of police-state intimidation by tending first to accuse or impugn the motives of the person making the allegation.

4. Establish and enforce policies and procedures that permit and encourage legitimate dissent and constructive criticism and protect dissenters from retaliation.

Many public employees take an oath of office to uphold, obey, and enforce the law in accordance with their sworn responsibilities. Therefore, perceived violations of that oath which result in differences of opinion about wrongdoing should be viewed as manifestations of accountability, rather than as rejections of supervisory authority, unless proven otherwise.

5. Create and support dissent channels to permit contrary or alternative views on policy issues to be reviewed at a higher level. Where disaffection grows not from allegations of wrongdoing

(continued)

(continued)

but from honest professional disagreement over policy decisions, what converts the grieved dissenter into an angry whistle blower is often the lack of any channel for additional senior review of the policy dispute. Good public administration in any institution includes provision for such open review at higher levels. Equating productive dissent or constructive criticism with disloyalty violates democratic principles of free speech and tends to discourage accountability, creativity and standards of excellence.

6. *Establish and enforce policies and procedures that require management to focus on the message rather than the messenger when an employee expresses either substantive dissent as a professional difference of opinion or makes an allegation of wrongdoing.*

In most instances, whistle blowing may be averted by giving serious consideration to the merits of the message and by taking appropriate and timely action. By focusing only on the assumed motivations of dissenters or whistle blowers, attention is diverted from the substance of their dissent or the merits of their allegations, to the detriment of the organization, its mission, and the general public.

7. *Create and use program evaluation, monitoring and other oversight methods to increase and improve the availability of reliable information for decision making.*

Top management needs accurate and timely information produced by competent staff who are encouraged to make recommendations and to energetically advocate them without fear of reprisal. Since an organizational pattern of absent, distorted, or unnecessarily suppressed information tends to produce demands for such information on the grounds of accountability, the systematic collection, analysis, dissemination, and use of verified facts should help to diminish or eliminate the motivation to blow the whistle.

Prohibitions on Political Activities

Political neutrality has traditionally been considered important to effective democratic governance. President Jefferson, for example, issued an early order against federal government employee partisanship, an order whose essence was repeated by Presidents Grant and Hayes. Legislative action occurred with the adoption of the Pendleton Act in 1883, which "prohibited political assessment, solicitations, subscriptions or contributions from or by any employee of the United States." The most sweeping ban on political activity, however, occurred during Theodore Roosevelt's administration. He declared that classified civil service employees "shall take no active part in political management or in political campaigns" (Masters & Bierman, 1985, p. 519). Later, Congress passed the Hatch Political Activities Act in 1939, stating that "no officer or employee of the executive branch of the federal government, or any agency or department thereof, shall take any active part in political management or in political campaigns." (A set of amendments passed in 1940 extended the ban on political management and campaigning to state and local employees whose programs were financed fully or in part by federal funds.)

Under the Hatch Act, public employees can register to vote, contribute money to campaigns, assist in voter registration drives, and express opinions about candidates and issues; however, certain other activities are prohibited:

1. Endorsing partisan candidates
2. Listing or raising money for political action committees
3. Participating in partisan voter registration and get-out-the-vote drives
4. Distributing campaign material on behalf of candidates
5. Serving as a delegate to a political convention
6. Making campaign speeches
7. Seeking public office in partisan elections (Masters & Bierman, 1985, pp. 519–520)

Although the Hatch Act seeks both to protect public employees from political harassment and the political process from special influence, it has been subject to various interpretations and has proven confusing in its application. Moreover, many have claimed that it unduly restricts public employees' political freedoms by essentially disenfranchising them from important political activities during the time they hold government employment. For this reason, there have been recent efforts in Congress to change the Hatch Act to permit a greater range of political activities by those in government. Many supported the proposed legislation, especially those in public employee unions, who felt that public employees should be able to run for office and solicit campaign funds on their own time. Others, however, argued that the Hatch Act was still necessary to prevent coercion of political officials. According to the Justice Department, which argued against the proposed legislation, "Two principles central to the operation of the Executive Branch— the nonpartisan administration and enforcement of federal laws and the advancement in the federal service based solely on merit—would certainly be threatened and could well be extinguished" (*Washington Post*, April 14, 1989). The legislation did not pass in 1989, but most people expect similar proposals to surface again.

MANAGING ETHICS

How does a manager promote more ethical practices in an organization? First, of course, there are a variety of formal controls, including legal, on the behavior of those in public organizations—the courts may direct public officials to undertake specific actions or to "cease and desist" from certain courses of action. They may also be required, on behalf of their agencies, to provide individuals with damages or other compensation. And, of course, any public employee may be prosecuted for breaking the law. But what if you are sued as an individual for actions you have undertaken in the course of your official duties?

Actually, this question has been the subject of considerable legal debate throughout our country's history. Whereas early interpretations of the law generally protected public officials against suits, claiming they violated an individual's rights in the course of one's duties, more recent interpretations have severely limited the immunity granted to public officials. Speaking broadly, there are two types of immunity—absolute immunity and qualified (or "good faith") immunity. Absolute immunity, which means that an official is not liable for damages under any circumstances, has been granted to certain legislative and judicial officers and, in limited cases, to members of the executive branch. (The president has been granted absolute immunity but state governors have not.)

Most other officials have only qualified immunity—they may be sued, but can defend themselves by showing they were acting in good faith to carry out their duties. That is, they must show that they were unaware of the impropriety of an act at the time they were carrying it out and that any reasonable person might have acted similarly. Although the current legal position allows most officials to be sued, relatively few suits have been successful—that is, most public managers have been found to have acted in good faith. In any case, knowing something about public officials' liability for their actions will better enable you and those in your organization to avoid problems in the first place, or respond to them when they arise.

Besides legal proceedings, other formal devices protect against waste or fraud on the part of public officials or the private individuals or groups with which they interact. For example, most major federal agencies have an Office of the Inspector General to investigate possible cases of fraud, waste, and abuse in government. The inspectors general are charged with looking into situations in which federal employees or funds are being used improperly. Targets of investigations may be either public employees or private individuals, such as contractors, who might attempt to defraud the government.

Through their internal investigations of federal agencies, the inspectors general have occasionally revealed major problems. A recent Air Force inspector general's report charged that hundreds of millions of dollars may have been wasted paying for faulty parts and work not done. The inspector general pointed out significant weaknesses in the system of internal controls, including no written contracts, no documentation of the need for consulting services, and no justification of the levels of fees charged (Moore, 1988, p. 32). An inspector general's investigation in the Department of Agriculture cited a California couple's illegally redeeming food stamps—over $1.8 million worth. Similarly, an inspector general's audit revealed that over 75 percent of the vendors for the Women, Infants, and Children (WIC) food program were overcharging the government an average of 28 percent.

Failure to follow an inspector general's advice may have been partly to blame for the scandals that rocked the Department of Housing and Urban Development in the late 1980s. Charles Dempsey, a former HUD inspector general, was quoted as saying that he warned HUD Secretary Samuel Pierce about the lack of internal controls as early as 1981. "We told them, 'You've got a lousy accounting system; you have to strengthen it.' They didn't do anything. How can you correct poor accounting systems when you're cutting the staff?" (Kurtz, 1989, p. 31). Six years later, Dempsey's successor made similar criticisms of HUD's handling of property sales, a key concern in the rash of allegations of fraud, embezzlement, and theft in HUD during Pierce's tenure as secretary.

Partially in response to situations like these, the Office of Management and Budget in the Bush administration has developed plans to monitor certain departments considered "high risk." For the most part, these programs involve large cash flows, high net transactions, and inadequate checks and balances. According to OMB head Richard Darman, "There are too many people in positions of political responsibility who are infatuated by the lure of glitter and lights and the often-illusory chance to make policy rather than in solid nuts and bolts management" (PA Times, October 13, 1989, p. 3).

Establishing an Ethical Climate

In addition to formal controls, you can help promote ethical behavior by providing strong ethical leadership, creating a climate in which ethical behavior is valued, and encouraging free and open communications throughout the organization. Kathryn G. Denhardt, author of The Ethics of Public Service, writes that "managing ethics involves more than making public statements espousing a particular set of values and more than selecting employees with good moral character. Managing ethics also involves careful analysis of the organizational culture, working to develop a cultural environment that places high value on ethical integrity and developing policies and procedures and systems that enable organization members to act with ethical integrity" (Denhardt, 1989, p. 1). Unfortunately, most organizations, including most public organizations, have not undertaken active programs to promote ethics (see Box 4.3).

127

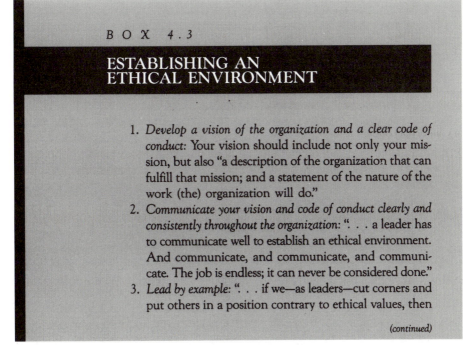

BOX 4.3

ESTABLISHING AN ETHICAL ENVIRONMENT

1. *Develop a vision of the organization and a clear code of conduct:* Your vision should include not only your mission, but also "a description of the organization that can fulfill that mission; and a statement of the nature of the work (the) organization will do."
2. *Communicate your vision and code of conduct clearly and consistently throughout the organization:* ". . . a leader has to communicate well to establish an ethical environment. And communicate, and communicate, and communicate. The job is endless; it can never be considered done."
3. *Lead by example:* ". . . if we—as leaders—cut corners and put others in a position contrary to ethical values, then

(continued)

(continued)

what we're doing, in effect, is asking them to erode their own value as human beings. And no employer has that right."

4. *Monitor those areas where there is risk:* One part of our organization has high potential for favors and kickbacks. "I've found that simply poking my nose into this area from time to time, with an occasional sharp question, shows that I care what's going on."

5. *Be ruthless in applying your values:* "When infractions occur—and they will—a leader has to be ruthless in applying his values—regardless of the cost and the risk of bad publicity."

SOURCE: Excerpted from Phillip L. Smith, "Establishing an Ethical Environment," *Ethics Resource Center Report* (Summer 1988): 5.

128

Many organizational members feel that, in the absence of an ethics program, the requirements of large bureaucracies tend to promote unethical, dishonest, and inhumane behavior. "Managers perceive that the bureaucratic environment is less ethical than their own values and beliefs, that they are under pressure to compromise personal standards to achieve organizational goals, and that their supervisors are interested only in results not how they were obtained" (Bowman, 1983, p. 74).

A first step in promoting more ethical practices in your organization is to analyze the basic ideas, beliefs, and attitudes that guide the behavior of the organization's members. The Environmental Protection Agency, for example, has long held to a set of beliefs about its mission, including

1. Support for vigorous regulation of pollutants;
2. A belief that engineering standards were the most effective way to control pollution;
3. A healthy skepticism of the value industry placed on the protection;
4. A belief that pollution control costs were not excessive and were far outweighed by the benefits of regulations; and
5. A belief that regulation was an adversarial process. (Meier, 1985, p. 163)

These beliefs were formed when the agency was established and became more thoroughly ingrained over time. By acting in accord with these beliefs, members felt they were acting with integrity.

Interestingly enough, the Reagan administration disagreed strongly with these beliefs and sought to change them through the appointment of Anne Burford. Her pronouncements about the value of deregulation, however, did not change the organization's beliefs; in fact, members responded by leaking information that eventually led to her resignation. In doing so, these members felt they were acting ethically; that is, in a way consistent with the organization's values. The EPA experience is an excellent illustration of the difficulty of balancing organizational values with responsiveness to changing political leadership.

One device for assessing the prevailing beliefs of your organization is an **ethics audit,** an assessment of the value premises that guide action in the organization. The audit provides a methodical review of the organization's activities and the implicit values that underlie the activities. Importantly, these values may not turn out to be those contained in public pronouncements, which has led one student of organizational behavior to conclude, "the key to learning the ethics of individuals or organizations is simple: *do not listen to what they say about ethics, observe what they do*" (Pastin, 1988, p. 92). By clearly establishing the values that guide behavior in the organization, you and other members can more consciously and clearly begin to alter those that seem inappropriate.

As an example, after numerous incidents of defense contract violations, the General Dynamics Corporation brought in an outside consultant to help establish an ethics program. The consultant conducted an ethics audit, which helped members of the organization recognize that they shared a basic, though unstated, assumption that the government was their adversary and that taking advantage of an adversary was quite acceptable. Once this assumption was understood, it could be addressed openly and replaced with more appropriate assumptions about the relationships between government and its contractors.

Following an ethics audit, your organization may wish to develop a clearer statement of values to guide individual behavior. That statement should include general moral guidelines, but it should also articulate a vision of the organization's mission—what it stands for, what it seeks to achieve, and how it plans to go about its business. Developing such a statement should involve many members of the organization and have the full support of the top management team. (We will examine statements of values in more detail in chapter 9.)

Besides developing a statement of management philosophy for your organization alone, you may also wish to employ more general codes of ethics developed by other organizations. The federal government, for example, has promulgated a Code of Ethics for Federal Service, and many state and local government organizations have developed similar codes. Professional organizations such as the International City Management Association also have codes of ethics related to members of their profession. Perhaps the most comprehensive code of ethics for public sector managers is that of the American Society for Public Administration. The ASPA Code of Ethics and accompanying guidelines illustrate the variety of ethical concerns public managers face and provide guidance for resolving ethical issues (see Appendix 4.A).

After assessing values and adopting statements to express the desired values, you might wish to develop training programs or other devices for communicating these ideals within the organization. The Office of Government Ethics, for example, conducts frequent seminars for federal managers on ethics in the public service. Similarly, organizations such as ASPA and ICMA have developed training programs that are available nationally or can be adapted to local circumstances. Training programs are also available for executives in nonprofit organizations.

As a manager, however, you should not neglect the fact that your own actions will be taken as a "model" of appropriate behavior. The example you set will be one of the most important "training" devices to members of your organization. If you wish them

129

to take the moral "high road," you must demonstrate by example that ethics is a substantial concern and that unethical conduct will not be tolerated.

SUMMARY AND ACTION IMPLICATIONS

As we move from the context of public administration to the ethics of public service, we also move from areas where abstract knowledge is helpful to areas where the ability to act is important. In dealing with the many ethical dilemmas that confront public officials, you must know not only what the correct action is, but be able to act in a way consistent with that judgment. Understanding something about how ethical choices are made is helpful, as is recognizing the importance of deliberation in making ethical decisions. But what will ultimately make the difference will be your willingness to act on the basis of moral principles.

The particular ethical issues you may face range from matters of individual integrity to those that derive from the special value commitments associated with working in the public interest. Most of the latter are associated in some way with the tension between efficiency and responsiveness that seems to pervade public organizations. That tension, as well as issues of accountability and responsiveness to public demands, are especially intense in the relationship between administrators and the legislative branch.

Many of the concerns you may encounter as a public manager are similar to those other managers face, but some are especially conditioned by the fact that you are operating "in the public interest." In either case, you must exhibit the virtues of benevolence and justice (including honesty, trustworthiness, and fairness) in your behavior. In any case, as you face some of the difficulties that arise, careful self-reflection and dialogue with others about ethical concerns will be especially helpful.

It is within your power as an administrator to undertake programs to encourage and facilitate a more ethical climate within your organization. Conducting an ethics audit, developing a statement of organizational philosophy or a code of ethics, and establishing training programs to deal with ethical issues will help improve your organization's ethics. As a manager, however, perhaps the most important message you can send is that communicated by your own actions. If you seem to attach great importance to ethical concerns, others in the organization will attach similar importance. The model you provide can make an important difference in the ethics of your organization.

TERMS AND DEFINITIONS

Cooptation: Situations in which citizens are given the feeling of involvement while exercising little real power.

Deontology: Belief that broad principles of rightness and wrongness can be established and are *not* dependent on particular circumstances.

Ethical (or moral) relativism: Belief that moral judgment can be made only by taking into account the context in which action occurs.

Ethics: Process by which we clarify right and wrong and act on what we take to be right.

Ethics audit: Evaluation of the value premises that guide action within an organization.

Morality: Practices and activities considered right or wrong and the value those practices reflect.

Neutral competence: The belief that a neutral public bureaucracy following the mandates of a legislative body will meet the requirements of democracy.

Objective responsibility: Assurance of responsiveness through external controls.

Subjective responsibility: Assurance of responsiveness based on an individual's character.

Utilitarianism: Philosophy of the greatest good for the greatest number of people.

STUDY QUESTIONS

1. Although ethics and morality are similar, what is the distinction between the terms?
2. Discuss the steps in ethical deliberation.
3. Compare the two approaches commonly used in moral philosophy.
4. Discuss the three levels of moral development devised by psychologist Lawrence Kohlberg.
5. What is meant by an "ethics of virtue"?
6. Discuss the conflict between efficiency and responsiveness.
7. Explain the limitations on administrators' discretion with regard to responsiveness and efficiency.
8. Discuss some of the ethical problems individuals who work in public organizations encounter and how they can deal with them properly.
9. The Hatch Act defines prohibited activities of public employees. Explain the significance of these prohibitions with regard to an individual's political actions.
10. Explain ways to improve the ethical behavior of those in a public organization and provide examples of managing ethics.

131

CASES AND EXERCISES

1. To illustrate various aspects of ethical deliberation, read and discuss the following case:

There is a raging River which can be crossed only by means of a boat. The only boat is owned and operated by a person we shall call A (in order to protect the innocent as well as the guilty). On the same side of the River is a person, X, who is deeply and sincerely in love with a person C on the other side of the River. X goes to A asking to be taken across the River, offering to pay whatever the charge for the service. A declines any money, but agrees to take X across the River if X will sleep with A. Person X refuses, of course (!), but argues and then pleads with A to name some other price. A, however, remains firm.

Person X leaves, but returns a second day to seek a way across the River. A remains as adamant as before. In frustration, X seeks out a third person, B, who hears the situation sympathetically, agreeing that A is certainly a rogue. But B says, "I have other matters concerning me just now and am not able to help you."

In desperation, X goes to A a third time, only to be met with the same offer for the trip across the River. X finally agrees to the price and sleeps with A, who then delivers X across the River as promised.

X and C are joyously reunited, until C asks how X got across the River. X truthfully replies, "I had to sleep with A to earn the trip across the River." C replies indignantly, "Out of my life!! I will have nothing to do with one who holds honor and principle so lightly!"

X, of course, is frustrated and desperate again, and appeals to Person D, who replies, "I understand and am deeply sympathetic. I'd do anything I can to help you." (The curtain falls.)

SOURCE: Excerpted from American Society for Public Administration, *Ethical Dilemmas*, no date.

Following your discussion of the case itself, consider to what extent the discussion reflected moral relativism, utilitarianism, or deontology. Then, reconsider the case, following the steps of ethical deliberation presented in this chapter: clarify the facts, find basic principles, and analyze the arguments. How could you establish a moral action?

2. A recent random check of long distance telephone calls at the Department of Housing and Urban Development, a study conducted by the agency's inspector general, indicated that some 30 percent were personal calls (though charged to the government). The cost of the calls was estimated at $73,000 for the sample and, by extrapolation, $290,000 for the agency as a whole. Many calls were placed to the homes of employees or their relatives, while others were calls to prerecorded messages, such as time and temperature, horoscopes, and financial information. Penalties for unauthorized use of federal telephone lines include fines, suspension, and dismissal.

Why do you think employees at HUD, and presumably elsewhere, misuse official telephone lines? What, if anything, should be done to limit such excesses? How do you respond to employees who argue that using agency telephone lines for personal business is necessary from time to time? What about those who argue that telephone use is an essential benefit the organization should provide? If you crack down on unauthorized calls, what will happen to morale in the agency?

To put the case in a more intense, real-world setting, imagine that you are Secretary of Housing and Urban Development. You have just finished testifying at a congressional hearing. On your way out the door, a senator corners you and waves a copy of the inspector general's report in your face saying, "This is an outrage! These people are stealing from the public and you've been letting it happen! I want some action on this right away!" Next, a reporter, who has seen the report and heard the exchange with the senator, points a microphone toward your mouth and asks, "Well, what are you going to do?" What is your response—both immediately and over the next several days?

3. Consider the following cases:

Sidney Franklin knew that one of his most valued employees, Anderson Hayes, was stealing from the organization—not much, and in a way that no one but Sidney would ever know—but he was stealing. Sidney also knew that without Anderson, his unit could never complete a newly assigned task on time. He decided to do nothing about the stealing incident and secretly hoped that success in the new assignment would bring about a long desired promotion and get him out of this awkward situation.

George Cave was a former CIA station chief in Teheran. When he heard that the Reagan administration was working with Manucher Ghorbanifar on an "arms for hostages" deal, he was horrified. "But what could he do? The project had the backing of CIA director William J. Casey and the White House. Cave bit the bullet and traveled to Iran in May 1986 as the translator for former national security adviser Robert C. McFarlane" (Ignatius, 1987, p. 15).

Shirley House, a recently appointed city manager in a small community in Tennessee, arrived at work one morning to find an envelope filled with receipts from a recent trip the mayor took to an economic development conference. Included were receipts from a four-day vacation the mayor and his wife took at a resort near the conference city. It was clear that the mayor wanted the city to reimburse him for everything included in the envelope.

Analyze and discuss each of these three cases in terms of the moral position that the individual involved should have taken. Then consider the nature of your own ethical reasoning. What types of moral philosophy, moral psychology, or moral action have you been using?

4. Reread the case in Box 4.1. Ask who in the class thinks the administrator, Gordon Chase, overstepped "the limits of administrative discretion" and who thinks he acted properly. Debate the issue, paying particular attention to the ethical justification for each position. What is the basis on which you build your argument? What assumptions are you making?

5. As a class, conduct an ethics audit (or survey) of your college or university and recommend ways the institution might begin to develop higher standards of ethical conduct.

Begin by considering in detail what might be expected from such an audit (or survey) in any organization and what is practical and *ethical* to expect from such a project conducted by *students* within the institution. Recognize your available resources, but also the limitations on your work. (You might even want to discuss your project with several university officers before going too far.)

As a practical matter, consider basing your work primarily on interviews with important decision makers throughout the institution, including administrators, deans and department chairs, members of the faculty (especially members of the faculty council or faculty senate), representatives of the school's athletic programs, and staff support in areas such as budget and accounting and personnel or human resources. Also consider interviews with members of the school's governing board. You might also want to collect material based on public record—newspaper reports, magazine articles, editorials, and so forth. The *Chronicle of Higher Education* and other materials dealing with higher education show what kinds of efforts other schools have undertaken.

Throughout your interviews and other research, you should first seek to determine the major ethical concerns facing institutions of higher education. Topics you will likely encounter are plagiarism and other forms of academic dishonesty (on the part of both faculty and students), the integrity of the research process, matters of institutional governance, questions of equal opportunity and affirmative action, institutional policies toward drugs and alcohol, the school's position on certain political issues (support for businesses in South Africa, etc.), and athletic recruiting policies—just to name a few. In going through these matters, you may find that your institution has taken strong moral positions in some areas (perhaps many); you may even find parts of the institution that have undertaken serious and detailed appraisals of their ethical positions—but you may also find that many of these issues simply haven't been considered, at least in terms of ethical implications.

If you can simply develop an inventory of ethical issues that should receive greater attention from members of the institution, you will have done a great service. But you may also identify cases where actual behavior seems to imply an ethical position different from the position espoused by those with whom you talk. If you do discover such cases, be prepared not only to document your findings, but also to present your report in such a way that will be helpful and constructive. Remember that you are seeking to provide a service to the institution, not an exposé.

Based on your research and analysis, prepare a written report for the school's president or chancellor and offer to have a delegation meet with him or her (or a representative) to discuss your findings. Again, your approach should be to provide preliminary findings that will be helpful in terms of institutional ethics. It may be helpful to think of yourselves as members of the president's or chancellor's staff, developing a report upon which constructive action can be taken. As in any such situation, you should be prepared to suggest specific action steps that will enable the school to give serious and sustained attention to its ethical posture.

After you finish your work, spend some time considering as a class what you have learned from this exercise: what you have learned about institutional ethics, about the administrative process, and what will make you a more effective and responsible administrator in the future. Try to develop specific action-oriented statements to guide your actions in the future. Finally, consider whether there were any ethical questions *you* faced in the course of this project. How did you resolve them? Or did you?

FOR ADDITIONAL READING

Burke, John P. *Bureaucratic Responsibility*. Baltimore, MD: Johns Hopkins University Press, 1986.

Cooper, Terry. *The Responsible Administrator*. Port Washington, NY: Kenikat Press, 1982; rev. ed., New York: Associated Faculty Press, 1986.

Denhardt, Kathryn G. *The Ethics of Public Service*. New York: Greenwood Press, 1988.

Fleishmann, Joel, Leibman, Lance, and Moore, Mark H. (eds.). *Public Duties*. Cambridge, MA: Harvard University Press, 1981.

Gutmann, Amy, and Thompson, Dennis (eds.). *Ethics and Politics*. Chicago: Nelson-Hall, 1984.

Kellar, Elizabeth (ed.). *Ethical Insight/Ethical Action*. Washington, DC: ICMA, 1988.

Rohr, John. *Ethics for Bureaucrats*. New York: Marcel Dekker, 1978.

Rohr, John. *To Run a Constitution*. Lawrence: University Press of Kansas, 1986.

Tong, Rosemarie. *Ethics in Policy Analysis*. Englewood Cliffs, NJ: Prentice-Hall, 1986.

Code of Ethics and Implementation Guidelines of the American Society for Public Administration

Demonstrate the highest standards of personal integrity, truthfulness, honesty and fortitude in all our public activities in order to inspire public confidence and trust in public institutions.

Perceptions of others are critical to the reputation of an individual or a public agency. Nothing is more important to public administrators than the public's opinion about their honesty, truthfulness, and personal integrity. It overshadows competence as the premier value sought by citizens in their public officials and employees. Any individual or collective compromise with respect to these character traits can damage the ability of an agency to perform its tasks or accomplish its mission. The reputation of the administrator may be tarnished. Effectiveness may be impaired. A career or careers may be destroyed. The best insurance against loss of public confidence is adherence to the highest standards of honesty, truthfulness and fortitude.

Public administrators are obliged to develop civic virtues because of the public responsibilities they have sought and obtained. Respect for the truth, for fairly dealing with others, for sensitivity to rights and responsibilities of citizens, and for the public good must be generated and carefully nurtured and matured.

If you are responsible for the performance of others, share with them the reasons for the importance of integrity. Hold them to high ethical standards and teach them the moral as well as the financial responsibility for public funds under their care.

If you are responsible for your own performance, do not compromise your honesty and integrity for advancement, honors, or personal gain. Be discreet, respectful of proper authority and your appointed or elected superiors, sensitive to the expectations and the values of the public you serve. Practice the golden rule: doing to and for others what you have done to and for you in similar circumstances. Be modest about your talents, letting your work speak for you. Be generous in your praise of the good work of your fellow workers. Guard the public purse as if it were your own.

Whether you are an official or an employee, by your own example give testimony to your regard for the rights of others. Acknowledge their legitimate responsibilities, and don't trespass upon them. Concede gracefully, quickly, and publicly when you have erred. Be fair and sensitive to those who have not fared well in their dealings with your agency and its applications of the law, regulations, or administrative procedures.

Serve in such a way that we do not realize undue personal gain from the performance of our official duties.

The only gains you should seek from public employment are salaries, fringe benefits, respect, and recognition for your work. Your personal gains may also include the pleasure of doing a good job, helping the public, and achieving your career goals. No elected or appointed public servant should borrow or accept gifts from staff or any corporation which buys services from, or sells to, or is regulated by, his or her governmental agency.

If your work brings you in frequent contact with contractors supplying the government, be sure you pay for your own expenses. Public property, funds and power should never be directed toward personal or political gain. Make it clear by your own actions that you will not tolerate any use of public funds to benefit yourself, your family, or your friends.

Avoid any interest or activity which is in conflict with the conduct of our official duties.

Public employees should not undertake any task which is in conflict or could be viewed as in conflict with job responsibilities.

This general statement addresses a fundamental principle that public employees are trustees for all the people. This means that the people have a right to expect public employees to act as surrogates for the entire people with fairness toward all the people and not a few or a limited group.

Actions or inactions which conflict with, injure, or destroy this foundation of trust between the people and their surrogates must be avoided.

Ironically, experience indicates that conflict of interest and corruption often arise not from an external affront, but as a result of interaction between persons who know each other very well. To strengthen resistance to conflict of interest, public employees should avoid frequent social contact with persons who come under their regulation or persons who wish to sell products or services to their agency or institution.

Agencies with inspectional or investigative responsibilities have a special obligation to reduce vulnerability to conflict of interest. Periodic staff rotation may be helpful to these agencies.

136

Individuals holding a position recognized by law or regulation as an unclassified or political appointment (e.g., Cabinet level and Governor's appointment positions) have a special obligation to behave in ways which do not suggest that official acts are driven primarily or only by partisan political concerns.

Public employees should remember that despite whatever preventive steps they might take, situations which hold the possibility for conflict of interest will always emerge. Consequently, the awareness of the potentiality of conflict of interest is important. Public employees, particularly professors in Public Administration, have a serious obligation to periodically stimulate discussion on conflicts of interest within organizations, schools, and professional associations.

Support, implement, and promote merit employment and programs of affirmative action to assure equal employment opportunity by our recruitment, selection, and advancement of qualified persons from all elements of society.

Oppose any discrimination because of race, color, religion, sex, national origin, political affiliation, physical handicaps, age, or marital status, in all aspects of personnel policy. Likewise, a person's lifestyle should not be the occasion for discrimination if it bears no reasonable relation to his or her ability to perform required tasks.

Review employment and personnel operations and statistics to identify the impact of organizational practices on "protected groups." Performance standards should apply equally to all workers. In the event of cutbacks of staff, managers should employ their criteria for selection of employees for separation, and humane strategies for administering the program.

Any kind of sexual, racial, or religious harassment should not be allowed. Appropriate channels should be provided for harassed persons to state their problems to objective officials. In the event of a proven offense, appropriate action should be taken.

Eliminate all forms of illegal discrimination, fraud, and mismanagement of public funds, and support colleagues if they are in difficulty because of responsible efforts to correct such discrimination, fraud, mismanagement or abuse.

If you are a supervisor, you should not only be alert that no illegal action issues from or is sponsored by your immediate office, you should inform your subordinates at regular intervals that you will tolerate no illegalities in their offices and discuss the reasons for the position with them. Public employees who have good reason to suspect illegal action in any public agency should seek assistance in how to channel information regarding the matter to appropriate authorities.

All public servants should support authorized investigative agencies, the General Accounting Office in the federal government, auditors in the state or large local governments, C.P.A. firms or federal or state auditors in many other cases. We should support the concept of independent auditors reporting to committees independent of management. Good fiscal and management controls and inspections are important protections for supervisors, staff, and the public interest.

In both government and business, inadequate equipment, software, procedures, supervision, and poor security controls make possible both intentional and unintentional misconduct. Managers have an ethical obligation to seek adequate equipment, software, procedures and controls to reduce the agency's vulnerability to misconduct. When an agency dispenses exemptions from regulations, or abatement of taxes or fees, managers should assure periodic investigatory checks.

The "whistle blower" who appears to his/her immediate superiors to be disloyal, may actually be loyal to the higher interests of the public. If so, the whistle blower deserves support. Local, state, and federal governments should establish effective dissent channels to which whistle blowers may report their concerns without fear of identification.

Supervisors should inform their staff that constructive criticism may be brought to them without reprisal, or may be carried to an ombudsman or other designated official. As a last resort, public employees have a right to make public their criticism but it is the personal and professional responsibility of the critic to advance only well founded criticism.

Serve the public with respect, concern, courtesy, and responsiveness, recognizing that service to the public is beyond service to oneself.

Be sure your answers to questions on public policy are complete, understandable and true. Try to develop in your staff a goal of courteous conduct with citizens. Devise a simple system to ensure that your staff gives helpful and pleasant service to the public. Wherever possible, show citizens how to avoid mistakes in their relations with government.

Each citizen's questions should be answered as thoughtfully and as fully as possible. If you or your staff do not know the answer to a question, an effort should be made to get an answer or to help the citizen make direct contact with the appropriate office.

Part of servicing the public responsively is to encourage citizen cooperation and to involve civic groups. Administrators have an ethical responsibility to bring citizens into work with the government as far as practical, both to secure citizen support of government, and for the economies or increased effectiveness which will result. Respect the right of the public (through the media) to know what is going on in your agency even though you know queries may be raised for partisan or other non-public purposes.

Strive for personal professional excellence and encourage the professional development of our associates and those seeking to enter the field of public administration.

137

Staff members, throughout their careers, should be encouraged to participate in professional activities and associations such as ASPA. They should also be reminded of the importance of doing a good job and their responsibility to improve the public service.

Administrators should make time to meet with students periodically and to provide a bridge between classroom studies and the realities of public jobs. Administrators should also lend their support to well planned internship programs.

Approach our organization and operational duties with a positive attitude and constructively support open communication, creativity, dedication and compassion.

Americans expect government to be compassionate, well organized, and operating within the law. Public employees should understand the purpose of their agency and the role they play in achieving that purpose. Dedication and creativity of staff members will flow from a sense of purpose.

ASPA members should strive to create a work environment which supports positive and constructive attitudes among workers at all levels. This open environment should permit employees to comment on work activities without fear of reprisal. In addition, managers can strengthen this open environment by establishing procedures ensuring thoughtful and objective review of employee concerns.

Respect and protect the privileged information to which we have access in the course of official duties.

Much information in public offices is privileged for reasons of national security, or because of laws or ordinances. If you talk with colleagues about privileged matters, be sure they need the information and you enjoin them to secrecy. If the work is important enough to be classified, learn and follow the rules set by the security agency. Special care must be taken to secure access to confidential information stored on computers. Sometimes information needs to be withheld from the individual citizen or general public to prevent disturbances of the peace. It should be withheld only if there is a possibility of dangerous or illegal or unprofessional consequences of releasing information.

Where other governmental agencies have a legitimate public service need for information possessed by an agency, do all you can to cooperate, within the limits of statute law, administrative regulations, and promises made to those who furnish the information.

Exercise whatever discretionary authority we have under law to promote the public interest.

If your work involves discretionary decisions you should first secure policy guidelines from your supervisor. You should then make sure that all staff who "need to know" are informed of these policies and have an opportunity to discuss the means of putting them into effect.

There are occasions when a law is unenforceable or has become obsolete; in such cases you should recommend to your superior or to the legislative body that the law be modernized. If an obsolete law remains in effect, the manager or highest official should determine if the law is or is not to be enforced, after consultation with the agency's legal advisor.

There are occasions where a lower level employee must be given considerable discretion. Try to see that such employees are adequately trained for their difficult tasks.

Tell yourself and your staff quite frequently that every decision creates a precedent, so the first decisions on a point should be ethically sound; this is the best protection for staff as well as for the public.

138

Accept as a personal duty the responsibility to keep up to date on emerging issues and to administer the public's business with professional competence, fairness, impartiality, efficiency and effectiveness.

Administrators should attend professional meetings, read books and periodicals related to their field, and talk with specialists. The goal is to keep informed about the present and future issues and problems in their professional field and organization in order to take advantage of opportunities and avoid problems.

Serious mistakes in public administration have been made by people who did their jobs conscientiously but failed to look ahead for emerging problems and issues. A long list of washed out dams, fatal mine accidents, fires in poorly inspected buildings, inadequate computer systems, or economic disasters are results of not looking ahead. ASPA members should be catalysts to stimulate discussion and reflection about improving efficiency and effectiveness of public services.

Respect, support, study, and when necessary, work to improve federal and state constitutions and other laws which define the relationships among public agencies, employees, clients and all citizens.

Familiarize yourself with principles of American constitutional government. As a citizen work for legislation which is in the public interest.

Teach constitutional principles of equality and fairness.

Strive for clear division of functions between different levels of government, between different bureaus or departments, and between government and its citizens. Cooperate as fully as possible with all agencies of government, especially those with overlapping responsibilities. Do not let parochial agency or institutional loyalty drown out considerations of wider public policy. (Adopted by ASPA National Council, March 27, 1985)

139

PART TWO

THE

TECHNICAL

FIELDS

BUDGETING
AND
FINANCIAL
MANAGEMENT

Public budgeting and financial management are concerned with   *143*
the allocation of limited resources to the problems governments and
other public organizations face. Just as you may establish a personal
budget to track your income and expenses and just as businesses create
budgets to aid in decisions affecting profits and losses, so do public
organizations of all types employ budgets to help in planning and
management. Beyond the budget process, however, public organizations
must carefully and responsibly manage large amounts of money and
other resources—taking in taxes and other revenues, purchasing
innumerable goods and services, and investing surplus funds or managing debt wisely.

From the point of view of the manager or the citizen trying to
influence public policy, the budget is an extremely important tool for
planning and control. To manage public programs effectively, you must
be able to manage resources, both practically and politically. In this
chapter we focus on the budget process from the standpoint of the
individual public manager, examining how budget decisions are made
and how you can influence budgetary outcomes. Although much of
the budget process is highly charged politically, specific technical
knowledge about budgeting systems will give you a distinct advantage.

The elaborate systems that public organizations have developed to
manage their fiscal affairs are relatively recent. Prior to the turn of
the century, revenues were easily sufficient to cover the expenses of
government, and financial management was merely record keeping.
But as the scope of government grew and new demands were placed

on its resources, the need for more sophisticated systems of decision making became apparent. Moreover, repeated instances of corruption and waste made more effective control over the public's resources necessary.

In establishing its executive budget process through the Budgeting and Accounting Act of 1921, the federal government was actually following the lead of several local and state governments that had already taken similar actions. The municipal reform movement emphasized the budget process as a means of bringing order to public spending; consequently, by the 1920s, most big cities had established a formal budget process. Similar developments were also occurring at the state level. In 1910, Ohio became the first state to require an executive budget; within the next decade, similar actions took place in most other states. At the federal level, a special Commission on Economy and Efficiency, known as the Taft Commission, recommended establishing an executive budget in 1912; the recommendation was implemented nearly a decade later.

Since the 1920s, the federal budget has grown in both size and complexity, as have budgets at the state and local levels. This growth means that budgeting and financial management have come to involve far more than keeping a record of income and expenses. Today, how government spends its money affects many other areas of the economy; consequently, the budget is an instrument of fiscal policy. Moreover, the budget is a primary expression of government priorities; it constitutes a record of the decisions that are made concerning various public policies.

144

THE BUDGET AS AN INSTRUMENT OF FISCAL POLICY

Budgets express the public policy choices of governments and others. Among these are choices with respect to the impact of the public sector on the economy. **Fiscal policy** is concerned with the impact of government taxation and spending on the economy generally. Before the Great Depression, little attention was paid to how the federal budget affected the economy; the economy was presumably regulated by what is called the **business cycle.** Periods of economic growth, featuring inflation and high employment, were followed by periods of recession or depression, featuring deflation and unemployment, and so on. Meanwhile, the federal government sought to balance its budget each year; that is, to make revenues and expenditures approximately equal.

Economists soon began to realize, however, that this pattern of government spending was in fact influencing the economy in a negative way. In periods of economic growth, government revenues naturally increased, so that, in an effort to balance the budget, taxes could be lowered to the level of expenditures; in periods of economic decline, the budget was balanced by lowering spending to meet the lower revenues. The unanticipated result of these actions was to increase citizens' income during good times and decrease their income in bad times—just the opposite of what would be desirable. Government taxation and spending had the effect of accentuating economic instability (Pechman, 1983, p. 8).

Economists such as the British scholar John Maynard Keynes argued, in contrast, that all else being equal, positive government action could lead to greater economic stability. A key to Keynes's analysis was the relationship between inflation and unemployment.

Keynes noted that periods of rapid economic growth are typically accompanied by high inflation, which is harmful to individuals because it lowers their purchasing power, especially if they are on fixed incomes. On the other hand, periods of economic decline are typically accompanied by high unemployment, which not only hurts individuals, but also lowers revenues for government. In either case, government action aimed at achieving greater stability might be both possible and desirable.

There are many ways the federal government can influence the economy, but one important way is simply by varying its own spending or, somewhat more indirectly, by raising or lowering taxes. The capacity of government spending patterns to influence the economy so dramatically is not hard to understand if you recognize the enormous role of government in the economy. The Gross National Product (GNP), the rate of inflation, and the rate of unemployment are the key indicators of economic health. The **Gross National Product,** a measure of total spending in the economy, comprises personal consumption, private investment, and government purchases. About two-thirds of our current Gross National Product is private in nature, but the remaining third is based on government spending. Based on revenues, the federal government is the single largest organization in the world, almost ten times the size of General Motors or Exxon. Obviously, decisions at the federal level play an important role in the health and stability of the economy generally.

The key relationships are these. If the economy is experiencing rapid growth—with high inflation and low unemployment—then the government might seek to "cool off" the economy by taking money out of the economy through lowering spending, raising taxes, or both. These actions have the effect of limiting private demand and slowing economic growth. On the other hand, if the economy is experiencing recession or depression—with falling prices and high unemployment—then the government might want to stimulate the economy by putting more money into circulation, through increasing spending, lowering taxes, or both. These actions have the effect of stimulating private demand and increasing economic growth. Creating a surplus, as might occur in the first case, would help restrain private spending during prosperity; creating a deficit, as in the second case, might stimulate spending during a recession (LeLoup, 1977, p. 28).

Cumulative state and local spending also affects the economy. State and local government expenditures constitute close to fifteen percent of the Gross National Product and must be taken into account in discussions of fiscal policy. If the federal government seeks to cut taxes, but also cuts aid to states and localities, those governments may find it necessary to raise taxes themselves, thus offsetting any economic gains caused by lower taxes at the federal level (Bahl, 1984, pp. 17–30).

Patterns of spending in many states and in major cities do have some effect on the local economy and, consequently, state and local officials are becoming more cognizant of their role in fiscal policy and especially economic development. These governments, however, often don't have the tools or authority to make certain kinds of decisions. For example, nearly all the states have either constitutional or statutory provisions requiring a balanced budget. (Both President Reagan and President Bush have called for a balanced budget amendment at the federal level as a way to eliminate deficit spending; however, such a proposal, though attractive in a symbolic sense, would obviously limit both the budgetary and the fiscal capacities of the federal government.) In any case, it is clear that the budget process has important effects on the economy that must be anticipated in structuring overall patterns of public spending.

THE BUDGET AS AN INSTRUMENT OF PUBLIC POLICY

Although the overall pattern of spending represented in a government budget has an important effect on the economy, the many individual entries in the budget represent important choices with respect to public policies of all types. The budget is, essentially, a measure of support (or lack of support) for specific programs. Those in favor are funded; those that are out of favor are not. For this reason, discussions of budgetary priorities are of special importance to political leaders, to government officials at all levels, and to representatives of various interests in society. As a manager, you will need to understand both where the money comes from and where the money goes (see Boxes 5.1 and 5.2).

Where the Money Comes From

Governments obtain the funds they need to operate the programs deemed important either from their own sources or through transfers from other governments. There are a variety of ways governments can raise their own revenues, including levying taxes and charging individuals or groups for specific services. Because all public programs are affected by the way governments raise revenues, and because revenue administration is itself an important part of public administration, you will find it helpful to understand the way taxes are structured.

Obviously, developing tax policies requires attention not only to the level of taxes being taken from individuals or groups, but also to the fairness, efficiency, and simplicity of the tax system. Everyone agrees that the tax system should be fair and that everyone should pay his or her "fair share." But what exactly does that mean? Some argue that each should pay according to the benefits they receive; others argue that those who have a greater ability to pay should in fact pay more (Musgrave & Musgrave, 1984).

One way to approach the issue is to think in terms of the relationship between one's tax rate and one's income. A tax is said to be **proportional** if it taxes everyone at the same rate. If a tax rate of 10 percent is applied to a $20,000 income (yielding $2,000) and the same rate is applied to a $200,000 income (yielding $20,000), even though the amounts differ, the tax is proportional. A tax is said to be **progressive** if it taxes those with higher incomes at a higher rate. A progressive tax might apply a 10 percent rate to a $20,000 income (yielding $2,000) and a 50 percent rate to a $200,000 income (yielding $100,000). Finally, a tax is said to be **regressive** if it taxes those with lower incomes at a proportionally higher rate than those with higher incomes. If an individual with a $20,000 income and one with a $200,000 income both pay a $400 tax on the same new car, the tax is regressive, taking 2 percent of the first individual's income but a much smaller proportion of the second individual's income (LeLoup, 1977, pp. 193–194).

Individual income tax   All methods of taxation involve application of a *tax rate* to a particular *tax base*; the product of the two yields *tax revenue*. The individual income

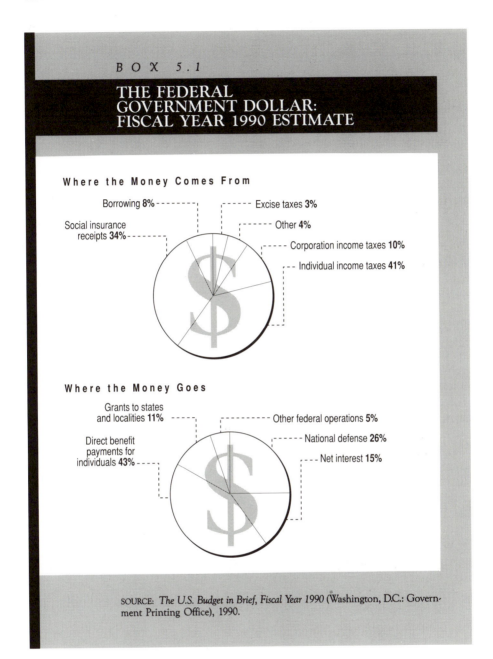

BOX 5.1

THE FEDERAL GOVERNMENT DOLLAR: FISCAL YEAR 1990 ESTIMATE

Where the Money Comes From

Borrowing **8%**

Excise taxes **3%**

Social insurance receipts **34%**

Other **4%**

Corporation income taxes **10%**

Individual income taxes **41%**

Where the Money Goes

Grants to states and localities **11%**

Other federal operations **5%**

Direct benefit payments for individuals **43%**

National defense **26%**

Net interest **15%**

SOURCE: *The U.S. Budget in Brief, Fiscal Year 1990* (Washington, D.C.: Government Printing Office), 1990.

tax, the single most important tax in our country, calls for the individual to add up all income from taxable sources, reduce that amount by certain deductions or exemptions, then apply a tax rate to that base to arrive at the individual's income tax. The current federal income tax, for example, allows a standard deduction of $5,000 for a married couple filing a joint return and applies rates of 15 and 28 percent to two income brackets.

BOX 5.2

THE STATE AND LOCAL DOLLAR

Where the Money Comes From

Charges and
miscellaneous **24.2%** ----   ------ Other taxes **5%**

                                                 ------ Intergovernmental revenues **17.6%**

Sales and gross
receipts taxes **21.1%** --   ----- Property taxes **17.5%**

                                                 --- Income taxes **14.7%**

Where the Money Goes

                                                 Interest on
Administration **5.1%** ---------   general debt **6.7%**

Housing and urban renewal **5.5%** -------   ---- Education **38.4%**

Parks and recreation and
natural resources **3.5%** ---------   --- Highways **8.9%**

Public safety **8.6%** --------

Health and welfare **23.3%** ------

SOURCE: *Statistical Abstract of the United States, 1989,* 109th Edition
(Washington, D.C.: Bureau of the Census), 1989.

All advanced industrial nations use some form of income tax. In the U.S., the income
tax is the primary source of revenue for the federal government and is used to a lesser
extent in many states and some cities. In most cases, a higher rate is applied to higher
incomes, making the income tax a progressive tax. For nearly thirty years after its passage
in 1913, the federal income tax applied only to a fairly small number of high-income

people; however, with the advent of World War II, deductions were reduced significantly and higher rates applied.

Managing the task of collecting an income tax from everyone in the country is obviously difficult; yet, despite occasional mishaps, the Internal Revenue Service has developed a remarkable mechanism for collection and does so at a cost of less than one half of one percent of the revenues produced (Pechman, 1983, p. 61). One key to the system is the requirement that each individual calculate his or her own tax liability. The Internal Revenue Service then selectively audits a relatively small number of returns, concentrating on those with unusual features. The extent of compliance with tax regulations in this country, though far from complete, is considered comparatively high.

Corporation income tax   The corporation income tax actually predates the individual income tax by several years and, for most of this century, was a key source of federal revenue. Also a progressive tax, the corporation income tax is justified by its proponents as a way of taxing capital accumulation that is not specifically distributed to individuals. Moreover, the corporation income tax is needed to support the individual income tax; without it, individuals could simply keep their income in corporations and avoid paying income taxes. Though most states have corporation income taxes, the tax is far more substantial at the federal level. Yet even here, the corporation income tax is declining in contrast to other sources of revenue. Where it once yielded more revenue than the individual income tax, the corporation income tax has declined to only about a tenth of federal revenues.

149

Payroll taxes   Taxes on payrolls support a variety of social security and other social insurance programs, such as unemployment compensation and medical care for the aged. (These specific taxes should not be confused with the general income taxes that may be deducted from a payroll check.) These programs are primarily financed by taxes paid either by the employer or by the employer and employee in equal amounts. Because there is a flat rate, with no deductions or exemptions, and maximum amounts above which taxes are not required, payroll taxes overall are regressive. Payroll taxes at the federal level now constitute the second largest source of federal revenue.

Sales and excise taxes   Both sales and excise taxes are applied to goods and services. *Sales taxes* are applied to a broad range of goods and services at either retail or wholesale levels and are a popular source of income at state and local levels. There are, however, significant variations in both sales tax rates and items covered by sales taxes; for example, some jurisdictions exempt food, clothing, and medicine from sales tax. **Excise taxes,** on the other hand, are applied to the sale of specific commodities, such as gasoline, tobacco or alcohol, and are the primary form of consumption tax at the federal level. Typically, excise taxes are applied at specific rates (e.g., 2 cents per gallon), but may also be applied to the total sales price. Some excise taxes are, in effect, user charges that help support particular activities. Gasoline taxes, for instance, are typically used to support highway construction and maintenance.

A major issue concerning sales and excise taxes is that of equity. Since the poor consume a greater portion of their income than the rich, the burden of consumption taxes tends to fall more heavily on the poor; that is, the taxes are regressive. These taxes also tend to penalize certain groups, such as those with large families or those just starting a household. On the other hand, these taxes tend to provide more stable revenues, something that is especially important at state and local levels.

Property taxes   Taxes on personal property are widely used at the local level and provide about half of local government revenues. Administration of a property tax involves assessment of an individual's property, most often land and buildings, then the application of a tax rate. About half the revenue generated by the property tax derives from residential property and half from businesses. Although the property tax is progressive in its effect (those who spend more on housing pay more), administration is difficult and has often not been highly professional. Moreover, recent tax limitations, such as Proposition 13 in California, have severely restricted the capacity of local governments to raise additional revenue through the property tax.

Other revenue sources   There are, of course, a variety of other sources of government revenues. Whereas public organizations have often charged fees for the use of specific government services, recent limitations on other tax revenues have made such charges increasingly attractive, especially at the local level. For example, fees for the use of parks and recreational facilities are becoming increasingly important. Another recent development in terms of revenues at the state level is the use of lotteries. Nearly half the states and several local governments now conduct lotteries, which provide a highly visible, but relatively small and unstable source of funds. Lotteries are also highly regressive in their effect (since poorer citizens tend to play the lotteries more); indeed, they are more regressive than even the sales tax (Mikesell & Zorn, 1986, pp. 318–319).

150

Nonprofit organizations, which lack the power to tax, derive revenues from quite different sources and, indeed, engage in a wide variety of efforts to support their programs. Obviously, membership organizations depend in large measure on member dues for revenue, but such organizations, along with many others, have recently sought to diversify revenues. While grant funding remains an important source of revenue for many nonprofit organizations, recent reductions in federal social service programs have seriously limited grant opportunities for many nonprofits. Additional sources of funds include donations (from individuals, corporations, and foundations), sales of goods and services (from books to coffee cups), and joint enterprises involving commercial firms (such as insurance plans or "affinity" credit cards).

Patterns of government revenues   As we have seen, different levels of government vary in their dependence on specific revenue sources. Box 5.1 shows the distribution of receipts at the federal level. The president's budget for 1989 estimated total revenues of $965 billion, including the following major categories:

Individual income taxes: $412 billion
Payroll taxes: $355 billion
Corporation income taxes: $118 billion
Excise taxes: $35 billion

Although the federal government relies heavily on the income tax, state governments are much more dependent on sales taxes and local governments are primarily dependent on property tax as a revenue source. All state and local governments combined generated $641 billion in revenues in 1986, with $135 billion coming from sales taxes of one kind or another and only $94 billion coming from various income taxes. In addition to tax receipts, the combined governments counted as revenues $113 billion in intergovernmental (primarily federal) transfers. At the local level, the property tax accounts for some $112 billion in revenues.

Where the Money Goes

These revenue figures are staggering, but they hardly match up to the demands on governments at all levels. There simply isn't enough money to meet every need or cure every problem, even if money alone were the solution. Instead, difficult choices must be made each year about which programs will be funded and at what levels. The choices made through the public policy process are reflected in the government's budget. The budget, therefore, stands as a record of the government's priorities.

But government priorities are always shifting. As new conditions arise, new programs are proposed and old programs are expanded or contracted. The emphasis the federal government gives to various areas, as one example, has reflected the condition of the country and the world at various times, as in the large percentage of national resources devoted to national defense during periods of international conflict.

We can also trace budgetary changes over shorter time spans, thus indicating the policy priorities of various presidents, governors, mayors, or other public officials. Certain restrictions, however, have been built into the federal budget over the years that somewhat limit the choices any president or Congress can make. Over the past twenty years, for example, Congress has passed a variety of **entitlement programs** that provide specified benefits to those who meet certain eligibility requirements. For example, legislation might provide benefits to all persons above a certain age or all persons below a certain income level. The implication, supported by several judicial rulings, is that individuals are entitled to or have a right to certain benefits (primarily social welfare benefits). Examples include old age and survivor's insurance (part of social security), unemployment compensation, food stamps, Medicare, and Medicaid (Weaver, 1985, pp. 307–308).

For these programs, Congress essentially agrees to provide whatever money is necessary from year to year to assure a certain level of benefits to all eligible people. Legislation is typically written so that new action is not required each year to keep the program going. Only a projection of likely beneficiaries is needed to determine the level of expenditures for a given year. Unless Congress takes specific steps to limit benefits or eligibility—something that legislators are reluctant to do—funding of these programs is practically automatic.

But these programs obviously vary in size over time. In a recession, for example, unemployment would be high, and spending for unemployment compensation would rise. Similarly, the changing character of the population—for example, a larger number of older Americans—would also change the amount of money required to provide benefits to that group. Moreover, most entitlement programs have now been *indexed* to the cost of living (or related measures), so that benefit levels automatically rise with inflation.

(Indeed, over the past several years, Congress has passed major expansions of indexing in social security and Medicare.) Expenditures for entitlement programs thus increase almost every year.

Such programs constituted about 43 percent of the 1989 federal budget. When they are combined with farm price supports (also indexed), with interest on the national debt (which must be paid), and with expenditures based on previous commitments, these so-called *uncontrollable expenditures* constitute almost 77 percent of the federal budget. If one further assumes that defense spending must not be cut appreciably, an assumption clearly made during the Reagan years (although it is being challenged early in the Bush administration), the remaining **discretionary spending,** that portion of the budget still open to changes by Congress, is only slightly above 10 percent.

The Reagan Budgets

Even though all these programs—entitlements, defense, and so on—represent the result of policy choices, it is becoming increasingly clear that the choices remaining at the federal level are limited. Yet there are still important choices to make. The Reagan years illustrate how presidential efforts to affect certain areas of public policy succeed or fail. President Reagan came into office with a clear ideological agenda: to strengthen our national defense, to limit the federal presence in domestic programs, and to reduce the size of government generally.

152

Comparing Reagan's last (1989) budget to expenditures in his first (1980), one is struck by the fact that the size of government outlays nearly doubled, from $590.9 billion in 1980 to $1094.2 billion (over a trillion dollars) in 1989. Even taking into account the effects of inflation, federal expenditures increased by 23 percent during the Reagan years. President Reagan can claim, however, to have slowed the growth of government, which had grown just under 37 percent in the seventies and at an even higher rate in the fifties and sixties (Caiden, 1988, p. 4).

On the other hand, in broad terms, President Reagan generally succeeded in his goals of increasing defense and decreasing domestic spending, with defense up by 52 percent (after adjustment for inflation) and discretionary domestic spending down by 35 percent (Blustein & Kenworthy, 1988b, p. 328). At the same time, however, the Reagan administration was not able to eliminate the major social welfare programs of the Great Society as the president had hoped. For example, projected 1989 spending for Medicare and Medicaid was 70 percent above the 1980 level, after adjustment for inflation (Blustein & Kenworthy, 1988a, p. 31). Overall, entitlements have remained at about the same level, with increases offset by cuts in other areas. Finally, aid to state and local governments for revenue sharing and other grant programs was sharply reduced during the Reagan years (37 percent), with only part of the reductions offset by new spending at the state and local levels.

Although President Reagan broadly reshaped the federal budget in line with his own priorities, there was one significant failure—his promise to balance the budget by 1984. As noted, traditional economic theory does not necessarily disapprove of public borrowing; indeed, there may be benefits to deficit spending in particular years. But at some point, a growing deficit becomes unmanageable, especially as interest payments become such a substantial part of government spending. Large deficits are generally thought to limit both short-term and long-term economic recovery, especially because they limit private investment. Moreover, large deficits contribute to an understandable lack of public confidence concerning their political leaders' ability to deal effectively with the budget.

The budget deficits of the Reagan years were substantial. Indeed, the administration's accumulated debt exceeded that of all previous administrations combined. By 1984, it became clear that, if no further actions were taken to reduce the deficit, by the end of the Reagan years, the deficit would total over $2.6 trillion and interest payments alone would require one out of every six federal dollars (Palmer & Sawhill, 1984, p. 9). Facing this prospect, Congress passed the Gramm-Rudman-Hollings Act of 1985. This legislation set a target for the next five budget years, progressively reducing the deficit amount in each year to zero in 1993. In any year in which the budget deficit exceeds the target, automatic across-the-board spending cuts are required to reach the required deficit level.

At the end of the Reagan term, the projected deficit (for 1989) was about $130 billion, an amount in line with the Gramm-Rudman-Hollings target of $136 billion, and far less than the $200 billion plus deficits of several previous years. Yet the deficit for 1989 still remained nearly twice as large as in 1981. Fourteen percent of the 1989 federal budget is required simply to pay the interest on the national debt!

153

The Bush Budget

An interest in expressing policy choices and doing something about the deficit were also central to the development of President Bush's first budget, the 1990 budget. The 1990 budget, of course, was prepared by administration officials during the last year of President Reagan's term, so that when he came into office in January of 1989, President Bush had to immediately suggest to Congress any changes he desired in the document that had already been prepared. He did so in a speech to Congress early in February; the speech outlined the priorities of the new administration.

Broadly speaking, the Bush approach was to propose a few limited spending increases above inflationary adjustments, then rely on reductions in selected areas and increased revenue that would come from economic growth to reduce the deficit. In defense, President Bush slightly reduced the amount that appeared in the budget prepared by the Reagan administration to the point that the Defense Department would basically stay even with inflation. On the other hand, the president slightly increased funding in education, suggesting new programs to reward excellent schools and teachers. The Education Department would also wind up staying even with inflation.

In the human services, the president restored funds for Medicaid, which President Reagan had proposed to cut from the budget, and sought greater support for the homeless and for child care programs. He also endorsed several new programs in science, technology, and environmental protection. In one particularly visible area, President

Bush proposed a 21 percent increase over the previous year for antidrug programs, primarily education, treatment, and drug-law enforcement. To help offset these increases, President Bush endorsed a Reagan administration proposal to cut a variety of specific programs, among them, reducing Amtrak and mass transit subsidies.

As the president and his budget director, Richard Darman, worked with congressional leaders over the following months to pass the budget, a key issue was what would happen to the deficit. For the 1990 budget, the Gramm-Rudman-Hollings law had targeted a deficit of no more than $110 billion. By October, when the fiscal year began, there was still no agreement on the budget. (As we will see, it is not unusual for a federal fiscal year to begin before the year's budget is approved.) Consequently, automatic, across-the-board spending cuts were applied to all federal agencies.

Finally, in late November, a deficit reduction plan was approved that would bring the projected deficit below the Gramm-Rudman-Hollings target. The plan that was agreed to, however, contained a number of provisions that appeared to be budgetary "smoke and mirrors." For example, part of the plan would save money by having the government lease rather than buy buildings, something that would obviously save up-front costs within 1990, but would likely increase costs in the long run. Similarly, certain payments to doctors under Medicaid were shifted to the following fiscal year. The biggest reduction item, however, was to simply maintain for another 130 days the across-the-board cuts that had been imposed in October, something that many observers read as a failure of the administration and the Congress to come to grips with the hard choices that deficit reduction requires. (The budget turmoil of October 1990 demonstrated that little had been learned from the earlier experience.)

State and Local Expenditures

Expenditure comparisons at the state and local levels are complicated by our system of intergovernmental transfers. In education, for example, the federal government provides some money directly to individuals (e.g., student grants and loans), but it also transfers large sums to state and local governments. States also spend some money directly (e.g., colleges and universities), but they also transfer some money received from the federal government and some raised at the state level to local governments, primarily to support education. Consequently, while local governments provide only about 31 percent of the money spent on education in this country, they actually are involved in spending 68 percent of that money (Wright, 1988, pp. 194–197). If we include intergovernmental transfers spent at the state and local levels in our calculations of state and local spending, the following patterns emerge: states spend the greatest portion of their funds on education, with public welfare next, and highways and natural resources somewhat less. At the local level, the largest amount again is spent on education, with health, public works, and social welfare next (see Box 5.2).

THE BUDGET AS A MANAGERIAL TOOL

As a public manager, you will find that the budget process is critical to your success and that of your agency, quite simply because the budget process establishes the level of funding for your programs and those of others. A variety of steps are required to enable a particular agency to spend money. Legislation must first be passed and signed by the chief executive to authorize the program. This **authorizing legislation** permits the establishment or continuation of a particular program or agency. (Authorizing legislation usually covers multiple years or is even open-ended, though some programs, such as the space program, require new authorization each year.) Next comes **appropriations,** whereby the legislature sets aside funds and creates budget authority for their expenditure. Only after both steps have been taken can an agency spend money in pursuit of its stated objectives.

In most cases, governments use a **fiscal year** as their basic accounting period. The federal fiscal year begins on October 1 and runs through September 30 of the following year. The fiscal year carries the name of the year in which it ends; thus, fiscal year 1991, or FY 91, begins October 1, 1990, and ends September 30, 1991. States and localities differ widely in terms of fiscal years; some follow the federal pattern and run from October through September, others start July 1 (as did the federal government until 1976), and others match the fiscal year to the calendar year. Kentucky and a few other states actually have a two-year-long fiscal year because their legislatures meet and pass a budget only every other year.

The fiscal year is the key period in which money is spent, but a variety of steps must be taken both before and after the fiscal year that can affect an agency's expenditures. The budget must be developed, typically by the chief executive (president, governor, mayor), and transmitted to the legislature; it must be approved by the legislature prior to the beginning of the fiscal year; it must be executed during the fiscal year; and it must be reviewed and audited following the fiscal year. At any given point in the *budget cycle*, there are actually several budgets being worked upon. While one budget is being executed (say, FY 90), formulation and approval of another (FY 91) is taking place, as are audits of the previous budget (FY 89) (see Box 5.3).

155

Budget Formulation

In the federal government and in many state and local jurisdictions, the chief executive has primary responsibility for preparation of the budget. The budget cycle typically begins with a letter from a central budget office to the various agencies outlining the timetable for preparation of the budget, transmitting forms for use in the process, and indicating any policy concerns of special priority for the fiscal year. The agencies then prepare their own budget requests and forward them to the central budget office for review. Often a series of meetings (or sometimes hearings) are held to negotiate differences in the views of the central budget office (reflecting the priorities of the chief executive) and the agencies. Finally, the budget document is prepared by the central budget office and transmitted by the chief executive to the legislature for approval.

In some jurisdictions, responsibility for preparing the budget may not lie completely with the chief executive, and the budget cycle may vary accordingly. In many states, for example, responsibility for budget formulation may be shared among the governor, other elected officials, and members of the legislature. Indeed, until recently, a legislative commission rather than the governor prepared the budget in Mississippi. At the municipal level, responsibility for preparing the budget varies according to the type of government.

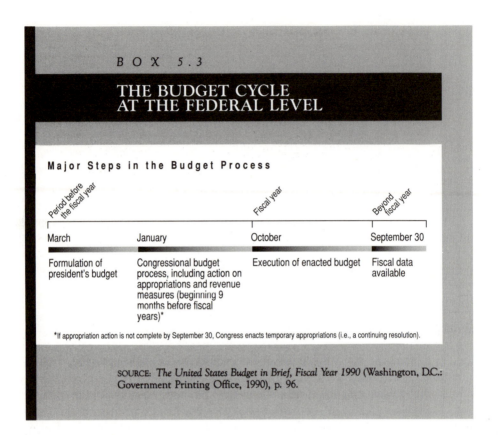

Cities with a strong mayor form usually give responsibility to the chief executive, whereas cities that operate under other forms tend to disperse budget authority. The city manager usually prepares the budget in council-manager cities, though typically with substantial input from the mayor and other council members.

The Office of Management and Budget is the central budget office at the federal level, and has evolved from an office established in 1921. Originally called the Bureau of the Budget, President Nixon renamed the Office of Management and Budget in 1970 to reflect an emphasis on management concerns in addition to budgetary responsibilities. At the outset of the budget process, OMB collects information on projected revenues for the coming fiscal year, as well as information on the outlook for the economy. In addition, OMB develops information on the progress of the current year's budget, as well as the budget being considered by Congress. After a beginning consultation with the agencies to assess their program priorities, OMB works with the president to establish basic policy guidelines for developing the budget.

These guidelines are communicated to the agencies, along with detailed forms for budget requests. In turn, managers in the various agencies assess their program priorities and decide the necessary level of funding for accomplishing objectives in the next fiscal year. Starting about September, a period of negotiation occurs with OMB. The central budget office represents the president's policy concerns and usually takes a generalist perspective, in contrast to the more narrow, specialized interests of the agency representatives. About November or December, the president becomes more actively involved in the budget process and makes final decisions with respect to both revenue and fiscal considerations and individual program needs.

For example, during the fall of 1989, President Bush persuaded Secretary of Defense Richard Cheney to agree to a series of reductions in the defense budget targeted to begin in FY 91. The president's action came at a time in which the Warsaw Pact countries were experiencing tremendous change, and the possibilities for a land war in Europe seemed to be diminishing. (At that time, 60 percent of the defense budget was targeted toward such a war.) Changing international conditions, combined with increasingly difficult deficit reduction problems, caused the president to break sharply with the defense buildup the country experienced during the Reagan years. (Of course, only a few months later military action in the Middle East required substantial spending.)

The final budget document, which is submitted to Congress early in the new year, represents the culmination of a long process of analysis and interaction among a wide variety of groups. As you can imagine, the difficulty of completing such an enormously complicated process in a relatively short time means that budget decisions are often less rational and precise than one might hope. In a candid interview with the *Washington Post*, David Stockman, Director of OMB early in the Reagan administration, described the impact of rushing through the process in 1981: "We were working in a twenty or twenty-five day time frame, and we didn't think it all the way through. We didn't add up all the numbers. We didn't make all the thorough, comprehensive calculations about where we really needed to come out and how much to put on the plate the first time, and so forth" (Axelrod, 1988, p. 84). Although Stockman was more revealing than many budget directors, others would surely recognize the difficulty of developing a careful and analytical process in a rapidly changing, highly charged political environment.

Obviously, given the magnitude and complexity of the federal government, the process of budget formulation at that level is the most complex in this country. But the difficulties of reconciling different and competing interests in the budget process are significant at all levels of government. In addition, chief executives at the state and local levels face constraints not found at the federal level. For example, most governors are required by constitution or statute to submit a balanced budget to the legislature, making it essential that they project anticipated revenues as closely as possible.

Budget Approval

The budget approval phase begins with submission of the budget to the legislature and ends with approval of the budget. The legislature, in most cases, can approve, disapprove, or modify the chief executive's budget proposal; it can add programs or eliminate programs; and it can alter methods of raising revenues. Remember that programs must first be authorized, then money appropriated for their implementation. In some cases, appropriations are contained in one bill that is debated, amended, and passed by the legislative body. In other cases, appropriations may be divided among several different appropriations bills.

In any case, the budget submitted to the legislative body is first sent to the committee or committees responsible for appropriations. These committees review the submitted document and hold hearings involving agency personnel, representatives of interest groups, other legislators, and private citizens. After consideration by the full legislative body, the bill as amended is passed and sent to the chief executive for signature (where approval is required), or, in the case of bicameral legislatures, sent to the other legislative body for similar consideration. If there are differences in the bills produced by the two houses of the legislature, the differences are worked out in a conference committee, and the bill is passed again by the two houses and sent to the chief executive.

Again, there are wide variations in the approval process from jurisdiction to jurisdiction. At the federal level, granting budget authority—the authority to obligate funds for immediate or future *outlays* (government spending)—can come about in several ways. Budget authority for most programs must be granted annually through passage of an appropriations bill. Congress has voted permanent budget authority for some programs, however, so that funds become available each year without further congressional action. In addition, within any given fiscal year, some outlays will be based on obligations made in previous years. Thus, total budget outlays for any fiscal year include the total of previously granted budget authority, authority granted through appropriations for the current year, and money obligated in previous years for spending in the upcoming fiscal year, minus outlays deferred to later years.

158

Under procedures established by the Congressional Budget Act of 1974, Congress considers budget totals before considering individual appropriations measures. Based on work by the Budget Committees of both houses, a first *concurrent resolution* (a resolution of both houses not requiring the president's signature) is passed by May 15, establishing targets for total revenues and total spending authority within various functional areas for the upcoming fiscal year. Although the president is not formally involved in this part of the budget process, consultation frequently occurs so that all parties will be informed of developments in the approval process. In December 1987, for instance, in response to the stock market crash that October, congressional leaders met with the president to work out a cooperative agreement that would demonstrate a "good-faith" effort to reduce the deficit. The various parties agreed upon a set of budget totals to be honored by both the president in his budget submission and the Congress in its approval process.

Congressional review of appropriations requests begins in the House of Representatives, where the Ways and Means Committee considers revenue estimates and the Appropriations Committee (through various subcommittees) reviews spending recommendations. Appropriations are considered within thirteen different appropriations bills covering groups of departments and agencies within related functional areas. After initial passage by the House, all tax bills and the thirteen appropriations bills are forwarded to the Senate for consideration. Differences in the appropriations measures coming from the two houses are worked out in conference committee and, following approval by both houses, are forwarded to the president for signature. The two Budget Committees are charged with drawing up a second concurrent resolution, this one binding in nature, setting limits on total spending; finally, a separate **reconciliation bill** attempts to reconcile individual actions in taxes, authorizations, or appropriations with the totals.

If action on appropriations for the fiscal year is not completed by the beginning of the fiscal year (October 1), the Congress enacts a **continuing resolution,** which permits the government to keep operating until an appropriations measure is passed. None of the thirteen appropriations bills for FY 88 had been passed by the beginning of the fiscal year, and, following several short-term continuing resolutions, a full-year resolution was enacted on December 22, nearly three months into the fiscal year.

Throughout its consideration of the budget, the Congress is aided by the work of Budget Committee staff members (whose numbers have grown substantially in recent years) and by the Congressional Budget Office. This agency provides basic budget information and its own economic forecasts and indicates to Congress how its conclusions differ from those of the executive branch. Such differences have, in several years, led the Congressional Budget Office to predict a more substantial budget deficit than that anticipated by the administration.

An increase in staff capabilities has been among the most important developments in the legislative approval process in most states and in some larger cities. Legislative budget staffs vary in structure and composition (i.e., partisan or nonpartisan, centralized or decentralized, joint (both houses) or single house, etc.); however, their responsibilities usually include analyzing the governor's budget, forecasting revenues and expenditures, and developing alternatives to the executive budget (Axelrod, 1988, p. 17). In all cases, greater staff capabilities have considerably aided the resurgence of state legislative involvement in the budget process.

One important feature of the approval process at the state level is the existence of the **item veto** in most states. (The item veto allows the governor to veto specific items in an appropriations bill rather than decide between "all or nothing.") Several recent presidents, including Presidents Reagan and Bush, have argued for line-item veto authority at the federal level, suggesting that such authority would lead to reductions in expenditures. There is considerable doubt, however, that the line-item veto would have such a result. In the first place, Congress, unlike state legislatures, often appropriates larger lump sums (rather than specific items) in order to give administrators flexibility. In doing so, the Congress can protect its own interests, because these sums would be far more difficult to veto. Moreover, as we have seen, the large percentage of uncontrollable expenditures in the federal budget would limit veto power to a narrow range of programs. Finally, the line-item veto would clearly alter the balance of power between the executive and the legislature, giving the president another bargaining tool—or threat—to employ in negotiations with Capitol Hill (Botner, 1988b).

Budget Execution

The budget execution stage, generally coinciding with the fiscal year, is that part of the budget cycle in which the agencies of government carry out agreed-upon programs and policies. Obviously, the execution stage involves public administrators in all aspects of the management process—planning, analysis, personnel management, communication, and other interpersonal skills.

Basic financial controls are exercised during the budget execution phase through the mechanism of **apportionment,** a process by which funds are allocated to agencies for specific portions of the year. Typically, the central budget office asks for submission of spending plans indicating what money the agencies anticipate spending in each quarter of the year. Because the agencies may not have received all they wanted in the appropriations process, the apportionment mechanism also acts as the basis for required changes in programs and policies. As soon as there is agreement between the central budget office (acting on behalf of the chief executive) and the agencies on the changes embodied in the apportionment plan, agencies begin receiving **allotments** to spend within a given period.

To assure that funds are in fact expended for the purposes for which they were intended and that there is indeed enough money budgeted to cover a proposed expenditure, some sort of **preaudit** (a review in advance of an actual expenditure) is usually required. Depending on the jurisdiction, the preaudit may be conducted by an agency's own budget office, by an independent agency, or even by an elected state official. Once approval has been given, however, the treasurer will "write a check" for the expenditure.

Even though budgets are not passed until just before (or even well into) the fiscal year, important changes may occur during the year that require changes in an agency's budgeted expenditures. Some changes may require greater funding; for example, when an unexpected natural disaster, such as a drought, places special burdens on farmers. If it is felt that the need must be met prior to the next budget cycle, the president and Congress can work together to provide a **supplemental appropriation,** a bill passed during the fiscal year to add new money to an agency's budget for that fiscal year. Such a bill may simply provide more money for existing programs or money for a newly authorized program.

There are also devices, used primarily by chief executives as a matter of administrative discretion, to restrict agencies' spending below budgeted amounts. Presidents throughout the nation's history have sought to limit agency spending by **impoundment**—withholding funds authorized and appropriated by law, typically in the case of emergencies or where the purpose of the money had been achieved and budgeted funds still remained. Similarly, at the state level, governors regularly withhold agency funds to meet revenue projections below those upon which the budget was based.

At the federal level, the impoundment issue became especially intense in the early 1970s, when President Nixon asserted his right to impound funds wherever he felt appropriate to achieve his fiscal goals. Especially annoying to Congress was his refusal to spend money for water pollution control; the money had been passed by Congress over a presidential veto (Pfiffner, 1979, p. 4). Many felt that Nixon's use of impoundment amounted to an unconstitutional item veto.

Consequently, the 1974 Budget Act sought to clarify matters by defining two types of legal impoundments. The first, a **deferral,** is a decision by the president to withhold funds for a brief period. In such circumstances, the president must inform the Congress, and either house of Congress may veto the action. The second, a **rescission,** is a presidential decision to withhold funds permanently; a rescission must receive the positive approval of both houses of Congress. Through these devices, Congress has sought to maintain its involvement in budget execution while at the same time allowing some administrative discretion to the president.

Because situations change, public managers are often accorded some flexibility in the use of allocated funds. Money originally allocated for salaries and wages, for example, might be shifted (with appropriate approvals) to an equipment and expense category. On a broader scale, some agencies engage in *reprogramming*—that is, taking money appropriated for one program and diverting it to another that emerges as a higher priority. This strategy must be undertaken with great care, however, not only because of legal and ethical implications, but because efforts to subvert the legislature's intention are likely to incur retribution in the next year's budget process.

Audit Phase

The final phase of the budget process is the *postexecution* or audit phase. *Postaudits* take place following the end of the fiscal year and are concerned with verifying the correctness and propriety of agency operations. These audits were originally designed to assure financial control; as such, they focused on accuracy of record keeping, on compliance with statutes, and on uncovering fraud, waste, and mismanagement. More recently, the concept of auditing has been broadened to include **performance auditing**—analyzing and evaluating the effective performance of agencies in carrying out their objectives. Three purposes are served by postaudits: (1) financial viability, as indicated by efficient use of resources; (2) compliance with statutes and other limitations; and (3) program performance, including the results of program operations (Brown, Gallagher, & Williams, 1982, p. 6).

161

Agencies themselves can carry out audits; indeed, we have already seen how the auditing work of inspectors general has revealed waste and fraud in some agencies. There is a clear trend, however, toward broader use of independent agencies. Moreover, to maintain detachment in their review of executive agencies, the postaudit function is increasingly being attached to the legislative rather than the executive branch. In 1921, for example, the federal government created the General Accounting Office as a support agency of the Congress, although President Wilson had previously vetoed such legislation on the grounds that the officers of such an agency should be answerable to the executive rather than the legislature (Mosher, 1979). As we saw, the GAO was originally concerned primarily with the financial auditing of selected federal agencies; however, more recently, it has extended its activities to include program evaluations as well.

At the state level, organizational arrangements vary; however, the trend toward having postaudit agencies attached to the legislature is clear. In 1938, there were five states in which the audit function was part of the legislative branch; in 1960, there were fifteen; today, there are over forty (Brown et al., 1982, p. 5). A large number of states retain an elected state auditor, however, whose office often goes beyond detached analysis and becomes embroiled in political controversy. Finally, a number of large cities, including Dallas and Seattle, have developed legislative postaudit functions.

APPROACHES TO PUBLIC BUDGETING

To be an effective tool in management and decision making, the budget must present information about the purposes of the proposed activity and the resources to be expended.

There are a variety of different ways to present such information. Some approaches to budgeting, for example, are based on the assumption that budget decisions are (and should be) largely *incremental*—policy makers start with the given situation (last year's budget) as a base and make only marginal adjustments to that base. Following this approach, managers build budgets by asking for limited increases in spending rather than focus on major programmatic concerns. Similarly, the legislature focuses on individual expenditures rather than the "big picture." According to proponents of incrementalism, this approach is not only an accurate representation of the actual behavior of decision makers, it is an appropriate way to maintain balance among the many different interests represented in the budget. In contrast, other budget theorists argue for a more rational, comprehensive, and programmatic approach.

Budgets can be categorized according to the purposes they serve. Allen Schick, a leading scholar in the field of budgeting, has suggested that budgets can have at least three different purposes, all of which are reflected in any approach to budgeting. These purposes are planning, management, and control. *Planning* involves the determination of organizational objectives and the development of strategies to meet those objectives; *management* involves the design of organizational means by which approved goals can be translated into action, as well as developing the staffing and resources necessary for execution; *control* refers to "the process of binding operating officials to the policies and plans set by their superiors" (Schick, 1987, pp. 41–42). According to Schick, each attempt at budget reform changes the balance among the three purposes—sometimes inadvertently, sometimes deliberately. Understanding how budgets are put together will help you present an effective case for program changes.

162

The Line-Item Budget

Those who established the first systematic governmental budgeting schemes were concerned primarily with assuring the public that expenditures were properly made and accounted for. Consequently, the systems they designed emphasized the control function. Because all agencies purchase essentially the same kinds of goods and services, it was argued, account classifications could be designed that would be broadly applicable to various agencies or departments. It would then be possible for auditors to apply uniform criteria to evaluate the expenditures of all (Lyden & Lindenberg, 1983, p. 67).

Accordingly, in what is called a **line-item** or *objects of expenditure* budget, categories of expenditures are listed along with amounts allocated to each. Typically, line-item budgets are organized by departments, so that the budget for one agency might look something like this:

	1991	1992
Salaries and wages	$75,300	$94,400
Utilities	12,320	13,750
Supplies and materials	13,500	13,950
Travel	950	750
Printing	1,200	1,350
Telephone	1,550	1,900

The cost of each object of expenditure is generally based on the agency's past experience and analysis of expected changes during the budget year. Since personnel costs (salaries, wages, and other personal services) typically constitute over half the budget, special attention is given to projected staffing changes, and such changes are often appended to the budget. (Our example projects, among other things, the addition of one clerical person during the upcoming year.)

The line-item budget continues to be widely used, partly because it is easy to understand and partly because it offers political leaders the more palatable option of reducing items (such as travel) rather than eliminating "programs." Moreover, it is well suited to incremental decisions, which make only minor modifications in the previous budget. However, because in the line-item budget the focus is on expenditures, not on their results, it is of little benefit to planning or management. Consequently, budget reformers have sought to balance the line-item budget's advantage of effective control with attention to other purposes as well.

The Performance Budget

The 1930s proved a turning point with respect to public budgeting. The federal budget grew tremendously, the Bureau of the Budget became attached to the White House, and, in general, greater attention was paid to the executive management of government agencies. This interest in management was paralleled at the state and local levels, where efforts to relate budget presentations to programmatic activities had been underway for some time. The result was a new approach to budgeting, the performance budget.

The **performance budget** is organized around programs or activities rather than departments and includes various performance measurements to indicate the relationship between the work actually done and its cost. As the Hoover Commission described it, a performance budget "would analyze the work of government departments and agencies according to their functions, activities, or projects. It would concentrate attention on the work to be done or the service to be rendered, rather than the things to be acquired" (Lyden & Lindenberg, 1983, p. 69). By focusing on the relationship between available resources and the work to be done, performance budgeting is well suited to the purposes of management.

To construct a performance budget, the manager must first determine appropriate program categories, such as highway safety, then break that program down into appropriate subprograms, such as school visitations or advertising programs. It is then necessary to establish detailed work measures for each activity; for example, a highway safety program might anticipate twenty-seven school visitations during the course of the year. These data would then be related to the cost of making such visits. In its most detailed presentation, a performance budget requires identifying the work activity, establishing an output unit, calculating the cost of each unit, and projecting the units required and the associated costs for the coming year.

Although performance measures are obviously helpful in making budgetary decisions, not all organizations can easily develop such information. A license bureau can report the number of licenses issued and fairly easily calculate the cost per license issued; a research unit or a group promoting civil rights would find its work much more difficult to measure. Performance budgeting also tends to concentrate on quantity of work rather than quality.

163

Finally, performance budgeting somewhat diffuses organizational responsibility, because one program or function may be located in several different units. "Public information," for example, may involve work in the mayor's office, police department, fire department, and elsewhere. To sort out costs by department, one would need to construct a *crosswalk* or matrix of expenditures. A matrix might place various activities on one dimension and departments on another:

| | Activities | | | Totals |
	1	2	3	
Division A	$10,000	$20,000	$15,000	$45,000
Division B	12,000	16,000	10,000	38,000
Division C	5,000	12,000	13,000	30,000
Totals	27,000	48,000	38,000	

A matrix could also be constructed relating activities to traditional objects of expenditure; such calculations are typical in performance budgets.

Program Budgeting

164   Another approach to budgeting had its origins in the Department of Defense in the early 1960s. Soon after taking office as Secretary of Defense, Robert McNamara discovered that his ability to manage the department was severely restricted by the lack of coordination between planning and budgeting. Each service (Army, Navy, Air Force) prepared its own annual budget, reflecting its own priorities, then submitted the documents to the secretary. Obviously, this plan failed to give proper attention to systemwide issues. But, equally important, because the budgeting system was based on a one-year time frame, it bore little, if any, relation to the multiyear projections of the department's planning and analysis staff. The development of major weapons systems, for example, involves research and development, assembly, and operations over many years, yet this fact was not clearly reflected in the annual budget submissions.

Consequently, McNamara instituted a new approach, which came to be known as the **planning-programming-budgeting system (PPBS),** an effort to connect planning, systems analysis, and budgeting in a single exercise. In the Defense Department, PPBS began with the identification of nearly a thousand program elements, each grouped under one of nine major programs or missions, that is, strategic retaliatory forces, continental air and missile defense forces, civil defense, and so on. Not only was extensive study required to identify the right combination of program elements to support each mission, but, once having established the combinations, units in the department were required to submit detailed analyses of proposed program changes. In addition, the new budget system was designed to cover a nine-year period and to show detailed projections for the first six years.

President Johnson was so impressed with the operation of PPBS in the Defense Department that he ordered the new system extended to all federal agencies. Each cabinet-level department was asked to identify a limited number of purposes to be served by the agency, then to organize budget requests around those themes. The Department of Health, Education, and Welfare, for example, chose topics such as "social and rehabilitation services" that cut across several agencies within HEW. Costs for each program element were projected five years into the future and extensive documentation justifying each element was required, especially in areas undergoing significant changes. Most agencies were able to develop their budgets using the new approach, but there was considerable confusion in the implementation of PPBS. As a result of this confusion and for a variety of other political reasons, PPBS was formally terminated by President Nixon in 1971.

During its relatively short tenure, PPBS attracted great attention, with many cities, states, and other countries embracing the new technique. PPBS not only emphasized the planning aspect of budgeting, but it appeared to bring greater rationality and comprehensiveness to the budget process. These goals, however, were accomplished at great cost. Substantial numbers of new staff members were needed, both in the central budget office and in the various agencies to provide the kind of analysis PPBS required. All in all, the process proved extraordinarily time-consuming. Consequently, very few full-blown PPBS systems remain, although many of the principles of PPBS have been incorporated into other approaches, often under the more general label *program budgeting.*

There are important differences between performance budgeting and program budgeting. "As a general rule, performance budgeting is concerned with the *process of work* (what methods should be used) while program budgeting is concerned with the *purpose of work* (what activities should be authorized)" (Schick, 1987, p. 53). Where a performance budget might define the operations of a city garbage department in terms of collecting and disposing of garbage, a program budget might focus instead on the purpose served by collecting the garbage—to prevent infectious disease or to protect property values (Lyden & Lindenberg, 1983, pp. 92–93).

Moreover, although both systems urge measurement of work being done, performance budgeting is more likely to employ measures related to the work (for example, the number of tons of garbage collected) and a program budget might concentrate instead on measures related to the purpose of the work (for example, the rate of infectious disease in the community). Performance data are of great interest to individual managers who seek to improve productivity, but legislators and other policy makers are more likely to be interested in the purposes of various activities.

Zero-Base Budgeting

One of the most recent budget reform efforts is **zero-base budgeting (ZBB),** a technique developed by Texas Instruments and first applied in government by Jimmy Carter while he was governor of Georgia. As president, Carter mandated the use of ZBB in all federal agencies. ZBB does not mean that agencies must simply start over with each budget cycle, building and rebuilding justifications for all their programs; rather, ZBB seeks to structure the budget so as to present information about the efficiency and effectiveness of existing programs and also highlight possibilities for eliminating or reducing programs (Pyhrr, 1977, p. 1). In contrast to the program development emphasis in program budgeting, the emphasis in ZBB is on cutting back.

The ZBB process begins with identifying a *decision unit*, the lowest organizational unit at which significant program decisions are made. The manager of the decision unit is asked to prepare one or more *decision packages*, which explain each proposed program and contain the purpose, a description of the action to be undertaken, costs and benefits, and workload and performance measures. Top management and the legislature use the decision packages to compare various programs and rank the highest priorities.

As part of developing the decision packages, managers must provide two other types of information. First, they must identify alternative measures for accomplishing the work and indicate why these alternatives were not chosen. For example, an air quality laboratory might recommend using a centralized laboratory to conduct tests rather than conducting tests at regional locations or contracting with a local university (Pyhrr, 1977, p. 4). Second, managers must identify various funding levels: (1) a minimum level; (2) the level necessary to continue current operations; and (3) an improvement level. In each case, the manager must indicate the effects of the funding level on program performance. For example, a minimum level of $140,000 might permit testing 37,000 air samples, meeting the minimum requirements of those who use the tests, and covering 70 percent of the state's population. An improvement level might require $246,000, but add additional urban areas and cover 90 percent of the population (Phyrr, 1977, p. 4).

ZBB has been criticized for generating too much paperwork and for failing to provide effective criteria for ranking decision packages. In addition, the minimum funding level requirement has proven difficult to establish; many jurisdictions equate minimum funding with a certain percentage of the current level (e.g., 75 percent). For these and other reasons, ZBB was discontinued by President Reagan, though many agencies still employ some of its elements in their budget process. The current federal budgeting system, like most at the state and local levels, is a combination of elements from several of the approaches we have discussed.

BUDGETARY STRATEGIES AND POLITICAL GAMES

Despite all attempts to rationalize the budget process, public budgeting is an inherently political activity. The changing demands on government and its programs, the shifting interests that are brought to bear in policy decisions, and the many different actors (and personalities) that are part of the budget process mean that budget decisions will always occur in a highly charged political environment. As one student of the budget process described the situation, "Budgeting in this environment is a matter of negotiation, persuasion, bargaining, bluff and counter-bluff" (Caiden, 1985, p. 498). Because agency managers typically (and properly) believe in the programs they operate and would like to see the programs be of even greater benefit to the public, they tend to become advocates of an agency position, often seeking to expand the size and scope of the agency's work.

If you can deal effectively with the political environment in which budgeting occurs, you will likely be more successful in expanding, or at least maintaining, your agency's programs. (There are, of course, many cases in which you will be judged on your capacity to hold the line on expenditures or to manage program reductions.) Whatever your intent, understanding the politics of the budgetary process will be helpful.

In discussions of budgetary strategies, two basic concepts will help orient your thinking. The first is the notion of program base. The *base* refers to those elements of an agency's program that everyone expects will be continued from year to year. Under normal circumstances, the program's base is assumed to remain pretty much the same from one year to the next and is not subject to special scrutiny. Having an activity approved for one year is one thing; having that activity considered a part of your agency's base budget is far more important. A second and related concept is that of receiving a *fair share* of the overall budget. Managers often measure success in terms of whether their program receives a proportionate amount of any increases or decreases that the government generally supports. Agency personnel often work for years to build a base that they consider a fair share of the overall budget (Wildavsky, 1988, p. 83).

As we saw earlier, budget requests typically originate with the agencies. They are then reviewed and often changed by a central budget office (acting in behalf of the chief executive) and submitted to the legislature for approval. In constructing a budget request, you need to take into account several different types of expenditures. Many departments at the federal level have a large budget component that is essentially *uncontrollable*. The Department of Health and Human Services, for example, which administers many entitlement programs, has a large percentage of its budget that is essentially fixed. A second part of an agency's budget is likely to be devoted to *adjustments for inflation*. The rising cost of utilities, telephones, postage, and other essential services must be taken into account, either absorbed in the base or covered by increased expenditures. Finally, some part of the agency's budget is *discretionary*, subject to increase or decrease according to the agency's priorities. The discretionary portion of the budget allows you to decide both which new programs to propose and which existing activities to recommend for more (or less) funding. Understanding these categories will help you argue for changes in a particular budget.   167

Strategies for Program Development

These choices lead to strategic questions you must answer in building a budget—including the important question of what total amount to request. Although an overall budget is likely to differ only incrementally from that of the previous year, some agencies are clearly more assertive in their requests than others. That is, they are more willing to request large increases rather than small ones. But how assertive to be is conditioned by several factors.

Obviously, support from the chief executive (the president, governor, mayor, etc.) is highly important, whether the support is specific in terms of advocacy for a particular program or more generally an expression of interest in a particular field, such as law enforcement. Similarly, legislative support is also highly important. Agency personnel, in fact, work hard throughout the year to maintain contact with key legislative leaders and to build the kinds of alliances that will be helpful in supporting programs of mutual interest. Finally, your personality—especially your willingness to take risks and defend risky choices—will play a strong role in deciding how much to request.

Aaron Wildavsky, who wrote a landmark study of the politics of the budgetary process, suggested three other strategic elements that not only affect the nature of the request, but also help build political support for it (Wildavsky, 1988, pp. 100–119). The first of these is *clientele support*. Obviously, the support of client groups and other associations interested in the agency's work will be helpful in developing testimony and lobbying in behalf of programs. An agency that is confident of the testimony of "satisfied customers" or able to show support for proposed changes will likely fare much better than others. Obviously, the most effective way to build support is to serve a client group well, but agencies may also try to stimulate supportive clientele to communicate with legislators about the agency's good work.

A second element of political support is the *confidence* of higher executives and legislative officials in your character and ability. The magnitude of government budgets is so great that higher officials or legislators simply cannot know all the necessary details for a purely rational analysis. At some point, they must simply trust the manager. Managers who enjoy a good reputation are typically more successful, especially in dealings with the legislature (see Box 5.4). One administrator commented, "If you have the confidence of your (appropriations) subcommittee your life is much easier and you can do your department some good; if you don't have confidence you can't accomplish much and you are always in trouble" (Wildavsky, 1988, p. 105). There are many ways to build confidence, but highly successful managers seem to agree that a reputation for integrity (telling the whole truth) and responsiveness (keeping in touch and responding completely to inquiries) are particularly important.

BOX 5.4

PLAY IT STRAIGHT

Everyone agrees that the most important requirement for confidence, at least in a negative sense, is to be aboveboard. As Rooney once said, "There's only two things that get me mad. One is harebrained schemes; the other is when they don't play it straight." A lie, an attempt to blatantly cover up some misdeed, a tricky move of any kind, can lead to an irreparable loss of confidence. A typical comment by an administrator states, "It doesn't pay to try to put something over on them [committee members] because if you get caught, you might as well pack your bags and leave Washington." And the chances of getting caught are considerable because interested committeemen and their staffs have much experience and many sources of information.

Administrators believe that punishments for failure to establish confidence are greater than the rewards for achieving it. But at times they do slip up, and then the roof falls in. When Congress limited the amount of funds that could be spent on personnel, a bureau apparently evaded this limitation in 1952 by subcontracting out a plan to private investors. The House Subcommittee was furious:

> *Representative Jensen:* It certainly is going to take a house-cleaning . . . of . . . all people who are responsible for this kind of business.
> *Official:* We are going to do it, Mr. Chariman.
> *Representative Jensen:* I do not mean "maybe." That is the most disgraceful showing that I have seen of any department.
> *Official:* I am awfully sorry.

SOURCE: Excerpted from *The New Politics of the Budgetary Process* by Aaron Wildavsky. Copyright © 1988 by Aaron Wildavsky. Reprinted by permission of Harper Collins Publishers.

Third, agency officials can take certain *tactical positions* to attempt to develop or protect their favorite programs. One approach, verging on the unethical but nonetheless common, is **budget padding**—that is, proposing a higher budget than is actually needed, on the assumption that after the central budget office and legislature cut it, you will have what you wanted in the first place. (One city manager described including "radio" items in his budget—a radio item was one that "makes a lot of noise but can be unplugged easily." The radio item would attract controversy and deflect attention from other items that were actually more important to the manager.) Another strategy is one Wildavsky terms the *camel's nose.* The manager asks for a small amount to begin a program, then later treats this program as part of the base and argues that it would be unfortunate to lose the money already invested by not finishing the job (Wildavsky, 1988, p. 115).

As we have seen, over the past ten years, many programs at all levels of government have experienced lower revenues and more limited funding. In some cases, such as in the social services, programs have been reduced or eliminated; in other cases, changes such as the termination of revenue sharing at one level of government have resulted in lower revenues at another; in still other cases, popular efforts to limit either revenues or expenditures, such as Proposition 13 in California, have limited government funds. In any case, many public managers have had to turn their attention from developing new programs to maintaining or even reducing existing ones. This effort has been variously referred to as *managing fiscal stress* or, where serious reductions have occurred, *cutback management.*

As you would expect under retrenchment conditions, many managers have used budgetary tactics of the sort outlined by Wildavsky to lessen the impact of fiscal stress on their agencies (Wildavsky, 1988, p. 113). Any attempt to resist cuts is risky, however, in part because it can quickly undermine the manager's credibility. Moreover, under conditions of long-term fiscal limitations, resistance to cuts is simply not a realistic option for many managers (Levine, 1980, p. 20). Several other ways of dealing with fiscal stress have been tried with some success:

- Following a *multiyear plan* so as to preserve the administrative capacity and the capital investment of the jurisdictions
- *Targeting* cuts in specific programs rather than cutting across the board (all programs cut at the same percentage)
- *Smoothing out* the impact of the cuts (lessening their immediate effect) (Levine, Rubin, & Wolohojian, 1981, p. 210)

Smoothing out may occur either through improvements in productivity, so the organization can accomplish more with less, or by generating new revenues, through such moves as imposing new user charges for services.

ASPECTS OF FINANCIAL MANAGEMENT

Although those in public organizations need to budget their resources, they must also attend to other aspects of managing the public's money. They must be concerned with the long-term financing of buildings, roads and highways, and equipment; they must carefully plan and manage borrowing; they must ensure against future losses; and, in all cases, they must try to get the most for the money they spend.

Capital Budgeting

In addition to budgeting annual expenditures, public policy makers and managers need to invest in facilities and equipment that will be used over a period of time. For example, government is primarily responsible for developing and maintaining the country's public works *infrastructure*—streets and highways, tunnels and bridges, sewers and water treatment facilities, and so on. In addition, governments invest in a variety of other major facilities, including schools and universities, hospitals and mental health centers, public housing, and correctional institutions. Finally, innumerable equipment purchases (especially military equipment at the federal level) are intended for long-term use. Expenditures on items that will be used over a period of several years are called **capital expenditures.**

Budgeting for capital expenditures is similar to the process of budgeting for annual expenditures, but it also differs in some ways. In most jurisdictions, with the federal government as the most notable exception, capital expenditures are treated in a separate budget called a *capital budget*. Most states have a separate capital budget, and nearly all give special treatment to capital expenditures in budget presentation; nearly all major cities and most other local governments use a capital budget. For many years, the federal government treated capital spending merely as part of the regular budget; only recently has it begun to provide a special analysis of capital spending. There is still not a separate capital budget at the federal level.

The primary argument in favor of separate consideration of capital items is that the benefits of these items are spread over future generations, and it is therefore not unreasonable to share the burden of repaying the money borrowed. A separate capital budget may also encourage more long-term thinking—the lack of which is often decried in the annual budget process. On the other hand, the capital budget can become a political "pork barrel," in which each legislator seeks to gain his or her share of projects (and their funding). Moreover, a capital budget can become a device for avoiding fiscal responsibility, by pushing expenditures that should be faced immediately into an indefinite future. In any case, whether a separate budget is developed or not, one should keep in mind the relationship between capital and operating expenditures. Building a new swimming pool, for example, implies that annual expenditures will be forthcoming in future years to keep it operating.

Ideally, a capital budget develops in the context of a fairly comprehensive planning process, undertaken either for the government as a whole or by the various agencies within their functional areas (such as health or criminal justice). Whether or not a planning process is in operation, an important intermediate step (and one followed by nearly all governments considering capital projects) is development of a *capital investment program*—a timetable indicating various projects to be undertaken, schedules for their completion, and methods of financing. A capital investment program is usually written to cover at least five years and is moved forward each year. New York, for example, recently prepared a five-year capital plan projecting nearly fifteen billion dollars of expenditures for construction and renovation of the state's capital facilities (Axelrod, 1988, p. 109).

To undertake such a plan, government decision makers often solicit proposals from the various agencies, then try to bring order to the resulting submissions. Among the criteria decision makers might use would be the essentiality of the project, especially for health and safety; whether the project fills a gap in existing services; whether it builds effectively on existing services; and whether it meets an unforeseen emergency need (Lyden & Lindenberg, 1983, p. 185). Because financing for capital projects is usually spread over many years, as are the benefits, complete analysis of each project is likely to involve detailed consideration of both costs and benefits over time.

Debt Management

One part of the capital budgeting process is careful consideration of the source of funding. Some jurisdictions try to operate on a "pay-as-you-go" basis, paying in full for all projects during the fiscal year in which they are authorized. (One variation of this idea is the accumulation of money in a *sinking fund*, something like a Christmas Club account, which is then used to pay for the needed improvement.) Other jurisdictions may be willing to borrow money for a project, either because waiting to accumulate funds would simply take too long or because, philosophically, it is felt that the costs as well as the benefits of the project should be spread over a period of years—a "pay-as-you-use" approach.

Borrowing is often used to finance capital improvement projects; but borrowing may be employed to meet a variety of other needs as well. In some cases, anticipated revenues will simply not be available at the time spending is necessary. To solve the resulting "cash-flow" problem, governments undertake short-term borrowing. (In more questionable cases, money is borrowed from future years' revenues to pay operating expenses within the current year. Such a practice was partly responsible for the financial crisis in New York City in the mid-1970s.) Borrowing is also used for emergency needs, for example, a natural disaster, such as fire or flood, might require funds far beyond the capacity of the annual budget. Especially when such spending will be used to reconstruct facilities that will have long-term benefits, borrowing may well be justified. Finally, at least at the federal level, borrowing is sometimes justified as a way of stimulating the economy.

Governments may undertake various types of borrowing; however, the primary mechanism for financing government debt is the issuance of a **bond**—that is, a promise to repay a certain amount (*principal*) at a certain time (*maturity date*) at a particular *rate of interest.* One of the most common bonds is the *general obligation bond,* which pledges the "full faith and credit" of the jurisdiction—in other words, the government provides as security all its revenues and resources. In contrast, *revenue bonds* promise as security the anticipated revenues that a capital project will produce. Revenue bonds might be issued based on the future toll receipts of a new highway or on the gross receipts of a new municipal sports complex.

Both from the standpoint of a jurisdiction, and from the standpoint of potential investors who might purchase the bonds, it is helpful to know something about the jurisdiction's **debt capacity**—if a city, the value of the city's resources combined with the ability of the city government to draw on the city's resources to provide payment. As a service to investors, several firms provide bond ratings for cities and other jurisdictions. The ratings are also important to the jurisdiction, because a lower rating means higher costs of borrowing for the government. Standard and Poor rates bonds in descending quality from "AAA" to "AA" to "A" to "BBB" to "BB," and so on. Cities or other government units that carry high ratings will be more successful than others in selling their bonds.

172

Risk Management

Public organizations are subject to a variety of risks that can prove extremely costly. A few years ago, for example, an individual who was driving through a particular city lost control of his car, which bounced off a guardrail into a ditch. The driver suffered serious injuries, then sued the city for several million dollars, arguing that the guardrail had been improperly placed. Similarly, a city employee, with no previous health problems, began to suffer back pains on the job. After several operations, high medical bills, and physical therapy, he was given disability retirement at age twenty-six (Lynch, 1985, p. 316). Another city was sued by residents who lived near the municipal airport, because the noise of aircraft landing and taking off supposedly lessened the value of their property. Over the years, cases such as these involving civil damages, breach of contract, worker's compensation, and related legal problems have cost cities, states, and other jurisdictions millions of dollars.

Risk management concerns how public organizations anticipate and cope with these risks. Obviously, a first step in risk management is to identify potential areas of loss and then to attempt to reduce the probability of losses occurring. Risk reduction programs might include improved work safety, periodic inspections of physical property owned by the city, and employee health programs. But whatever the success of risk reduction efforts, losses do occur. The government has a variety of options for meeting losses, including payment from operating funds or financial reserves, levying special taxes to cover the loss, or even floating bonds.

In anticipation of losses, however, many public organizations purchase insurance, often from private firms. In recent years, this option has become more difficult, as insurance rates for governments and other public organizations have risen dramatically and put many traditional forms of insurance beyond reach. (The difficulty of purchasing insurance has also led some jurisdictions to eliminate uninsured services, such as some recreation programs.) Another possibility, however, is *self-insurance*, the development of an insurance pool by the jurisdiction itself. After all, many governments are larger than insurance companies, so such an undertaking is not only financially feasible, but provides some administrative control and flexibility that is not present when private firms are used. An increasingly popular means of self-insurance involves pooling risks in a shared program operated by several municipalities.

Purchasing

A final aspect of financial management in public organizations is the purchase of goods and services. Because public organizations are typically not equipped to produce all the goods and services they require (and in most cases would not find it financially feasible to do so anyway), they must acquire some goods and services from the private sector. Like individuals and businesses, public organizations want to get the most for their money (see Box 5.5). But at the same time, because government purchasing involves such substantial sums of money and is capable of influencing the structure of the market generally, public purchasing must also take into account social and political goals.

BOX 5.5

A BUREAUCRACY BUSTER AT THE POST OFFICE

Boston native John J. Davin, who arrived in Washington 13 months ago, already has done the unlikely in a city where bureaucratic regulation is as much a part of life as the Irish are in Boston.

A former corporate purchasing executive, Davin, 59, has presided over what is probably one of the deepest reductions in red tape Washington has seen in recent years, slashing the U.S. Postal Service's two-volume, 1,327-page purchasing manual to two slim volumes totaling 460 pages.

The project is part of a Postal Service effort to radically alter the way it spends more than $4 billion each year—purchases that make it second only to the national defense establishment in federal buying power.

The rules, which become effective during the coming months, call for the service to abandon its policy of seeking low-bid

(continued)

(continued)

contracts in most cases and substitute a negotiated bidding procedure that will hand contracting officers much greater authority.

Too often, major postal contracts have become flawed or stalled
when low-bidding firms were unable to deliver the quantity of
goods that the service needed, Davin says.

SOURCE: Excerpted from *The Washington Post National Weekly Edition* (October
17, 1987), p. 33. © 1987 The Washington Post. Reprinted by permission.

Governments have often found that centralizing purchasing in one agency, rather
than having each agency buy what it needs, results in considerable savings. For one
thing, a central purchasing unit can buy in sufficient volume to get better prices; for
another, those in the purchasing unit can develop expertise with respect to pricing,
business conditions, and market practices. Finally, experts in purchasing are likely to
be more successful in the negotiating process. Although individual agencies occasionally
complain that their specific needs are not met by the purchasing unit, most state and
local jurisdictions use centralized purchasing operations.

174   The amounts they spend are sometimes surprising. One midwestern state, for example,
spends some $4 million a year for groceries and $3 million a year for drugs to supply
residents of state institutions. The state buys several hundred cars each year, and last
year spent $43,000 on pens, $8,000 on pencils, and over $3,000 on rubber bands. It
also spent over $1 million on toilet paper. In addition to supplies and materials, the
state's purchasing division bought a wide range of personal services, from aerial
photography to interpreters for the deaf and blind to embalmers. According to experts,
the division saves the state hundreds of millions of dollars each year (Levine, 1985).

In most cases, a purchasing unit circulates and advertises the government's needs
and solicits bids for the required goods and services. The resulting bids are evaluated in
terms of cost, and the lowest bid is usually, though not automatically, chosen. Consideration is also given to the quality of the product and to the ability of the firm to actually
deliver the goods or services in a timely fashion. In addition, purchasers are often required
to give special preference to certain groups, such as minority firms or in-state companies.
Several jurisdictions often join together to cooperate in purchasing activities. In some
instances, several local governments may form a common purchasing unit; in other cases,
prices negotiated by the state purchasing office are available to local governments as well.

ACCOUNTING AND COMPUTER-BASED
INFORMATION SYSTEMS

Keeping track of the revenues and expenditures of government and other public organizations is an enormously complex task. Not only are there billions of dollars to record

and report, but the presentation of financial information must serve several purposes at once. Certainly financial data should be developed and reported in such a way that public officials can be held accountable for the use of public funds, but at the same time, the accounting and reporting system should provide managers with information they can use to operate their organizations more efficiently and effectively. This dual requirement means that financial information should correlate closely with other managerially relevant material, such as personnel data or productivity measures.

Government Accounting

Accounting, whether in the public or private sector, is simply "the process of identifying, measuring, and communicating economic information to permit informed judgment and decision making by users of the information" (Berne & Schramm, 1986, p. 12). But because the purposes of public organizations differ from those of private organizations, accounting practices also differ. Those in public organizations, for example, are generally not concerned with making a profit; rather, they tend to focus on achieving a balance between revenues and expenditures—what comes in and what goes out. There are some exceptions, such as public corporations, hospitals, and water companies, which are somewhat more like profit-seeking groups; however, in nearly all public organizations, accountability is more important than profit maximization.

Governmental accounting systems reflect these different purposes. The cornerstone of accounting in the public sector is the allocation of resources to various *funds*, each of which is designed to record transactions within a particular functional area and assure that funds are used in accord with the purposes sought. (Use of such funds is uncommon in the private sector.) The various funds typically reflect policy makers' intent in authorizing certain activities and appropriating funds for them. The legislature may decide, for example, that certain gasoline taxes should be used exclusively for highway maintenance, in which case a separate fund might be created to keep track of money produced by the tax and spent for highways. In all cases, a primary concern is that the accounting system show whether the organization's activities have been consistent with the purposes for which it was created. There are several broad types of funds that are used in public organizations.

1. *General government funds* are used to account for most of the ordinary or routine functions of government. Most important among the general government funds is what is called the **general fund,** which handles the "unrestricted" funds of government, those not restricted to specific purposes (and typically allocated to other funds). The general fund is the dominant fund in most jurisdictions, and handles most of the government's operational activities. Related general government funds might include those that account for special revenues, like a dedicated gasoline tax, or those that monitor expenditures for capital projects.

2. **Proprietary funds** are used to account for government activities or enterprises that more closely resemble private business in their orientation toward profit. This does not mean that all agencies employing proprietary funds are required to make a profit; indeed, they may break even or perhaps require a subsidy. What is implied is that a measure of profit is possible and usually desirable in such operations; examples include a local transit system or a state printing operation.

3. Finally, **fiduciary funds** are used when the government must hold assets for individuals (e.g., those in a pension fund) or when the government holds resources to be transmitted to another organization (e.g., property taxes that a county collects for a city) (Berne & Schramm, 1986, pp. 14–15).

Within each fund there is an accounting of the resources available and the flow of funds in and out of the account. On the one hand, there are *assets*—what the organization *owns*; on the other hand, there are *liabilities*—what the government *owes*. Assets include items such as cash, capital facilities, equipment, and money owed to the government; liabilities include items such as bills that the government has yet to pay. When the organization's liabilities are subtracted from its assets, the remainder is called a *fund balance* (and may be expressed either in positive or negative terms). An organization with $2,525,000 in assets and $2,300,000 in liabilities has a fund balance of $225,000. Note that a fund balance does *not* mean the amount of "cash on hand," but rather signifies a relationship between all assets (including cash) and all liabilities. Broadly, the fund balance is the key measure of the viability of the operation monitored by the fund and is one of many items contained in financial reports issued by governments and other public organizations.

Both accounting practices and financial reporting are guided by standards referred to as "generally accepted accounting practices," or GAAP. The Governmental Accounting Standards Board was established several years ago to develop standards for accounting and financial reporting at the state and local levels. In its work, the GASB has been especially attentive to multiple users of public financial information, including citizens, taxpayers, legislative bodies, upper-level executives, labor and employee groups, interest groups, contractors, and the press. Again, an important characteristic of governmental accounting is that it must serve multiple purposes, including accountability within a democratic system.

Computer-Based Information Systems

The emergence and widespread use of computers in tracking financial data as well as other program-relevant information has led to what one writer has called a "quiet revolution" in the analysis and use of information in public organizations (Botner, 1983). Not only do computers make easier the accumulation and manipulation of vast amounts of data, they also greatly facilitate analysis of that data in terms that are meaningful to decision makers at all levels. Computers have also increased the probability that provision of information can occur on a timely basis—the decision maker can have information when it is needed, not weeks later. Consequently, a great deal of attention is being given to design and implementation of computer-based information systems in the public sector and to the political and organizational implications of such changes. Applications in the area of financial management have often led the way in these efforts.

A distinction is often made between management information systems and decision support systems. *Management information systems* collect and summarize routine information as a basis for structured decision making. Relevant data bases might include budgetary information, expenditures for salaries and wages, and personnel data. The system might be asked, for example, to produce a list of employees eligible for salary increases based on length of service in the agency (McGowan & Lombardo, 1986, p. 581).

Decision support systems, on the other hand, are interactive systems that can assist in the solution of unstructured or nonroutine problems (Rubin, 1986, p. 541). These systems can range in capabilities from one that allows the manager to manipulate data within the system to produce a specific analysis for a particular decision to one that provides optimization models to use in analyzing a particular policy recommendation. Although most public organizations are developing management information systems of various sorts, the development of decision support systems remains somewhat behind, though we can expect increasing attention to this area in the future.

Applications of computer-based information systems are as wide-ranging as the work of public organizations; however, most organizations are quickly becoming familiar with the use of spreadsheets and statistical packages for budget analysis, with financial management packages for revenue and expenditure forecasting, and with accounting packages for fund accounting and analysis. But far more extensive applications of information technology have been developed in government agencies. A recent survey indicates that federal agencies vary considerably in use of computer-based information systems, but in the area of financial management, some agencies have developed quite sophisticated systems. The Department of State, for example, has developed and implemented a comprehensive system designed to operate in the department's financial management centers around the world. Other federal agencies have yet to develop agencywide financial management information systems, though all seem to be moving in that direction. In the meantime, all agencies report extensive and varied applications of information technology throughout their organizations (Botner, 1988a, pp. 2–3).

At the state and local levels, one of the most interesting developments in information technology has been the design and implementation of information systems integrating budgeting, accounting, personnel, performance reporting, and auditing. In Maryland, for example, the Statewide Accounting and Reporting System (STARS) began by integrating budgeting and accounting data; personnel and performance information are now being incorporated into the system as well (Botner, 1983, pp. 134–135). Similar developments in most other states have important management implications. To the extent that budgetary and performance data are made available to the chief executive and other top managers on a timely basis, more effective management decisions will be possible. In addition, freeing budget analysts from the more mundane aspects of budgetary procedures should allow more attention to planning and analysis.

Similar developments have occurred at the local level, especially since the advent of microcomputers has made advanced information technology available to even the smallest communities. Applications at the local level, as elsewhere, have typically taken place first in the area of financial management; however, a variety of other uses of information technology have been reported (Kraemer et al., 1981). Some applications are relatively mundane, such as keeping track of traffic tickets, but others involve fairly sophisticated computer models to develop routing patterns for police patrols or to simulate natural disasters and other emergencies. (We will discuss other computer applications in government in chapter 8.)

177

SUMMARY AND ACTION IMPLICATIONS

Budgeting and financial management in public organizations share much in common with those activities elsewhere. But there are also important differences, most of which flow from the necessity for public organizations to be accountable to elected officials and, ultimately, to the people.

The centrality of the budget to any organization can hardly be underestimated; if you want to know what's going on in an organization, look at where the money is going. Establishing budget processes that reflect the organization's priorities, while securing appropriate levels of involvement from all those who will want to affect the budget, is thus extremely important. Finding ways to present budgetary information clearly and comprehensibly is a great aid to decision makers and to the public. Finally, developing mechanisms to assure that the public's money is being spent both efficiently and responsibly is essential. You will find that knowing the technical side of the budget process—being able to follow the budget process and clearly understanding preparation, administration, and review—will be extremely helpful as you try to influence the operations of your organization.

If you work in a central budget office, you will find that the period during which the budget is formulated is intense, and your technical expertise will be put to the test. But you will also recognize that you are playing an important role in shaping public policies. Similarly, if you are managing an agency, you will place your imprint on the policies and directions of your organization through the budget process. Your skill in presenting and supporting requests for programs may determine whether or not they are undertaken.

The budget process at the federal level, and in some state and local jurisdictions, is integrated with a process for long-range planning. Federal agencies are asked to provide certain projections for the two-year period following the year for which the budget is being prepared, thus adding an element of long-range planning to the process.

Budgets and financial management systems are important tools for planning, prioritizing, and operating public programs, as well as important mechanisms for accountability and control. Public access to budgets and financial statements allows citizens to see how their interests are reflected in the actual conduct of government. Budgets and other financial documents that clearly show what is happening in an agency are a necessary part of operating in the public interest.

TERMS AND DEFINITIONS

Accounting: The process of identifying, measuring, and communicating economic information to permit informed judgment and decision making.

Allotments: Amounts that agencies are authorized to spend within a given period.

Apportionment: Process by which funds are allocated to agencies for specific portions of the year.

Appropriation: Legislative action to set aside funds and create budget authority for their expenditures.

Authorizing legislation: Legislative action that permits establishment or continuation of a particular program or agency.

Bond: Promise to repay a certain amount (principal) at a certain time (maturity date) at a particular rate of interest.

Budget padding: Proposing a higher budget than is actually needed.

Business cycle: Periods of economic growth featuring inflation and high employment followed by periods of recession or depression and unemployment.

Capital expenditures: Spending for items that will be used over a period of several years.

Continuing resolution: Resolution permitting the government to continue operating until an appropriation measure is passed.

Debt capacity: Value of resources combined with the ability of the government to draw on them to provide payment.

Deferral: Decision by the president to withhold expenditure of funds for a brief period.

Discretionary spending: That portion of the budget still open to changes by the president and Congress.

Entitlement programs: Programs that provide a specified set of benefits to those who meet certain eligibility requirements.

Excise tax: Tax applied to the sale of specific commodities.

Fiduciary funds: Funds used when government must hold assets for individuals or when government holds resources to be transmitted to another organization.

Fiscal policy: Public policy with respect to the impact of government taxation and spending on the economy.

Fiscal year (FY): Government's basic accounting period.

General fund: Fund that handles the "unrestricted" funds of government.

Gross National Product (GNP): Measure of total spending in the economy; includes total personal consumption, private investment, and government purchases.

Impoundment: Withholding of funds authorized and appropriated by law.

Item veto: Allows a governor to veto specific items in an appropriations bill.

Line-item budget: Budget format for listing categories of expenditures along with amounts allocated to each.

Performance auditing: Analysis and evaluation of the effective performance of agencies in carrying out their objectives.

Performance budget: Budget format organized around programs or activities, including various performance measurements that indicate the relationship between work actually done and its cost.

Planning-programming-budgeting system (PPBS): Effort to connect planning, systems analysis, and budgeting in a single exercise.

Preaudit: Review in advance of an actual expenditure.

Progressive tax: One that taxes those with higher incomes at a higher rate.

179

Proportional tax: One that taxes everyone at the same rate.

Proprietary funds: Used to account for government activities that more closely resemble private business.

Reconciliation bill: Legislative action that attempts to reconcile individual actions in taxes, authorizations, or appropriations with the totals.

Regressive tax: One that taxes those with lower incomes at a proportionally higher rate than those with higher incomes.

Rescission: Presidential decision to permanently withhold funds.

Risk management: Ways that public organizations anticipate and cope with risks.

Supplemental appropriation: Bill passed during the fiscal year adding new money to an agency's budget for the same fiscal year.

Zero-base budgeting: Budget format that presents information about the efficiency and effectiveness of existing programs and highlights possibilities for eliminating or reducing programs.

STUDY QUESTIONS

1. Discuss how government uses the budget to affect fiscal policy.
2. Describe some of the ways government obtains funds for operation. Identify the various types of taxes that governments use.
3. How does the government spend the money it collects?
4. The budget cycle consists of four major phases. Discuss government's role in the budget cycle and the components of each phase.
5. Allen Schick suggests three different purposes of the budget. Identify and define these purposes.
6. Compare and contrast the different types of budgeting processes.
7. Explain the two basic concepts of budgetary strategies.
8. Political influence has a major impact on the budgetary process. What are some of the strategies managers use to influence the budget process?
9. Financial management is also an important part of fiscal activities. Discuss some of the concerns fiscal managers deal with, including capital budgeting, debt management, risk management, and purchasing.
10. Discuss the broad types of funds that public organizations use.

CASES AND EXERCISES

1. Revenues, especially at the state and local levels, can vary dramatically from year to year or even month to month, depending on both public actions and economic fluctuations. A *Wall Street Journal* article (June 1, 1988, p. 50) described the following shifts in revenue expectations:

What a difference a year makes.

Last May, California state government was unexpectedly awash in excess tax revenue. Eventually the state rebated some $1.1 billion to taxpayers.

Today, California is staring at an annual revenue shortfall of $1 billion for this year and a similar amount next year. Shocked state officials are now trying to figure out ways to cut spending and raise revenue. The turnaround, says state finance director Jesse Huff is "mind boggling."

The nation's most populous state isn't alone in its predicament. After a big surplus last year, New York faces a $900 million shortfall in its current budget. Massachusetts is looking at about $200 million less than expected for its coming fiscal year. Other states are faced with similar problems.

Assume that you are Director of Motor Vehicle Registration for your state. Your agency, with offices scattered all across the state, is responsible for registration and licensing of cars, trucks, and other vehicles. About six months into the fiscal year, the governor announces that all state agencies will have to finish the fiscal year with expenditures 5 percent less than originally budgeted. You have already spent half your yearly allocation, so the reduction means you actually have to cut spending by 10 percent over the next six months. How would you go about complying with the governor's order?

2. On December 1, 1988, Larry Rice, the City Manager of Lakewood, Colorado, submitted the 1989 budget to the mayor and city council of Lakewood. Part of that budget dealing with activities in the public works area is shown in Figure 5.1. A public works summary page shows the 1987 actual, 1988 budgeted and estimated, and 1989 proposed expenditures, first by program, then by category of expenditure, then by source of funds.

Following the summary page, there are two pages detailing public works activities in the area of snow and ice removal (line 9 of the summary). Information is provided about performance standards, current services, and program objectives. Although the 1989 budget assumes a relatively flat revenue projection, several new budget initiatives are included, one of which is removal of snow from all residential streets when snow depth reaches six inches. (Note the increase in start-up and annual costs this item involves.)

Analyze these budget pages from the perspective of (1) a city council member who will have to make decisions about which city services to fund; (2) the public works department director who wants to improve services to the community; and (3) an average citizen interested in seeing whether the city's tax dollars are being put to good use. For the purposes of each viewpoint, how complete and clear is the information? Does the budget tell you what you want to know in order to act? Does it present a convincing case for the initiative it contains? How might the budget presentation be improved?

3. Consider the following case. You are Mike Smith, Chief Procurement Officer for a major university. Work generated by your staff of 20 procurement specialists includes writing proposals to vendors and evaluating the vendors' bids. To write those bids, the procurement specialist works with someone from the university agency who is knowledgeable about the project. Tom Drake, a procurement specialist, is currently working with

PROGRAM	1987 ACTUAL	1988 BUDGET	1988 ESTIMATED	1989 BUDGET
Public Works Administration	$ 251,388	$ 212,983	$ 199,369	$ 196,298
Traffic Signals	788,913	957,404	1,182,739	934,777
Traffic Control	592,166	648,585	594,926	661,744
Street Lighting	808,501	945,752	901,500	920,652
Design Inspections and Survey	813,850	929,998	816,879	838,401
Development Review	342,080	366,324	354,618	368,022
Street Maintenance	1,604,400	1,561,003	1,607,462	1,592,208
Street Cleaning	423,154	484,322	483,094	497,097
Snow and Ice Removal	417,428	285,397	283,322	409,817
Street Resurfacing/Concrete Rehab.	2,611,102	2,000,342	2,720,000	2,003,384
Drainage Maintenance	379,232	351,007	315,382	304,545
Drainage Improvements	621,173	1,317,500	252,500	600,000
Capital Improvements:				
Street Construction	3,085,010	4,580,205	2,898,500	505,000
Fleet Management	(1,093,554)	(1,169,483)	(1,140,596)	(1,149,398)
Water Utility	400,086	--	558,154	500,333
Sewer Utility	1,385,950	2,852,892	2,165,168	2,731,163
TOTAL	$ 14,524,433	$ 17,493,714	$ 15,333,613	$ 13,063,441

CATEGORY	1987 ACTUAL	1988 BUDGET	1988 ESTIMATED	1989 BUDGET
PERSONAL SERVICES	$ 3,503,068	$ 3,552,303	$ 3,435,311	$ 3,512,808
OPERATING AND MAINTENANCE SUPPLIES	665,666	644,114	655,276	656,050
CHARGES AND SERVICES	3,802,154	4,136,768	4,397,995	5,051,861
CAPITAL OUTLAY	6,553,545	9,160,529	6,845,031	3,842,722
TOTAL	$ 14,524,433	$ 17,493,714	$ 15,333,613	$ 13,063,441

FUNDS	1987 ACTUAL	1988 BUDGET	1988 ESTIMATED	1989 BUDGET
GENERAL	$ 6,141,818	$ 6,325,775	$ 6,160,866	$ 6,323,561
CAPITAL IMPROVEMENT FUND	4,173,076	4,654,592	4,743,738	3,508,384
GRANT CAPITAL FUND	845,269	--	390,000	--
CENTRAL GARAGE REVOLVING	(1,093,554)	(1,169,483)	(1,140,596)	(1,149,398)
STREET BOND	1,578,234	--	1,315,687	--
NONREVENUE INTERGOVERNMENTAL RESOURCE	--	3,660,455	--	--
WATER AND SEWER FUNDS	1,786,036	2,852,892	2,723,322	3,231,496
TOTAL	$ 14,524,433	$ 17,493,714	$ 15,333,613	$ 13,063,441

Figure 5.1   City of Lakewood: Department of Public Works budget summary

Kathy Kline of the Communications Department to develop a bid proposal to purchase a new campuswide telephone system that includes a quick-dial feature. The university's current telephone system was installed 15 years ago by Regional Telephone, and over

182

DEPARTMENT: Public Works   PROGRAM: SNOW AND ICE REMOVAL

FUNCTIONAL DESCRIPTION:

This program provides for the removal of snow and ice from the City street system (not including State Highways) and selected bikeways and sidewalks by plowing and sanding.

SERVICE STANDARDS: Services are standard when:

1. All plows and sanders are hooked up within 90 minutes after notification of a coming storm and before every weekend and holiday through winter for faster deployment.

2. 75% of crews are on their routes within 1-1/2 hours of being called.

3. Plowing begins on priority #1 and #2 streets when snow depth reaches 2". Plowing/sanding continues until all priority streets are cleared within 48 hours after the end of the storm.

4. All residential streets (not priority 1 or 2) are plowed when snow depths reach 6". Plowing is completed within 48 hours after the end of the storm.

5. Plowing or sanding requests received from citizens are written up for completion by snow removal crews and completed within 72 hours after the end of the storm, except during extremely heavy snowfalls when this time is increased.

CURRENT SERVICE EVALUATION:

1. Met.

2. Met and exceeded.

3. Met. Plowing starts at 2". Priority 1 and 2 streets are cleared within 48 hours after the end of a storm.

4. Not met. Non-priority residential streets are currently not plowed except in storms of over 18" - 24".

5. Met.

PROGRAM OBJECTIVES FOR THE COMING YEAR:

1. Meet service standard #4 to plow all residential streets when snow depth reaches 6 inches, at an annual cost of about $38,000 and $28,000 in initial start up costs.

2. Computerize record keeping.

3. Replace worn out sanders and plows in kind.

STATISTICS:	1983	1984	1985	1986	1987	1988 Estimated	1989 Budget
Number of deployments	24	19	21	17	19	15	15
Tons of sand/salt used	7905	3816	8493	4186	11,542	5,000	5,000
Inches of snow	151	118	76	78	107	75	75
Number of complaints	2385	249	528	583	1,648	500	500
Man Hours	13,836	7378	10,363	7053	13,900	8,000	8,000

183

Figure 5.1 continued

the last few years, Regional and one other vendor have sold add-on equipment to five of the university's fifteen departments. This add-on equipment is expensive and represents a major investment to the five departments, one of which is the Communications

DEPARTMENT: Public Works   PROGRAM: SNOW AND ICE REMOVAL

PROGRAM EXPENDITURE SUMMARY:

	1987 ACTUAL	1988 ESTIMATED	1989 BUDGET
PERSONNEL	$ 133,491	$ 119,727	$ 136,709
SUPPLIES	103,970	50,298	52,298
SERVICES	153,904	113,297	167,310
CAPITAL OUTLAY	26,063	--	53,500
TOTAL	$ 417,428	$ 283,322	$ 409,817

PROGRAM FUND SOURCES:

GENERAL FUND	$ 417,428	$ 283,322	$ 409,817

PERSONNEL ASSIGNED:

	1987 ACTUAL	1988 ESTIMATED	1989 BUDGET
Maintenance Operations Manager	.10	--	.10
Maintenance Supervisor	.40	.30	.30
Maintenance Crew Leader	.40	.40	.40
Clerk III	.25	.25	.25
Maintenance Specialist III	.50	.50	.50
Maintenance Specialist II	1.00	1.00	1.00
Maintenance Specialist I	.70	.60	.60
Maintenance Worker II	.80	.70	.70
TOTAL	4.15	3.75	3.85
Part Time	--	--	3,652 hr.

GENERAL COMMENTS:

The Snow and Ice Control Program has two shifts that are on rotation for 12 hours. There are ten priority #1 routes consisting of 247 lane miles and 6 zones of priority #2 routes with 265 lane miles.

In 1989 smaller units throughout various City Departments will be equipped with plows and used to clear residential streets when snow depth reaches 6 inches. Existing City employees will be utilized to operate the plow units.

Figure 5.1 continued

Department. Departments that have the quick-dial equipment are pleased with the results; departments that do not have quick-dial cannot afford it and are unhappy with Regional.

Tom has updated you on the status of the proposal. The communications office has insisted throughout the proposal process that the new phone system must be capable of using the existing quick-dial equipment. Tom tells you that if that is the case, only Regional and two or three other vendors would be able to bid on the system. Six other vendors with their own quick-dial equipment would not be able to respond to the bid. Tom explains that in some cases, a whole new system was less expensive than hooking up one of Regional's systems to existing quick-dial equipment. Tom also tells you he has heard that several staff members from the Communications Department have threatened to quit if the bid goes to a company other than Regional. After 15 years, they feel Regional is the best and only qualified vendor. Tom wants to know how he should proceed to satisfy both the university's needs and the vendors' rights to a fair bidding process.

1. How should Tom proceed to ensure that all bidders have an equal chance to participate in the bid process?
2. How can the procurement office avoid the practice of vendors helping buyers to write a bid proposal?
3. What about Tom's responsibility to taxpayers? (Several thousands of dollars would be wasted if the quick-dial equipment already purchased was scrapped.)

SOURCE: This case was provided by Bill Carney.

4. The following is an exercise in zero-base budgeting: As Superintendent of the Highway Patrol, you have been advised by your department head that only $13,950,000 will be available the next fiscal year for expenditure by the Highway Patrol. You have four decision units that could each achieve several performance levels with different funding levels. Rank your decision packages in order of decreasing benefit.

Function: Enforcement Activities, Highway Patrol

Decision units
A. Traffic patrol
B. Criminal investigations
C. Checking of trucks
D. Citizen education

Decision packages	Increments	Cost per increment
A–1	1,000,000 miles	$8,000,000
A–2	500,000 miles	4,000,000
A–3	500,000 miles	4,000,000
B–1	3,000 investigations	600,000
B–2	1,000 investigations	200,000
B–3	1,000 investigations	200,000
C–1	10,000 truck checks	500,000
C–2	5,000 truck checks	250,000
C–3	5,000 truck checks	250,000
D–1	500 seminars	100,000
D–2	250 seminars	50,000
D–3	250 seminars	50,000

SOURCE: This case was provided by Stanley Botner of the University of Missouri–Columbia.

5. The following simulation reenacts a series of budget discussions held at the University of Southern Anonymous (USA) during a time of significant budget reductions. To conduct the simulation, divide the class into five groups, each of which will represent one character in the simulation. All students in the class should read the following general description of the situation facing USA. Then members of each group should read *only* the character description assigned to their group. (It is important that you read *only* the description assigned to you.) The role descriptions of the following characters begin on page 187.

Vice President Cooper
Dean Berryderry, College of Liberal Arts
Dean Stevens, Dean of Science
Dean Dudley, Dean of Education
Dean Dollar, Dean of Business

After everyone has had a chance to read the general description of the situation and the specific information pertaining to their character, each character group should meet separately for fifteen to twenty minutes. During this period, the group should (1) select a representative of the group to play the character at a meeting to be held in Vice President Cooper's office, and (2) develop detailed strategies and information for that person to use in representing your group's interests in the meeting.

Following the individual group meetings, the five individuals selected to play the five characters should meet around a table near the middle of the room. Vice President Cooper will call the meeting to order, present any opening remarks he or she wishes to make, then preside over the remainder of the discussion. All other students should remain quiet during this part of the simulation. During the course of the meeting, any member may request a recess to consult with his or her group (for no longer than five minutes). When the meeting in Vice President Cooper's office reconvenes, the person who called the recess will have the floor. The meeting should continue until a consensus is reached concerning the reductions or until Vice President Cooper feels the meeting is stalled and he or she will have to make a decision independently. Enjoy the discussion!

General Description of the Situation

The University of Southern Anonymous (USA) has been informed by the state administration that its budget for the current year will be reduced by several million dollars. The President of the University, I.M. Fearless, has informed Vice President for Academic Affairs Cooper that the various colleges in the university will be required to reduce their budgets by an average of 8 percent. In turn, Vice President Cooper has chosen not to implement across-the-board cuts of 8 percent for all colleges, but has discussed different target percentage reductions with each of the deans of the four colleges—Liberal Arts, Science, Education, and Business. In response to a request from several of the deans, Vice President Cooper has called a meeting of the four deans to get their reactions to his targeted amounts for each college and to find out how each college plans to implement the required reduction.

By way of background, USA is a medium-sized midwestern university with the mission of providing students with a broad-based liberal arts education as well as limited graduate programs, primarily in business and education. The school serves a regional constituency in the southern part of the state, though it draws students from around the country, many of whom first heard of USA because of its reputation as a leader in intercollegiate billiards. (In fact, some cynics refer to USA as "Cue U.")

Though the university has traditionally enjoyed a good relationship with the governor and members of the legislature, President Fearless has antagonized many in the state capitol with his rough and abrasive manner. Similarly, many on campus see the president as bringing the university the same administrative style he employed as a colonel in the Marine Corps. Despite these difficulties, most academic programs at the university are considered sound, with some exceptions. Similarly, many feel some programs are not suited to the mission of a regional midwestern university, notably the school's long-standing program in oceanography, which some feel is out of place because the university is 700 miles from the nearest ocean.

Character Descriptions

Vice President Cooper

Though you have been vice president at USA for five years, you have never faced such a difficult situation. You recognize that the university's president is in some political trouble and may be asked to resign soon. As a ploy to reduce the heat on his office, he has passed on the largest part of the budgetary reductions to you. If you can come through this situation in good shape, you will receive considerable notoriety and be a likely candidate for the presidency should the president be forced to resign. You will, however, need to be sure that you maintain the support of all the deans of the colleges, for their support is essential for your promotion. On the other hand, a major disruption at the university, in which you might lose support of the deans, would end any chances of your attaining your ambition. In fact, you might be fired along with the president!

Given the instructions from the president, there seems to be little you can do other than to assign reductions to the colleges. After reviewing the various programs within the colleges, however, you have decided that across-the-board cuts would be inappropriate and that some colleges could indeed stand to be cut more than others. You have, therefore, assigned differential reductions to each college, with Education receiving the greatest reduction (20%), Liberal Arts receiving the second greatest reduction (10%), Science next (7%), and Business last (2%). You have chosen these figures based on your assessment of the quality of programs, the quantity of students (faculty/student ratios), the nature of the programs, and their suitability to the mission of your university.

The total reductions you have assigned to the deans exceeds the total the president has required you to complete. Your reasons for this strategy are twofold: (1) if any of the deans complain too loudly, you can fall back to the figure you actually need as a compromise, and (2) if you persuade all the deans to accept the assigned reduction, then you will have some money available for internal reallocations, which you would like to achieve anyway.

For the most part, you are willing to let the various deans assign reductions within their colleges as they see fit, so long as each seems to be doing a thorough job in the assignment. Later, if there is money available, you can make other needed reallocations to add needed new programs or strengthen others.

However, you are personally interested in a couple of particular areas. First, your favorite uncle chairs the oceanography program. Second, your own degree is in Higher Education Administration, and you have enjoyed periodic classroom visits to that department. Third, the governor has expressed a strong interest in the integrity of the public administration program.

Dean Berryderry

College of Liberal Arts (target reduction—10%). You approach the meeting with the vice president with some trepidation, for you realize that your college is likely to be high on the list of cuts. Obviously you would prefer across-the-board cuts that would not place a special burden on your college. Several of your programs, however, are of minimal quality and simply have not been attracting students over the years. For example, your program in German has graduated an average of two majors a year over the past several years, while having a faculty of three. Several other programs, such as anthropology and geography, are showing similar results. These programs, however, are important to a broad-based liberal arts education. You feel that students should at least have the opportunity to enroll in such programs if they see fit.

On the other hand, there are some programs currently housed in your college you would just as soon see ended. For example, the graduate program in public administration is a professional program that you feel is inconsistent with the liberal arts perspective of the college. The total faculty salaries in this department would just about equal the total by which you need to reduce your budget. This is an obvious area to eliminate.

Next, it has occurred to you that your staff of professional advisors could be eliminated and all academic advising performed by members of your faculty. This could be accomplished with no faculty or program reductions.

You feel a natural alliance with the College of Science and would prefer to see reductions occur in either Education or Business rather than in Liberal Arts or Science. However, Dean Stevens of the College of Science has always been somewhat antagonistic toward you, perhaps because of your critical remarks about the oceanography program, which you think should be eliminated.

Finally, several personal considerations enter into your thinking. First, if the vice president were to become president, you would probably be the leading candidate for the vice presidency. You would find that very attractive. Second, though you don't want to appear to favor any department, your home department, the Department of Political Science, is putting strong pressure on you to support expansion of the program. Across-the-board cuts *within* your college would make that impossible. Third, a member of your faculty was recently offended by sexual advances from the dean of the School of Business, Dean Dollar.

Dean Stevens

Dean of the College of Science (target reduction—7%). You have conducted a thorough analysis of the possibilities for reduction within your college. You feel that by eliminating one visiting professorship, four graduate teaching assistantship positions, and two staff positions, you'll be able to accommodate the reductions. You are quite aware, however, that others see your Department of Oceanography as a primary target for elimination. This is, however, one of your oldest and strongest programs, certainly one of the leading oceanography programs in the midwest. You want to protect the program as it is; however, even if you are required to reduce that program, you wish to do so only by eliminating several faculty positions rather than the entire department. You also feel this program will be protected because the chair of that department is the vice president's uncle.

Several other personal considerations affect your thinking. First, you feel that the entire College of Education could be eliminated with no real loss to the university. Other programs within the state clearly produce enough graduates in that field. Eliminating the entire college would mean no reductions would be needed in any other college. Second, you think Dean Berryderry is an idiot. You were especially incensed by Berryderry's comments about oceanography. If Berryderry can't run his own college, why try to run yours? Third, one of your faculty members recently was offended by sexual advances from the Dean of the School of Business, Dean Dollar.

Dean Dudley

Dean of the College of Education (target reduction—20%). You know you are in trouble! Over the past several years, enrollments have been dropping in Education to the point that you are considerably overstaffed. At the same time, other programs in the state have developed and now have better reputations. This is especially true of the Department of Higher Education Administration. The main campus of the university boasts one of the country's leading programs in this area. Your best hope is to argue for across-the-board cuts that would affect all colleges equally. Your suspicion is that the College of Business will receive the lowest reduction and the College of Liberal Arts and the College of Science will be somewhere above. One of them would probably benefit from across-the-board cuts as opposed to targeted reductions; the other would probably lose—but you don't know which one.

In addition, several personal considerations guide your thinking. First, nearly all the athletes who are part of the school's winning billiards program are students in your college. You doubt if they could pass their coursework elsewhere. Second, the chair of the Department of Higher Education Administration has been one of your strongest critics over the years, and eliminating that department would eliminate one of your biggest problems. Third, a member of your faculty was recently offended by sexual advances from the Dean of the School of Business, Dean Dollar.

Dean Dollar

Dean of the School of Business (target reduction—2%). Though you realize that your college will have to take a token reduction, you are certain that your reduction is far less than that required from other schools. Consequently, you are highly supportive of the vice president's selective reduction and opposed to across-the-board cuts. Your college has grown by leaps and bounds in the past several years, and you are in desperate need of more faculty, not less. At the same time, salaries have increased dramatically in your field, and retention of capable faculty is a problem. You can probably accommodate the reductions assigned to you through minimal staff changes and will not have to fire faculty.

You see all this as a possibility for considerable reorganization of programs. One program that you would particularly be interested in bringing into the college is that in public administration. This program is viewed with great favor by the governor and consequently by those higher in the university's administration. Moreover, the program would seem to be consistent with the interest of your college in management. You wonder if perhaps somewhere in all of this redistribution of money you might be able to acquire a new program. If you can discredit Dean Berryderry's interest in public administration and champion that field, you should stand a good chance of receiving support from the higher administration. All in all, you see this process as opening the possibility of adding to your college rather than reducing it. This result, however, depends on selective reductions rather than across-the-board cuts and upon reallocations *beyond* the amount required for the president's stated budget reduction.

You also have several personal concerns. First, you think both the College of Education and the Department of Oceanography (in the College of Science) could be eliminated outright . . . and you could use the money. Second, you have heard that the chair of the Department of Oceanography is the vice president's cousin. Third, you have just met a very attractive person who is an advisor in the College of Liberal Arts. You think you are falling in love, again!

Do Not Read This Paragraph Until After the Simulation

190

Following the simulation, the entire class should discuss each group's strategies and tactics. Sometimes it is helpful to ask first what others thought each dean was trying to do, then ask that group to describe its strategy. Pay particular attention to strategies of cooperation and competition, as well as to strategies that have little to do with actual budget reductions. (For example, shifting a program from one location to another doesn't save the university any money.) Note also the inevitable lack of information, as well as the roles of rumor and false impressions in the budget process. Both these features are more typical of budget decisions than you might imagine! Finally, just for fun, have Dean Berryderry read the last line of his or her description; then have Dean Stevens do the same; then Dean Dudley; then Dean Dollar.

FOR ADDITIONAL READING

Axelrod, Donald. *Budgeting for Modern Government.* New York: St. Martin's Press, 1988.

Bahl, Roy. *Financing State and Local Government in the 1980s.* New York: Oxford University Press, 1984.

Levine, Charles H., ed. *Managing Fiscal Stress.* Chatham, NJ: Chatham House, 1980.

Levine, Charles H., Rubin, Irene S., and Wolohojian, George G. *The Politics of Retrenchment.* Beverly Hills, CA: Sage, 1981.

Lyden, Fremont J., and Lindenberg, Marc. *Public Budgeting in Theory and Practice.* New York: Longman, 1983.

Lynch, Thomas D. *Public Budgeting in America.* 2nd ed. Englewood Cliffs, NJ: Prentice-Hall, Inc., 1985.

Mikesell, John L. *Fiscal Administration.* 2nd ed. Pacific Grove, Calif.: Brooks/Cole, 1986.

Musgrave, Richard A., and Musgrave, Peggy B. *Public Finance in Theory and Practice.* 4th ed. New York: McGraw-Hill, 1984.

Pechman, Joseph A. *Federal Tax Policy.* 4th ed. Washington, DC: The Brookings Institution, 1983.

Rabin, Jack, and Lynch, Thomas D., eds. *Handbook on Public Budgeting and Financial Management.* New York: Marcel Dekker, 1983.

Rubin, Irene S., ed. *New Directions in Budget Theory.* Albany: State University of New York Press, 1988.

Rubin, Irene S. *The Politics of Public Budgeting.* Chatham, NJ: Chatham House, 1990.

Wildavsky, Aaron. *The New Politics of the Budgetary Process.* Glenview, IL: Scott, Foresman, 1988.

THE MANAGEMENT OF PUBLIC PERSONNEL

Nothing is more critical for an administrator than to effectively manage the people who work in his or her organization. Yet the hiring and treatment of public employees often seem so bound up in rules, regulations, and "red tape" that effective management is extremely difficult. Many managers feel that civil service systems (and central personnel offices), originally designed to attract and retain competent personnel, exist merely to complicate the manager's life and make it more difficult to manage. Instead of simply hiring someone for a job, the manager must advise an applicant to take a competitive examination and join many other candidates on a register for the position (some of whom may be given special preferences in the hiring process) and then to wait until all the paperwork clears. After someone has been hired, the manager finds there are limits to the "rewards and punishments" that can be offered to encourage improved job performance; and, should the person fail to perform adequately, the paperwork and justifications required to terminate his or her employment seem endless. You may wonder how anything else gets done!

But there are good reasons for the way personnel management in government has developed. Even though it is true that some civil service systems have become overly rigid, even "fossilized," most of the requirements relating to government employment are deeply rooted in important political and ethical principles. So an understanding of how government personnel systems operate not only includes knowledge of personnel techniques, but also a sensitivity to the values that underlie personnel systems in public organizations.

Nowhere is the contest between the competing values of efficiency and responsiveness played out more clearly than in the area of personnel. On the one hand, it is obvious that staffing government agencies with the most competent people available is essential to effective management. On the other hand, it is equally clear that those who staff the offices of government should be responsive to the citizenry. In any case, the personnel system for any public organization ultimately reflects the political priorities of the particular public involved. In some cases or in some periods, managerial concern for efficiency may receive preference; in others, the democratic concern for responsiveness may be uppermost.

MERIT SYSTEMS IN PUBLIC EMPLOYMENT

Because the Constitution made little mention of either administrative structures of government or how they would be staffed, early leaders at the federal, state, and local levels experimented with many different approaches to hiring, treatment, and firing. In the late 1800s, however, growing concern about the composition of the civil service led to a new focus on competence and professionalism and, in turn, to legislation establishing the **merit principle** in public employment. The merit principle, though widely varied in its application, generally means that selection and treatment of government employees should be based on merit or competence rather than on personal or political favoritism. Despite the apparent simplicity and appeal of this notion, the development of public personnel systems has been infused with controversy.

Spoils versus Merit

Most of the early American presidents followed George Washington's lead in seeking persons of high competence and integrity—what he called "fitness of character"—to hold governmental positions. This approach resulted in a stable and fairly skilled government work force, but not without several problems. Because there were few well-educated persons in society and because those with education tended to be from the wealthier classes, the newly formed civil service soon took on a somewhat elitist character. Moreover, partisan considerations began to enter into the process as well. Presidents and members of Congress began to recognize not only that government employees needed to be loyal to the new government (and presumably the party in power) but also that public offices (and salaries) could be rewards to the party faithful. Finally, there was the question of tenure—should civil servants hold office for life, thus providing experience and continuity, or should they change with each administration, providing loyalty (and jobs) to the incoming party?

All these concerns were dramatically illustrated in the administration of Andrew Jackson. Jackson was swept into office on a strong wave of democratic sentiment and was especially concerned with making government more accessible to those previously excluded, the "common people." Though Jackson was not the first to employ the **spoils system** (the notion that "to the victor belongs the spoils"—in this case, the ability to give government jobs to the party faithful), his administration was notable for its expansion of the system and for his elaborate justification of it. Jackson not only argued that

193

the common people had as much right to government jobs as the wealthy, but that most government jobs could be done without special training.

Jackson is sometimes portrayed as something of a villain for his defense of the spoils system, though far greater abuses occurred later at all levels of government. At the same time, however, Jackson made several rather positive contributions to democratic government; for example, there is no question that he democratized the civil service of his era and set a tone for greater representativeness within government agencies for decades to come.

Even Jackson could not have foreseen the corruption and abuse that would soon become associated with the spoils system (see Box 6.1). Succeeding presidents went far beyond Jackson in applying the system, as did political bosses at the state and local levels. The quality of the civil service rapidly declined, and even those who found jobs in government became disenchanted with the financial contributions exacted from them each election year. The system also became a problem for each new president, as thousands of office-seekers came to press their claims for patronage positions, and presidents soon grew weary of the long lines of people seeking jobs.

BOX 6.1

THE EARLY SPOILS SYSTEM

By the late 1800s, the spoils system was firmly a part of political life in most jurisdictions. One aspect of the system was collecting funds from appointees to help sustain the party in power. Although such practices persisted in some jurisdictions well into the 1950s and even 1960s, they were hardly as blatant as the tribute requested in this letter from a state party committee in 1870.

Dear Sir:

(We) have great and imperative need of funds at once, to carry the campaign to successful issue. An assessment of one per cent on the annual gross receipts of your office is therefore called for, and you will please inclose that amount, without delay, to the treasurer, E. S. Rowse, in the envelope inclosed.

This assessment is made after conference with our friends at Washington, where it is confidently expected that those who receive the benefits of Federal appointments will support the machinery that sustains the party which gives them pecuniary benefit and honor. The exigencies are great, and delay or neglect

> will rightly be construed into unfriendliness to the Administration. We do not look for such a record from you, and you will at once see the propriety and wisdom of the earliest attention to the matter.
>
> Isaac Sheppard
> Chairman of Committee
>
> SOURCE: Leonard D. White, *The Republican Era: A Study in Administrative History 1869–1901* (New York: The Free Press, 1958), p. 332.

These factors began to set the stage for reform, but even more important in eventually bringing about change was the increasing corruption in government. There were kickbacks from contractors, private sales of surplus public property, skimming of tax receipts, and many other abuses. Corruption was becoming a normal way of doing government business.

The various ills that grew from the spoils system eventually led to a strong and active reform movement, spearheaded by such groups as the National Civil Service Reform League. The reformers made both vigorous and eloquent appeals, but their eventual success was assured more by a historical accident, the assassination of President Garfield, than by eloquence. Though Garfield had hardly been a proponent of civil service reform and had indeed drawn criticism from the reform groups for his failure to support a reform bill, the fact that he was killed by a disappointed office-seeker made him a martyr for the reform cause.

A man named Charles Guiteau had hoped to be consul to Paris. After weeks of making his case and after repeatedly being turned away from Garfield's office, he followed Garfield into a train station and shot him twice in the back. As he did so, he shouted that now Chester Arthur, a noted spoilsman, would be president. The reformers capitalized on this comment, portraying the situation as the obvious result of the evil spoils system and, in a sudden change of heart (and reality), they described Garfield as a proponent of reform. After two more years of pressure, the Republican Congress finally acknowledged the rising sentiment for reform and passed the Pendleton Act, which was signed into law in January 1883.

The Pendleton Act is one of two landmark pieces of legislation in federal personnel administration (the other being the Civil Service Reform Act of 1978). The Pendleton Act was primarily an effort to eliminate political influence from administrative agencies and, secondarily, an effort to assure more competent government employees. It pursued these aims through the following major provisions:

1. A bipartisan commission, the U.S. Civil Service Commission, was created within the executive branch to establish and implement personnel rules and procedures for the federal government.

195

2. Open and competitive examinations to test job-related skills were developed wherever practical within the agencies covered by the law and were to become the primary basis upon which to make hiring decisions.

3. Employees were given protection against political pressures, such as assessments (mandatory contributions) or "required" participation in campaign activities.

4. **Lateral entry** into government positions (that is, entry at any level as opposed to entry only at the beginning level) was encouraged, thus maintaining an important element of Jacksonian openness.

5. Positions in Washington offices were to be apportioned among the various states, in an effort to provide geographical representation in the civil service.

6. The president was given the authority to extend coverage to other groups of government employees beyond the approximately 10 percent of federal employees covered by the Act.

These provisions, especially the last, provided the basis for the gradual extension of the idea of a *merit system* throughout most of the federal government as well as state and local governments. A respected writer on public personnel provides the following definition of the civil service system that emerged: "Throughout its history, the civil service idea has rested on three basic principles: (1) that the selection of subordinate government officials should be based on merit—the ability to perform the work rather than any form of personal or political favoritism; (2) that since jobs are to be filled by weighing the merits of applicants, those hired should have tenure regardless of political changes at the top of organizations; and (3) that the price of job security should be a willing responsiveness to the legitimate political leaders of the day" (Heclo, 1977, p. 20). The concept of "merit" is so central to the American approach to public personnel administration that "merit system" and "civil service system" have become almost synonymous.

The Pendleton Act, although it was important in establishing the notion of a merit system of public employment, merely provided a framework within which a more full-blown system might develop. Unfortunately, the development of the system was not well coordinated. Although the merit system was gradually extended to more and more government employees, the values of the system were not always the primary motivation for extension. For example, one unlikely set of agents for the extension of personnel reforms turned out to be out-going presidents, many of whom sought to "blanket in" those they had appointed to patronage positions by making their positions subject to the merit system. In this way, merit coverage was extended from its original 10 percent of all federal employees in 1883 to approximately 70 percent by the end of World War I and some 90 percent today.

Other changes in the system also occurred slowly. The Pendleton Act contained provisions for examinations, but other devices for improving the quality of the work force, such as position classification, standard pay schedules, and objective performance appraisals, had not yet been developed. Over the next decades, however, these ideas too became a part of the federal system of civil service. The Classification Act of 1923, for example, established a system for classifying jobs according to qualifications needed to carry them out and tying them to various pay grades, thus providing uniformity throughout the system.

196

Changes were also required to respond to a newly professionalized work force and a larger and more activist government. In the early days, the main jobs in government were essentially clerkships, but as government grew and entered new fields, there was a need for more professional and more highly specialized people. Similarly, especially through the Roosevelt years, a multitude of new agencies were created, each placing different demands on the personnel system. Prior to this time, the Civil Service Commission had assumed the role of the government's central personnel agency; now it was necessary to decentralize personnel responsibilities to the various agencies, with the Commission setting regulations and monitoring implementation.

In any case, the merit system has now become firmly established at the federal level. Nine out of ten federal employees are covered by either the general merit system or by one of several special systems created by law to pursue merit principles within specific agencies—the Postal Service, the Federal Bureau of Investigation, the Foreign Service, and so on. The remaining positions are exempt because they are not amenable to competitive selection or to regular personnel procedures; they include seasonal workers, those in intelligence, and a limited number of policy-making/confidential positions. Any incoming president now has only about 2,500 positions to fill on a purely political basis—a number that many think is still too high.

Many questions have been raised in recent years about whether there are too many political appointees in the federal government—or, in other words, whether the federal bureaucracy has become too highly politicized. This issue was especially pronounced during the first Reagan term, when the number of career executives decreased by 18 percent and the number of political appointees rose by 169 percent (Levine, 1986, p. 201). The growth in numbers of political appointees was accompanied by increasing centralization of the appointment process in the White House. At present, nearly all the several thousand political appointments that occur at the federal level—executives, members of boards and commissions, ambassadorships, and judgeships—are cleared through the White House personnel office.

The Civil Service Reform Act and Its Aftermath

For nearly a hundred years, the Pendleton Act provided the primary statutory basis for federal civil service. That changed with the passage and implementation of the Civil Service Reform Act of 1978. During the sixties and seventies, it became increasingly clear that there were serious problems in the federal personnel management system. The problems were in large part a result of the fairly haphazard pattern through which the system had been established. Responsibilities for various aspects of personnel management were spread among the president, the Congress, the courts, the Civil Service Commission, and the various agencies; but there was often not agreement on the basic principles that should guide the development of the system.

Even within the Civil Service Commission itself, there was confusion about the direction of personnel policy. On the one hand, the Commission existed to execute the president's personnel directives; on the other hand, it was also responsible for protecting employees from political abuse. At times, the two objectives came into conflict. As a result, the numbers of federal personnel rules and regulations were not only excessive, they often directly conflicted with one another.

President Carter made reform of the personnel system one of the central themes of his administration and targeted at least five problem areas.

1. *Technical overkill:* Critics charged that those in charge of the personnel function had, in their drive to achieve political neutrality, created overly detailed regulations for recruiting, testing, selecting, classifying, and releasing employees. In many cases, these technical rules became a maze that prevented rather than aided action, and sorting through the procedures to replace a key manager could take as long as two years. Firing one $8,000-a-year Commerce Department employee who consistently failed to show up for work without valid reasons took twenty-one months!

2. *Excessive protection of employees:* Similarly, many felt that the drive to achieve political neutrality created excessive protections for employees. Although these protections were initiated for the best of reasons—so that employees would not be unduly or arbitrarily punished or dismissed—they sometimes resulted in incredible outcomes, such as an award of almost $5,000 in back pay to a postal employee who had been fired for shooting a co-worker in the stomach! On the other hand, protections were needed in other areas; for example, employees who pointed out cases of waste, fraud, and abuse in public agencies—"whistle blowers"—were often subjected to harassment or even dismissal.

3. *Lack of management flexibility:* Managers, especially political appointees, claimed that civil service regulations were so inflexible that they could not manage effectively. In an effort to counter this tendency, one official in the Nixon administration prepared a document, known as the Malek Manual, suggesting 130 ways that managers could subvert the intent of the merit system and do what they wanted to do. One entry described how to get rid of someone who doesn't enjoy traveling: "[He] is given extensive travel orders criss-crossing the country to towns (hopefully with the worst accommodations possible) of a population of 20,000 or under. Until his wife threatens him with divorce unless he quits, you have him out of town and out of the way. When he finally asks for relief you tearfully reiterate the importance of the project and state that he must continue to obey travel orders or resign."

4. *Inadequate incentives to eliminate inefficiencies:* It was also charged that a system that seemed to grant raises according to longevity rather than performance and that made raises and promotion appear almost automatic encouraged inefficiency. Over 99 percent of the nearly three million federal employees regularly received satisfactory performance ratings that entitled them to raises. Alan Campbell (1978), a leading advocate of reform, wrote: "The current system provides few incentives for managers to manage or for employees to perform."

5. *Discrimination:* Many—notably women and minorities—felt the federal personnel system was not adequately promoting their representation within the bureaucratic ranks. They wanted to make sure that any new system would be more attentive to their interests and better able to cope with the increasing number of complaints in this area.

The Civil Service Reform Act was proposed to "restore the merit principle to a system which has grown into a bureaucratic maze" (Carter, 1978). (See Box 6.2.) The Act sought to deal with the often contradictory roles of the Civil Service Commission by creating a new Office of Personnel Management responsible for policy leadership and a Merit Systems Protection Board to handle investigations and appeals. OPM is "the President's principal agent for managing the federal work force"; it has responsibility for human resource management and enforcement of personnel regulations (Campbell, 1978, p. 100). The Merit System Protection Board, on the other hand, is the "watchdog" of the personnel system, hearing and resolving complaints, as well as protecting whistle blowers from reprisals. The previously conflicting responsibilities of the Civil Service Commission were split between the two new agencies.

BOX 6.2

CIVIL SERVICE REFORM: A NEW COMMITMENT

On January 19, 1978, in his State of the Union message, President Carter stated that he considered the reform of the civil service "to be absolutely vital." This marks the first time that an American president has included civil service reform among his major legislative priorities. The President is convinced that this reform is necessary to fulfill his promise of "a government that is efficient, open and truly worthy of our people's understanding and respect."

Consistent with his commitment, the President has forwarded to Congress two major initiatives aimed at better execution of the laws governing federal personnel management, and at better management of the people who operate within those laws. The first initiative is a Reorganization Plan, which would reassign the functions performed by the U.S. Civil Service Commission to two separate agencies: the Merit Systems Protection Board and the Office of Personnel Management. The reorganization plan provides the organizational framework necessary to carry forth the second initiative, the Civil Service Reform Act. This legislation, the product of the most comprehensive review of the civil service system since its inception nearly a century ago, will, as the President pointed out, "restore the merit principle to a system which has grown into a bureaucratic maze. It will provide greater management flexibility and better rewards for better performance without compromising job security."

Specific provisions of the reorganization plan and Civil Service Reform Act can best be described within the context of those conditions from which they emerged. Despite the fact that the views of federal managers and staffers, careerists and non-careerists, union members and nonunion members, frequently

199

(continued)

(continued)

are at odds, all agree that the personnel system within which they operate needs change. All of these groups complain of serious problems in the system, yet, to balance their competing interests in reform proposals has been very difficult to accomplish. How, for example,

- can widespread manipulations of the merit system be prevented without imposing constraints which would stymie the system;

- can an appeals system be designed to guarantee the procedural rights of employees without making managers reluctant to initiate legitimate adverse actions;

- can managers be given the authority with which to manage and employees the protection from abuses of that authority; and

- can efforts to bring about a federal work force representative of the American population be accelerated?

SOURCE: Excerpted from Alan K. Campbell, "Civil Service Reform: A New Commitment," *Public Administration Review*, 38 (March/April, 1978): 99. Reprinted with permission from *Public Administration Review*, © 1978 by the American Society for Public Administration (ASPA), 1120 G Street NW, Suite 500, Washington, D.C. 20005. All rights reserved.

Beyond establishing the two new agencies, perhaps the most striking feature of the Civil Service Reform Act was the creation of the Senior Executive Service (SES). Following ideas that had been discussed for nearly forty years and specifically proposed but not adopted in the Nixon years, the SES created a separate personnel system for the highest ranking civil service officials, permitting greater flexibility in assignments and establishing a new system of incentives for top-level managers. Basically, eligible managers would apply for positions in the SES and, if accepted, would hold SES rank as individuals, rather than being limited to the rank of a particular position. This meant that, within certain limitations, SES managers could be moved from agency to agency depending on their talents and the needs of the agencies. A new system of performance evaluations and pay increases closely tied to performance was also developed, along with an elaborate system of bonuses for exceptional executives.

In addition to these major features, the Civil Service Reform Act made several other changes: giving agencies greater flexibility to administer their own personnel systems, establishing a new and more sophisticated performance appraisal system, creating a merit pay system for managers just below the SES range, providing protection for whistle blowers, assigning the federal Equal Employment Opportunity program (previously with the Civil Service Commission) to the Equal Employment Opportunity Commission, and creating a more independent Federal Labor Relations Authority.

A number of questions have been raised about the Civil Service Reform Act directed primarily toward the possibility for greater political manipulation. There is no question that the Act sought to create greater responsiveness to the policy directives of the administration. Several actions of recent administrations seemed to go beyond the effort to assert policy direction, however, and to constitute attempts to politicize the civil service system. As one example, Edwin Meese, then counsel to President Reagan and later attorney general, distributed a memo indicating the possible use of political considerations in performance evaluations, which he described as important to ensure that the president's objectives were accomplished. Even more alarmingly, there were reports of "hit lists" of civil servants established within certain agencies. It remains to be seen whether President Bush will become involved in such activities. On the one hand, he has thus far been highly supportive of the career service; on the other hand, the Bush administration has been accused of politicizing certain presidential appointments, such as giving ambassadorships to relatively unqualified campaign supporters.

Since passage of the Civil Service Reform Act, there have also been questions about protection of employees under the Act. From the outset, there were concerns about the wisdom of having separate agencies responsible for personnel management and for the protection of the civil service. Bernard Rosen, a former Executive Director of the Civil Service Commission, argues that, despite the separation, responsibility for investigating both effectiveness and legal compliance would reside in OPM, an agency dominated by political appointees. Without the protection of a bipartisan commission, "the [Merit Systems Protection Board] is left with using reports of inspections made by a White House-controlled Office of Personnel Management and the protection of merit principles would range from quite modest to superficial. The watchdog would have a patch over one eye" (Rosen, 1978, p. 303). Rosen's fears seem to have been at least partially justified, as the Merit Systems Protection Board has been less than vigorous in its protection of employees.

201

A final criticism of the Reform measures is that they are based on an unnecessarily dim view of human nature, one that suggests senior managers are motivated primarily by greed (thus, rewards) and fear (thus, punishments). Such a view contrasts with much of modern management theory, which argues that such extrinsic motivators may actually "backfire," creating animosity and distrust (Thayer, 1978). Many members of the SES apparently agree, and express serious questions about the viability of the Senior Executive System pattern of rewards (Colby & Ingraham, 1981). The use of money alone as a motivator may be of limited effectiveness.

After more than a decade, the Civil Service Reform Act is still receiving mixed reviews. The most favorable opinion is that there is little wrong with the Act itself, but that implementation has been flawed by lack of funding and administration pressures to increase the number of political appointees. Others continue to suggest that the Act was based on questionable assumptions about the nature of the federal work force and was doomed from the beginning. In any case, the Civil Service Reform Act represented the first major change in personnel policy at the federal level since the Pendleton Act. Its confirmation of the principle of merit, its effort to sort out the multiple responsibilities of the personnel system, and its attempt to produce greater managerial flexibility have been significant. It remains to be seen whether those efforts are undercut by lack of funding from Congress and by presidential partisanship.

STATE AND LOCAL PERSONNEL SYSTEMS

Many of the same problems that led to institution of the federal civil service system in the late 1800s also existed at the state and local levels—indeed, the problems were often even more severe. Although the federal government was certainly influenced by politicians interested in maintaining power through patronage, it was never so completely dominated by political bosses and machines as were the states and, especially, the cities.

Even after the federal government created its civil service system, states and localities were slow to follow. New York adopted the first state civil service law in 1883, followed by Massachusetts the next year. It was twenty years, however, before another state joined these two. By 1935, only twenty states had adopted merit systems. Even today, only about 60 percent of state government employees are covered by merit systems.

The story is much the same at the local level: Albany, New York, was the first city to adopt a civil service system (1884), and a few other cities and counties followed prior to the turn of the century, but reform came slowly at the local level. Moreover, even where formal systems were adopted, patronage practices and political manipulation of the government work force continued. Chicago and Cook County were among the first to adopt civil service systems; yet even today, mayoral candidates often run on a platform of reducing machine control in Chicago. In any case, today almost 90 percent of local jurisdictions over 50,000 population have some type of merit system on the books.

202

In recent years, a primary motivator for adopting merit systems at state and local levels has been the number of federal laws requiring such systems in order for states and localities to receive federal funds. By 1980, every state and thousands of local governments had federal grants that required personnel systems that met a set of federal standards. The result has been that most state agencies receiving large amounts of federal funding are now covered by merit systems; those that receive limited or no federal funds are much less likely to have a merit system. In addition to these requirements, the courts have extended due process protections to many public employees and have supported affirmative action and other personnel-related actions that place greater burdens on state and local governments for detailed testing, classification, and reporting. Many states have thus found it advisable to establish or to extend merit concepts for their own protection.

Though the Reagan and Bush administrations have somewhat relaxed these regulations, it seems unlikely that state and local governments will return to massive use of the spoils system. Indeed, there is some evidence that governments are pursuing many of the same reforms pursued at the federal level in the late 1970s, which some charge have led to greater politicization of the public work force. For example, states and localities are experimenting with decentralization of personnel functions, greater responsiveness of managerial and political authority, and closer ties between performance appraisals and merit pay. Whether elected officials at state and local levels will be subject to the same temptation as were those at the federal level to employ the new devices in a more politicized approach to public personnel remains to be seen.

HIRING, FIRING, AND THINGS IN-BETWEEN

Most provisions of public personnel systems exist to protect public employees from excessive political interference; however, in some cases, they appear to make public personnel actions unduly complicated. Knowing the "rules of the game" will be a considerable help in your administrative work and will also be of help if you are looking for a job in a government agency.

Classification Systems

The key to most public personnel systems is the notion of **position classification,** the arrangement of jobs on the basis of duties and responsibilities and the skills required to perform them. A position classification system usually begins with a set of job descriptions, each based on a thorough analysis of the work and the required capabilities. A **job description** typically contains the following elements: job title, duties required, responsibilities associated with the position, and qualifications needed to carry out the job. A clerk-typist position, for example, might be described as including duties such as typing reports, maintaining correspondence records, answering telephone and walk-in inquiries, arranging for meetings and conferences on behalf of the supervisor, and other duties "as assigned." Qualifications might include such things as a high school degree or the equivalent, typing speed of 40 words a minute, and two years' secretarial experience.

Typically, sets of jobs that are closely related are then grouped together in classes that indicate increasing levels of difficulty—Clerk-Typist I, Clerk-Typist II, Clerk-Typist III, and so forth. In larger jurisdictions, such as the federal government, various classes may also be grouped into grade schedules that group jobs of varying levels of difficulty. For example, the federal General Schedule, which covers clerical and professional positions, lists within one grade, GS-11, a variety of different occupations.

Organizations use personnel classification systems for several reasons: to maintain an objective inventory of positions, to provide equity across similar jobs, to connect tasks and the skills required to perform them, and to provide standards for judging the work of specific employees. Historically, such systems developed out of a concern for objectivity and equity consistent with the idea of protecting employees from political abuse. The Position Classification Act of 1923, for example, required grouping jobs into classes on the basis of duties and responsibilities and, in language sounding much more contemporary, committed the federal government to providing "equal compensation for equal work, irrespective of sex." With this early impetus, most public organizations have developed rather sophisticated classification systems that are usually more advanced than their private sector counterparts.

The Recruitment Process

Having objective statements of duties, responsibilities, and qualifications makes it possible to recruit personnel based not on who one knows, but on what one knows and what

203

one can do. Recruitment efforts in the public sector must also be concerned with assuring fairness, openness, and representativeness. Typically, the recruitment process involves

1. Advertising or giving notice of a vacancy to be filled
2. Testing or otherwise screening applicants
3. Preparing a list of qualified candidates
4. Selecting someone to fill the position

In most jurisdictions, a personnel officer within a particular agency or someone from a central personnel department is significantly involved in the first three steps.

Testing or screening processes have been subject to special scrutiny in recent years. Screening can occur through a review of written applications and recommendations, aptitude or ability testing, performance examinations, interviews, or assessment centers. Of the various aptitude or ability tests that public organizations use, some measure general knowledge, others measure personality characteristics, and still others measure specific job-related knowledge or abilities. Performance examinations, such as typing tests, measure specific job capabilities.

The method of testing should relate to the job to be filled. Though individual interviews are a common part of the hiring process, for example, they tend to be poor predictors of eventual job performance. Generally speaking, **structured interviews,** in which a previously developed set of questions is used with each applicant, and *panel interviews* involving more than one interviewer are preferable. Similarly, carefully constructed assessment centers using several independent raters may be used. (An *assessment center* involves putting several job applicants through a series of job-related simulations to observe their performance under nearly "real-life" conditions.)

For almost a decade, the primary examination for entry-level administrative and professional positions in the federal government was the Professional and Administrative Career Examination (PACE). In 1982, however, the Reagan administration bowed to repeated challenges from groups charging that the test unfairly discriminated against minority applicants and discontinued use of the test. (Over the years, only 5 percent of blacks and 13 percent of Hispanics who took the PACE exam passed it.)

Through most of the eighties, the federal Office of Personnel Management has advised agencies to promote from within, to use noncompetitive appointments, or to use temporary appointments to fill vacancies—an approach that has obvious limitations in attracting and retaining "the best and the brightest" for government service. Recently, OPM has made efforts to develop a new hiring plan that would involve either a certain college grade-point average or successful completion of a newly designed achievement test.

In any case, after testing or screening, a small number of eligible applicants are certified and forwarded to the hiring agency, often with rankings based on the candidates' qualifications. Most merit systems require that at least the top three names be forwarded to the agency, so that the manager has some flexibility to consider personal or subjective characteristics in the final selection. This **rule of three** provision has proven controversial, however; many claim that it has been used as a device to discriminate against women and minorities. (Under this provision, a sexist employer could hire a white male even if a woman or a minority candidate were objectively more capable.) An equally controversial provision of many merit systems requires that veterans (or sometimes even relatives of veterans) receive extra points in the ranking system. Obviously, such a provision works against the interests of nonveterans, most of whom are women; as you might imagine, however, it is strongly supported by veterans' groups.

Pay Systems

Naturally, both the recruiting process and the individual's performance on the job are affected by compensation patterns, including both wages and benefits. Generally speaking, pay is determined by the nature of the work and the quality of performance in the job. But pay plans in the public sector are difficult to construct, for they must embody two often contradictory principles. On the one hand, to be fair and equitable, they must be highly structured; on the other hand, to be competitive, they must be responsive to changing political and economic conditions (Hays & Reeves, 1984, p. 142).

Most large personnel systems in government (including states and big cities) base their pay plans on their classification systems, which usually define a series of grades, each containing a set of jobs that are generally comparable in terms of difficulty, and a number of steps within each grade. These *steps* represent approximately equal increments of pay, with the highest generally about 20 to 30 percent above the lowest. In most cases, the grades are slightly overlapping, so that the first step in one grade is equal to one of the higher steps in the grade below. Individuals are assigned to a particular grade and step depending on how the position is described and on their individual qualifications for the position.

Employees in this type of system may receive pay increases in several ways. One way is to change grades; however, for an employee to change grades, either the particular position would have to be reclassified or all equivalent positions would have to be moved to a higher range. For an employee to receive increases within grade, either the entire pay plan can be adjusted upward, for example, through a legislative action to improve overall pay (e.g., through cost of living increases), or the individual can receive a raise. Raises can be based on several factors, ranging from seniority to merit pay, or pay for performance.

The idea of **merit pay** is simply that increases in salaries and wages should be tied to the actual quality of the work being done, so that those who perform better or more productively receive greater rewards. Although governments have used various merit pay systems, such systems have not always worked well. In many cases, the money available for merit raises for a few is spread so thinly that meritorious employees aren't differentiated from others. Part of the reason for this development is the difficulty of objectively measuring an individual's performance and the fact that many managers find it awkward to evaluate their employees' work.

As noted, the Civil Service Reform Act of 1978 sought to remedy this situation by requiring merit pay based on formal performance appraisal systems. Although agencies have been given considerable flexibility as to what systems they adopt, efforts have been made to base evaluations on critical elements of the individual's job or to develop results-oriented systems that tie evaluation to specific job outcomes. Any system of performance appraisal must be both accurate and fair:

> Performance-appraisal systems must be based on the *real* requirements of the task. They must reflect *realistic* levels of performance, and couched in terms that the workers

205

understand, while at the same time providing workers with some insights on where and how performance improvements need to be made. (Siegel & Myrtle, 1985, p. 337)

One aspect of compensation policy that has received substantial attention over the years is the comparability of wages and salaries in the public and private sectors. Though nearly all efforts to make such comparisons have been plagued by the difficulty of comparing apples and oranges, early studies tended to show public sector salaries considerably below those in the private sector (though the difference seemed to be partially offset by benefits packages offered in the public sector).

As a result, and in an effort to attract more capable people to the public service, the Federal Pay Comparability Act of 1970 and similar pieces of legislation at state and local levels were passed. The federal law, requiring pay rates comparable to those in the private sector for white collar employees, worked well until 1978, when raises were less than required to achieve comparability, a situation permitted under the law in cases of emergencies or poor economic conditions. Raises since 1978 have continued below comparable levels, to the point that the pay gap between federal employees and those in the private sector now averages about 22 percent. A similar situation exists at the state and local levels; indeed, pay differences are often even more pronounced here.

Conditions of Employment and Related Matters

206

There are several contemporary issues in personnel management that relate either to the conditions under which employees are hired or the conditions under which they must work. One of the most dramatic and widely publicized concerns of the past several years focuses on drug testing in the workplace. More and more employers, in both the public and private sectors, are recognizing that substance abuse is responsible for greater absenteeism, higher accident rates, and generally lower productivity. Consequently, programs have been established to identify and to aid or dismiss employees who have problems with drugs or alcohol.

Testing for drugs, primarily through urinalysis, has become quite common. Despite the fact that such programs violate personal dignity and have a variety of technical problems, a substantial number of private companies now use drug testing. Whereas in 1983 only about 3 percent of private firms used drug testing, today over 35 percent do so. Employees in private firms have little protection from testing and, in the absence of collective bargaining agreements to the contrary, may be tested at management discretion (Klingner, O'Neil, & Sabat, 1987, p. 1). Because public employees (at least civilian employees) are more clearly protected against illegal search and seizure and are guaranteed equal protection and due process, programs to test public employees have frequently been challenged in the courts. For the most part, the courts have held that random mandatory testing is a violation of employee rights, but that testing may be required where there is reasonable suspicion of abuse or where testing is made a part of the hiring process. But questions continue to be debated; for example, what type of testing is appropriate for those in "sensitive positions," such as air traffic controllers or those in contact with nuclear or chemical weapons (see Box 6.3).

This question has been central to recent efforts at the federal level to extend drug testing to many if not most federal employees. The federal program began with a presidential directive in 1986 requiring a drug-free workplace and urging the development

BOX 6.3

GUIDELINES FOR DRUG TESTING IN THE PUBLIC SECTOR

Although each organization may approach drug testing in a different way, there are a number of common questions that must be addressed in any drug testing program.

1. *Why does my organization need to test employees for illegal drug abuse?* There must be legitimate organizational reasons for embarking on employee drug testing. Employers may be prepared to support their program based on a well-grounded job-related rationale. Common justifications thus far have included:

   a. Concern for employee health and well being
   b. Concern for public safety
   c. Concern for safety of fellow employees
   d. Concern for maintaining a high level of integrity and public confidence
   e. Concern for conduct inconsistent with the essential mission of the agency
   f. Concern for high levels of productivity and performance

2. *Which specific positions within the organization will be subjected to testing?* Once an appropriate rationale has been determined, the next logical inquiry focuses on the composition of the relevant workforce. It is unlikely that all employees within the organization will need to be subjected to mandatory drug testing.

3. *Who should be tested—only current employees, applicants for positions or both?* Are you more concerned with the changing nature of the relevant recruitment pool than you are with the current job incumbents holding identified drug testing positions? If so, then applicant testing may be more important than testing only job incumbents. If your main concern is drug abuse among current employees, then applicant testing may not be necessary. It may be that the answer to the above question is "both."

4. *What set of circumstances will trigger the implementation of the testing program?* Testing programs are normally

(continued)

207

(continued)

conducted under any of the following sets of conditions: a. unannounced random testing; b. testing based on cause or impaired job performance; or c. following an accident.

5. *What drugs will be tested for?* An employer must answer this question based on an earlier analysis of the rationale behind the drug testing program and the perceived problems within the organization. Cost factors are also relevant here since the number of drugs screened will have an impact on the costs.

6. *Who will do the actual testing?* One of the most important decisions to be made in drug testing is the choice of the laboratory. Most organizations do not have the in-house capability to perform such testing so contracting-out becomes a necessity. Accuracy, reliability, promptness in reporting results, and costs are all important considerations in making a choice of testing laboratories.

7. *Should any personnel decision be made based on the results of a single test result?* According to the overwhelming consensus of medical authorities, the answer is a resounding "no!"

8. *What actions should be taken following a positive screening and a positive confirmatory test?* Sooner or later employers must determine what actions will result from their drug testing program. Will employees be reassigned, suspended, terminated, or given some chance at rehabilitation? Earlier it was stated that positive concern for the employee should be an important factor in modern personnel policies. Punishment and termination should be actions of last resort.

SOURCE: Copyright 1989 by the Institute of Public Affairs, University of South Carolina; all rights reserved. Reprinted by permission of the *Review of Public Personnel Administration* and Robert B. Elliott, "Drug Testing and Public Personnel Administration," Vol. 9, Summer 1989.

of testing programs, the conduct of training programs to help supervisors recognize symptoms of drug abuse, and the creation of counseling programs for problem employees. The testing provision was at first extended only to those in "sensitive" positions, while the courts sorted out the limitations that might be placed on more extensive random tests. Even so, hundreds of thousands of public employees are tested each year. Workers who test positive can be fired immediately; however, most are sent to rehabilitation programs.

At the state level, more than half the states have developed testing programs, either through legislation, executive order, or collective bargaining agreements. Most state programs limit testing to those in "sensitive" positions and regulate the number and kind of tests that can be used. Many permit testing job applicants even where persons already working in the same agency cannot be tested. Kansas, for example, requires drug testing at the time of hiring for state law enforcement officers who are authorized to carry a gun and for state corrections officers. Current employees may be tested if there is reasonable suspicion of drug use or concern that the employee may not be able to perform his or her duties safely. Although programs such as this are being implemented in many public agencies, legal challenges are still before the courts, and public managers are still trying to more clearly establish ways to treat those who may have problems with substance abuse.

Sexual harassment   Another contemporary concern is establishing a work environment that is supportive of all persons and sensitive to their needs, regardless of gender. One aspect of this concern is sexual harassment. **Sexual harassment** may be defined as any unwarranted and nonreciprocal verbal or physical sexual advances or derogatory remarks that the recipient finds offensive or that interfere with job performance. Sexual harassment especially includes (though is not limited to) situations in which one in a position of power or influence uses his or her position to encourage or coerce a subordinate or co-worker into undesired sexual activity. The courts consider sexual harassment a type of inequality that employers must deal with, both in terms of eliminating offensive behaviors and creating a less hostile or intimidating work environment for both men and women.

209

Despite attention to sexual harassment in many public organizations, a survey by the Merit Systems Protection Board found that 42 percent of all women working for the federal government said they had been sexually harassed in the past two years. Incidents cited included actual or attempted rape, pressure for sexual favors, deliberate touching, suggestive looks, and sexual remarks. Daniel R. Levinson, chairman of the board, estimated that the practice cost the federal government $267 million over two years in lost productivity and turnover (Havemann, 1988b, p. 31).

Although there appear to be many instances of sexual harassment, many remain unreported; for instance, the Office of Personnel Management reports only a handful of actual complaints. One reason for this situation may be the complex and often ambiguous procedures many organizations have for dealing with complaints, which are often lengthy, expensive, and psychologically draining. For this reason, many public organizations are currently reviewing their policies on sexual harassment, establishing more clearly the seriousness of the offense, and developing strong enforcement and disciplinary measures, including dismissal. The goal is not only to eliminate specific instances of harassment, but also to create a work environment that is fully supportive of the potential of all employees, both men and women.

AIDS policy   Related issues having to do with creating a positive work environment arise as public organizations, like others, struggle to deal with the AIDS epidemic. On the one hand, antidiscrimination laws appear to afford AIDS-infected employees the same protections as other handicapped employees; on the other hand, the organization may, in some cases, be held liable if someone contracts AIDS in the workplace.

The first concern was dealt with in a federal Office of Personnel Management directive issued in 1988. The policy prohibits discrimination against employees with AIDS and allows managers to take disciplinary action against anyone who refuses to work with an AIDS-infected employee. Among other things, the guidelines say that employees with AIDS "should be allowed to continue working as long as they are able to maintain acceptable performance and do not pose a safety or health threat to themselves or others in the workplace." Moreover, because there is no medical basis for someone to refuse to work with employees with AIDS, where managers feel that employees' refusal is "impeding or disrupting the organization's work, [the manager] should consider appropriate corrective or disciplinary action against the threatening or disruptive employees" (Havemann, 1988a, p. 34).

Removing Employees

For whatever reason, things occasionally don't work out on the job. An employee may not live up to expectations or may become unproductive. In cases such as these, your first step as a manager is to try to improve the individual's work (a strategy that is, of course, far easier than recruiting and training a replacement). You may encourage or counsel the employee, either personally or, better, through an employee assistance program. Or, in a surprising number of cases, you may be able to restructure the job so as to better motivate the employee. Concerns about an employee's work can often be addressed in positive and productive ways that are helpful to both the individual and the organization.

But if your efforts to help the employee fail, you may have to resort to disciplinary action, which might include formal reprimands, reduction of pay, suspension without pay, or outright dismissal. In all cases, it is important to be able to demonstrate that there is adequate cause for disciplinary action. Simply firing someone for personal reasons unrelated to the job opens both you and the organization to possible lawsuits; and, of course, firing someone for political reasons is contrary to the whole concept of merit employment in the public sector.

At the federal level, the Civil Service Reform Act encourages development of performance appraisal systems that make it easier for managers to document employee incompetence and remove them from the organization (although the managerial flexibility implied here has also made it easier to fire someone for political reasons). At the state and local levels, various court cases have indicated that employees being terminated have certain due process rights, such as advance notice and the opportunity for a hearing. In any case, if you decide to pursue disciplinary action, you should build a clear case to demonstrate the underlying reasons for your action.

THE CHANGING CHARACTER OF LABOR–MANAGEMENT RELATIONS

An interesting issue that cuts across the field of public personnel management is the rise and decline of public sector unions. At the federal level, many rather narrow issues,

210

having primarily to do with working conditions, are resolved through collective bargaining, though more controversial issues, such as compensation and hiring practices, are rarely considered. At state and local levels, there is a patchwork of labor relations practices, ranging from highly restrictive to extremely permissive labor legislation.

The early development of public sector unions was tied to the reform of the patronage system. With the establishment of merit principles in public employment, employees had greater protection from political intrusions, but they also had fewer direct ways to get the attention of political leaders. To combat the possibility that they might simply be ignored, public employees began organizing in the late 1800s and early 1900s. At first, political leaders strenuously opposed these efforts; at least two presidents issued *gag orders* to prevent federal workers from pursuing wage demands except through departmental channels. In response, the newly organized employees, led by the postal workers, pressed Congress for recognition, which they finally received in the Lloyd–LaFollette Act of 1912. The only statutory basis for public sector unionization for more than half a century, this act permitted federal employees to join unions (that did not advocate the right to strike) and to appeal directly to Congress.

With the early emergence of unions at the federal level, a few agencies, such as the Tennessee Valley Authority, developed rather advanced patterns of labor-management relations; elsewhere, however, public unions emerged relatively slowly, especially in comparison to their counterparts in the private sector. The slow development of public unions can be explained in part by the several difficult questions that public sector unionization raised for those in public organizations.

First there was the issue of sovereignty, the notion that the ultimate power to decide issues of public policy in a democracy lies with the people or their elected representatives and cannot properly be delegated, even partially, to some nongovernmental group such as a union. Illustrating this position, President Franklin Roosevelt wrote, "The process of collective bargaining, as usually understood, cannot be transplanted into the public service. . . . The very nature and purpose of Government makes it impossible for administrative officials to represent fully or bind the employer in mutual discussions. The employer is the whole people who speak by means of laws enacted by their representatives in Congress" (Klingner & Nalbandian, 1985, p. 292).

A second set of factors restricting the growth of public unions concerns the nature of governmental services, which are often considered either essential to the community (police, fire, national defense) or relatively unprofitable (systems of mass transportation). In the case of essential services, the ultimate union weapon—the strike—may be seen as holding the public interest hostage and can backfire; in the case of low-profit undertakings, the balancing factor of the market—the fact that a company may go out of business if pressed too far—does not appear to operate. In either case, the private sector model of collective bargaining seems to apply only loosely.

A third factor limiting the growth of public sector unions through much of this century is the varied nature of government employment and the difficulties this presents for unionizing. Traditionally, for example, unions have organized around occupational groups, such as truck drivers or garment workers. But government employs people in thousands of occupational groups; to have a union for each group would lead to endless and unsuccessful bargaining for both sides. The federal government is also characterized by geographic dispersion (only about 10 percent of the federal work force is located in

211

the Washington area), and the fact that there are so many white collar workers in government, who have been historically reluctant to organize. Thus, the question of finding an appropriate focus for union activity has been especially difficult at the federal level.

Yet unions have been able to organize. Sparked at least partly by the success of unions in the private sector, where the right to bargain collectively was never seriously questioned after passage of the Wagner Act in 1935, public employees continued to press for recognition of their right to negotiate labor-management disputes (see Box 6.4). Soon even the sovereignty argument was eroded; Secretary of Labor Willard Wirtz commented, "This doctrine is wrong in theory; what's more, it doesn't work" (Levitan, 1983, p. 6). Bills providing recognition for unions in the public sector were introduced (although unsuccessfully) in every session of Congress from 1949 to 1961.

BOX 6.4

EIGHT FACTORS THAT CONTRIBUTED TO THE GROWTH AND ACTIVISM OF PUBLIC EMPLOYEE ORGANIZATIONS

1. The inability of individual workers in a large bureaucracy to be heard by their employers unless they speak in a collective voice;
2. A growing sentiment within the less mobile, unskilled, semiskilled, and clerical labor force that concerted organized action is needed to increase their earning power and to protect their rights;
3. A greater appreciation by public employee organizations of the collective bargaining techniques used in the private sector;
4. An awareness among many unions that their strength in private industry is on the wane, and that the public service represents a virtually untapped field for productive organizational efforts;
5. The financial resources and expertise of national unions in assisting public employee groups to organize and present their demands to management;
6. The aggressiveness of public employee unions which has caused many long established associations to adopt a more belligerent stance;
7. The spillover effect in state and local governments of Executive Order 10988 which gave strong support to the principle of the public employees' right to organize;

> 8. Finally, and perhaps most importantly, the "head in the sand" attitude of many public employers, rooted in the traditional concept of the prerogatives of the sovereign authority and distrust of the economic, political, and social objectives of unions, an attitude which has made the question of whether employee organizations will be recognized for the purpose of discussing grievances and conditions of work with management the second most frequent cause of strikes.
>
> SOURCE: Carl W. Stenberg, "Labor Management Relations in State and Local Government: Progress and Prospects," *Public Administration Review,* 32 (March/April 1972): 103. Reprinted with permission from *Public Administration Review,* © 1972 by the American Society for Public Administration (ASPA), 1120 G Street NW, Suite 500, Washington, D.C. 20005. All rights reserved.

Just as another such bill seemed stalled in Congress, President Kennedy took the initiative in reforming public labor-management relations by issuing Executive Order 10988 in 1962. Kennedy's order affirmed the right of federal employees to form and join unions, set up conditions under which unions would be recognized for purposes of "meeting and conferring" (*discussing,* not necessarily *negotiating*) with management on certain issues, and established limits on the kinds of issues that could be discussed. Though the order placed a great deal of administrative authority in the hands of the various agencies, it did seek some uniformity in application through the Civil Service Commission.

213

The Kennedy order was expanded somewhat by several executive orders during the Nixon and Ford administrations. Principally, Executive Order 11491, issued in 1969, sought a more coherent labor policy at the federal level through establishment of the Federal Labor Relations Council and slightly expanded the scope of bargaining. The essential items of wages and benefits, however, remained outside the bargaining process.

The next landmark in federal employee unions was the Civil Service Reform Act of 1978. Though the CSRA did little to expand areas of bargaining or to alter administration of federal labor practices (other than replacing the Federal Labor Relations Council with a Federal Labor Relations Authority separate from the Office of Personnel Management), the Act was important in that it based federal labor relations on a single, comprehensive statute rather than a series of executive orders.

Currently, some three out of every five federal workers are represented by unions, the largest of which is the American Federation of Government Employees (AFGE), a part of AFL-CIO. But because Congress has refused to permit a "union shop" among federal workers, though it exists in the private sector, the actual membership of federal unions is significantly less than it might otherwise be. (A *union shop* is an arrangement under which all members of an agency are required to join the union that represents them.) The AFGE, for instance, negotiates agreements that apply to three times its actual membership. Despite that fact, however, the percentage of federal workers who pay dues to unions compares quite favorably to that among workers in the private sector; public unions have done quite well in terms of membership (Levitan, 1983, pp. 14–20). Indeed, overall, public sector union membership is higher than that in the private sector.

At state and local levels, there is incredible variety in the kinds of labor-management relations permitted by law. Though there has been occasional talk of uniform federal statutes to govern state and local practices, the case of *National League of Cities v. Usery* (1976) seemed to indicate that states have considerable sovereignty over public employees. More recently, however, the case of *Garcia v. San Antonio Metropolitan Transit Authority* (1985) again opened the possibility of further federal intervention. But until federal legislation is passed, states will continue to exercise control over labor relations in widely varying ways. At present, some states follow the "meet and confer" model of the Kennedy program, while others establish a "negotiations" process similar to the private sector model. Some states differentiate between state and local employees, while others differentiate among various occupational groups as well. Some states require enforced arbitration of one kind or another, and eight states permit strikes by public employees.

In all, forty-three states have comprehensive labor relations laws, most of which are more favorable to unions than the existing federal legislation. In 1980, some 14,000 state and local governments were conferring or negotiating with more than 30,000 bargaining units representing employees in education, police and fire, health and social services, and other areas. Between 1960 and 1985, in fact, the two most rapidly growing unions in this country were the American Federation of State, County, and Municipal Employees and the American Federation of Teachers, both of which operate exclusively at the state and local levels (Klingner & Nalbandian, 1985, p. 295).

214

Steps in the Bargaining Process

The first and major steps in the bargaining process are recognizing the union's right to exist, determining the type of bargaining permitted, and the scope of bargaining. Scope of bargaining is a source of continuing debate in many jurisdictions. Legislation may prescribe areas where negotiation is permitted, areas where it is prohibited, and areas where it is required. But the applicable legislation may range from a prohibition on negotiating wages and salaries (as exists at the federal level) to situations in which wages and salaries are at the heart of the process (as in many states and localities). Even beyond these questions, many other issues are less clear. For example, does inclusion of "work methods and procedures" in a bargaining arrangement for public schools mean that teachers can negotiate class sizes?

The typical procedure requires that organizers who wish to represent employees petition the administrative authority to establish a **bargaining unit** that will represent the employees in conferring or negotiating various issues. (The decision to include or exclude certain groups in the bargaining unit is called **unit determination.**) Whereas the traditional standard for setting unit boundaries has been to establish a "community of interests," governments have loosely applied this concept, in some cases recognizing agency-based units (the Department of Social Services or the Department of Mental Health) and in others recognizing units based on occupational classes (nurses, custodians, or security officers). After deciding on the bargaining unit, some mechanism must be established to assure coordination among the various groups and to prevent **whipsaw tactics** (arguing that pay or benefits negotiated by one group should apply to others as well).

A similar concern is where to draw the line between managers and workers; for example, are first-line supervisors part of the bargaining unit or part of management? The importance of this issue was illustrated in the case of *NLRB v. Yeshiva University* (1980), in which it was determined that faculty at Yeshiva University, a private university, are management personnel, participating in decisions such as curricula and scheduling, and therefore outside the coverage of federal labor laws. Similar questions are raised in almost any unit determination; inclusion or exclusion of supervisors in the bargaining process varies greatly from place to place.

After appropriate bargaining units have been established, the administrative authority may either voluntarily recognize a particular union, essentially by petition, as representing a group of employees, or it may conduct an election to determine which, if any, union will represent the employees in that area. Once a union has been recognized, it is usually granted exclusive representation of employees in the unit, including the ability to bargain on all issues required or permitted by law. (The reverse of this process, *decertification*, is rare, though it can occur, as in the PATCO case.)

Bargaining may then begin, typically with both sides bargaining in *good faith*—attempting to resolve the issues at hand even while following the strategy they feel will be most advantageous to them. In most cases, the bargaining process results in an agreement; occasionally it does not. Where an *impasse* occurs, there are several possibilities for resolving the issue: mediation, fact finding, and arbitration.

1. *Mediation* involves the use of a neutral third party to attempt to work out a settlement. The work of the mediator is to assist the parties in communicating and clarifying their positions, but not to impose solutions. Though the mediator's recommendations are not binding, professional mediators are remarkably successful in helping parties reach agreements.

2. *Fact finding* employs the third party in a somewhat more investigatory and judicial role, to examine evidence on both sides of the issue, present the evidence, and, in most cases, make specific recommendations with respect to a settlement. Some jurisdictions require making the recommendations public, on the assumption that public pressure will then lead toward an agreement.

3. *Arbitration* is a form of impasse resolution involving fact finding followed by specific recommendations that are usually binding on the parties. One form of arbitration that has received attention recently is **final-offer arbitration,** a technique in which both parties must present their best offer with the understanding that the arbitrator will choose one or the other without modification. Presumably, since both parties know that unreasonable proposals will lead to the arbitrator's choosing the opposing proposal, it is in the interest of both parties to submit their most reasonable position.

To Strike or Not to Strike

If impasse resolution fails, the employee organization may consider a strike. Although most governmental jurisdictions prohibit strikes by public employees, they do occur. There are usually several hundred work stoppages in public agencies each year. These strikes raise difficult questions for public sector labor-management relations. Certainly public employees have the right to form associations, and one might argue that they should have the right to withhold services just as employees in the private sector do. On the other hand, the importance of public services, especially those such as fire or police protection, may justify different standards in the public sector.

Experts make the following arguments against public employee strikes:

1. Strikes violate sovereignty (conceding authority to any special interest group contravenes the public interest).
2. Public services are essential and cannot be interrupted. In effect, all government services are vital.
3. Traditional channels of influence on public policy exist for unions: lobbying and voting.
4. Whereas strikes in the private sector are usually of an economic nature, those in the public service are political. They are strategies that use the leverage of public inconvenience to cause a redirection of budgetary priorities. (Siegel & Myrtle, 1985, pp. 377–378)

On the other hand, advocates of public employees' right to strike make these points:

1. Public employee strikes occur whether or not they are illegal and regardless of heavy penalties prescribed by law.
2. In strike situations, labor-management conflict becomes channeled and socially constructive—both labor and management gain greater understanding of each other and of the consequences of work stoppages.
3. The right to strike enhances a union's strength as a bargaining agent. Lack of the ultimate ability to withdraw services weakens labor's position at the bargaining table.
4. Many private workers doing the same work that public employees do (for example, in transit, health care, garbage collection, and communications) have the right to strike, and for many other public employees (clerks, for instance), the public consequences of striking would be little different than they are when private sector clerks strike.

216

Though strikes at the state and especially at the local level are more frequent, two landmark strikes at the federal level were especially dramatic. The postal workers' strike of 1970 occurred when members of the Manhattan Bronx Branch of the National Association of Letter Carriers voted to strike against the U.S. Postal Service. The immediate issue was the low wage scale for carriers—a scale that left a substantial number of postal workers on welfare. Beyond this concern, the postal workers desired the right to negotiate wages and benefits, especially if the Nixon administration followed its plans to make the post office a government corporation. The strike began with about 25,000 postal workers in New York City, but soon spread up and down the east coast and to several major cities around the country, ultimately involving some 200,000 union members. As the situation became more intolerable, President Nixon sent 27,500 National Guardsmen into New York to sort and deliver the mail. He also broke a long-standing precedent, however, and agreed to permit postal workers to bargain for wages. Following this agreement, the postal workers returned to work, most claiming victory in the strike. Eventually the Postal Reorganization Act was passed, setting up the government corporation Nixon sought, and also providing for a bargaining pattern similar to that in the private sector.

A quite different result occurred when members of the Professional Air Traffic Controllers Organization went on strike in August 1981. PATCO had earlier established itself as one of the most powerful and most militant of the public unions, boasting 90 percent of the FAA's air traffic controllers as members (probably the highest percentage among federal level unions at the time). Early in the year, the FAA was pressured into negotiating with the union concerning issues of wages and working conditions, even though it had no statutory power to do so and could only recommend wage increases to Congress. The union, arguing that the controllers were underpaid and subject to severe job stress, presented several demands, including a $10,000 across-the-board annual salary increase for the controllers and a four-day, thirty-two-hour work week. Although the FAA did not meet these demands, Secretary of Transportation Drew Lewis agreed to support a $40 million package of improvements, including a $4,000 wage increase. However, 95 percent of the union membership rejected this proposal.

After a final round of negotiations was unsuccessful, the union decided to strike; union leader Robert Poli declared, "The only illegal strike is one that fails" (Steele, 1982, p. 38). As it turned out, this strike was to fail. What had begun as a confrontation between the union and the FAA now became a confrontation between the union and the White House. President Reagan acted decisively, fining the union and firing nearly 11,500 striking controllers for participating in an illegal strike. Although there was severe disruption in the air transportation system for several days, new controllers were hired, airline schedules were altered, and training programs were accelerated. The situation soon gave at least the appearance of a return to normalcy. Beaten in the strike and decertified by the FLRA, less than a year later PATCO filed for bankruptcy.

In the wake of the short-lived PATCO strike, there has been somewhat of a decrease in public sector union activity; membership growth, for instance, has more or less leveled. It is clear, however, that unionization in the public sector is an established fact. The chief issue still remaining is whether the traditional private sector model of bargaining can be fully applied in the public sector (Rosenbloom & Shafritz, 1984, pp. 215–321). Certainly the prohibition against strikes is a major problem for public unions seeking to follow the private sector model; on the other hand, public unions have made substantial gains for members through lobbying efforts and use of the court system. It remains to be seen which direction the development of public unions will take; however, a more carefully constructed system of labor-management relations in the public sector appears necessary. As one authority on labor unions in the public sector puts it, "Orderly procedures for determining the conditions of federal employment—including meaningful opportunities for worker participation and recourse to neutral arbiters—would go a long way toward improving morale in the civil service and ensuring that disputes are resolved in a fair and efficient manner" (Levitan, 1983, p. 138).

CORRECTING PATTERNS OF DISCRIMINATION IN PUBLIC EMPLOYMENT

Whereas civil service systems have traditionally emphasized the concept of "merit" in public employment, other values have become increasingly important. Most prominent is a concern for correcting patterns of discrimination in hiring and treatment of workers in public agencies. The two terms that have been central to that debate are "equal employment opportunity" and "affirmative action." **Equal employment opportunity** refers to efforts to eliminate employment discrimination on the basis of race, ethnic background, sex, age, or physical handicap; it simply seeks to ensure that all persons have an equal chance to compete for and hold positions of employment based on their job qualifications. **Affirmative action,** on the other hand, involves the use of "positive, results-oriented practices to ensure that women, minorities, handicapped persons, and other protected classes of people will be equitably represented in the organization" (Hall & Albrecht, 1979, p. 26).

The concept of equal opportunity has a firm basis in constitutional and legal history, but the primary piece of federal legislation guiding current practices is the Civil Rights Act of 1964. (Many states had passed equal employment legislation in advance of the federal act.) Title VII of the Civil Rights Act banned employment discrimination in areas such as selection, promotion, and training based on race, national origin, sex, or religion and created the Equal Employment Opportunity Commission to investigate complaints of discrimination in the private sector. In 1972 the Act was amended through the Equal Employment Opportunity Act to extend coverage to all public sector employees (at the federal, state, and local levels) and to provide for stronger actions, including filing suits, against those who did not comply with the Act.

The original Civil Rights Act did not require affirmative action to correct past patterns of discrimination; this requirement was included in an Executive Order issued by President Johnson. Executive Order 11246 sought to secure compliance with the Civil Rights Act by requiring that federal contractors not discriminate on the basis of race, creed, or national origin and that they develop affirmative action programs leading to equal employment practices. President Johnson's Executive Order 11375 later added women to the list of protected groups and specified requirements for affirmative action plans. Currently, some 73,000 private facilities employing 23 million people are covered under provisions of these executive orders (PA Times, Oct. 1, 1985, p. 4).

These requirements were first applied to federal contractors, but were soon adopted elsewhere in government and the private sector. The Civil Rights Act of 1964 had declared "that it shall be the policy of the United States to ensure equal employment opportunities for federal employees," but it was an executive order issued by President Nixon in 1969 that required agency heads to create "affirmative programs" in eliminating patterns of discrimination (Shafritz, Hyde, & Rosenbloom, 1981, pp. 185–186). Similarly, state and local governments were brought under the provisions of the Civil Rights Act in 1972 and were threatened with loss of federal funds in the event of noncompliance. Title IX of the Higher Education Act of 1972 was interpreted to require universities to provide equal athletic opportunities for both sexes in intercollegiate sports; the penalty was withdrawal of federal funds from universities found not in compliance.

There is reason to speculate, however, as to whether the trend toward further extension of equal employment opportunity has slowed. In 1986, for example, the Reagan administration seriously considered revising the Johnson executive order in a way that would effectively eliminate affirmative action requirements for federal contractors. The draft revision, proposed by the attorney general, would have eliminated numerical goals applied to recruitment and other employment practices and would have made it more difficult to prove discrimination. Presidential advisors argued that the existing rules had

218

not significantly helped minorities, had discriminated against white males, and had proven excessively costly to businesses.

In a related area, Supreme Court efforts to limit the applicability of civil rights legislation have been the source of considerable controversy. In the case of *Grove City v. Bell* (1984), the Court narrowly interpreted the law as it regarded sex discrimination to mean that federal funds were to be restricted from the particular program receiving funds rather than from an educational institution as a whole. This meant that if an English department were found guilty of discrimination, its federal funds would be cut off, but funds to other parts of the institution would not be.

Obviously, the effect of the Grove case was to severely limit enforcement power of the federal legislation dealing with sex discrimination, and, by implication, similar legislation dealing with discrimination based on race, age, or handicap. Barely a week after the Grove ruling, for example, the Department of Education dropped charges against the University of Maryland's athletic programs because they did not receive federal aid— though the institution as a whole received substantial federal funding in scholarships, research money, and so on. Not surprisingly, legislation was soon introduced in Congress to put teeth back into the various civil rights laws. The Civil Rights Restoration Act, passed by an overwhelming bipartisan majority, applies not only to educational institutions, but to a wide range of other public and private organizations receiving federal funds. Though President Reagan vetoed the bill, the veto was overridden easily and the bill became law (Marcus, 1988, p. 31).

Questions of Compliance

Early efforts to prove discrimination against an employer required proof of "evil intention"—evidence that the employer was knowingly discriminating. The difficulty of proving intent led to a new focus on "unequal treatment"—proof that an employer used different selection procedures for different groups or used the same procedure in different ways. Still, under this definition, minorities made little progress entering the work force.

In 1971, however, the Supreme Court, in *Griggs v. Duke Power Company*, settled on a new definition, **adverse or disparate impact.** The Griggs decision held that it was no longer necessary to prove discriminatory motive or differential treatment; it was simply necessary to show that employment practices affect one group more harshly than another. The Court stated, "practices, procedures, or tests neutral on their face, and even neutral in terms of intent cannot be maintained if they operate to 'freeze' the status quo of prior discriminatory practices" (Hays & Reeves, 1984, p. 354).

The notion of adverse impact has been articulated more fully in a set of *Uniform Guidelines* agreed upon by federal agencies. Under the Uniform Guidelines, employers are required to keep records indicating the relationship between those hired and minorities, including women, available in the community and the comparative success of various groups in selection for a position. If, for example, women constitute 50 percent of the labor market, yet only 20 percent of the work force are women, there is evidence of adverse impact. (Actual figures show that about 55 percent of employees in local government are women, 45 percent of employees in state government are women, and only 34 percent of employees in federal government are women. And, of course, women are disproportionately represented in lower-paying positions, such as secretarial or clerical jobs.)

The guidelines also follow another aspect of the Griggs case in requiring employers whose practices are found to have adverse impact to demonstrate the *job relatedness* of tests or procedures used in hiring or promotion decisions. That is, if a screening test cannot be shown to relate specifically to job performance, then it cannot be used as a criterion in making employment decisions. Elimination of the Professional and Administrative Career Examination (PACE) is a classic case of the job relatedness issue. In a court challenge, it was ruled that the PACE exam, at that time the primary test given to applicants for federal managerial positions, was not related to the eventual jobs these persons would hold and had an adverse impact on blacks and Hispanics. For this reason, the exam was shelved.

Affirmative Action and Reverse Discrimination

To correct past patterns of discrimination against minorities and women, many employers are now required to implement *affirmative action programs*. Such plans typically include (1) a statement of policy indicating a commitment to correct discrimination with respect to employment practices; (2) an analysis of existing practices and their results; and (3) a statement of goals to improve those practices (see Box 6.5).

220

B O X   6 . 5

EXAMPLES OF AFFIRMATIVE ACTION PROGRAMS

- The establishment of a long-term goal and short-range, interim goals and timetables for the specific job classifications, all of which should take into account the availability of basically qualified persons in the relevant job market;

- A recruitment program designed to attract qualified members of the group in question: re-design jobs in ways that provide opportunities for persons lacking "journeyman" level knowledge or skills to enter and, with appropriate training, to progress in a career field;

- Revamping selection instruments or procedures which have not yet been validated in order to reduce or eliminate exclusionary effects on particular groups in particular job classifications;

- The initiation of measures designed to assure that members of the affected group who are qualified to perform

> the job are included within the pool of persons from which the selecting official makes the selection;
>
> - A systematic effort to provide career advancement training, both classroom and on-the-job to employees locked into dead end jobs; and
>
> - The establishment of a system for regularly monitoring the effectiveness of this particular affirmative action program, and procedures for making timely adjustments in this program where effectiveness is not demonstrated.
>
> SOURCE: *Uniform Guidelines on Employment Selection Procedures* (1978) 43 FR 38,290.

Unfortunately, a great deal of popular and legal confusion has developed around the notion of goals and quotas, often resulting in charges of *reverse discrimination* against white males. Although quotas require hiring specific numbers of people from specific groups (and are rarely used in actual practice), goals or timetables are intended to be flexible and are to be established internally by the employer. Both goals and quotas may involve numbers (and this causes some of the confusion), but the goals are merely intended to show a direction in which an employer wishes to move; generally, a good faith effort in that direction will be viewed as satisfactory in terms of providing opportunities for equal employment.

Even the Supreme Court has found it difficult to clarify exactly what is acceptable and what constitutes reverse discrimination. In *Bakke v. The Regents of the University of California* (1978), the Supreme Court ruled that it was illegal for a university to reserve a specific number of slots in its medical school for minority applicants who were less qualified than other students who were rejected. The Court agreed that race could be considered one factor in an admissions decision, but only one among several.

On a slightly different issue, the Court held in *United Steel Workers of America v. Weber* (1979) that a training program that admitted black workers before white workers with more seniority was acceptable. The key here seemed to be that the company initiated the program voluntarily to eliminate obvious patterns of discrimination and that it did not necessitate the discharge of white workers (Stewart, 1983). On the other hand, in *Firefighters Local Union #1784 v. Stotts* (1984), the Court held that a lower court could not order an employer to lay off more senior employees in favor of less senior employees on the basis of race to preserve a specific percentage of minority employees. The emerging consensus, reflected in such recent cases as *United States v. Paradise* (1987) and *Johnson v. Transportation Agency* (1987), seems to be that affirmative action programs will be limited to specific needs and circumstances. Broad-scale programs are not likely to be accepted.

Studies are beginning to document the effects of affirmative action on public employment (Dometrius & Sigelman, 1984). It seems apparent that the debate over affirmative action will continue, however, especially as a conservative Supreme Court seeks to narrow the basis on which charges of discrimination can be made. For the manager in a public organization, the responsibility of developing programs to eliminate employment discrimination seems clear. As the American Society for Public Administration has stated, "the merit system becomes truly meritorious when qualified persons of all races are meaningfully employed at all levels of responsibility in public services" (PA Times, Oct. 1, 1984, p. 4).

The Emerging Debate over Comparable Worth

One more aspect of the affirmative action question focuses on what has come to be called **comparable worth.** The idea of comparable worth is that men and women in jobs that are not identical but require similar levels of skill and training should be paid equally. To understand this distinction, consider two questions:

1. Studies have shown that female electricians make less money on the average than male electricians doing the same work. In situations like this, should employers be required by law to increase women's pay to equal that of men?
2. Studies have shown that nurses, who have greater job skills and more extensive responsibilities than electricians, make less money on the average than electricians. Most nurses are women and most electricians are men. In situations like this, should employers be required by law to increase nurses' pay to match their job skills and responsibilities?

222

The first question raises the familiar issue of equal pay for equal work; the second rests on the concept of equal pay for *comparable* work.

The comparable worth issue has its roots in Title VII of the Civil Rights Act of 1964, which prohibited discrimination based on sex, and in the Equal Pay Act of 1963, which provided for equal pay "on jobs the performance of which requires equal skills, effort, and responsibility, and which are performed under similar working conditions." These two pieces of legislation (primarily the former) provide the basis upon which action can be taken to redress past patterns of discrimination.

Here's how it works. Persons in a female-dominated field seeking to prove discrimination would have to convince a court that their work requires equal skills, effort, and responsibility, and is performed under working conditions similar to those in a comparable male-dominated field. If these matters could be proven, the defendant company or agency would then have to convince the court that the reason for the difference was not sex discrimination but rather something that occurred under one of the Equal Pay Act's exceptions. These exceptions permit paying workers of different sexes different wages where there is (1) a seniority system, (2) a merit system, (3) a system that measures earnings by quantity and quality of production, or where the differential is based on a factor other than sex; for example, where there is a scarcity of people to fill a particular job.

Although the comparable worth issue has been debated for many years, it gained much of its present visibility through a court case involving the state of Washington. The issue was opened when a state-commissioned study of pay policies in state government indicated that male-dominated occupations paid about 20 percent more than female-dominated occupations requiring similar knowledge, skills, mental demands, accountability, and working conditions. The study showed, for example, that clerical supervisors ranked considerably higher on factors such as these than did chemists, yet chemists were paid 41 percent more. A similar comparison was made between electricians and beginning secretaries, who were found to require comparable knowledge and skills and greater responsibility. Truck drivers were ranked at the bottom, well below telephone operators and retail clerks, yet truck drivers received 30 percent more than telephone operators and were even further above retail clerks (PA Times, May 1, 1984, p. 12).

Based on these findings, the American Federation of State, County, and Municipal Employees brought suit, alleging discrimination and demanding restitution. In December 1983, a federal district court ruled in their favor, holding that the state owed some 15,500 employees back pay that could amount to as much as $550 million. In its ruling, the court declared that "there has been historical discrimination against women in employment in the state of Washington" and the discrimination has been "direct, overt and institutionalized" (Chi, 1984, p. 35).

Following the ruling, the state appealed the case to the U.S. Circuit Court of Appeals, which, in September 1985, overturned the ruling of the federal district court and held in favor of the state. The court in this instance held that the state did not create the general market conditions that led to wage disparities and therefore was not responsible for the resulting differences. "The State did not create the market disparity and has not been shown to have been motivated by impermissible sex-based considerations in setting salaries" (PA Times, September 15, 1985). The case, now considered "classic" in the field of comparable worth, was appealed to the Supreme Court, but was settled out of court before being heard. Under the agreement between the state of Washington and AFSCME, some 35,000 workers in Washington government will receive pay equity increases averaging 4 to 5 percent a year for five years (Washington Post, August 28, 1986).

Despite the prominence of this case, the issue of comparable worth is certain to be debated in labor negotiations at all levels of government and in private industry for some time to come. Since 1982, for instance, the U.S. Congress, at least thirty-five states, and a variety of local governments have considered legislation to study or implement comparable worth policies. Among these, Minnesota voluntarily paid roughly $22 million in the 1984 and 1985 fiscal years to achieve pay equity. The state's action came after a task force found that clerical positions, overwhelmingly filled by women, were paid as much as $350 less per month than groundskeeping positions requiring comparable skills and filled mostly by men. Senior groundskeepers were making more even than nurses performing jobs that required considerably higher skills (PA Times, April 15, 1984, p. 5). According to one estimate, similar action to correct pay inequities within the federal government would cost between $2.5 and $5 billion annually (Emmert & Lewis, 1985, p. 51).

Those who argue against the concept of comparable worth hold that even the best available job analyses cannot properly compare apples and oranges and that, even if they could, it would be improper (as well as excessively costly) to intervene in wage-setting. It is much better, they contend, to let the market decide prevailing wages in various occupations and for women who desire higher pay to train for different jobs. On the other hand, those who favor the notion of comparable worth point out that the full-time earning power of women has consistently been about 60 percent of that of men over the past decade and that where pay differentials are clearly the result of patterns of sex discrimination, corrective action should be taken. An AFSCME attorney in the Washington case said, "An employer who discriminates in compensation on the basis of sex owes the workers back pay as clearly as the thief owes money wrongfully taken" (PA Times, April 1, 1984, p. 12).

Again, regardless of the outcome of specific court cases, it is clear that managers in public and private organizations need to be attentive to shaping employment policies so as to eliminate discrimination from the workplace. Whether in the area of affirmative action generally or in the area of comparable worth, a manager is well advised to understand the issues clearly and to take positive measures to create more equitable circumstances in the public workplace.

POLITICAL APPOINTEE– CAREER EXECUTIVE RELATIONS

The tension between political responsiveness and managerial effectiveness that characterizes public management is especially well illustrated in the relationship between political appointees and career executives. Each newly elected administration, whether at the federal, state, or local level, has a certain number of top-level managerial positions to fill with persons of its choosing. These appointees become the "bosses" of career civil servants who staff the various agencies of government. As you might imagine, there is occasionally some tension between the two groups. The political executive wants to move in new policy directions, but often has little experience in government operations; the career executive, on the other hand, has both knowledge and expertise, but, aware of potential problems, may appear reluctant to change.

The inevitable tension between political executives and careerists has become even more pronounced in recent years. Many argue that both the Carter and Reagan administrations came into office with a serious misunderstanding of the role of civil servants and consequently encountered difficulties in their relationship with the career service. Both presidents had, in a sense, run "against the bureaucracy," pledging to "clean up the mess" in Washington. Consequently, during the early days of their administrations, both presidents seemed mistrustful of career bureaucrats and felt that civil servants were inflexible and tied to the policies and programs of previous administrations. Unfortunately, this antagonism toward civil service limited both administrations' effectiveness. Representative Pat Schroeder comments, "had the Reagan people or the Carter people understood the nature of the bureaucratic mind, they could have accomplished more change" (Schroeder, 1984, p. 20). (These lessons were not lost on President Bush, who entered office expressing strong support and admiration for the career service.)

In any case, sorting out the relationship between politically appointed executives and career executives returns us to the old question of politics and administration. One interpretation suggests that the role of the career executive is solely to execute orders given by superior authorities—elected officials and their appointees. In the most extreme formulation of this view, the career executive should be isolated from any involvement in policy development and should concentrate on implementing policies handed down from above. This view was expressed in 1981 by the incoming Director of the Office of Personnel Management, Donald Devine, who argued that "the honor of the civil servant is vested in his ability to execute conscientiously the order of superior authorities" (Lorentzen, 1984, p. 5). It is not surprising that many career executives took this proclamation as relegating the civil service to the role of "robots." They were naturally resistant to such a view, which seemed to give them little credit for their experience, expertise, and interest in policy development.

In contrast to this extreme position, career executives and many others find another interpretation of the politics-administration issue more appealing. This view holds that there are important reasons for career executives' involvement in policy development (see Box 6.6). Certainly career executives have the background and expertise to contribute substantially to developing practical and effective public policies. In addition, these

BOX 6.6

EDUCATION OF POLITICAL APPOINTEES

I recall an instance in which I was instructed by a new cabinet secretary to award a sole source contract of substantial dollar value to an individual who had been active in the presidential campaign which had just ended. The contract would have provided a service for which many other firms were qualified, and one clearly could not make a reasonable case of unique capability which would justify a sole source procurement. I indicated to the secretary that while a sole source procurement in this instance violated federal procurement regulations, he possessed the authority to approve it. I further advised, however, that to award the proposed contract would be a serious error since it would be perceived as political favoritism which would only embarrass him and undermine his credibility.

[In another case], I had pointed out to an assistant secretary, who had been an executive with a major bank, the advisability of consulting with, or at least providing advance notice to, the chairman of the appropriate congressional committees on action to be taken. In rejecting my advice, I was told "at the bank when we decided to change minimum deposit requirements, we merely posted an announcement. We'll decide and then tell them what we've done." Needless to say, throughout the assistant secretary's tenure, he never had good relations with the Congress.

SOURCE: Excerpted from Alfred M. Zuck, "Education of Political Appointees," *The Bureaucrat* 13 (Fall 1984): 17. Reprinted by permission.

executives are likely to be more effective in implementing policy if they have been involved in developing it, if they understand the need for policy changes, and if they feel some sense of "ownership" of the new policies.

Political appointees, on the other hand, generally come to government with relatively little knowledge about their subject matter (at least compared to career bureaucrats) and certainly with little understanding of how policies are developed in a governmental setting. There is a high degree of turnover among political executives; executives last an average of only 18 to 22 months. If the stereotype of the bureaucrat is one of hostility to any change, the stereotype of the political appointee is someone brash, inexperienced and intent on "quick and flashy change" (Lorentzen, 1985, p. 411).

The Relationship between Political and Career Executives

Assuming that political appointees and career executives are going to work side by side, how might their relationship be improved and their work together be made more effective and more responsible? Paul Lorentzen, a former federal executive, summarizes the major problems in the relationship:

1. The new political appointee's lack of knowledge of and prior experience in the public sector;
2. The need of career staffs to learn about the new leadership's policy goals and directions; and
3. The joint need of the political appointees and executives to understand each other's perceptions, attitudes, role perspectives and values. (Lorentzen, 1984, p. 8)

There have been several efforts to define a more effective relationship between political appointees and career executives. Al Zuck, a former career official in the Department of Labor and elsewhere emphasizes the responsibility of the career executive. Zuck (1984, p. 18) writes, "Career executives have a distinct advantage and, therefore, a distinct educational responsibility, as it relates to the substantive knowledge of program content and history, as well as the knowledge of government processes to get things done. They possess invaluable institutional knowledge which can be of great assistance to political executives." Based on this perspective, Zuck makes the following suggestions as to how the career executive can relate most effectively to the political appointee:

1. A successful relationship between career executives and political appointees must begin with the career person's recognition that policy changes can and will occur and that the career staff will be used as an instrument of change.
2. Career executives need to act professionally—the career executive should offer the best advice, information, and insight that his or her experience has provided.
3. The career executive must be careful not to be too "bureaucratic"—so bound by procedures and processes that nothing gets done.
4. Options or alternative courses of action should be provided to political officials so they have full and complete information about their various choices.
5. The career executive should expect to have one's advice ignored or rejected. "Not only is it likely that one's advice is not always sound, but also each administration and political appointee has the right to fail." (Zuck, 1984, p. 18)

The interface between political and career executives will continue to be a source of some tension. There is no question, however, that the Bush administration has created a more cooperative climate than its recent predecessors. By virtue of President Bush's long experience in government and his respect for career officials, the relationship between political appointees and career officials in the Bush administration seems to be much improved. (We will examine this changed climate in chapter 12.)

There appear to be at least three areas in which still further improvements might be made in the relationship between political appointees and career executives. First, political appointees must receive the training and orientation they need to effectively manage public organizations and to work with career executives both in developing and implementing policies. Second, an exchange of views between political leaders and careerists, including team building sessions between politically appointed executives and career executives, may help to develop greater understanding between the groups and forge more effective working relationships. Third, Congress should reassess the structure of executive management in government and make whatever structural changes are needed to establish a more balanced political–career interface. But the basic dilemma continues: the political appointee must make sure that the bureaucracy is responsive to the policy directives of the current president; the career executive must maintain high standards of professionalism so that the work of the organization is carried out in the best way possible.

227

SUMMARY AND ACTION IMPLICATIONS

Personnel systems in the public sector have evolved in response to a variety of competing demands. Much of the earliest personnel legislation at the federal level was directed toward assuring a neutral and competent bureaucracy protected from the potentially corrupting influences of politics. More recent efforts have sought greater responsiveness on the part of the bureaucracy to political leadership. Personnel systems in the public sector—like systems of budgeting and financial management—reflect important, though sometimes changing, values.

The development of merit systems of public employment reflects such concerns. At the root, policies governing recruitment and classification in the public sector reflect the fact that public organizations must, by definition, operate in the public interest. Similar concerns significantly affect the way contemporary issues such as conditions of employment (drug testing, etc.), labor-management relations, and comparable worth are played out in the public sector.

As a manager, you must obviously be concerned with recruitment, training, and retention of the best possible people to work in your organization. You may often feel that public personnel systems and the people who monitor them are simply roadblocks to effective management. Fortunately, in many jurisdictions, the relationship between manager and personnel officer is shifting in a more positive direction.

Obviously, personnel managers have been given the responsibility of protecting the merit system from abuse, by maintaining detailed records of personnel transactions and enforcing personnel rules and procedures. Personnel officers have thus often been placed in the position of exercising control over the activities of program managers. But public personnel officers, like their private sector counterparts, have always had another role as well—that of helping managers employ and utilize personnel effectively.

Although this service aspect of the personnel officer's role has often been treated as a secondary function, there is every reason to believe that the more progressive personnel systems will increasingly emphasize this aspect. More and more personnel officers are shifting from the traditional emphasis on compliance to a new emphasis on consultation. In this role, those in personnel will be available to help with human resource management questions of all kinds; for example, a personnel specialist might be called in to help develop a productivity improvement program or to advise on legal questions. As this new orientation becomes established, line managers will tend to view the personnel officer more as an ally than a protagonist.

Consequently, you are likely to be more effective as a public manager if you are able to develop a good understanding of the technical details of personnel transactions *and* an effective working relationship with the personnel professionals in your agency. The support of trained experts in the field of personnel management can help improve your organization's performance and, in turn, its service to the public.

TERMS AND DEFINITIONS

Adverse or disparate impact: Criterion for showing that employment practices affect one group more harshly than another.

228

Affirmative action: Use of positive, results-oriented practices to ensure that women, minorities, handicapped persons, and other protected classes of people will be equitably represented in an organization.

Bargaining unit: The organization that will represent employees in conferring and negotiating various issues.

Comparable worth: Notion that men and women in jobs that are not identical but require similar levels of skill and training should be paid equally.

Equal employment opportunity: Refers to efforts to eliminate employment discrimination on the basis of race, ethnic background, sex, age, or physical handicap; ensures that all persons have an equal chance to compete for employment and promotions based on job qualifications.

Final-offer arbitration: Technique in which both parties must present their best offer with the understanding that an arbitrator will choose one or the other without modification.

Job description: A thorough analysis of the work to be done and the capabilities for a job; typically contains these elements: job title, duties required, responsibilities, and job qualifications.

Lateral entry: Entry into government positions at any level.

Merit pay: Increases in salary and wages that are tied to actual quality of work performed.

Merit principle: Concept that selection and treatment of government employees should be based on merit or competence rather than personal or political favoritism.

Position classification: Analyzing and organizing jobs on the basis of duties, responsibilities, and knowledge and skills required to perform them.

Rule of three: Provision of most merit systems that requires at least the top three applicants' names to be forwarded to the hiring official to allow some flexibility in selection.

Sexual harassment: Any unwarranted and nonreciprocal verbal or physical sexual advances or derogatory remarks that the recipient finds offensive or that interfere with his or her job performance.

Spoils system: The ability to give government jobs to the party faithful; "to the victor belongs the spoils."

Structured interviews: Those in which a previously developed set of questions is used with each applicant.

Unit determination: Decision to include or exclude certain groups in a bargaining unit.

Whipsaw tactics: Argument that pay or benefits negotiated by one group should be applied to others.

STUDY QUESTIONS

1. "To the victor belongs the spoils" was a phrase used to define the spoils system for filling vacancies of government jobs. Discuss the historical use of this system and its contemporary manifestations.
2. What was the Pendleton Act, and how did it help to reform federal personnel procedures?
3. Explain the basic principles of the civil service system.
4. Discuss some of the basic problems President Carter faced regarding personnel/civil service reform.
5. The Civil Service Reform Act provided for various changes in personnel procedures. Explain the importance of this legislation and discuss the impact of major provisions on the civil service system.
6. What are some of the criticisms of the Civil Service Reform Act?
7. List the steps in recruiting for a government position.
8. Identify various methods of testing and screening applicants.
9. Discuss government methods to combat discrimination in employment activities.
10. What are some of the tools governments use to ensure compliance with equal employment opportunity regulations?
11. Discuss the pros and cons of comparable worth in pay systems.
12. With changing labor-management relations, public unionization has become an issue. Explain the factors public managers must recognize to unionize the public sector.
13. Discuss the major components of the bargaining process.
14. Identify arguments against strikes by public employees and give a few examples of strikes that have occurred.
15. Discuss the relationship between political appointees and career executives and how it might be improved.

CASES AND EXERCISES

1. Consider the following case: You are Steve Style, a programming director in a large city's Data Processing Department. You manage five sections of computer programmers, each made up of a senior programmer and 3 to 4 trainees. The department generates computer systems for the other city departments, thus requiring you and your staff to spend a lot of time with the users of the systems. Your staff has a reputation throughout the city for being highly professional. For some time, your boss, Tom Traffic, has been talking about the need to expand the programming staff by adding a data base administrator.

A few months ago, a new police chief was hired, brought in from another city. In the past, when a new department head came in, if he or she were married, the spouse also found a job somewhere in city government. You had heard that the police chief's wife has a degree in computer science. On Monday, Tom calls to tell you he has just hired Muffy Mann as the data base administrator in your area. Tom is happy to get someone with Muffy's education and background, which includes working for several software companies. Tom also tells you that Muffy is the police chief's wife and that she will be making more money than any of your current senior programmers.

Excited about the addition of a data base administrator, you go to tell the staff about the program expansion. Rather than the positive reaction you had expected, theirs is quite negative. David Denman, the most experienced programmer, is upset for two reasons. First, isn't she the police chief's wife? It sounds to him like a deal was made. And, second, why didn't any of the current staff have a chance to interview for the new position? Another staff member leaves the meeting grumbling about how much money Muffy will be making in comparison to the other senior programmers.

You go back to your office trying to figure out how to deal with this problem. You're looking forward to having a data base administrator, and from what Tom tells you, Muffy is well qualified. You are concerned about the staff's reaction. You know you will face an uphill battle to convince the users that Muffy is qualified for the position.

- As a practical matter, how does an administration deal with the problem of a "qualified spouse"?

- How do you justify to your staff the fact that Muffy is making a higher salary than any of them and that they didn't have the chance to interview for the position?

- How does the personnel office handle this problem in light of the city's civil service system?

SOURCE: This case was provided by Perri Lampe.

2. Through contacts with the U.S. Office of Personnel Management, the state's personnel office, and the city's personnel office, learn as much as you can about finding employment in a government agency in your area. Address such questions as

- What kinds of positions are typically available?

- What should you expect in terms of the salary range for entry at the bachelor's or master's level?

- What benefits and salary increments are associated with these positions?
- What is the hiring process (how do you apply, what types of tests or interviews are required, who makes the final decision)?

In addition, contact a variety of nonprofit organizations in your community or a representative of the American Society of Association Executives to discuss career possibilities in the nonprofit sector. Make your report available to students on campus through your academic department and through your school's placement center.

3. Obtain a copy of your school's policy (or policies) on sexual harassment regarding administrators, faculty, staff, and students. Based on conversations with knowledgeable faculty and other school officials, as well as your own reading and research, analyze the policy in terms of the following questions:

- Does the policy define sexual harassment in terms that are generally understandable?
- Does the policy specify particular types of actions that will be considered harassment?
- Are there clearly defined procedures through which charges of harassment can be brought and heard?
- Are there specific penalties, including dismissal from the school, for prohibited actions?
- Has the policy been employed in actual cases with success?
- Does the policy act as a deterrent to sexual harassment?
- Are there training programs or other educational materials available to help administrators, faculty, and students understand the issue of sexual harassment specifically and gender sensitivity more generally?
- What would you suggest to strengthen, to clarify, or to more easily enforce the policy?

4. Form small groups to complete the following exercise.

You have just accepted membership on the Energy Resources Commission Recruitment Task Force. This task force was recently created by the newly elected governor. The purpose of the task force is to develop recruitment strategies to staff the ERC, which has just been established to fulfill the following functions:

- Determine the future energy needs for the state.
- Develop strategies to meet these needs.
- Provide technical assistance to the public utilities and agencies involved in meeting these needs.

Special recruitment problems are anticipated because this is a completely new agency that will require a significant number of professional and technical personnel. The Task Force has been charged with the responsibility for developing specific action plans to recruit the required manpower over the next three years. The ERC will require approximately 250 employees by the end of this three-year period, in the following categories:

1. Management and management staff (50 employees)
2. Clerical support staff (65 employees)
3. Professional/technical personnel (100 employees)
4. Blue collar/maintenance-type personnel (35 employees)

Factors that may or may not complicate the recruitment effort include the following:

1. The primary sources of employment in the state are in agriculture, mining, and transportation.
2. The population of the state totals 10 million, but almost 40 percent of the population resides in a single upstate metropolitan district.
3. The political environment has traditionally been characterized by conflict between upstate Democrats and downstate Republicans.
4. This political competition has produced extensive reliance on patronage as the means for staffing most public agencies.
5. Control of state government has just shifted to the Republicans after twelve years of Democratic control, but one of the new governor's major campaign promises was to professionalize the personnel system and expand civil service coverage to most state employees.
6. During the campaign, the governor also committed himself to hiring within the state whenever possible.
7. The state is currently involved in two employment discrimination law suits: one brought by the National Organization for Women, and the other by the NAACP.
8. Racial minorities comprise 15 percent of the population, but most of these individuals reside in the upstate metropolitan area.
9. Of the total state work force, 22 percent are women and 4 percent are classified minority.
10. The unemployment rate for the state is 12 percent, but most of the unemployed reside in the upstate area.
11. The unemployment rate by occupational class is as follows: 18 percent blue collar, 7 percent white collar, and 3 percent professional/technical.
12. The unemployment rate for minorities is 21 percent, and the rate for women is 16 percent.
13. Public sector unionization is in its early stages of development in the state. Unions are competing for membership and becoming more and more militant. A key demand, which is currently before the legislature, is to establish an "agency shop" for public utility employees.
14. Citizens' groups and professional associations actively lobbied for the creation of the ERC.
15. The ERC is being partially funded by a federal grant-in-aid program that, in addition to requiring 50 percent matching funds from the state, also requires establishment of a merit system to ensure nondiscrimination in employment.

The task force is to design a specific recruitment strategy to meet *all* the staffing needs of the new Energy Resources Commission. Besides paying particular interest to the characteristics delineated above, you might also consider the following in your deliberations:

232

1. Need and approach for determining the commission's specific staffing requirements.
2. Characteristics of the labor market—geographically and by occupational field.
3. Level and availability of the state's labor resources.
4. Extent of search process for candidates—geographically; occupationally; type of institutions/organizations/agencies to be covered in recruitment process.
5. Qualification standards (education, training, work experience, residency, physical characteristics, etc.) that should be required for each occupational category in the commission.
6. Implications of these standards for the recruitment effort.
7. Selection devices (tests, practical or aptitude type; credentials examination; interviews, etc.) and their effect on recruitment.
8. Whether recruitment should be for specific jobs, or for a career (and the implication of this decision for qualification standards, selection devices, etc.).
9. Recruitment approaches for each occupational category; e.g., job announcements, written brochures and materials, recruitment visits (and institutions that will be covered, if any), use of professional/collegial contacts (whose?), etc.
10. Consideration of the factors to emphasize to prospective candidates (i.e., what would be the attractive aspects of a job/career in this agency in this locale).

SOURCE: This exercise was adapted from material provided by Charles Sampson of the University of Missouri–Columbia.

FOR ADDITIONAL READING

Cayer, N. Joseph. *Public Personnel Administration in the United States.* 2nd ed. New York: St. Martins Press, 1986.

Cohen, Michael, and Golembiewski, Robert T. *Public Personnel Update.* New York: Marcel Dekker, 1984.

Elliott, Robert H. *Public Personnel Administration: A Values Perspective.* Reston, VA: Reston, 1985.

Hays, Steven W., and Kearney, Richard, eds. *Public Personnel Administration.* 2nd ed. Englewood Cliffs, NJ: Prentice-Hall, 1990.

Hays, Steven W., and Reeves, T. Zane. *Personnel Management in the Public Sector.* Boston: Allyn and Bacon, 1984.

Ingraham, Patricia, and Ban, Carolyn, eds. *Legislating Bureaucratic Change: The Civil Service Reform Act of 1978.* Albany: State University of New York Press, 1984.

Klingner, Donald E., and Nalbandian, John. *Public Personnel Management.* 2nd ed. Englewood Cliffs, NJ: Prentice-Hall, 1985.

Levitan, Sar. *Working for the Sovereign.* Baltimore, MD: Johns Hopkins University Press, 1983.

Rabin, Jack, Vocino, Thomas, Hildreth, W. Bartley, and Miller, Gerald J., eds. *Handbook on Public Personnel Administration and Labor Relations.* New York: Marcel Dekker, 1983.

Shafritz, Jay M., Hyde, Albert C., and Rosenbloom, David H. *Personnel Management in Government.* 2nd ed. New York: Marcel Dekker, 1981.

Siegel, Gilbert B., and Myrtle, Robert C. *Public Personnel Administration: Concepts and Realities.* Boston: Houghton Mifflin, 1985.

PLANNING, IMPLEMENTATION, AND EVALUATION

Developing policies and programs, putting them into operation, and measuring their success or failure constitute an important and recurring cycle for public managers. A new policy toward shipping in the Persian Gulf is established. Soon the Navy organizes a fleet of vessels to patrol those waters, while political and military leaders assess the operation and decide what to do next. Similarly, a new policy involves sending literature on AIDS to all households in the United States. A group in the surgeon general's office is convened to monitor the operation. Both the efficiency of getting the mailing out and its effectiveness as an educational device are discussed. Meanwhile, a local parks and recreation department develops a program for handicapped athletes. After staff and money are acquired to support the program and it begins operations, the department director asks whether the program is worth the time and energy it seems to be taking from other tasks. Over and over, plans are made, policies and programs are implemented, and the work of the organization is evaluated.

While planning, implementation, and evaluation all require knowledge of the political and ethical context of public administration and certain personal and interpersonal skills, certain technical aids have been developed to assist the manager in each of the three areas. These techniques range from strategic planning to specific quantitative methods for evaluating programs.

STRATEGIC PLANNING

On a daily basis, all managers engage in planning. But organizations, and indeed entire governments, engage in more formal planning processes, often involving a wide range of participants and the development of considerable data and other information. Planning typically leads to the development of alternative courses of action that must each be examined to decide which way to go. Depending on the level of the problem, the process of examining and choosing from among alternatives may involve the manager in either "policy analysis" or "program design."

Strategic planning is one approach that has been increasingly employed in the public sector. A number of writers have commented on the rapidity of the social and technological changes we are now experiencing and on the turbulence and complexity that such changes generate (Naisbitt, 1982). In an effort to recognize and respond to such changes, many private corporations began programs in the 1960s and 1970s to systematically plan for future development. The success of these programs is now confirmed by the fact that more than half of publicly traded companies use strategic planning in some form. Studies show that companies employing strategic planning are more successful than their competitors and that those that begin strategic planning become more successful than they were before using such planning (Glueck, 1980).

What is strategic planning? A dictionary definition indicates that military strategy, the obvious root of the term, is the art of deploying one's forces so as "to impose upon the enemy the place, time and conditions for fighting preferred by oneself" (Cannon, 1968). Strategy suggests designing today's actions to enable us to face the future on our own terms, not on those imposed from the outside. As Peter Drucker (1974) puts it, the relevant question is not simply what shall we do tomorrow, but rather what shall we do today to get ready for tomorrow?

Strategic planning helps an organization match its objectives and capabilities to the anticipated demands of the environment so as to produce a plan of action that will assure achievement of objectives. William Glueck (1980, p. 9) points out that a strategy is a plan that is unified (ties all the parts of the enterprise together), comprehensive (covers all aspects of the enterprise), and integrated (all parts are compatible with one another and fit together well). Similarly, Robert Shirley (1982, p. 262) writes that "strategy (1) defines the relationship of the total organization to its environment and (2) gives guidance to administrative and operational activities on an ongoing basis."

We can differentiate strategic planning from more familiar long-range planning activities in several ways. Long-range planning primarily concerns establishing goals or performance objectives over a period of time; it is less concerned with specific steps that must be undertaken to achieve those goals. Strategic planning, on the other hand, implies that a series of action steps will be developed as part of the planning process and that these steps will guide the organization's activities in the immediate future. Strategic planning takes the future into account, but in such a way as to improve present decisions.

A second way that strategic planning differs from long-range planning is its special attention to environmental complexity. The organization is not assumed to exist in a vacuum; rather, both the organization's objectives and the steps to achieve them are seen in the context of the resources and constraints presented by the organization's environment.

A final distinction between the two types of planning is that strategic planning, especially in the public sector, is a process that must involve many individuals at many levels. As most managers know quite well, effective changes in organizational practices are most readily accomplished by involving all those who will be affected by the change. This general rule is especially applicable to changes generated through a process of strategic planning.

Public organizations undertake strategic planning efforts for many reasons—to give clarity and direction to the organization, to choose from among competing goals and activities, to cope with expected shifts in the environment, and to bring together the thoughts and ideas of all participants in the work of the organization. Most importantly, planning activities provide an opportunity for the widespread involvement of leaders and citizens in defining the direction of the community or the agency as it moves into the future, thus building trust and commitment.

Planning for Planning

As a manager, you may wonder whether such activities are appropriate for your jurisdiction or agency. Whatever your work—at any level of government or in a nonprofit organization—you will find precedents for planning. Many federal, state, and local agencies have begun strategic planning programs over the past several years, as have voluntary associations, human service organizations, and job training programs. The key seems to be that any organization is a candidate for strategic planning if, by allocation of resources, it can significantly influence either formulation or implementation of public policy.

You may, of course, question whether strategic planning is worth the costs—in terms of consultant fees, research and data analysis, and time away from other duties. The best gauges for assessing costs are (1) is it likely that careful planning will lead to reduced operating costs or increased productivity over the long run? and (2) what might the organization lose in the absence of a more comprehensive and integrated approach to the future?

The latter question has become increasingly important to those in local governments, who now realize that they must compete with other communities in attracting industry, providing amenities, and maintaining the population base. The issue, however, must be treated differently when an administrative agency such as a state government department is considering planning. Although strategic planning might make the agency more competitive in attracting resources from the executive or legislature, this clearly should not be the purpose of planning. Rather, the agency should use strategic planning to involve all important "stakeholders" in assessing the unit's work and the possibilities for improving its services (Ackoff, 1981). The process may indeed lead to requests for further funding, but it may also suggest ways to more effectively utilize existing resources or even ways to reduce the scope of activities.

You may also question, because of budgetary uncertainties, whether the time is right for planning activities. Some say that planning can't take place without solid information about funding levels. But the opposite argument is compelling—that planning is most essential in times of uncertainty, for these are exactly the times when you most need to be in control of your own destiny. Times of uncertainty do not mitigate the need for planning, they intensify it.

Managers in the public sector voice a related argument—that periodic changes in political leadership make planning more difficult than in private industry. Again, the opposite argument is compelling: in times of transition, planning can provide continuity. Even when the new leadership wishes to change the directions specified in an earlier planning effort, changes can be made with greater clarity and aimed more readily toward critical concerns if a plan is in place.

Finally, you may wonder whether strategic planning efforts are consistent with your organization's commitment to democratic or participatory processes. Here lies the most significant difference between strategic planning in the public and private sectors. Whereas planning in the private sector may involve many people throughout an organization, it remains centered and directed at the top, because that is where the private interests of the firm are most clearly articulated. In the public sector, however, every effort must be made to significantly involve all those who play an important role in the jurisdiction or the agency. For example, a local government planning effort should involve not only elected leadership and city staff, but also many others with a stake in the outcome— unions, neighborhood associations, chambers of commerce, civic organizations, and so forth. Similarly, a state government agency's planning effort should involve persons from all levels of the organization, members of constituent groups, elected officials, persons from other agencies and other levels of government, and representatives of the general citizenry.

237

Strategic planning in the public sector must be a highly participatory process, but this participation opens the possibility of building new understanding among various groups. Many communities that have engaged in strategic planning have found that the process brought together various groups in a way not previously possible. Strategic planning may therefore be undertaken to achieve both direction and commitment.

Organizing for Planning

The planning process can proceed in a number of different ways, but the most common approach is to form a central planning group to work closely with an outside consultant to obtain information and make commitments to various new directions. In a local community, the group might include the city's political leadership, representatives of city administration (for example, the city manager), representatives of business, industry, labor, members of neighborhood associations, and so on. For a federal or state agency, on the other hand, the major planning group might comprise the agency director, mnagers from the next organizational level below, and selected program directors. The planning group in a nonprofit organization might include the executive director, members of the board, staff members, and representatives of constituent groups.

Steps in Planning

Once it has been brought together, the planning group will want to give its attention to four primary concerns: (1) the organization's mission or objectives, (2) an assessment of the environment in terms of both opportunities and constraints, (3) an examination of the organization's existing strengths and weaknesses, and (4) the values, interests, and aspirations of those important to the organization's future (see Box 7.1). Consideration of these issues will lead to several strategic alternatives, perhaps stated as "scenarios for the future," and to the choice of a particular direction in which the organization should move. Finally, a set of action steps or implementation items will be developed to indicate what must be done immediately to put the organization in the proper position to face the future most effectively.

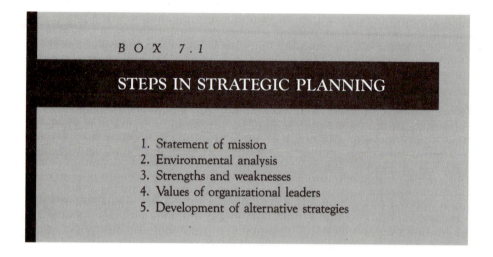

B O X   7 . 1

STEPS IN STRATEGIC PLANNING

1. Statement of mission
2. Environmental analysis
3. Strengths and weaknesses
4. Values of organizational leaders
5. Development of alternative strategies

1. Statement of mission   Arriving at a concise yet inclusive statement of the mission of the organization is a difficult step in the planning process. Although most organizations have a general sense of their mission, questions often arise that cannot be readily answered in terms of stated objectives. Having a specific mission statement, however, provides an identity for the organization, as well as a guideline for future decisions and a standard against which to measure specific actions.

Because arriving at a mission statement may imply certain strategies, care should be taken to consider alternative approaches to the organization's goals. A statement of mission might indicate, for instance, whether a city wishes to seek a broad industrial base or focus on particular types of businesses, such as tourism or high tech industries. Similarly, a university mission statement might indicate whether the institution seeks a broad range of programs in all areas or a limited number of exceedingly high-quality programs. The mission statement of a state agency might comment on the desired range of clientele, responsiveness to changes in the environment, or quality of service. If there is doubt or debate about items, they should be carried forward as elements of strategy for later consideration.

2. Environmental analysis   After developing a mission statement, the planning group should move to an analysis of the environment within which the organization operates. This assessment should include legal and political considerations, social and cultural trends, economic circumstances, technological developments, and, where appropriate, the organization's competitive or "market" position. Each area should be examined in terms of the present environment and how it is likely to change in the future. This assessment leads the group toward identifying possibilities for reducing constraints and extending opportunities.

3. Strengths and weaknesses

At this point, the planning group can turn its attention toward assessing the organization's existing capabilities—its strengths and weaknesses. The analysis should be as forthright and inclusive as possible, taking into account financial resources (including changing patterns of funding), human resources (including political and managerial strengths and weaknesses), the operation of both technical and organizational systems, and quality of work. This assessment of capabilities should relate as directly as possible to the stated mission of the organization. For example, an agency involved in facilities design and construction might want to consider the age and condition of facilities, the number and abilities of architects and engineers, the number and frequency of design projects, and the unit's standing among other similar organizations. Examining strengths and weaknesses should be accompanied by some attention to programs that might significantly improve capabilities in one or more areas.

4. Values of organizational leaders

A final step in preparing to develop strategic alternatives is to take into account the values, interests, and aspirations of those who will guide the organization into the future. People will respond to the same environmental and organizational analysis in different ways. In business, for example, some will be perfectly satisfied with the security of a stable market share, while others will be willing to take greater risks in the hope of greater payoffs. Leaders vary in terms of creativity, energy, and commitment. Yet to effectively implement a plan, it must reflect the concerns and interests of those who will play major roles in shaping the future of the organization.

5. Development of alternative strategies

At this point, the planning group can move to formulate alternative strategies. These strategies can take several forms; however, one useful way to proceed is to draw up alternative "scenarios of the future," indicating what the organization might look like five, ten, or twenty years into the future. The scenarios should indicate new directions the organization might take; pessimistic, realistic, and optimistic interpretations of its future; and factors likely to influence these future patterns. It is helpful to develop more than one scenario, then use them as competing viewpoints from which to debate the merits of various alternatives. From a thorough discussion of the scenarios, one or more strategies will emerge. The strategy should be chosen that most effectively moves the organization toward its mission, given environmental opportunities and constraints, organizational strengths and weaknesses, and the values, interests, and aspirations of the leadership. After developing the strategic orientation, the planning group should be pressed to identify specific action steps for implementing the strategy. A local job training program, for example, went through an extensive planning exercise involving thorough analysis of environmental opportunities and constraints as well as organizational strengths and weaknesses. Based on the information developed, and especially on expectations of future funding patterns, the program's directors chose to deemphasize subsidies for local businesses to

239

employ those without work and to try for longer-term benefits through skills training and job preparation.

The Logic of Policy Analysis

One possible outcome of a formal planning process is that the need for new policies will be identified. (The need for new policies can be generated in other ways as well, many of which we discussed in chapter 2.) A local group considering economic development issues might recognize the need for new tax incentives for industries interested in locating in the community. A state welfare department planning group might focus on the relationship between providing day care and job training. Or a nonprofit organization might decide there was a need for a new publications program. In each case, a problem is identified and the question arises as to whether a new approach to the problem—a new policy—might help.

Many issues may come up. Exactly what is the nature of the problem? What would we be trying to achieve with the new policy? What might be alternative approaches? What might we expect from each alternative? What criteria would we use to evaluate alternatives? Which alternative would best meet our criteria? Answering questions like these is the basis of analysis of public policies. We can therefore define **policy analysis** as the process of researching or analyzing public problems to give policy makers specific information about the range of available policy options and the advantages and disadvantages of various approaches.

240

There are several ways you might become involved in policy analysis. All managers engage almost daily in a sort of informal analysis of public policies; they encounter new problems and consider alternative policies. But often a more formal review of policy options is called for. Sometimes staff members can do the analysis; many public organizations employ policy analysts to work on just such problems. In other cases, another governmental agency may be able to help; for example, the Office of Management and Budget, as well as its counterparts in many states, develops policy reports. Policy analysis might also be performed by legislative staff or legislative research groups. Finally, many analyses are performed by consultants, including university consultants, where the public manager acts as a client, issues the contract, monitors the work, and receives the final report. Even though, as a manager, you may perform the analysis yourself, you must be able to distinguish between high quality analysis and work of limited usefulness.

Broadly speaking, most policy analyses attempt to follow a "rational" model of decision making, involving five major steps: formulating the problem, establishing criteria for evaluation, developing policy alternatives, considering the expected impact of the various alternatives, and ranking the alternatives according to the established criteria (see Box 7.2). One author illustrates these steps by considering the question of what would be the best route from home to work (Quade, 1989, pp. 33–34). If we assume at the outset that the "best" route is the shortest, then we could simply lay out the alternative routes on a map and select the shortest. (Using a map would in effect create a "model" that would help in our analysis.) As in almost all policy analyses, however, there may be more than one criterion involved. For example, the shortest route might involve more traffic and take longer to drive. The shortest travel time might then constitute a second criterion, but would require a more sophisticated model than a map, taking into account

BOX 7.2

STEPS IN POLICY ANALYSIS

1. Problem definition
2. Setting objectives and criteria
3. Developing alternatives
4. Analyzing various policies
5. Ranking and choice

traffic congestion and perhaps other variables. Just thinking through the various complications that might arise in this "simple" example, you can get some sense of the difficulties you might encounter in moving through the five stages of a more comprehensive policy analysis.

Problem definition   There are obviously many problems facing any public organization and, correspondingly, many opportunities to analyze policy alternatives. Someone, however, must decide about the problem to be analyzed and about how the analysis will proceed. This someone—the *sponsor* of the analysis—may be a legislator, an elected chief executive, or an agency manager. But, in any case, the one who will perform the analysis—the *analyst*—should seek as clear a statement of the problem as possible and as much information about the nature of the problem and the range of solutions. Why has the problem surfaced? Who is affected? How does this problem relate to similar problems? What policy options have already been tried? What is the range of policies that would be feasible, both economically and politically? What resources are available to support the analysis?

Obviously, how the question is initially formulated will guide the analyst toward certain possibilities and away from others, so it is important at the outset to be as clear as possible, without unnecessarily cutting off alternatives. The sponsor might ask, for example, "How can we provide adequate shelter for the homeless in our community this winter?" This statement of the issue permits exploring alternatives ranging from subsidizing existing shelters to building new shelters. If, however, certain options, such as building new shelters, are clearly out of the question, by reason of time or money, then the analyst should be advised of these limitations.

Sometimes the problem is only vaguely understood at the outset, and part of the analyst's job is to develop a background statement or issue paper formulating the problem. In some cases, gathering information at the library will be helpful, especially in laying out the history of the problem, discovering approaches used in other jurisdictions, and in becoming aware of technical developments in the field. Additionally, the analyst may want to talk with other people, perhaps in other jurisdictions, to see what their experience has taught them. People in other governments, other levels of government, and other agencies at the same level can be helpful. The analyst can also gather information from those involved. In our example, the analyst would probably want to talk with those already involved in providing shelter. A statistical survey might even be possible. Finally, agency records and statistics might be helpful. Throughout these initial information gathering efforts, the analyst wants to develop an idea of how different people and different groups perceive the problem and possible solutions.

Setting objectives and criteria   As we have seen, establishing objectives for a new policy or criteria for judging alternatives is often quite difficult. In some rare agencies, the existing values and preferences are clear enough to guide choices. The manager might be able to say, "It's worth much more to our agency to achieve result A than result B, C, or D. Therefore, whenever the choice presents itself, choose A." But in most policy areas, there are likely to be multiple and often conflicting objectives. To route a highway through an urban area, for example, one must consider factors such as the cost of the project, how many and who might use the highway, the number of houses and other properties that might be displaced, and the impact of noise and pollution on adjacent neighborhoods. How does one begin to rank all the factors?

There are other problems in selecting criteria. For example, criteria may differ among different levels of the organization. A constant problem for decision makers is to be sure that criteria used at one level are consistent with those at another level. A particular course of action might fit the criteria developed at one level, but so distort the use of resources at the next higher level as to make the choice inappropriate. Criteria must also be stated as completely as possible. An analyst might be told to seek a solution that maximizes output at minimum cost, then discover that no single alternative can meet both criteria. Which is more important?

Finally, choosing criteria depends on individual perspective. Most policy areas have many different **stakeholders**—many different people who are involved in the policy decision and affected by the result. These may include legislators, agency personnel, client groups, and other interest groups, and each group may feel quite differently about what is most important. In the design of a new highway, for example, a neighborhood association might place highest value on environmental concerns, while someone who lives in the suburbs might be most concerned with finding the shortest, quickest route to work. Many different criteria are likely to compete for prominence in any policy analysis. And, often, which criteria receive greatest prominence is a political decision of legislators or high-ranking administrators.

Developing alternatives   Developing alternative policies is without question the most creative phase of policy analysis, for it is here that the analyst must move beyond easy solutions and develop innovative approaches to public problems. Different alternatives often derive from different assumptions about the problem. For example, should the welfare system be oriented toward providing support at home for impoverished mothers or should it enable mothers to work by providing day care (Majchrzak, 1984, p. 30)? Should day care be addressed by building new centers or by providing tax credits or vouchers to subsidize attendance at existing centers? Obviously, answers to questions

242

about alternative approaches to child support depend on interpretation of both the causes of poverty and the motivations of the mothers. To develop a complete range of alternatives, the analyst must assume the perspectives of many different stakeholders.

Another way to develop far-ranging alternatives is to consider the relationship between the particular problem and other similar issues. For example, adequate care for the homeless ties to issues of health care, financial support for housing, welfare policy, and perhaps such areas as mental health and social security. Again, alternatives that take the various interrelated concerns into account are likely to be generated if the analyst takes into account the views of many different stakeholders. Rather than saying "How can my organization solve this problem," the analyst should ask "How can this problem be solved?"

Analyzing various policies   Having generated a number of realistic policy alternatives, the analyst must now assess the likely impact each alternative will have. Obviously, how one analyzes impacts will vary according to the particular type of policy. In some policy areas, including some of major importance, only limited information about possible impacts will be available. The analyst can only make intuitive judgments based on his or her experience and the experience of others. In other cases, however, one can gather specific data and analyze it by means of quantitative techniques. In the urban highway example, data could be gathered and analyzed to determine cost per mile, load-bearing capabilities, travel time for users, and a variety of other factors.

Occasionally, actual experiments with several policy options may be possible, sometimes with an experimental design similar to that used in the natural sciences. That is, the behavior of a particular target population may be compared to that of a control group when only one variable (the policy) is changed. A classic experiment of this type occurred in the late 1960s when researchers tried to measure the impact of a negative income tax on low-income target populations in urban and rural areas (Kershaw, 1980). Applied to large-scale social problems, such experiments may be quite costly, but they may also save considerable time and money in the long run. Sometimes it is appropriate to spend millions to save billions. (We should also note the ethical problems associated with providing a treatment expected to be beneficial to one group, but intentionally denying it to another "control" group. Is it ethical to deny some persons a treatment you think will be beneficial?)

A less formal means of policy experimentation occurs when one state or locality tries a particular policy approach and makes the results available to other communities. Sometimes this form of experimentation is simply the result of different groups trying different programs, but sometimes it is conscious. When state and local groups pressured the Carter administration to move the administration of the small cities portion of the Community Development Block Grant program to the states, two states—Wisconsin and Kentucky—were asked to run the program on an experimental basis. Their success in tailoring programs to local needs led to legislation in 1981 allowing all other states to assume administration of the program (Jennings, Krane, Pattakos, & Reed, 1987).

Ranking and choice   The final step in the analytic process is to compare the impacts associated with various alternatives and the criteria for evaluation established earlier. Alternatives can then be ranked in terms of their respective impacts. When both the

243

criteria and the impact levels are fairly straightforward, a simple comparison of possible effects may readily show which choice should be made; other cases may be more complex. The highway construction example, for instance, might yield three or four alternative proposals and as many as twenty criteria by which to evaluate the alternatives. One way to treat such cases is to simply lay out the expected results of each alternative in terms of the various criteria, leaving the task of comparing the data and ranking the alternatives to the decision maker. Sometimes more sophisticated quantitative techniques are available to the analyst.

Costs and Benefits

One of the most straightforward quantitative techniques is the *cost-effectiveness* approach, which "permits analysts to compare and advocate policies by quantifying their total costs and effects" (Dunn, 1981, p. 250). Costs are usually measured in monetary terms, but effects may be measured in units of any type.

Typically, the cost-effectiveness approach takes one of two forms. First, the level of effectiveness can be fixed, and one can search for the alternative that achieves this level at the least cost. If, for example, we want to increase the number of houses in a community tested for radon by 25 percent, would it be cheaper to hire inspectors or to spend money on advertising so that homeowners would do the inspection themselves? A second approach fixes the budget amount, then asks which alternative will provide the highest level of effectiveness for that amount. If we want to spend no more than $50,000 a year on radon inspections, which of our two approaches will result in a higher number of inspections?

The cost-effectiveness model is widely used because it is quite flexible and does not demand the same degree of precision as other approaches. Cost-effectiveness is especially useful when the relative merits of competing proposals, such as different child care delivery mechanisms, are being debated. It is not as useful in comparing questions of absolute merits, however, such as whether to allocate resources to early childhood programs or to radon testing. Moreover, the cost-effectiveness approach may be somewhat limited where criteria and impacts are more complex.

A closely related approach is cost-benefit analysis. Essentially, the **cost-benefit** approach involves identifying and quantifying both negative impacts (costs) of a proposal and positive impacts (benefits), then subtracting one from the other to arrive at a measure of net benefit. In contrast to cost-effectiveness analysis, the cost-benefit approach seeks to establish both the total monetary costs and total monetary benefits of a proposal (Dunn, 1981, p. 244). The logic of cost-benefit analysis is obvious, but applying it to policy proposals that involve large expenditures and produce difficult-to-measure results can be quite complicated.

There are several advantages to cost-benefit analysis (Sylvia, Meier, & Gunn, 1985, pp. 48–49). If programs can be evaluated in terms of costs and benefits, the approach can result in rather precise recommendations. But even if it is difficult to calculate costs or benefits, focusing on the two areas may help clarify the manager's thinking about

244

a proposal. Legislation often requires that cost-benefit analysis precede particular policy changes, especially in environmental or regulatory policy.

Several factors make it difficult to assess the costs and benefits of a particular program. First, the analyst will be asked to come up with measures of both costs and benefits and reduce them to a common unit of measure (usually money). But in analyzing a proposed new highway, can we accurately portray the fatality rate for similar highway segments as a measure of safety? And, if so, how can we translate the rate of fatalities into dollars? Second, we should always remember that the final calculated cost-benefit ratio is not the only basis for choosing one alternative over another. Despite the ratio of costs and benefits in our highway example, a particular level of fatalities may simply be considered too high, either politically or ethically.

Typically, costs are thought of as inputs and benefits as outputs. *Costs* might include one-time items such as research and development, buildings and facilities, land acquisition, equipment purchases, and so on, and recurring budgetary items such as personnel, rent, maintenance, administrative overhead, insurance, and so forth. Because these expenditures take place over time, calculations usually take into account the *time value of money*—the fact that people generally are not as willing to pay for something in the future as in the present. Although the particular calculations are beyond the scope of this text, taking time into account enables us to answer questions such as whether Project A with low initial cost but high maintenance is better than Project B with high initial cost but low maintenance (McKenna, 1980).

Benefits, based on outputs, include both positive and negative effects. (The negative effects of a program obviously might be calculated either as increases in cost or decreases in benefits. They are usually the latter.) Positive benefits might include reduction in disease or improved drinking water or increased highway safety; negative benefits might include increased noise and pollution from constructing a new airport. Again, some effort to translate positive or negative benefits into monetary terms would have to be made.   245

Obviously, measuring outputs and translating them into dollars are exceedingly difficult. For example, eliminating a disease might increase productivity, which could be measured, but also reduce pain and suffering, which would be more difficult to measure. Omitting these factors because they are hard to measure biases the analysis, but assigning a dollar value to them might do the same. Alice Rivlin, for many years director of the Congressional Budget Office, pointed out the difficulties of putting the benefits of social programs into dollar terms—comparisons that are often "shaky and unrewarding" (Rivlin, 1971, p. 60). Consequently, the quantitative presentation of costs and benefits is often accompanied by an explanation of additional qualitative considerations.

Other quantitative techniques   In addition to cost-effectiveness and cost-benefit analysis, there are many other techniques to aid policy analysis. It is not necessary to examine the mathematical formulas, but it is helpful to understand the logic they depend on. Let us examine the following *payoff matrices* with that goal in mind. Assume a simple example: hiring an office worker who will need proficiency in computer operation and budgeting. After interviewing two applicants, A and B, you feel that A is stronger than B in both areas. Your thoughts might be modeled like this:

	Value measures	
Possible actions	Computers	Budgeting
Choose A	+	+
Choose B	−	−

Your choice here is simple, because one candidate is clearly superior in both respects. But what if your decision appears to be structured like this:

	Value measures	
Possible actions	Computers	Budgeting
Choose A	+	−
Choose B	−	+

Now there is no clear choice. Even if you thought computer skills were more important than budgeting skills, you couldn't choose, because candidate A might be a little better with computers, but candidate B may be much better in budgeting. To decide, you need either more sophisticated measures of ability or a way to weight the two factors, as we do in our next example:

246

	Computers	Budgeting	Combination
Choose A	.9	.5	.8
Choose B	.5	.8	.6
Weight	.7	.3	

Here we are assuming that we can measure ability in the two areas on a ten-point scale and that we have established that computer skills are more important than budgeting skills. By multiplying the scores by the weights, we obtain a combined value measure for the two candidates, thus enabling us to choose the better candidate. (This example is adapted from Latane, 1963.)

We could extend the logic of the payoff matrix even further. One way is to combine scores under differing working conditions. Indeed, following the logic of the payoff matrix, we could accommodate large numbers of weighted variables, as might be involved in a large-scale policy analysis; the logic remains much the same. Remember that one can adopt different decision rules and that the choice of criteria is subjective.

Another tool of policy analysis is **decision analysis,** a technique for use where decisions are likely to be made sequentially and with some degree of uncertainty. Decision analysis is applicable to a variety of complex problems, such as choosing airport sites or developing plans for commercial breeder reactors, but the underlying logic is fairly straightforward and often quite helpful. Consider the following case:

> The officer in charge of a United States Embassy recreation program has decided to replenish the employees' club funds by arranging a dinner. It rains nine days out of

ten at the post, and he must decide whether to hold the dinner indoors or out. An enclosed pavilion is available but uncomfortable, and past experience has shown turnout to be low at indoor functions, resulting in a 60 percent chance of gaining $100 from a dinner held in the pavilion and a 40 percent chance of losing $20. On the other hand, an outdoor dinner could be expected to earn $500 unless it rains, in which case the dinner would lose about $10. (Stokey & Zechauser, 1978, p. 202)

Using decision analysis to structure the officer's dilemma involves first constructing a **decision tree** to show the various possible outcomes, given the risks associated with each (see Figure 7.1).

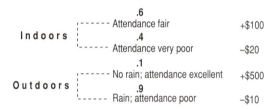

Figure 7.1   Decision tree

Obviously, the decision tree drawn here merely lays out the options, the probabilities of various occurrences, and the anticipated outcomes in much the same way as a payoff matrix. It is easy to imagine how much more complicated the situation could become, however, with the addition of other variables or other decision options. Even in this simple case, matters might be complicated by other variables, such as whether the weather will be hot or cold, whether there are other ways to increase attendance (advertising, etc.), and whether the commanding officer prefers indoors or outdoors. You can imagine the sequences and variables involved in a decision concerning location of a nuclear facility.

And, as if this weren't enough, consider what happens when you take into account competition from others. Let's imagine a chess match in which we have decided upon some evaluation criterion, such as king safety or center control, that we can measure. That is, we have identified a way to place a value on each outcome that might result from a given set of moves. Let's say that White is ready to move and has two options, W1 and W2, leading to the following decision tree. (If we move W1, then Black can move either B1 or B2; if we move W2, then Black can move either B3 or B4; etc. We will take the values across the bottom to be the outcomes.)

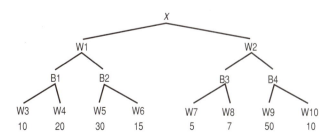

We would obviously prefer to choose W2, then have Black choose B4, so that we could choose W9, the alternative with the highest value for us. But taking into account what Black is likely to do, we recognize that if we take W2, then Black will take B3, leading us to the two lowest payoffs. Recognizing this probability, we will instead take W1, expecting that Black will take B1, and we will have a satisfactory outcome.

Although our examples have been quite simple, their logic can support far more sophisticated applications of policy analysis. Moreover, the discipline these techniques imposes makes them useful for even relatively simple applications. The models force us to examine our assumptions, structure the problem clearly and logically, and consider the full range of available options. The models also allow us to more effectively communicate our analysis to others.

That brings us to one final point. No matter how sophisticated the analysis and how rational its conclusions, a policy analysis must be effectively communicated to the actual decision makers. Communication is often quite difficult, because decision makers are extremely busy and have a variety of conflicting demands on their time and interests. Sometimes even those who are invited to do a policy analysis find themselves and the analysis swept aside by political or other considerations and, indeed, that is the prerogative of major decision makers. A noted sociologist, Amitai Etzioni, spent several years as a senior advisor to the White House during the Carter administration. After trying unsuccessfully to interest the administration in a reindustrialization program, he wrote with some frustration: "Outsiders who seek to promote policy ideas uninvited, especially without the backing of an organized societal group, lobby, or pressure group, will usually find the process tortuous. Those who choose to travel this road should understand that as a rule they are in for a long haul" (quoted in Majchrzak, 1984, p. 92). A rational analysis is helpful in the decision process, but political considerations, in the positive sense, must also be taken into account before actions are taken.

IMPLEMENTATION

In the cycle of planning, implementation, and evaluation, implementation is the action phase. Once plans have been made and policies decided upon, you must put them into operation. Financial and human resources must be allocated and mobilized, organizational structures and systems must be devised, and internal policies and procedures must be developed. During implementation, you may be involved in issuing and enforcing directives, disbursing funds, awarding grants and contracts, analyzing programmatic and operational problems, taking corrective action, and negotiating with citizens, business, and those in other public and nonprofit organizations.

Recently, a body of literature dealing with the implementation process has emerged. Some of the literature merely uses new terms to talk about the general processes of administration in the public sector, whereas other parts of the literature focus on the relationship between policy development and program implementation, specifically alerting us to the difficulty of effective implementation and to how implementation of programs may distort or even subvert the intent of policy makers. Most pointedly, one commentator has written, "It is hard enough to design public policies and programs that look good on paper. It is harder still to formulate them in words and slogans that resonate pleasingly in the ears of political leaders and the constituencies to which they are responsive. And it is excruciatingly hard to implement them in a way that pleases anyone at all, including the supposed beneficiaries or clients" (Bardach, 1977, p. 3).

A classic study of the relationship between policy and implementation was suggestively titled *Implementation: How Great Expectations in Washington Are Dashed in Oakland; or Why It's Amazing that Federal Programs Work At All* (Pressman & Wildavsky, 1973). *Implementation* described a particular economic development program in the Oakland, California, area that was less than successful. Pressman and Wildavsky conclude that "what seemed to be a simple program turned out to be a very complex one, involving many participants, a host of different perspectives, and a long and tortuous path of decision points that had to be cleared" (p. 94). Implementation was characterized by multiple and conflicting interests, each trying to influence the program's direction to suit their many and divergent needs. The major recommendation of the study seemed to be that persons involved in designing public policies "pay as much attention to the creation of organizational machinery for executing a program as for launching one" (pp. 144-145).

This lesson has been clearly recognized in the literature of strategic planning. Plans remain sterile without implementation, so there has always been a close connection between planning and execution. As noted, planning is most beneficial where it can help make immediate decisions in light of future impact. Thus, a final step in any planning process is to arrive at a series of specific actions to take in the near future—the next six months, or the next year or two years—who does what, when, and to what effect. These steps, which may detail new policy positions or new organizational processes, will form a new action agenda for the community or the agency.

Organizational Design

Some of the classic approaches to implementation, or what was formerly called simply "organization and management," focused on the structure and design of new organizations and their work processes or flows. The traditional organization chart expresses both the division of labor within an organization and the structure of command or control.

In the late 1930s, Luther Gulick advised managers developing new organizations that there were several ways they could divide work (Gulick, 1937, pp. 21-29). Among these were (1) purpose, (2) process, (3) persons or things, or (4) place. Dividing work according to purpose might result in distinctions such as that between providing education or controlling crime, while dividing it according to process might lead to a legal unit, a medical unit, or an engineering unit. One could also divide work according to the persons served or the things being dealt with; for example, the Veterans Administration deals with all problems that veterans face, whether legal, medical, and so on. Finally, one may organize according to geographic area, as would a state welfare department that has regional or county offices.

Gulick and his contemporaries also talked about the number of levels that would be appropriate to an organization. Obviously, many organizations are fairly "tall"—they have many levels; others are "flat"—they have relatively few levels. The number of levels is guided to a degree by the type of work and by the number of people who report to any one manager. The term *span of control* signifies the number of people that one individual supervises; though there are significant variations depending on type of work, it is generally considered difficult to supervise more than six to ten people.

In addition to developing organizational structures, early writers urged charting work processes as an aid to organizational design. **Process charting** or **flow charting** can provide a graphic demonstration of the various steps in an operation, the people performing each step, and the relationships among these elements. Box 7.3 shows a simple illustration of process charting, though charts can become far more sophisticated in actual applications. This process chart uses a variety of symbols to indicate different activities. The vertical lines set the basic framework of the chart. The columns show the flow of work from one unit or person to another and vary depending on the complexity of the process and the degree of analysis desired. The column headings indicate the elements under study. In this example, the larger circles on the chart refer to a specific task (filling out a form, testing a sample, etc.); the smaller circles indicate transportation of the work

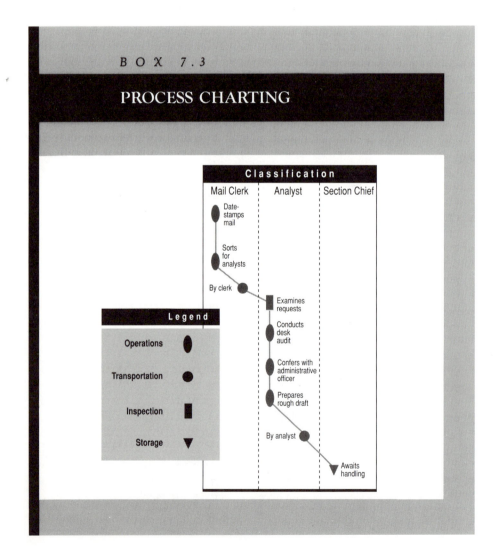

BOX 7.3

PROCESS CHARTING

from one unit or person to another. The triangles indicate storage, a period in which the item or operation is stationary. Finally, the square indicates an inspection of the work item, usually to check for quality or quantity. As illustrated here, one can make notations on the chart to indicate the nature of particular steps in the process.

Process charting is most useful where a considerable number of clerical or nonprofessional employees perform the same general classes of work and follow the same general sequence of operating steps. Although process charting is less useful in analyzing the work of professionals, there are possible applications here as well. For example, charting a professional operation may reveal bottlenecks, excessive periods of review, or excessive check points that inhibit the flow of work. As with other techniques, process charting can become quite complex, but its logic is both simple and compelling. Process charting simplifies analysis because it sharply points out backtracking, excessive detail, unnecessary repetition, poor distribution of functions, and other administrative defects.

Systems Analysis

Recently, far more sophisticated devices have been developed for analyzing the design and operations of both public and private organizations. Many of the approaches are based in **systems theory,** an effort to identify, in logical fashion, the interactions of various internal and external elements that impinge on an organization's operations. The systems approach has been used in a variety of fields, including physics, biology, economics, sociology, and information science, but the basic concepts are much the same regardless of discipline. Generally speaking, a **system** is a set of regularized interactions configured or "bounded" in a way that differentiates and separates them from other actions that constitute the system's environment; thus, we can speak of a biological system, a physical system, an economic system, or a political system. Any such system receives *inputs* from its environment, then translates these through some sort of *conversion process* into *outputs* that are returned to the environment. These outputs in turn affect future inputs to the system through a *feedback loop.* Presumably, if the outputs of a system are valued by the environment, new inputs will be forthcoming and the organization will survive. (A basic systems model is illustrated in Box 7.4.)

251

Following that model, consider the operation of a thermostat. The thermostat takes in information about the heat in a room, then measures the heat against some standard. If the level of heat is below the standard, the thermostat causes more heat to be put out into the room. The additional heat becomes part of the environment and creates new information (feedback), which becomes part of the next input into the system.

The systems concept works similarly in human organizations. A business might receive input from its environment that customers are demanding more red shoes. A decision might be made to produce more red shoes, and those shoes would be part of the organization's output. The new red shoes become part of the environment and affect new inputs into the system, which might range from comments about the quality of the shoes or information that the demand has not yet been met. This new information guides the operation of the system in the future.

Like many of the other models we have discussed in this chapter, the systems approach has been used in highly sophisticated applications ranging from analysis of organizational design and processes to creation and modification of major weapons systems. Indeed,

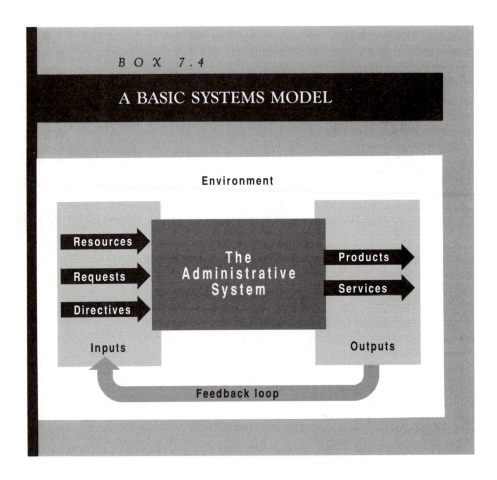

BOX 7.4

A BASIC SYSTEMS MODEL

the first major applications of systems analysis occurred in the military during and soon after World War II. For some time thereafter, the Department of Defense was the major user of systems analysis, depending on a variety of contractors, most notably the Rand Corporation. This is why techniques such as PPBS (discussed in chapter 5) found their earliest and warmest reception in the Department of Defense. Yet it is possible to apply systems logic to a variety of problems public organizations face, and, as with other techniques, the systematic discipline that the approach brings to problem solving is perhaps its greatest strength.

Systems analysis emphasizes the relationship between the organization and its environment, suggesting that public managers carefully consider factors in the environment that impinge on their operations. These factors include legal and political matters, support and opposition generated by interest groups and client organizations, human and financial resources, and applicable technology. Naturally, the environment also includes a large number of other organizations with which the agency interacts, such as the chief executive's office, the legislature, the budget office, related agencies at the same level of government, parallel agencies at other levels of government, and a variety of private and nonprofit groups and associations.

Many systems analysts tend to ignore what occurs within the system itself, preferring to think of it as a "black box" into which inputs go and from which outputs come. Others speak of several different subsystems that carry forward the organization's work. The **institutional subsystem** is responsible for adapting the organization to its environment and for anticipating and planning for the future. People involved in this activity generally constitute the organization's leadership cadre. The **technical subsystem,** on the other hand, is concerned with the effective performance of the organization's actual work. If the work of the organization is building rockets, the technical subsystem is the people who actually build the rockets. Finally, the **managerial subsystem** is concerned with providing the necessary resources for accomplishing the technical task, as well as mediating between the technical and institutional subsystems (Thompson, 1967, pp. 10–11).

Outputs of public organizations range from goods (such as highways or buildings) to services (such as student loans or employment counseling), but also include regulations, adjudication, and support for other programs. To know the effect of their efforts, managers need some sort of feedback mechanism. Feedback often occurs naturally: clients write letters of appreciation; legislators inquire about program operations; a program may even become an issue during an election campaign. Sometimes, however, you will want to secure more systematic and accurate feedback, for which you can use devices such as questionnaire surveys, field testing, or spot checks of service provision. Recall that systems analysis helps focus on how an organization interacts with its environment; developing effective feedback mechanisms helps the manager in that process.

253

PERT/CPM

Another technique for guiding implementation of public programs is the *Program Evaluation Review Technique (PERT)* or the *Critical Path Method (CPM).* (The two techniques were developed separately and have minor differences, but we can treat them as one, using the title PERT.) **PERT** is a system for organizing and monitoring projects that have a specific beginning point and a specific ending point. NASA used the system extensively in developing the manned spacecraft program; it can accommodate quite substantial projects. We will focus on the basic logic underlying the system.

A *PERT chart* uses a series of circles, designating events, and arrows, designating time or costs, to indicate various activities for completing a project and the necessary sequence. One circle might show the beginning of a particular effort and be connected by an arrow to another circle, which might show the end of the first activity and the beginning of a second. Any activity that must be completed before the start of another activity should appear to the left of that activity. Thus, the key elements in a PERT chart might look like this:

Put on socks $\longrightarrow$ Put on shoes

Activities that are independent of one another are shown in separate sequences; for example, if you could put on your shirt while you are putting on your shoes, that activity could be parallel to putting on your shoes.

A more complex PERT chart appears in Box 7.5, showing a variety of activities that might be undertaken to hold a conference. As in all PERT charts, no activity can take

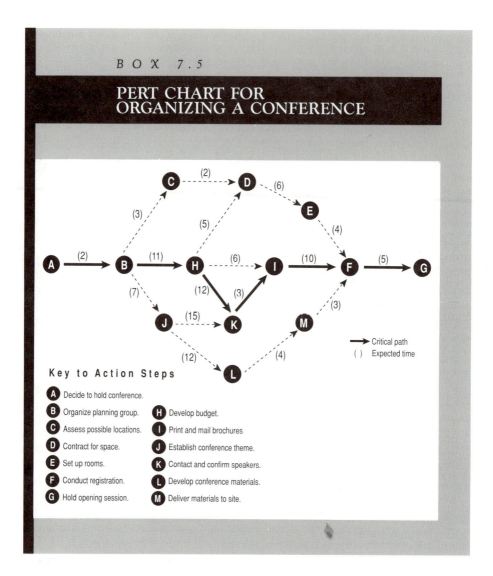

BOX 7.5

PERT CHART FOR ORGANIZING A CONFERENCE

Key to Action Steps

- **A** Decide to hold conference.
- **B** Organize planning group.
- **C** Assess possible locations.
- **D** Contract for space.
- **E** Set up rooms.
- **F** Conduct registration.
- **G** Hold opening session.
- **H** Develop budget.
- **I** Print and mail brochures.
- **J** Establish conference theme.
- **K** Contact and confirm speakers.
- **L** Develop conference materials.
- **M** Deliver materials to site.

place until all events logically prior to that event occur. For instance, to print and mail the brochures (I), it is necessary to develop a budget (H), contract for the space (D), and identify the conference speakers (K). Each event is necessarily preceded by others. Time estimates for each activity are entered above each line. (Some PERT charts give a normal, an optimistic, and a pessimistic time projection, but we give one figure—the expected time in days. PERT charts can also be constructed with cost estimates substituted for time estimates.)

Various paths lead from the decision to hold the conference (A) to the opening session (G). If you add the times required to complete all the steps along any particular path, you arrive at an expected time to complete that path—ABCDEFG requires 22 days; ABJKIFG requires 42 days. The path that takes the most time is the *critical path* (in this case, path ABHKIFG) and is usually highlighted in some way. Any delay in the critical path will delay the entire project. Other paths may have built-in slack times, where small delays will not cause that path to exceed the time required for the critical path. The critical path in this example tells us that the conference organizers have 43 days to complete their project. If for some reason the conference must be held sooner, they must find some way to decrease the time required to complete the critical path.

In summary, program implementation involves the full range of administrative skills and concepts, but implementation can occasionally be facilitated by using certain techniques. Our examples are simplified to illustrate the logic of the technique. All the techniques, however, can be applied to projects of much greater magnitude and complexity. Regardless of the complexity of the application, the result should be the same— a more disciplined and precise view of the implementation of one's program.

PROGRAM EVALUATION

Many of the analytic techniques used in policy development can be applied after a program has been implemented to evaluate its efficiency and effectiveness. There are, however, differences in both the rationale for evaluation and in application to ongoing programs. As with policy analysis, program evaluations seek to provide appropriate and relevant information to those who will decide about the program's direction or whether it continues. Such information not only assists in the decision process, it improves the accountability of public programs and facilitates legislative oversight and administrative control.

Several legislative groups conduct or "sponsor" program evaluations at the federal level. These include the General Accounting Office (GAO), the Congressional Budget Office, the Congressional Research Service, and the Office of Technology Assessment, as well as the various legislative committees, primarily those concerned with the budget and with oversight of specific programs. Executive agencies, such as the Office of Management and Budget and the Executive Office of the President, also conduct evaluations. Many evaluations, however, are sponsored by the various agencies themselves, as managers seek to determine how they can better manage or improve existing programs. Obviously, each group's primary interest varies; some are more interested in whether or not a program should continue, be modified, or be terminated, and others are more concerned with the technical details of program management.

There is also great interest in program evaluation at the state and local levels, although resources to support such activities have often been limited. State governments have often developed analytic capabilities within the executive branch, often through the budget office. In addition, legislative research staffs or commissions and legislative postaudit units conduct evaluations for use in legislative decision making. Finally, state auditors (often an elective office) conduct a variety of program reviews. Similarly, at the local level, both executive and legislative capabilities in evaluation have grown over the past decade, primarily in the largest cities.

Again, at the state and local levels and in most nonprofit organizations, as at the federal level, a great deal of evaluation is done as part of the agency or program manager's ongoing responsibilities. This work may not be as detailed or sophisticated as major

255

evaluations, but it is extremely important in determining program direction and changes in program management. Many agencies, especially at local and state levels, do not have permanent evaluation staffs, but often hire consultants from outside the organization to conduct program evaluations.

Types of Evaluations

There are a variety of ways to classify the approaches to program evaluation. There are, for example, outcome evaluations and process evaluations. *Outcome evaluations* focus on the results of program activity, the extent to which a program meets its objectives in terms of impact on the environment. If the work of the organization is to pave and repair city streets, then an evaluation might measure the number of miles of streets paved and repaired. That information would likely then be related to program inputs to show, in a cost-benefit ratio, the number of miles paved per thousand dollars spent. In general, an outcome evaluation seeks to determine whether X causes Y, where X is the activity of the program and Y is the desired outcome or goal. As you can imagine, outcome evaluations are particularly valuable to legislators and others concerned with continuation or elimination of various programs.

A distinction is sometimes made between outputs and outcomes: *outputs* are the actual goods or services produced by an organization and *outcomes* are the desired objectives. As an illustration, one unit of the postal service produces stamps; its outputs—stamps—are straightforward and measurable. Evaluation of the work of this organization might focus simply on the quantity (and perhaps quality) of the stamps produced. On the other hand, the Federal Aviation Administration issues regulations, which are its outputs. But someone measuring the work of this organization would be only moderately interested in the number of regulations it issues. More important would be the effect of the regulations on desired goals, such as improved air safety. Improved air safety would be an outcome. (Generally speaking, objectives are likely to be narrow and specific, directly tied to the particular activities the organization engages in; outcomes, on the other hand, are related to the larger purposes to be served by the agency's work.)

In contrast to outcome evaluations, **process evaluations** focus on ways program implementation might be improved to better meet the program's objectives. The question here is what can be done to X, the program's management, to improve Y, the desired outcome. Where an evaluator interested in outcomes might spend a great deal of time developing systematic measures of program results, someone interested in process evaluation would analyze the organization and management of the agency's activities, including distribution of financial and human resources and design of service delivery mechanisms (Sylvia, Meier, & Gunn, 1985, p. 136). Process evaluations also determine if legally proscribed processes are being followed and assure that individual rights are not violated.

Relevant measures here would fall more on the "input" side, and might include such items as workload measures or data on resource allocation. In such studies it may be important to distinguish between efficiency and effectiveness. **Efficiency** is concerned with the relationship between inputs and outputs, usually expressed in a ratio per unit of input. For example, a measure of streets paved per thousand dollars spent would be a measure of efficiency. **Effectiveness,** on the other hand, is concerned with the extent to which a program is achieving or failing to achieve its stated objectives (Poister,

256

McDavid, & Magoun, 1979, p. 3). Effectiveness measures are outcome-oriented; they focus on the real changes the program produces, such as a decrease in airline deaths.

Sometimes process evaluations occur "after the fact," that is, upon completion of the program; but often they occur during program operation. Indeed, some process evaluations are almost continuous in their ongoing review of program operations (Poister, 1983). In either case, the information that emerges in the course of a process evaluation is likely to be of greatest interest to the program manager who hopes to improve his or her organization's performance.

Program evaluations may therefore be directed toward many different audiences and serve many different purposes. The specific kinds of information required vary from evaluation to evaluation. Eleanor Chelimsky, head of the General Accounting Office's Program Evaluation and Methodology Division, lists the following types of information that may be developed retrospectively:

- Information on program implementation (such as the degree to which the program is operational, how similar it is across sites, whether it conforms to the policies and expectations formulated, how much it costs, how stakeholders feel about it, whether there are major problems of service delivery or of error, fraud and abuse, etc.);

- Information on program management (such as the degree of control over expenditures, the qualifications and credentials of personnel, the allocation of resources, the use of program information in decision making, etc.); and

- Ongoing information on the current state of the problem or threat addressed by the program (is the problem growing? is it diminishing? is it diminishing enough so that the program is no longer needed? is it changing in terms of its significant characteristics?).

- Information on program outcomes (what happened as a result of program implementation?);

- Information on the degree to which the program made, or is making, a difference (that is, what change in the problem or threat occurred that can be directly attributed to the program?); and

- Information on the unexpected (as well as the expected) effects of the programs (e.g., was a program of drug education accompanied by an increase in the use of drugs?). (Chelimsky, 1985, pp. 8–9)

Evaluation Designs and Techniques

Approaches to the evaluation of public programs range from historical analysis to sophisticated experimental designs. Indeed, over the years, there has been a recurring debate over the proper approach to evaluation. Some argue that such research should be primarily qualitative, concerned with tracking program development and indicating forces that helped shape the program. Advocates of this approach tend to be most interested in "process" questions, such as reasons for success or failure and unanticipated consequences of the program; they ask "What happened?" Others argue that program evaluations should, wherever possible, employ the most rigorous scientific methods appropriate to the subject matter, including the design and execution of formal experiments. These analysts tend to be more interested in program "outcomes"; they ask "Does it work?" (Chelimsky, 1985, p. 14).

Whatever the approach, those involved in program evaluation must confront two challenges to the validity of their work. The first question, concerning *internal validity*, asks whether the approach measured what was intended. Was the design consistent with the goals of the program and the needs of the "sponsor"? Were the methods most appropriate for answering the questions that needed to be asked? Were the results as free from bias as possible? A second question, concerning *external validity*, asks to what extent the findings may be applicable to more general circumstances. What does the study say about similarly situated programs? Can the study be replicated and expected to produce similar results? These and other questions can be directed toward the various techniques employed in evaluation research.

Qualitative techniques   Many program evaluations depend on qualitative information, derived from reading about the program, interviewing important actors (including agency personnel, clients, and others), and sometimes from actually participating in the work of the program. The initial step in a qualitative evaluation project is usually to read everything available about the program and the subject matter, including background material on the subject of the program (flu vaccines, child nutrition, rapid transit systems, etc.), agency documents, operating procedures, internal memoranda, newspaper and magazine articles, articles on similar programs elsewhere, and reports issued by various concerned groups. The researcher would also likely make a few phone calls to identify the significant actors in the program and determine where the most important activities are taking place.

258

Following an initial reconnaissance, the analyst settles on a limited number of sites (schools, hospitals, highway systems, etc.) as the focus of the investigation. Most qualitative evaluations are largely **exploratory,** designed to explore a variety of hunches or intuitions about the program's operation. For these cases, the analyst will probably try to select sites that vary widely along several crucial dimensions. Some evaluations, however, are *hypothesis-guided*, designed to demonstrate the plausibility of a particular hypothesis, so the analyst might choose a limited number of crucial sites that are especially illustrative of the issue under investigation (Murphy, 1980, pp. 38–47).

Once the research sites have been chosen, the analyst may choose to gather most of his or her information through *intensive interviews*, detailed information-gathering sessions involving major actors both inside and outside the agency responsible for the program. Interviewing skills include establishing the interviewer's credentials, setting the proper climate, arranging questions effectively, asking reasonable but challenging questions, and keeping a good record of all that is said. Perhaps most important, the interviewer must keep the discussion on the subject, in a way that is neither obvious nor embarrassing to either party. Immediately following the interview, the interviewer should review and expand upon the notes taken during the interview session. These notes will form an important basis for drawing conclusions about the program.

An alternative means of gathering qualitative information is the use of a **participant–observer,** someone involved in either the target population or the agency itself who makes observations and draws conclusions based on that firsthand data. For example, an evaluation of an antipoverty program in eastern Kentucky some years ago employed a participant–observer who lived in the community, talked daily with others in the community about the program, and reported back to the overall evaluation staff.

Either technique can be questioned with respect to both internal and external validity. Biased information and questions about internal validity can arise if the wrong people are chosen to interview or if those interviewed provide misleading information, intentionally or unintentionally. Participant–observers can affect the program's operation through their own presence, leading to outcomes far different from what would otherwise have happened. Questions concerning external validity (or generalizability) might be raised with either technique based on the choice of only a limited number of sites for investigation.

Quantitative techniques   Policy evaluations often endeavor to approximate the scientific methods of the physical sciences, though such efforts are extremely difficult. In its classic formulation, an *experimental design* involves examination of two or more groups under carefully controlled conditions. One group, the *experimental group*, receives a treatment or intervention; in the case of program evaluation, members of the experimental group receive the benefits of the program being evaluated. Another group, the *control group*, consists of individuals who are as similar as possible to those in the experimental group and who act under the same general conditions, yet do not receive the intervention. Members of both groups are tested before and after the experimental intervention (pretest and posttest measures) and the results are compared. If the program has had either a positive or negative effect, the differences should show up in the data.

259

We can illustrate the difficulties in designing a rigorous experimental design with respect to social programs by imagining that we are interested in analyzing the effectiveness of a new approach to mathematics education in the fourth grade. One classroom might be designated an experimental group and taught using the new approach; another classroom might be designated the control group and taught using traditional methods. The mathematical abilities of all students would be measured both before and after the period in which the new program was being taught. If the new technique is indeed more effective in educating children in mathematics, the posttest scores of the children in the experimental group should be higher than those of the children in the control group.

Very generally, this is an application of an experimental design to a social program, and you can easily imagine how similar designs might be used to measure other programs, ranging from immunizations to welfare incentives to highway designs. But we can readily observe the difficulties in such designs, some of which relate to questions of internal validity. One might respond to the study by saying that the students in the experimental group were smarter to begin with, or that the absence rate was higher among those in the control group. Or you might suggest that one teacher was better than the other, and that made the difference. Or, even if the same teacher taught both groups, you might speculate that he or she taught the new material with more enthusiasm. Similar questions might be raised about external validity. For instance, if the results were obtained in a rural school, would they apply as well to an urban setting?

Some, if not all, of these questions could be anticipated by slightly altering the research design. For example, students could be randomly assigned to the two groups, thus eliminating any possibility of bias in group composition. But questions such as these show the difficulty of achieving true experimental conditions in measuring social programs. For this reason, most evaluations of social programs are called "quasi-experimental."

Quasi-experimental designs retain the requirement for systematic data gathering that should be part of any quantitative approach, but free the researcher from some of the difficulties of developing experimental designs, such as the need for random assignment of subjects to various groups. Here again, different groups may be compared, but an essential task for the researcher is to separate the effects of a treatment from effects of other factors (Cook & Campbell, 1979, p. 6). Only the effects caused by the treatment are of interest.

Quasi-experimental approaches are not only more adaptable to social situations; they also better fit the situation in which program evaluators often find themselves—assigned to the evaluation long after the program began and having little way to influence patterns of intervention. In such a case, a historical approach may be of special value. For example, one quasi-experimental design, **time series analysis,** involves making a number of observations about the target population both before and after the program intervention. (These observations may even be made retrospectively, by gathering historical data.) In one case, basic information about neighborhood crime was developed for a period of years prior to the introduction of a new patrol pattern, then similar data followed after the new approach was introduced.

260   *SUMMARY AND ACTION IMPLICATIONS*

As a public manager, you will become quite familiar with the cycle of planning, implementation, and evaluation. In practice, the phases of the cycle will rarely appear as distinct as in our discussion, but you will still find that you must devote a portion of your time to each phase. In middle and upper management, the planning, implementation, and evaluation cycle will become especially complex, because you will find yourself engaged in all three phases almost simultaneously. That is, you will be planning for one project at the same time that you are implementing a second and evaluating a third . . . and so on. Obviously, maintaining a good sense of the timing of the various projects and knowing when and how to shift from one to the next will be extremely important.

As we have seen, techniques have been developed to help you work through the typical problems you will encounter in each phase of the cycle. Although many of the techniques can be elaborated in highly complex ways, the logic upon which they are based can be helpful in dealing even with fairly simple and immediate problems.

Throughout the planning, implementation, and evaluation cycle, you should remember that, whereas we have focused on technical aids to your administrative work, each of the three areas will be strongly affected by how you interact with the *people* in your organization (and elsewhere). Planning, implementation, and evaluation are human processes, and are thus subject to people's shifting values, attitudes, and behaviors. In planning, implementation, and evaluation, as with budgeting, financial management, and personnel, techniques are only successful when you use them with full regard for democratic values, clear leadership, and humane management.

TERMS AND DEFINITIONS

Cost-benefit: Identifying and quantifying both negative impacts (costs) and positive impacts (benefits) of a proposal, then subtracting one from the other to arrive at a net benefit.

Decision analysis: Technique wherein decisions are likely to be made sequentially and under some degree of uncertainty.

Decision tree: Technique that identifies various possible outcomes, given the risk associated with each.

Effectiveness: Extent to which a program is achieving or failing to achieve its stated objectives.

Efficiency: Relationship between inputs and outputs.

Exploratory evaluation: Investigating a variety of hunches or intuitions about program operations.

Institutional subsystem: Responsible for adapting the organization to its environment and for anticipating and planning for the future.

Managerial subsystem: Concerned with providing necessary resources for accomplishing a technical task and mediating between the technical and institutional subsystems.

Participant–observer: Someone in either the target population or the agency who makes observations and draws conclusions based on firsthand experience.

PERT: A way to monitor the time or costs of various activities required to complete a project showing the sequence in which the activities must be completed.

Policy analysis: Process of researching or analyzing public problems to provide policy makers with specific information about the range of available policy options and advantages and disadvantages of different approaches.

Process evaluations: Seeking ways to improve program implementation so as to better meet program objectives.

Process/flow charting: Graphically demonstrating the various steps in an operation, the people who perform each step, and relationships among those elements.

Stakeholders: The many different persons who are involved in policy decisions and are affected by the results.

Strategic planning: Matching organizational objectives and capabilities to the anticipated demands of the environment so as to produce a plan of action that will assure achievement of objectives.

System: Set of regularized interactions configured or "bounded" in a way that differentiates and separates them from other actions that constitute the system's environment.

Systems theory: Effort to identify the interactions of various internal and external elements that impinge on an organization's operations.

261

Technical subsystem: Concerned with effective performance of an organization's actual work.

Time series analysis: Making a number of observations about the target population both before and after program intervention.

STUDY QUESTIONS

1. Planning is one aspect of the policy process. Discuss the various types of planning and their objectives.
2. In organizing a planning process, what are the primary concerns of the planning group?
3. Discuss the necessary steps for comprehensive policy analysis.
4. Identify some of the quantitative techniques used for policy analysis.
5. The second phase of the policy process is implementation of plans. Discuss some of the techniques available to help in the beginning stages of the implementation process.
6. Compare and contrast the several different subsystems that carry forward an organization's work.
7. What are the different types of evaluation approaches? Discuss the distinctions among them.

262

CASES AND EXERCISES

1. As a class or working in small groups, assume the role of a task force that the governor has asked to develop plans for a new university the legislature has created in a rapidly expanding area in the corner of your state. Your plan should be based on whatever assumptions you wish to make by explicitly stating them in writing; however, all your assumptions should be consistent with the following guidelines:

    a. Assume that you have full legal authority to develop the university, including the power to develop a full range of undergraduate programs and a limited number of graduate programs in areas of special interest to the state. Assume a high degree of political support within the corner of the state where the university will be built, and general support throughout the state, but assume major opposition from the state's leading public university.

    b. Assume that the area where the new university is to be located already houses a community college, which the university will take over, and a couple of small, private liberal arts colleges. Assume that the community college has two thousand freshmen and sophomores and operates in two large buildings on a large tract of otherwise undeveloped land, which will be sufficient to accommodate the new university.

    c. Assume that the area in which the university will be built has traditionally had an agricultural and tourist-based economy, but is experiencing rapid growth in high tech industry, primarily because companies are attracted to the area's natural beauty and comfortable climate.

d. Assume that you can anticipate a budget starting at twelve million dollars for the first year of operations (this is inclusive of the community college budget), but rising at a rate of seven million dollars a year for the next nine years. Assume also that, in addition, there is adequate financing available for whatever new construction will be required during the first ten years of the university's existence.

e. Assume that you have full control over the curriculum of the university and authority to propose to the Coordinating Board on Higher Education any new program offerings. Assume, however, that the major university in the state will fight hard to protect its engineering and computer science programs from competition.

You should create a plan for development of the new university over the next ten years. You should take into account all aspects of development, including all academic programs, student services, administrative support (including the physical plant, personnel, and financial and accounting systems), capital construction, and intercollegiate athletics. You may wish to establish subcommittees or task forces to work on particular areas; however, all reports should be combined into one single planning document to be submitted to the governor's office.

2. Imagine that your city council is considering a proposed ordinance to require a five-cent deposit on each beverage container sold in the city. Each beer can, soft drink bottle, or other container would carry a city sticker or imprint. Retailers would collect the deposit on each container sold and would be required to pay five cents for each empty container returned to the store. Proponents of the bill argue that it would help clean up the city and provide better recycling of containers. Opponents argue that the bill would be difficult for stores to adhere to and a nightmare for the city to enforce. Develop a research design—that is, a plan for conducting research—that would enable you to report to the city council on the potential costs and benefits of the proposed ordinance.

3. Complete the following exercise: The newly-elected governor of a large Middle Atlantic state has asked you to assist in developing a plan to revise the method of patrolling the highways. The problem stems from a report by the federal Department of Transportation showing that an independent sampling of traffic in the state indicates far too many motorists are exceeding the federally mandated speed limit. The report goes on to threaten a cutoff of all federal highway funds to the state if something is not done. Perhaps of greater urgency, however, is the finding that the number of accidents per 1,000 miles driven is rising dramatically.

The governor's office has provided you with a set of alternative strategies for patrolling the highways and the associated costs and probable reductions in both accidents and speeders. Also included in the materials is a study of the revenue generated by the issuance of citations. You are asked to write a report indicating the various "payoffs" associated with each strategy.

The types of patrols are:

stationary radar trap patrol
cruising car patrol
airplane/chase car patrol

The costs per shift for each patrol type are:

stationary = $600 per patrol
cruising = $800 per patrol
airplane = $1,500 per patrol

The cost of servicing each accident that occurs during a patrol is $250. The likelihood of accidents, however, differs depending on the type of patrol; the stationary patrol results in a .50 probability of two (2) accidents; the cruising patrol results in a .30 probability of two (2) accidents; and the airplane patrol results in a .25 probability of two (2) accidents. Finally, the number of citations issued varies by type of patrol: stationary patrols issue 8 citations on average; cruising patrols issue 5 citations on average; and airplane patrols issue 3 citations on average.

A previous study indicated that accident rates of *less* than an average of one (1) per patrol were typical of states where the Department of Transportation found acceptable levels of speeding.

In a concluding paragraph, the governor indicates that it costs the state $50 to process a citation (which averages a fine of $85), but—the governor goes on to say—that may not be relevant to the choice of patrol type since the whole idea is to prevent accidents by slowing traffic to the legal speed limit (and preventing a cutoff of federal money).

How would you go about developing the report to the governor?

264

SOURCE: This case was adapted from material provided by Barry Hammond of Slippery Rock University.

4. Complete the following exercise: You have been hired by Expert Analysis consulting firm to work on a project for New York City. The city has hired the firm to analyze the advisability of "contracting out" garbage collection, expanding city garbage collection capacity, or going to a 24-hour collection system.

The city currently operates a sanitation department of 2,538 people using 781 garbage trucks of two different sizes. The large trucks carry 35 tons per trip and make two trips per day. The small trucks carry 15 tons and make three trips per day. There are 537 small trucks and 244 large trucks. The cost of one day for a large truck is $720 in wages for three people (eight-hour shift) and $200 for maintenance. The cost of one day for a small truck is $480 for wages for two people (eight-hour shift) and $150 for maintenance. The collective bargaining contract calls for a "shift differential" of 15 percent above the standard $30 per hour for the truck crews, if the crews work other than 6:00 A.M. to 3:00 P.M. The contract has three years to go before it expires. A recent study indicates that the amount of garbage to be collected in the city will increase 14 percent in the next year and 18 percent in the following year. The study also shows that many of the larger firms in the city are contemplating using a private garbage service (We-Haul, Inc.), which has recently begun competing with the city. The study concludes that, although the amount of garbage to be collected will rise, the amount the city will be required to collect might fall slightly or remain steady.

A quick check of the maintenance records for the large trucks indicates that you can expect a 20 percent increase in maintenance costs if you operate the trucks 24 hours a day and a 30 percent increase for the small trucks. You call the Tidy-Truck manufacturer and get a quote of $82,000 for a new large truck and $59,000 for a new small truck if you order this year. They expect a 6 percent price increase next year.

Just as you put down the phone, your liaison with the city calls to tell you that the private contractor (We-Haul, Inc.) has offered to collect the additional garbage at a "special rate" for the city of $18 per ton for the first year and $20 per ton for the second year.

Making reasonable assumptions about information you may need, develop a recommendation as to whether the city should expand its service by buying more trucks and hiring more people, operate its service 24 hours a day, or contract with the private service to pick up the increase.

SOURCE: This case was adapted from material provided by Barry Hammond of Slippery Rock University.

FOR ADDITIONAL READING

Bryson, John. *Strategic Planning for Public and Nonprofit Organizations.* San Francisco: Jossey-Bass, 1988.

Chelimsky, Eleanor. *Program Evaluation: Patterns and Directions.* Washington, DC: American Society for Public Administration, 1985.

Cook, Thomas D., and Campbell, Donald T. *Quasi-Experimentation.* Boston: Houghton Mifflin, 1979.

Dunn, William N. *Public Policy Analysis.* Englewood Cliffs, NJ: Prentice-Hall, 1981.

Edwards, George, ed. *Public Policy Implementation.* Greenwich, CT: JAI Press, 1984.

House, Peter W., and Shull, Roger D. *The Rush to Policy.* New Brunswick, NJ: Transaction Books, 1987.

Majchrzak, Ann. *Methods for Policy Research.* Beverly Hills, CA: Sage Publications, 1984.

McKenna, Christopher K. *Quantitative Methods for Public Decision Making.* New York: McGraw-Hill, 1980.

Nagel, Stuart. *Public Policy: Goals, Means, and Methods.* New York: St. Martin's Press, 1984.

Nakamura, Robert T., and Smallwood, Frank. *The Politics of Policy Implementation.* New York: St. Martin's Press, 1980.

Poister, Theodore H. *Performance Monitoring.* Lexington, MA: Lexington Books, 1983.

Pressman, Jeffrey, and Wildavsky, Aaron. *Implementation.* 3rd ed. Berkeley: University of California Press, 1984.

Quade, E. S. *Analysis for Public Decisions.* 2nd ed. New York: North-Holland, 1989.

Starling, Grover. *Strategies for Policy Making.* Pacific Grove, CA: Brooks/Cole, 1988.

Stokey, Edith, and Zechauser, Richard. *A Primer for Policy Analysis.* New York: Norton, 1978.

Sylvia, Ronald D., Meier, Kenneth J., and Gunn, Elizabeth M. *Program Planning and Evaluation for the Public Manager.* Pacific Grove, CA: Brooks/Cole, 1985.

IMPROVING PUBLIC PRODUCTIVITY

O

ver the past few years, you have probably heard concerns about the declining productivity of American business. Especially as Japanese corporations have made impressive gains in the international marketplace, companies in the U.S. have been taken to task for alleged inefficiency and lack of responsiveness to market demands. Books like *In Search of Excellence* suggest that many, perhaps even most, American corporations are not well-focused in their work and lack the capacity to adapt to changing social and economic conditions. Many have voiced the feeling that American industry simply has not kept pace with international competition. A key issue seems to be lagging productivity.

Public organizations in this country compare favorably to those around the world, and, indeed, to the surprise of many, are more productive than private organizations. (For example, over the past twenty years, governmental productivity has increased at double the national average.) Still, for somewhat different reasons, questions have been raised about governmental productivity. For this reason, it is important that you know something about the ways quality and productivity can be improved in public agencies.

Concern about government productivity centers around issues of efficiency and accountability. These issues have, of course, been debated throughout the country's history; modern expression is typically dated back to the passage of Proposition 13, a tax limitation amendment passed by California voters in the late 1970s. Following the California example, other states and localities also began efforts to limit what voters perceived as the excessive cost of governmental services.

We have already seen some implications of the "no new taxes" mood of the voters. At the federal level, the desire to avoid new taxes meant reduction or elimination of numerous domestic programs, especially during the Reagan years. Many of these programs provided aid to state and local governments. When the reductions were combined with the desire to limit state and local taxation, many governments were severely constrained to provide sufficient revenues to support important, even basic, services. But despite these limitations, these governments were often asked to do more—that is, to provide increased services—with the same or even with reduced funding.

We examined some of the implications of this situation in chapter 5 with respect to budgeting and financial management, as many governments were forced to search for alternative financing methods, including privatization, coproduction, user fees, and so forth. But the same governments also sought new ways to improve both the quality and quantity of work without extra cost. Many governments and agencies at all levels began new or at least intensified efforts to increase governmental productivity.

There are a variety of definitions of public productivity, which are tied in part to the somewhat ambiguous purposes of government and the difficulty of precisely measuring progress toward those purposes. Whereas private organizations can readily point to increases or decreases in the "bottom line," public organizations must take a broader view. In government, considerations of quality and productivity are inevitably intertwined. (See Box 8.1.)

Productivity in public organizations must be defined broadly so as to include the full range of public concerns, from delivering the mail to assuring equal employment

267

BOX 8.1

The federal government's productivity improvement program uses the following definition of productivity:

The *efficiency* with which resources are used to provide a government service or product at specified levels of *quality* and *timeliness*.

Efficiency is achieved by reducing unit costs (total dollar value of inputs divided by total number of outputs) associated with a product or service.

Quality is the extent to which a product or service meets customer requirements.

Timeliness implies meeting schedule for design, development and delivery of a product or service.

SOURCE: Presentation at the University of Missouri by Carolyn Burstein, U.S. Office of Management and Budget (November 1988).

opportunity, and consideration of both quality and quantity of services. Basically, however, public productivity is concerned with how organizations can achieve their objectives as efficiently and effectively as possible—how they can improve their performance. We will focus on productivity improvement efforts that seek to "(1) increase service levels while holding costs constant, or (2) decrease costs for current service levels, or, ideally, (3) increase performance and service levels while simultaneously reducing costs" (Jarrett, 1982).

IMPLEMENTATION ISSUES IN PRODUCTIVITY IMPROVEMENT

Some productivity improvement programs simply require you to undertake new efforts to motivate your employees. Others are more programmatic; for example, you might emphasize greater responsibility on the part of lower-level personnel through a job enrichment strategy or you might develop a recognition program within the unit. You might also work with a broader program, such as undertaking a quality circles program throughout a state government or establishing a governmentwide employee suggestion award system (see Box 8.2).

268

B O X   8 . 2

BUREAUCRAT WORKS WAY OUT OF JOB

Twenty-seven years of federal employment have made Robert G. Halstead realistic enough to know that changing the bureaucracy in a place as ponderous as the Agriculture Department is akin to trying to move a polar ice cap.

But that doesn't mean he thought it wasn't worth trying.

As a result, in a development that seems to run counter to centuries-old wisdom about the nature of bureaucratic self-perpetuation, Halstead has just about worked himself out of a job.

The USDA's Office of Management Reform, which Halstead was chosen to head in 1984, has finished its work and disbanded. To denote the finality of it all, Halstead and Co. held a ceremonial burning of the secretarial memo that set up the short-lived operation.

"The easiest thing in the world would have been to keep it going," Halstead said. "The idea was for us to work a year and then quit. But it was extended another year at the request of the department's top managers, who agreed to fund it out of their own budgets."

Now, no one at USDA is rash enough to claim that polar caps have been moved. But Halstead said that the effort produced savings of at least $4.6 million in USDA operations and gave some of the department's 115,000 employees a new sense of participation in USDA decision making.

"Lord, no, we haven't improved everything," said John J. Franke, Jr., assistant secretary for administration, "but we have had some remarkable success in instilling a top-down, bottom-up approach aimed at finding ways that we could work smarter and work better."

"Can we change the bureaucracy?" Halstead asked rhetorically. "Yes, it can be done, and I think we have made some impact."

His formula: Have a "champion" at the top who wants it done; involve bureaucrats who are "risk-takers," eager to effect change, and "ask the troops what's wrong. . . . They have a share in all of this. And try to make it fun."

If nothing else, the exercise may have set records for saving paper. Halstead's file of nearly two years of correspondence with Franke, his boss, contains two—repeat—two memos. One from Halstead proposed an agenda; Franke's answer told him to get cracking.

SOURCE: Excerpted from Ward Sinclair, *The Washington Post* (Friday, November 28, 1986). © The Washington Post. Reprinted with permission.

Steps to Productivity Improvement

Whatever the level or organization of the productivity improvement effort, there are certain basic issues to consider (Holzer, Rosen, & Zalk, 1986, pp. 9–15).

1. Identify areas that are "ripe" for productivity improvement.

Any program, however great its ambitions, must start small. It makes sense to start where you are most likely to achieve immediate gains, because you will identify savings most quickly here, and because a few early successes will encourage productivity improvement efforts elsewhere. To identify areas, managers should be particularly attentive to:

- Functions continually faced with large backlogs of work or slipping deadlines
- Operations where visible problems have already been hinted at (citizen complaints, high employee turnover)
- Operations that appear to be using an unusually large percentage of resources
- Operations where large numbers of employees perform essentially repetitive tasks (payoffs will be especially evident here because of the effect of multiplying any increase by the number of employees)
- Availability of new techniques or technology already proven workable elsewhere (e.g., computer installation to improve police response time)
- Receptivity of managers and supervisors to new ideas coupled with an ability to follow through (Holzer et al., 1986, p. 10)

2. Locate models in other jurisdictions.   Whatever your organization, it is likely that there are others like it and that others have experienced similar problems. Having some idea of how others approached the issues you are now confronting is especially helpful. Fortunately, such information is readily available, either through publications such as the *Governmental Productivity News* or through professional organizations such as the American Society for Public Administration or the International City Management Association. From these sources, you may discover new approaches to productivity improvement or you may find that approaches you are considering have either been successful or have failed elsewhere.

3. Define the roles of those who will be involved in planning and implementing the program.   Some programs are oriented to a particular department, while others cut across several departments within a jurisdiction; in either case, some staffing for the productivity effort will be necessary. Staffing at the department level will provide a specific focus to the productivity program and will allow you to build technical expertise (e.g., in fire or police work); a centralized productivity staff will enable you to give broad impetus to the program and to build general expertise in productivity techniques. Presumably, this general knowledge can then be applied in various departments.

4. Set realistic goals and objectives.   As noted, productivity programs in public organizations have been stimulated by public demand for "doing more with less." You may thus be tempted to set high expectations for a new productivity improvement effort; resist the temptation. Setting realistic goals and objectives and actually meeting them is more helpful in the long run than setting too-high expectations and falling short.

5. Choose among alternative programs.   Different approaches range from changes in management style to technological innovations to specific productivity efforts, such as quality circles or incentive programs. In implementing a productivity program, it is advisable to fit the solution to the problem rather than the other way around. Though this advice seems obvious, you may find yourself tempted to pursue an immediate

270

opportunity rather than engage in more careful planning. For example, a vendor might herald a new telecommunications system as the solution to all your problems. Even though you may not view communications issues as your highest priorities in terms of productivity improvement, you may be tempted to adopt the new technology "just because it's there." A more reasonable approach, of course, is to establish a prioritized list of problems, then seek to develop solutions that match *your* most important concerns.

6. Anticipate problems.   Many problems can arise in implementing a productivity improvement program, especially one of high visibility. Many of the problems are based on misconceptions about what productivity improvement is all about and can be anticipated and dealt with early in the program. Employees might feel that a quality circles program will lead to elimination of jobs, or they may feel that safety standards will be lowered; in fact, neither outcome is likely. But these are serious concerns that should be thoroughly discussed as the program is begun. To the extent possible, all participants and all persons likely to be affected by the program should have a chance to learn about and comment on the proposed program. Dealing with questions up front minimizes confusion and disruption later.

7. Implement the program.   After carefully analyzing the need for a productivity improvement program and deciding upon a course of action that will address the identified needs, you will face the difficult task of implementation. Implementation may, in fact, be the most difficult phase. Expectations may be too high; needed legislation may be difficult to pass; organization "turf" issues may interfere; there may not be enough money to invest in the program.

271

You can avoid some of the difficulties by starting the program on a modest basis, then expanding to other areas. Limiting objectives at the outset can help keep expectations from rising too high and will make it easier to demonstrate the viability of the effort. Beginning the program in an area where you might reasonably expect quick and identifiable gains will enable you to claim early success and in turn make the program more likely to be adopted elsewhere. Similarly, keeping a low profile for the program in its early days will make it less threatening to labor and management. Whatever publicity is accorded to the program (and many political leaders will want high-profile efforts), you should monitor the program carefully in its early days to avoid misconceptions.

The most serious limitations, however, are the difficulties in institutionalizing the program. Implementation is not merely a short-term concern; you should be concerned from the beginning about how durable the program is likely to be. Several factors work against institutionalization of productivity improvement programs. Programs may be dependent on a particular individual, such as a governor or mayor or a particular department head, and may be discontinued when that person leaves office. Many programs lack an organizational home and thus find it difficult to sustain support over a period of years (Bailey, 1987, pp. 19–20).

8. Evaluate the program.   Most productivity improvement programs require an initial investment of money and time; you have to spend money to save money, and many people may be skeptical of the program's value. Skeptics are likely to be unconvinced by general statements of program advocates; they will want to see specific, objective data.

Types of information you should collect from the beginning are documented cost savings, increased output that has been achieved at a similar or reduced cost, or increased citizen satisfaction with the agency's services. This information can be made public through periodic reports to legislators or other decision makers or through press conferences or news releases.

An aspect of evaluation that needs special attention is the development of an appropriate measurement system to assure that the proper information is being acquired at an appropriate time. You must be sure that information is gathered on a timely basis and that it is accurate. The information must also be fully relevant to measuring the improvement effort. It is difficult to develop a measurement system, but it may be critical to sustaining your program over time.

We have already discussed ways to measure objectives. (Indeed, much of our discussion of more general issues involving program evaluation are applicable here.) For example, a social service agency might measure the number of clients served, a police department might measure response time, or a public works department might measure numbers of miles of streets and highways paved. Matters are complicated, of course, by the fact that most organizations seek several objectives simultaneously. The social services agency is not concerned only with screening clients, but may also make referrals to other agencies or distribute money to certain clients. Each of these multiple objectives, and each of the activities that contribute to the objectives, may require its own separate measure.

Even more important, those who measure the effects of productivity improvement programs need to be attentive to what properly reflects the *quality* of work performed. Obtaining an increase in cost savings at the expense of courtesy or promptness is questionable at best; responding to requests for information or help "when it is convenient" to the agency may be less costly, but will probably not be acceptable in terms of quality. You may wish to consider either a separate measure of quality or implementation of a quality control system. You might also be able to develop composite measures that combine considerations for output and quality. For example, the streets department might measure repairs made within a certain number of working days, or the revenue department might measure the number of tax returns processed without error.

Three conditions appear to be required for productivity improvements to occur: "(a) the performance of individuals or groups must be assessed in a valid, objective manner, emphasizing the public purposes of the services provided by those employees, (b) such assessment should be closely linked to some type of reward or penalty, whether monetary or nonmonetary, and (c) there should be both early meaningful involvement by employee organizations as well as adequate advance participation and training for those affected, including supervisory as well as nonsupervisory employees" (Greiner et al., 1981, p. 411). Developing programs with these considerations in mind will help assure not only early successes in productivity improvement, but will also help sustain the program through the years.

TECHNOLOGICAL INNOVATIONS AND PRODUCTIVITY IMPROVEMENT

Productivity in public organizations, as in others, can often be improved through technological innovations. Many areas of federal, state, and local governmental activity

272

rest on a strong technical base. In areas such as the design and construction of waste-to-energy plants, development of pollution control devices, including hazardous waste treatment centers, or building of public housing, new technologies may help governments to be not only more effective in meeting their objectives, but also to be more cost efficient.

Think for a moment about the changes that are likely to occur in the country's transportation system over the next twenty years. In the not-too-distant future, high-speed intercity rail systems or vehicles that move on cushions of air may well displace planes, cars, and trains as the primary means of transportation between major urban areas. Designing the systems, regulating them, coordinating among various systems, providing communications and control—all these and many more functions will fall at least in part to government, and all will benefit from advanced technology.

Computer-Based Systems

Much of the advanced technology now employed in public agencies—and the technology that presents the most difficult managerial questions—is computer-based. (We examined the use of computer-based management information systems in financial management in chapter 5.) Applications of computer-based systems have not been restricted to the financial arena. In 1985, federal civilian agencies alone had over 20,000 mainframe and minicomputers, and over 200,000 microcomputers. In addition, related technological developments in telecommunications and office automation have had enormous impact on the work of those in all public organizations. (How many managers have asked, "Do we need to buy a FAX machine?" or "Should I install a cellular phone in my car?")

Computer applications   The advantages of computer applications in merely processing the enormous amounts of data generated by public agencies are obvious. Just to illustrate the complexity of information required, in public organizations, we might examine the development of a new information system in a relatively small (twenty people) community mental health agency. An outside consultant was asked to develop a new information system, based on a thorough review of the agency's existing and future information needs. The consultant identified five basic kinds of data required.

> These were background data on the client including name, address, demographic characteristics, and medical history; initial analysis and diagnosis data obtained during the intake session; transaction data on the characteristics of each visit, including the type of visit, recommended treatment, length of visit and staff member; transaction data concerning the discharge of the client from the mental health center; and agency data providing the name, identification number, and other information on the agency's professional staff. It is also estimated that the agency would process approximately 15,000 client-based transactions during the course of the fiscal year. (Rubin, 1986, p. 549)

Having such detailed data immediately available for review and analysis would obviously be helpful to the agency staff and would be impossible without a computer-based system. But, of course, this agency's information demands are miniscule compared to those of data-based agencies such as a state motor vehicle license bureau or the Internal Revenue Service. Computer-based systems have made it possible for agencies like these to process large amounts of data at far greater speed and considerably less cost to the public. Whereas such applications have become an accepted part of modern life, installing and continually refining them represent substantial efforts in productivity improvement.

Computer-based systems have helped in other quite different productivity improvement efforts. For example, in the mid-1970s, San Francisco implemented a new fire command system. Previously, when an alarm was received, a coded bell signal was sent to all fire stations. The station commander would determine the particular response based on whatever information was available concerning personnel and equipment at that station and at all others. In a sense, each office had to keep track of the operations of the entire department. The new computerized system, on the other hand, is able to keep track geographically of all activities and assignments and determine and display the proper assignment for the incoming alarm. An alarm is then sounded at the appropriate fire house and a teletype printout of the location along with routing information is generated. As units arrive on the scene, the commanders feed new information into the system, which may in turn lead to a higher level of response. By improving the accuracy of assignments, the new system clearly helps the department provide better fire protection (McKenna, 1980, pp. 378–379).

Some of the most interesting applications of computer technology in public organizations involve *artificial intelligence* or *expert systems*. **Expert systems** are computer programs that mimic the decision-making processes that human experts use in a particular field. These programs have the ability to accept information and infer conclusions based on decision hueristics (or "rules of thumb"). Doctors, for example, use a program called MYCIN to provide a greater knowledge base against which to check their judgments. Through this program, doctors literally have a "second opinion" close at hand (Coursey & Shangraw, 1989, p. 246). Similarly, General Electric developed a program named DELTA to help solve repair problems in diesel locomotives. Before development of the expert system, one person had to travel to different locations to work on different locomotives; with DELTA, the experience and expertise of this one individual is available to people in various parts of the country (Coursey & Shangraw, 1989, p. 252).

There have been applications of artificial intelligence in the Environmental Protection Agency, the Department of Agriculture, NASA, and a few state and local governments. An example will illustrate some of the properties of expert systems (Dilworth, 1988). A particular personnel support unit of the U.S. Army has the responsibility for determining whether individuals are fit for continued military service and, if not, what percentage of disability should be provided. This evaluation occurs in four different offices around the country. Over a period, it was discovered that the four centers were quite consistent in their recommendations except in the area of psychiatric evaluation. The differences were easily explained by the fact that the headquarters unit had a psychiatrist on staff, while the other units did not.

To make a psychiatrist's expertise available to the other offices without actually hiring a psychiatrist in each location, an expert system was developed. The system, designed to help evaluate mental disorders, proceeds through a series of questions regarding hospitalization, mental capacities, psychological predispositions, and so forth to arrive at an evaluation of the disorder and the appropriate percentage of disability. The computer's preliminary judgment is later confirmed by a human expert; in the meantime, considerable savings in time and money have resulted. Since the program can be asked at any point to explain its rationale for a particular choice, it also is an excellent device for training individuals who perform evaluations.

Another set of computer applications with fascinating implications for the conduct of public programs involves what has been termed "electronic democracy," the use of computer-based information systems and related technology to facilitate interaction between citizens and their governments. Interactive cable television programming is already becoming quite familiar in some parts of the country and, some say, provides great potential for citizens to directly influence the work of government. In other applications, both Kansas City, Missouri, and Hillsborough County, Florida, have received some attention for efforts to establish "around-the-clock" information/access centers. Kansas City's "City Hall in the Mall" concept features electronic "kiosks" (or cabinets) located in local shopping centers. The kiosks will eventually allow a citizen to obtain information, request services or register complaints, and conduct certain transactions with the city. In this and similar applications, the hope is that computer technology will enable the government to provide better service to its "customers"—that is, its citizens.

The Human Side of Technological Innovation

Whether in designing new vehicles for collecting garbage, developing new techniques for space exploration, or creating broad-based management information systems, the technical questions are always accompanied by a related set of "human" concerns, most having to do with how human beings work together to solve technical problems. For example, what is the proper relationship between government and industry in supporting research and development activities? How can technological innovations be transferred from one jurisdiction or organization to another? What are the human consequences for a particular organization in adopting particular approaches? How can people in the organization be helped in adapting to the new technology?

One group that has been deeply involved in responding to questions such as these is Public Technology, Inc. PTI began in 1969 when a group of local government managers joined together to establish a way to apply technologies developed by NASA to problems encountered by local governments (Mercer & Philips, 1981). (Throughout most of its history, NASA has had a special mandate to support civilian applications of space technology.) For example, local officials were concerned about inadequate or bulky air supply for firefighters. As a result of conversations with NASA people who designed life support systems, the local officials gained access to high-pressure, lightweight air tanks, devices that see through smoke, and other similar tools (Toregas, 1988, p. 3).

In addition to specific technical contributions, Public Technology, Inc. focused on the human element of technology transfer. PTI felt that what came to be called *orgware*, that combination of human and interpersonal skills needed to cope with the frustration and fear associated with new technologies, was more important than the technical hardware or software (Toregas, 1988, p. 3). Emotional issues can often get in the way of applying improved technology; for example, fire fighters viewed a new, automated, radio-controlled nozzle for fire trucks as such a threat to their jobs and their normal way of fighting fires that it was abandoned almost immediately.

Experiences such as this led Public Technology to adopt a formula for technology management: for every five dollars spent on hardware, fifteen dollars must be spent on

275

software, and eighty dollars must be spent on "orgware"—training, organization develop-ment, and so on. Organizational members' concerns about introduction of new tech-nologies can be dealt with effectively, but implementing a change to new technologies is time-consuming and costly. In any application of new technology, you must keep the human element very much in mind.

Other dimensions of the human side of advanced technology, especially advanced information technology, are also important. The first has to do with the impact of infor-mation technology on day-to-day work patterns. As we will see in later chapters, managers' work is not only information-based, but highly interpersonal as well. There is no question that computer networking, for example, will increase the information available to managers and decrease the time spent waiting for it. Moreover, extensive networking should improve managers' capacity to more effectively integrate the work of various groups within the organization. On the other hand, managers with access to computer networks may spend much less time in face-to-face conversations or in visits to various locations where the work is done, and these interpersonal tasks are essential.

Second, we should expect greater dependence on advanced information technology to raise several very personal concerns for those who work in or deal with public organiza-tions. The depersonalized nature of computerized control and evaluation systems may prove highly stressful for either employees or clients. In the private sector, for instance, there have already been experiments with automated systems of accountability—measuring the number of keystrokes a typist generates or the number of calls a salesperson makes. Similar applications in the public sector could well lead to the same negative reactions that have often occurred in the private sector applications.

Third, the use of advanced information technology raises questions about how organizations of the future are likely to be structured. Networking can simultaneously allow for greater centralized control or for greater decentralization. Some argue that "knowledge is power," and that making more information available to top officials on a timely basis will permit them to accumulate even greater power (perhaps to the detriment of others). Some argue instead that new technology will spread information throughout the organization and, consequently, power will be decentralized. The latest studies take a different position—that information technology in and of itself does not necessarily lead an organization toward either more or less central control. Rather, the organization's initial structure, history and culture, and the behavior of its managers are the deter-minants. Information systems, it seems, can be designed to either centralize or decentralize.

HUMAN RESOURCES AND PRODUCTIVITY IMPROVEMENT

Whereas advanced technology can improve productivity, far greater improvements are possible through more effective use of human resources. Many approaches for improving the commitment, motivation, and creativity of employees (including managers) have been developed over the years. Most today are considered merely good management practice, but many specific techniques are more often used in formal productivity improve-ment programs than as ongoing managerial processes. We will review four techniques:

management by objectives (MBO), quality of work life programs (especially job enrichment), quality circles (or similar group approaches), and incentive programs.

Management by Objectives

One of the oldest productivity improvement techniques to be used systematically in business and government is **management by objectives** (MBO). Management by objectives became especially popular in the late 1960s and through the 1970s. President Nixon extended MBO concepts throughout many federal agencies, a pattern that was soon followed in a large number of state and local organizations. Although MBO has fallen into some disfavor in government agencies, many of its key elements, such as objective setting and performance appraisal, remain in place in many agencies.

Essentially, management by objectives is a highly participatory approach to establishing clear and measurable objectives throughout an organization. First, MBO assumes that the organization as a whole will benefit by clarifying its broad range goals and by targeting the work of all organizational units and all individuals in pursuit of those goals. Second, MBO assumes that all elements of the organization, from top to bottom, will benefit from establishing realistic objectives each year and measuring progress toward the objectives as the year goes by. Third, MBO assumes that the process of establishing goals and objectives should involve a broad spectrum of organizational members, both to solicit the fullest range of ideas and to build patterns of effective communications and commitment.

Management by objectives is based on an image of the organization as a hierarchy of linked goals and objectives. The organization's broad goals are developed at the top of the hierarchy and become the basis for negotiating more specific objectives at the next level down. These objectives in turn become the basis for negotiating objectives at the next level and so on down through the organization, even to the level of setting objectives for each individual employee. In a fully developed MBO system, the broad agency goals theoretically provide a framework within which everyone in the organization—including both managers and other employees—has before him a set of performance objectives to guide one's work during the course of the year (Jun, 1976, pp. 15-16).

Note that the objective-setting process is not one in which objectives decided "from above" are merely handed down to each successive level. Rather, MBO involves a highly decentralized objective-setting process, in which each supervisor works with each subordinate manager or employee to arrive at a reasonable set of objectives. Ideally, this process of negotiation involves face-to-face conversations in which objectives at various levels are worked out; however, in many applications of MBO, the objective-setting process occurs through an exchange of memos and written forms.

For objectives to most effectively guide the work of those throughout the organization, you must pay special attention to the type of objectives being developed (Morley, 1986, p. 186). The most useful objectives are those that are:

Clear and specific: The objectives should state exactly what is to be done (e.g., to reduce response time to three minutes), rather than vague and subjective (e.g., to respond in the shortest possible time).

277

Realistic: The objectives should be challenging to the unit or the individual, but not beyond reach. It also should be clear that the resources and support necessary to meet the objectives will be available.

Measurable (or otherwise verifiable): There must be some way for both the supervisor and subordinate to know when the objective has been met.

Prioritized: Both the superior and subordinate should agree on which objective is most important, which is next most important, and so on.

The resulting objectives may be stated in several ways: in terms of amount of work (cases processed per week), effectiveness of work (applicants placed each month), quality of work (a minimum error rate), completion dates and target costs, or some combination of these (Morley, 1986, p. 186). You should follow the objective-setting process with a more detailed examination of what must be done to meet the objective. Usually an action plan is developed, indicating how, when, and by whom the actual work will be done to meet the objectives. (At this point, of course, it is important to agree on the resources and support necessary to attain the objective.) Finally, managers must assign specific responsibility to those in their units for completing the necessary task.

As mentioned, MBO has been tried in many different government and nonprofit organizations here and abroad. Recently, MBO has been widely criticized, largely because of the extremely detailed paperwork that many organizations required as part of their MBO system, but many places still use important features of MBO. For example, setting of goals and objectives and the accompanying action plans are central to more contemporary strategic management efforts. Similarly, one of the most important features of MBO systems, which has been retained in many organizations long after the demise of a full-blown MBO system, is the frequent review and revision of objectives, accompanied by detailed **performance appraisal**—that is, a specific evaluation with respect to an individual's progress in completing specified tasks. By setting a standard against which to measure performance (which is often especially difficult at the professional or managerial level), MBO-based performance appraisal systems provide a base against which results can be measured. Finally, the emphasis in MBO on frequent communications up and down the organizational ladder has clearly been maintained in other approaches to productivity improvement, as well as in management practice more generally.

Quality of Work Life/Job Enrichment

For a period, management by objectives took on the aura of a "movement," complete with classic texts, disciples and other advocates, and strong commitment to "the cause." Much the same is true of the recent concern for Quality of Work Life (QWL). The quality of work life "movement" traces its ancestry back to the development of child labor laws, passage of worker's compensation legislation, and more general concerns for human relations arising in the 1930s. Its more recent impetus, however, has come primarily from a group of European scholars and practitioners associated with the Tavistock Institute for Human Relations in London.

The Tavistock group was initially concerned with how organizations might become more adaptive to a society engaged in a shift from a production base to a service base, one expected to exhibit a high degree of social change and "turbulence." According

278

to the Tavistock researchers, most organizations reflect their technological bases; that is, their organizational structure models their technology. Unfortunately, such a structure limits adaptability. The Tavistock group urged attention to the interaction of social *and* technical systems.

For at least some QWL advocates, creating a work environment of high quality was even more important than improving productivity. The most important question to ask, they argued, is whether a particular organization is doing all it can to contribute to a more humane and progressive work environment. Others, however, felt that one didn't have to trade productivity for quality. Rather, by improving the quality of work life, the productivity would rise as well. Indeed, studies seemed to show that improving the quality of work life led to decreased absenteeism and turnover, greater job satisfaction, and greater commitment to the organization and its goals—all features that should improve an organization's productivity as a whole.

There are several ways to define a high quality work environment. (As an exercise, before reading further, you might try listing those values or characteristics you would seek in a job—those that would define for you personally a "good place to work.") As one response to this question, Richard Walton of the Harvard Business School offered eight categories for judging the quality of work life: (1) adequate and fair compensation; (2) safe and healthy working conditions; (3) immediate opportunity to use and develop human capacities; (4) the opportunity for continued growth and security; (5) social integration in the work organization; (6) "constitutionalism" in the workplace; (7) a balance between work and the rest of one's life; and (8) social relevance (1975, pp. 93–97). (See Box 8.3.)   279

BOX 8.3

JUDGING THE QUALITY OF WORK LIFE

Adequate and fair compensation: Compensation for one's work should meet general standards for the work involved and should bear an appropriate relationship to the pay provided for other work.

Safe and healthy working conditions: The conditions of work should include reasonable hours and should not be detrimental to the health of the worker.

Immediate opportunity to use and develop human capacities: The job should allow for substantial autonomy and self-control, it should permit use of a wide range of capacities, and it should be meaningful to the worker.

(continued)

(continued)

> *Opportunity for continued growth and security:* The job should allow for and indeed encourage personal growth and development on the part of the employee, as well as opportunities for meaningful advancement in a career.
>
> *Social integration in the work organization:* The personal side of one's organizational involvement, one's interaction with others on the job, should be a source of satisfaction.
>
> *Constitutionalism in the work organization:* The rights of the individual, including rights to privacy, free speech, equal treatment, and due process, should be protected.
>
> *Work and the total life space:* One's work life should be adequately balanced with the other spheres of one's life, especially one's family life.
>
> *The social relevance of work life:* If the organization is not seen as being socially responsible (for example, in its employment policies or approaches to energy conservation or waste disposal), workers will think less of their work and their careers.

SOURCE: Richard E. Walton, "Criteria for Quality of Working Life." Reprinted with permission of The Free Press, a Division of Macmillan, Inc. from *The Quality of Working Life Volume I: Problems, Prospects and the State of the Art*, Louis E. Davis and Albert B. Cherns, Eds. Copyright © 1975 by Louise E. Davis and Albert B. Cherns.

280

Obviously, any movement directed toward concerns as broad as these may lack some focus—and that has been a problem with efforts to improve the quality of work life; the term has become so embracing as to be unclear. Some scholars, however, have focused on three paramount concerns—the autonomy, the responsibility, and the authority granted to individual workers. "The general objective is to arrange organizations, management procedures, and jobs for the maximum utilization of individual talents and skills, in order to create more challenging and satisfying work and to improve organizational effectiveness" (Jenkins, 1983, p. 2). Another writer puts the objective of QWL efforts in this question: "How can jobs be designed so that effective performance is linked with meaningful, interesting, and challenging work?" (Suttle, 1977, p. 1).

This question leads to a specific productivity improvement effort—*job enrichment*, which is concerned with designing or redesigning particular jobs so that workers experience greater meaning and satisfaction from the work and consequently can be more productive. Job enrichment efforts usually assume that people will perform better (1) where they perform a diverse array of tasks; (2) where they have a high degree of autonomy in their work; and (3) where they get clear feedback on the quality of their work.

Diversity, autonomy, and feedback in a particular job can be enhanced through a variety of mechanisms. For example, you might combine tasks so that instead of a series of individuals each involved in only one part of an assembly process, each individual would be responsible for the entire product. Jobs might also be enriched through *vertical loading*—that is, giving individual workers responsibilities and controls previously reserved for management, such as responsibility for deciding on work methods or for training new workers (Hackman, 1983, p. 249). Presumably, workers in enriched jobs not only find the quality of work life improved, but also become more productive.

Quality Circles

The "quality circles" concept has been widely used over the past decade, and hundreds of reports of documented savings and solutions to work-process problems—some involving public sector organizations—have appeared in the popular and business press. A **quality circle** is a small group of people who do similar or connected work and meet regularly (usually an hour a week) to identify, analyze, and solve work-process problems. Quality circles involve six to twelve employees, who are led by their first-line supervisor (often called a *team leader*) and assisted by a trained facilitator, usually from outside the work unit. The circle chooses its own problems to work on and approaches them through a structured, problem-solving process. Resulting recommendations are usually presented to the team leader's immediate supervisor, who in turn may carry the recommendations further up the hierarchy.

Since quality circles offer front-line employees the opportunity to get involved in decisions affecting their work, circles have proven popular among employees (as well as employers) in many organizations. In some places, employees have never been asked how they think work processes might be improved, yet they are the experts—in providing patient care, processing tax returns, or developing procedures to remove hazardous wastes. The benefits for these employees are thus twofold: first, they are given time to solve problems that cause frustrations and that keep them from completing their jobs; and second, by taking greater responsibility for work process problems, they gain a greater awareness of solutions and may have greater interest in the success of those solutions.

The team leaders, facilitators, and circle members receive training in quality circle operations and in group dynamics and problem solving. Despite this preparation, however, those initially involved often see the process as cumbersome and confusing. This is especially true for the new team leader, who is suddenly an "expert" in the problem-solving process (after only a few days of training). As a result, it is important for the facilitator to meet with the team leader before each of the early meetings to prepare an agenda, answer questions about the process, and provide reassurance as to the leader's ability.

Labeling some of the participants "facilitators" is crucial as a visible indication of the organization's support of the circle program. The symbolic value of trained facilitators may be almost as important to instituting a circle program as their actual contributions in helping circle leaders understand group dynamics, the problem-solving process, and the leader's role in the circle meeting. The facilitators also fill the role of advocates for the circle program with many constituencies in the organization, a role that is particularly critical during the early phase of circle implementation. As advocates, facilitators can play a linking-pin role between circles and managers elsewhere in the organization. And, they can make sure that managers receive enough information about the circles' activities. An open atmosphere concerning circle activities helps managers to feel comfortable with the circle concept, a natural step toward acceptance and institutionalization of the entire program.

A key ingredient in the success of a quality circle program is the support of top management. This factor needs careful attention at the beginning stages of a quality circle program. Without active support from the top, quality circle members may feel their recommendations will not be taken seriously, and managers elsewhere in the organization may see no incentive to start quality circles in their work areas. Although quality circles are a bottom-up approach to problem solving, the implementation process is very much top-down; information about the concept must be presented to those at all levels of the organization.

Upper- and middle-level managers need to understand the benefits they will receive by supporting quality circles. A visit to a quality circle actually in operation can be helpful. On-site visits can be designed to answer questions managers may have about the process and to reduce their skepticism by providing specific examples of how quality circles have been successful in similar work areas. The message to convey to managers is that the quality circle will make recommendations through the existing chain of command, and no changes in work processes will be made until the appropriate level of management has approved. Building support from the top takes time, but all the efforts to train supervisors and front-line workers in circle procedures and techniques are ultimately wasted if top and middle managers are not supportive.

282

Although managerial support is necessary for long-term success, the real core of any circle program is the participants themselves; without a large proportion of highly motivated and properly trained circle leaders and members, the circle program cannot succeed. Presentations to front-line supervisors and employees need to focus on the benefits they will receive by getting involved in quality circles. For the front-line supervisor, who will probably be the circle leader, you must demonstrate that the quality-circle program will provide an opportunity to solve some of the production, quality, and cost problems he or she encounters each day.

After all members of the organization have been introduced to the notion of quality circles and team leaders, facilitators, and group members have been trained in problem-solving techniques, the real work of the quality circles begins. Normally, circles meet regularly, perhaps once a week, for a specified time, usually an hour. The first task is choosing a problem to solve. Generally, circles choose a problem by *brainstorming*— generating long lists of topics without evaluation or comment. The group reviews the list and selects one problem to focus on. (This same process is used when the cycle is completed and a new topic is chosen.)

The circle members then analyze the problem and develop solutions. Analysis typically involves some data collection or information gathering, followed by efforts to identify both the causes of the problem and potential solutions. Each solution is examined with respect to its effectiveness in dealing with the problem and feasibility of implementation. Some solutions may be considered ineffective, others too costly, and others inconsistent with agency policies. When a solution has been settled on, the circle members prepare and make a formal presentation of the problem and their recommended solution to management. In most cases, management finds the solution acceptable and works with the circle members to implement it.

Although quality circles are usually employed to solve specific work-process problems, and are more frequently used in units where such problems are found, the basic quality circle principles of widespread participation and group problem-solving are applicable elsewhere. For example, **task forces** (groups brought together to work on specific organizational problems) may consist of members from different parts of the organization. They may address work-process problems or issues of organizational policies or broader public policies; however, the approach to problem solving may be much like that modeled by quality circles.

Incentive Programs

Many if not most personnel systems in public agencies emphasize merit considerations in deciding which employees receive larger and smaller raises. This is an effort to build into the system a reward or incentive for high-level performance. In addition to pay increases, there are several other types of incentive plans that reward extraordinary performance. The rewards are usually money, but may sometimes be nonmonetary incentives such as merchandise or time off. The incentives seek to reward increased output (measured quantitatively), improved performance (measured qualitatively), or improved behavior (such as reduced absenteeism or fewer accidents) (Morley, 1986, p. 118).

A variety of incentive plans are currently used in public agencies (Greiner et al., 1981, pp. 28–29). Among the most common are performance bonuses, piecework bonuses, gainsharing plans, suggestion awards, behavioral awards, and employee recognition.

Performance bonuses are one-time monetary awards based on superior performance on the job generally or in a particular task. Often used to reward professional or managerial employees, bonuses may be presented annually or upon completion of a specific task. There are, however, several difficulties with bonus systems in the public sector. Many people, including many legislators, seem to feel that performance evaluation is so difficult to manage that there is no fair basis for deciding which employees receive bonuses and which do not. Consequently, bonus systems may become mechanisms for rewarding friends and favorites in the organization. Although these concerns can be addressed in several ways, they have led, in many jurisdictions, to legislation prohibiting bonus systems.

Piecework bonuses are performance incentives that tie the worker's productivity in a given task to monetary rewards. These systems may either tie the monetary reward directly to the numbers of units produced or use some formula to determine which workers are exceeding a standard level of performance. For example, keypunch operators in many jurisdictions are paid according to number of entries. Similarly, painters and electricians in some areas are paid according to what degree they meet or exceed a standard of performance set in advance. The effectiveness of piecework bonuses depends on arriving at specific measures of performance that will be clear to all concerned.

Gainsharing plans provide a monetary award for a group of employees based on savings the group generates. Based simply on the idea of rewarding those who produce more, this kind of plan is easy for both employees and citizens to understand. Washington, for example, has operated such a program for nearly a decade; through the state's Teamwork Incentive Program, employees in groups that develop significant savings can receive up to 25 per cent of the documented savings. State employees have received as much as $6,273 per employee (Government Productivity News, April, 1989, p. 1).

Gainsharing can also be combined with a quality circles program. If, for example, a quality circle designed a new computer program that saved a state government $6,000 a year, it might split as much as $600 among the circle members. Again, this system depends on careful documentation of the savings generated by the work of the group.

Suggestion award programs provide incentives for employees who make specific suggestions that result in savings for the organization. Such systems are widely used in American industry; firms such as General Motors have major suggestion "contests" that result in thousands of dollars, even hundreds of thousands, in awards to individuals— and, of course, even greater savings for the companies. Suggestion programs have only recently become widespread in public agencies and are still less well established than in the private sector.

Such programs typically involve extensive advertising encouraging employees to participate. Suggestions are carefully scrutinized as to originality and applicability to the organization. If a proposal seems workable, the savings to be generated are documented and an award, usually a percentage of the savings, is granted. Most systems limit the maximum award, but the limits can be quite high: in British Columbia, for example, the maximum award is $25,000. Suggestion systems can help increase productivity; in Phoenix, for example, a recent suggestion to reduce pavement thickness by one inch, which could be done while maintaining quality, saved the city $1.2 million in one year.

Behavioral awards reward specific behaviors that management wishes to encourage. If absenteeism is a problem, a system might be designed to reward good attendance; if workplace accidents are a problem, a system might be designed to reward excellent safety records. Again, it is important to establish clear standards for performance and relate them to specific benefits.

Employee recognition programs, although they do not provide monetary incentives, are often an effective way to acknowledge special contributions of certain employees or groups. An employee-of-the-month program, for example, allows top management (the governor, a department head, or a city manager) to recognize individuals who have done work "above and beyond the call of duty." Similarly, special recognition of groups of employees involved in quality circles or interdepartmental task forces is a good way to highlight work of exceptional quality. At little or no real cost, such programs provide a surprisingly good incentive for employees and emphasize the high quality work that most employees of public organizations do. As one productivity leader pointed out, "You always hear about the bad things that happen in government. An employee-of-the-month program gives us an opportunity to talk about the good things that happen!"

All in all, incentive programs are effective mechanisms for encouraging employees to make more significant or more appropriate contributions to the organization. You must be careful, however, to identify specific behaviors that will lead to improved productivity, devise specific measures so you know when the objective has been met, and provide an appropriate and meaningful incentive. As the success of employee recognition programs testifies, incentive programs do not work merely because employees need more money. Employees also respond because they take pride in their work and in their contributions to the organization's success.

284

RECENT EXPERIENCES IN PRODUCTIVITY IMPROVEMENT

Public organizations at all levels have experimented with formal productivity improvement efforts. Some emphasize technological innovation, while others emphasize human resources management; some operate through centralized productivity improvement staffs, while others are more decentralized. But most have successfully demonstrated the value of sustained attention to productivity concerns.

Productivity Improvement at the Federal Level

In 1982, President Reagan announced a series of management improvement efforts called "Reform '88," a designation coinciding with the anticipated length of the president's term. Reform '88 actually brought together a number of existing programs under one umbrella and charged the Office of Management and Budget with overseeing the various efforts. Among these were efforts to improve financial management systems; to eliminate fraud, waste, and abuse in government; to utilize appropriate new technologies in the public workplace; and, consistent with the philosophy of the Reagan administration, to further "privatize" public services. Many efforts were quite successful; for example, new cash management procedures were developed to deal with the federal government's $1.5 trillion cash flow, resulting in nearly a billion dollars in additional interest income each year. Similarly, the government's 320 different financial management systems were reduced to less than twenty, and its 190 payroll systems reduced to ten.

One of the more controversial aspects of Reform '88 was the appointment of the President's Private Sector Survey on Cost Control, known as the Grace Commission. The commission was first appointed to obtain advice from business leaders on ways to improve management of the federal government. However, the commission and its outspoken chairman, J. Peter Grace, soon alienated managers throughout the federal government with its callous and antagonistic approach to managers and other employees. Whereas the commission identified thousands of areas where it was alleged that greater efficiencies could be obtained, many had already been dealt with by managers in government, some actually would have violated the law, and others required legislative rather than administrative action. Yet Grace blamed federal managers and an ill-defined "bureaucracy" for waste and inefficiency.

A more important and certainly more sensitive effort was a new Productivity Improvement Program, initiated by executive order in February 1986. An earlier General Accounting Office report had suggested several ways in which previous federal productivity efforts had been limited: the programs were seen as having a narrow focus, as having neither top-level commitment nor cohesion, as failing to integrate productivity into the management process, and as lacking a specific organizational focus (Dineen, 1986, p. 10). The new program was designed to provide just such a focus.

The overall objective of the federal productivity improvement program was "to provide high-quality, error-free, and timely products and services to the American public, using service delivery systems that are responsive to customer needs and make the most effective use of taxpayer dollars" (Burstein, 1988). This statement of objectives brings together

285

the traditional concerns of productivity programs for reducing unit costs with new concerns for quality and timeliness, concerns especially well-suited to the public sector. (Quality here refers to the ability of the program to meet "customer" requirements; timeliness refers to meeting appropriate schedules for design, development, and delivery of a product or service.) The federal productivity improvement staff began by identifying almost 700 different programs or functions of the federal government. From this inventory, a small number became the focus for the first year's activities, with the idea of expanding the program to other functions in later years. Managers in the selected program areas were encouraged to identify problems of efficiency, quality, and timeliness, then to under-take programs to solve the problems. Specific instructions were provided with respect to measuring and evaluating productivity efforts in the selected programs. Many of the results were rather dramatic (Dineen, 1986, p. 11):

- In one year the Department of State reduced the time required for issuing passports from almost four weeks to ten days, even though there was a twenty percent increase in applications.

- Similarly, the U.S. Geological Survey cut the number of days required to process customer orders for maps in half, from twenty days to ten days.

- The U.S. Customs Service changed the entry procedure at Houston Interconti-nental Airport, reducing the time for most people to go through customs from an hour-and-a-half to fifteen minutes.

286

As a result of these early efforts, there was a growing emphasis on quality in the federal program. Quality improvement prototypes (possible success stories) were identified, productivity conferences and other educational programs were developed to extend the concepts of quality and productivity, and there was a new emphasis on Total Quality Management (TQM). TQM is basically oriented toward building a "culture of quality" within federal agencies (see Box 8.4). TQM is a broad-based program emphasizing such notions as quality of service, a customer orientation, and excellence in all aspects of program operation. Such concepts are pursued through high levels of employee involve-ment, effective and renewed communications, reliance on standards and measures, and extensive training and recognition. The Office of Management and Budget will require all major agencies to submit yearly reports on how they are implementing Total Quality Management beginning in 1991. (We will discuss the concept of Total Quality Manage-ment in chapter 9.)

Some of the ideas being discussed under the rubric of TQM might indeed reshape federal service delivery. One proposal envisions the creation of several Federal Service Centers, locations designed as an initial point of contact for citizens dealing with a variety of related agencies (such as licenses and permits, labor and industrial development, etc.). These centers could be electronically tied to central processing systems that would respond to citizen inquiries on a real-time basis. In all cases, the centers would provide the coordi-nation; it would not be necessary for the citizen to work out questions of where to go next.

Developments in State Government

Many of these exciting developments at the federal level were paralleled or even preceded by actions at the state level. Several governors elected in the mid-seventies to the early

BOX 8.4

TOTAL QUALITY MANAGEMENT

Total quality management means creating a culture of excellence where agency executives, managers, and employees continuously strive to:

- Meet customer expectations
- Do the right things right the first time
- Achieve ever-higher standards of quality, timeliness, and efficiency

SOURCE: Presentation at the University of Missouri by Carolyn Burstein, Office of Management and Budget (November 1988).

287

eighties placed management improvements high on their list of state priorities. Governor James B. Hunt of North Carolina spoke of preparing state government to meet the changes of modern society; Governor John Y. Brown of Kentucky talked about "running government like a business" (in his case, the fried chicken business!). With this emphasis, management issues generally and productivity improvement specifically moved to a prominent place on the states' agendas.

One review of state government productivity improvement efforts suggests several distinct characteristics of such programs (Jarrett, no date). First, most state programs have been initiated by the executive branch rather than the legislature. Although legislative actions have sometimes been required, as in providing funding for special productivity initiatives, the primary impetus has come from the executive branch. Second, many programs have employed temporary task forces of private sector executives to advise government, though the savings resulting from such approaches have often been exaggerated (similar to that of the Grace Commission at the federal level). Third, most early efforts focused on direct cost reduction rather than quality improvements, though the latter emphasis seems to be increasing. Several state programs now find it advantageous to speak of "quality and productivity" as equal objectives.

The results have often been impressive. During Richard Thornburg's administration, Pennsylvania developed a sustained cost reduction program. Documented savings ranged from a $1,500 reduction in magazine subscriptions in one agency to a $740 million gain through more efficient collection of state revenues (Jarrett, p. 8). Other savings resulted from reduction in the use of sick leave, from controlling the number of vacant positions filled, and from providing incentive funds for productivity improvements.

The incentive idea had been tried earlier in New Jersey and involved establishing a fund to support agency-based productivity improvement efforts, primarily technological innovations. The fund supports one-time improvements that will repay their cost within a relatively brief period, usually no more than three years. Agencies that have needed to "spend money to save money," typically for new equipment, have been able to do so through the investment fund.

Other efforts in New York also proved "productive." For example, the State Insurance Fund implemented an alternate-year auditing schedule that saved $390,000; the Department of Transportation reduced painting costs on highways by using chlorinated rubber paint, which lasts longer; and the Department of Labor centralized numerous employee and benefit programs in a "one-stop" facility (Government Productivity News, April, 1989, p. 3). An interesting aspect of the New York program is a joint labor-management program that has led to many new ideas such as a day care program, an employee assistance program, and new efforts in safety training. Although such programs might, at first glance, seem to benefit the employees more than the state, the savings are easier to recognize when you consider the costs of replacing and retraining employees that leave state government. As evidence to this point, a recent survey by the Administrative Management Society indicated that, among private firms, 40 percent offer alcohol/drug abuse programs, and about 25 percent offer marital, financial, and legal counseling (Government Productivity News, October, 1988, p. 4).

Developments at the Local Level

288

Similar success stories are being told at the local level, where productivity improvement efforts have expanded greatly in the last couple of decades. Many improvements involve the use of new technology. For example, several cities now use minipumpers to put out smaller fires. These units run at only a fifth the cost of a regular pumper and extend the life of the larger machines. Similarly, many cities now use new all-weather street-patching materials, which is far more cost-effective. Other productivity gains are being made by reorganizing services for more effective delivery. For example, five Texas cities contributed to a unified police dispatch system, which none of the cities could have afforded alone. One county government decentralized building inspections by creating nine field offices. Inspectors now report to the office nearest their inspection sites, thus significantly reducing travel time between inspections (Barbour, 1976, pp. 3–4).

Cities have also experimented with programs designed for increasing employees' motivation. One major study indicates, however, that cities, like states, have encountered several difficulties in providing incentives, especially monetary, for workers (Greiner et al., 1981, p. 409). Among these problems, civil service regulations and existing union contracts have proven especially difficult to alter. Despite the barriers to incentive programs, several cities have introduced them, such as suggestion systems, while others have tried job enrichment, especially in police departments.

An interesting experiment that has been tried primarily at the local level involves hiring an interim manager, who takes on an especially difficult job for a specific period, makes needed changes, then leaves, taking all the "heat." In a New Jersey township, for example, an interim manager was selected to head a community development department for a period. He completely revamped the department by installing new project control systems and by managing several particularly volatile projects. Similarly, in Florida, a city manager hired an interim director to develop a brand new agency, while simultaneously recruiting the person who would be the permanent director (Government Productivity News, July/August, 1989, pp. 1, 4).

IMPLEMENTING QUALITY
CIRCLES IN STATE GOVERNMENT

To clarify some issues you might face in implementing a productivity improvement program, let's examine in some detail the implementation of a major quality circles program in Missouri state government. During the summer of 1982, Governor Christopher (Kit) Bond and Commissioner of Administration John Pelzer began a new and broad-based productivity improvement program for Missouri. While that program led to several important initiatives, including a Governor's Advisory Council on Productivity, an Employee Suggestion Award system, and a Manager's Roundtable program, the primary thrust of the productivity program over the first four years was to establish quality circles in state agencies.

The initial impetus for the quality circle program came from Commissioner Pelzer, a former city manager, based on his understanding of the success of quality circles in Dallas, Texas. After securing the governor's support for the program, the Office of Administration contracted for a consultant to supervise the initial presentation and implementation. At the same time, Pelzer visited each of the fourteen state department directors, explaining the quality circle program and asking for their participation. As a result of the conversations, six department directors agreed to sponsor a total of ten quality circles. Departments in the pilot program included Revenue, Social Service, Corrections and Human Resources, Natural Resources, Mental Health, and the Office of Administration.

In September 1982, the consultant made an initial presentation on quality circles to the department directors and to the newly created Governor's Advisory Council on Productivity (a group of primarily private sector representatives with experience in productivity improvement efforts). Although reaction to the presentation was quite positive on the part of the six department directors who had already committed to the concept and on the part of the council members, three other directors were firmly opposed to the concept, and the remainder assumed a "wait and see" attitude.

It was felt that for the quality circle concept to have a chance of success, it would be necessary to have the full support of managers in the various agencies. So, on the following day, division directors reporting to the six department directors attended a similar overview and participated in exercises based on the quality circles problem-solving approach. The response to this session was overwhelmingly positive, to the point that, when the department directors met again to discuss implementation, they agreed that the pilot program should be expanded from ten to twenty-five circles. They believed a broader experience would help establish the program in such a way that it might continue across a change in administration two years later.

To further build managerial support, the consultant continued presentations with middle-level managers for each of the six departments. The reaction continued to be favorable, but many more questions were raised at this level. Many managers were not familiar with the quality circles concept, and the consultant felt a need to "sell" the idea, which was made difficult by a lack of state government examples. Managers quite understandably wondered whether a technique developed in production-oriented private industries would suit their more service-oriented agencies.

At about that time, the state's first productivity improvement coordinator was hired in the Office of Administration and began to work with the consultants in training facilitators and team leaders, thus adding a greater sense of permanence to the program. Each training session took five days and included commentary on the history of quality circles, what might be expected of quality circles in state government, group dynamics, and the problem-solving process. Each participant practiced leading the group through a problem-solving module. Case studies were included, although again the training was hampered by lack of public sector (especially state government) examples. (Later training sessions, using examples drawn from the work of the pilot circles, were far more successful.) Twelve facilitators, most with some training experience but drawn from the agencies themselves, were trained, as were twenty-five team leaders.

Following team leader training and before the actual start of circle operations, each circle leader, working with a facilitator, led a session for employees elsewhere in his or her own organization who were not involved in the actual circles. These overview sessions were designed to inform those outside the circles about the process, assure them that the circle members were actually going to be talking about work-related items, and invite them to submit suggestions for consideration.

Though there was some initial skepticism about the quality circle program, especially among middle-level managers and among employees not involved in the program, several early successes seemed to spur interest, and soon many requests came for creating new circles. The productivity staff in cooperation with the state training office trained new facilitators and team leaders. Generally, managers recruited potential team leaders, though some first-line supervisors initiated contacts themselves. Candidates were told they would not be required to begin circles, but were invited to a training session to learn more about the circle concept and to decide whether circles would be appropriate for their areas. Again, once the leader became committed to the program, employees were introduced to the idea and given opportunities to participate. As training progressed, many who were trained were given "training the trainers" sessions so as to multiply the resources available for extending the program to new areas. By 1986, all circle-related training was conducted by state employees, much of it (leader and facilitator training) on a regular monthly schedule.

By the late 1980s, over 125 circles were operating in Missouri state government, and, indeed, extended well beyond the six agencies that began the program. Results of the program have been positive in several ways, and it seems likely that new circles will continue to develop. Whereas the early circles tended to focus more on work-process issues than on cost savings issues, several circles have now demonstrated direct cost savings as a result of their work. These are some of the many successes of the quality circles:

1. *Department of Revenue, Division of Taxation:* The key entry staff of the Central Processing Bureau had a problem meeting the deposit deadline on sales tax returns. The circle devised a way to key enter returns in smaller batches so that errors could be found more readily. The processing deadline was also extended past the deposit deadline of 2:30 P.M. to permit processing more returns and depositing additional funds

each day. The benefit of this solution was not only that the deadline pressure was eliminated, thus reducing data-entry errors, but on a yearly basis, an additional $1 million was deposited one day earlier, thus earning an additional $10,000 in interest each year.

2. *Office of Administration, Division of General Services (the Printshop):* Ten printing press operators spent one-half hour each day searching for printing and binding materials in an unorganized storage area. The quality circle's solution to the problem was to purchase metal shelves to store the printing materials (at a cost of $2,130). The benefit of this solution was that the 1,230 hours per year spent searching for materials could be used in operating the presses. Since management estimated the lost time could be recovered at $21.50 per hour, savings totaled $26,445. The result was a net savings of $24,315.

3. *Department of Social Services, Division of Family Services (Claims and Restitutions):* Erroneous payments entered in the Claims and Restitutions System for food stamps and AFDC were not being classified properly to facilitate recapture. The quality circle (the "Sports Cars") designed a system for entering claims before they are paid. Now the claims are classified, and the state can recapture funds. As a result of the changed policy and changed computer programming, $50,000 was recaptured initially; it was estimated that an additional $3,000 a month would be saved as well.

4. *Office of Administration, Division of EDP Coordination (Systems Maintenance and Support):* The computer run time for financial programs on the automated accounting system took too long. Current fnancial data was not available on a daily basis because of the length of time required for the daily run. The daily job series required 8 hours of computer run time; the monthly series required 72 hours. Quality circle members began to examine "optimization" techniques for the computer program. They studied methods of coding, data flow, and file organization. With technical assistance from the State Data Center, the computer program was changed and run time was greatly reduced. The result was that the computer run time per day was reduced by 50 to 70 percent. This prompted similar changes in the monthly run. The reduced run time was calculated at $160 daily, which translates to approximately $40,000 in annual savings. In addition, users now have online systems available at the beginning of the work day, resulting in increased user productivity. Late-night maintenance has been reduced significantly.

A major part of a successful quality circle program is recognition for circle members, leaders, facilitators, and middle managers. Recognition is provided in the form of presentations to managers, visits from the department director to circle meetings, letters from directors to the circle following a successful presentation, and articles in the productivity newsletter about a circle's project.

In several Missouri departments, the department director visited an early circle meeting, both to learn more about the program and to demonstrate interest in quality circles. Because in several cases these were the first times the director had taken the time to meet directly with front-line employees, the meetings were quite significant. They proved to be enjoyable for the department directors, good motivators for circle members, and an indication to all employees of the director's interest in both the employees and the quality circles.

Each department that is using quality circles in the Missouri program has chosen to recognize the accomplishments of its circles' members in various ways, including awards luncheons and other recognition ceremonies. The Department of Social Services hosted a quality circle conference for circle members and managers. Circle members attended workshops on management presentations, data gathering, and problem analysis. Managers saw actual presentations that had already solved a problem and were given additional information about how quality circles might work in their areas. In addition, top-level managers from the department made speeches about the circles in their division. Five circles were recognized for outstanding achievements, and one was chosen the Quality Circle of the Year. Awards were presented at a dinner at the end of the conference.

Also, near the end of his term, Governor Bond held an Employee Recognition Day to honor those who had participated in the quality circle program or other productivity improvement efforts. An awards ceremony was followed by a brief reception, again emphasizing the weight the governor placed on productivity improvement and the involvement of those present in improving productivity. Bond's successor, John Ashcroft, continued the tradition, adding emphasis to the effort to improve quality and productivity in the state.

SUMMARY AND ACTION IMPLICATIONS

Technical innovations are often dramatic in their impact, sometimes saving thousands, even millions, of dollars. But technological innovations do not occur independently of the skills and attitudes of those who work in an organization. Innovations seem to flourish in a climate where human creativity is encouraged and usually require human changes— what one group calls "orgware"—to be successfully implemented.

Improved productivity appears to depend at least in part on a shift from the traditional authoritarian approach to management to a more open and participatory approach. This shift has been especially apparent in implementing productivity improvement programs at all levels of government. In many cases, but especially in the federal government's emphasis on Total Quality Management, we find a shifting orientation toward management that places greater emphasis on the involvement of all employees. (The resulting orientation was perhaps best expressed by the head of a state productivity council, who described his philosophy this way: "Those who do the work know the work best and know best how to improve the work.") The result is an approach to management that seems not only more human in scale and perspective, but that many authorities are coming to believe is far more productive as well.

A recent study by the Canadian government of "well-performing" governmental organizations in that country outlines some of the basics of this new approach. That study identified five factors leading to organizational success, which we may take as recommended patterns of action for managers to seek in trying to improve productivity.

Emphasis on people. People are challenged, encouraged and developed. They are given power to act and to use their judgment. There is a belief that high performance is a product of people who care rather than systems that constrain. People do not preoccupy themselves with the risk of failure, but are confident they can tackle virtually any challenge.

Participative leadership. Leadership is not authoritarian or coercive, but participative whenever possible. The leaders envision an ideal organization, define purpose and goals, then articulate these and foster commitment. Staff communicate easily.

They feel comfortable consulting peers as well as those above and below them. Although formal levels exist for administrative purposes, there are no boundaries that inhibit collaboration in achieving goals.

Innovative work styles. Staff reflect on their performance. They learn from the effects of their actions. They seek to solve problems creatively. They maintain strong monitoring, feedback and control systems as useful tools. They are self-reliant, rather than dependent on control from an outside authority.

Strong client orientation. These organizations focus strongly on their clients, deriving satisfaction from serving the client rather than the bureaucracy. There is an alignment of values and purpose between the well-performing agency and their political and central agency masters.

A mindset that seeks optimum performance. People hold values that drive them to always seek improvement in their organization's performance. When conditions change, they adjust their methods, not their values. Because of this orientation toward performance and adaptability, the organization performs well even in a changing environment. This mindset may be the most important feature of all. (Government Productivity News, December, 1989, p. 4)*

As a manager, one of the primary technical concerns you will face is improving your organization's productivity. Whereas you may be able to accomplish great gains through technological innovations, the most significant long-term gains will come from a proper emphasis on the human factors in organizational effectiveness. To be judged successful, you will always have to balance your concern for the technical side of your agency's work and your attention to the human side of the organization, a topic to which we will turn in the next several chapters.

293

TERMS AND DEFINITIONS

Behavioral awards: Used to reward specific behaviors that management wishes to encourage.

Employee recognition program: Effective way to acknowledge special contributions of certain employees or groups to the organization.

Expert systems: Computer programs that mimic the decision-making processes of human experts within a particular field.

Gainsharing plan: Monetary award for a group of employees based on savings generated by the group.

Management by objectives: Participatory approach to establishing clear and measurable objectives throughout the entire organization.

Performance appraisal: Specific evaluation with respect to an individual's progress in completing specified tasks.

*SOURCE: Extract originally from the Report of the Auditor General of Canada to the House of Commons for Fiscal Year ending 31 March 1988, Chapter 4: "Attributes of Well-Performing Organizations." Reproduced with permission of the Minister of Supply and Services, Canada, 1990.

Performance bonus: One-time monetary award based on superior performance on the job or in a particular task.

Piecework bonus: Incentive that ties the worker's productivity in a given task to the monetary rewards he or she receives.

Quality circle: Small group of people who do similar or connected work and meet regularly to identify, analyze, and solve work-process problems.

Suggestion award programs: Incentives for employees who make specific suggestions that result in savings for the organization.

Task forces: Groups brought together to work on specific organizational problems.

STUDY QUESTIONS

1. Discuss the relationship between the growing use of computer-based systems and the human element involved in technology transfer.
2. What is management by objectives and how can this approach benefit an organization?
3. Identify the eight categories for judging the quality of work life.
4. Discuss the variety of incentive plans currently used in public agencies. Explain the usefulness of each approach.
5. Productivity improvement has become a major concern of public managers. What basic issues should one consider when undertaking a productivity improvement program?
6. Compare and contrast productivity improvement activities at various levels of government.

CASES AND EXERCISES

1. Review the criteria in Box 8.3 for evaluating the quality of work life. Working in groups of five to seven, choose two or three jobs that members of the group have previously held and analyze the quality of work life in those jobs. In each case, members of the group should interview the person who held the job, asking questions about each category in the chart. When everyone has a complete understanding of the nature of the job, the group as a whole should draw conclusions with respect to the quality of work life for someone holding that job.

Following this activity, choose two or three jobs to which members of the group might reasonably aspire in ten to fifteen years. Have one individual imagine in detail what the job would be like from day to day, then follow the same procedure to interview the "job holder" and draw conclusions about the quality of work life. In what ways do you expect that future jobs will be of higher "quality" than those in the past? Why should there be any differences?

Finally, choose one job from the "jobs already held" and one from those "to which you aspire." Then consider these jobs from the standpoint of the person to whom the individual job holder would report. How could the manager improve or "enrich" the particular job? Specifically, could adjustments in authority or responsibility improve the quality of work life for the job holder? How would those changes affect the individual's productivity? Report your conclusions to the class.

2. Divide the class into groups ranging from seven to ten members each. Have each group select a reasonably small public agency—federal, state, local, or nonprofit. Based on interviews with several top managers and a sampling of employees throughout the organization, analyze the organization's existing system of incentives. Design a new incentive program you think would result in improved quality and productivity. (If you have difficulty locating or gaining access to a particular organization, simply develop a research design through which you might test an incentive system. Assume an organization of two hundred people engaged in manual processing of tax receipts for a state government. What kinds of questions would you ask of which individuals in the organization?)

3. Academic departments, like other organizations, can benefit from information and advice from employees and clients (faculty, staff, students, alumni, potential employers, etc.). Consider the department of your major. How would you design a comprehensive program of employee and client involvement that would help the department improve the quality of its offerings? (After designing a program, you might interview the department chair to find out what mechanisms are already in place.)

4. There has been considerable attention to "Japanese management" in recent years. Based on materials available in your school's library, develop a list of "principles" of Japanese management and assess the impact of these ideas on the operation of public agencies in this country.

295

FOR ADDITIONAL READING

Greiner, John M. *Productivity and Motivation.* Washington, DC: The Urban Institute Press, 1981.

Holzer, Marc, and Halachmi, Arie. *Strategic Issues in Public Sector Productivity.* San Francisco: Jossey-Bass, 1986.

Holzer, Marc, and Nagel, Stuart, eds. *Productivity and Public Policy.* Beverly Hills, CA: Sage Publications, 1984.

Kolodny, Harvey, and van Beinum, Hans, eds. *The Quality of Work Life and the 1980s.* New York: Praeger, 1983.

Matzer, John, Jr., ed. *Productivity Improvement Techniques.* Washington, DC: International City Management Association, 1986.

Mercer, James L., and Philips, Ronald J. *Public Technology.* New York: American Management Association, 1981.

Morley, Elaine. *A Practitioner's Guide to Public Sector Productivity Improvement.* New York: Van Nostrand Reinhold, 1986.

Stevens, John M., and McGowan, Robert P. *Information Systems and Public Management.* New York: Praeger, 1985.

Wholey, Joseph S., Abramson, Mark A., and Bellavita, Christopher. *Performance and Credibility: Developing Excellence in Public and Nonprofit Organizations.* Lexington, MA: D. C. Heath, 1986.

PART THREE

PERSONAL

AND

INTERPERSONAL

SKILLS

MANAGING IN A POLITICAL CONTEXT

A public administrator needs a good understanding of the values and principles underlying work in the public sector, knowledge of how public policy is developed and executed, and familiarity with a number of administrative techniques peculiar to the public sector. But the real key to managerial success in public organizations is not what you *know*, but what you can *do*. How effectively and how responsibly can you deal with the seemingly endless series of problems and opportunities that confront you? A legislator calls to ask for an immediate report on a matter you know will require a week to examine properly; a subordinate confesses that he has grown dependent on drugs and needs your help; someone in a meeting becomes outraged over what you perceive as a minor matter and threatens to have you fired; your boss asks your assistance in designing a completely new program, and asks if you would be interested in running it—these situations and many more like them constitute the real challenges of public administration.

Your response to each event, of course, is spontaneous; yet your actions will soon add up to a pattern that reflects your knowledge, values, and most of all, skills in dealing with other people. If, time after time, you can act effectively and responsibly in situations that arise unexpectedly and require immediate answers with little time to think through the "theoretical" possibilities, you will likely be considered a highly successful manager.

Fortunately, the skills required for managerial effectiveness can be developed over time. In this and the following chapters, we will examine how your knowledge and values can be brought to bear in real-world situations. We will focus on the specific personal and interpersonal skills a manager requires and on some ways you might further develop those skills. In this chapter, we will look at several broad approaches to understanding the structure and design of public organizations as well as people's behavior in those organizations.

IMAGES OF ORGANIZING IN THE PUBLIC SECTOR

All managers carry ideas or images of how public organizations should operate and how individual managers should act. These images, built up through experience, reading and discussion, and reflection, include notions about the most effective structures for public agencies, the best way to manage employees, and the proper relationship between elected and appointed officials. Depending on your particular view of public organizations, you will tend to look for and emphasize certain things and ignore others. The images you carry in your head will lead you to emphasize certain aspects of organizational life and deemphasize others.

Some of these images derive from our experiences in our families; others derive from school experiences; still others derive from our work in other organizations. Some are general lessons we learned about topics such as power and authority, communications and cooperations, and so forth. Others are more specific to the world of work or the world of public service. Some are fairly conscious, others lie far beneath the surface.

300

Whatever their form, these images direct our actions in specific ways. They cause us to see the world in a particular way and, correspondingly, to act in a particular way. So it is important to carefully consider how each of us thinks about public organizations. What images do we have, and how do they direct us to think about public organizations? Which images allow us to be most successful? Which images hold us back or get in our way?

As you begin to think more carefully about the images that shape your work in public organizations (or elsewhere), and especially as you begin to accumulate experiences in public organizations, you will begin to identify areas where your insight (and consequently your actions) might be improved. One way to sharpen your images of public organizations is to consider what scholars and practitioners in the field of management generally and public management in particular have said and written. Fortunately, there is a considerable and growing body of material to draw upon that offers many categories and approaches you might use in thinking about your involvement in public organizations.

For the most part, this literature has developed out of the experiences of practicing managers. Reflective practitioners and thoughtful academics have asked over and over how public managers can be helped to select those features of organizational life that will be most helpful to them. Many students and practitioners of public administration have contributed to our understanding of the management of public agencies. They have developed "word pictures" (often simply called *theories*) to suggest what will be most helpful when you approach similar problems.

Each theoretical approach directs attention toward certain topics or ideas and away from others. It is up to you to select the most relevant and most helpful approaches to your particular situation. In this chapter, we will review some of the most influential ways of thinking about management in the public sector. Some early approaches focused on fairly obvious points; more recent approaches seem more complex and sophisticated.

THE FUNCTIONS OF MANAGEMENT

Writing early in the 20th century, French management theorist and practitioner Henri Fayol (1949) identified five general functions managers should perform: planning, organizing, commanding, coordinating, and controlling. Several years later, Luther Gulick arrived at a similar list. Gulick, at the time an advisor on federal government reorganization, described the functions of public management in terms of an acronym, POSDCORB: Planning, Organizing, Staffing, Directing, Coordinating, and Budgeting (Gulick, 1937). To Fayol and Gulick, these activities were the essence of management and identified functions that had to be performed if organizations were to be managed effectively. They constituted advice to managers as to what they should be doing.

Planning involves preparing yourself and your organization to move effectively into the future. All managers engage in planning at least to some extent, and for some managers, such as those on strategic planning staffs, planning is almost a full-time activity. Some managers make plans for the entire organization, others make plans for the units they directly supervise, and all managers plan for their own activities. Unfortunately, as we noted earlier, planning is one managerial function that is often easy to overlook. Managers get caught up in the hectic pace of conversations, meetings, and deadlines and often neglect planning. Yet the most effective managers are aware that time taken out for planning, whether for the organization or for oneself, pays rich dividends.

Planning is closely related to decision making, an aspect of managerial work that cuts across many of the other areas. The ability to make thoughtful decisions seems to distinguish the more successful managers. Because decision making is so fundamental to managerial work, it has been studied intensively for many years. In most organizations, decision making is a central activity.

Organizing refers to many different activities, including division of the organization into different departments, creating levels in the organization's hierarchy, and deciding who reports to whom. In a specific department or division, organizing also includes the task of defining specific positions and jobs. Note that organizing includes job design, but the assignment of individuals to specific jobs involves the staffing rather than the organizing function.

Staffing is the process of acquiring, training, and developing the personnel to conduct the organization's activities. Staffing is today more generally described as "personnel management" or sometimes "human resources management." As we saw in chapter 6, specific tasks such as hiring, training, firing, and so forth are examples of the staffing or personnel function. Obviously, dealing with people involves important skills in communication and motivation, as well as the ability to make sound decisions about who you hire to work with you.

Directing is often the most dynamic and most visible management function. It includes three critical management activities: leading, motivating, and changing things when necessary. Providing direction to an organization is a subtle and complex task that involves the full range of personal and interpersonal skills.

301

Coordinating the work of many different people in many different places is also a central managerial function. The complexity and diversity of most modern organizations means that a great deal of time must be spent making sure that all the "pieces" fall into place at the right time. Coordinating involves special skills in problem solving—how to make things work—but also skills in communicating and negotiating.

Budgeting involves managing the organization's resources, especially financial. Budgeting involves securing, planning for, and managing the organization's funds. As we saw in chapter 5, budgeting is a technical field, but it also involves considerable human skills, especially those of developing funding for one's programs and allocating scarce resources among many different competing programs and people.

In addition to these standard management functions, there are also a number of *miscellaneous tasks* that are usually considered managerial work. One of the most important is dealing with people from outside the organization. Skills in presenting your organization and point of view to others is becoming an increasingly important activity as the relationships among organizations at many different levels become more intense. Representing your organization before outside groups and organizations has come to be known in the literature on management as **boundary spanning.**

The importance of effective management has been presented prescriptively to management students since the founding of management as a discipline (sometime in the late nineteenth century). The prescription was and usually is presented as an article of faith or as an assertion based on experience; however, there is a much more solid basis for arguing that these management functions are crucial. That basis is a classic study conducted at the University of Michigan in the late 1940s and early 1950s (Kahn & Katz, 1953).

The Michigan researchers studied supervisors in three industries: insurance, railroading, and tractor manufacturing. An important question was the extent to which the performance of basic managerial functions made any difference to organizational outcomes. To investigate this question, the supervisors of work sections in each industry were asked a version of the following question: "How much of your time do you usually spend in supervising the men, and how much in other things, like planning the work, making out reports, and dealing with people outside your section?" Data about the productivity of each responding supervisor's section were also collected, which made it possible to compare how much time supervisors spent performing managerial tasks in high-productivity units to the amount of time supervisors spent on managerial tasks in low-productivity units.

Similar results were obtained from all three industries, but they are clearest in the insurance industry sample. There, 75 percent of the supervisors of high-productivity units spent half their time or more on managerial tasks, in contrast to 59 percent of the supervisors of low-productivity units, who spent less than half their time on managerial work. Thus, managerial work seems to make a difference: as more management is done, the better the outcomes. There was even some evidence that individuals in work sections where supervisors were doing too little managerial work would spontaneously attempt to perform some of the managerial tasks (Kahn & Katz, 1953, p. 615).

THE EARLY WRITERS: A CONCERN FOR STRUCTURE

The question of how managers might be guided in their work has occupied theorists and practitioners for many years. Early writers on public administration thought of management in highly mechanical terms and considered questions of organizational structure and design of paramount importance. Recall that the birth of public administration as a separate field of study occurred during a time of impressive gains in science and industry; new ideas and new products were changing society almost overnight, as were the industrial and organizational processes that made them possible. It was a time of rigid control by "captains of industry"; it was also a time of fostering the birth of the assembly line.

In such an era, the machine became the leading image for how to organize technical and human processes. Just as the machine was precise, mechanical, and efficient, so should the organizations that built machines show the same characteristics. The result was a highly mechanical approach to organization that valued the idea of developing proper structures and operating them with great efficiency.

This orientation was epitomized in the influential work of Frederick W. Taylor, who developed what he termed **scientific management,** an approach based on carefully defined "laws, rules, and principles" (1923, p. 7). Taylor focused first on the individual worker, designing detailed measurements of time and motion to discover how the worker might become more efficient. For example, one might measure the distance from where a particular piece of equipment was stored to where it was used, then try to reduce that distance and the time and motion required to use the equipment. (In one example, Taylor sought to develop a "science of shoveling" based on the premise that the size of each individual shovel load would affect the daily output of "first-class shovelers." After careful and detailed experiments, it was determined that the greatest tonnage per day would be achieved with an average shovel load of about twenty-one pounds!)

Obviously, Taylor's approach could be applied to a wide variety of work-process problems, from the design of assembly lines to the arrangement of items on one's desk. But beyond these efforts to turn workers into highly tuned machines, Taylor's work provided guidance for managers throughout the organization. The manager's role became that of making the organization more efficient through the application of detailed "scientific" information. The smooth-running organization was to be highly mechanical, with the human elements strictly controlled so as to contribute to overall efficiency. The manager's job was to assure the efficient operation of the system.

Just as Taylor and others emphasized the efficient operation of industrial systems, others soon applied this emphasis in public administration. Leonard White wrote, "The objective of public administration is the most efficient utilization of the resources at the disposal of officials and employees" (1926, p. 2); "In the science of administration, whether public or private, the basic 'good' is efficiency," Luther Gulick concurred (1937b, p. 192). Though several writers objected, pointing out that other values, such as responsiveness, need to come into play in public organizations and that mechanical efficiency is "coldly calculating and inhuman" (Dimock, 1936, p. 120), efficiency was clearly the primary interest of most early public administrationists.

From the field of business, the early writers in public administration transferred other lessons about the design and structure of organizations, specifically the importance of establishing single centers of power controlling basically top-down structures. At the top of the organization there was to be one single authority to whom all subordinate personnel ultimately reported. Though the organization would be characterized by many managers and perhaps many organizational units, the ultimate responsibility and authority lay at the top.

303

To reconcile this view with the democratic requirement that public organizations should be responsive to the popular will, the early writers suggested that the organization's head, the single source of power and authority, should simply be accountable to the legislative body in much the same way a corporate chief executive officer is accountable to a board of directors. (Recall this idea as "the doctrine of neutral competence.") In describing the role of an agency chief executive, the advice of the early writers was to vest all administrative authority in a single executive, who would be given appropriate powers to carry out the work and responsibility for seeing that it was done. According to W. F. Willoughby, this was the first step in making the executive branch a "single, integrated piece of administrative machinery" (1927, p. 37). (This advice was at odds with the standard political practice of that period, the election of many administrative officers and the use of many, large executive boards. As we saw earlier, even today, most states elect officers such as secretary of state or treasurer rather than having such officers report to a single chief executive, in this case the governor.)

The early writers who put forth the administrative management viewpoint were practical people who drew on their experience in managing public agencies. Consequently, when they described their work, they tended to emphasize how organizational structures might be built. Luther Gulick, for example, wrote extensively about the formation of agencies. After the agency was created and an executive chosen, Gulick saw the next question as one of dividing the work necessary to the organization, then establishing proper means of coordination and control. In other words, the new organization would move through four phases in which the legislature or chief executive would (1) define the job, (2) select a director, who would (3) determine the nature and number of required units, and (4) establish a structure of authority through which he or she would coordinate and control activities of the units (1937a, p. 7).

The division of labor, which amounted to creation of an organizational structure, was a critical element. The logic was compelling: since people differ in knowledge and skills and since the amount of time any one person can contribute to solution of large-scale problems is limited, it is necessary to divide the work of the organization into manageable portions. As we saw earlier, division of labor could be accomplished in a limited number of ways. (Recall that Gulick suggested organizing on the basis of (1) the major *purpose* served (education, welfare, etc.), (2) the *process* (engineering, medicine, etc.), (3) the *persons or things* being dealt with by the unit (veterans, convicts, etc.), or (4) the *place* or geographic location where the work is done (1937a, pp. 21–29).)

Having established a division of labor, the next problem facing the new director or manager was to create a structure of authority to coordinate and control the various parts of the organization. Gulick's answer to this question, like others during this period, was again drawn from orthodox practice in business—the organization should feature unity of command exercised through a hierarchical structure of authority. By the turn of the century, hierarchical organizations, like those symbolized in the standard organization chart (see Box 9.1), had become models for industry (as they had previously been in the military and the Catholic Church). Gulick and many other early scholars and practitioners in public administration suggested a similar approach in the public sector.

Guidance for creating such structures was given by two former General Motors executives, James Mooney and Alan C. Reiley (1939). Mooney and Reiley described four main principles for structuring large organizations. The first, coordination through *unity of command*, emphasized the importance of strong executive leadership exercised through

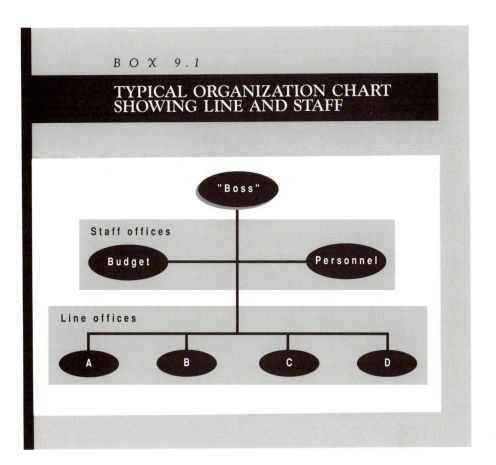

BOX 9.1

TYPICAL ORGANIZATION CHART SHOWING LINE AND STAFF

a specific and formal chain of command. In this structure, each person would have only one boss, and each boss would have a limited *span of control*—that is, a limited number of people reporting to him or her. Mooney and Reiley argued that there should be no question about whose orders to obey. The second principle was the **scalar principle,** which described the vertical division of labor among various organizational levels. (In military terms, the difference between a general and a private reflects the scalar principle.) Third was the **functional principle,** describing a horizontal division of labor. (Again, in military terms, the difference between infantry and air force would be a functional difference.) Finally, Mooney and Reiley discussed the relationship between *line and staff*, with line offices representing the direct flow of authority, and staff offices (such as personnel or finance) available to advise the chief executive, but not exercising direct authority over line offices.

The language of hierarchical structures became somewhat standard. And, just as distinctions were often drawn between line and staff, managers were (and are today) often classified as top, middle, or supervisory. Supervisory managers are at the bottom of the hierarchy, top managers at the peak, and middle managers in between. A supervisory manager directly manages the people involved in producing the organization's output. The supervisory level is the first level of management, so supervisors are sometimes called first-line managers. There are normally *no* managers below the supervisory level. An example of a supervisory manager is the person to whom your mail carrier reports at the post office.

Supervisors report to middle managers, usually defined as "managers who manage other managers." If the organization is small, there may be only one level of middle managers; large organizations usually have more than one middle-management level. The highest level of management, the top level, usually has the fewest managers of the three levels. Top managers, often called "executives," are responsible for entire organizations, whereas middle and supervisory level managers focus on smaller and smaller sections of it. Top managers are usually the most involved in relationships with other groups and agencies.

It is easy to distinguish supervisory-level from middle-level managers, but it is often ambiguous as to where middle management stops and top management begins. Titles often confuse things more than they help. The title of vice-president, for example, indicates a top manager in some organizations; in others, the vice-president is only a middle manager. Banks are particularly well known for having many vice-presidents, most of whom are obviously not part of top management. Similarly, titles in public organizations, such as division director, branch chief, and department head, are used in many different ways and are usually only meaningful if you understand the conventions of the particular organization.

306

Independently of the American writers we have mentioned, German sociologist Max Weber examined the concept of bureaucracy early in this century, though Weber's work was not well known to the earlier public administrationists. Weber used the term *bureaucracy* to refer to any large organization, public or private, characterized by a clearly defined hierarchy of impersonal offices to which persons are appointed based on technical qualifications and through which they are subject to strict discipline and control (Weber, 1947, p. 328). Though we now often use *bureaucracy* pejoratively, Weber's more technical use carries no negative connotation. Indeed, Weber argued that bureaucracy is an attractive way to organize because it is so efficient: "Experience tends to universally show that the purely bureaucratic type of administration . . . is . . . capable of attaining the highest degree of efficiency and is in the sense formally the most rational known means of carrying out imperative control over human beings" (p. 337).

In any case, early writers on public administration generally sought to apply what they saw as the correct "principles" of administrative management to the conduct of public organizations. In doing so, they implied that the problems facing government and their solutions were much the same as those in industry—centralization of authority and the development of hierarchical structures. But this assumption sidestepped several important issues essential to the operations of *public* agencies. Was the criterion of efficiency the only criterion by which the work of public organizations should be evaluated? Is it incompatible to create highly authoritarian structures to carry out the work of a democracy?

There were also questions about whether approaches to organization based on structural analyses alone were even the most efficient. In both the public and private sectors, for example, managers and researchers began to ask whether the rigid structures described in the principles of administrative management could effectively adapt to change. And, perhaps most important, where does the individual human being enter into the equation, other than as a potential machine? The structural lens through which many early scholars and practitioners viewed the world proved to be somewhat limiting; something else was needed.

RECOGNIZING HUMAN BEHAVIOR

In the mid-1920s, an impetus to further investigation of the informal or human factors in organizational life came from studies conducted by a group of Harvard researchers at the Hawthorne Works of the Western Electric Company. The studies, which began in a way largely consistent with the scientific management tradition, were designed to measure the relationship between working conditions (such as lighting, temperature, and humidity) and worker productivity (including monotony and fatigue). In the experiment, certain groups were isolated from their co-workers and placed in carefully controlled environments where conditions could be varied systematically. But, as the experiment developed, regardless of the changes in environmental conditions—lighter or darker, hotter or colder, more or less humid—the productivity of the experimental group tended to increase. Can you guess why?

The researchers' answer was that the experimental group was responding not to the conditions around them, but to the fact that they had been singled out for special attention. As a result, the researchers developed a new interest in the human aspects of organizational life. Those involved in the Hawthorne study began to see organizations as not only meeting the stated goals of producing goods or services but as being concerned also, even if implicitly, with the distribution of "satisfactions"—some monetary, others social and psychological—to the members of the organization. The *informal organization*, the human interactions that paralleled those prescribed by the organizational structure, was viewed as important or even more important than the *formal organization*. If this were the case, then it made sense that the manager's role involved attention to both the formal structure of the work process *and* the pattern of informal relationships among the workers. Either one could affect efficiency and effectiveness.

There was, of course, abundant advice on how to manage the formal structure, but only speculation about how to manage the informal or the human side of organizations. Consequently, a number of studies were undertaken that dealt with the critical human relationship between manager and worker. Many of the studies suggested that changes in one's approach to managing, or *management style*, could lead to important differences in productivity. By treating workers differently, you could affect the work they did.

An example of this orientation was Douglas MacGregor's discussion of Theory X and Theory Y. After reviewing other work on management, MacGregor suggested that a better theory of human behavior (not structure) might make it possible to more effectively control workers in organizations. Specifically, MacGregor contrasted a set of assumptions about human behavior that appeared to form the basis for traditional management techniques (Theory X) with a set of assumptions he felt would underlie a new and more enlightened approach (Theory Y). Traditionally, MacGregor argued, managers seemed to assume that human beings are lazy and dislike work, that they must therefore be coerced to produce, and that most in fact *want* such direction. MacGregor suggested in contrast that work is quite natural, that people do not need to be coerced, that they will devote energy to objectives to which they are committed, and that they will make commitments to objectives that, when completed, will lead to rewards. As a consequence, MacGregor suggested that most workers were not being utilized to their full potential. The lesson was straightforward: managers must take care to determine the needs and desires of their employees, then help orient the individual's objectives so that they are met by work toward the organization's objectives.

Two Classic Works

Two writers on organizational behavior, both stimulated by the new attention to human factors in organizational life, wrote "classics" on the subject during the forties and fifties. One author, Herbert Simon, came from the field of public administration; the other, Chris Argyris, began his work in the field of industrial psychology. Both have influenced all fields of management even to the present.

Simon began by suggesting that the reason we have large organizations in the first place is that individual human beings are limited or "bounded" in their rationality or capacity to solve the complex problems we face in the modern world. "The capacity of the human mind for formulating and solving complex problems is very small in comparison with the size of the problems whose solution is required for objectively rational behavior in the real world—or even for a reasonable approximation to such objective rationality" (1957, p. 198). Organizations are seen as devices for molding our sometimes erratic behavior to rational patterns of obtaining our objectives.

In the abstract, it's really not difficult to design a rational system for reaching organizational objectives. The difficulty comes when human beings, with all their emotions and interests, are inserted into the system. Because they are human, they often appear "irrational" *in terms of the system,* even though what they are doing, from their point of view, may be perfectly rational. The chief problem for Simon, therefore, became how to understand and direct human behavior in such a way that it aids in pursuit of the organization's objectives in a rational (that is, efficient) way.

Simon described the organization as a decision-making system involving two primary sets of decisions on the part of the individual—the decision to be a part of an organization and the decision to contribute desired behaviors to the organization. Simon approaches each problem through a rational calculation of costs and benefits. For example, a person may be expected to remain a member of an organization as long as the benefits provided by the organization appear to exceed those that might be obtained elsewhere.

The same approach is used with respect to the individual's contributions to the organization, an issue closely tied to the question of authority. Simon argued that each individual establishes an **area of acceptance** within which the subordinate is willing to accept the decisions made for him by his superior" (Simon, 1957, pp. 74–75). But since it is in the interest of the organization to have the "zone" as wide as possible, the organization, through its managers, offers certain "inducements" designed to increase the individual's "contributions." Inducements obviously include money and status, but they also involve creating a state of mind in which individuals will tend to obey rather than disobey.

In establishing this state of mind, Simon argues that you cannot expect people to make perfectly rational decisions. Indeed, most human beings act with **bounded rationality**—

they seek the best possible solution, though not necessarily the one that is most rational from a purely economic standpoint. The member can be made to fall in line with the organization's expectations by means of inducements that are just good enough to elicit the desired contributions. In this way, what Simon terms *administrative man* (in contrast to "economic man") becomes a part of a rationally-behaving system.

Chris Argyris, rather than focusing on the design of rational systems, focused on the interaction of the individual and the organization, and suggested, much like MacGregor, that formal organizational structures and traditional management practices were inconsistent with a natural human striving for growth and development. Individuals in our society, Argyris concluded, develop from infancy through adulthood along several important dimensions: from passivity to activity, from dependence to independence, from a limited to a greater range of behaviors, from shallow to deeper interests, from a shorter to a longer time perspective, from a position of subordination to a position of equality or superordination, and from lack of awareness to greater awareness. Movement along each dimension contributes to what we know as the healthy adult personality.

Yet, argued Argyris, these goals are exactly those that traditional management practices prevent. For example, standard patterns of management give the individual little control over his or her work. Workers are expected to be passive, submissive, and limited in the range of their responses. They are basically expected to behave like children. Moreover, if individuals express frustration at such a situation, managers often see their behavior as hostile and dysfunctional. The typical managerial response is to crack down, to assert even more severe methods of control.

A healthier approach, suggests Argyris, would be to understand the basic tendencies of the human personality for growth and development, then to "fuse" these tendencies with the objectives of the organization. Achieving this congruence or fusion is the task of the manager. This requires that the manager develop "skill in self-awareness, in effective diagnosing, in helping individuals grow and become more creative, in coping with dependent-oriented . . . employees, and in surviving in a competitive world of management" (1962, p. 213).

In the work of both Simon and Argyris, there is a dramatic shift from concerns with structure to concerns with human behavior. Each offers a new way of looking at organizations and the people in them. The manager, according to this new view, needs to take structure into account (for that will affect human behavior), but the "bottom-line" is how people behave. And, of course, the behavior of human beings is affected by much more than the structures in which they reside. In these works, the attention of the manager is redirected from structure to behavior. In this new view, the job of the manager is to mold human behavior toward the purposes of the organization.

THE ORGANIZATION AND ITS ENVIRONMENT

Both the early emphasis on structure and the later emphasis on human behavior proved helpful in focusing attention on important aspects of life in complex organizations. But neither viewpoint even considered the relationship between the organization and its environment. This missing element began to appear, however, as writers in the field of public administration returned to issues of structure, though they viewed it in a quite different way. The new concern for structure was stimulated by two emerging approaches to public organizations—systems theory and the political economy approach. The **systems approach** suggested that public (or other) organizations could be viewed in the same general way as biological or physical systems—as whole "organisms," independent of their parts and pursuing specific purposes within a complex environment; the **political economy approach** focused on politics and economics as categories for analyzing organizational behavior.

Systems Theory

We discussed the basic ideas associated with systems theory in chapter 7. Recall that the systems model suggests that the organization receives from its environment the human and material resources it requires to function, as well as requests and directives about how it should operate; these resources, requests, and directives are processed through the organization and transformed by it; the resulting outputs (products, services, etc.) are transmitted back into the environment. In turn, these outputs are taken into account as new inputs are developed, and, over time, a balancing point is reached that makes possible the survival of the organization.

In addition to its application in organizational design, the systems approach led those in public administration to think more carefully about the environment in which they worked and to begin to consider what influences were most important. A classic study of the relationship between an agency and its environment was Selznick's analysis of the Tennessee Valley Authority in the 1940s. Selznick argued that, in contrast to the closed, mechanical systems implied in many approaches to public organizations, those organizations are in fact *open systems*. That is, they exist within an institutional framework, which includes political parties, pressure groups, and special interests, and, though the groups' demands may appear "irrational" from the perspective of the organization, they simply cannot be ignored.

The Tennessee Valley Authority sought to involve already existing local agencies in planning power distribution systems and other programs. One reason was to enable the TVA to anticipate potential demands and be prepared to respond. A second reason was to try to get local groups committed to the TVA program by making them feel part of the organization. By bringing outside groups into the structure of the organization (by placing persons on advisory groups or negotiating service contracts with them), TVA sought support for its own programs. You will recall this idea as *cooptation*, a term Selznick defined as "the process of absorbing new elements into the leadership or policy-determining structure of the organization as a means of averting threats to its stability or existence" (Selznick, 1949, p. 13).

Another study examining the influence of environmental factors on the operations of public agencies was Herbert Kaufman's analysis of the United States Forest Service. The Forest Service faced the problem of how to secure compliance and consistency from forest rangers scattered across the country and subject to all kinds of pressures from their local communities. Rangers often served, of course, in isolated locations. Whereas they sought to carry out the policies of the Forest Service, they also developed loyalties to their local communities. They often had to carry out regulations that would adversely affect their friends and neighbors in the local areas and, in such cases, might be tempted to deviate from central office directives. The agency's response was to devise a series of training programs, procedural devices, inspections, and sanctions as efforts to reduce the influence of the local environment and to ensure that central office orders were actually carried out in the field.

Looking at how environmental factors influence public organizations led other writers to characterize public agencies as interdependent systems operating in a complex environment. No longer could one agency's work be viewed in isolation from other public and private agencies; one would simply not be able to understand how an agency operated without understanding the myriad external influences on the agency. Imagine, for example, the difficulty of implementing a new set of standards for water quality in a city such as Cincinnati, located on a state boundary. Think of all the agencies, public and private, that would have to be notified and would wish to express their views. Think of the various political jurisdictions—states, cities, counties, and possibly many special districts. Think of the various bodies within each jurisdiction that might want input— the mayor, legislature, and administrative agencies.

The complexity of administrative activities (as in this example) have led some scholars to suggest that it is no longer even meaningful to focus on a specific agency's contribution to implementing a particular policy, but to think instead in terms of *programs*. We have already noted that many federal programs operate through a pattern of funding in which money, rules, and guidelines are established for programs that are actually delivered at the state and local levels through both public and private agencies. In vocational education, for example, the Bureau of Adult and Occupational Education gives grants to state and local vocational institutes to provide training, which the institute then subcontracts to public and private groups, such as Goodwill Industries (Rainey & Milward, 1983). The money goes to fund programs, not specific agencies, so that these public programs operate through rather diffuse networks of loosely joined groups rather than through traditional hierarchical structures. In such ill-structured "structures," older notions of organizational control necessarily give way to new emphasis on bargaining and negotiation, in which the systems perspective has much to offer.

311

Political Economy

Interest in interorganizational policy networks was further stimulated by the emergence of the political economy approach to understanding public organizations. Wamsley and Zald suggest that public organizations can best be understood in terms of the conjunction of political and economic factors influencing their operation. These factors affect the organization both internally and externally, leading to four categories through which we might view organizations. First, the external political environment involves the interplay of various interest groups and other organizations that affect the organization's political climate. Second, the external economic environment consists of market exchanges that influence the available supply of resources. Third, the internal political category focuses on the distribution of power and authority; and fourth, the internal economy concerns the allocation of resources and how they are used.

The Wamsley-Zald approach is related to a more sophisticated and complex approach most often associated with Vincent Ostrom. Ostrom's *public choice* approach begins with examining how individuals might make choices if they were free to act rationally and in their own self-interest. Under some circumstances, people might be expected to engage in collective action, especially where "public goods" are involved, or where situations are neither purely public nor purely private. (Public goods are distinguished from private goods—those that can be measured, marketed, and maintained—by the fact that they are highly *indivisible*; a public good—such as the national defense—is available to all once it is provided for one.)

Following this logic, Ostrom sees public organizations as "a means for allocating decision-making capabilities in order to provide public goods and services responsive to the preferences of individuals in different social contexts" (Ostrom & Ostrom, 1971, p. 207). Ostrom argues that the best structures for satisfying individual preferences are not centralized bureaucratic agencies, but rather more fragmented, multiorganizational arrangements.

CONTEMPORARY APPROACHES TO MANAGEMENT

Although earlier behavioral studies like Simon's and Argyris's were important in countering the field's dependence on a structural interpretation of organizational life, they were limited in certain ways. First, most of the behavioral literature failed to question the top-down pattern of organizational authority, so many thought it merely provided more sophisticated mechanisms for managerial control. Second, there seemed to be little interest in organization change processes at a time that rapid social change was becoming a dominant feature of the landscape. Third, as the open systems theorists pointed out, the perspective failed to comprehend the complexity of interorganizational bargaining and negotiation.

Among major critics of earlier approaches were a group of scholars in the early 1970s whose collective work came to be known (and, despite the passage of time, is still known) as "the New Public Administration." In contrast to older approaches that emphasized efficiency and control, the New Public Administration heralded openness and change, equity and involvement. In a rapidly changing society populated by diverse groups, the New Public Administrationists felt that the key element in the survival of organizations— indeed, of the society—was the capacity to adapt to rapid social change. Organizations would have to find ways to deal with an increasingly "turbulent" environment.

Doing so would require stimulating the creativity of everyone involved in any public program, both within the agency and in the environment. Involving the organization's members and its clients in the decision-making process would, the New Public Administrationists felt, foster creativity. Moreover, such an approach seemed far more consistent with democratic norms and practices than operating through top-down structures of control. The key words in the New Public Administration were *equity* and *involvement*.

Many of those associated with the New Public Administration became students of organizational change processes and sought ways to help organizations implement needed changes. One of the most important approaches they employed was **organization development**, a process-oriented approach to planned change. Organization development suggests many techniques for change, which we will examine in chapter 10, but it also offers another approach through which to view the work of organizations.

Robert Golembiewski, a leader in the application of organization development strategies and techniques to the public sector, points out that organization development represents a particular philosophy of management that is considerably at odds with traditional top-down tendencies. It values

1. Mutual accessibility and open communications
2. A willingness to experiment with new behaviors and to choose those that seem most effective
3. A collaborative concept of authority that emphasizes cooperation and willingness to examine conflicts openly
4. Creating mutual helping relationships involving a sense of community and acceptance of responsibility for others
5. Authenticity in interpersonal relationships (Golembiewski, 1972, pp. 60–66)

(A more complete statement of the commitments of organization development appears in Box 9.2; we will discuss organization development further in the context of strategies for organizational change.)

BOX 9.2

MAJOR OBJECTIVES OF TYPICAL OD PROGRAMS

- To create an open, problem-solving climate throughout the organization so that members can confront problems rather than fight about or flee from them
- To build trust among individuals and groups throughout the organization, whether through vertical linkages between superiors and subordinates, horizontal linkages among peers, or diagonal linkages among individuals of different ranks in different units
- To supplement the authority of role or status with the authority of knowledge and competence
- To locate decision-making and problem-solving responsibilities as close as possible to the information sources
- To make competition, where it exists, contribute to meeting work goals (organization units compete to produce a good or service more efficiently and effectively) as opposed to win/lose competition
- To maximize collaboration between individuals and units whose work is interdependent

(continued)

(continued)

- To develop a reward system that recognizes both achievement of the organization's mission (profits or service) and human development (growth of people)

- To increase the sense of ownership of organization objectives throughout the work force

- To help managers manage according to relevant objectives rather than according to "past practices" or to objectives that do not make sense for one's area of responsibility

- To increase self-control and self-direction for people within the organization

- To create conditions where conflict is brought out and managed

- To increase awareness of group "process" and its consequences for performance—that is, to help people become aware of what is happening between and to group members while the group is working on the task (e.g., communication, influence, feelings, leadership styles and struggles, relationships between groups, how conflict is managed, etc.)

From Organizational Culture to Strategic Management

Beyond work in organization development, many recent discussions of management, especially in the private sector, have emphasized the importance of understanding the "culture" of the organization. Most writers refer to **organizational culture** as the basic pattern of attitudes, beliefs, and values that underlie the organization's operation. An organization's culture consists of the shared assumptions that members of the organization hold. Edgar H. Schein (1987, p. 6) notes that culture can be manifested in many ways, including the following:

1. *Observed behavioral regularities* when people interact, such as the language used and the rituals around deference and demeanor.
2. The *norms* that evolve in working groups, such as the particular norm of "a fair day's work for a fair day's pay" that evolved in . . . the Hawthorne studies.
3. The *dominant values espoused* by an organization, such as "product quality" or "price leadership."
4. The *philosophy* that guides an organization's policy toward employees and/or customers.
5. The *rules* of the game for getting along in the organization, the "ropes" that a newcomer must learn in order to become an accepted member.

6. The *feeling* or *climate* that is conveyed in an organization by the physical layout and the way in which members of the organization interact with customers or other outsiders.

The notion of organizational culture is closely related to what has recently been called strategic management. Contemporary works such as Peters and Waterman's *In Search of Excellence* (1982), analyzing the implicit philosophies that guide the most successful American companies, have gained enormous popularity. Peters and Waterman suggest the importance of establishing a core set of values that comprise the mission of the organization and shape decisions throughout the structure. Beyond this, they suggest the importance of constant interchange between managers and workers, the organization and its clients. "MBWA," or Management by Walking Around, is recommended to managers who need to keep in close contact with the thoughts and ideas of their workers; similarly, the importance of "putting yourself in the position of your clients" is stressed—for example, the owner of a particular hotel chain stays at various hotels all over the country just to get an idea of how people experience their stays there.

Beyond these general orientations, Peters and Waterman (1982, pp. 13–16) argue that the best companies have other features in common:

1. *A bias for action*: a willingness to experiment and to take risks
2. *Close to the customer*: a near obsession with service and quality
3. *Autonomy and entrepreneurship*: companies allow a freedom to develop new ideas and to compete with other parts of the company
4. *Productivity through people*: treating people as adults, giving them trust and respect
5. *Hands on, value driven*: companies pay attention to their values and managers work hard to express those values
6. *Sticking to the knitting*: do what you know best, don't diversify excessively
7. *Simple form, lean staff*: avoid top-heavy and complex organizational structures
8. *Simultaneous loose–tight properties*: the coexistence of firm central direction and maximum individual autonomy

These criteria for excellence can be translated into a public sector context without great difficulty. For example, the International City Management Association and the Center for Excellence in Local Government adapted the Peters and Waterman criteria to define "excellence in local government":

1. *Action orientation*: excellent local governments identify problems and deal with them quickly, fighting through structural political, legal, and environmental constraints that make action more difficult than in the private sector.
2. *Closeness to citizens*: this criterion includes establishing and maintaining a variety of close links with citizens who are served by the local government—including those who are regulated against their will. Excellent local governments listen, and are sensitive and responsive to public input.
3. *Autonomy and entrepreneurship*: excellent local governments have developed climates conducive to conceiving ideas and doing new things to solve problems. They have track records for implementing creative solutions, even in the face of declining resources.

315

4. *Employee orientation:* this criterion demands more than lip service to employees and their needs. Excellent local governments insist on intensive, pervasive treatment of employees as human beings and adults.

5. *Values:* excellent local governments have a defined set of values. Their overall focus is on being the best by providing superior quality service to the public. Their values are communicated clearly and demonstrated regularly to employees. Those values also provide the source of enthusiasm and pride among employees.

6. *Mission, goals, and competence:* mission is the underlying premise of the organization. Excellent local governments have evaluated their missions based on changing resource levels and citizen demands, and have used mission statements as the foundation for establishing community and organizational goals. Within their defined mission, excellent local governments provide consistent, uniform service levels.

7. *Structure:* in excellent local government, the potential negative effects of antiquated, bureaucratic structures have been minimized. These organizations have fewer management levels and fewer centralized support staffs. They provide firm central direction, while giving maximum autonomy to employees.

8. *Political relationships:* political relationships refer to more than how the elected governing body and management staff work together. In excellent local governments, managers and policy makers are tuned in to the political environment, have established positive, open, and respectful relationships with each other, and have established political stability.

SOURCE: Barbour et al., *Handbook: Excellence in Local Government Management*, 1984, p. 2. International City Management Association, Washington, D.C. Reprinted with permission.

Total Quality Management

Many of the themes in the organizational culture literature and that dealing with strategic management are coming together under the heading of Total Quality Management (TQM). As we saw in chapter 7, TQM is a broad-scale approach to changing an organization's entire culture so as to focus on establishing and maintaining high standards of quality, especially with respect to meeting "customer" expectations. The key of TQM is to serve the "customer," whether the "customer" is internal to the organization or someone outside. (Many government agencies serve citizens directly, but some serve other government agencies.)

The OMB circular describing TQM for federal executives calls it "a comprehensive management approach for meeting customer needs and expectations that involves all employees in improving continuously the organization's processes, products, and services." (A more detailed description of TQM drawn from the OMB circular appears in appendix 9.A.) Specifically, TQM involves bringing together everyone in the organization in such a way as to create a new "culture of excellence" that emphasizes:

- Top management leadership and support
- Strategic planning and implementation geared to long-term success
- Focus on the customer
- Commitment to training and recognition
- Employee empowerment and teamwork

- Reliance on measurement and analysis of process and outputs
- Quality assurance (OMB Draft Circular A–132, 1990)

The emphasis in TQM is first on improving quality, not productivity. Indeed, the assumption is that if the quality of the organization's work is improved, its productivity will also improve. Improvements in quality are sought through a variety of tools or techniques, each tailored to the specific work of the organization. One organization might develop a series of quality control teams to oversee and control quality throughout its delivery of services; another organization might choose to develop a more detailed measurement system to pinpoint errors in its production processes. In all cases, however, the commitment to quality must be strongly expressed by top management and throughout the organization. It should also be long-term; TQM is not seen as a quick fix but as a never-ending process of improvement.

As mentioned in chapter 8, Total Quality Management is now being adopted in many federal agencies and will soon be required of all federal agencies (see Box 9.3). Similarly, many state and local agencies are undertaking TQM projects. While TQM is an amalgam of many other approaches to management reform and in many ways may be merely the latest "fad" in management, the attention it is receiving makes it worthy of study.

BOX 9.3

NORFOLK NAVAL SHIPYARD: A TQM SUCCESS STORY

How do you make sure that a shipyard older than the country itself will still be a leader in the ship repair industry in the 21st century? This is the problem that Captain Edward S. McGinley faced when he took command of the Norfolk Naval Shipyard in Norfolk, VA, in 1987.

To McGinley, TQM was the answer. In September 1987 he sequestered the shipyard's top managers in a local hotel for two days. They devised a list of objectives for the shipyard, ranging from reducing the cost of overhauls by at least 25 percent to improving compliance with environmental regulations.

To implement the goals, Norfolk uses a highly structured TQM program. At the top is the shipyard's Quality/Productivity Improvement Council, chaired by McGinley and composed of top managers and representatives of two of the shipyard's eight employee unions. The council creates overall quality initiatives and monitors their implementation.

(continued)

(continued)

Council recommendations for process improvements are turned over to a Quality Management Board for action. These boards are permanent groups of managers and union representatives. There are currently 16 such boards at the Norfolk shipyard. Each oversees a different aspect of the repair and overhaul process.

Quality Management Boards recommend that specific processes be examined and improved by Performance Action Teams. This is where TQM gets down to the nitty gritty. Each team is made up of people who actually work on the process designated for improvement. The team recommends specific improvements and implements them. "You could easily have a thousand teams," says Fred Porter, a TQM adviser at Norfolk.

The TQM process has been applied in the shipyard's sheet metal shop, where designs for equipment such as ventilation systems are turned into working sketches. Before TQM, as many as 23 percent of such sketches were going to the shop floor with errors—even after workers were given eye exams and the lighting in the sketch area was improved.

So a Performance Action Team was appointed. Under its guidance, every completed sketch was inspected. Different types of errors were categorized and posted on charts in the sketch area. In addition, individual errors were noted and shown to employees. Managers did not see these personal evaluations.

Larry Kiser, who works in the sketch area, says it worked. "I knew where I was making errors, so the next time I did something I was aware of the problem." Fred Mullins, a supervisor, says that checking every sketch took time, but every 15–20 minutes spent in checking saved 15–20 hours on the shop floor. In the sketching of ventilation systems, the error rate dropped to eight percent.

Efforts like this have made Norfolk one of the federal government's most prominent TQM success stories. In 1989 the shipyard won an award from the Office of Management and Budget for its TQM program. The award noted that all eight of the ships repaired at the shipyard from April 1988 to March 1989 were completed at or under estimated cost, and that seven were returned to the fleet early or on time.

Still, like virtually all other managers who have started to implement TQM in government, McGinley says the process is just starting. "I'm going to be long gone before this thing ever comes to complete fruition," he says. "It's going to be at least five years before we can say we've got something."

SOURCE: Excerpted from "Norfolk Naval Shipyard: A TQM Success Story," *Government Executive*, (March 1990) p. 21. By Tom Shoop. Reprinted with permission.

TQM may be required in some agencies, but its spirit and philosophy have already been heralded by many public organizations. For example, in an effort to implement, in a practical way, the types of commitments we have just reviewed, many public organizations have recently developed statements reflecting their philosophy and the commitments to which they wish to aspire. One organization, Missouri's Office of Administration, recently reviewed its guiding values and developed a Statement of Management Philosophy. A new commissioner of administration felt that the organization had been too focused on controlling other agencies (with respect to purchases, expense vouchers, personnel requirements, etc.) and had not paid enough attention to serving other agencies. In addition, the new commissioner also wished to establish a more open organizational climate in which individual members would feel valued and free to express their concerns.

After working with a consultant over a period of months, the commissioner and his top management team arrived at a new Statement of Management Philosophy (see Box 9.4). This statement was then communicated to all members of the organization

BOX 9.4

STATE OF MISSOURI OFFICE OF ADMINISTRATION STATEMENT OF MANAGEMENT PHILOSOPHY

We are *proud* of our role in providing *effective* and *responsible* government to the citizens of the State of Missouri.

As the chief agency responsible for the management and operations of state government, the Office of Administration plays an important role in serving the line agencies of state government and in assuring the accountability of governmental operations. Despite the fact that the Office of Administration provides less direct services to the public than some

(continued)

(continued)

agencies, we are constantly reminded of the public nature of our activities and our ultimate responsibility to the citizens of Missouri.

We *respect* the elected officials of the State and will perform our responsibilities in a way consistent with their direction.

As the management arm of state government, we provide leadership in various policy areas and, more generally, we seek to improve the managerial effectiveness of state government. In these areas, we will seek not only to be responsive to the political leadership of the State but to build the kind of professional competence those leaders and the citizens of the State can depend on.

In our relationships with other agencies, we will seek to be *sensitive* to and *supportive* of the special needs of those agencies.

We will provide the highest quality service to other agencies. In our dealings with those elsewhere in state government, we will be helpful, courteous, and respectful; in our decisions and recommendations, we will be open and flexible, but also fair and consistent. We recognize that our own effectiveness is directly related to the service we provide others.

We *care* about our employees and we *respect* and *value* their work.

In our internal operations, we will place first the worth and dignity of each individual member of our organization. Through programs enhancing the quality of work life, we will seek to develop a more humane and caring organization. We care about those who work in the Office of Administration and we wish that caring to show; we also appreciate the excellent professional work being done by those in the Office of Administration and we will remember to say "thank you" more frequently.

We will seek to improve *communications* and *coordination* throughout the organization.

We recognize that in an organization as diverse as ours, communications and coordination are of special importance and we will give priority to ways of improving our capabilities in these areas. As managers, we will seek to establish a clear direction for the development of the organization, but within that framework we will seek mechanisms for the involvement of all employees in building a more effective department. We will listen carefully to their ideas and, where possible, we will act promptly on their suggestions.

320

We recognize the importance of personal *growth* and organizational *development* and will seek ways of constantly extending our capabilities.

We recognize that as individuals we must always be attentive to our own growth needs and to the many ways we might extend our capabilities; we also recognize that improvements can always be made in the quality of service and in the productivity of all organizations, including our own. For these reasons, we will be attentive to the developmental needs of our members and to building programs to improve the work of the organization.

We value our participation in the *public service* and will strive for *high quality* in all our activities.

Though we come from many different professional backgrounds, we are brought together in the public service. We take seriously the special responsibility the notion of the public service implies and we value our participation in the work of government. We want our agency to be one of the recognized leaders in Missouri state government, one to which others will look for professional, technical, and moral guidance. With the full cooperation and involvement of all members of a caring and concerned organization, we are confident this goal is attainable.

through public meetings, postings on bulletin boards, and publication in the organization's *Newsletter*. Members soon came to understand more clearly the shift in perspective that the statement expressed. Their behavior, in turn, became more consistent with the new set of values established in the statement.

Some Concluding Guidelines for Practice

What lessons can you draw from these various perspectives that might guide your actions as a public manager? One way to begin to answer that question is to summarize some of the thinking about management in terms of guidelines for practice. The recent literature on strategic management seems to suggest the following guidelines:

1. *Maintain clarity about organizational priorities, goals, and objectives.* Although some ambiguity is often unavoidable in stating organization priorities, goals, and objectives, most organizations are far too confused on these issues. This confusion leaves people throughout the organization, including people who are required to make frequent decisions about organizational direction, without an appropriate basis for making such

decisions. The direction of the organization should be stated as clearly as possible and widely communicated to all members.

2. *Make decisions today in terms of the most likely future circumstances.* Strategic management implies making all organizational decisions in terms of "futurity"—that is, how they will meet expected changes in the environment. It suggests taking every action in light of anticipated conditions, thus putting the organization in the best position to take advantage of future opportunities.

3. *Be attentive to the context in which you operate, especially relationships with other actors in the governmental system.* There is a natural but unfortunate tendency toward "tunnel vision" in most organizations. Actions are viewed in immediate terms, without fully considering who will be affected by the action. Acknowledging the importance of the environment is essential to strategic thinking.

4. *Understand clearly the organization's capacities and limitations.* New programs and policies can be effectively implemented only if they fall within the existing capacity of the organization or provide sufficient opportunity to build capacity. There are dangers in both underutilization of resources and becoming overextended.

5. *Balance program goals with attention to organizational values and processes.* It is important to state programmatic objectives clearly; however, the organization's culture and the prevailing norms, beliefs, and values of its members are equally important. Organizational processes, such as leadership, communications, motivation, group dynamics, and so forth, need constant attention, because they are essential to goal accomplishment.

6. *Create diverse mechanisms, both temporary and permanent, for constantly renegotiating programs and processes.* Both programmatic concerns and organizational processes are constantly changing in ways that affect persons throughout the organization. Thus, clarity with respect to priorities, goals, and objectives must not lead to rigidity. Mechanisms must permit and, in fact, encourage the entire membership of the organization to contribute regularly to refining programs and processes.

7. *Build trust and commitment through open communications and genuine participation.* Guidelines by which we might measure the degree of participation the organization encourages include members' access to information and to forums of decision making, their ability to open any issue without fear of retaliation, and their feeling that their ideas will at least be considered by major decision makers. (Redford, 1969, p. 8)

PUBLIC MANAGEMENT AND DEMOCRACY

Much of the work reviewed here applies equally to management in the public and private sectors. It is interesting to note that some of the most recent general trends in management have been anticipated in public sector management. Public organizations' dependence on pluralistic decision processes—that is, processes through which many different people and groups are likely to be involved in any particular decision—makes the process of managing change in the public sector quite complicated. It also means that a high degree of ambiguity and uncertainty is likely to surround most efforts to implement or alter programs, and that managers must be especially skillful in negotiating across organizational boundaries rather than expecting to control circumstances "from the top." In addition, public organizations must have a service orientation—specifically, an understanding of and an attempt to act in accord with the public interest. We noted that organizations seeking public purposes must operate openly, be cognizant of client interests, and must understand the political context within which they operate.

Under these circumstances, it is not at all surprising that the values and perspectives that now seem so much a part of "modern management," such as those associated with strategic management or Total Quality Management, have always been central (if not dominant) in public administration theory. Thus, for example, Marshall Dimock's (1936, p. 120) comment that "successful administration is warm and vibrant. It is human" sounds very much like a quotation from Peters and Waterman. One might thus argue that, in contrast to Woodrow Wilson's admonition that public agencies should operate like businesses, it seems that public organizations and the values and interests they represent today should be and are becoming models for organizations of all types (see Box 9.5).

BOX 9.5

EMPOWERING AN ORGANIZATION

Because I like to think I have learned a few things in 25 years (in the field of urban management), hopefully there are also some things I now do differently. At the front end of my career, for example, my concern was in making sure everybody in the organization knew I was in charge. Reorganization, replacement of key personnel, and formal control mechanisms were the hallmarks of my early days. They were meant to define me as a "take charge" person and to signal that change had occurred. My guess also is that this behavior reflected a need to overcome the insecurity associated with immaturity.

In reflecting on my earlier approach, I have now come full circle. The kinds of changes I made back then were clearly visible and so probably satisfied those who wanted to see change. I have learned, however, that it is relatively simple to bring about physical, visible change but that to cause actual improvement in the way an organization functions is a far more difficult trick. It is easy to make things look different; it is not so easy to make things substantively better. Obedience as the basis for organizational success has given way in my mind to the need for trust. A successful relationship is based upon mutual give and take rather than on "you give and I take." When blind obedience

(continued)

324

(continued)

is the operative concept, the "boss" gathers all the power. In the trust relationship, the boss shares power with everyone else.

What impresses me as more productive now is to figure out how you get those in the organization to feel confident about what they do, to move the organization where it needs to go. The values that permeate an organization have the power to override, at least in the long run, any other changes that may be made. What is new for me now in the second half of my career is an understanding that if dysfunctional and counter-productive values do not change, not much else of importance will either. And if management is not trying to improve the organizational culture's value system, no one else will.

A related lesson I have learned is that management cannot "order" values to change. This kind of change takes place relatively slowly, and it occurs only if management talks a lot about what is expected, sets the right example, creates the right kind of organizational climate, and uses the personnel and compensation system to support the right behavior.

So I am preaching. I am talking about organizational values important to success—customer responsiveness, treating people right, supporting city policies, being a good source of information, getting and giving "more bang for the buck," and providing anticipative rather than reactive management. I reward those who join in to support these expectations and "unreward" those who do not. And, yes, here and there a little organizational change may be in order, as well.

The point of all this is to empower the people in the organization to exert themselves by their own volition, in the right direction. A manager can indicate the proper direction. A manager can encourage needed values and can create the climate in which employees will choose to make the organization's success their goal. Managers used to see success as a function of the assertion of their own power. Now they see the empowerment of others as a more likely avenue to success.

SOURCE: Excerpted from Roy R. Pederson, "Empowering an Organization," *Public Management* (August 1989), pp. 2–3, International City Management Association, Washington, D.C. Reprinted with permission.

The question we encounter once again is, "How can we balance efficiency and responsiveness in the operation of public programs?" The field of public administration has generally leaned toward the efficiency side of the equation. Now, however, there is growing evidence that emphasizing responsiveness is not only consistent with democratic principles, but, in the long run, may also be the most effective way of operating. Whereas a structural view of organizations tends to emphasize internal efficiency, it is apparent that greater attention to external relationships—and the ability to negotiate across organizational boundaries—will become more and more necessary in our increasingly complex society, as will an organizational environment that fosters creativity.

Developing a "democratic" approach to management has often been attractive to public administration theorists because it seems only proper that government institutions in a democracy should operate democratically. What we are finding more and more is that such an approach is not only appealing but necessary for organizations of all types—not only those in the public sector—to survive.

SUMMARY AND ACTION IMPLICATIONS

As we have seen, your behavior is guided by the images you carry around in your head. Some of these images will have to do with the role of public agencies in a democratic society, others will have to do with the most effective and responsible way to run a complex public organization, and still others will have to do with the relationships you establish with other actors, both within and outside the governmental system. Over your career, you will develop and refine your images based on experience and on careful reflection and self-critique. You will also benefit from comparing your images (and approaches) to those that others recommend.

Through the years, students and practitioners of public administration have spent considerable time reflecting on the nature of their work and sorting out the many factors that make for successful public management. Each resulting "theory" represents an attempt to suggest where you should cast your attention. Because you can't attend to all things at once, a certain amount of selectivity goes into theory-building. Each theory implies evaluating what is most important to be aware of and do so as to manage successfully.

Early writers thought that issues of organizational structure were most important, so they spent considerable time detailing concerns for structure. Later theorists (some of them practitioners) felt that structural issues should be balanced, if not outweighed, by a concern for the behavior of individuals in the organization. Still others sought further refinements, moving from behavior to structure and back again. Contemporary approaches tend to emphasize the organization's culture or value structure, but these approaches will probably, in time, yield to still others.

For the time being, however, we should note the special sensitivity that those in public organizations have always shown for value questions. We have seen time and time again how the values of public service—the pursuit of the public interest—affects the work of those in public organizations. The concern of contemporary writers in business and related fields for service and human values is something that those in public administration have always had to contend with, especially as they have been challenged to find a form of management compatible with the requirements of a democratic society.

TERMS AND DEFINITIONS

Area of acceptance: Area within which the subordinate is willing to accept the decisions made by the supervisor.

Boundary spanning: Representing an organization to outside groups and organizations.

Bounded rationality: The best possible solution, but not the most rational from a purely economic standpoint.

Functional principle: Horizontal division of labor.

Organization development: Process-oriented approach to planned change.

Organizational culture: Basic patterns of attitudes, beliefs, and values that underlie an organization's operation.

Political economy approach: Focusing on politics and economies as categories for analyzing organizational behavior.

Scalar principle: Vertical division of labor among various organizational levels.

Scientific management: Approach to management based on carefully defined "laws, rules, and principles."

Systems approach: Suggestion that public (or other) organizations can be viewed in the same general way as biological or physical systems.

STUDY QUESTIONS

1. Discuss the approaches to public management espoused by early writers in the field.
2. Explain Douglas MacGregor's Theory X and Theory Y management concepts.
3. Compare the management approaches of Herbert Simon and Chris Argyris.
4. Two management approaches combine the human element with the structural aspect of the organization. Discuss the differences between the systems approach and the political economy approach.
5. What shared assumptions, as outlined by Edgar H. Schein, seem consistent in organizational cultures? What features do Peters and Waterman contribute to the list?
6. What basic philosophies underlie recent work in strategic management, organizational culture, and Total Quality Management?

CASES AND EXERCISES

1. Divide the class into four small groups (or multiples of four). Have each group analyze *your class* as an organization, taking into account questions of power and authority, communications, motivation, group dynamics, and so on. One group should employ *only* a structural perspective; the second group should employ *only* a behavioral perspective; and the third group should employ *only* a systems perspective. The fourth group should employ whatever perspective (or combination of perspectives) that its members consider most modern and most complete.

Have each group (or a representative of each type of group, depending on the numbers) report their conclusions to the entire class. Think of each perspective as allowing you to see certain things and preventing you from seeing others. What do you see from the "structure" perspective? What about the "behavior" perspective? The "systems" perspective? The combination perspective is likely to seem most complete, but consider the possibility that this modern viewpoint also overlooks a great deal, and that, though we think it is complete (as those using earlier perspectives considered them complete), there may be much left to understand about organizations—even small ones. What other questions might we encounter in the future?

2. As a class, study the interorganizational relationships of one small organization. The organization might be a unit at the university (either an academic or a staff unit), a unit in city, state, or federal government, or a local nonprofit organization. Pick an organization that is clearly identifiable and, if possible, that appears to have considerable autonomy. Based on interviews with its top administrators and top staff people, develop a chart showing the organization's relationships with others in its environment. (A model something like one of a molecular structure might be appropriate.) Indicate the importance of each relationship, the degree to which that relationship is considered positive or negative, and the degree to which it is considered essential. Try to develop some sense for how much time administrators and staff members spend on external relations versus internal organizational work.

3. The following statement expresses the philosophy of management of the Greensboro, NC, District of the Internal Revenue Service:

> Our first priority as managers will be to identify and focus on eliminating the barriers to our employees doing their work with the highest degree of quality. We will communicate in such ways as to provide information which will enhance understanding and involvement by our employees in the district decision-making process. We will encourage our employees to speak out and we will be receptive to their questions and/or criticisms of management directions. We will support, guide, and develop our employees to assist them in reaching maximum potential. We will promote positive feelings among our employees toward each other and their work. We will do everything possible to enhance the professional image of the IRS. (Government Productivity News, June, 1989, p. 3)

First, this statement deals with internal operations of the district; it is primarily concerned with the relationship between managers and employees. What elements would you wish to add to the statement?

Second, think about the relationship between a tax collection agency and its clients. What statements of philosophy dealing with the relationship between agency and clients would be appropriate to add?

Third, given the statement and your modifications, what *specific* steps would you recommend to the managers of the agency for putting their commitments (and yours) into practice?

FOR ADDITIONAL READING

Denhardt, Robert B. *Theories of Public Organization.* Pacific Grove, CA: Brooks/Cole, 1984.

Fredrickson, H. George. *New Public Administration.* Tuscaloosa: University of Alabama Press, 1980.

Golembiewski, Robert T. *Humanizing Organizations*. Mt. Airy, MD: Lomond Publications, 1985.

Harmon, Michael M., and Meyer, Richard T. *Organization Theory for Public Administration*. Boston: Little, Brown, 1986.

Morgan, Gareth. *Images of Organization*. Beverly Hills, CA: Sage Publications, 1986.

Ouchi, William. *Theory Z*. Reading, MA: Addison-Wesley, 1981.

Peters, Thomas J., and Waterman, Robert H. *In Search of Excellence*. New York: Harper & Row, 1982.

Schein, Edgar H. *Organizational Culture and Leadership*. San Francisco: Jossey-Bass, 1987.

Description of Total Quality Management (TQM)

Total Quality Management is a total, integrated organizational approach for meeting customer needs and expectations that involves all managers and employees and uses quantitative methods and employee involvement to improve continuously the organization's processes, products and services. TQM is based on the principles taught by W. Edwards Deming, Joseph Juran, and Philip Crosby (among the most well-known authorities on quality) and the practical experience over the past 10 years of numerous private and public sector organizations which have implemented quality improvement. This collective body of knowledge and experience has been integrated into a total management approach that is best described under seven headings. The description provided below presents TQM as it would exist in an advanced phase in an organization.

Top management leadership and support   Top managers are directly and actively involved in the TQM process. They take the lead in establishing an environment and culture that encourage change, innovation, risk-taking, pride in work, and continuous improvement on behalf of all customers. They exhibit a highly visible, personal leadership and communicate the organization's quality vision, goals, and values to all members. Managers provide the resources, time, and training necessary for the organization to improve quality and productivity. They show by example that open communication (vertically and horizontally) and information sharing are the organizational norm. They understand that quality improvement is a long-term process, not to be compromised by short-term considerations. Managers remove barriers to improvement; e.g., they delegate authority to the lowest feasible level, deregulate work, and discourage the "quick-fix" mentality that seeks short-term results at the expense of long-term goals. Managers establish trust, encourage cooperation among organizational units to achieve better service, and reward behavior that reflects the organization's TQM goals. They establish an organization structure that fosters effective implementation of the quality improvement process.

Strategic planning   Strategic planning drives the organization's improvement efforts. Short- and long-term goals for quality improvement are established across the organization and are integrated into the strategic plan. Customer needs and expectations as well as issues relating to improved supplier relationships are considered and incorporated into the strategic plan. Resources are allocated to support the quality improvement objectives the organization wants to achieve. Periodically-revised business plans at sub-organizational levels provide the who-what-when details for the strategic plans. Business plans include quality improvement projects with measurable goals for each organizational unit and managers are held accountable for their achievement. A dynamic organizational plan is in place to assure that structural changes and people capabilities are able to accommodate changes in the organization's environment.

Focus on the customer   Management actively seeks ways to make all employees aware of customers and their needs. Employees can identify both the internal and external customers of all their products and services. They understand that their primary task is to satisfy customer requirements and expectations. Communication with customers, as with suppliers, is open, continual and two-way to ensure that clear definitions of needs and expectations are received and problems and concerns are understood. Customer perceptions of performance are continually measured, evaluated, and reported to responsible managers and employees. Feedback data are used to improve processes and services and provide input for strategic planning. Access by customers to information about the organization's products or services is easy and trouble-free. Complaints about aspects of the organization's services are solicited and corrected. Trends in customer satisfaction indicators are positive. The validity and objectivity of monitoring methods is ensured. Where expectations, desires and perceptions of different customer groups are in conflict with each other, the organization strives to achieve a balance among them that best fulfills the organization's mission.

Satisfying public service customers is constrained by the public policy process and the need to base many decisions on law rather than on individual desires. However, the organization uses several ways to reconcile the differences between what customers want and what the system allows. First, laws often recognize differences among groups of people and different circumstances within those groups. These differences are recognized and respected in dealing with people. Second, there are well established standards for informing people about services and providing due process for their grievances. The organization uses every opportunity to volunteer information and let people voice their concerns. Third, the organization pays attention over time to what customers identify as important. This becomes an important data base of information for the organization to use in modifying or changing the law. Finally, public employees are people dealing with other people. The organization provides responsive, courteous behavior which is always within the bounds of law.

Commitment to training and recognition   Managers and employees receive ongoing training to enable them to keep abreast of changing job requirements and prepare for greater responsibilities. A key element of training for all managers and employees is quality awareness and the use of tools, technologies, and techniques to support continuous improvement. The scope, intensity, and timing of training depend on organization level, the nature of work, and specific processes under review for improvement. Training is tailored to support the vision and goals of the organization; it is objectively assessed and documented, and periodically updated. Training plans are fully integrated into overall strategic planning. Training investment shows clear evidence of the priority placed on human resource development.

Employees are motivated to achieve total quality through trust, respect and recognition. Managers believe that employees want to do a good job; they personally, regularly, and fairly recognize individuals and teams for measurable contributions to quality improvement. Rewards and recognition are broad-based and innovative, encompass all levels of the organization, are centered on team quality and productivity improvement, and include peer recognition as a part of the reward structure. Celebration of small successes is common. Performance plans for managers include measurable quality improvement objectives. Evaluations focus on the degree to which the objectives are met.

Employee empowerment and teamwork   Management provides an environment that supports employee involvement, contribution, and teamwork. Where unions exist, union leaders are involved in high-level policy and decision-making groups, such as Quality Councils or Policy Boards. Teamwork is the vehicle for cooperation and communication among managers, supervisors, unions, and employees in addressing quality improvement issues. The demands of quality, cost, schedule, and mission that cross organizational units are met through cross-functional team cooperation. Employees have clear avenues for participation and involvement; e.g., as members of self-regulating work teams responsible for an entire process or group of customers, contributors to developing and implementing improvement plans, suggestors of ideas for improvement, participators in establishing work unit performance measures and goals, evaluators of processes, and decision-makers in many aspects of their work and work environment. Hierarchies are reduced in favor of cooperative teams and networks. Employees have a strong feeling of empowerment and team ownership of work processes because sufficient power, rewards, information and knowledge are moved to the lowest levels of the organization to enable everyone to accomplish their work with excellence. As a result, everyone feels "ownership" of quality improvement and exhibits personal pride in the quality of their work.

331

Measurement and analysis of processes and outputs   All information required to support total quality of processes and products/services is complete, timely, accurate, useful, and clearly communicated to those who need it. The scope of the data includes: customers and suppliers (both internal and external), internal operations, products/services, employees, comparisons or benchmarks of other organizations, and safety/environmental considerations (if appropriate). This information is the basis for developing quality measures that cover all aspects of work processes and all products and services provided a customer. Customer satisfaction measures are used extensively. These measures are used by employees to identify problems, determine root causes, identify solutions and verify that proposed remedies produce the expected results. Structures methodologies that employ quantitative methods and statistical techniques are used to improve processes. The emphasis on prevention, measurement and analysis applies equally to all the organization's processes—administrative, research, accounting, human resource, legal, policy development, or service-based. Measurement and analysis support continuous improvement.

Quality assurance   Products, services, and processes are designed and verified to meet customer needs and expectations. Processes which produce the organization's products and services are controlled, optimized and maintained. There is sufficient standardization within the organization to ensure compatibility. Comprehensive assessments of the quality assurance system as well as of products/services are performed at appropriate intervals. An approach exists for translating assessment findings into quality documentation supporting quality assurance. Quality assurance systems are updated to keep pace with changes in technology, practice and quality improvement. Product and service performance standards are set for internal support functions such as finance and accounting, personnel and administrative support. There is an established method to verify that the organization's quality requirements are being met by suppliers and other providers of goods and services. The organization compares (benchmarks) its products, services and internal operations with the "best" in the private or public sectors (e.g., other Federal agencies, state and local governments, and the governments of other countries).

SOURCE: Excerpted from Office of Management and Budget, Draft Circular A-132, 1990.

PERSONAL SKILLS IN PUBLIC MANAGEMENT

T he broad perspective that theories of public management
provide is not merely helpful, but essential in approaching managerial
work correctly. But the perspective is sterile without the personal and
interpersonal skills to put theory into practice. A manager must be
able to size up a situation and take appropriate action often within
a matter of seconds. A division director to whom you report calls to
tell you that the president is getting ready to announce a new
breakthrough in a disease treatment your unit has been working on
unsuccessfully for years. Or you hear on the radio that asbestos has
been found in a building your organization recently pronounced
"clean." Or your boss, the head of the state mental health department,
calls to tell you he has just resigned in protest over the legislature's
failure to support a new appropriation—and you are in charge. In all
these cases, you will necessarily and appropriately analyze and understand the situation in terms of your own approach or theory. But you
will also have to act. You may have to talk with certain people; you
may have to motivate others to act; you may have to judiciously exercise
the power of your office.

All these examples test your skills as a manager. If you can communicate well, and if you can make decisions and motivate others to follow
your lead, you will quite likely be judged effective. If you lack these
skills, you will be judged ineffective. Managerial success is based largely
on managers' ability to exercise various "interpersonal" skills.

Interestingly, however, effectively exercising interpersonal skills
depends on several essential "personal" skills that are a part of one's

social and psychological makeup. Some of these personal skills reflect your approach to the world, others have to do with your capacity for creativity or effective decision making, still others have to do with how you deal with ambiguity or lack of clarity. For example, the manager suddenly promoted to the directorship of the mental health department will certainly have important (and immediate) decisions to make, perhaps involving creative solutions to organizational problems left by the departing director. The new manager will also have to be able to operate, perhaps for months, in a highly ambiguous situation.

In this chapter and chapter 11, we will examine the "personal" and "interpersonal" skills that underlie managerial effectiveness. Personal skills include management of stress and time, creativity and problem solving, individual decision making, and issues of power and leadership.

THE MANAGER'S DAY

What, specifically, do public managers do? Most important, how would you spend your time as a public manager? Obviously, the answer depends on your job and level in the organization. Nevertheless, several recent studies give us some idea of a typical manager's day. Colin Hales (1986) discusses five aspects of managerial work: (1) the elements of managerial work; (2) distribution of managers' time between work elements; (3) interactions with other people; (4) the informal elements of managerial work; and (5) the themes of managerial work.

Elements of managerial work   Hales's review of what managers actually do at work closely parallels the classic descriptions of what managers "should" do, with some contemporary variations. Hales identifies nine elements as common, nearly universal, activities of managers.

1. *Playing the role of figurehead and leader* of an organizational unit. The manager symbolizes the organization to the outside world.
2. *Acting as liaison.* Liaison or boundary spanning is performed with individuals outside of the organization as well as with other organizational units and with managers of units higher and lower in the hierarchy.
3. *Monitoring.* Managers monitor affairs both internal and external to the unit, including the tasks of filtering and disseminating information.
4. *Allocating resources.* Managers make decisions with respect to appropriate distribution and use of human, financial, and physical resources.
5. *Handling disturbances.* Managers are frequently called upon to deal with disruptions in the flow of work in the organization.
6. *Negotiating.* Reaching agreement with a variety of parties, both inside and outside the organization, is an important part of the manager's work.
7. *Innovating.* Where there is the need to change, the manager often acts as a creative center or catalyst for change.
8. *Planning.* Managers must always be attentive to the future, especially as probable future conditions affect the work of the organization today.

9. *Directing subordinates.* The manager must spend considerable time developing a direction for the organization and securing the support and activities of the many individuals required to move the organization in that direction.

Like the classic descriptions noted earlier, these elements of managerial work identify a variety of activities. Nearly all the classic functions are included in the list (depending on how one classifies the elements), but several aspects deserve emphasis. First, note the wide diversity of activities in managerial work. Second, note the number of activities that involve other people. And, third, note the emphasis on change and innovation. Indeed, one might even say that the ability to handle change is a hallmark of *modern* management.

Distribution of time among work elements   Studies of how managers spend their time often use terms such as *tactical, frenetic, reactive, troubleshooting,* and *constant interruptions.* They describe the frequency of short, face-to-face meetings that move constantly from topic to topic. These findings, however, do not necessarily mean that the image of the manager as one who plans, thinks, and formulates strategy is a myth. To the contrary, effective managers have general agendas that enable them to quickly gather large amounts of information and make the correct decisions to further those agendas. Furthermore, managers work within networks that must be both developed and activated. These tasks require many interactions with people in the networks, and the interactions must of necessity be sporadic and informal (Kotter, 1982, p. 166).

What appears to be an absence of planning may sometimes be illusory; for some managers, planning is something that happens constantly. The seemingly disjointed nature of managerial interactions with others does not so much indicate disorganization, but rather the wide range of problems that must be handled. General agendas allow managers to deal with many situations opportunistically within the context of a larger framework or agenda that provides guidance for specific decisions.

335

Managerial interaction and communication   Descriptions of managerial time usage have identified the importance of interactions with other people, which typically involve some sort of communication. Hales found that between two-thirds and four-fifths of a manager's day is spent giving or receiving information, and that most of this giving and receiving takes place in face-to-face interactions. Communication is clearly a dominant activity in a manager's day.

Interestingly, and again despite appearances to the contrary, patterns of communication are not random. A majority of managerial communication is with managers of the same rank *(lateral communication).* Among the remaining communication, how much is *vertical* (i.e., up and down the hierarchy) varies widely with the manager's position, but regardless of position, the predominant pattern of communication is lateral.

Since much of their day is spent responding to requests for information, managers are often described as reactive. They spend more time responding to information requests than to initiating requests. To the casual observer, these interactions would appear extremely diverse, and often informal rather than official, but there is more to informal communication than meets the eye.

Informal aspects of managerial work   Unfortunately, it is difficult to provide universal descriptions of the informal aspects of management. There is, for example, considerable debate over whether the informal aspects of the manager's role are "good" or "bad"—that is, whether they contribute to or detract from the organization's goals. As in many such debates, it is probable that the informal work sometimes enhances and at other times detracts from the organization's goal achievement. For example, informal activities are often political in nature and involve negotiation; as such, these activities are extremely relevant. In any case, what is formal and what is informal is often a specific manager's perception as to what is actually part of his or her job—that which is really considered a part of the job is defined as formal, and that which is not is defined as informal.

Themes of managerial work   Hales draws a number of general conclusions about managerial work, one of which is that managerial work is extremely diverse and variable in terms of the different activities managers perform in a typical day. A manager may work on literally dozens of distinct topics during the course of the day and bring to bear a wide range of skills in dealing with those topics. A second conclusion is that managerial jobs are loosely enough defined to allow significant variation and choice by the specific manager in regard to both job content and style of performance. Two jobs that appear identical on an organizational chart are not necessarily composed of exactly the same tasks, nor will they necessarily be carried out in the same way. A central part of the work of managers is "the management of their work" (Hales, 1986, p. 101).

336

Hales's third conclusion is that managerial work is pressured and conflictual. There are many demands on the manager, and these demands are often contradictory. Consequently, there may be competing claims on the same resources of time, energy, personnel, and equipment. Moreover, competing claims often occur simultaneously or within a short period, creating even more pressure and conflict. Fourth and finally, Hales reports that managerial work tends to be action-oriented, with emphasis on action rather than on reflective contemplation. So many problems arise so quickly that managers often develop a preference for concrete action to address problems and opportunities.

We can conclude that the manager's job is one of life's more challenging in the world of work. It is diverse, and that diversity implies the need for diverse skills. The need for many skills is compounded by the pace of managerial work and its unending stream of conflicting demands for action. (See Box 10.1 for a review of the diversity and complexity of a local government manager's job.) Fortunately, managers often have considerable latitude in building their positions and in developing their working styles.

STRESS MANAGEMENT

Our examination of the general nature of managerial work in chapter 9 emphasized the skills, especially interpersonal, that are required to manage successfully. But effective use of interpersonal skills is predicated on a number of personal qualities and characteristics that form the basis for action.

Although not all managerial positions in public organizations are stress-filled, "pressure-cooker" jobs, there are certainly moments of tension, just as in management jobs elsewhere. The pressure of deadlines, questions about who is responsible for a particular

B O X   1 0 . 1

A TYPICAL (?) MANAGER'S DAY

A typical local public manager's daily agenda might look something like this:

8:00 a.m.	Arrives at work to polish off leftover paperwork/dictation from yesterday.
9:15 a.m.	Meets with mayor to review next week's council agenda prior to its publication.
10:00 a.m.	Local business group offers ideas on newly proposed industrial park on east side.
10:45 a.m.	City engineer and city treasurer join group to brief them on construction/financial details of site development.
11:30 a.m.	Police chief and personnel officer review a pending grievance against the department by a member of the city employees' union.
12:15 p.m.	Leaves ten minutes late for luncheon speech at League of Women Voters' monthly meeting to urge their help with the water bond campaign.
1:30 p.m.	Back again for more discussion with the police chief on the same topic discussed in the morning.
2:15 p.m.	Rides with public works director to inspect north side residents' complaints of "smells" from nearby city dump—mentally drafts responses to their council members and neighborhood group on return to office.
3:15 p.m.	Returns stacked-up phone calls at office.
3:45 p.m.	Talks with local newspaper reporter about the importance to the city of next month's special water bond vote.
4:10 p.m.	Free time that was scheduled to review several pending budget items is interrupted by visit from two council members.

(continued)

(continued)

5:20 p.m.   Goes home for dinner.

7:10 p.m.   Leaves to attend meeting of south side citizen association, a predominately poor black group that the manager wants to involve more closely in community public housing planning.

11:00 p.m. Home to bed at last!

NOTE: Several managers from all levels of government, upon reviewing this schedule, commented that this particular day appeared rather "light"!

SOURCE: Excerpted from Wayne F. Anderson, Chester A. Newland, and Richard J. Stillman, II, *The Effective Local Government Manager* (Washington, DC: International City Management Association, 1983), p. 35. Reprinted with permission.

problem, an angry flare-up at a staff meeting—these and other stressful situations arise in the course of the manager's job.

338   A variety of organizational factors can contribute to stress. (See Box 10.2.) In public organizations, stress is especially likely in situations of role conflict or role ambiguity. **Role conflict** occurs when there are two different and incompatible sets of demands on the individual—for example, if one is asked to complete two different projects simultaneously. **Role ambiguity** occurs when one does not clearly understand the rights and responsibilities of one's job. These two conditions seem to be especially prominent in public organizations.

BOX 10.2

ORGANIZATIONAL FACTORS THAT PROMOTE BURNOUT

- Continuously high stress levels
- A norm of constantly giving to others
- Discouragement of hierarchical staff interaction
- Constant demands for perfection
- Expectations of extra effort with minimal rewards

- No reinforcement for suggestions on improving morale
- Repetitive work activities
- Minimal additional resources available for extra-effort tasks
- Lack of encouragement for professional development
- Discouragement of mutual participation
- Evangelistic leadership styles
- Policy changes unrelated to problem priority
- Policy changes too frequent to be evaluated
- Rigid role typing for workers
- A belief that playfulness is unprofessional
- Pervasive "isms" (ageism, sexism, nepotism, etc.)
- Emphasis on past success
- Constant shifting of ground rules for policy
- Minimal emphasis on positive feedback
- Minimal emphasis on comfort of environment
- High instance of work overload
- High number of dead-end jobs
- Poor communication and feedback

SOURCE: Excerpted from Linda Hopper, "Unstressing Work," reprinted with permission from the November 1988 issue of *Public Management* magazine, published by the International City Management Association (ICMA), Washington, D.C.

Stress of any type, or continued stress over time, can be quite damaging to both the individual (mental or physical ill health can result) and the organization (managers operating under excessive stress are typically less competent in interpersonal relations and less productive generally). To prevent these problems and to have a happier, more satisfying work experience, public managers are finding it increasingly helpful to understand the nature of job-related stress and develop programs for reducing its negative consequences.

Hans Selye, the "father" of stress research, defines *stress* as the "nonspecific response of the body to any demand made upon it" (Selye, 1974, p. 27). Selye points out that stress can be good or bad, depending on the situation and the individual; stress can produce positive responses, such as joy and excitement, as well as harmful effects such as depression or ill health. Our concern is with excessive or continued stress leading to psychological or physiological impairment. Note, however, that people respond differently to sources of stress (or *stressors*)—a situation that one person may react to calmly may be a crisis for another.

Selye suggests that individuals respond to stress through a set of defense reactions that occur as a general syndrome. The first response phase is *alarm*, marked by increases in anxiety, fear, or depression (depending on the nature of the stressor). Muscles tense and heart rate and blood pressure increase. There is usually also a marked increase in psychological defensiveness. If the stressor is only momentary, the body soon returns to normal. But if the stressor continues, the individual may move to the next stage, *resistance*, wherein one engages in a variety of defense mechanisms to counter the stressor. These may range from (psychologically) attacking the stressor itself, attacking oneself or others, denying the stressor, or withdrawing either actually or symbolically from the situation (Whetten & Cameron, 1984, pp. 92–93). These mechanisms may reduce the level of stress, but where the stressor overwhelms the individual's defenses, a pathological state—which Selye terms *exhaustion*—may result. Exhaustion can lead to physical or mental difficulties, such as depression, alcoholism, or heart problems, or interpersonal problems, such as trouble with one's superiors or subordinates or one's family.

Fortunately, there are signals to help you recognize patterns of behavior that lead to excessive stress and specific techniques to reduce stress levels.

Type A / Type B behaviors   During the past twenty-five years, there has been growing interest in the relationship between various patterns of human behavior and the health problems that may result. A substantial part of medical and psychological research on this issue has focused on cardiovascular disease, the leading cause of death in this country. Coronary heart disease (CHD), a form of cardiovascular disease characterized by an inadequate supply of oxygen to the heart, has been shown to be related to certain patterns of behavior often exhibited by managers in public and private organizations. Researchers have labeled these behaviors "Type A."

In the 1950s, cardiologists Meyer Friedman and Ray Rosenman became aware that many of their patients' illnesses could not be explained by the traditional factors related to CHD (heredity, high blood pressure, and high levels of cholesterol). Other factors seemed to be playing a major role in contributing to CHD. They began to describe this set of factors as the *Type A behavior pattern*, which included (1) an intense, sustained desire to achieve; (2) a profound eagerness to compete; (3) a persistent drive for recognition; (4) seemingly continuous involvement in many activities that were subject to deadlines; (5) a habitual propensity to accelerate the rate of execution of all mental and physical functions; and (6) an extraordinary mental and physical alertness (Price, 1982, p. 7).

In contrast, people who exhibit more relaxed, easy-going patterns are referred to as having "Type B" behavior. Studies indicate that Type A individuals are two to three times more likely to suffer CHD than Type B individuals.

Life-style changes   Type A personalities, "workaholics," or others especially vulnerable to stress-related problems should obviously be attentive to ways of altering their behavior patterns to reduce the possibility of impairment (either illness or reduced effectiveness). Research shows that even those who are less vulnerable can improve the quality of their lives and the effectiveness of their work through sustained programs designed to reduce stress. Some involve merely recognizing and eliminating undesirable characteristics, such as Type A behaviors; others involve more specific efforts to alter one's life-style. For example, greater self-awareness—understanding oneself and how one reacts to different situations—allows one to anticipate and moderate reactions. One study showed that "receptive managers," those concerned with detail, are most affected by time pressures or information overload, whereas "preceptive managers," those who concern themselves with the "big picture" or the whole, are most stressed by role conflict or role ambiguity. Similarly, "systematic managers," who prefer logical solutions, are most affected by problems requiring creativity, whereas "intuitive managers" are most stressed by problems requiring logic and objectivity (Whetten & Cameron, 1984, p. 102). Obviously, if you can anticipate what problems will cause you the most difficulty, you can marshal your psychic resources to deal with them, enlist the help of someone better attuned to the particular type of problem, or simply avoid the issue.

Understanding the context of your work and how your work life relates to the rest of your life is also helpful in reducing the negative effects of stress. Having a sense of the meaning of your work, as opposed to just doing a job, provides a helpful way to assess what is really important and what is merely irritating. Similarly, exploring the relationship between your work life and family life will provide a clearer "grounding" for work activities. *Life-work planning* activities, offered either in groups or in one-on-one relationships with career counselors, give you an opportunity to step back from your work and develop an improved picture of where your career and your life may generally lead. Finally, developing a **support system,** a network of people with whom you can talk about problems you face, can be a great help.   *341*

Relaxation techniques   Specific relaxation techniques can help moderate either immediate or long-term stress. Deep-breathing exercises, visualizing and rehearsing upcoming situations, or diverting your attention to more pleasant times are primarily techniques to deal with fairly immediate stressors. More long-term stress reduction can be accomplished through techniques such as meditation.

Benson suggests that, just as the fight-flight syndrome is associated with overactivity of the nervous system, another response—the *relaxation response*—brings about a quieting of the nervous system. The relaxation response can be brought about through traditional techniques of religious meditation or more secular means, but the essentials are much the same. Four essential elements elicit the relaxation response:

1. A quiet environment
2. A mental device such as a word or phrase that should be repeated in a specific way over and over
3. Adoption of a passive attitude (perhaps the most important of the elements)
4. A comfortable position

Practicing these four elements for ten to twenty minutes once or twice daily should markedly enhance one's well-being (Benson, 1975, p. 19). Regular use of any relaxation technique will help reduce tension and improve one's ability to handle stressful circumstances.

Exercise   The benefits of exercise to physical health are well known; researchers have found that individuals who exercise regularly are less tense and more self-confident as well.

Cardiovascular conditioning, which strengthens the heart and lungs, is especially important in reducing stress and increasing one's sense of well-being (Cooper, 1978, p. 77).

Stress and the Organization

Many public organizations, like their counterparts in the private sector, recognize the tremendous drain on resources that stress can cause. Stress not only causes managers and employees to perform poorly because of distraction, poor concentration, and exhaustion, but can lead to more severe mental and physical problems and addictions. Consider the following facts:

- A smoker costs an employer more than $600 per year, for a national total of more than $27.5 billion annually.
- Over 1 million workers call in sick each day, resulting in over 330 million lost workdays.
- Losing an executive at 41 years of age to death or disability can cost between $600,000 and $1 million. . . . (Hopper, 1988, p. 4)

In addition to the direct costs of illnesses, through diminished productivity or having to replace workers, organizations suffer in other ways. For example, temporary workers or replacement personnel are not likely to be as effective as full-time permanent employees, thus limiting service delivery.

Many organizations have developed employee assistance programs to help employees through difficult times. The programs may deal directly with mental or physical problems, through drug and alcohol counseling, smoking cessation sessions, hypertension control, and so on, or they may use a preventive approach, seeking to promote a healthier work force through exercise and fitness programs, health screening, or nutrition and weight control. Many smaller organizations are not able to afford employee assistance efforts on their own, but there are abundant resources in most communities to provide needed help. The point is that if you or one of your employees could benefit from such a program, you shouldn't hesitate to become involved; both you and your organization will benefit.

TIME MANAGEMENT

Obviously, your ability to use time effectively will be one determinant of your success as a manager. It will be difficult to manage others' affairs if you cannot manage your own, especially because your activities will directly affect the people you will manage (see Box 10.3). It is not surprising that strategies and techniques for more effective time management have evolved and that time management training programs are popular today. (The techniques taught in such programs are as helpful to students facing the many demands of college life as they are to managers in public or private organizations.)

Time management begins with establishing goals. Goals are the heart of time management; everything else is just a tactic or a technique. Most approaches to time management tell you to set your own goals (though in some organizations, supervisors are involved

342

BOX 10.3

LEARNING THE BALANCING ACT IN PUBLIC LIFE

If Sheryl Sculley ever thought being Kalamazoo City Manager meant sitting behind a desk all day, she since has learned otherwise.

Take the time she inspected the inside of the Blakeslee Water Tank, which holds 3 million gallons of water in two compartments underground.

"Dressed in a suit, I stuffed my skirt in the oversized hip boots, size 11, and walked, as best as I could, to the entrance," she told an audience of Kalamazoo Network members at a recent meeting.

"Sticking out of a hole were two wooden ladders tied together in the middle extending to the bottom of the 30-foot tank. I stepped into the chlorine solution to sanitize my boots and reluctantly proceeded with no safety belt, in size 11 boots, down a slippery wooden ladder.

"I was as nervous as ever, but I couldn't retreat in front of all those employees."

When she returned from the bottom of the tank, Sculley recalled, "the employee holding the ladder must have noticed the look of relief on my face. He leaned over and quietly said, 'That's OK. It took me two days to develop the courage to climb down that ladder.'

"Needless to say, I had a few words for our utilities director as we drove back to city hall that morning—the first having to do with safety for our employees, the second about setting me up for such an experience with no advance warning."

Sculley came with her husband to Kalamazoo after they married and in the fall of 1974 was hired as a research writer in the city's planning department. She was named assistant city manager in 1977, deputy city manager in 1979, and acting city manager in 1984.

The mother of two children—6-month-old Collin and 2-year-old Courtney—supports parental leave as an individual but does not champion it as a city spokeswoman.

"The highest increase in the rate of labor force participation has been in women with children under 3 years of age," she told the Network audience. "The number of mothers returning to

(continued)

343

(continued)

work while their infants were less than 1 year old increased by 95 percent between 1970 and 1984. At this rate, by the year 2000, four out of every five American infants will have a mother in the labor force."

Sculley's work as city manager consumes an average of 60 hours per week, so her time with her children is planned. "Our time together includes more than mere presence," she said. "We bike, ride, read, walk in the woods, paint, take swimming classes at the YMCA, and Courtney even comes to city hall with me on Saturday mornings—and that's one of the highlights of her week."

SOURCE: Excerpted from "Sculley Learns the Balancing Act in Public Life," *Public Management* 70 (November 1988), p. 19, International City Management Association, Washington, D.C. Reprinted with permission.

344

in setting goals). Although your own goals may or may not equate with the goals of the organization, they will probably overlap at least to some extent.

Remember also that you do not necessarily set a goal for a lifetime; goals change, they are modified or abandoned, and this is normal, even desirable. One should consciously set goals, but reevaluate them periodically. New goals can replace old goals or goals that have been accomplished. Most people have more than one goal, which creates a potential problem if they are not managed properly. Not all goals are equally important; we constantly have to choose which goals to give priority. Many choices favor one goal at the expense of others, so if one's goals are not ranked, at least roughly, it will be difficult to use them to make choices.

Once you have established goals and your priorities among them, you can genuinely begin to manage your time better, which means you will be managing your work better. You can even answer the constant question, "What am I going to do today?" Part of your day is primarily under your control, but part of it is not. Effective time management can help you manage both parts.

You can manage the part of your day that is primarily under your control by using a "To Do" list, one of the older time management technologies. Even as a student, you may currently be using some version of it. One of the best examples of an earlier manifestation of a "To Do" list involves Charles Schwab, the president of Bethlehem Steel early in the twentieth century (LeBoeuf, 1979, pp. 52–54). Schwab evaluated his work performance as president of the company and decided he was not doing as good a job as he should be. He hired Ivy Lee as a consultant to advise him on how to do a better job, and the two struck a rather unique agreement on how they would proceed. Lee was to observe Schwab at work and recommend ways Schwab could improve. Schwab would do whatever Lee told him, and he would pay Lee whatever he thought the recommendations were worth after trying them.

Lee's major recommendation was for Schwab to begin each workday by writing a list of everything he could think of that he might do that day. Schwab was then to examine the list and identify the *most important* thing he might do and begin work on that item immediately. If he completed the task during the day, he was to pick the second most important task to work on, and so forth. The next day, Schwab was to write out a completely new list, pick out the most important task on it, go to work on it, and proceed as he had on the preceding day. Schwab tried this recommendation for a few weeks, and he must have thought it was valuable, because he sent Lee a check for $20,000 (and that $20,000 was in 1910 dollars!). Lee's advice was basically what we know today as the "To Do" list.

The "To Do" list is simply a list of the things you intend to do during the day, usually ranked in some order of importance. Since Schwab and Lee's time, a number of systems have been developed to rank activities. One popular system is the ABC system (Lakein, 1973). Each activity is placed into one of three categories on the basis of how important it is (this is where your overall goals come into play). A activities are essential to complete; B activities, less so; and C activities are those that can wait. Another popular system is a five-category scale where 1 = Important and urgent, 2 = Important but not urgent, 3 = Urgent but not important, 4 = Busywork, and 5 = Wasted time.

Whatever system you use, the important thing is to prioritize your activities to identify which are most important. You should then plan to devote more time and energy to the important activities. Prioritized goals can serve as criteria for placing a particular activity in one category or another. Without prioritized goals, you will have to create a new criteria system for each "To Do" list you write.

345

We have described the "To Do" list as a daily time management system. It is actually very flexible, and some people create weekly or monthly "To Do" lists in addition to or in place of a daily list. Charles Schwab wrote his list at the beginning of each day, but many people write theirs at the end of one day for the next, and some people write a tentative one at the end of the day and revise it when they get to work the next morning. Regardless of when you write the list, it is crucial that it be written down and the activities prioritized in some way. In this way, you are really managing your work as you manage your time.

We said earlier that a prioritized set of goals will help you manage the parts of your time that are not primarily under your control just as they will help you deal with the parts of the day that are under your control. This is because the goals will help you determine how to respond to the uncontrolled parts of the day. They will help you decide how to react in terms of energy and concern about events beyond your control, and in this way manage some important internal resources.

CREATIVITY AND PROBLEM SOLVING

One of the most important personal skills for managers is the capacity for creative problem solving. There are many approaches to problem solving; indeed, if a random sample of people is given an identical problem or situation, individuals in the sample will approach the problem differently and often arrive at very different decisions about what to do. A psychological model developed by Carl Jung provides a compelling explanation for this phenomenon and for why the differences will be systematic. Jung's model of psychological types is a way to classify people according to differences in their psychological makeup. The model describes various psychic functions based on how we take in and process information.

Jung identified two fundamental ways in which people acquire information or perceive things and labeled the two modes *intuition* and *sensation*. Perception by *sensing* is information acquired directly by means of the senses (seeing, hearing, touching, etc.); sensing is a conscious form of information acquisition. Information acquisition through *intuition* is mainly an unconscious process, in which ideas are added indirectly to perceptions made through the senses and associations are made between elements perceived by the senses. A genuine hunch or insight (not a guess) is an example of an intuitive perception. Emphasis on one mode of perception or the other may lead the individual to different ways of approaching the world; some approaches may help in some situations, and other approaches may help in other situations. The sensing individual tends to see the details of a situation, whereas the intuitive person tends to see the whole, but not the parts. Similarly, the sensing person will be clear about what is actually occurring at the moment, while the intuitive person will look more creatively at the possibilities that lie ahead.

After information is acquired, it must be processed; decisions must be made about what to do. Jung's model identifies two major modes of information processing and evaluation. Making choices based on *thinking* is the rational and logical way of dealing with information; one attempts to develop logical, objective conclusions. *Feeling*, on the other hand, emphasizes making a value judgment, deciding according to what is right or wrong, or based on a preference about what is better or worse. The evaluation is not necessarily illogical, but its basis is always a human value and thus ultimately subjective. There are advantages in each approach. An individual who relies on thinking will be careful and objective, though he or she may appear cold and uncaring. The person who relies on feeling will appear friendly and engaging, but may not be as exact or objective as some might want.

Jung argued that all people employ all four psychic functions from time to time, but over the years, each person comes to rely on some functions more than others. Some people tend to emphasize sensing, others emphasize intuition; some people emphasize thinking, others emphasize feeling. (Although we are discussing categories, when the dimensions are actually measured, people seem to differ more in degree rather than categorically.) Based on the combination of preferences, we can arrive at four different psychological "types," illustrated in Box 10.4. Certain personal characteristics or predispositions have been found to be associated with each of the four types of information acquisition/evaluation.

The upper left-hand cell in our illustration is the sensing/thinking combination, which combines the realistic view of the sensing function with the logical and objective capacities of the thinking function. The sensing/thinking person is likely to be good at handling data and solving problems logically. People like this tend to gravitate toward occupations such as accounting, computer programming, and engineering.

In many ways, the lower right-hand corner is the opposite of the sensing/thinking combination, as it combines intuition and feeling. The intuition/feeling combination draws on the creativity of the intuitive function and the strong emotional sense of the

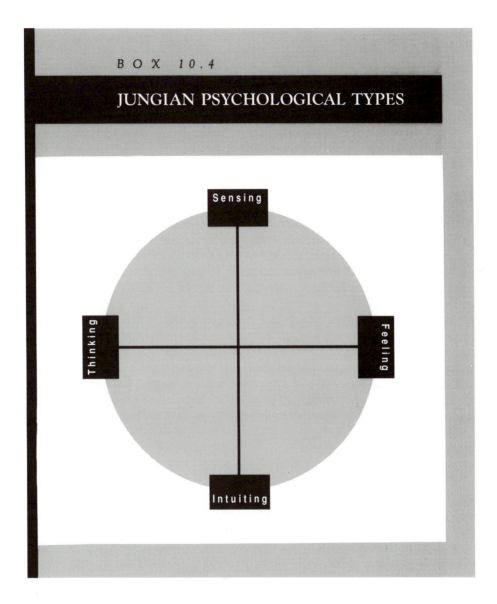

BOX 10.4

JUNGIAN PSYCHOLOGICAL TYPES

feeling function. The intuitive/feeling person is likely to be concerned with the future and with creativity, but, at the same time, be sensitive to and caring about the needs of individuals. Characteristic occupations here are art, advertising, public relations, and personnel management.

The lower left-hand cell combines intuition and thinking. The intuitive/thinking combination brings together the creativity of the intuitive function with the logical, problem-solving ability of the thinking function. The intuitive/thinking person is likely to be creative with respect to problem solving but is also likely to work out the details of a particular solution logically and objectively. Many scientists and architects share these preferences, and, indeed, many middle and upper managers are found here. Top managers must be careful and objective, but are also relied upon to plan the work of the organization, a task that requires the future orientation that comes with intuition.

The upper right-hand cell combines sensing with feeling. The sensing/feeling combination brings together the preference of the sensing function for immediate data and the feeling preference for values and emotions. A sensing/feeling person sees the world in terms of immediate sense data, but is also concerned about the human implications of action based on that data. Teaching, counseling, and sales are associated with this combination, as are, again, significant numbers of managers.

The point is not that one or the other of these combinations is "better" than the other, but that they are different. Consequently, we would expect an individual's approach to solving problems to differ according to how the individual acquires and processes information. Presenting "identical" situations to a random sample would not seem at all "identical" to the people in the sample. Because the subjects would tend to use different modes of acquisition and evaluation, they would "see" very different things and reach very different conclusions. At least one result of the differences would be different decisions. How one sees things makes all the difference in the world when it comes to solving problems.

The implications of these differences for management are profound. We have already emphasized the diversity of situations in which managers find themselves. We can now say that different situations may require the use of different psychic functions. As an illustration, imagine two individuals who are about to buy a house looking in the window of that house. One, emphasizing the sensing function, might say, "This house is a wreck—the carpet is torn up, the ceiling is falling down, the walls are dirty." On the other hand, an intuitive person looking in the same window at the same time might say, "We could do great things with this room; if we fixed the carpet and the ceiling and if we painted the walls, this could be a real showcase." The two people see things quite differently.

Translating these differences in viewpoint into daily activity, you would surely acknowledge that the activity of balancing one's checkbook is not one where you want a great deal of creativity; instead you want to be careful about the immediate data and work with those data in the most logical and objective way possible. On the other hand, there are situations where you will need especially creative solutions to problems. In those situations, the intuitive capacity is very helpful. (Remember that we all have all the functions at our disposal, but we may have to work a little harder at those we don't ordinarily rely upon.)

Similarly, different management activities draw on different psychic functions. For example, monitoring work and performance is likely to be facilitated by carefully observing performance data. On the other hand, the planning function is likely to be aided by the creative potential of the intuitive function. Depending on the situation, you may be required to emphasize one psychic function or another. If your normal preference is to emphasize the sensing function, you may wish to call more consciously on your intuitive capacities where long-term planning is required. You may sometimes want to bring together different people who typically rely on different functions to help solve various problems. You may, for example, want to bring in people you recognize as having strong sensing and thinking capacities to help solve accounting problems. Or, you may wish to bring in individuals noted for strong intuitive and feeling capabilities to help solve human resource planning issues.

348

MODELS OF INDIVIDUAL DECISION MAKING

One could argue that decision making is the most universal managerial activity because it is involved in all the other functions of management. It is impossible to plan, control, staff, direct, organize, or perform any of the miscellaneous management functions without making decisions. All management involves either explicit or implicit decisions. We will examine decision making at the individual level and explore several models of how decisions *should* be made and how decisions are *actually* made.

A great deal of research has been conducted concerning rational processes for decision making, some of which we discussed in terms of rational policy analysis. In its purest form, the rational model of decision making suggests the following steps:

1. Find an occasion for decision making ("decide to decide") and then formulate the problem in the best way possible.
2. Develop as many alternative solutions as possible.
3. Choose the alternative that maximizes the possibility that we will attain our goals or standards.

In essence, analyze the problem, generate alternative solutions, and choose from among the solutions. For our purposes, the most important lesson of the rational decision model lies at the beginning—becoming aware that a problem exists and correctly defining the problem. If you are not aware of a problem, you will not go through the rest of the process to solve it. Your chances of solving the problem are obviously low. (The probabilities are not zero, however, since problems are sometimes solved by accident.) Even if you are aware that a problem exists, your chances of solving it do not increase much if you do not identify it correctly.

Definition of the situation is one's perception of reality. Human beings need to make sense of things. We do not tolerate chaos well, and thus are continually defining and redefining situations we find ourselves in. Aside from our need to make sense of things, defining the situation is important because it is the basis upon which we act and make decisions to act. All mentally healthy individuals behave in a way consistent with their definitions of situations.

When it comes to problem solving, incorrect diagnosis of the problem (that is, an incorrect definition of the situation) can be disastrous; the correct definition is half the battle. An example from the Cold War days of the early 1960s illustrates this point. During this period, the U.S. and its allies had installed long-range radar systems to monitor the Soviet Union and to give warning of any Soviet attack by either missile or bomber. Soon after the radar systems were installed, the commander of an installation in England was made aware of a set of images on the station's screens that looked as if the Soviet Union were launching a massive missile assault against the U.S. It was the commander's job to evaluate the information, report it to Washington, and include a recommendation and evaluation of the accuracy of the information.

Obviously, since missiles travel pretty fast, the commander did not have a great deal of time to contemplate the situation. But, being a calm and collected individual, the commander thought things over a few moments before he made his report. He remembered that Nikita Krushchev, then premier of the Soviet Union, was in New York City addressing the United Nations that day and thought it would be an unlikely time for the Soviets to attack. He also took into consideration the fact that the radar system was new, and that new systems sometimes have "bugs" in them. Putting all this together, he made his report, including in it his relatively low confidence in the information on his screens. He stated that he believed there was a malfunction somewhere in the system and recommended that the radar images not be interpreted as an attack on the U.S. Obviously he was correct; there was no major attack by the Soviet Union. But what was actually happening?

It turned out that the radars were so powerful that some of the radiation they broadcast traveled far out into space. The system operated smoothly for about a week, but then the moon orbited into position to be hit by some of the radiation, which was reflected back to the radar antennas, in turn creating images on the screens that looked much like a flight of missiles heading toward the U.S. The computers in the radar system had not been programmed to disregard the radiation coming back from the moon.

The commander was presented with a problem: the decision of interpreting the images and making his report. He had two interpretations. One was that the Soviet Union had started World War III; the other, that he had a malfunctioning system. One definition of the situation might have actually started World War III; the other avoided that catastrophe. You can easily see why correct definition of the problem is so critical in a problem-solving situation.

The rational decision model is often presented as the way people actually go about making decisions (or at least the way they should), and this is probably true to a certain extent. It is also clear that, in many cases, solutions to problems are arrived at in a far different way. The basis of the rational problem-solving process is the economic assumption that people attempt to *maximize* their outcomes when they make choices (i.e., decisions). Theoretically, people select a criterion, such as income or profit, then evaluate all decision alternatives in terms of that criterion, and select the alternative that will produce the best results.

Herbert Simon has studied decision-making behavior, especially in organizations, and concludes that the classic "economic man" assumption is seldom an accurate description of human problem-solving or decision-making behavior in real life. Simon (1957, p. xxvi) argued that maximizing outcomes is simply not possible in most situations and identified several reasons that it is usually impossible. All the reasons Simon offers add up to constraints on human beings' abilities to acquire and process information. There are time limits for making most decisions, and there are only so many resources available to gather information. Moreover, because we care more about some problems than others, our motivation to solve problems varies. We are willing to spend more mental and physical energy on some problems than on others.

Even if we had access to unlimited information about any problem, there are cognitive limits to how much information we can process at any given time. Furthermore, particularly in managerial situations, we seldom have the luxury of being able to deal with just one problem at a time. Other problems compete for our attention, time, and energy, which further taxes our cognitive limits.

Putting all these constraints together, Simon argues that human beings are rational and attempt to be rational, but they can only be rational within certain limits or bounds. What Simon calls "bounded rationality" (see Chapter 9) suggests that choices will be evaluated, but only within the bounds of these constraints. This results in a satisficing criterion for evaluating alternatives, rather than in a maximizing one.

A **satisficing decision** is one that is just "good enough" in terms of some criterion. Bounded rationality leads to satisficing decisions, and the process, in its pure form, operates as follows. When an individual faces a choice situation in which a decision must be made, rather than attempting to gather all possible information, generate all possible alternatives, and choose the alternative likely to produce the best results, the decision maker decides what level of outcome (in terms of some criterion) will be satisfactory or "good enough." The individual then examines choice alternatives one at a time and selects the first one that equals or exceeds the minimal ("good enough") criterion level. The process stops at this point, and the choice becomes the decision. No attempt will be made to examine other, potentially better, options.

That human beings vary in attempts to maximize suggests something of a continuum between satisficing and maximizing. But Simon's work suggests that most decisions, most of the time, fall much closer to the satisficing end of the continuum than the maximizing end, even where we are making important (and potentially costly) decisions. Marketing research shows, for example, that people tend to seek out most of the information they acquire about new cars after they purchase a new car rather than before.

Thus, the rational decision-making process can be considered a *prescriptive* model that tells us what we should do to make better decisions, but it does not give us an accurate picture of how human beings actually make decisions. Because we tend to satisfice rather than maximize, a modified and more limited version of this process, the satisficing model, provides the more accurate description. Hence, we can call it a *descriptive* model, which attempts to describe how things actually happen without regard to how they should happen. Given the nature of managerial work, satisficing may be the only way a manager can deal with the constant stream of problems and choice situations that arise daily.

Interestingly, one alternative model of decision making in the public sector claims to be both prescriptive and descriptive. Charles Lindblom's incremental model of decision making assumes that most governmental decisions (and others) usually begin by analyzing the existing situation and then move marginally or incrementally away from that position. In making a case for new programs, for example, managers often talk about how a new idea "builds on" existing strengths. This descriptive aspect of the model has a familiar ring. But, in a curious twist, Lindblom also suggests that the incremental model may even make sense normatively—because incremental proposals focus on well-known experiences, they reduce the number of alternatives to be considered and thus reduce the complexity of the problem at hand (Lindblom, 1968, p. 27).

351

POWER AND LEADERSHIP

The capacity to understand power, especially the capacity to recognize and use the resources one has available to influence others, is essential in modern organizations of all types. But power is a far narrower term than leadership. We will consider power as one aspect of the larger question of how one might develop greater skills in public leadership.

Many commentators have argued that improved leadership is essential for us to successfully meet the challenges of the coming century. Public opinion data reveal widespread loss of faith in the leadership of business, government, labor, and other private and public institutions. But many argue that the problem relates not merely to formal positions of power; rather the failure of leadership is pervasive throughout society. John Gardner, the former cabinet secretary and founder of Common Cause, stated, "In this country leadership is dispersed among all the segments of society and down through all levels, and the system simply won't work as it should unless large numbers of people throughout society are prepared to take leaderlike action to make things work at their level" (Gardner, 1987).

In this view, leadership is a pervasive phenomenon, occurring in families, work groups, businesses, and at all levels of government, society, and culture. Leadership, then, should be seen not merely as a position someone holds, but rather as something that happens in a group or organization, something that comes and goes, something that ebbs and flows as the group or organization does its work. Anyone can be a leader, no matter how briefly.

As we have seen, modern society can be described as (1) highly turbulent, subject to sudden and dramatic shifts; (2) highly interdependent, requiring cooperation across many sectors; and (3) greatly in need of creative and integrative solutions to problems. Under such circumstances, ambiguity is increasingly a hallmark of decision making, and the involvement (rather than the control) of many individuals in group decisions will be necessary. "Leadership . . . will become an increasingly intricate process of multilateral brokerage, including constituencies both within and without the organization. More and more decisions will be public decisions; that is, the people they affect will insist on being heard" (Bennis, 1983, p. 16). Leadership for the future cannot be equated merely with the exercise of control by those in formal positions of power.

352   What do we know about leadership, especially shared or public leadership? What do we know about leadership in the increasingly common situations where no one is really "in charge"—student organizations, churches, political groups, and so on. Often, much of their work is done through committees or other even less formal groups. And those committees seem to waste a lot of time and energy, partly because of lack of leadership. Even though one person may be designated the "leader," rarely does he or she exercise much control. Usually, things drift for a while—maybe a long while—until someone finally puts forth a suggestion that people pick up on and begin to get excited about. At that point, we can say that someone has exercised leadership.

Somewhat more formally, then, we can define leadership as "the character of the relationship between the individual and a group or organization that stimulates or releases some latent energy within the group so that those involved more clearly understand their own needs, desires, interests, and potentialities and begin to work toward their fulfillment." Where leadership is present, something occurs in the dynamics of the group or organization that leads to change. What is central to leadership is the capacity of the leader—whether or not called a leader—to "energize" the group.

Leadership involves helping the group become aware of a new direction in which to move. The leader merely taps and reshapes the "consciousness" of the group. Acts of leadership express a new direction, but one that is determined by the emerging interests of all members of a group. We can say that one exercises public leadership who (1) helps the group or organization understand its needs and potential; (2) integrates and articulates the group's vision; and (3) acts as a "trigger" or stimulus for group action.

The essence of leadership, therefore, is its "energizing" effect. But often the people we formally refer to as leaders don't really lead; at best, they "manage" things successfully, by keeping the group running more or less smoothly.

Although power may be an important resource to the leader, one need not exercise power to bring about change (see Box 10.5). Efforts to control a group are often ultimately destructive of leadership. On the other hand, when the direction of the group or organization is selected through a developmental process that gives priority to group members' needs and desires, leadership is much more likely to be enduring. Leadership for the future will require much more than a formal position.

BOX 10.5

BASES OF SOCIAL POWER

Power is really much more complex than we often think. For example, the power we exercise is based on a number of different factors that operate in social situations. A classic research article describes the following "bases of social power."

1. *Reward power*: the ability to meet the needs of another, or control the other by rewarding the desired behavior. Pay, promotions, or bonuses may be ways that organizations exert reward power over employees.
2. *Punishment power*: coercive power, or the ability to deliver a painful or punishing outcome to others, and hence control them by their desire to escape the punishment. Firing, ridiculing, or disciplining an individual are common techniques of punishment.
3. *Expert power*: power based on the ability to understand, use, and deliver information that others need. Engineers or scientists may exert great influence in an organization based on their knowledge of scientific techniques for manufacturing a product, etc.
4. *Legitimate power*: control or influence exerted by virtue of one's holding a particular position in the organizational structure. The "power" is vested in the rights and responsibilities of the position, not the person. Thus, a company president or chairman of the board has power by virtue of the rights and responsibility given to whoever holds the office. Compliance with legitimate power occurs because other individuals in the organization respect the organizational structure and the rights and responsibility that accompany particular positions.

(continued)

353

> *(continued)*
>
> 5. *Referent power:* liking, charisma, or the desire to comply
>   with someone's wishes because you are attracted to him
>   or her are examples of referent power. Control based on
>   referent power depends upon the power-holder's ability
>   to have others like and be attracted to him or her, and
>   to follow his or her leadership because of this attraction.
>
> SOURCE: Adapted from John R. P. French, Jr., and Bertram Raven, "The Bases
> of Social Power," in *Group Dynamics,* 2nd ed., Dorwin Cartwright and Alvin F.
> Zander. Copyright © 1962 by Dorwin Cartwright and Alvin F. Zander.
> Reprinted by permission of HarperCollins Publishers.

What skills will you need to be successful as a leader? They begin with those we ordinarily associate with effective management—the ability to use power and influence effectively, the ability to communicate with and motivate others, and the ability to work in and among diverse groups of people. (We will discuss most of these skills in the next chapter.) But leadership builds on these skills in some interesting ways.

To energize the group, for example, the leader must know how to "sense" its underlying desires, sometimes even before those desires are clear even to the group members. The leader must also be able to act in ambiguous situations and to take risks; leadership involves change, and change is often difficult for both group and leader. Developing the personal strength to face change is important.

Leadership has often been viewed in terms of the exercise of power by one person or group over another—getting people to do what one wants them to do by manipulating power and influence. Leadership in the future will be more and more independent of power, and the most critical leadership skills will be the personal (rather than interpersonal) skills associated with correctly empathizing with and "reading" a group, acting with a sense of direction in the presence of ambiguity, and having the courage to take risks when change is warranted.

SUMMARY AND ACTION IMPLICATIONS

Public management is a complex and diverse career. One moment you may be developing a budget for your agency; the next moment you may be leading a meeting on sick leave policy; and the next, you may be counseling an employee who is feeling burned out. The diversity of the work and its occasional intensity mean that you not only need to understand the ethical and political context of your work, but also to develop the personal and interpersonal skills to bring about action.

Skills based in the individual personality—management of stress and time, creativity in solving problems, capacity for decision making, and skills in public leadership—are played out in social settings, but each skill is deeply rooted in your own identity and character. Because they are so personal, these skills underlie nearly everything you do.

Thus, understanding yourself is an essential prerequisite to acting effectively and responsibly in public organizations. Moreover, to the extent that you are able to learn about yourself, your strengths and weaknesses, your desires and frustrations, you will be much more effective in your work with others. If you are able to reflect on your experiences and share them with others, and to learn from others' experience as well, you will be a much more effective learner—and a much more effective manager.

Nowhere is this admonition more appropriate than in the area of leadership. To lead others, you must first know yourself. Leadership involves more than power or control. Whereas power may be a resource, leadership capabilities are more likely to arise from the ability to understand the emerging desires of a group, to articulate the vision or direction the group wishes to follow, and to stimulate the group to action. Leadership unquestionably requires social or interpersonal skills, but it is based in empathetic understanding, the ability to express the aspirations of the group, and the confidence to undertake the risks associated with change. Nowhere is this more true than in the realm of *public* leadership.

TERMS AND DEFINITIONS

Role ambiguity: Occurs where the rights and responsibilities of the job are not clearly understood.

Role conflict: Occurs where one faces two different and incompatible sets of demands.

Satisficing decision: One that is just "good enough" in terms of some criterion.

Support system: Network of people with whom one can talk about problems.

STUDY QUESTIONS

1. Discuss the activities involved in a typical managerial day.
2. Discuss the concept of "stress management." What are some specific techniques for reducing stress levels?
3. The ability to effectively use the time available is one determinant of a successful manager. How do time management practices help improve success?
4. Explain how individuals vary in terms of creativity and problem-solving skills.
5. What features are present in rational decision making?

CASES AND EXERCISES

1. Chapter 1 listed management skills developed by the U.S. Office of Personnel Management. Part of that list is reproduced here. Go through the list and assess your level of development in each of the skills. You might want to verify your evaluations by talking with others who know you well and have seen you operate in groups and organizations. After you have a sense of your own level of skill development, try to identify the activities (classes, workshops, readings, etc.) that would help you improve your skills in areas that need some work.

The "How" of Management Effectiveness Characteristics

Broad perspectives: Broad, long-term view: balancing short- and long-term considerations

Strategic view: Collecting/assessing/analyzing information; diagnosis; anticipation; judgment

Environmental sensitivity: "Tuned into" agency and its environment; awareness of importance of non-technical factors

Leadership: Individual; group; willingness to lead and manage, and accept responsibility

Flexibility: Openness to new information; behavioral flexibility; tolerance for stress/ambiguity/change; innovativeness

Action orientation: Independence, proactivity; calculated risk taking; problem solving; decisiveness

Results focus: Concern with goal achievement; follow through, tenacity

Communication: Speaking; writing; listening

Interpersonal sensitivity: Self-knowledge and awareness of impact on others; sensitivity to needs/strengths/weaknesses of others; negotiation; conflict resolution; persuasion

Technical competence: Specialized expertise (e.g., engineering, physical science, law, accounting, social science)

2. This instrument will help you determine, very roughly, your psychological preferences. After completing and scoring the questionnaire, note your preferred functions. In a small group, discuss the extent to which your personality tends to mirror the characteristics of your type.

Personal Style Inventory

Just as every person has differently shaped feet and toes from every other person, so we all have differently "shaped" personalities. Just as no person's foot shape is "right" or "wrong," so no person's personality shape is right or wrong. The purpose of this inventory is to give you a picture of the shape of your preferences, but that shape, while different from others' personality shapes, has nothing to do with mental health or mental problems.

The following items are arranged in pairs (*a* and *b*); each member of the pair represents a preference you may or may not hold. Rate your preference for each item by giving it a score of 0 to 5 (0 meaning you *really* feel negative about it or strongly about the other member of the pair, 5 meaning you *strongly* prefer it or do not prefer the other member of the pair). Scores for *a* and *b* must add up to 5 (0 and 5, 1 and 4, 2 and 3, etc.). Do not use fractions such as 2½.

I prefer:

1a. _____ being called imaginative or intuitive.

1b. _____ being called factual and accurate.

2a. _____ making decisions about people in organizations based on available data and systematic analysis of situations.

2b. _____ making decisions about people in organizations based on empathy, feelings, and understanding of their needs and values.

3a. _____ using methods I know well that are effective to get the job done.

3b. _____ trying to think of new methods of doing tasks when confronted with them.

4a. _____ drawing conclusions based on unemotional logic and careful step-by-step analysis.

4b. _____ drawing conclusions based on what I feel and believe about life and people.

5a. _____ thinking about possibilities.

5b. _____ dealing with actualities.

6a. _____ being thought of as a thinking person.

6b. _____ being thought of as a feeling person.

7a. _____ the abstract or theoretical.

7b. _____ the concrete or real.

8a. _____ helping others explore their feelings.

8b. _____ helping others make logical decisions.

9a. _____ possible views of the whole.

9b. _____ the factual details available.

10a. _____ using common sense and conviction to make decisions.

10b. _____ using data, analysis, and reason to make decisions.

11a. _____ ideas.

11b. _____ facts.

12a. _____ convictions.

12b. _____ verifiable conclusions.

13a. _____ carrying out carefully laid, detailed plans with precision.

13b. _____ designing plans and structures without necessarily carrying them out.

14a. _____ logical people.

14b. _____ feeling people.

15a. _____ imagining the nonexistent.

15b. _____ examining details of the actual.

16a. _____ experiencing emotional situations, discussions, movies.

16b. _____ using my ability to analyze situations.

357

Personal Style Inventory Scoring

Instructions: Transfer your scores for each item of each pair to the appropriate blanks. Be careful to check the *a* and *b* letters to be sure you are recording scores in the right blank spaces. Then total the scores for each dimension. These scores are rough approximations of your psychological preferences as outlined in our discussion of the Jungian psychological types.

Perception Dimension		Evaluation Dimension	
Intuiting	Sensing	Thinking	Feeling
Item	Item	Item	Item
1a. ___	1b. ___	2a. ___	2b. ___
3a. ___	3b. ___	4a. ___	4b. ___
5a. ___	5b. ___	6a. ___	6b. ___
7a. ___	7b. ___	8a. ___	8b. ___
9a. ___	9b. ___	10a. ___	10b. ___
11a. ___	11b. ___	12a. ___	12b. ___
13a. ___	13b. ___	14a. ___	14b. ___
15a. ___	15b. ___	16a. ___	16b. ___
Total	Total	Total	Total
Intuiting ___	Sensing ___	Thinking ___	Feeling ___

SOURCE: Adapted from R. Craig Hogan and David W. Champagne, "Personal Style Inventory," © Organization, Design, and Development, Inc., King of Prussia, PA 19406. Reprinted by permission.

3. The following "classic" exercise in group problem solving will illustrate several important aspects of the decision-making process.

Your spaceship has just crash-landed on the moon. You were scheduled to rendezvous with the mothership 200 miles away on the lighted surface of the moon, but the rough landing has ruined your ship and destroyed all the equipment on board, except for the 15 items listed below.

You and four to seven other people should take this test individually, without knowing one another's answers, then take the test as a group. Share your individual solutions and reach a consensus—one ranking for each item that best satisfies all group members.

Your crew's survival depends on reaching the mothership, so you must choose the most critical items available for the 200-mile trip. Your task is to rank the fifteen items in terms of their importance for survival. Place a 1 by the most important item, a 2 by the second most important, and so on through 15, the least important.

___ Box of matches
___ Food concentrate
___ Fifty feet of nylon rope
___ Parachute silk
___ Solar-powered portable heating unit
___ Two .45-caliber pistols
___ One case of dehydrated evaporated milk
___ Two 100-pound tanks of oxygen
___ Stellar map (of the moon's constellation)
___ Self-inflating life raft

____ Magnetic compass
____ Five gallons of water
____ Signal flares
____ First-aid kit containing injection needles
____ Solar-powered FM receiver-transmitter

NASA experts have determined the best solution to this task. Their answers appear in appendix 10.A.

SOURCE: Jay Hall, "Decisions, Decisions, Decisions," *Psychology Today* (November 1971), 5, pp. 51–88. Reprinted with permission from *Psychology Today Magazine*. Copyright © 1971 (PT Partners, L.P.).

4. *Stress profile*: Place your answer to each of the following questions in the space provided before each number. Answer with: (a) almost always true; (b) often true; (c) seldom true; (d) almost never true.

    ____ 1. I hate to wait in lines.
    ____ 2. I often find myself "racing" against the clock to save time.
    ____ 3. I become upset if I think something is taking too long.
    ____ 4. When under pressure I tend to lose my temper.
    ____ 5. My friends tell me that I tend to get irritated easily.
    ____ 6. I seldom like to do anything unless I can make it competitive.
    ____ 7. When something needs to be done, I'm the first to begin even though the details may still need to be worked out.
    ____ 8. When I make a mistake, it is usually because I've rushed into something without giving it enough thought and planning.
    ____ 9. Whenever possible I will try to do two things at once, like eating while working or planning while driving or bathing.
    ____ 10. I find myself feeling guilty when I am not actively working on something.

Scoring: a = 4, b = 3, c = 2, d = 1   Score: ____

This exercise tests "Type A" behavior, characterized by impatience with delays, urgency, competitiveness—and stress-related illness. A total score of 26 or above indicates that you tend toward this type.

SOURCE: Daniel A. Girdano and George S. Everly, Jr., *Controlling Stress and Tension: A Holistic Approach*, © 1979, pp. 108–109. Adapted by permission of Prentice-Hall, Inc., Englewood Cliffs, New Jersey.

5. Although power should not be equated with leadership, it can certainly be an important resource to public managers. To illustrate some of these types of power, think back over the past week or two as you attended class and worked in various groups and organizations, and answer the following questions:

    a. Who were the two or three people during this period who exercised the greatest power over you?
    b. Who were the people during this period over whom *you* exercised the most power?

Now return to the "Bases of Social Power" in Box 10.4. What was the basis for the power that others exercised over you? What was the basis for the power that you exercised over others? How might you most effectively build up your power base in groups and organizations to which you belong?

FOR ADDITIONAL READING

Bennis, Warren, and Nanus, Burt. *Leaders: Strategies for Taking Charge.* New York: AMACOM, 1985.

Burns, James MacGregor. *Leadership.* New York: Harper & Row, 1978.

Cleveland, Harlan. *The Knowledge Executive.* New York: E. P. Dutton, 1985.

Hall, Richard H., and Quinn, Robert E. *Organization Theory and Public Policy.* Beverly Hills, CA: Sage Publications, 1983.

Lakein, Alan. *How to Get Control of Your Time and Your Life.* New York: Signet Books, 1973.

Meyers, Isabel Briggs. *Gifts Differing.* Palo Alto, CA: Consulting Psychologists Press, 1980.

Price, Virginia Ann. *Type A Behavior Pattern.* New York: Academic Press, 1982.

Selye, Hans. *Stress without Distress.* Philadelphia: J. B. Lippincott, 1974.

Whetten, David A., and Cameron, Kim S. *Developing Management Skills.* Glenview, IL: Scott, Foresman, 1984.

"Lost on the Moon" Exercise: Answers from NASA Experts

1. *Two 100-pound tanks of oxygen:* most pressing survival need
2. *Five gallons of water:* replacement for tremendous liquid loss on lighted side
3. *Stellar map of the moon's constellation:* primary means of navigation
4. *Food concentrate:* efficient means of supplying energy requirements
5. *Solar-powered FM receiver–transmitter:* for communication with mothership; but FM requires line-of-sight transmission and short ranges
6. *Fifty feet of nylon rope:* useful in scaling cliffs, tying injured together
7. *First-aid kit containing injection needles:* needles for vitamins; medicines, etc.; will fit special aperture in NASA spacesuits
8. *Parachute silk:* protection from sun's rays
9. *Self-inflating life raft:* CO bottle in military raft may be used for propulsion
10. *Signal flares:* distress signal when mothership is sighted
11. *Two .45-caliber pistols:* possible means of self-propulsion
12. *One case of dehydrated evaporated milk:* bulkier duplication of food concentrate
13. *Solar-powered portable heating unit:* not needed unless on dark side
14. *Magnetic compass:* magnetic field on moon is not polarized; worthless for navigation
15. *Box of matches:* no oxygen on moon to sustain flame; virtually worthless

INTERPERSONAL SKILLS AND GROUP DYNAMICS

The ability to work effectively with other people is absolutely central for the public manager. To persuade people on issues, to encourage and motivate your employees, to represent your organization well before external groups—these and many other interpersonal skills contribute to your success as a public manager. Whereas it was once thought that managers were "born, not made," we now know that the skills managers need can be learned and improved. By carefully considering and constantly practicing good management skills, you can become more effective.

COMMUNICATIONS

As we saw in chapter 10, most of a manager's typical day is spent in some form of communication activity; some days are devoted almost exclusively to communications. The ability to communicate well is necessary for any adult to function successfully in American society. Rankin (1929) discovered that, on the average, adult Americans spend 70 percent of the waking day in some form of communication activity. He classified how people spent their communication time, and found that 9 percent of the time was spent writing, 16 percent reading, 30 percent speaking, and 45 percent listening.

More recent studies confirm Rankin's findings, although there is some evidence to suggest that we now spend even more time listening—to television! We will discuss the communication modes of listening, speaking, and writing. (We will not address reading, except to note that the special skill known as "speed reading" is probably one a manager would find useful.)

Listening

We do more listening than we do any other form of communication. Recent research focusing exclusively on managers reveals that managers spend a greater than average portion of their time listening—about 63 percent of the day. Recall that the studies of managerial activities we discussed in chapter 10 indicate that a majority of a manager's communication interactions are initiated by others. Because most are in the form of face-to-face interactions, this finding implies a lot of listening.

But doing a lot of listening does not mean that managers listen well. Listening is not the same as hearing, and, although hearing cannot be altered without medical or technical intervention, one can substantially improve the quality of one's listening with proper motivation and training. Let us first review some basics of effective listening (see Box 11.1).

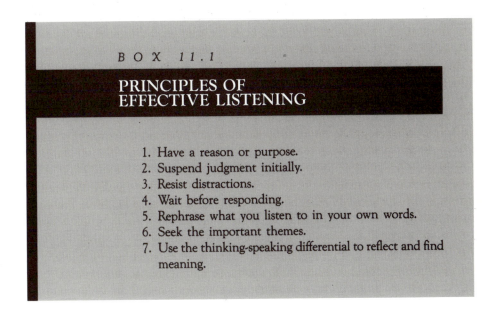

B O X   1 1 . 1

PRINCIPLES OF EFFECTIVE LISTENING

1. Have a reason or purpose.
2. Suspend judgment initially.
3. Resist distractions.
4. Wait before responding.
5. Rephrase what you listen to in your own words.
6. Seek the important themes.
7. Use the thinking-speaking differential to reflect and find meaning.

Have a reason or purpose.   This is the most important principle of those we will discuss. Having a purpose or a reason to listen provides the motivation to listen, and, generally speaking, anything you are motivated to do, you will do better than if you are not motivated. Listening is no exception. One must be motivated to listen well; it does not just happen. Without motivation, you will not use the other six principles, or you will not use them as well as you could.

But, you ask, what if I don't have a reason to listen? Then find one. Actively search for a reason to listen to what is being said. Ask yourself, "How can this information help me do my job better?" Or, "How can I use this information in some way, on the job or elsewhere?" Finding a reason to listen will provide the motivation to use all the other principles and techniques.

Suspend judgment initially.   The key word in this phrase is "initially." You will obviously need to evaluate the material you listen to, but you should wait until you hear the entire message before you begin the evaluation. This can be difficult. In an election year, for example, if we know a particular candidate's party, we are likely to evaluate what the candidate is going to say before he or she even begins speaking. It is not coincidental that television and radio advertising for many candidates does not prominently identify the candidate's party. The advertisers want to increase the chances of having the message heard rather than losing half the audience immediately by identifying the speaker as a Democrat or Republican. To make a judgment before listening carefully to what someone is saying is the opposite of the "suspension" principle.

Resist distractions.   Many things can distract us when we are trying to listen. The "distraction" principle tells us to fight back, to actively resist whatever may be distracting us. Among the many things that distract us, various sounds are usually the most powerful. The sound may be a nonverbal noise, such as the siren from a passing fire engine or ambulance, or the voices of several people speaking at once, or something about the way the speaker talks. Regardless of what type of sound is creating the distraction, the remedy is to resist, to try harder.

In this case, "trying harder" means that you should increase your concentration. If you are in a face-to-face situation with a speaker, make sure you maintain constant eye contact. You can also lean a little bit in the direction of the speaker. By increasing your level of concentration, you can resist distractions you would have thought impossible to overcome. And that is the problem with distractions—they become an excuse for not even trying to listen, because "It's impossible to hear what she's saying."

A common classroom demonstration in listening skills illustrates the "distraction" principle (as well as others). Two volunteers read a short paragraph to the class. The volunteers are positioned in front of the class, about 15 feet away from each other. Each has a sheet of paper containing a short (30–40 seconds) paragraph. Each student in the class is assigned to listen to one or the other of the two volunteers, but not to both. The students are instructed not to take notes while the paragraphs are being read, but, at the end of the reading, to write down something about each of the major points their speaker has read.

The trick is that each volunteer has a different paragraph and they read the paragraphs simultaneously! After the first round of the exercise, checking usually reveals that only a small number—and sometimes none—of the students in the class are able to write down something about every major point their speaker read. The instructor then reviews the eye-contact and leaning points, picks two new volunteers, gives them two new paragraphs, and repeats the exercise. The second time around it is not unusual to find that 20 to 25 percent of the class has written down something about each major point.

This exercise demonstrates that there is variability in the quality of listening, both between and within individuals. It also demonstrates that it is possible to resist even a major distraction. The effectiveness of the demonstration lies in the fact that it shows that our ability to resist distractions is much higher than we realize, and that we can overcome a great deal to improve the quality of our listening.

Some distractions are less obvious, perceived only semiconsciously. One such distraction for many Americans is English spoken with a foreign accent or with a different regional accent. Allen Bluedorn recalls learning this lesson while he was in the U.S. Army and was taking part in a listening course. The course made the same point about distractions that we have made, and he wondered if he had been allowing the fact that people spoke with different accents to become excuses not to listen. (He was stationed at Ft. Bliss in El Paso, Texas, at the time, and he had ample opportunities to hear English spoken with a Hispanic accent.)

The approach he used to test the principle was to simply concentrate harder the next time he encountered someone who spoke with a Hispanic accent. To his surprise, by concentrating harder, he was able to understand completely what the person said. He concluded that he had indeed been succumbing to the distraction of the accent, and it had become an excuse not to listen well. This lesson is important in today's increasingly multicultural organizations, where English is often spoken with a wide variety of accents. But the larger and more important lesson is that even substantial distractions can be overcome.

Wait before responding.   The "response" principle suggests that one relax and wait for natural opportunities to speak, instead of jumping into the conversation immediately. When we are burning to contribute to a discussion or conversation, we become too excited about getting into the conversation; we concentrate on whatever it is we want to say and stop concentrating on and listening to what the speaker is saying. The "response" principle suggests that one wait for a natural opportunity to contribute; try to flow with the conversation as an event rather than disrupting it by speaking at the wrong time.

365

Rephrase what you listen to in your own words.   The "rephrasing" principle suggests an incredibly simple, yet powerful, way to check one's understanding. The idea is merely to take something you hear (an idea, instructions, etc.) and put it into your own words. You then repeat it to the person who gave you the information and ask if that is what was meant. As easy as it seems, this is an excellent way to check understanding and avoid mistakes. When you give instructions, you can ask the person who is receiving them to do the same thing. You can say, for example, "I'm not sure I explained that very well. Please tell me what you got out of that."

Seek the important themes.   The "thematic" principle indicates that the main ideas are more important than facts—so important that they are the general keys to understanding and retaining what is said. Understanding the main ideas provides a framework for organizing the facts, which makes the facts themselves easier to remember.

The man usually credited with starting the listening movement over thirty years ago, Ralph Nichols, demonstrated this point in his research. He discovered that A and B students reported different listening habits than C and D students. In surveys of hundreds of students, he discovered that the A and B students gave a much different response to the question, "What do you listen for first when you attend a lecture?" than did the C and D students. The A and B students predominantly gave a response like, "I listen for the main ideas first," whereas C and D students said "I listen for the facts." (This finding probably does not entirely explain the differences in these students' GPAs, but it is undoubtedly part of it.)

Use the thinking-speaking differential to reflect and find meaning. The "meaning" principle reflects the fact that people think faster than they speak. Although it varies by region, people in the U.S. speak at a rate of about 150 words per minute, but in terms of language, they think at a rate of about 500 words per minute. Thus, we normally think more than three times faster than we speak. This differential creates an opportunity to listen more effectively, but the opportunity can also be a temptation to do things that interfere with our listening. The extra time can also be used for things that distract from the listening process—concentration lapses, daydreaming, thinking something other than what the speaker is saying, and so forth. All these things interfere with good listening, so the extra time is a two-edged sword—both opportunity and temptation.

Listening is both the most widely used and the most widely misused communication skill. It is also the skill least often taught in the American education system, from kindergarten through graduate school (Steil, Barker, & Watson, 1983).

Speaking

Most of the speaking managers do is informal, one-on-one or small group communications—in their offices, on the phone, and in meetings. To show how we can improve our speaking, we will focus on giving instructions, because a significant amount of manager-initiated communication consists of giving instructions to others. The managerial activity of delegation, in fact, would be virtually impossible without instruction giving. The key to giving instructions successfully is the ability to put yourself in the position of the person who will receive the instructions. Ideally, you want to give exactly the right amount of information—neither too much nor too little; however, if one must depart from the ideal, it is usually better to give too much rather than too little.

Two questions help you put yourself in the position of the individual who will receive the instructions:

1. What does the person *need* to know to carry out the instructions?
2. What does the person *want* to know to carry out the instructions?

The ability to decide what information is really needed is, incidentally, a justification for promotion from within—making managers out of the people who have done the jobs they will be managing. People who have done the job should be able to determine more accurately what their subordinates need to know when they receive instructions. Unfortunately, not everyone who is promoted to the management level takes full advantage of this knowledge.

To demonstrate how difficult it is to identify what information to transmit, let's consider another classroom exercise to illustrate how you can put yourself in the position of the person who will be receiving the instructions. Students form pairs, and one member of each pair is given a diagram. The students are seated back-to-back, and the one with the diagram gives the other one instructions for drawing the diagram on a piece of paper. Only the instruction giver is allowed to speak, and the instruction giver is not allowed to look at the copy as it is drawn. After the copy is completed, the diagram is evaluated according to a set of scoring rules. Roles are then exchanged in the pairs, a new diagram is distributed, and instructions are again given to produce copies of the diagram, all rules remaining the same.

It is common for the scores in the second round to be higher than those in the first, even if the second diagram is more complex. Why? The answer seems to be that the instruction giver in the second round has been in the position of the instruction receiver during the first round and, thus, has a better idea of what information is really needed. Furthermore, the instruction givers during the second round know the scoring rules and can focus on what elements of the diagrams will be scored when the copies are evaluated. Most important, however, the instruction giver who understands what information someone needs is better able to provide that information.

Writing

Writing is a less common form of managerial communication than speaking and listening, but it is important nevertheless. Most managerial writing is brief, often one or two pages. The memo is the most common type of written communication for many managers. Sussman and Deep (1984) offer six rules for effective managerial writing—the "Six C's."

367

Clarity: To be clear, one must put oneself in the reader's position much as the instruction giver must put himself or herself in the receiver's position. Write in the active voice (i.e., Dave painted the house) rather than the passive (i.e., The house was painted by Dave); avoid jargon; and try to use the simple format of introduction, body, and conclusion.

Courtesy: Courtesy involves knowing your readers, adapting to their mood, and writing at their level, providing neither too much nor too little information. Again, there are clear parallels with instruction giving.

Conciseness: This is the rule of brevity, to be short and to the point. Sometimes you may want to repeat something for emphasis, but the general rule is, the shorter the better. Think of it this way: which are you more likely to read, a fifty-word memo or a ten-page report? You are likely to read the fifty-word memo on the spot; the ten-page report goes into the pile you will "get to when I can."

Confidence: Always write with confidence. Confidence is really a matter of judgment on the writer's part, based on one's knowledge of one's readers. Judgment is especially important in avoiding two extremes: overbearing (too confident) and wishy-washy (not confident enough).

Correctness: You *must* be correct in grammar and composition, the technical rules of writing which include spelling and punctuation. Inaccurate spelling is especially conspicuous.

Conversational tone: To achieve a conversational tone, try to write in about the same way you talk, and try to imagine one specific person to whom you are writing. Thinking of a specific individual rather than an abstract category makes it much easier to write. It is much easier to write to John Jones than to "all economics professors." Occasionally, conversational writing calls for violating some formal rules of grammar, but this breach often makes things smoother, and thus more understandable and easier to follow.

Communications will affect nearly every aspect of your work as a public manager. Your ability to persuade others of your position, your clarity in sharing ideas, and your ability to deal effectively with difficult people will shape your image as an administrator (see Box 11.2). Fortunately, you can improve your ability to listen, to speak, and to write. So, practicing your communication skills whenever possible will pay dividends whatever your career.

BOX 11.2

SECRET WEAPONS FOR ORGANIZATIONAL COMMUNICATION

Here are several methods for dealing with difficult situations in the work setting. (1) Remember that people do things for their own reasons, not yours. Someone's anger may mean he or she actually sees the situation from a completely different perspective, so try to understand that view. (2) When under attack, use a calm, even tone of voice and low-key body language. The content of what you say can be the same, just modify your delivery—in face-to-face communication, words carry 7% of your message, tone of voice 38%, and body language 55%. (3) Use conversational fantasy to anticipate a really sticky situation by saying exactly what you want to say. Then tone it down to what you know you should say. (4) Remember to rehearse so that you are prepared to cope with the situation when it arises. Practice receiving and returning "verbal hardballs." (5) If necessary, use emotional jujitsu. The principle of jujitsu is to flow with your opponent's strength, to turn his own force against him by redirecting it rather than resisting it. Rather than defending yourself, agree. Your critic will be instantly disarmed, and then you can begin to deal with the causes of the emotion rather than the emotion itself.

SOURCE: Excerpted from "Personal Productivity: Organizational Communication," *Government Productivity News* 3 (September 1989), p. 4.

DELEGATION AND MOTIVATION

Management can be defined as "the process of getting things done through others." To get things done through others, it is necessary to communicate with others and, often, to motivate them as well. Much of the time, those "others" are the people you supervise. After all, if you can do all the work yourself, you should just go ahead and do it. As a manager, however, you are not there to do the actual work but to do the managerial work, as illustrated in this case study:

After a long and distinguished career as a research scientist, Fraser Parks became manager of a well-known research and development laboratory. Soon after his appointment, a major new project was assigned to the lab. The task was clear in Fraser's mind; as a good scientist he knew how to do the work and how to ensure a high-quality, technically flawless piece of equipment. With a couple of years alone in the lab, he knew he could do the whole project by himself and do it well. The problem was that the equipment was needed in less than three months. Fraser knew that most of the work would have to be delegated to newly hired and reassigned staff, but he knew these people would never be able to do the high-quality job that he alone would have done. After two and a half months of trying to get the job done right, Fraser collapsed in his office one night and was immediately hospitalized.

Delegation is the process of assigning tasks to others. Like so many other managerial tasks, it may be done poorly or it may be done well. As Fraser Parks discovered, poor delegation can be nearly fatal. To delegate well, you need to try to delegate an equal amount of authority and responsibility for a job. Authority is the legitimate power to do the job, and responsibility is the accountability the individual has to you for getting the job done. The idea that an individual should have equal amounts of both is the **parity principle.** Managers often complain that they will be held responsible for something, but have not been given enough authority to get the job done. Less frequent, but equally troublesome, is an individual who has authority but is not held responsible for its use.

369

Generally speaking, you should delegate jobs with complete and clear instructions, and you should delegate tasks to the appropriate level. Holding everything else equal, the appropriate level is the lowest level in the hierarchy where the task can be accomplished competently. You should also provide support for the delegated tasks. This support can take many forms, including delegation of authority in a public statement (such as saying at a meeting, "Betty is in charge of inspections in the northern district now").

It is often helpful to involve subordinates in the process of delegation, encouraging them to make suggestions about the kind of work they can or should be doing. Delegation should be a two-way process. On the other hand, do not fall victim to the *upward delegation* phenomenon. Upward delegation occurs when subordinates bring problems to their managers that the subordinates should be solving themselves. This is the opposite of effective delegation. You should refuse to accept these problems. An effective technique is to insist that any subordinate who wants advice about a problem (the way the upward delegation attempt is often presented) should first think of at least one potential solution before they come to you to discuss the problem.

To allow for creativity and motivation in the delegation process, it is best to hold subordinates accountable for results and leave the "how" up to them. This principle assumes, of course, that the "how" will be within the constraints of legal and ethical behavior as well as the constraints of public or organizational policies. Finally, tasks should be delegated consistently—when the workload is light as well as heavy and when the jobs are fun as well as nasty.

Besides getting things done through others, delegation helps to develop employees, thereby making them more valuable to you and to the organization. Some managers are threatened by the idea that they may be developing possible replacements (i.e., competitors). But there is another way to look at this situation. Unless you are at the very top of the organization, you probably want to be promoted. But you cannot be promoted if you cannot be replaced. Developing your subordinates through delegation is a way of providing, to your advantage, your own potential replacements!

Motivation

Whether members of an organization perform well depends partly on ability and partly on motivation. A person must have or be able to call upon the right mix of skills and abilities to do a job and must be motivated to do the job well. Whereas you can help develop your employees' skills through instruction, training programs, and so forth, you are likely to have a significantly greater impact on their motivation.

Pay and job satisfaction
When one thinks of motivation in a managerial context, pay is a subject that naturally comes to mind. Frederick Taylor based the entire incentive system of his scientific management program on economic factors. Contemporary thinking about motivation is more sophisticated than Taylor's, however, as pay is seen to interact with other motivators in complex ways.

Even as early as the 1950s, Frederick Herzberg developed a model of motivation known as the **two-factor theory.** Herzberg (1959) argued that two sets of variables were relevant to the question of motivation. One set, "hygiene factors," related to job *dis*satisfaction; the other set, "motivators," related to job satisfaction.

Hygiene factors included variables such as pay and working conditions; motivators were factors such as chances for achievement, recognition, and advancement. Herzberg argued that improvements in hygiene factors such as pay would not increase job satisfaction; instead, any improvements would simply reduce dissatisfaction. If an individual's pay got worse or did not increase fast enough, dissatisfaction would increase. Conversely, motivators such as achievement or advancement would not affect dissatisfaction, but would increase or decrease job satisfaction. The lesson for managers was that motivating employees is a far more complex task than simply changing salary levels.

Other approaches to motivation were based on psychologist Abraham Maslow's theory of human development, the assumption that everyone has a need to grow and develop and to establish a sense of meaning in their lives. Maslow (1954) suggested a hierarchy of needs that all human beings must fulfill. At the first level, we must meet our *physiological* needs for food, clothing, and shelter. Next we have a need for *safety and security*. Beyond these basic needs, we have *social needs*, which we meet by being a part of a group. Next, we have a need for *ego satisfaction and self-esteem*. Finally, at the highest level, we have a need for development or *self-actualization*. This final level, which can only be reached after the other four levels have been achieved, describes that state of psychological development through which we reach our greatest human potential.

Controversy about the effect of job satisfaction goes back as least as far as the Hawthorne studies conducted during the mid-1920s and early 1930s. Recall that these studies began as a research project to investigate the effects of physical working conditions, such as lighting, on workers' productivity. Given some unexpected findings early in the studies, the investigators changed the focus of the research to investigate the impacts of social and supervisory variables on performance.

Some authors interpreted the results of the later studies as indicating that higher levels of job satisfaction led to higher levels of worker performance, a conclusion that some argue was never present in the original research reports and is thus a misinterpretation (Organ, 1986). But misinterpretation or not, the Hawthorne studies are usually credited for the "discovery" that a "happy worker is a productive worker." Other studies of the job satisfaction-performance relationship produced mixed results. Some theorists argued that the job-satisfaction-leads-to-better-performance thesis was wrong in terms of the causal ordering—that it was actually the other way around, with higher levels of performance causing higher levels of job satisfaction.

Although there is still not complete agreement on this issue, support is accumulating for a third interpretation of the job satisfaction-performance relationship—that there will only be a relationship between job satisfaction and performance if the rewards one receives are based on one's performance. If rewards are based on performance, there should be a positive correlation between job satisfaction and performance (the higher the performance, the higher the job satisfaction) because higher performance will lead to higher rewards, which will produce higher job satisfaction. If this is true, one part of the manager's job will be to make sure that performance is directly linked to rewards—pay as well as others. One method to achieve this linkage is reinforcement theory.

Reinforcement theory Reinforcement theory and related approaches have been given various labels, including behaviorism, operant conditioning, stimulus-response psychology, and Skinnerian psychology. The labels all refer to more or less the same thing, an approach to explaining behavior based on Thorndike's law of effect: "Of several responses made to the same situation, those which are accompanied or closely followed by satisfaction (reinforcement) . . . will be more likely to occur; those which are accompanied or closely followed by discomfort (punishment) . . . will be less likely to occur" (Daft & Steers, 1986, p. 51).

The law of effect has been studied for over a century, as it relates to learning in both animals and human beings. Results of this research have produced a number of generalizations about the specifics of reinforcement. There are four basic scenarios or results that may follow a specific behavior. If a reward follows the behavior, the individual is more likely to repeat the behavior; this is called *positive reinforcement*. Reinforcement will also occur when behavior is followed by the removal of something unpleasant, called *negative reinforcement*.

On the other hand, if an unpleasant event or *punishment* follows the behavior, the individual is less likely to repeat it. Note that negative reinforcement is not the same as punishment, even though the terms have become synonymous in ordinary usage.

371

From the standpoint of the recipient, punishment would be considered a bad outcome, whereas negative reinforcement would be considered a good outcome. The final possibility is that nothing will happen following a behavior, or at least no reinforcement will occur in connection with it. When this is the case, the individual is less likely to repeat the behavior and will eventually stop repeating it altogether. This cessation of behavior is called *extinction*.

Regardless of which of the four possibilities one is considering, a common theme, and one of the key principles of the reinforcement approach, is that whatever response is given to the behavior, the response should follow the behavior as soon as possible. If there is too long a delay following the behavior, the response (reward, removal of an unpleasant situation, etc.) may be misinterpreted and associated with other behaviors that have occurred in the interval.

Other important considerations of the reinforcement approach are the patterns, frequency, and basis for providing the response. In terms of frequency, responses can be given every time the behavior occurs (continuous reinforcement schedule) or for only a certain proportion of occurrences (partial reinforcement schedule). The basis for making the responses can be either the number of times an event occurs (ratio schedules) or the passage of time (interval schedules). The pattern of responses can be either consistent (fixed schedules) or random (variable schedules). Research indicates that fixed schedules lead to faster learning, but to quicker unlearning or forgetting when the schedule is abandoned. Conversely, variable schedules lead to slower learning, but once the behavior is learned, the unlearning or forgetting is much slower when the schedule is abandoned.

372

This description of reinforcement approaches probably conjures up images of laboratory animals running through a maze to earn food pellets or to avoid electric shocks, and these are indeed how reinforcement has been studied in the laboratory. An obvious and natural parallel applying reinforcement theory in a managerial context is to link pay in some way to an individual's performance. This can be done, but pay (wages or salaries) tends to be set only once a year, and, since organizational policies often dictate pay levels, many managers have only a partial impact on establishing their subordinates' pay levels. This limits the extent to which the manager can use pay as a motivational tool.

Kenneth Blanchard and Spencer Johnson (1982) have developed a way to apply reinforcement principles in managerial situations that do not involve pay: the One-Minute Praising and One-Minute Reprimand, both based on reinforcement principles. The praise or reprimand is contingent on the behavior, it *follows* the behavior, and it should follow the behavior as closely as possible. Blanchard and Johnson recommend saying something immediately, being specific, telling people how you feel about their actions, stopping for a moment to let your feeling sink in, then bringing the session to closure, ending by shaking hands or touching them to let them know of your support.

Before you implement this system, be aware that you must be genuine in your presentation of either praise or reprimands. It is unethical to present either one falsely, and most of us are not good enough actors to pull it off successfully anyhow. You will end up in worse shape if you come off as a phony than if you had done nothing at all.

Second, Blanchard and Johnson's last guideline suggests shaking hands or touching in some other way at the conclusion of the praise or reprimand episode. There will not be much of a problem with the advice to shake hands, but a strong caveat is in order with any other form of touching. American society, in general, is a nontactile culture, and hand shaking tends to be the only form of touching (outside one's family) whose interpretation is well understood and accepted. Many people do not want to be touched in any other way, and this is their right, which should be respected. Given the ambiguity associated with any other form of touching, you should be aware of possible misinterpretations and the possibility of sexual harassment charges as a result. The hand-shake is the safe, unambiguous route to take in most situations.

Goal setting Goal setting is another method of motivating that can be used by itself or in conjunction with reinforcement techniques. In fact, you can use it to motivate yourself as well as other people. A goal is a desired state of affairs one attempts to realize, and, as research has shown, merely setting goals seems to increase the probability of attaining them. But some ways of setting goals are better than others in terms of motivational impact. Research indicates at least eight necessary characteristics for a goal to have maximum motivational impact.

First, it is best to write down a goal rather than to just keep it in mind. In a technical sense, one does not "do" a goal—one achieves a goal; therefore, the proper way to write a goal statement is with the word "to" followed by an action verb—for example, "To finish this chapter by five o'clock today." Something about writing down a goal creates greater commitment on the part of the writer. It is harder to ignore, and seeing it on your desk or in your notebook constantly makes the goal harder to forget. Writing down a goal can also facilitate planning, as you consciously identify the actions you must take to achieve the goal.

Second, because specific goals are much better motivators than general goals, a properly stated goal should be as specific as possible. A field experiment on goal setting at the Weyerhauser Lumber Company several years ago tested the relative impacts of general and specific goals. The objects of the experiment were truck drivers who hauled logs from one location to another in Oklahoma for processing.

The federal government established safety standards for how much weight the truckers could carry, and this amount was taken to be the maximum capacity of the trucks, 100 percent. The researchers and managers at Weyerhauser noted that the truckers normally only hauled about 62 percent of capacity. The first part of the experiment consisted of management informing the truckers that they wanted more weight to be carried on each load and that the truckers were to "Do your best" to achieve this goal.

The truckers' performance was tracked for the next three months and there was little or no improvement (one or two percent at most). The truckers were then informed that a goal had been set for them; the goal was to haul 94 percent of capacity on each load—a much more specific goal than "Do your best." After three months, the truckers were averaging over 90 percent of capacity per load, very close to the ninety-four percent goal the managers had set for them.

No pay increases were given for the increase in weight hauled, although the truckers were told they would not be asked to make any more runs than they normally did as a result of hauling more weight. This remarkable change in behavior saved Weyerhauser over $250,000 annually, and subsequent checks on the truckers have found this level of performance to have been maintained for many years. A specific goal indeed makes a difference.

373

Third, the means for verifying whether a goal has been achieved should be specified. In the study at Weyerhauser, the truckers weighed in at the delivery location for the logs, which provided a precise way to measure the amount of weight they were hauling and, in turn, how close they were to the goal. (Incidentally, the weigh-in procedure was not added by the experiment; the truckers had been following it for many years as part of their job.)

Fourth, a date or time by which the goal is to be accomplished should be specified. The presence or absence of a deadline is a critical attribute of any goal-setting exercise. Deadlines stimulate action, and the closer the deadline, the more motivation to act. The absence of a deadline makes the urgency of the goal indefinite and hence less motivating. For example, there are a disproportionately large number of plays during the last few minutes of a football game because the team that is behind faces a deadline for scoring more points or losing the game. Similar increases in activity occur toward the end of the trading period each day on the New York Stock Exchange. Think of your own behavior as a test date approaches and you begin to increase your preparation activities. These examples illustrate the motivational force of a deadline, a crucial ingredient in any goal statement.

Fifth, a goal should be perceived as attainable. Impossible goals often are demotivating because there is no reason to try if they cannot, by definition, be attained. (Problems may occur, however, if the goal is *too* attainable.)

Sixth, although a goal should be attainable, it should also be challenging. There is little or no satisfaction in achieving a goal that presents too little challenge. The best goal in terms of motivation is one that is perceived as attainable yet challenging—as one that can be achieved, but only with significant effort. Psychologist David McClelland demonstrated this phenomenon many years ago. Children were asked to throw bean bags into a box from various distances, including a position located right next to the box. After they had thrown from various distances, they were asked from which position they preferred to throw. Very few picked the location next to the box; most picked a position farther away, a decision consistent with the properties of attainability and challenge. In effect, the children were setting their own goals, and the goals they set were challenging but attainable.

Seventh, when setting a goal for someone else, the goal must be understandable to the people for whom you are setting them. If they cannot understand the goals, how can you expect them to achieve them? As in so many areas, clarity is highly important.

Finally, it was originally thought that if the people did not take part in setting goals, they would reject them. Subsequent research, such as the Weyerhauser study in which the truck drivers did not take part in establishing the goals, has shown that people are quite willing to accept goals that others set for them. This does not mean, however, that involving people in establishing goals is a waste of time. Among other things, if the people who will actually be trying to accomplish the goals take part in formulating them, there is a greater chance that they will more completely and accurately understand the goals. And although people may be willing to accept goals established by others, there may be greater motivation if they participate.

Managers often worry about involving subordinates in decision making, including decisions about goals and goal levels. A study comparing goals that managers set for

374

their subordinates to goals for the same activities set by the subordinates themselves revealed that the subordinates set the more difficult goals (Hitt, Middlemist, & Mathis, 1983, p. 289). Although this may not happen all the time, it is an intriguing finding that supports the notion of including subordinates in the goal-setting process.

CONFLICT, BARGAINING, AND NEGOTIATION

Differences and conflicts inevitably arise in public organizations. Finding a way to equitably resolve differences is a key interpersonal skill for public managers. Some problems are relatively minor; others are quite substantial. Two employees raise a concern about which one is to manage a particularly valued program. A labor union demands increased wages and changes in working conditions for city workers. The secretary of state discusses arms control with his counterpart from the Soviet Union. Where differences exist, some means of resolving them is necessary.

Roger Fischer and William Ury of the Harvard Negotiation Project have suggested that negotiation is a natural process that occurs where two parties share certain interests but are opposed with respect to others. Negotiations often move quickly to positions that are held by one party or another. For example, a union representative requests a ten-percent raise, while the city negotiator takes the position that only a two-percent raise is possible. Moving quickly to a position and allowing it to become hard and fast tends not only to produce undesirable results, but to damage the continuing relationship between the parties. Positional bargaining seems to move participants to one of two postures: a soft posture that tends to emphasize the ongoing relationship and seeks agreement among participants, or a hard posture that assumes an adversarial relationship and in which each party seeks victory over the other.

Fischer and Ury suggest an alternative method called "principled negotiation." Principled negotiation is based around four elements of negotiation: people, interests, options, and the criteria for solution. Four guidelines emerge from these elements (see Box 11.3).

B O X   1 1 . 3

GUIDELINES FOR SUCCESSFUL NEGOTIATIONS

1. Separate the people from the problem.
2. Focus on interests, not positions.
3. Generate a variety of possibilities before deciding what to do.

(continued)

> *(continued)*
>
> ### 4. Insist that the result will be based on some objective standard.
>
> SOURCE: Roger Fischer and William Ury, *Getting to Yes* (Boston: Houghton Mifflin, 1981), pp. 3–98.

According to Fischer and Ury, following these guidelines leads to negotiated settlements that are more equitable and more likely to lead to continued effective working relationships than are more traditional modes of bargaining. Remember that negotiations occur in all kinds of situations, from deciding which movie to see to resolving matters of war and peace; however, the same general guidelines may be employed in all negotiations to generate more effective and responsible solutions.

GROUP DYNAMICS

Individuals acting alone make a majority of organizational decisions, but sometimes two or more people combine efforts to solve a problem or make a decision. Research has shown that sometimes a group should make a decision and that certain advantages come from group decision making, but there are also disadvantages. Similarly, studies of group dynamics have established fairly predictable patterns of interactions.

Advantages of Group Decision Making

An old cliché has it that two heads are better than one—probably because two heads hold more information than one. Put any two people together, and each one will know something the other does not. Create a group of five or six, and there is even more information available. We have already seen that generating alternatives is one of the fundamental steps in the rational decision-making process, even under satisficing conditions. Because there is more information in a group, there is greater potential for generating more alternative solutions to a problem than could be generated by a single decision maker. But these advantages will surface only if the group is managed properly.

Groups may also benefit from *synergy*, the notion that the whole is greater than the sum of the parts. Synergy can occur in a group, but it is a precious commodity that is not easy to create. Consider the following case: Three people get together to solve a problem. Bob proposes a solution, then Allen proposes a different solution. Betty has been listening to the proposals, which stimulates an idea to solve the problem in a completely new way. The idea represents something new that was not present before in the group. If it were possible to quantify the information in the group at the beginning of the discussion, the total information would equal the sum of the information held by the individual members. With Betty's new idea, an idea stimulated by the group discussion, the sum is now greater than the sum of the individual parts.

How much and how often synergy occurs in a group is often a function of the nature of the group's communications. In small groups (ten or fewer), a number of characteristic communication patterns or *networks* tend to develop, some of which promote synergy more than others. A fundamental way communication networks differ from one another is in terms of how centralized the networks tend to be. The more centralized a communication network, the more one or a few people are at or near its "center." In such a group, the people near the center of the network are involved in receiving and transmitting all or most of the messages that are communicated within the network. The less centralized or more decentralized a network is, the more everyone can communicate with everyone else without having to transmit the message through intermediaries.

As shown in Box 11.4, the Wheel is the most centralized of the networks, the All-Channel is the least centralized, and the Circle and the Chain fall between the two extremes. Research has shown that decisions are made more quickly in centralized networks when a simple problem is being handled, and that groups with centralized networks also tend to produce more accurate solutions to simple problems than do decentralized groups.

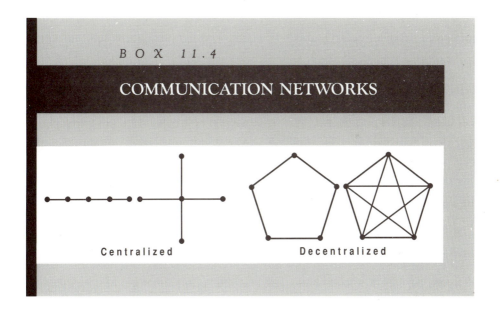

BOX 11.4

COMMUNICATION NETWORKS

Centralized   Decentralized

Decentralized networks, however, are both faster and more accurate in reaching decisions about complex problems, and they will also produce more accurate solutions. Complex problems, by their nature, involve more information, and the decentralized networks make it easier to tap and process the information held by each member. Complex problems also tend to benefit more from synergy in developing solutions, and the ability of everyone to be involved in the discussion and to listen to the discussions of others promotes synergy. Thus, decentralized communication networks tend to promote synergy more than do centralized networks.

There is also evidence that centralized, one-way communication also tends to promote information loss. A well-known study followed messages sent from the boards of directors in 100 companies to see what happened to them as they worked their way down the hierarchy in each company. The messages passed from the board of directors, to vice-presidents, to division managers, to plant managers, to supervisors, and finally to the operating managers. By the time the messages reached the operating managers, only 20 percent of the original content was left!

We want to do more than just make a good decision. The final step in the decision-making process is always implementation. Especially if the people who make the decision are the same who will be implementing it, commitment to the decision should help with implementation. Research also reveals that satisfaction with the group and its processes increases as the networks become more decentralized. Satisfaction is not exactly the same thing as commitment, but the two are closely related. In most cases, then, as participation in making the decision increases, so should commitment to the final decision.

An interesting property of group decision making, the risky shift, can be either an advantage or a disadvantage. The **risky shift** refers to how daring the decisions would be if made as a group compared to the average risk of the same decision if each member made it alone. It was originally thought that groups would always make riskier decisions than would individual members. As more research was conducted, however, it was discovered that sometimes the shift will be in the opposite direction—that groups sometimes make decisions that are less risky than the decisions of the group's members working alone.

Sometimes a daring decision produces better results, but sometimes it makes things worse. Since the same can be said about more conservative decisions, the dilemma is that it is often impossible to predict whether a more conservative or more daring decision will yield better results. The most we can say is that a group decision will normally be either more daring or more conservative than the average riskiness of a decision made by each member acting individually.

Disadvantages of Group Decision Making

In addition to the several advantages that are possible with group decision making, there are potential problems too. One of the obvious constraints on human beings that results in our "bounded rationality" is the constraint of time. Time not only limits the efforts of individual decision makers to acquire and process information, but it also limits the possibilities for groups to make decisions. Normally, it takes a group much longer to make a decision than it takes an individual to make a decision about the same problem. Time thus becomes an important constraint on a manager's ability to use group decision making.

Another constraint may be cost. Even if group decision making and individual decision making were equally fast, the group is still more expensive. Compare a single decision maker, whose pay amounts to $100 per hour, taking one hour to reach a decision to a committee of five managers, each of whose salaries amount to $100 per hour. The cost to the organization for the single decision maker is $100, whereas the cost of the committee is $500.

Another property of groups, which is the opposite of synergy, is *groupthink*. If synergy is the notion that the whole is greater than the sum of the parts, groupthink makes the whole (the group) less than the sum of the parts. Groupthink was first defined and analyzed by Irving Janis as "a mode of thinking that people engage in when they are deeply involved in a cohesive in-group, when the members' strivings for unanimity override their motivation to realistically appraise alternative courses of action" (Janis, 1983). Because the group is so cohesive, greater emphasis is given to conformity than to making good decisions.

Janis identified characteristics of groups victimized by groupthink and cautioned managers to interpret the presence of these characteristics in a group carefully. For example, groups experiencing groupthink have an illusion of morality, a belief that the group's position, whatever it may be, is inherently ethical and moral in comparison to positions held by other individuals and groups. Such groups also engage in negative stereotyping of other people and groups, often viewing outsiders as the "enemy" and as being too different to negotiate with. Groupthink tends to produce an illusion of invulnerability, which makes decisions seem less risky than they really are. Rationalization is commonly employed as a way to discredit information critical of the group or its decisions, and there is frequent self-censorship of dissenting views, which minimizes the amount of critical or contrary information to which the group is exposed. A strong conformity pressure permeates the group and puts further pressure on group members to agree with the dominant position. Finally, an illusion of unanimity results in the belief that everyone in the group believes in the group's decision and judgment. Obviously, groups that are victimized by groupthink are limited in their constructive abilities.

Interpersonal Dynamics in Groups

Interpersonal relationships affect the work of groups or teams. To illustrate the problems that can arise, imagine that two people who despise each other are assigned to the same committee. Obviously, these two individuals will not work as well together as two people who are neutral toward each other or who like or respect each other. Even if the conflict is not manifest, personal animosity may contribute to building a **hidden agenda,** where privately held goals and priorities motivate actions more directly than the overt and publicly stated reasons. Obviously, the operation of hidden agendas disrupts the group and diminishes its effectiveness.

But the interpersonal dynamics of groups in action are much more subtle and complex than these examples suggest (Gardner, 1974, pp. 8–11). For example, groups often follow a fairly predictable pattern of development. Typically, at the outset of the group's work, its members are highly *dependent* on the leader of the group. They ask for direction and become quite frustrated if specific direction is not given. If the leader allows the group to become overly dependent, however, its effectiveness will suffer in the long term. The leader can resist dependency by referring questions back to the group's members for input.

Often, however, a period of *counterdependence* will follow, in which members may show hostility toward the leader. Still wanting some direction, the group's members are now also experiencing a need for independence, just as an adolescent may simultaneously love and hate his or her parents. Counterdependency seems especially likely to occur in authoritarian work environments, where members' actions are too closely regulated.

On the other hand, in a group where members feel they can openly express themselves and their ideas without fear of retaliation, feelings of *interdependence* may develop. At this stage, group members recognize the purposes they hold in common and come to have greater trust and respect for one another. The group will probably be most effective when it reaches this stage.

As the group moves through these stages of development, certain patterns of behavior are likely to occur. Early in the group's development, some members may seek *flight*, through actual withdrawal from the work of the group or through silence, irrelevant comments, or self-serving remarks. Most flight behavior is an implicit attempt to say that nothing significant will happen unless the leader gives in to the group's desire for explicit direction. In the counterdependent stage, members may engage in *fight* behavior or in *pairing*. Fighting the group's leader in some symbolic fashion is, of course, a fairly straightforward act of rebellion; pairing or breaking off into small groups or alliances is somewhat more subtle, yet expresses the same emotion. Finally, as the group reaches the stage of interdependence, the actual *work* of the group can be accomplished in reasonable and satisfying ways.

At this stage, a variety of leadership functions must occur for the group to maintain its effectiveness (see Box 11.5). These functions can all be performed by a single person, typically the group's formal leader, but they can also be performed by a variety of different people active at different times in the group's development. In either case, if you wish to help the group meet its objectives, you should be attentive both to the stages of group development and to the extent to which the various leadership functions are being fulfilled.

BOX   11.5

LEADERSHIP ROLES
IN GROUP DYNAMICS

1. *The coordinator role:* Communicate to all members about meetings, schedules, tasks, procedures, and similar matters; act as an information clearinghouse for all group members and as a contact person with other groups or outsiders.

2. *The facilitator role:* Set up procedures and a structure for group work; assist members in identifying problems, defining issues, summarizing progress, and working together. (This role involves minimal direct influence on the group task. It concentrates on establishing an interpersonal network that helps members work together to solve problems.)

3. *The trainer role:* Teach group members ways of approaching problems; provide the group with methods of learning from their own experiences; arrange for outside consultants to train the group.

4. *The observer role:* Be alert to how the group is functioning and particularly to which functions are not being met; describe to members what is happening in terms of the group process; show the group areas in which change might facilitate their work.

5. *The gap filler role:* Fulfill those functions that are not being handled by anyone else, particularly the functions of summarizing, clarifying, synthesizing, or facilitating compromise.

6. *The monitor role:* Once the group has determined a procedure to follow or a solution to a problem, see to it that the group is reminded of responsibilities, functions, and assignments necessary for implementation of the decision; provide copies of budgets, schedules, assignment sheets, and agendas to members so they can complete their work on schedule.

SOURCE: Excerpted from Ernest Stech and Sharon Ratliffe, *Working in Groups* (Lincolnwood, IL: National Textbook Company, 1976), pp. 220–221. Reprinted by permission.

381

Changing the Composition of the Group

An *open group* is one that experiences a great deal of turnover among its membership, whereas a *closed group* has a stable membership (Ziller, 1965). Because of their stability, closed groups tend to become very cohesive, but this feature often makes it difficult for a newcomer to become integrated with the group. Whereas lack of acceptance of a newcomer is a group property, it may be perceived as the result of unsatisfactory interpersonal relationships between the newcomer and individual group members.

American organizations are becoming more multicultural in composition at both the managerial and nonmanagerial levels. As more and more women and members of minority groups come to be included in what were previously relatively homogeneous groups, other types of problems, often interpersonal, will tend to occur, and the people involved will often not consciously know the reasons for them. Rosabeth Kanter (1977) explains what happens when a previously homogeneous group is joined by a newcomer who differs in some socially salient way from the group members as the "theory of relative numbers." The insights it provides can be useful to managers working in multicultural environments.

The theory of relative numbers is proposed as a universal explanation for the phenomena that occur when a homogeneous group is joined by someone who differs from the existing group members. Groups defined by occupation, age, religion, political preference, marital status, and many other characteristics all fit the theory and its explanation. The theory then presumably applies to many situations other than groups defined by race or gender, although these are the characteristics with which we are concerned. The theory begins by asking what happens when an all-white group is joined by a black member, or when an all-male group is joined by a female member.

When a group is homogeneous in terms of a characteristic such as race or sex, members may differ in terms of individual personalities, but they will not stand out, by definition, because of race or gender differences. Kanter illustrates such a group with the letter "X" and calls all of the group members X's (members of a single race).

$$X \; X \; X \; X \; X \; X \; X \; X \; X \; X \quad (1)$$

Kanter represents a member of a different race with the letter "O"; when an individual of this race joins the group, the group is diagrammed as follows:

$$X \; X \; X \; X \; X \; O \; X \; X \; X \; X \quad (2)$$

This new group, new in terms of composition, will experience different dynamics now that O is present. Diagram (2) illustrates what happens in this situation. Which letter sticks out in row (2)? It is the O, who experiences extra visibility as a result of the racial difference. The extra visibility itself, to say nothing of prejudicial attitudes that may prevail in the group, will create problems for O. Because always standing out is inherently stressful, O faces more personal stress. Moreover, O will also have problems with informal aspects of the organization because X's tend to become involved with other X's rather than O's. This makes it harder for O's to become part of the informal networks that exist in organizations. It also means that O's tend to be unsponsored or unmentored, since X's tend to mentor other X's.

One of the more intriguing things that happens to O is a form of stereotyping. As we have mentioned, human beings do not tolerate chaos well and create order by defining and redefining situations to explain what is happening. This is especially true in trying to understand human behavior, as we all tend to develop explanations for why other people behave as they do. Explanations for O's behavior will tend to take the form "O is behaving that way because that is the way all O's behave." Explanations for O's behavior will often be based on O's status as an O. These attributions are often detrimental to O's standing because, among other things, they tend to depersonalize O.

In terms of solutions or remedies, adding more O's to the group may be helpful. Kanter suggests that the extra visibility and its attendant effects tend to diminish as the proportion of O's in the group increases to about 15 percent, but she believes they do not become inconsequential until the group is composed of about 40 percent O's. The key is the proportion of X's and O's in the group, not absolute numbers; for example, two O's in a group with ten members will experience the same visibility as four O's in a twenty-member group.

It is not always possible to solve or significantly reduce many of these problems by increasing the proportion of O's. African-Americans, for example, compose about 15 percent of the American population, which means that, on the average, only enough blacks could be added to a predominantly white group to *begin* to reduce the visibility-created problems. Thus, having managers become aware of the visibility phenomenon and acting appropriately in their own behaviors toward O's will become particularly important as more diverse types of people become part of organizations.

Managing Groups in Action

After examining the pros and cons of group decision making, the manager's strategy should be obvious: if a group is to make a decision, it should be managed so as to enhance the advantages of the group technique and minimize the disadvantages. How, exactly, does one manage the group to accomplish this? Because most group decision making takes place in meetings, one answer would seem to be in good meeting management (see Box 11.6).

The meeting has nearly the worst reputation of any managerial tool, and much of this reputation is probably justified. Most of the blame should not be on the meeting as a

B O X   1 1 . 6

HOW TO BE AN EFFECTIVE GROUP LEADER

Effective group leadership requires:

1. A solid knowledge of and dedication to the history, goals, values, achievements, and current directions of the organization.
2. An ability to keep issues in focus and matters in perspective; to demonstrate emotional stability in times of stress and conflict.
3. To value the opinions of each member, to judge each on its merits alone and not be persuaded or intimidated by displays of emotion or aggressiveness.
4. A willingness to give credit to others and to accept the blame for failures without being overly dramatic or obvious.
5. A good sense of humor, the ability to keep meetings lively and interesting, will contribute as much as anything to good attendance, morale, and overall achievement.
6. To find enjoyment in the meeting and be able to infect others with enthusiasm.
7. To be responsive to the individual members but to be firm when necessary in order that the members know where they stand.

SOURCE: Excerpted from Bill D. Schul, *How to Be an Effective Group Leader* (Chicago: Nelson-Hall, 1975). Reprinted with permission.

technique, however, but on the way meetings are usually managed (or mismanaged). The first point in improving the effectiveness of meetings is that they are activities that require active management: a successful meeting does not just happen, it requires a lot of work.

Not surprisingly, the fundamentals of managing a meeting are similar to the fundamentals of management generally. For example, a meeting must be *planned*. When will we have it? Where? What do we intend to accomplish? These questions should be answered well before the meeting begins.

A meeting must also be *staffed*. Who do we want to attend? Who will we invite? These questions often depend upon the intent of meeting, which further emphasizes the importance of planning, but there are other factors in selecting participants. Are there people who might have hidden agendas, or who might not work well together? How well did the people you are considering work together last time? How productive were they?

An effective meeting manager must *organize* the meeting, which also involves a substantial amount of planning. What roles will you create at the meeting? Will you have anyone serve as parliamentarian? In what order will topics and problems be discussed? Will you divide the group into subcommittees to work on special projects? If so, should they work on them before, during, or after the meeting?

Directing the meeting—providing the actual leadership of the ongoing meeting—is itself complex. Some necessary skills are obvious, such as starting the meeting on time; others are subtle, such as the ability to inhibit a too-vociferous participant. If you have planned well, you will have a good general idea of what the meeting is intended to accomplish and will try to move the meeting in that direction.

As meetings often produce decisions, the manager must also see that the decisions are *implemented*. This is often achieved through a form of delegation at the meeting, when assignments for future action are made. Indeed, it is often a good idea to review assignments as part of the meeting's conclusion. Finally, conducting a critique of the meeting after it is over, perhaps introspectively, may prove helpful in moving the manager closer to the goal of better meeting management.

Specialized Techniques for Group Decision Making

Brainstorming is a technique that was developed to enhance the alternative-generation portion of the decision-making process. The goal is to generate as many ideas about some problem as possible, while suspending judgment about each idea. The task before the group is to develop ideas about a problem, or even solutions to the problem, and the more that are generated, the better.

Once the assignment is announced, group members begin to generate ideas. The ideas are described orally, and someone records each idea on a blackboard or flipchart for everyone to see. No evaluations of ideas are permitted during brainstorming, and the session continues until everyone is out of ideas or the leader feels the session has lasted long enough. The purpose is to bring out the information held by different group members and to encourage synergy by stimulating new ideas.

While brainstorming helps enrich the alternative-generation portion of the decision-making process, the **nominal group** technique generates both alternatives and solutions. A major purpose of the design is to avoid groupthink. A nominal group is a face-to-face meeting that allows only very limited interaction among participants. A problem is presented, but unlike brainstorming, the group is expected to make a decision about how to solve the problem. After the problem has been presented, each member, working alone, writes down as many solutions to the problem as he or she can formulate. When everyone is finished writing, the leader calls for the solutions. Each person in the room presents one solution until all the possible solutions have been heard.

The solutions are recorded publicly as they are presented, again usually on a blackboard or a flipchart. Other members may ask questions for clarification if they do not understand a solution, but only clarifying questions are allowed. Members may not debate the merits of particular solutions. After every solution has been presented and all questions answered, the group makes a decision by means of a written poll, taken as a secret ballot. Each member rank-orders the different solutions from best to worst. The rankings are submitted to the meeting leader without any identifying material on the ballot. The leader or someone assisting the leader tabulates the ballots, and the solution that receives the highest average preference becomes the group's decision.

In many ways, *quality circles* are the most comprehensive specialized technique for group decision making in that they are explicitly concerned with every step in the decision-making process, from recognition that a problem exists through implementation of solutions. Quality circles also incorporate other specialized techniques such as brainstorming. (We reviewed techniques for operating quality circles in chapter 8.)

Now that we have examined the advantages and disadvantages of group decision making, how do we know when to use group decision making rather than an individual decision maker?

385

Participation in Decision Making

The Vroom–Yetton model of participation in decision making focuses on the manager's decision concerning the extent to which subordinates should participate in making a specific decision (Vroom & Yetton, 1973; Vroom & Jago, 1988). The most impressive study supporting the model was an investigation of 200 actual managerial decisions. Managers made these decisions as part of their jobs without the aid of the model; the model was then applied, after the fact, to determine the effectiveness of various patterns of involvement in decision making.

Vroom and his associates identified the 200 decisions and gathered data about how much subordinate participation was involved in making each decision. The researchers were also able to gather information about the consequences of each decision—specifically, whether each decision produced successful results. When decisions were made using a level of subordinate participation consistent with levels that would have been recommended by the Vroom–Yetton model (remember, none of the managers knew anything about the model at the time they made the decisions), 68 percent of the results or outcomes were judged to have been successful. When the amount of participation by subordinates was not at a level consistent with the model's recommendations, only 22 percent of the outcomes were judged to have been successful.

This is a remarkable difference. In both relative and absolute terms, the managers who involved subordinates to a degree consistent with the model's recommendations had extremely good results. In relative terms, the outcomes were more than three times better than the decisions whose level of subordinate participation was inconsistent with the model. In absolute terms, 68 percent success is excellent, because factors other than how a decision is made determine whether it produces good results. We would not expect any decision-making method to produce successful outcomes 100 percent of the time, so the results in the study were quite impressive.

The Vroom–Yetton model involves the choice of various levels of involvement in decision making; the choice is not merely between a single individual and an entire group. These are two alternatives that frame a continuum with several other levels of participation in between. As Vroom and Yetton conceptualized them, there are five levels of participation along this continuum (see Box 11.7). The Vroom–Yetton model indicates which level of participation is appropriate in a particular situation. (Note that for some situations, two or more participation levels are equally likely to produce decisions that will generate successful results.)

BOX 11.7

TYPES OF MANAGEMENT DECISION METHODS

Symbol	Definition
AI	You solve the problem or make the decision yourself using the information available to you at the present time.
AII	You obtain any necessary information from subordinates, then decide on a solution to the problem yourself. You may or may not tell subordinates the purpose of your questions or give information about the problem or decision on which you are working. The input provided by them is clearly in response to your request for specific information. They do not play a role in the definition of the problem or in generating or evaluating alternative solutions.
CI	You share the problem with the relevant subordinates individually, getting their ideas and suggestions without bringing them together as a group. Then *you* make the decision. This decision may or may not reflect your subordinates' influence.
CII	You share the problem with your subordinates in a group meeting. In this meeting you obtain their ideas and suggestions. Then *you* make the decision, which may or may not reflect your subordinates' influence.
GII	You share the problem with your subordinates as a group. Together you generate and evaluate alternatives and attempt to reach agreement (consensus) on a solution. Your role is much like that of chairperson, coordinating the discussion, keeping it focused on the problem, and making sure that the critical

Symbol	Definition
	issues are discussed. You can provide the group with information or ideas that you have, but you do not try to "press" them to adopt "your" solution, and you are willing to accept and implement any solution that has the support of the entire group.

SOURCE: Reprinted from *Leadership and Decision-Making*, by Victor H. Vroom and Phillip W. Yetton, by permission of the University of Pittsburgh Press. © 1973 by University of Pittsburgh Press.

To use the model, you must understand (1) how to identify the different situations, and (2) how to match different situations with the appropriate levels of participation. Both issues are resolved by the use of two tools in combination: (1) the set of alternative courses of action listed in Box 11.7 and (2) the decision tree shown in Box 11.8.

The decision tree initially appears complex but is simple to use. One begins under point A by answering question A (all questions must be answered either "yes" or "no"; no "maybe's" or "sometimes" are allowed.) Depending on the answer, you proceed to either question D (for a "no" response to A) or to question B (for a "yes" response to A). One continues answering the questions as indicated by the decision tree until you reach an end point.

Each end point is numbered, with a set of participation levels listed after each end point. These are *feasible sets*; all the participation levels listed in a feasible set are equally likely to result in a successful outcome. This does not mean, however, that there is no reason to pick one style over another within the feasible set. The decision styles are arranged in the order of the amount of time it will take to reach a decision using the styles. The style listed first is the fastest, followed by the second fastest, and so on. In most situations, one should choose the fastest style in the feasible set.

Again, the answers to the questions along the path reaching the particular end point define the situation, and the participation levels indicated in the feasible sets provide guidance as to the appropriate level of involvement. Although the model, even as presented here in simplified form, may initially seem cumbersome and complex, managers who practice it for several days seem to be able to utilize it without notes thereafter.

ORGANIZATION CHANGE AND DEVELOPMENT

The capacity to bring about needed changes effectively and responsibly may be the key determinant of success or failure as a public manager. Change is ubiquitous in public organizations; some changes are small and little noticed, others are major and widely publicized. New programs and procedures must be developed, new organizational arrangements are required, and new attitudes and behaviors must be encouraged. Especially

BOX 11.8

DECISION TREE GOVERNING GROUP PROBLEMS

A. Does the problem possess a quality requirement?
B. Do you have sufficient information to make a high-quality decision?
C. Is the problem structured?
D. Is acceptance of the decision by subordinates important to effective implementation?
E. If you were to make the decision by yourself, is it reasonably certain that it would be accepted by your subordinates?
F. Do subordinates share the organizational goals to be attained in solving this problem?
G. Is there likely to be conflict among subordinates over preferred solutions?

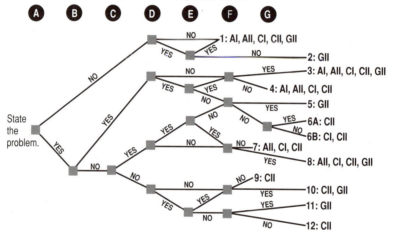

SOURCE: Reprinted from *Leadership and Decision-Making*, by Victor H. Vroom and Phillip W. Yetton, by permission of the University of Pittsburgh Press. © 1973 by University of Pittsburgh Press.

as the pace and complexity of modern life impinges on those in public organizations, a high degree of flexibility, creativity, and adaptability on the part of the organization and its members is increasingly required.

But change does not come easily in modern organizations, so it is important to understand the nature of the change process and the reasons that people sometimes accept and support changes and sometimes resist. Some people are simply more open to change than others. The intuitive person, for example, is attracted by the future and is eager to embrace new ideas and concepts; the sensing person, on the other hand, lives more in the here and now and may need more convincing that a proposed change is a good idea. But regardless of personal differences, there are things managers can do to increase the likelihood that organization members will agree to a particular change. If people trust the person who is proposing the change, either based on his or her skill and expertise or his or her record in past change efforts, then they will be more likely to accept the change. Similarly, if people fully understand the implications of the change, and if they have been involved in developing the new idea, they will be more likely to accept the change. Finally, if the manager is sensitive to the implications of the change for individuals in the organization and for their relationships with one another, people will be more likely to accept the change.

Unfortunately, these basic guidelines for implementing change are regularly violated, often leading to confusion and turmoil. Take the following case as an example:

Jane Sanford knew the work of the health services agency better than anyone else; she also knew the importance of employee involvement in organizational changes. As she listened to proposals from her staff for ways to implement a new immunization program, however, she knew that the plan she had formulated earlier in her office was far superior. Just as consensus seemed to be building around one particular suggestion, Jane jumped in and announced her plan, asking for quick implementation. To Jane's surprise, the members of her staff were furious.

Obviously, as Jane Sanford discovered, if a change is ordered abruptly and dictatorially with little advance notice or preparation, the chances of its ready adoption are severely reduced. Moreover, if some perceive a proposed change as threatening, its chances of success are lessened. These outcomes are especially likely when the organization is already marked by poor working relationships; the proposed change may become a target for other real or imagined frustrations and will not be considered on its merits at all.

Diagnosing the Need for Change

Ideas for change often occur in response to a feeling that something is wrong with the existing situation. As a manager, you will often scan the organization for "blips" or trouble spots that need attention; from these reviews, you may recognize symptoms of underlying problems. Sometimes you may wish to undertake a more thorough and detailed analysis that could possibly lead to a major change activity. These are standard topics to consider.

1. *Context:* What is the purpose and history of the organization? What have been major strengths and weaknesses over the years? What are the political and economic constraints on operations?
2. *Outputs:* At the organizational level, what are the levels of citizen satisfaction, efficiency, and productivity? At the group and individual levels, what is the satisfaction level of the employees and their commitment to the organization?
3. *Organizational culture:* What are the dominant beliefs, attitudes, and values in the organization? Are there different values in different parts of the organization? Are some sets of values in conflict with others?

4. *Task requirements:* What are the principal tasks that members of the organization must perform? Do employees clearly understand organization goals? How highly developed (or overdeveloped) are organizational rules and procedures?

5. *Formal organization:* How is the work organized? What is the organization structure? How many levels of management are there? How is work planned and coordinated? What are the forml modes of communication through the organization?

6. *People:* How many employees does the organization have and where do they work? What is the mix of skills and abilities among employees? How many managers are there, and how do they relate to other employees?

7. *Physical setting and technology:* What is the condition of the organization's buildings and equipment? How does the physical environment affect the work being done? What is the level of technology, and how effectively is it employed? (Lippitt, Langseth, & Mossop, 1985, pp. 6–13)*

Strategies for Organizational Change

Having diagnosed the need for changes, the manager may wish to undertake a fairly broad-scale effort to revitalize the organization. As we saw earlier, one set of approaches to change efforts is generally termed *organization development*. Those involved in organization development, or "OD," tend to focus on the human side of the organization, though their work may lead to recommendations about physical or programmatic matters as well. OD practitioners see the primary problem in most organizations as restrictive patterns of behavior, often based on misunderstanding and mistrust, that limit the capacity of the organization and its members to deal effectively with a complex and changing environment. The problem then becomes one of "unfreezing" past patterns of behavior, replacing them with more open and trusting relationships, and "freezing" these in place. Because these behavior patterns are largely based on the implicit images or "theories" of organization that guide our eventual behaviors, it is important not only that behaviors change, but that real learning—that is, adjustment of one's "theories"—occur.

Most students of organization development find that efforts to change established patterns of behavior are easier with the help of an outside educator or **interventionist,** an external consultant brought in to work with members to reveal dysfunctional behaviors and to try to develop more effective working relationships. It is important to have changes develop internally rather than be imposed from outside. Chris Argyris suggests that the interventionist's role involves three efforts: "(1) to help generate valid and useful information; (2) to create conditions in which clients can make informed and free choices; and (3) to help clients develop an internal commitment to their choice" (Argyris, 1970, pp. 12–13).

A variety of techniques are available to the interventionist, including the following:

Team building: Much of an organization's work is done in groups; a program of team development may help improve group effectiveness. Usually, one begins

*SOURCE: Reprinted with permission from Lippitt, G. L., P. Langseth, and J. Mossop. *Implementing Organizational Change*, San Francisco, Jossey–Bass, Inc., 1985.

with a careful review of how team members communicate and work together. Following a diagnosis of interpersonal group problems, the facilitator leads the group in designing an action plan to overcome those difficulties. Many of these "interventions" can be accomplished without an outside facilitator.

Intergroup problem solving: Occasionally conflict or competition arises among groups; for example, two divisions of a small organization may fight over resources and prestige, or overlapping responsibilities, or over confusion about allocation of responsibilities. An interventionist might bring the groups (or representatives) together to identify problem areas and begin to devise ways to deal with the problems. As you might expect, confrontations are often difficult—sometimes even tumultuous—but a trained group facilitator can help keep the group focused on resolving the real issues that divide them.

Goal setting and planning: In goal-setting efforts, superior-subordinate pairs or groups throughout the organization are asked to systematically assess their capabilities and set specific targets for future performance. After a specific period, the individuals or groups meet again to evaluate their work and establish goals for the next period. (As we have seen, one broad approach to organizationwide efforts to engage in formal planning and goal setting is described as management by objectives or MBO.)

Sensitivity training: As we saw in chapter 9, the values heralded by students of organization development emphasize openness and trust among people at all levels of the organization. One way to significantly improve openness and trust is to help individuals and groups identify and explore their deep-seated feelings about their work and, perhaps, about one another. A trained facilitator is almost essential here, for serious personal and interpersonal issues often emerge and must be handled with great care.

SUMMARY AND ACTION IMPLICATIONS

All the knowledge, values, and skills you possess are expressed in the moment of action. Whether you are a manager or a policy analyst, or hold some other position in a public organization, your ability to act effectively and responsibly "in the real world" will determine your success. Your actions will usually occur in social settings and require working with others. Especially in a managerial position, you will engage in almost constant interaction with other people. So, no matter how much you know or how proper your values, your effectiveness will be limited if you cannot work well with others.

Today we recognize that interpersonal skills, like other skills, can be developed and improved over time. Just as artists or athletes can improve proficiency, so can you improve your skills in areas of communications, delegation, negotiation, and group dynamics. The key to improving your skills in public management, as in other areas, is practice and repetition, accompanied by self-reflection and self-critique.

If you want to be a better communicator, for example, you should seek opportunities to practice communicating with others. Find opportunities to make presentations; practice listening with special concentration and sensitivity; try to develop your writing skills. As you practice, be conscious of your own and others' reactions. Reflect upon your successes and failures and try to learn from both. Over time, you'll improve your skills and find yourself far more effective.

Throughout this book, we have described public management as involving cognitive, conceptual, technical, and human skills. In the moment of action, however, the areas cannot be separated. Indeed, your capacity to bring together knowledge, technique, and interactive skills at the moment of action will determine success or failure in most situations. Public management can be studied in the abstract, but it must be lived in the real world—a world of stress, complexity, and uncertainty. In few other fields do so many aspects of the human personality have to come together. But it is this very difficulty that makes public service so challenging and rewarding.

TERMS AND DEFINITIONS

Brainstorming: Technique for enhancing the alternative-generation portion of the decision-making process.

Delegation: Assigning tasks to others.

Hidden agenda: Privately held goals and priorities.

Interventionist: External consultant brought in to reveal dysfunctional patterns of behavior and to try to develop more effective working relationships.

Nominal group: Face-to-face meeting that allows only limited interaction among participants.

Parity principle: Idea that individuals should have equal amounts of authority and responsibility.

Risky shift: Difference in the daringness of decisions group members make as a group compared to the average risk of the same decision if each member made it alone.

Two-factor theory: Model of motivation involving two variables: job satisfaction and job dissatisfaction.

STUDY QUESTIONS

1. What are the seven basics of effective listening?
2. Why is speaking an important interpersonal skill?
3. Discuss the "Six C's" for effective written communication.
4. Management can be defined as "the process of getting things done through others." Discuss how delegation and motivation enable the work of management to occur.
5. Explain reinforcement theory and its four basic scenarios or results.
6. Goal setting is another motivation technique. Discuss what characteristics a goal should have for maximum motivational impact.
7. What are the elements of "principled negotiation"?
8. Discuss advantages and disadvantages associated with group decision making.
9. Explain the fundamentals of managing group dynamics.

10. Identify and discuss various techniques for group decision making.

11. Change is an important aspect of administrative work. Discuss the necessary steps for organizational change and development.

12. Define the techniques available to interventionists involved in organizational change and development.

CASES AND EXERCISES

1. Divide your class into groups of three. Taking turns, have one person choose a topic from the list below and begin a conversation with the group. Try to follow the rules of effective communication.

    a. You are short of cash and want to take a winter vacation to an island off the coast of Mexico. You need to borrow at least $300 for the trip. You are pretty sure you can pay it back in three months.

    b. The two classmates you are talking with have been working with you on a class project. Actually, the problem is that they *haven't* been working! You have to do something to get them busy, or your grade will suffer. You need at least a "B" in the course to graduate.

    c. You have been working in behalf of the homeless in your community for the past two years. A march on Washington has been scheduled for next week, and a bus has been chartered to take people from your community to Washington, at a cost of $83 each. The problem is that unless you can find two more people to make the trip, the bus won't go. You want to convince your two friends to go with you.

2. Imagine that you are an administrative assistant to the director of the Department of Social Services in your state government. The director is interested in starting a new quality circles program and wants to send a letter to all the managers and employees in the department describing the new program and enlisting their support. You have been asked to draft the letter. Using the information about quality circles in chapter 8, draft an appropriate letter.

After everyone in the class has drafted a letter, each draft should be shared with and analyzed by at least one other student. Your analysis should take into account the specifics of the situation (what should be said, how much should be said, how it should be said) as well as the more general Six C's of effective communications listed in this chapter.

3. Divide the class into task groups of five persons each, with three observers assigned to each group. The task groups should complete the following task:

List what you consider the five most important guidelines for effectively managing a large organization.

After the task group completes its work, the observers should lead a discussion of the group dynamics they observed in the work of the task group.

393

For observers only: During the discussion, you should silently watch the discussion and take notes about the operation of the group. Try to identify patterns of group development such as those presented in the chapter. Pay special attention to shifting patterns of leadership and communications. If this same group were to perform a similar task, what would you suggest to improve its effectiveness?

4. Divide the class into groups of three. Have one person in each group play the role of Chris, the supervisor, and another play the role of Lynn, the employee. (Each person should read only his or her own role description and not that of the other person.) The third person in each group should observe the discussion between Chris and Lynn, then comment on the motivation strategies employed. The scene begins as Lynn walks into Chris's office and says, "Someone said you wanted to see me."

Chris: You are twenty-eight years old and recently received your MPA from a fairly prestigious school in the East. You have worked for the federal government for four years, moving rapidly from a Presidential Management Internship to your current position supervising a small unit that produces health and safety brochures for industry. Lynn has worked with the agency for twenty-three years as a design specialist. Throughout this period, from what you understand, Lynn has done an excellent job. In the few months you have been with the agency, however, you have noticed a decided drop in both the amount and quality of Lynn's work. With a heavy workload anticipated over the next several months, you decide that you have to do something to improve Lynn's performance. You have asked that he come in to visit.

Lynn: You have worked for twenty-three years as a design specialist for a small federal government unit that produces health and safety brochures for industry. Throughout your career, you have taken great pride in your work and have done an excellent job. Over the last few months, however, you have been increasingly troubled by painful back spasms, the source of which you have not been able to identify. The problem with your back has triggered a lot of concerns—about your health, your age, your work. Although you haven't shared these concerns with anyone, you find that you spend long periods daydreaming about them. Even drinking a few martinis each evening hasn't calmed your fears. You still enjoy your design work, but somehow the projects you have had recently just don't seem all that exciting. What's worse, your supervisor, a kid probably half your age, has been hinting that your work may not be up to par.

5. Consider the following case. You have recently been appointed head of a new agency established to monitor pollution emissions from coal-based power plants throughout the Midwest. The data you collect will have a direct impact on an anticipated presidential decision concerning "acid rain" in the Northeast and Canada. You must try to develop the most comprehensive and precise measures possible, then monitor as many plants as you reasonably can during the relatively short period prior to the presidential decision.

Your staff, most of whom have been in the pollution control field much longer than you and are highly committed to the goals of your agency, have been arguing that a new piece of equipment, an Emission Systems Monitoring Instrument (ESMI), is the only device that is capable of precise measurements of the particular pollutants with which you are concerned. The problem is that the ESMI is both extremely costly and would require nearly half the time you have available just to be delivered. You are skeptical that the ESMI is worth the cost, but even more concerned that its limited availability will mean that you will fail to meet your deadline. You also think—though you are not sure—that the rough estimates generated by the existing equipment will be sufficient for the purposes of your report to the president. Do you go ahead with the existing equipment or do you buy the ESMI?

Using the Vroom–Yetton model for decisions about delegation, work through the various aspects of this problem to determine the appropriate level and pattern of delegation.

FOR ADDITIONAL READING

Daft, Richard L., and Steers, Richard M. *Organizations: A Micro/Macro Approach.* Glenview, IL: Scott, Foresman, 1986.

Fischer, Roger, and Ury, William. *Getting to Yes.* Boston: Houghton Mifflin, 1981.

Gortner, Harold F., Mahler, Julianne, and Nicholson, Jeanne Bell. *Organization Theory: A Public Perspective.* Pacific Grove, CA: Brooks/Cole, 1987.

Hersey, Paul, and Blanchard, Kenneth. *Management of Organizational Behavior.* 4th ed. Englewood Cliffs, NJ: Prentice-Hall, 1982.

Hitt, Michael A., Middlemist, R. Dennis, and Mathis, Robert L. *Management Concepts and Effective Practice.* St. Paul, MN: West, 1983.

Kolb, David A., Rubin, Irwin M., and McIntyre, James M., eds. *Organizational Psychology.* 4th ed. Englewood Cliffs, NJ: Prentice-Hall, 1984.

Lippitt, Gordon L., Langseth, Peter, and Mossop, Jack. *Implementing Organizational Change.* San Francisco: Jossey-Bass, 1985.

Luthans, Fred. *Organization Behavior.* 4th ed. New York: McGraw-Hill, 1985.

Steil, Lyman K., Barker, Larry L., and Watson, Kittie W. *Effective Listening.* Reading, MA: Addison-Wesley, 1983.

Vroom, Victor H., and Jago, Arthur G. *The New Leadership.* Englewood Cliffs, NJ: Prentice-Hall, 1988.

THE
FUTURE
OF
THE
PUBLIC
SERVICE

F or those considering work in the public service, whether for a relatively short period or for an entire career, several consid-erations may shape your thinking. As we have noted, the rewards of public service are not likely to be primarily financial. Salaries in most public organizations lag somewhat behind comparable salaries in business or industry. At the same time, however, those in public organizations are likely to be given a broader range of responsibilities earlier in their careers than their counterparts in business or industry. Moreover, the challenges and complexities of public service provide a special excitement that comes from being a part of unfolding major events—local, state, national, or even international.

    If you want to be a part of what's happening in a changing society, then the public service is the place for you. Think about the incredible variety of work in the public sector. Public managers are key actors in foreign affairs, the human services, environmental policy, educational reform, the space program, and an endless variety of other important areas. Indeed, it is fair to say that every major local, state, national, or international issue now being discussed will provide challenges and opportunities for public managers in the future. If you are interested in meaningful work—work that makes a difference in people's lives—then you should find involvement in the public service quite appealing.

THE CHANGING IMAGE
OF THE PUBLIC SERVICE

Throughout most of our country's history, public service has been recognized as an important undertaking that contributes to the betterment of society, supported by citizens and politicians alike. Unfortunately, for the past twenty years or so, support has wavered. From the late 1960s through the middle 1980s, the public service seemed to be under fairly constant attack. Through the candidacies of both Jimmy Carter and Ronald Reagan, national politicians of both parties organized their campaigns at least in part around attacks on Washington and the bureaucracy. Public administrators were criticized as both unresponsive and overly responsive—unresponsive to the common citizen and overly responsive to special interests. Public organizations were accused of being highly ineffective and inefficient, failing to achieve their objectives and wasting enormous sums of public funds.

Much of this attack was a response to the rapid growth of government in the 1960s and 1970s—public budgets had expanded rapidly, and the range of phenomena touched by government had greatly increased. One need only consider a partial list of the many programs initiated and regulatory statutes adopted during this period to realize how much things had changed within two decades. Two major civil rights acts (1964 and 1965) were adopted; legislation to protect the handicapped and to promote equality in schools was approved. The "War on Poverty" had its beginnings in the Equal Opportunity Act of 1964, and was rapidly followed by a variety of legislative initiatives promoting employment and training. A substantial change in the government's role in promoting and protecting health was brought about through Medicare, Medicaid, medical school subsidies, and neighborhood health clinics. Major environmental protection legislation was enacted. Initiatives were undertaken to promote health and safety in the workplace. Laws were adopted to regulate toy safety, poisons, securities, lead-based paint, employment opportunities, consumer products, pesticides, noise, motor vehicle sales, hazardous materials transportation, pensions, credit, and so on.

Correspondingly, government budgets grew rapidly. Government spending at all levels increased from $136 billion in 1960 to $869 billion in 1980, an increase not solely attributable to inflation. Spending in constant (1972) dollars went from $146 billion in 1960 to $381.8 billion in 1980. In per capita terms, expenditures in constant (1972) dollars went from $810 in 1960 to $1,681 in 1980. Thus, real spending per capita doubled over the twenty-year period, representing an increase in government spending from 27 percent to more than 33 percent of the gross national product.

Such a substantial and sustained transformation in the responsibilities and activities of government was bound to lead to difficulties. Independent of the government's capacity to handle its new responsibilities, dislocations were inevitable. For every service that would meet a need, there was a cost that someone had to pay. For every benefit produced by regulation, there was also a cost. The costs that we had been paying in terms of human suffering, poor health, and reduced productivity would now be more specifically reflected in government budgets and in the expenses of private firms and citizens. In addition, the new initiatives would redistribute costs among institutions, groups, and individuals. Behavior would have to change; old ways of doing things would be replaced by new methods.

Even if there had been widespread agreement on the necessity for action, the dislocations would surely have led to disenchantment, complaints, and protests. Those who were adversely affected challenged the new developments and brought their anger to bear on everyone involved in implementing the programs and enforcing the regulations. Curiously, they were also joined by supporters of the new activities, who either felt their programs were being implemented improperly or too slowly or who came to recognize negative consequences of their favored policies that they had not anticipated.

The more natural conservative opposition to expansion of government was joined by moderates and liberals, who also raised questions. Had expansion gone too far? Had government become too active and too intrusive in private affairs? Had a mistake been made?

Critics of new programs and regulations often targeted their complaints as much at the agencies responsible for implementing the laws as toward those who created the laws. Whether the agencies performed poorly or well was almost irrelevant to the criticisms hurled at them. As Charles Goodsell (1985) pointed out, those in government agencies were often criticized for policies or actions over which they had no control. The image of a misguided bureaucracy bound up in red tape became part of the conventional wisdom.

Not surprisingly, political leaders were quick to capitalize on this public sentiment. President Carter campaigned against a generalized "mess in Washington," then sought, through the Civil Service Reform Act and other measures, to create a bureaucracy more responsive to political leadership (a goal sought by most recent presidents). President Reagan and leading members of his administration directed their attacks at public managers themselves. A Heritage Foundation report specifically assigned responsibility for the "mess in Washington" to "the bureaucrats," whom it described as persons for whom political executives should feel "legitimate hostility." Similarly, Donald Devine, Director of the Office of Personnel Management, called for a sharp division between politics and administration, assigning to civil servants the role of automatons. Finally, the Grace Commission was created to purge the bureaucracy of alleged waste and inefficiency. Thus, generalized discontent with the massive growth of government in the 1960s and 1970s was transposed by a conservative administration into an attack on the public service itself.

A Changing Climate

Fortunately, the environment of the public service has changed considerably over the past several years, leading us to be somewhat more optimistic about its future image. Part of this change is the result of policy and program shifts brought about in response to questions about government activism; part reflects a growing acceptance of the initiatives that gave rise to dissent; and part is the reemergence of a positive view of government. In addition, the emergence of state and local governments as both significant and professional in their dealings with the public has had a positive effect.

In policy areas, over the past decade, Americans have seen tax reductions and tax reform at the federal level, as well as tax limitations at the state and local levels. These actions have helped to mitigate the view that the government tax machine is running wild (though obviously concerns about the huge federal deficit remain). Similarly, beginning in the Carter administration and continuing through the Reagan years, there was a move to deregulate certain activities. Some areas (such as transportation) were significantly deregulated, while others were put under special scrutiny by the Office of Management and Budget. In general, an impression developed that excessive government intervention was being brought under control.

At the same time, other programs were changing. A series of block grants shifted responsibility from the federal to the state level in many program areas, such as social services, elementary and secondary education, maternal and child health care, and small cities community development. Because of the Reagan administration's efforts to reduce federal activism and because the federal budget deficit made it difficult for the national government to maintain, let alone expand, domestic responsibilities, the perceived locus of responsibility for many government programs shifted from the federal level to states and localities, especially the states. The shift, even though the actual dollars involved constituted only a small share of total federal expenditures, contributed to a new public impression that the federal government was being reduced.

In addition to policy shifts, programs and policies that generated reaction against government in the 1970s and early 1980s were reaffirmed. Despite continued conservative resistance, civil rights laws and affirmative action policies are now widely accepted; in fact, much of the business community has come to view them as essential to social progress and economic development. Moreover, despite efforts of the Reagan administration, most programs of the Great Society remain viable today. Programs such as Medicare and Medicaid, Head Start, community health services, and job training and development, though modified in some ways, are still regarded as important contributors to the public welfare.

400

At the same time, political leaders have become more supportive of the bureaucracy, as one would expect when the "outs," who were so critical, became the "ins." Over time, both the Carter and Reagan administrations, like others before, found that they not only needed the support of federal bureaucrats to achieve their objectives, but that, by working cooperatively with civil servants, they could obtain that support. Significantly, in its efforts to build a cooperative relationship with federal bureaucrats, the Reagan administration began to change its rhetoric dramatically—for example, calling for "quality" improvements rather than eliminating waste.

Finally, the political climate has been changing, even to the point that we might suggest the reemergence of a positive view of government. Such a view has been most evident at the state and local levels. Even while the Reagan administration put the clamps on a wide range of domestic policy initiatives, in several important areas—notably education, economic development, and environmental concerns—the states were taking positive actions. And, at the same time, public confidence in state and local governments was growing.

Moreover, with growing national concern about such problems as AIDS, hazardous waste, ocean dumping, the greenhouse effect, drugs, foreign competition, the homeless, and child care for working families, we might even speculate that a new era of national action is on the horizon. During the 1988 presidential election, both George Bush and Michael Dukakis were willing to support federal action in such areas as education and the environment and, perhaps not by coincidence, both were also supportive and appreciative of the public service (see Box 12.1). And, of course, as president, George Bush has continued to proclaim his support for and appreciation of the men and women who constitute the public service.

BOX 12.1

ON THE FEDERAL SERVICE

During his presidential campaign, George Bush addressed the following letter to a number of public service organizations, including the American Society for Public Administration:

My experience as vice president, and as director of the CIA, has given me a very high regard for the overall competence of career civil servants and for the vital role they have in our democratic form of government.

How well the tasks of government are done affects the quality of the lives of all our people. Moreover, the success of any political leadership in implementing its policies and objectives depends heavily upon the expertise, quality, and commitment of the professional career employees of government.

So, despite our determination to cut the size and costs of government, we recognize that the nation needs a highly skilled and dedicated civil service to perform those governmental services that we, as a people, decide we want.

For those reasons, improving the quality, morale, and performance of the public service will be a high priority of my administration. My appointees will work closely with career civil servants to provide the teamwork needed to implement my policies, and to manage more effectively necessary programs across the government.

One of the things we will do is to provide a White House orientation program for all new appointees without previous federal experience. That orientation will have firm objectives: to show them how to be effective in the federal environment; to be sure they understand the limitations our democratic system places upon executive branch officials; to help them lead their agencies skillfully; and to urge them to build teamwork among the political and career officials in the agency they lead.

Through that kind of teamwork, we will launch a vigorous effort to achieve excellence in governmental programs and the delivery of services to the public. Many of the past failures of government have occurred—not because federal employees lack talent and energy—but because byzantine rules and procedures imprison talents and sap morale.

(continued)

(continued)

It has been my observation that most federal workers are like most other American workers. They have the same desire for pride in their work, the same drive for accomplishment, and the same work ethic that has made the American work force one of the most effective in history. It will be our objective, therefore, to remove impediments to effective management and to encourage work force creativity.

Because of the rigidities now existing in the federal pay structure, many agencies are finding it difficult to retain and recruit high-quality employees. This is especially true in hard-to-hire occupations and locations. Working with both federal professional associations and federal employee unions, we will seek to improve federal recruiting efforts and to make federal jobs more challenging and more satisfying.

As examples, we will experiment with "honors" programs to attract top professional and law school graduates, with new types of inservice professional development, and with tuition assistance for work-related courses.

Several major studies of the federal service are now being conducted by such distinguished groups as the National Commission on the Public Service (which is headed by Paul Volcker) and the National Academy of Public Administration. The objective of these studies is to advise the next president on ways of solving the problems of the public service, and they have been assured of my interest in their recommendations.

The Office of Personnel Management (OPM) must be a vital center for human resource planning for the federal work force. The director I choose for OPM will be a person with both the managerial and professional experience needed to fill that role. Responsibility for personnel operations, however, will be delegated to the departments, and to their field installations to the maximum degree feasible. Overregulation *within* the federal government is as unwise as overregulation *by* the federal government.

Beyond these specifics, my administration will work cooperatively and continually with your group and with other friends of the public service, to make it more efficient, more effective, and more productive, as well as a more satisfying place to work.

SOURCE: George H. W. Bush, "On the Federal Service," *The Bureaucrat* 17 (Winter 1988–1989), p. 7 (complete). Reprinted with permission.

These efforts in support of the public service return our country to a long-standing tradition. At other periods—and even today in other countries—the public service has been considered a proud and honorable profession. John F. Kennedy's inaugural statement continues to have relevance today. Recall that Kennedy said, "Ask not what your country can do for you, ask what you can do for your country." In another speech, Kennedy amplified the point: "Let the public service be a proud and lively career. And let every man and woman who works in any area of our national government, in any branch at any level, be able to say with pride and honor in future years: I served the United States Government in that hour of our nation's need." Those who work in the field of public administration at all levels of government carry forward that long and proud tradition.

EFFORTS TO SUPPORT THE PUBLIC SERVICE

Despite recent attacks on the public service, more and more people are coming to recognize its tradition of excellence. Recognition of the importance of public service has been fostered by several groups and organizations, among them the American Society for Public Administration. Always a defender, ASPA recently developed a "National Campaign for the Public Service," to promote the dignity and worth of the public service. Activities of ASPA's National Campaign for the Public Service have included joining with other groups, such as the Public Employees Roundtable, in publicizing the benefits and contributions of public servants, developing award programs and other forms of recognition for outstanding public officials, and developing curriculum projects at elementary and secondary school levels to introduce young people to the public service and the benefits of public service careers.

403

Consider the following:

- During the past twenty years, governmental productivity has increased 1.5 percent a year, almost double the national average.
- The U.S. is tied with Germany for the fewest public-sector administrative employees per capita in the industrialized nations.
- Government employees invented lasers, computers, titanium (and other stronger and lighter materials), the Catscan, plastic corneas, teflon, and plastic wrap.

One particularly prestigious body that actively supports the public service is the National Commission on the Public Service, chaired by former Federal Reserve Board chairman Paul A. Volcker. The Commission was formed in 1987 following a symposium in Washington, D.C., on "A National Public Service for the Year 2000." Those at the symposium concluded that a private, nonprofit organization should be assembled to prepare action recommendations to the president and Congress on what many saw as a "quiet crisis in government." The group felt that "too many of the best of the nation's senior executives are ready to leave government, and not enough of its most talented young people are willing to join." Moreover, conferees felt that "this erosion in the attractiveness of the public service at all levels—most specifically in the federal civil service—undermines the ability of government to respond effectively to the needs and aspirations of the American people, and ultimately damages the democratic process itself" (National Commission, 1989). Following a period of study and deliberation, the Commission made the following general recommendations (see also Box 12.2):

- First, the president and Congress must provide the essential environment for effective leadership and public support.
- Second, educational institutions and the agencies of government must work to enlarge the base of talent available for, and committed to, public service.
- Third, the American people should demand first-class performance and the highest ethical standards, and, by the same token, must be willing to provide what is necessary to attract and retain needed talent.

BOX 12.2

MAIN CONCLUSIONS OF THE VOLCKER COMMISSION

The central message of this report of the Commission on the Public Service is both simple and profound, both urgent and timeless. In essence, we call for a renewed sense of commitment by all Americans to the highest traditions of the public service— to a public service responsive to the political will of the people and also protective of our constitutional values; to a public service able to cope with complexity and conflict and also able to maintain the highest ethical standards; to a public service attractive to the young and talented from all parts of our society and also capable of earning the respect of all our citizens.

A great nation must demand no less. The multiple challenges thrust upon the Government of the United States as we approach the twenty-first century can only reinforce the point. Yet, there is evidence on all sides of an erosion of performance and morale across government in America. Too many of our most talented public servants—those with the skills and dedication that are the hallmarks of an effective career service—are ready to leave. Too few of our brightest young people—those with the imagination and energy that are essential for the future—are willing to join.

Meanwhile, the need for a strong public service is growing, not lessening. Americans have always expected their national government to guarantee their basic freedoms and provide for the common defense. We continue to expect our government to keep the peace with other nations, resolve differences among our people, pay the bills for needed services, and honor the people's trust by providing the highest levels of integrity and performance.

At the same time, Americans now live in a stronger, more populous nation, a nation with unprecedented opportunity. But they also live in a world of enormous complexity and awesome risks. Our economy is infinitely more open to international competition, our currency floats in a worldwide market, and we live with complex technologies beyond the understanding of any single human mind. Our diplomacy is much more complicated, and the wise use of our unparalleled military power more difficult. And for all our scientific achievements, we are assaulted daily by new social, environmental, and health issues almost incomprehensible in scope and impact—issues like drugs, AIDS, and global warming.

Faced with these challenges, the simple idea that Americans must draw upon talented and dedicated individuals to serve us in government is uncontestable. America must have a public service that can both value the lessons of experience and appreciate the requirements for change; a public service that both responds to political leadership and respects the law; a public service with the professional skills and the ethical sensitivity America deserves.

SOURCE: Excerpted from The National Commission on the Public Service, *Leadership for America: Rebuilding the Public Service* (Washington, DC: 1989), pp. 1–2.

405

Specifically, the Commission called upon the president and the Congress to:

- Take action now by word and deed to rebuild public trust in government;
- Clear away obstacles to the ability of the president to attract talented appointees from all parts of the society;
- Make more room at senior levels of departments and agencies for career executives;
- Provide a framework within which those federal departments and agencies can exercise greater flexibility in managing programs and personnel; and
- Encourage a stronger partnership between presidential appointees and career executives.
- Develop more student awareness of, and educational training for, the challenges of government and public service;
- Develop new channels for spreading the word about government jobs and the rewards of public service;
- Enhance the efforts to recruit top college graduates and those with specific professional skills for government jobs;

- Simplify the hiring process; and
- Increase the representation of minorities in public service.
- Build a pay system that is both fair and competitive;
- Rebuild the government's chief personnel agency to give it the strength and mandate it needs;
- Set higher goals for government performance and productivity;
- Provide more effective training and executive development; and
- Improve government working conditions.

With the efforts of groups such as ASPA and the Volcker Commission, and with renewed support of political leaders at the national, state, and local levels, we can expect the reemergence of a greater sense of respect and appreciation for the work of those engaged in public service at all levels. The work of the public service, the work of building a better world, requires the best possible talent and deserves both commitment and support. As the Volcker Commission puts it, "A great nation must demand no less" (National Commission on the Public Service, 1989, p. 1).

TRENDS IN THE PUBLIC SERVICE

The challenges that will face those in the public service over the coming years are substantial, for they not only require resolving important public policy problems, but resolving them in a way that restores and then maintains public confidence. The efforts to restore meaning and integrity to the public service are much needed in our society, but they should be accompanied by a clear understanding of several important trends in our field that are reshaping the values and commitments of public service itself.

Future Trends

First, remember that a significant redefinition of the public service is now taking place. Note specifically that changing economic conditions are affecting both the mission and structure of the public enterprise. Our economy is shifting in several ways—from a production base to a service base, from a national base to a global base, and from a growing public commitment to a limited commitment. In each case, there are direct implications for those in the public service.

- Challenges face public managers in areas where traditional industries, such as steel or timber, have suddenly declined, as "high tech" and "high touch" have become banners for economic growth.
- Challenges face those at the state and local levels who must play new and important roles in economic development, including international economic development, which may require them to know as much about business decisions in Japan as in their own state capital.

- Challenges face those operating public programs, especially in the human services, who have found government spending severely restricted at a time when the need for the services seems ever-increasing.

Our economy is presenting important challenges to government, but in responding to these challenges, government is not alone. The challenges have led to new ways of thinking about public/private relationships in the provision of public services. As a result, public service work is no longer the work only of government, but an effort in which governmental agencies, nonprofit and third-sector organizations, and corporate and business interests participate. Consider these examples:

- In many states, the number of persons employed by private security forces exceeds the number employed by local police departments.

- In some cities, the chamber of commerce is so involved in public programs that it receives more funding from government than it receives from private business.

- In major urban areas, less than half of human services are delivered by government; the majority are delivered by nonprofit and private agencies.

Some of these trends, such as privatization and contracting for specific goods and services, are becoming familiar; others are quite distinctive, as they involve third parties' discretion in the use of public authority and in spending of public funds. This development suggests a significant reshaping of the public service and raises serious questions about equity and accountability in the management of public programs.

407

Second, changing economic conditions have combined with technological developments to make the international dimensions of public administration more important than ever. Understanding the activities of political and administrative officials in other countries is important not only for those who will spend part of their careers outside the U.S., but also for those who will work at home. More and more city managers, for example, find that to be effective in local economic development activities, they must be experts in international business. But global interdependencies will affect us in other ways as well; for example, deforestation in Brazil, Africa, and the Philippines will directly affect the quality of our own environment. And, of course, we cannot overlook our obligation to help reduce poverty and hunger throughout the world.

A *third* area of concern is the changing environment in which public servants work. New people and new values are entering the public workplace. More women and minorities in public agencies have had an important and positive impact on the values of those agencies. One hopes that present trends toward greater equity and involvement will continue.

Similarly, we have already felt the impact of changing technology on the workplace. The influence of computers and related information technology on how we conduct the public's business has been remarkable, and there is no reason to expect that the technological revolution is over. In addition, the human consequences of advanced technology should not be ignored. How technology affects the relationship between government workers and their clients, how to cope with the seemingly inevitable impersonality of the computer age, and how to resolve the difficult ethical questions related to privacy and abuse—these and many other issues will continue to confound us over the coming decades (see Box 12.3).

BOX 12.3

AN AGENDA FOR THE 21ST CENTURY

[In an effort to describe the most important issues facing the world in the twenty-first century, Rushworth Kidder of the *Christian Science Monitor* interviewed twenty-two leading thinkers from all over the world. In a speech to a group of federal government managers, Kidder discussed the results.]

There was, in fact, a tone of urgency—a desperate need to shake humanity awake to see man's inhumanity—that came out in interviews not only in this country but worldwide.

Japanese philosopher and writer Schuichi Kato pointed out that "most people are not very much concerned, seriously, with other people's suffering. By and large, it seems to me, the whole of society is geared to domination and manipulation rather than to compassion."

Abiding Faith

But most of the interviewees also had an abiding faith in mankind's flexibility, adaptability, and basic good nature. "I don't believe that any human being is absolutely and completely evil," said General Olusegun Obasanjo, who was the man who finally delivered Nigeria to its first civilian rule and was head of state. "There must be some good in him. Why don't we, through communication, find out what are the other man's fears, hopes, aspirations?"

What, then, were the common threads? What consensus were they driving towards? What were the issues that again and again bubbled to the surface?

The Problem of the Nuclear Threat

Predictable, and the only issue to which I could assign a clear priority. If you're talking to people about the twenty-first century, the first thing they want to make sure that you understand is the caveat, "if there is a twenty-first century!" And that depends on whether or not we have destroyed ourselves through nuclear disaster. The need for arms control was the greatest concern, although they also touched on nuclear energy. It's the first time, as many of them said, that man has had the power not only to wipe himself out but to take all of nature along with him.

The Population Crisis

In many ways, this is the only perfectly predictable crisis that we have. After all, everybody who is going to be middle-aged in the early years of the twenty-first century has already been born. We can count them: We know how many there are, and it's not guesswork.

The world now has about 5 billion people, heading for between 9 and 14 billion. Is this in itself a serious problem? Many of the people I talked to said, "No, not in and of itself." The world, most people felt, can handle 14 billion people; we have the resources to do that. The real problem, as Robert McNamara, former head of the World Bank, said, is the imbalance between population growth rates on the one hand and economic development on the other. You've got to get those two things in line, or you're in for some real disasters.

Many connect this problem of population growth with other problems—the environment, hunger, and so forth. So it's sometimes hard to tell when people are talking about a population crisis and when they're talking about something else.

The Environment

The president of West Germany, Richard von Weizsacker, is deeply concerned about the environment. "Every possible agenda item you're going to mention has to do with my primary concern—namely, to preserve nature," he told me. His argument is that our concern about the nuclear question, our concern about the population question, and our concern about most other questions can finally be traced back to what it is doing to the environment.

Many of those I talked to said that environmental degradation is second only to the nuclear threat in its capacity to destroy mankind. And they list real and significant problems: desertification, destruction of the rain forests, problems of the water table, the destruction of the ozone layer, the greenhouse effect.

(continued)

409

(continued)

The North–South Gap

This one is often described as the gap between the developing world and the developed world, or the industrial nations and the less developed nations. As University of Chicago President Hannah Gray asked, "How do you sustain a world economy and the hopes for democracy and humanitarian governments at the same time?" Or, as Abdus Salam put it, "Are the rich really getting richer and the poor poorer?"

Education Reform

"Our educational system is absolutely inadequate," said Mortimer Adler—and then he paused and said "not relatively but absolutely inadequate—for the purposes of democracy." He insists that democracy requires that educated capacity. That's as true in the developing world as in the West.

But what will happen in the future, when we get to the position where the best job many people can find occupies 20 hours a week? It may be some very menial task, but nobody will worry because the economy will be roaring along and everybody will be well fed and well housed. What are they going to do with their time? What are they going to think about? And what, for example, will be the health consequences, even the psychiatric consequences, for a society that is not equipped even to begin to ponder those kinds of questions?

Breakdown in Public and Private Morality

This one surprised me—particularly the fact that it came out as strongly as it did from so many quarters. When I asked historian Barbara Tuchman how she would describe our age, she said she would call it "an age of disruption"—sparked, she said, by the deterioration of public morality. She points, for example, to the ethical lapses in stock market dealings, to educational cheating, to marital infidelity, to weapons fraud, and to a whole range of other ethical issues.

Concluding Observations

Those, then, are the six issues. Norman Cousins, in a sense, summed them up by saying, "We move into the twenty-first century without a philosophy or a sociology or a politics that can keep the species going." That's a hard-nosed condemnation— something, it seems to me, that we need to think through carefully.

SOURCE: Rushworth M. Kidder, "An Agenda for the 21st Century," *The Bureaucrat* 17 (Fall 1988), pp. 3–7, and *An Agenda for the 21st Century* (MIT Press, 1987). Reprinted by permission of the author.

The Ethical Challenge

Establishing a proper ethical basis for public action is itself one of the most important challenges facing the public service. If your generation has one significant contribution to make to the development of the public service, it may be to identify and elaborate the moral and ethical dimensions of public administration and to assert moral leadership.

As we have seen, early writers in the field portrayed public administration primarily as a managerial concern with the technical processes of implementing public policy. Over the years, public administrators have developed considerable skill in managing public programs—probably more than they are usually given credit for.

Others soon came to recognize that public administration is also a political concern— that administrators at all levels are deeply involved in shaping public policy. Despite recent rhetoric in Washington, there is every reason to expect that those in public organizations will increasingly be called upon to do more than simply respond to legislative mandate; they will be asked to identify and to articulate important public interests.

Beyond a view of public administration as a managerial or a political concern, public administration today is more and more an ethical concern. Indeed, all the "spontaneous" little actions you will take as an administrator will carry important value implications. At the root of every act of every public servant, whether in developing or executing public policy, lies a moral or ethical question.

What does it mean, then, to recognize public service as not only a managerial and political concern but as a moral and ethical concern? For one thing, it means that public administrators must demonstrate in their own actions the highest standards of behavior. Beyond that, to see the public service as a moral and ethical concern requires recognition that every action an administrator takes involves an effort to discover or to clarify the public interest.

The future public servant will likely be both active in policy development and responsive to the public interest. Our constitutional structure not only permits but encourages an active executive and administrative role. Even more important is the implicit philosophical directive of the Constitution that the public service is a special calling in a democracy, and that those who participate in the public service, regardless of background or occupation, are guardians of a public trust.

This point is most critical at a time when our definition of public service is shifting. As we have noted, the public service is no longer merely that group of political and

411

administrative officials employed by government agencies. Public service today involves a wide range of private and nonprofit organizations in the delivery of public goods and services. This development raises managerial concerns, political concerns, and most of all, moral and ethical concerns. Under these conditions, public administrators must assume leadership in establishing a high moral tone for the public service generally. In contrast to the often-heard advice that public administrators should follow the model of business, we might propose just the opposite—that public organizations and the values and commitments they represent should become models for all organizations, at least those involved in the management of public programs.

For the public service to regain its proper role in our society, we will have to establish and maintain throughout government and the public service a true commitment to the values of democracy. Trust in the public service and the public willingness to partici-pate in the work of government will occur only if the public is convinced that those in office, whether political or administrative, seek the public interest (not merely their own), and that they do so with skill and responsibility. Only when our commitment to democratic practices and ideals is clear to all will we once again be able to establish public service as the highest calling in our society.

Commitment to democratic ideals involves concerns such as responsiveness and involvement, but also commitment to equity and justice. Think for a moment of the reasons that bring people to the public service. No doubt high on the list would be "concern for the well being of others." At one point in our history, we seemed to feel that the primary measure of success of the public service was the elimination of human suffering. Public officials are still at the forefront of dealing with the complex and difficult issues of homelessness, poverty, and drug addiction. Perhaps more than any other group, public administrators are uniquely situated to see and understand these concerns. They certainly should be able to pinpoint the failures of past policies, to suggest alternatives, and to work actively toward implementation with elected leaders. Indeed, they have a moral responsibility to do so.

A FINAL NOTE

The challenges to the public service are substantial and pose managerial, political, and ethical questions for all who participate in public programs. They will require careful analysis and effective action on the part of academics and practitioners in the field of public administration and beyond. Most of all, they are challenges that will require responsibility—both in the sense of acting responsibly and in the sense of accepting responsibility for our ideas and actions. The frontiers of public service will present quite difficult personal and professional choices. But the responsible public servant will find their solution very rewarding. Albert Schweitzer once said, "I don't know where you will go or what you will do, but the ones among you that will be most happy will be those who serve." I would only add that especially happy will be those who serve the public, well and faithfully.

STUDY QUESTIONS

1. Discuss some of the changes in the image of public service over the last thirty years.
2. What are some recommendations of the National Commission on the Public Service for attracting and retaining the "best and the brightest" in the public service?
3. Discuss future trends in the field of public administration.

CASES AND EXERCISES

1. By most objective measures, public agencies are, on the average, highly productive—at least in comparison to their private-sector counterparts. (Obviously, there are wide variations in both sectors, but the general conclusion seems valid.) The general public, however, seems to have exactly the opposite impression—that government agencies are hopelessly inefficient and unproductive. Part of the problem seems to be that people are more critical of government in the abstract than where it directly touches their lives. In fact, one study found most people highly critical of the coldness and inefficiency of government in general, but highly complimentary of specific government employees with whom they had dealt most recently.

In any case, there seems to be some disparity between image and reality—a disparity that is often quite damaging to the morale of the public work force. Write an essay explaining why you think governments are considered less productive and less efficient than they really are. Consider the issue from several viewpoints. How would the issue appear from the perspective of a legislator? A public manager? A citizen? On the basis of your analysis, what should be done to improve the image of the public service?

2. In this chapter, we have considered a number of trends that are likely to affect the public service over the next decade or more. What do these trends mean in terms of the skills that individual public managers will require? Review once more the set of public management skills in chapter 1, then, in small groups, discuss the following questions: What specific skills will public managers likely utilize more frequently in the future than in the past? What, if any, will be deemphasized? To what extent will the demands of the future public service change the mix of conceptual, technical, and human skills needed for effective public management? Finally, how will the *values* that underlie the work of public managers shift as we move through the coming years?

3. Read the following excerpt from *Megatrends*, by John Naisbitt.

> The political notion of governance is being completely redefined. Today's well-educated, well-informed citizen is capable and desirous of participating in political decisions to a greater extent than the present representative system permits. Hence the growth in referenda, initiatives, and recalls during the 1970s. Despite occasional outcries to the contrary, we do not want strong leadership in national affairs because we are basically self-governing. And we are gradually extending the ideal of democracy into corporations,

413

where we are demanding a greater voice as consumers, shareholders, outside directors, and (most importantly) employees.

This newly evolving world will require its own structures. We are beginning to abandon the hierarchies that worked well in the centralized, industrial era. In their place, we are substituting the network model of organization and communication, which has its roots in the natural, egalitarian, and spontaneous formation of groups among like-minded people. Networks restructure the power and communication flow within an organization from vertical to horizontal. One network form, the quality control circle, will help revitalize worker participation and productivity in American business. A network management style is already in place in several young, successful computer firms. And the computer itself will be what actually smashes the hierarchical pyramid: With the computer to keep track of people and business information, it is no longer necessary for organizations to be organized into hierarchies. No one knows this better than the new age computer companies.

SOURCE: John Naisbitt, *Megatrends* (New York: Warner Books, 1982), p. 251. Reprinted with permission.

Discuss how changes such as those discussed here (and in other studies of societal trends) will affect the work of those in public organizations.

FOR ADDITIONAL READING

414   Calista, Donald J., ed. *Bureaucratic and Governmental Reform.* Greenwich, CT: JAI Press, 1986.

Chandler, Ralph Clark. *A Centennial History of the American Administrative State.* New York: The Free Press, 1987.

Denhardt, Robert B., and Jennings, Edward T., Jr. *The Revitalization of the Public Service.* Columbia: University of Missouri, 1987.

Goodsell, Charles T. *The Case for Bureaucracy.* 2nd ed. Chatham, NJ: Chatham House, 1985.

National Commission on the Public Service. *Leadership for America.* Washington, DC: National Commission, 1989.

Newland, Chester A. *Public Administration and Community.* McLean, VA: Public Administration Service, 1984.

Chapter One

BLUMENTHAL, W. MICHAEL. "Candid Reflections of a Businessman in Washington." In *Public Management*, by James L. Perry and Kenneth L. Kraemer. Palo Alto, CA: Mayfield Publishing, 1983.

FLANDERS, LORETTA R., and UTTERBACK, DENNIS. "The Management Excellence Inventory." *Public Administration Review* 45 (May/June 1985): 403–410.

KATZ, ROBERT L. "Skills of an Effective Administrator." *Harvard Business Review* 52 (September-October 1974): 90–102.

RUMSFELD, DONALD. "A Politician-Turned-Executive Surveys Both Worlds." In *Public Management*, by James L. Perry and Kenneth L. Kraemer. Palo Alto, CA: Mayfield Publishing, 1983.

SIMON, HERBERT A., SMITHBURG, DONALD W., and THOMPSON, VICTOR A. *Public Administration*. New York: Knopf, 1950.

WHITE, LEONARD D. *The Study of Public Administration*. New York: Macmillan, 1948.

WILLOUGHBY, W. F. *Principles of Public Administration*. Baltimore, MD: Johns Hopkins Press, 1927.

WILSON, WOODROW. "The Study of Public Administration." *Political Science Quarterly* 2 (June 1887): 197–222.

Chapter Two

ABNEY, GLENN, and LAUTH, THOMAS P. "Councilmanic Intervention in Municipal Administration." *Administration and Society* 13, no. 4 (February 1982): 435–456.

ANDERSON, JAMES E., BRADY, DAVID W., and BULLOCK, CHARLES. *Public Policy and Politics in America*. Pacific Grove, CA: Brooks/Cole, 1984.

ARCHIBALD, SAMUEL J. "The Freedom of Information Act Revisited." *Public Administration Review* 39, no. 4 (July/August 1979): 311–317.

BEHN, ROBERT, and BEHN, JUDY. "The Governor as CEO." Washington, DC: Center for Policy Research, National Governor's Association, n.d.

BEHN, ROBERT D. "The False Dawn of Sunset Laws." *The Public Interest* 49 (Fall 1977): 103–118.

BOWMAN, ANN O'M., and KEARNEY, RICHARD C. *The Resurgence of the States*. Englewood Cliffs, NJ: Prentice-Hall, 1986.

CALDWELL, LYNTON. *Administrative Theories of Hamilton and Jefferson*. Chicago: University of Chicago Press, 1944.

COOPER, PHILLIP J. "Due Process, the Burger Court, and Public Administration." *Southern Review of Public Administration* 6, no. 1 (Spring 1982): 65–98.

COOPER, PHILLIP J. *Public Law and Public Administration*. Palo Alto, CA: Mayfield, 1983.

415

COOPER, PHILLIP J. "Conflict or Constructive Tension: The Changing Relationship of Judges and Administrators." *Public Administration Review* 45, special issue (November 1985): 643–652.

COOPER, PHILLIP J. "By Order of the President." *Administration and Society* 18, no. 2 (August 1986): 233–262.

CRENSON, MATTHEW A. *The Federal Machine.* Baltimore, MD: Johns Hopkins University Press, 1975.

DODGE, WILLIAM R. "The Emergence of Intercommunity Partnerships in the 1980s." *Public Management* (July 1988): 2–7.

ELLING, RICHARD C. "State Legislative Casework and State Administrative Performance." *Administration and Society* 12, no. 3 (November 1980): 327–356.

FISHER, LOUIS. "Judicial Misjudgments about the Lawmaking Process." *Public Administration Review* 45, special issue (November 1985): 705–711.

GILMOUR, ROBERT S. "Agency Administration by Judiciary." *Southern Review of Public Administration* 6, no. 1 (Spring 1982): 26–42.

HENRY, NICHOLAS. *Governing at the Grassroots.* Englewood Cliffs, NJ: Prentice-Hall, 1980.

HILL, LARRY B. "The Citizen Participation-Representation Roles of American Ombudsmen." *Administration and Society* 13, no. 4 (February 1982).

HODGKINSON, VIRGINIA A., and WEITZMAN, MURRAY S. *Dimensions of the Independent Sector.* Washington, DC: Independent Sector, 1984.

JOHANNES, JOHN R. *To Serve the People.* Lincoln: University of Nebraska Press, 1984.

JOHNSON, STEPHEN F. "The Legislative Veto in the States." *State Government* 56, no. 3 (1983): 99–102.

KARL, BARRY D. *Executive Reorganization and Reform in the New Deal.* Cambridge, MA: Harvard University Press, 1963.

KINGDON, JOHN W. *Agendas, Alternatives, and Public Policies.* Boston: Little, Brown, 1984.

LOWI, THEODORE. "Four Systems of Policy, Politics, and Choice." *Public Administration Review* 32 (July-August 1972): 298–310.

MCLAUGHLIN, CURTIS. *The Management of Nonprofit Organizations.* New York: Wiley, 1986.

MEIER, KENNETH J. *Politics and the Bureaucracy.* 2nd ed. Pacific Grove, CA: Brooks/Cole, 1987.

NELSON, MICHAEL. "A Short, Ironic History of American National Bureaucracy." *Journal of Politics* 44, no. 3 (August 1982) 747–778.

OGUL, M.S. *Congress Oversees the Bureaucracy.* Pittsburgh, PA: University of Pittsburgh Press, 1976.

REICH, ROBERT B. "Public Administration and Public Deliberation: An Interpretive Essay." *Yale Law Review* 94 (1985): 1617–1641.

RIPLEY, RANDALL B., and FRANKLIN, GRACE A. *Congress, the Bureaucracy, and Public Policy.* 4th ed. Pacific Grove, CA: Brooks/Cole, 1987.

ROURKE, JOHN T. "The GAO: An Evolving Role." *Public Administration Review* 38 (July/August 1978): 453–457.

STILLMAN, RICHARD J. "Status of the Council-Manager Plan." *Public Management* 67, no. 7 (July 1985): 3–6.

WALSH, ANNMARIE HAUCK. *The Public's Business.* Cambridge, MA: MIT Press, 1978.

WHITE, LEONARD D. *The Federalists.* New York: Macmillan, 1948.

WOLF, THOMAS. *The Nonprofit Organization.* Englewood Cliffs, NJ: Prentice-Hall, 1984.

YOUNG, DENNIS R. *If Not for Profit, for What?* Lexington, MA: Lexington Books, 1983.

Chapter Three

ALDRICH, HOWARD, and WHETTEN, DAVID A. "Organization-sets, Action-sets, and Networks: Making the Most of Simplicity." In *Handbook of Organizational Design*, vol. 1, by Paul C. Nystrom and William H. Starbuck. Oxford: Oxford University Press, 1981.

BEAM, DAVID R. "New Federalism, Old Realities." In *The Reagan Presidency and the Governing of America*, by Lester M. Salamon and Michael S. Lund. Washington, DC: The Urban Institute, 1984.

BECKMAN, NORMAN. "Developments in Federal-State Relations." In *The Book of the States, 1988–1989 Edition*. Lexington, KY: The Council of State Governments, 1988.

BOWMAN, ANN O'M., and KEARNEY, RICHARD C. *The Resurgence of the States*. Englewood Cliffs, NJ: Prentice-Hall, 1986.

BRUDNEY, JEFFREY L., and ENGLAND, ROBERT E. "Toward a Definition of the Coproduction Concept." *Public Administration Review* 43 (January/February 1983): 59–65.

CARRINGTON, TIM, and POUND, EDWARD T. "War Games." *The Wall Street Journal* (June 27, 1988): 1, 4.

DEHOOG, RUTH HOOGLAND. *Contracting Out for Human Services*. Albany: State University of New York Press, 1984.

DERTHICK, MARTHA. "American Federalism: Madison's 'Middle-Ground' in the 1980s." *Public Administration Review* 47 (January/February 1987): 66–74.

DOHERTY, EDWARD J. "Private Contracting in Municipal Operations." *Urban Resources* 2 (Summer 1985): 29–36.

FORESTER, JOHN. "The Effects of the Elimination of General Revenue Sharing on U.S. Cities." Unpublished manuscript, 1988.

HATRY, HARRY P. *A Review of Private Approaches for Delivery of Public Services*. Washington, DC: The Urban Institute, 1983.

HOWARD, S. KENNETH. "A Message from *Garcia*." *Public Administration Review* 45, special issue (November 1985): 738–741.

JENNINGS, EDWARD T., JR., KRANE, DALE, PATTAKOS, ALEX N., and REED, B. J., eds. *From Nation to States*. Albany: State University of New York Press, 1986.

KANE, VANCE. "State Aid to Local Governments." In *The Book of the States, 1988–1989 Edition*. Lexington, KY: The Council of State Governments, 1988.

KETTL, DONALD F. *The Regulation of American Federalism*. Baton Rouge: Louisiana State University Press, 1983.

KETTL, DONALD F. *Government by Proxy*. Washington, DC: CQ Press, 1988.

KOCH, EDWARD I. "The Mandate Millstone." *The Public Interest* 61 (Fall 1980): 42–58.

KOLDERIE, TED. "Two Different Concepts of Privatization." *Public Administration Review* 46 (July/August 1986): 285–291.

KURTZ, HOWARD. "In an Era of Reduced Federal Aid, Newark Stays Afloat." *The Washington Post National Weekly Edition* 5, no. 35 (June 20–26, 1988): 31–32.

LOVELL, CATHERINE, and TOBIN, CHARLES. "The Mandate Issue." *Public Administration Review* 41 (May/June 1981): 318–330.

MEESE, EDWIN, III. "Taking Federalism Seriously." *Intergovernmental Perspective* 13 (Winter 1987): 8–10.

MILWARD, H. BRINTON. "Interorganizational Policy Systems and Research on Public Organizations." *Administration and Society* 13, no. 4 (February 1982): 457–478.

MURRAY, SYLVESTER. "Privatization: Myth and Potential." *Urban Resources* 2 (Summer 1985): 3–5.

NATHAN, RICHARD P., DOOLITTLE, FRED C., and ASSOCIATES. *Reagan and the States*. Princeton, NJ: Princeton University Press, 1987.

NICE, DAVID C. *Federalism: The Politics of Intergovernmental Relations*. New York: St. Martins Press, 1987.

PA Times (April 28, 1988).

PETERSON, GEORGE E. et al. *The Reagan Block Grants*. Washington, DC: The Urban Institute Press, 1986.

RAFUSE, ROBERT W. "Fiscal Federalism in 1986." *Publius* 17 (Summer 1987): 35–53.

REAGAN, MICHAEL D., and SANZONE, JOHN G. *The New Federalism*. 2nd ed. Oxford: Oxford University Press, 1981.

REAGAN, RONALD. "Inaugural Address." Washington, DC, January 20, 1981.

SEADER, DAVID. "Privatization and America's Cities." *Public Management* (December 1986): 6–9.

STENBERG, CARL W. "States Under the Spotlight." *Public Administration Review* 45, no. 2 (March/April 1985): 319–326.

STONE, CHARLES F., and SAWHILL, ISABEL V. *Economic Policy in the Reagan Years*. Washington, DC: The Urban Institute, 1984.

WALKER, DAVID B. *Toward a Functioning Federalism.* Cambridge, MA: Winthrop, 1981.

WRIGHT, DEIL S. "A Century of the Intergovernmental Administrative State." In *A Centennial History of the American Administrative State,* by Ralph Clark Chandler, pp. 219–260. New York: The Free Press, 1987.

WRIGHT, DEIL S. *Understanding Intergovernmental Relations.* 3rd ed. Pacific Grove, CA: Brooks/Cole, 1988.

ZIMMERMAN, JOSEPH F. "Changing State-Local Relationships." In *The Book of the States, 1988–1989 Edition.* Lexington, KY: The Council of State Governments, 1988.

Chapter Four

ARENDT, HANNAH. *Eichmann in Jerusalem.* New York: Viking Press, 1963.

BAILEY, STEPHEN K. "Ethics and the Public Service." In *Public Administration and Democracy,* edited by Roscoe C. Martin. Syracuse, NY: Syracuse University Press, 1965.

BOWMAN, JAMES S. "Ethical Issues for the Public Manager." In *Handbook of Organization Management,* edited by William B. Eddy, pp. 69–102. New York: Marcel Dekker, 1983.

BOWMAN, JAMES S. "Whistle Blowing: Literature and Resource Materials." *Public Administration Review* (May/June 1983): 271–276.

BURKE, FRAN, and BENSON, GEORGE. "Written Rules: State Ethics Codes, Commissions, and Conflicts." *State Government* 62 (September/October 1989): 195–198.

DEGEORGE, RICHARD T. *Business Ethics.* New York: Macmillan, 1982.

DENHARDT, KATHRYN G. *The Ethics of Public Service.* New York: Greenwood Press, 1988.

DENHARDT, KATHRYN G. "Managing Ethics." Unpublished manuscript.

DIMOCK, MARSHALL E. "Criteria and Objectives of Public Administration." In *The Frontiers of Public Administration,* edited by John M. Gaus, Leonard D. White, and Marshall E. Dimock, pp. 116–134. Chicago: University of Chicago Press, 1936.

FINER, HERMAN. "Administrative Responsibility in Democratic Government." In *Bureaucratic Power in National Politics,* edited by Frances Rourke, pp. 165–175. Boston: Little, Brown, 1972.

FLEISHMAN, JOEL L., and PAYNE, BRUCE L. *Ethical Dilemmas and the Education of Policy Makers.* Hastings-On-Hudson, NY: The Hastings Center, 1980.

FRIEDRICH, CARL J. "Public Policy and the Nature of Democratic Responsibility." In *Bureaucratic Power in National Politics,* edited by Frances J. Rourke, pp. 176–186. Boston: Little, Brown, 1972.

GULICK, LUTHER. "Science, Values, and Public Administration." In *Papers on the Science of Administration,* edited by L. Gulick and L. Urwick, pp. 189–195. New York: Institute of Public Administration, 1937.

HILBERG, RAUL. *The Destruction of the European Jews.* Chicago: Quadrangle Books, 1961.

IGNATIUS, DAVID. "U. S. Civil Servants Are Cowed into Silence." *Manchester Guardian Weekly* (February 22, 1987): 15–16.

KOHLBERG, LAWRENCE. "From Is to Ought." In *Cognitive Development and Epistemology,* edited by T. Mishel, pp. 151–235. New York: Academic Press, 1971.

KURTZ, HOWARD. "The White House Used HUD as a Dumping Ground." *The Washington Post National Weekly Edition* (June 26–July 2, 1989): 31.

MASTERS, MARICK F., and BIERMAN, LEONARD. "The Hatch and the Political Activities of Federal Employee Unions." *Public Administration Review* (July/August 1985): 518–526.

MEIER, KENNETH J. *Regulation: Politics, Bureaucracy and Economics.* New York: St. Martin's Press, 1985.

MILGRAM, STANLEY. *Obedience to Authority.* New York: Harper & Row, 1974.

MOORE, MOLLY. "The Inspector General Calls the Air Force on the Carpet." *The Washington Post National Weekly Edition* (November 14–20, 1988): 32.

PASTIN, MARK. "The Thinking Manager's Toolbox." In *Ethical Insight, Ethical Action,* by International City Managers Association, pp. 91–104. Washington, DC: ICMA, 1988.

PA Times (October 13, 1989).

PRESIDENT'S COMMISSION ON FEDERAL ETHICS LAW REFORM. *To Serve With Honor: Report and Recommendations to the President.* Washington, DC: U.S. Department of Justice, 1989.

RAWLS, JOHN. *A Theory of Justice.* Cambridge, MA: Belnap Press of Harvard University Press, 1971.

REDFORD, EMMETTE S. *Democracy in the Administrative State.* New York: Oxford University Press, 1969.

REICH, ROBERT B. "Public Administration and Public Deliberation: An Interpretive Essay." *Yale Law Review* 94 (1985): 1617–1641.

RUBIN, HANK. "Dimensions of Institutional Ethics." In *The Nonprofit Organization*, edited by David Gies, J. Steven Ott, and Jay Shafritz. Pacific Grove, CA: Brooks/Cole, 1990.

TONG, ROSEMARIE. *Ethics in Policy Analysis.* Englewood Cliffs, NJ: Prentice-Hall, 1986.

TRUELSON, JUDITH A. "Protecting David from Goliath: On Blowing the Whistle on Systematic Corruption." *Dialogue* (Spring 1986): 1–23.

Washington Post (April 14, 1989).

WHITE, LEONARD D. *Introduction to Public Administration.* 3rd ed. New York: Macmillan, 1948.

Chapter Five

AXELROD, DONALD. *Budgeting for Modern Government.* New York: St. Martin's Press, 1988.

BAHL, ROY. *Financing State and Local Government in the 1980s.* New York: Oxford University Press, 1984.

BERNE, ROBERT, and SCHRAMM, RICHARD. *The Financial Analysis of Government.* Englewood Cliffs, NJ: Prentice-Hall, 1986.

BLUSTEIN, PAUL, and KENWORTHY, TOM. "Reagan May Wind Up Having Third Term After All." *The Washington Post National Weekly Edition* (February 29–March 6, 1988a): 31–32.

BLUSTEIN, PAUL, and KENWORTHY, TOM. "The Reagan Budget." *Congressional Quarterly Weekly Report* (February 20, 1988b): 327–331.

BOTNER, STANLEY B. "The Quiet Revolution in State Financial Management." *State and Local Government Review* 15 (Fall 1983): 134–139.

BOTNER, STANLEY B. "Impact of Data Processing Techniques in Budgeting and Financial Management in Federal Nondefense Departments and Agencies." Unpublished manuscript, 1988a.

BOTNER, STANLEY B. "A Presidential Item-Veto: Assessment of the Issues." *Economic and Policy Information* (University of Missouri) 31, no. 8, 1988b: 1–3.

BROWN, RICHARD E., GALLAGHER, THOMAS P., and WILLIAMS, MEREDITH C. *Auditing Performance in Government.* New York: Wiley, 1982.

CAIDEN, NAOMI. "The Boundaries of Public Budgeting." *Public Administration Review* 45 (July/August, 1985): 495–502.

CAIDEN, NAOMI. "The President's Budget for 1989." *Public Budgeting and Finance* 8 (Summer 1988): 3–20.

KRAEMER, KENNETH L., DUTTON, WILLIAM H., and NORTHROP, ALANA. *The Management of Information Systems.* New York: Columbia University Press, 1981.

LELOUP, LANCE T. *Budgetary Politics.* Brunswick, OH: King's Court Communications, 1977.

LEVINE, CHARLES H., RUBIN, IRENE S., and WOLOHOJIAN, GEORGE G. *The Politics of Retrenchment.* Beverly Hills, CA: Sage, 1981.

LEVINE, CHARLES H. "Organizational Decline and Cutback Management." In *Managing Fiscal Stress*, edited by Charles H. Levine, pp. 13–32. Chatham, NJ: Chatham House Publishers, 1980.

LEVINE, CHARLES H. "Big Spender." *Jefferson City News and Tribune* (Sunday, October 13, 1985): 22.

LYDEN, FREMONT J., and LINDENBERG, MARC. *Public Budgeting in Theory and Practice.* New York: Longman, 1983.

LYNCH, THOMAS D. *Public Budgeting in America.* 2nd ed. Englewood Cliffs, NJ: Prentice-Hall, 1985.

419

MCGOWAN, ROBERT P., and LOMBARDO, GARY A. "Decision Support Systems in State Government." *Public Administration Review* 46, special issue (November 1986): 579–583.

MIKESELL, JOHN L., and ZORN, C. KURT. "State Lotteries as Fiscal Savior or Fiscal Fraud." *Public Administration Review* 46 (July/August 1986): 311–320.

MOSHER, FREDERICK C. *The GAO: The Quest for Accountability in American Government.* Boulder, CO: Westview Press, 1979.

MUSGRAVE, RICHARD A., and MUSGRAVE, PEGGY B. *Public Finance in Theory and Practice.* 4th ed. New York: McGraw-Hill, 1984.

PALMER, JOHN L., and SAWHILL, ISABEL V. "Overview." In *The Reagan Record*, edited by John L. Palmer and Isabel V. Sawhill. Cambridge, MA: Ballinger, 1984.

PA Times (November 3, 1989).

PA Times (April 1, 1989).

PA Times (October 1, 1985).

PA Times (September 15, 1985).

PA Times (October 1, 1984).

PA Times (May 1, 1984).

PA Times (April 15, 1984).

PECHMAN, JOSEPH A. *Federal Tax Policy.* 4th ed. Washington, DC: The Brookings Institution, 1983.

PFIFFNER, JAMES P. *The President, the Budget, and Congress.* Boulder, CO: Westview Press, 1979.

PYHRR, PETER A. "The Zero-Base Approach to Government Budgeting." *Public Administration Review* 37 (January/February 1977): 1–8.

RUBIN, BARRY M. "Information Systems for Public Management." *Public Administration Review* 46, special issue (November 1986): 540–552.

SCHICK, ALLEN. "The Road to PPB: The Stages of Budget Reform." In *Perspectives on Budgeting*, 2nd ed., edited by Allen Schick. Washington, DC: American Society for Public Administration, 1987.

Washington Post (August 28, 1986).

WEAVER, R. KENT. "Controlling Entitlements." In *The New Direction in American Politics*, edited by John E. Chubb and Paul E. Peterson. Washington, DC: The Brookings Institution, 1985.

WILDAVSKY, AARON. *The New Politics of the Budgetary Process.* Glenview, IL: Scott, Foresman, 1988.

WRIGHT, DEIL S. *Understanding Intergovernmental Relations.* 3rd ed. Pacific Grove, CA: Brooks/Cole, 1988.

Chapter Six

CAMPBELL, ALAN K. "Civil Service Reform: A New Commitment." *Public Administration Review* 38 (March-April 1978).

CARTER, JIMMY. "State of the Union Address." January 19, 1978.

CHI, KEON S. "Comparable Worth." *State Government* 2 (1984): 34–45.

COHEN, MICHAEL, and GOLEMBIEWSKI, ROBERT T. *Public Personnel Update.* New York: Marcel Dekker, 1984.

COLBY, PETER, and INGRAHAM, PATRICIA. "Civil Service Reform: The Views of the Senior Executive Service." *Review of Public Personnel Administration* 1 (Summer 1981): 75–89.

DOMETRIUS, NELSON C., and SIGELMAN, LEE. "Assessing Progress Toward Affirmative Action Goals in State and Local Government: A New Benchmark." *Public Administration Review* 44 (May/June 1984): 241–246.

EMMERT, MARK A., and LEWIS, GREGORY B. "Pay Equity and Politics." *Review of Public Personnel Administration* 5 (Summer 1985): 50–64.

HALL, FRANCINE, and ALBRECHT, MARYANN H. *The Management of Affirmative Action.* Santa Monica, CA: Goodyear, 1979.

HAVEMANN, JUDITH. "The Government Takes a Stand on AIDS in its Office." *Washington Post National Weekly Edition* (March 28–April 3, 1988a): 34.

HAVEMANN, JUDITH. "Sexual Harassment." *Washington Post National Weekly Edition* (July 11–17, 1988b): 30–31.

HAYS, STEVEN W., and REEVES, T. ZANE. *Personnel Management in the Public Sector*. Boston: Allyn and Bacon, 1984.

HECLO, HUGH. *A Government of Strangers*. Washington, DC: Brookings Institution, 1977.

KLINGNER, DONALD E., and NALBANDIAN, JOHN. *Public Personnel Management*. 2nd ed. Englewood Cliffs, NJ: Prentice-Hall, 1985.

KLINGNER, DONALD E., O'NEIL, NANCY G., and SABAT, AMAL. *Drug Testing in the Public Workplace*. Florida International University and the American Society for Public Administration: The Clearinghouse on Drug and AIDS Testing, November, 1987.

LEVINE, CHARLES H. "The Federal Government in the Year 2000." *Public Administration Review* 46 (May-June 1986): 195–206.

LEVITAN, SAR. *Working for the Sovereign*. Baltimore, MD: Johns Hopkins Press, 1983.

LORENTZEN, PAUL. "A Time for Action." *The Bureaucrat* 13 (Fall 1984): 5–11.

LORENTZEN, PAUL. "Stress in Political-Career Executive Relations." *Public Administration Review* 45 (May/June 1985): 411–414.

MARCUS, RUTH. "Push Comes to Shove on Grove City." *Washington Post National Weekly Edition* (March 14–20, 1988): 31.

RABIN, JACK, VOCINO, THOMAS, HILDRETH, W. BARTLEY, and MILLER, GERALD J., eds. *Handbook on Public Personnel Administration and Labor Relations*. New York: Marcel Dekker, 1983.

ROSEN, BERNARD. "Merit and the President's Plan for Changing the Civil Service." *Public Administration Review* 38 (July-August 1978): 301–304.

ROSENBLOOM, DAVID H., and SHAFRITZ, JAY M. "Future Concerns of Public Sector Labor-Management Relations." In Robert T. Golembiewski (Ed.), *Public Personnel Update* (New York: Marcel-Dekker, Inc., 1984).

SCHROEDER, PATRICIA. "Is the Bridge Washed Out?" *The Bureaucrat* 13 (Fall 1984): 22–24.

SHAFRITZ, JAY M., HYDE, ALBERT C., and ROSENBLOOM, DAVID H. *Personnel Management in Government*. 2nd ed. New York: Marcel Dekker, 1981.

SIEGEL, GILBERT B., and MYRTLE, ROBERT C. *Public Personnel Administration: Concepts and Realities*. Boston: Houghton Mifflin, 1985.

STEELE, RANDY. "Strike Zone." *Flying* (March 1982): 34–41.

STEWART, DEBRA W. "Assuring Equal Employment Opportunity in the Organization." In *Handbook of Public Personnel and Labor Relations*, edited by Jack Rabin, Thomas Vocino, W. Bartley Hildreth, and Gerald J. Miller. New York: Marcel Dekker, 1983.

THAYER, FREDERICK. "The President's Management 'Reforms': Theory X Triumphant." *Public Administration Review* 38 (July/August 1978): 309–314.

ZUCK, ALFRED M. "Education of Political Appointees." *The Bureaucrat* 13 (Fall 1984): 15–18.

421

Chapter Seven

ACKOFF, RUSSLE L. *Creating the Corporate Future*. New York: Wiley, 1981.

BARDACH, EUGENE. *The Implementation Game*. Cambridge, MA: M.I.T. Press, 1977.

CANNON, J. THOMAS. *Business Strategy and Policy*. New York: Harcourt Brace Jovanovich, 1968.

CHELIMSKY, ELEANOR. *Program Evaluation: Patterns and Directions*. Washington, DC: American Society for Public Administration, 1985.

COOK, THOMAS D., and CAMPBELL, DONALD T. *Quasi-Experimentation*. Boston: Houghton Mifflin, 1979.

DRUCKER, PETER. *Management*. New York: Harper & Row, 1974.

DUNN, WILLIAM N. *Public Policy Analysis*. Englewood Cliffs, NJ: Prentice-Hall, 1981.

GLUECK, WILLIAM F. *Strategic Management and Business Policy*. New York: McGraw-Hill, 1980.

GULICK, LUTHER. "Notes on the Theory of Organization." In *Papers on the Science of Administration*, edited by L. Gulick and L. Urwick, pp. 1–46. New York: Institute of Public Administration, 1937.

JENNINGS, EDWARD T., JR., KRANE, DALE, PATTAKOS, ALEX N., and REED, B. J., eds. *From Nation to States.* Albany: State University of New York Press, 1986.

KERSHAW, DAVID N. "A Negative-Income-Tax Experiment." In *The Practice of Policy Evaluation,* edited by David Nachmias. New York: St. Martin's Press, 1980.

LATANE, HENRY A. "The Rationality Model in Organizational Decision Making." In *The Social Science of Organizations,* edited by Harold J. Leavitt. Englewood Cliffs, NJ: Prentice-Hall, 1963.

MAJCHRZAK, ANN. *Methods for Policy Research.* Beverly Hills: Sage Publications, 1984.

MCKENNA, CHRISTOPHER K. *Quantitative Methods for Public Decision Making.* New York: McGraw-Hill, 1980.

MURPHY, JEROME T. *Getting the Facts.* Santa Monica, CA: Goodyear, 1980.

NAISBITT, JOHN. *Megatrends.* New York: Warner Books, 1982.

POISTER, THEODORE H., MCDAVID, JAMES C., and MAGOUN, ANNE HOAGLAND. *Applied Program Evaluation in Local Government.* Lexington, MA: Lexington Books, 1979.

POISTER, THEODORE H. *Performance Monitoring.* Lexington, MA: Lexington Books, 1983.

PREBLE, JOHN F. "Anticipating Change: Futuristic Methods in Public Administration." *American Review of Public Administration* 16 (Summer/Fall 1982): 139–150.

PRESSMAN, JEFFREY, and WILDAVSKY, AARON. *Implementation.* Berkeley: University of California Press, 1973.

QUADE, E. S. *Analysis for Public Decisions.* 2nd ed. New York: North-Holland, 1989.

RIVLIN, ALICE M. *Systematic Thinking for Social Action.* Washington, DC: The Brookings Institution, 1971.

SHIRLEY, ROBERT C. "Limiting the Scope of Strategy." *Academy of Management Review* 7 (April 1982): 262–268.

STOKEY, EDITH, and ZECHAUSER, RICHARD. *A Primer for Policy Analysis.* New York: Norton, 1978.

SYLVIA, RONALD D., MEIER, KENNETH J., and GUNN, ELIZABETH M. *Program Planning and Evaluation for the Public Manager.* Pacific Grove, CA: Brooks/Cole, 1985.

THOMPSON, JAMES D. *Organizations in Action.* New York: McGraw-Hill, 1967.

Chapter Eight

BAILEY, MARY TIMNEY. "A Model System for Institutionalizing Productivity Improvement Efforts." *Public Productivity Review* 44 (Winter 1987): 19–28.

BARBOUR, GEORGE P., JR. "Improving Productivity for Better Service Delivery." *Management Information Service Report* 8, no. 6. Washington, DC: International City Management Association, 1976.

BURSTEIN, CAROLYN. Presentation to the Governor's Advisory Council on Productivity, State of Missouri, November, 1988.

COURSEY, DAVID H., and SHANGRAW, R. F., JR. "Expert Systems Technology for Management Applications." *Public Productivity Review* 12, no. 4 (Spring 1989): 237–262.

DILWORTH, ROBERT L. "Artificial Intelligence: The Time Is Now." *Public Productivity Review* 12, no. 2 (Winter 1988): 123–130.

DINEEN, CAROLE. "Productivity Improvement: It's Our Turn." *The Bureaucrat* 14 (Winter 1985–1986): 10–14.

GARDNER, WILLIAM L., and SCHERMERHORN, JOHN R. "Computer Networks and the Changing Nature of Managerial Work." *Public Productivity Review* 11, no. 4 (Summer 1988): 85–100.

Government Productivity News (December 1989).

Government Productivity News (October 1989).

Government Productivity News (July/August 1989).

Government Productivity News (April 1989).

GREINER, JOHN M. et al. *Productivity and Motivation.* Washington, DC: The Urban Institute Press, 1981.

HACKMAN, J. RICHARD. "Designing Work for Individuals and for Groups." In J. Richard Hackman, Edward J. Lawler, and Lyman W. Porter, *Perspectives on Behavior in Organizations,* 2nd ed. New York: McGraw-Hill, 1983, pp. 242–257.

HOLZER, MARC, ROSEN, ELLEN DOREE, and ZALK, CONSTANCE. "Steps in Productivity Improvement." In *Productivity Improvement Techniques*, edited by John Matzer, Jr. Washington, DC: International City Management Association, 1986.

JARRETT, JAMES E. "Strategies and Innovations in Productivity Improvement." Unpublished manuscript.

JARRETT, JAMES E. "Productivity." In *The Book of the States 1981–1982*. Lexington, KY: Council of State Governments, 1982.

JENKINS, DAVID. "Quality of Work Life." In *The Quality of Work Life and the 1980s*, edited by Harvey Kolodny and Hans van Beinum, pp. 1–32. New York: Praeger, 1983.

JUN, JONG S. *Management by Objectives in Government*. Beverly Hills, CA: Sage Publications, 1976.

MCKENNA, CHRISTOPHER K. *Quantitative Methods for Public Decision Making*. New York: McGraw-Hill, 1980.

MERCER, JAMES L., and PHILIPS, RONALD J. *Public Technology*. New York: American Management Association, 1981.

MORLEY, ELAINE. *A Practitioner's Guide to Public Sector Productivity Improvement*. New York: Van Nostrand Reinhold, 1986.

RUBIN, BARRY M. "Information Systems for Public Management." *Public Administration Review* 46 (November-December 1986): 540–552.

STEVENS, JOHN M., and MCGOWAN, ROBERT P. *Information Systems and Public Management*. New York: Praeger, 1985.

SUTTLE, J. LLOYD. "Improving Life at Work." In *Improving Life at Work*, by J. Richard Hackman and J. Lloyd Suttle, pp. 1–29. Santa Monica, CA: Goodyear, 1977.

TOREGAS, COSTIS. "Technology and Our Urban Communities: Who Shall Lead?" *Public Management* 17 (May 1988): 2–5.

WALTON, RICHARD E. "Criteria for Quality of Working Life." In *The Quality of Working Life*, edited by Louis E. Davis and Albert B. Cherns. New York: The Free Press, 1975.

423

Chapter Nine

ARGYRIS, CHRIS. *Interpersonal Competence and Organizational Effectiveness*. Pacific Grove, CA: Brooks/Cole, 1962.

BARBOUR, GEORGE, P., JR., FLETCHER, THOMAS W., and SIPEL, GEORGE A. *Handbook: Excellence in Local Government Management*. Washington, DC: ICMA, 1984.

DIMOCK, MARSHALL E. "The Criteria and Objectives of Public Administration." In *The Frontiers of Public Administration*, edited by John M. Gaus, Leonard D. White, and Marshall E. Dimock. Chicago: University of Chicago Press.

FAYOL, HENRI. *General and Industrial Management*, trans. by C. Storrs. London: Isaac Pitman and Sons, 1949.

GOLEMBIEWSKI, ROBERT T. *Renewing Organizations*. Itasca, IL: Peacock, 1972.

Government Productivity News (June 1989).

GULICK, LUTHER. "Notes on the Theory of Organization." In *Papers on the Science of Administration*, edited by Luther Gulick and L. Urwick, pp. 1–46. New York: Institute of Public Administration, 1937a.

GULICK, LUTHER, "Science, Values, and Public Administration." In *Papers on the Science of Administration*, edited by Luther Gulick and L. Urwick, pp. 189–195. New York: Institute of Public Administration, 1937b.

KAHN, ROBERT, and KATZ, DANIEL. "Leadership Practices in Relation to Productivity and Morale." In *Group Dynamics*, edited by Dorwin Cartwright and Alvin Zander. Evanston, IL: Row, Peterson, 1953.

MOONEY, ALAN, and REILEY, ALAN C. *The Principles of Organization*. New York: Harper & Row, 1939.

OFFICE OF MANAGEMENT AND BUDGET, OMB Draft Circular A-132 (1990).

OSTROM, VINCENT, and OSTROM, ELINOR. "Public Choice: A Different Approach to the Study of Public Administration." *Public Administration Review* 31 (March-April 1971): 203–216.

PETERS, THOMAS J., and WATERMAN, ROBERT H. *In Search of Excellence.* New York: Harper & Row, 1982.

RAINEY, HAL G., and MILWARD, H. BRINTON. "Public Organization: Policy Networks and Environments." In *Organization Theory and Public Policy*, edited by Richard H. Hall and Robert E. Quinn, pp. 133–146. Beverly Hills, CA: Sage Publications, 1983.

REDFORD, EMMETTE. *Democracy in the Administrative State.* New York: Oxford University Press, 1969.

SCHEIN, EDGAR H. *Organizational Culture and Leadership.* San Francisco: Jossey-Bass, 1987.

SELZNICK, PHILIP. *TVA and the Grass Roots.* Berkeley: University of California Press, 1949.

SIMON, HERBERT A. *Models of Man.* New York: Wiley, 1957.

TAYLOR, FREDERICK W. *Scientific Management.* New York: Harper & Row, 1923.

WEBER, MAX. *The Theory of Social and Economic Organization.* New York: Oxford University Press, 1947.

WHITE, LEONARD. *Introduction to the Study of Public Administration.* New York: Macmillan, 1926.

WILLOUGHBY, W. F. *Principles of Public Organization.* Baltimore, MD: John Hopkins Press, 1927.

Chapter Ten

BENNIS, WARREN. "The Artform of Leadership." In *The Executive Mind*, by Suresh Srivastya. San Francisco: Jossey-Bass, 1983.

BENSON, HERBERT. *The Relaxation Response.* New York: Morrow, 1975.

COOPER, KENNETH H. *The Aerobics Way.* Toronto: Bantam Books, 1978.

GARDNER, JOHN. Remarks to the National Conference of the National Association of Schools of Public Affairs and Administration, Seattle, October 23, 1987.

HALES, C. P. "What Do Managers Do? A Critical Review of the Evidence." *Journal of Management* 23 (1986): 88–115.

HOPPER, LINDA. "Unstressing Work." *Public Management* 17 (November 1988): 1–4.

KOTTER, JOHN P. *The General Manager.* New York: The Free Press, 1982.

LAKEIN, ALAN. *How to Get Control of Your Time and Your Life.* New York: Signet Books, 1973.

LEBOEUF, MICHAEL. *Working Smart.* New York: McGraw Hill, 1979.

LINDBLOM, CHARLES E. *The Policy-Making Process.* Englewood Cliffs, NJ: Prentice-Hall, 1968.

PRICE, VIRGINIA ANN. *Type A Behavior Pattern.* New York: Academic Press, 1982.

SELYE, HANS. *Stress Without Distress*, Philadelphia: Lippincott, 1974.

SIMON, HERBERT A. *Models of Man.* New York: Wiley, 1957.

WHETTEN, DAVID A., and CAMERON, KIM S. *Developing Management Skills.* Glenview, IL: Scott, Foresman, 1984.

Chapter Eleven

ARGYRIS, CHRIS. *Intervention Theory and Method.* Reading, MA: Addison-Wesley, 1970.

BLANCHARD, KENNETH, and JOHNSON, SPENCER. *The One-Minute Manager.* New York: Berkley Books, 1982.

DAFT, RICHARD L., and STEERS, RICHARD M. *Organizations: A Micro/Macro Approach.* Glenview, IL: Scott, Foresman, 1986.

GARDNER, NEELY. *Group Leadership.* Washington, DC: National Training and Development Service, 1974.

HERZBERG, FREDERICK. *The Motivation to Work.* New York: Wiley, 1959.

HITT, MICHAEL A., MIDDLEMIST, R. DENNIS, and MATHIS, ROBERT L. *Management Concepts and Effective Practice.* St. Paul, MN: West, 1983.

JANIS, IRVING. *Groupthink.* 2nd ed. Boston: Houghton Mifflin, 1983.

KANTER, ROSABETH MOSS. *Men and Women of the Corporation.* New York: Basic Books, 1977.

LIPPITT, GORDON L., LANGSETH, PETER, and MOSSOP, JACK. *Implementing Organizational Change.* San Francisco: Jossey-Bass, 1985.

MASLOW, ABRAHAM. *Motivation and Personality.* New York: Harper & Brothers, 1954.

ORGAN, DENNIS H. "A Review of *Management and the Worker.*" *Academy of Management Review,* 11, no. 2 (April 1986): 459–464.

RANKIN, PAUL. "Listening Ability." Proceedings of the Ohio State Educational Conference, Ninth Annual Session, 1929.

STEIL, LYMAN K., BARKER, LARRY L., and WATSON, KITTIE W. *Effective Listening.* Reading, MA: Addison-Wesley, 1983.

SUSSMAN, LYLE, and DEEP, SAMUEL. *Comex.* Cincinnati, OH: Southwestern, 1984.

VROOM, VICTOR H., and JAGO, ARTHUR G. *The New Leadership.* Englewood Cliffs, NJ: Prentice-Hall, 1988.

VROOM, VICTOR H., and YETTON, PHILIP W. *Leadership and Decision Making.* Pittsburgh, PA: University of Pittsburgh Press, 1973.

ZILLER, R. C. "Toward a Theory of Open and Closed Groups." *Psychological Bulletin* 64 (1965): 164–182.

Chapter Twelve

GOODSELL, CHARLES T. *The Case for Bureaucracy.* 2nd ed. Chatham, NJ: Chatham House, 1985.

NATIONAL COMMISSION ON THE PUBLIC SERVICE. *Leadership for America.* Washington, DC: National Commission, 1989.

JOURNALS

Administration and Society
Center for Public Administration and Public Affairs
Virginia Polytechnic Institute and State University
Blacksburg, VA 24061

Administrative Science Quarterly
Johnson Graduate School of Management
Malott Hall
Cornell University
Ithaca, NY 14853

American Review of Public Administration
L. P. Cookingham Institute of Public Affairs
Henry W. Bloch School of Business and Public Administration
University of Missouri—Kansas City
Kansas City, MO 64110

Bureaucrat
9 Pine Avenue
Takoma Park, MD 20912

Government Productivity News
P.O. Box 17435
Austin, TX 78755-0435

International Journal of Public Administration
Institute of State and Regional Affairs
Pennsylvania State University—Harrisburg
Harrisburg, PA 17057

Journal of Policy Analysis and Management
Association for Public Policy Analysis and Management
Graduate School of Public Policy
University of California
Berkeley, CA 94720

Journal of State Government
The Council of State Governments
P.O. Box 11910
Lexington, KY 40578

Journal of Urban Analysis and Management
W. Averell Harriman College for Urban
 and Policy Studies
State University of New York
Stony Brook, NY 11790

*New Directions in Public Administration
 Research*
School of Public Administration
Florida Atlantic University
220 S. E. Second Avenue
Fort Lauderdale, FL 33301

Policy Studies
Policy Studies Institute
100 Park Village East
London NW1 3SR

Policy Studies Journal
Policy Studies Organization
17 Lexington Avenue, Box 336
Baruch College
New York, NY 10010

Policy Studies Review
Policy Studies Organization
School of Justice Studies
Arizona State University
Tempe, AZ 85287

Public Administration Quarterly
Southern Public Administration Education
 Foundation, Inc.
Institute of State and Regional Affairs
Pennsylvania State University—Harrisburg
Harrisburg, PA 17057

Public Administration Review
American Society for Public Administration
University of Southern California
1201 J Street
Sacramento, CA 95814-2919

Public Budgeting and Finance
ASPA Section on Budgeting and Financial
 Management
Department of Public Administration
California State College
San Bernardino, CA 92407

Public Budgeting and Financial Management
Institute of State and Regional Affairs
Pennsylvania State University—Harrisburg
Harrisburg, PA 17057

Public Management
International City Management Association
1120 G Street, NW
Washington, DC 20005

Public Personnel Management
International Personnel Management
 Association
1850 K Street, NW
Suite 870
Washington, DC 20006

Public Productivity Review
APSA Section on Management Science
 and Policy Analysis
National Center for Public Productivity
John Jay College, City University of
 New York
445 West 59th Street
New York, NY 10019

Publius: The Journal of Federalism
Center for the Study of Federalism
Department of Political Science
North Texas State University
Denton, TX 76203-5338

Review of Public Personnel Administration
Institute of Public Affairs
University of South Carolina
Columbia, SC 29208

State and Local Government Review
Carl Vinson Institute of Government
University of Georgia
Terrell Hall
Athens, GA 30602

ORGANIZATIONS

Academy for State and Local Government
444 North Capitol Street NW, Suite 349
Washington, DC 20001

427

American Consortium for International Public
  Administration
1120 G Street NW, Suite 225
Washington, DC 20005

American Council on Education
One Dupont Circle NW
Suite 800
Washington, DC 20036

American Planning Association/American
  Institute of Certified Planners
1776 Massachusetts Avenue NW, Suite 704
Washington, DC 20036

American Public Health Association
1015 15th Street NW, 3rd Floor
Washington, DC 20005

American Public Power Association
2301 M Street NW, 3rd Floor
Washington, DC 20037

American Public Welfare Association
810 First Street NE, Suite 500
Washington, DC 20002

American Public Works Association
1313 East 60th Street
Chicago, IL 60637

American Society for Public Administration
1120 G Street NW, Suite 500
Washington, DC 20005

Council of State Governments
Iron Works Pike
P.O. Box 11910
Lexington, KY 40578

Education Commission of the States
1860 Lincoln Street, Suite 300
Denver, CO 80295

Government Finance Officers Association
180 N. Michigan Avenue, Suite 800
Chicago, IL 60601

International City Management Association
777 North Capitol Street
Washington, DC 20002

International Institute of Municipal Clerks
160 North Altadena Drive
Pasadena, CA 91107

International Personnel Management
  Association
1617 Duke Street
Alexandria, VA 22314

National Academy of Public Administration
1120 G Street NW, Suite 540
Washington, DC 20005

National Association of Counties
440 1st Street NW, 8th Floor
Washington, DC 20001

National Association of Schools of Public
  Affairs and Administration
1120 G Street NW, 5th Floor
Washington, DC 20005

National Association of State Budget Officers
400 North Capitol Street NW, Suite 295
Washington, DC 20001

National Civic League
1601 Grant Street, Suite 250
Denver, CO 80203

National Forum for Black Public
  Administrators
1301 Pennsylvania Avenue NW, Suite 801
Washington, DC 20004

National Institute of Governmental Purchasing
115 Hillwood Avenue, Suite 201
Falls Church, VA 22046

National League of Cities
1301 Pennsylvania Avenue NW, 6th Floor
Washington, DC 20004

Public Administration Service
1497 Chain Bridge Road
McLean, VA 22101

Public Technology, Inc.
1301 Pennsylvania Avenue NW, Suite 704
Washington, DC 20004

Accounting: The process of identifying, measuring, and communicating economic information to permit informed judgment and decision making.

Adverse or disparate impact: Criterion for showing that employment practices affect one group more harshly than another.

Affirmative action: Use of positive, results-oriented practices to ensure that women, minorities, handicapped persons, and other protected classes of people will be equitably represented in an organization.

Agenda setting: Phase in public policy process when certain problems come to be viewed as needing attention.

Allotments: Amounts that agencies are authorized to spend within a given period.

Apportionment: Process by which funds are allocated to agencies for specific portions of the year.

Appropriation: Legislative action to set aside funds and create budget authority for their expenditures.

Area of acceptance: Area within which the subordinate is willing to accept the decisions made by the supervisor.

Authorizing legislation: Legislative action that permits establishment or continuation of a particular program or agency.

Bargaining unit: The organization that will represent employees in conferring and negotiating various issues.

Behavioral awards: Used to reward specific behaviors that management wishes to encourage.

Block grants: Grants in which the money can be used for nearly any purpose within a specific functional field.

Bond: Promise to repay a certain amount (principal) at a certain time (maturity date) at a particular rate of interest.

Boundary spanning: Representing an organization to outside groups and organizations.

Bounded rationality: The best possible solution, but not the most rational from a purely economic standpoint.

Brainstorming: Technique for enhancing the alternative-generation portion of the decision-making process.

Budget padding: Proposing a higher budget than is actually needed.

Business cycle: Periods of economic growth featuring inflation and high employment followed by periods of recession or depression and unemployment.

Capital expenditures: Spending for items that will be used over a period of several years.

Capital grants: Grants for use in construction or renovation.

Categorical or project grants: Grants requiring that the money may be spent for only a limited purpose; typically available on a competitive basis.

Charter: Local government's equivalent of a constitution.

429

Cohesion: Degree to which members of a group are uniformly committed to the group and its goals.

Comparable worth: Notion that men and women in jobs that are not identical but require similar levels of skill and training should be paid equally.

Constituent policy: Policy designed to benefit the public generally or to serve the government.

Continuing resolution: Resolution permitting the government to continue operating until an appropriation measure is passed.

Cooperative federalism: Greater sharing of responsibilities between federal and state governments.

Co-optation: Situations in which citizens are given the feeling of involvement while exercising little real power.

Coproduction: Using volunteer activity to supplement or supplant the work of government officials.

Cost-benefit: Identifying and quantifying both negative impacts (costs) and positive impacts (benefits) of a proposal, then subtracting one from the other to arrive at a net benefit.

Councils of government: Oversight bodies representing various localities to help coordinate local affairs.

Cross-cutting requirements: Rules that apply to most grant programs.

Debt capacity: Value of a city's resources combined with the ability of the government to draw on them to provide payment.

Decision analysis: Technique wherein decisions are likely to be made sequentially and under some degree of uncertainty.

Decision tree: Technique that identifies various possible outcomes, given the risk associated with each.

Deferral: Decision by the president to withhold expenditure of funds for a brief period.

Delegation: Assigning tasks to others.

Democracy: A political system in which decision-making power is widely shared among members of the society.

Deontology: Belief that broad principles of rightness and wrongness can be established and are *not* dependent on particular circumstances.

Dillon's rule: Municipalities have only those powers granted in their charters; cities are creatures of the state.

Direct orders: Requirements or restrictions that are enforced by one government over another.

Discretionary spending: That portion of the budget still open to changes by the president and Congress.

Distributive policy: Policy involving use of general tax funds to provide assistance and benefits to individuals or groups.

Dual federalism: Pattern in which federal and state governments are struggling for power and influence with little intergovernmental cooperation.

Effectiveness: Extent to which a program is achieving or failing to achieve its stated objectives.

Efficiency: Relationship between inputs and outputs.

Employee recognition program: Effective way to acknowledge special contributions of certain employees or groups to the organization.

Entitlement grants: Grants that provide assistance to persons who meet certain criteria.

Entitlement programs: Programs that provide a specified set of benefits to those who meet certain eligibility requirements.

Equal employment opportunity: Refers to efforts to eliminate employment discrimination on the basis of race, ethnic background, sex, age, or physical handicap; ensures that all persons have an equal chance to compete for employment and promotions based on job qualifications.

Equality: The idea that all persons have an equal claim to life, liberty, and the pursuit of happiness.

Ethical or moral relativism: Belief that moral judgment can be made only by taking into account the context in which action occurs.

Ethics: Process by which we clarify right and wrong and act on what we take to be right.

Ethics audit: Evaluation of the value premises that guide an organization's action.

Excise tax: Tax applied to the sale of specific commodities.

Executive order: A presidential mandate directed to and governing, with the effect of law, the actions of government officials and agencies.

Expert systems: Computer programs that mimic the decision-making processes of human experts within a particular field.

Exploratory evaluation: Investigating a variety of hunches or intuitions about program operations.

Fiduciary funds: Funds used when government must hold assets for individuals or when government holds resources to be transmitted to another organization.

Final-offer arbitration: Technique in which both parties must present their best offer with the understanding that an arbitrator will choose one or the other without modification.

Fiscal policy: Public policy with respect to the impact of government taxation and spending on the economy.

Fiscal year (FY): Government's basic accounting period.

Formula grants: Grants that employ a specific division rule to indicate how much money any given jurisdiction will receive.

Franchise: Exclusive award to one firm (or a limited number) to operate a certain business within the jurisdiction.

Functional principle: Horizontal division of labor.

Gainsharing plan: Monetary award for a group of employees based on savings generated by the group.

General fund: Fund that handles "unrestricted" funds of government.

Grants: Transfers of money (and/or property) from one government to another.

Grantsmanship: Skills needed to compete successfully in the grant process.

Gross National Product (GNP): Measure of total spending in the economy; includes total personal consumption, private investment, and government purchases.

Hidden agenda: Privately held goals and priorities.

Home rule: Provision allowing cities greater autonomy over local activities.

Impoundment: Withholding of funds authorized and appropriated by law.

Independent agencies: Agencies intentionally created outside the normal cabinet organization.

Individualism: The idea that the dignity and integrity of the individual is of supreme importance.

Institutional subsystem: Responsible for adapting the organization to its environment and for anticipating and planning for the future.

Intergovernmental relations: A term encompassing all the complex and interdependent relations among those at various levels of government.

Interorganizational networks: Pattern of relationships within and among various groups and organizations working in a single policy area.

Interventionist: External consultant brought in to reveal dysfunctional patterns of behavior and to try to develop more effective working relationships.

Iron triangle: Term given to a coalition of interest groups, agency personnel, and members of Congress created to exert influence on a particular policy issue.

Item veto: Allows a governor to veto specific items in an appropriations bill.

Job description: A thorough analysis of the work to be done and the capabilities for a job; typically contains these elements: job title, duties required, responsibilities, and job qualifications.

Lateral entry: Entry into government positions at any level.

Legislative veto: Statutory provision that gives Congress the authority to approve or disapprove certain executive actions.

Liberty: The idea that individual citizens of a democracy should have a high degree of self-determination.

Line-item budget: Budget format for listing categories of expenditures along with amounts allocated to each.

Management by objectives: Participatory approach to establishing clear and measurable objectives throughout the entire organization.

Managerial subsystem: Concerned with providing necessary resources for accomplishing a technical task and mediating between the technical and institutional subsystems.

Mandate: Order requiring a government to do something.

Merit pay: Increases in salary and wages that are tied to actual quality of work performed.

Merit principle: Concept that selection and treatment of government employees should be based on merit or competence rather than personal or political favoritism.

Morality: Practices and activities considered right or wrong and the values those practices reflect.

Negotiated investment strategy: Bringing together representatives of all affected groups to set priorities for funding.

Neutral competence: The belief that a neutral public bureaucracy following the mandates of a legislative body will meet the requirements of democracy.

Nominal group: Face-to-face meeting that allows only limited interaction among participants.

Nonprofit organizations: Organizations prohibited by law from distributing surplus revenues to individuals.

Objective responsibility: Assurance of responsiveness through external controls.

Ombudsman: Permanent office that receives complaints and acts on behalf of citizens to secure information, request services, or pursue grievances.

Operating grants: Grants for use in development and operation of specific programs.

Organization development: Process-oriented approach to planned change.

Organizational culture: Basic patterns of attitudes, beliefs, and values that underlie an organization's operation.

Parity principle: Idea that individuals should have equal amounts of authority and responsibility.

Participant–observer: Someone in either the target population or the agency who makes observations and draws conclusions based on firsthand experience.

Performance appraisal: Specific evaluation with respect to an individual's progress in completing specified tasks.

Performance auditing: Analysis and evaluation of the effective performance of agencies in carrying out their objectives.

Performance bonus: One-time monetary award based on superior performance on the job or in a particular task.

Performance budget: Budget format organized around programs or activities, including various performance measurements that indicate the relationship between work actually done and its cost.

PERT: A way to monitor the time or costs of various activities required to complete a project showing the sequence in which the activities must be completed.

Picket fence federalism: Pattern of intergovernmental relations in which the horizontal bars represent levels of government and the vertical slats represent various substantive fields.

Piecework bonus: Incentive that ties the worker's productivity in a given task to the monetary rewards he or she receives.

Planning-programming-budgeting system (PPBS): Effort to connect planning, systems analysis, and budgeting in a single exercise.

Policy: Statement of goals and intentions with respect to a particular problem or set of problems.

Policy analysis: Process of researching or analyzing public problems to provide policy makers with specific information about the range of available policy options and advantages and disadvantages of different approaches.

Policy analysts: Persons who provide important information about public programs through research into the operations and impacts of the programs.

Policy entrepreneur: A person willing to invest personal time, energy, and money in pursuit of particular policy changes.

Political economy approach: Focusing on politics and economies as categories for analyzing organizational behavior.

Position classification: Analyzing and organizing jobs on the basis of duties, responsibilities, and knowledge and skills required to perform them.

Preaudit: Review in advance of an actual expenditure.

Privatization: Use of nongovernmental agencies to provide goods and services previously provided by government.

Process/flow charting: Graphically demonstrating the various steps in an operation, the people who perform each step, and relationships among those elements.

Process evaluations: Seeking ways to improve program implementation so as to better meet program objectives.

Program managers: Persons ranging from the executive level to the supervisory level who are in charge of particular governmental programs.

Progressive tax: One that taxes those with higher incomes at a higher rate.

Proportional tax: One that taxes everyone at the same rate.

Proprietary funds: Used to account for government activities that more closely resemble private business.

Public administration: The management of public programs.

Public corporation: An essentially commercial agency where work requires greater latitude and acquires at least a portion of its funding in the market place (e.g., Tennessee Valley Authority).

Public policy: Authoritative statements made by legitimate governmental actors about public problems.

Quality circle: Small group of people who do similar or connected work and meet regularly to identify, analyze, and solve work-process problems.

Reconciliation bill: Legislative action that attempts to reconcile individual actions in taxes, authorizations, or appropriations with the totals.

Redistributive policy: Policy designed to take taxes from certain groups and give them to another group.

Regressive tax: One that taxes those with lower incomes at a proportionally higher rate than those with higher incomes.

Regulatory commission: Group formed to regulate a particular area of the economy; usually headed by a group of individuals appointed by the president and confirmed by the Senate.

Regulatory policy: Policy designed to limit actions of persons or groups to protect all or parts of the general public.

Rescission: Presidential decision to permanently withhold funds.

Revenue sharing: Grant pattern in which the money can be used any way the recipient government chooses.

Risk management: Ways that public organizations anticipate and cope with risks.

Risky shift: Difference in the daringness of decisions group members make as a group compared to the average risk of the same decision if each member made it alone.

Role ambiguity: Occurs where the rights and responsibilities of the job are not clearly understood.

Role conflict: Occurs where one faces two different and incompatible sets of demands.

Rule making: Administrative establishment of general guidelines for application to a class of people or a class of actions at some future time.

Rule of three: Provision of most merit systems that requires at least the top three applicants' names to be forwarded to the hiring official to allow some flexibility in selection.

Satisficing decision: One that is just "good enough" in terms of some criterion.

Scalar principle: Vertical division of labor among various organizational levels.

Scientific management: Approach to management based on carefully defined "laws, rules, and principles."

Sexual harassment: Any unwarranted and nonreciprocal verbal or physical sexual advances or derogatory remarks that the recipient finds offensive or that interfere with his or her job performance.

Special districts: Local governments created for a specific purpose within a specific area.

Spoils system: The ability to give government jobs to the party faithful; "to the victor belongs the spoils."

Staff managers: Persons who support the work of program managers through budgeting and financial management, personnel and labor relations, purchasing and procurement.

433

Stakeholders: The many different persons who are affected by the results of a policy decision.

Strategic planning: Matching organizational objectives and capabilities to the anticipated demands of the environment so as to produce a plan of action that will assure achievement of objectives.

Structured interviews: Those in which a previously developed set of questions is used with each applicant.

Subjective responsibility: Assurance of responsiveness based on an individual's character.

Suggestion award programs: Incentives for employees who make specific suggestions that result in savings for the organization.

Sunset law: Provision that sets a specific termination date for a program.

Sunshine law: Provision that requires agencies to conduct business in public view.

Supplemental appropriation: Bill passed during the fiscal year adding new money to an agency's budget for the same fiscal year.

Supply-side economies: Argument that decreased taxes and spending will stimulate capital investment and economic growth.

Support system: Network of people with whom one can talk about problems.

System: Set of regularized interactions configured or "bounded" in a way that differentiates and separates them from other actions that constitute the system's environment.

Systems approach: Suggestion that public (or other) organizations can be viewed in the same general way as biological or physical systems.

Systems theory: Effort to identify the interactions of various internal and external elements that impinge on an organization's operations.

Task forces: Groups brought together to work on specific organizational problems.

Technical subsystem: Concerned with effective performance of an organization's actual work.

Time series analysis: Making a number of observations about the target population both before and after program intervention.

Two-factor theory: Model of motivation involving two variables: job satisfaction and job dissatisfaction.

Unit determination: Decision to include or exclude certain groups in a bargaining unit.

Urban renewal: Government program designed to provide cities with money for public housing and urban redevelopment.

Utilitarianism: Philosophy of the greatest good for the greatest number of people.

Whipsaw tactics: Argument that pay or benefits negotiated by one group should be applied to others.

Zero-base budgeting: Budget format that presents information about the efficiency and effectiveness of existing programs and highlights possibilities for eliminating or reducing programs.

INDEX

437

441

TO THE OWNER OF THIS BOOK:

We hope that you have found *Public Administration: An Action Orientation,* by Robert B. Denhardt, useful. So that this book can be improved in a future edition, would you take the time to complete this sheet and return it? Thank you.

Instructor's name: _____

Department: _____

School and address: _____

_____

1. The name of the course in which I used this book is: _____

_____

2. My general reaction to this book is: _____

_____

_____

3. What I like most about this book is: _____

_____

_____

4. What I like least about this book is: _____

_____

_____

5. Were all of the chapters of the book assigned for you to read?   Yes   No

    If not, which ones weren't? _____

6. Do you plan to keep this book after you finish the course?   Yes   No

    Why or why not? _____

7. On a separate sheet of paper, please write specific suggestions for improving this book and anything else you'd care to share about your experience in using the book.

Optional:

Your name: _____ Date: _____

May Brooks/Cole quote you, either in promotion for *Public Administration: An Action Orientation* or in future publishing ventures?

Yes: _____ No: _____

Sincerely,
Robert B. Denhardt

FOLD HERE

BUSINESS REPLY MAIL

FIRST CLASS   PERMIT NO. 358   PACIFIC GROVE, CA

POSTAGE WILL BE PAID BY ADDRESSEE

ATT: *Robert B. Denhardt*

Brooks/Cole Publishing Company
511 Forest Lodge Road
Pacific Grove, California 93950-9968

FOLD HERE